The
Decline and Fall
of the Soviet Empire

The
Decline and Fall
of the Soviet Empire

FORTY YEARS THAT
SHOOK THE WORLD,
FROM STALIN TO YELTSIN

FRED COLEMAN

ST. MARTIN'S PRESS
NEW YORK

Design by Ellen R. Sasahara

Map copyright ©1996 by Mark Stein Studios

Library of Congress Cataloging-in-Publication Data

Coleman, Fred.
    The decline and fall of the Soviet Empire : forty years that shook the world, from Stalin to Yeltsin / Fred Coleman. — 1st ed.
        p.   cm.
    ISBN 0-312-14312-5
    1. Soviet Union—History—1953–1985.   2. Soviet Union—Histo   985–1991.   I. Title.
DK274.C58   1996
947.085—dc20   96-1658
                                                                        CIP

First Edition: June 1996

10   9   8   7   6   5   4   3   2   1

To Nadya

CONTENTS

Part III   Mikhail Sergeyevich Gorbachev
(1985-1991)

Part IV   Boris Nikolayevich Yeltsin
(1991–1995)

INTRODUCTION

John Reed got it wrong. In calling his classic eyewitness book on the 1917 Bolshevik Revolution *Ten Days That Shook the World,* Reed was much too shortsighted. In fact, the revolution that brought communism to power in Russia triggered global shock waves for closer to ten decades.

Communism's ideological arm, Marxism-Leninism, rose up against every school of thought from democracy and capitalism to Christianity, Islam, and Buddhism. Its driving force, the Soviet Union, held the world to ransom with nuclear blackmail. For much of the century, the Soviet empire expanded as the prime mover, making all others react. Even in its death throes, from the fall of the Berlin Wall to the collapse of the U.S.S.R., communism set the crisis agenda. There is no longer any doubt. Communism was the great challenge of the twentieth century.

No other modern alternative to the established world order affected more lives more profoundly for more years in more countries. As a philosophy, as a state religion, as a political and economic system, and as a military threat, the Soviet-led Communist challenge spanned most of the century and played a key role in every watershed event, from two world wars to the end of colonialism to the Cold War.

When Nikita Khrushchev boasted, "We will bury you," millions of people all over the world feared that might be true. In every nation they ruled, the Communists always seized and held power by force of arms, rather than through the ballot box. Their ambition knew no limits. The Western democracies were absolutely right to draw the line of containment and resist Communist expansion, even at the risk of global war. Had they not, they too might have lost their freedom. In the end, Western resolve succeeded. The Communists buried themselves.

When communism died in Russia in 1991, its global empire collapsed as well. The century-long challenge to remake the world was over. Nothing could save what remained of communism, even in the handful of nations where the system survived—China, Cuba, North Korea, and Vietnam. There too the system would soon self-destruct, for many of the same reasons that killed communism in Russia. Nor do Communist dictatorship, ideology, and economics have much chance of returning to power anywhere in the world in their past discredited forms.

In Eastern Europe, where former Communists now win free elections, they do so as the candidates with the most experience in government service, running as social democrats or under some other more credible new label. They have no intention, or chance, of reviving the Communist past. As Czech president Vaclav Havel, a leading democrat in Eastern Europe, puts it: "The return of former Communists does not mean the return of communism."

Even Russia's reconstructed Communists, in their uphill struggle to regain power, know their only hope of reviving the economy is to abandon Marxism-Leninism and embrace free-market policies. Gennady Zyuganov, the Russian Communist Party leader, says he won't renationalize private industry if he forms a government. Hardheaded capitalists tend to believe him. Salomon Brothers, the investment banking firm, said in a 1995 report that Zyuganov's party leadership was "bourgeois in outlook." Zyuganov, of course, is capable of saying one thing while campaigning for the Russian presidency and doing just the opposite once in office. Communists could indeed take power in Russia again and try to reinvent the past, but their unworkable system, now largely discredited in Moscow itself, would be even less able to solve the nation's economic, political, and social problems the second time around.

Thus all over the world, the same result is already abundantly clear. By the end of this decade, communism will be recognized everywhere no longer as the great challenge but rather as the great failure of the twentieth century.

Now at last, in the 1990s, the time has come to analyze the decline and fall of the Soviet empire, to establish how and why communism failed. This book is one such exercise. It leads to some disturbing conclusions, among them:

- The collapse of communism was always inevitable.

- All attempts to reform the Communist system were doomed to failure.

- The United States could have done better in resisting the Communist challenge, short of risking nuclear war. It often overestimated the Soviet threat, missing opportunities to hasten the demise of the Communist system decades earlier.

- There are important lessons to be drawn from the mishandling of the Communist challenge. If they are learned in time, they could well help the world survive a future nuclear threat. So far, unfortunately, little progress has been made in this direction.

Above all, the lessons on how and why communism failed, and how the West could have done better, are to be found in Russia, since the death in 1953 of Josef Stalin, principal architect of the global Soviet threat. It is a story of chronic illness and failed cures as Nikita Khrushchev, Leonid Brezhnev, and Mikhail Gorbachev each unwittingly contributed essential steps in marching communism to its grave.

The Gorbachev reforms, which were intended originally to strengthen the Soviet system, eventually killed it. But those who focus only on the Gorbachev era miss the point. Gorbachev could not have conducted his reforms without the legacies Khrushchev and Brezhnev left behind. The unintended dismantling of the Communist system, largely by the Soviet leaders themselves in succession, took nearly forty years, from 1953 to the collapse of the U.S.S.R in 1991. That process of decline and fall, from Josef Stalin to Boris Yeltsin, and how it was often mishandled by the United States, is detailed for the first time in the pages of this book.

The narrative is based primarily on the author's personal experiences in Moscow at most key stages and on newly released, once-secret official Soviet documents. What John Reed did in chronicling the birth of Communist power, this book attempts to do for its death.

Reed's presence on the ground in Russia at the time and his reporting skills are taken as models, but not his political views. That point must be stressed at the outset. Reed was a true believer in communism, a faith that to me always looked fatally flawed. In my view, communism was doomed from the start because it promised the impossible. All of the world's other great religions offered their faithful paradise in the next life. Only communism claimed the ability to create heaven on earth—and it then manifestly failed to do so.

John Reed's account of the Bolshevik Revolution is far from perfect. Nevertheless, he was the only American journalist to watch it unfold, and he told what he had witnessed firsthand; in time, even the Russians accepted his book as definitive. As the only American journalist on the scene in Moscow from Khrushchev and Brezhnev to Gorbachev and Yeltsin, I feel a similar need to try to make sense of everything I saw and heard, watching and interviewing the major players. Any possible similarity with Reed, however, ends there.

Undoubtedly this work too will be imperfect. And it makes no claim to be as definitive as Reed's. But if it can increase understanding of communism as the dominant challenge of the twentieth century—and of how the West might have responded more effectively—then the effort will have been worthwhile.

I start with Nikita Sergeyevich Khrushchev, the first great Soviet reformer. His de-Stalinization began the long decline and fall of the Soviet empire, although that is hardly what he had in mind. Khrushchev is also the starting point because his humiliating forced retirement, in the only successful coup d'état in Soviet history, established the battle lines for all subsequent Kremlin power struggles, up to and including those involving the second great reformer in Soviet history, Mikhail Sergeyevich Gorbachev.

As a young reporter in Moscow, then twenty-six years old, I covered the 1964 coup against Khrushchev. For me, it became the seminal experience of a journalistic career. The fascination of watching a drama of historic importance unfold was mixed with the utter frustration of never knowing even the most basic elements of the plot, among them who acted first, exactly how, and why. Kremlin secrecy on this political sea change was total, and, at the time, looked permanent, yet I determined then and there to follow the case until the various mysteries were resolved. Three decades later, as a veteran foreign correspondent on my third tour of duty in the U.S.S.R., I finally obtained the once top-secret official Soviet records of Khrushchev's removal, as well as interviews with players in the plot. All the evidence from an inquiry spanning thirty years has been combined in this book into the fullest record of Khrushchev's fall from power ever published.

It is recounted at length because the 1964 coup was to be a major influence on both Brezhnev and Gorbachev. The very real threat that a similar putsch could occur at any time cast a shadow over all Kremlin leaders for the remainder of Soviet history. The message from Khrushchev's downfall could hardly be clearer. Let the reformer beware, it warned. In the Soviet Union, the system is stronger than the man. If a reform leader threatens the system, it will destroy him.

Leonid Brezhnev never forgot that lesson. For nearly two decades Brezhnev preserved the system, rejecting all attempts at meaningful reform, in order to safeguard his own leadership position. In the process he bankrupted the country and the worldwide Communist movement it supported. He also proved that no change was no answer either. Without the risk of essential reforms, the Brezhnev era showed, communism was doomed.

Histories profit from perspective. The passing of years helps to clarify events. So does geographical distance from the subject. This book, partly written in Paris long after the events described, benefits from both. But historic documents plucked from dusty archives years later on return trips to the U.S.S.R. provide only part of the story. Equally important material comes from the portraits of living, breathing Russians written in Moscow at the time they were playing key roles in the demise of Soviet communism. A primary aim of this book is to combine official documents and glimpses of everyday life into a closer look at the real Russia than the Western reader has had before.

In the pages that follow, readers will go behind the Kremlin's closed doors many times to see how Soviet leaders operated. This book will also take them into Andrei Sakharov's kitchen for tea, into KGB prison camps, onto a Soviet tank retreating from Afghanistan, inside the heads of ordinary Russians.

Through the Khrushchev and Brezhnev eras, the chapters ahead will build a mosaic of every aspect of Soviet life, so that by the time Gorbachev comes to power, the reader will have a broad knowledge of the enormous challenges that had to be faced—and that ultimately proved insurmountable.

More than a broad historical record is involved, however. Chapters are also designed to deepen knowledge as the reader goes along. For example, the initial on-scene account of Khrushchev's fall is limited to what was generally known in 1964. The fuller subsequent account, drawn from official archives eventually made available, provides insights into the inner workings of Kremlin power politics that no one outside the ruling Politburo knew in Khrushchev's day.

Similarly, the central arguments of the book are deepened through successive chapters, among them the conclusion that wiser Western diplomacy could have ended the Communist challenge decades earlier. Support for this view comes from analyses of several related factors, including the internal Kremlin power struggle, rebellion in Eastern Europe, dissent in Russia, the imploding Soviet economy, the military threat, and U.S.–Soviet relations. Evidence is added gradually in the belief that it becomes increasingly persuasive. The reader is asked to withhold judgment until the entire case is made.

Nowhere is this cumulative approach more important than in establishing that Soviet communism was always doomed. This can only be done by examining the experience of Khrushchev, Brezhnev, and Gorbachev in succession.

Certainly Mikhail Gorbachev could never forget the lessons of either Khrushchev or Brezhnev. He understood from the Khrushchev precedent the personal political risk for a Soviet leader in undertaking reform. But he also understood from Brezhnev's record that doing nothing was more dangerous in the long run for the country than risking reform. With great courage and tactical skill, Gorbachev went much further than Khrushchev had dared in implementing fundamental change.

In the end, however, Gorbachev too paid a high price. The hard-line defenders of the Communist system rose up against him in August 1991, much as they had against Khrushchev twenty-seven years earlier, right down to beginning their coup while the leader was on vacation on the Black Sea. Once again, they acted for much the same reason: change had gone too far; the reformer had to be removed to save the system. Once again, I had the good fortune to be a correspondent in Moscow watching the drama unfold.

This time was different, of course. Boris Yeltsin defiantly stood on a tank, and the nation supported him in defeating the hard-line attempt to turn the clock back toward Stalinism. Russia had changed too much over the past three decades for the old medicine to work. After the failed coup, not even Gorbachev could save communism or himself. He lost power, and the Soviet system he had led collapsed underneath him.

The claims that communism could somehow be strengthened, or even saved, were at last all seen to be without any foundation. Brezhnev had proved communism could not survive without reform. Gorbachev proved communism could not survive with reform. The fatal contradiction had finally been confirmed, once and for all. Communism was damned if it reformed and damned if it didn't. That same contradiction ultimately doomed the entire world movement. It killed communism in the Soviet Union. And without the U.S.S.R's driving force, communism elsewhere in the world lay terminally ill, destined to follow the Soviet model into the grave.

In the process, the collapse established this iron rule: sooner or later every Soviet-bloc nation has to choose between communism and reform. None of them can have both. Reform communism is an unworkable contradiction in terms.

It doesn't really matter which leader starts which reform with which tactics. Burdened by an unworkable economic system, every Communist regime reaches a crisis where it must reform or perish. And whatever reform is reluctantly handed down from the top only increases the public hunger for further progress toward both economic and political freedom. Eventually the pressure for change reaches revolutionary strength. At that point, either the regime declares war on its own people and forces them back to servitude, in a massive bloodbath, or it gives up and lets the revolution from below sweep communism away. The crucial question is always the same: how ruthless are communist leaders willing to be with their own people in order to save the system?

Only China so far, in Tiananmen Square, has been willing to slaughter its own citizens to save communism when a showdown came, but even that brutal massacre is likely to be only a temporary stay of execution for Communist rule in Beijing. It did nothing to resolve the inherent contradictions of the system, which continue to water the seeds of rebellion. China's approach has been economic reform only, replacing Marxism-Leninism with market Leninism, yet there is no way political reform there can be held off indefinitely. Inevitably, opposition will rise until communism is defeated in China too, perhaps soon after the current aged leadership passes from the scene.

In Eastern Europe, the leaders went the other way when the crunch came. They preferred to let the system collapse with the Berlin Wall rather than prolong it through a mass murder of their own people.

Even the Soviet Union's hard-liners made that choice. In August 1991, when thirty thousand people rallied to Yeltsin's side, risking their lives to stop tanks with only their bodies, coup leaders could not bring themselves to fire on their own people to save the Communist system. Instead, they gave up the ghost. Soviet communism collapsed.

Democracy did not win in Russia in August 1991. Communism lost. The distinction is vital.

The Russian people agreed on what they opposed. They were against a return to hard-line communism. But they have yet to agree on what they are for. The political struggle for Russia's soul continues, the age-old battle between the forces of repression and the forces of reform that has raged from the days of Tsar Peter the Great to Gorbachev. The ultimate outcome remains uncertain.

Nonetheless, the basic choices Russia faces are clear already. Yeltsin or a reformist successor may yet establish a lasting democratic, free-market society, competing economically and cooperating politically in a peaceful world. Or a conservative rival may reimpose the iron fist, this time without communism's unworkable economic system or discredited ideology. A new nationalist, militarist, or fascist dictatorship could emerge that again makes Russia an aggressive nuclear threat to the world.

One way or another, Moscow is poised to play a superpower role again by the early years of the next century. Russia's assets include two-thirds of the territory of the former Soviet Union, half its 280 million population, most of its mineral wealth, nuclear arms, and conventional military might. A highly educated elite has shown itself capable of outdoing the West, as when it orbited the first man in space, Yuri Gagarin. Freed from subsidizing a bankrupt Soviet empire, freed from communism's hopeless economic dead end, the new Russia alone has more territory, more natural resources, more economic potential, and more military power than any other country in Europe by far, including the newly reunited Germany.

Clearly the West has a vital interest in helping the new Russia make democratic reform irreversible and avoiding the outbreak of a second Cold War. Unfortunately, past Western attempts to influence Russian policy inspire little confidence. As subsequent chapters will make clear, the historical record is full of missed opportunities and serious mistakes. Whether the West can learn from past errors in time to help Moscow avoid a return to dictatorship is already very much in doubt. If the United States misses this chance, there may not be another one.

Moscow and Paris, 1992–1995

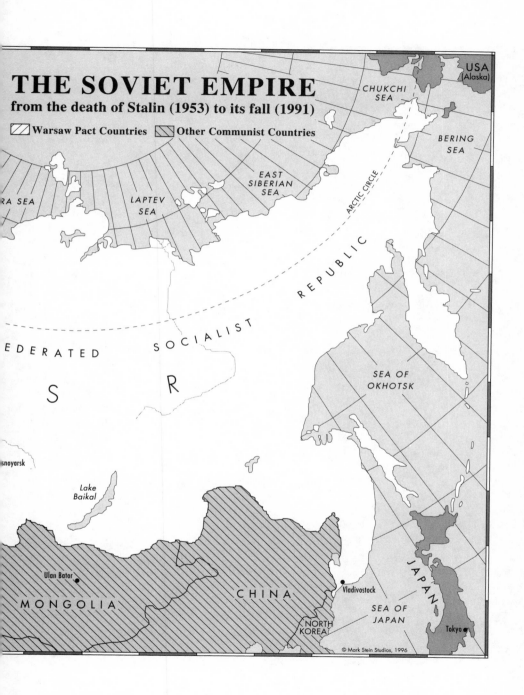

THE SOVIET EMPIRE
from the death of Stalin (1953) to its fall (1991)

Warsaw Pact Countries   Other Communist Countries

CHUKCHI
SEA

USA
(Alaska)

BERING
SEA

EAST
SIBERIAN
SEA

LAPTEV
SEA

RA SEA

ARCTIC CIRCLE

REPUBLIC

SOCIALIST

EDERATED

S   R

SEA OF
OKHOTSK

snoyarsk

Lake
Baikal

JAPAN

Ulan Bator

MONGOLIA   CHINA   Vladivostock

SEA OF
JAPAN

NORTH
KOREA

Tokyo

© Mark Stein Studios, 1996

PART I

Nikita Sergeyevich Khrushchev

(1953–1964)

1

The October Surprise

Nikita Sergeyevich Khrushchev bubbled with confidence that morning. He knew the date, October 12, 1964, would be historic. The Soviet Union had just launched the first spacecraft carrying an entire crew. Three Russian cosmonauts orbited the earth in a huge, new-generation satellite called *Voskhod* ("Sunrise"). Their flight dramatized their country's lead over the United States in the race to land the first man on the moon. For months, perhaps even years, smaller American satellites would still be able to launch only one astronaut at a time.

Communism was beating capitalism to the frontiers of outer space. The Communist system was showing the whole world its technological superiority. Khrushchev could hardly contain his excitement. This was the sort of moment he lived for. As usual, he alone expected to congratulate Russia's latest space heroes. It was his right as the undisputed leader of the Soviet Communist Party and government. Then, suddenly, strange things began to happen.

Impatiently, Nikita Sergeyevich[1] ordered a radiotelephone link established from his luxurious vacation dacha on the Black Sea to the orbiting spacecraft. Soviet journalists crowded into his ground-floor study to record the scene. When Khrushchev finally got the connection, he greeted the cosmonauts with characteristic gusto, promising them "a welcome stronger than the force of gravity" when they returned to earth. The bald, rotund Soviet leader smiled and joked nonstop for the cameras. Then, apparently still playing the clown, Khrushchev told the cosmonauts: "I am handing the telephone to Anastas Ivanovich Mikoyan. He is literally tearing the receiver out of my hand, and I cannot deny him."

To millions of Soviets listening to the radio or watching television, it seemed to be just another bit of exuberant Khrushchev horseplay, one more emotion-charged exaggeration at a triumphant moment. They should have known better. After all, who ever dared grab a telephone from Josef Stalin?

Only one small group of men in the Kremlin knew exactly what the

3

gesture meant when Mikoyan took control of that phone. Nikita Khrushchev had just spoken his last words in public.

Anastas Mikoyan was president of the Soviet Union. It was a ceremonial post. His real power came as one of the eleven members of the Soviet Communist Party's ruling Politburo,[2] the most important men in the country, including Khrushchev himself. The Politburo made all the key decisions, without any of the inconveniences facing democratic governments, like a parliamentary opposition or an investigative press. The Soviet Politburo was a law unto itself. It ran the Communist Party and the Soviet government, the army and the KGB secret police, the parliament, the press, the courts, and everything else in the U.S.S.R., down through a chain of command of privileged officials known as the *nomenklatura*. The unswerving loyalty of all such subordinates was assured by rewards—access to special stores, hospitals, and dachas—if they did what they were told, and the threat of prison or worse if they stepped out of line.

No Soviets said no to the Politburo. Whatever the Politburo majority wanted, it got, including the power to say which of its members would be the top leader, the first secretary of the Party.[3] That job was now held by Nikita Sergeyevich, who thought he would keep it for life. There was no legal restriction on his term of office. He had long ago outfoxed his enemies and replaced them in the leadership with his own loyal supporters. Only the Politburo could challenge Khrushchev, and no one there was strong enough for that, he thought. His closest colleagues were about to prove him wrong.

They had sent Mikoyan down to the Black Sea with Khrushchev to keep an eye on him. Some of the Kremlin's most ambitious rising power brokers needed their boss on vacation and out of the way for two weeks, while they stayed in Moscow and put the finishing touches on a secret plot to get rid of him.

Mikoyan was the ideal choice to accompany the leader, for one simple reason: Nikita Sergeyevich trusted Mikoyan. They had been close political colleagues for many years and were also intimate personal friends. They lived next to each other in government mansions on Moscow's Lenin Hills. Even their sons were good friends.

More important, Mikoyan was also the ultimate survivor. It took consummate skill at political maneuvering to last through Stalin's bloodiest purges, as he did, and serve a record thirty years in the Politburo. Admirers said he could walk between the raindrops and not get wet. Critics thought that only a ruthless set of priorities had kept him in the top leadership for so long. Anastas Ivanovich knew better than most when friendship had to be cast aside in the interest of political survival. Mikoyan had always known how and when to adjust his personal position to accommodate coming political change. October 1964 was no different. He knew Khrushchev had to go. So he would help the plotters keep Nikita Khrushchev in the dark until they were ready, then escort his old friend back to Moscow to the closed-door Kremlin meeting that would end the Khrushchev era. That was what the Politburo wanted. And Anastas Mikoyan was too good an old Bolshevik to disappoint the Politburo.

I was a young journalist in Moscow at the time, having arrived only three weeks before. Since then, I had managed to see Khrushchev up close twice, once at a diplomatic reception when he sought out a group of Western correspondents to announce that the Soviet Union had a powerful new missile "which can hit a fly in the sky," and a second time at an airport ceremony for departing President Sukarno of Indonesia at the end of an official visit. Like virtually everyone else on the planet, I had often seen Nikita Sergeyevich on television. Now at least I had seen a bit more than that. His boundless energy and robust health for a man of seventy, his sharp tongue, and his supreme confidence were even more impressive in the flesh. I had no idea at the time that my first two glimpses of Khrushchev in power would turn out to be my last.

On Monday, October 12, I wasn't even thinking about him. Like my older, more experienced colleagues, I was chasing the wrong story. All of us were scrambling for clues to what the space mission meant. Tass, the official Soviet government news agency, announced only that it would be "a long flight." But how long? What would the cosmonauts try to accomplish? Would one of them exit from the orbiting satellite by umbilical cord and become the first man to walk in space? How far ahead of the Americans were they? When would the Soviets try to land a man on the moon?

As usual, no responsible official would answer. The Soviet space program was so secret in 1964 that rocket liftoffs were never shown on television, no foreigner had ever visited the launch center at Baikonur, and its top scientist was known only as "the chief designer"; his name was officially classified as a state secret.[4] Any Soviet citizen leaking unauthorized information on the space program risked a death sentence on treason charges. So, not surprisingly, security held. All foreign correspondents in Moscow that October 12 spent a frustrating day digging fruitlessly for additional scraps of information on the latest space success. No one had time to think about Khrushchev. Indeed, there seemed to be no earthly reason to worry about him.

As he relaxed at his magnificent villa on the Black Sea near Pitsunda, fifteen hundred miles southeast of Moscow, the vacationing Khrushchev could be forgiven for feeling confident. Over the years he had outmaneuvered his great political rivals—Georgi Malenkov, Vyacheslav Molotov, Lavrenty Beria, Nikolai Bulganin, and all the other heirs of Stalin who at one time or another became pretenders to the throne. Nikita Sergeyevich had long ago mastered the art of keeping various factions at each other's throats and himself on top, all without spilling more blood. Once secure in the leadership, he had ended Stalin's terror, the purges that had killed more than twenty million Soviet citizens, and already assured himself a place in history. But there was still much more to do.

At Pitsunda, Khrushchev enjoyed the finest estate in the Soviet Union. I was one of the few foreign journalists ever allowed to see it.[5] Pine forests and a ten-foot-high concrete wall sealed off the huge seafront property from prying eyes. Hidden behind the walls were several guesthouses, each too far away to be seen through the trees from its neighbors. The main house, a two-story mansion, contained priceless oriental rugs, a Japanese garden on the roof, and an elevator running up an outside wall. Nearby was a glass-enclosed swimming pool where, in good weather, the roof slid away at the touch of a button to permit bathing in the open air. Telephones were fixed to trees along the garden paths where Nikita Sergeyevich liked to walk. Great care was taken to please his every whim. Pitsunda gave him time to think, and it was there that he dreamed up some of his more ambitious ideas for further reform.

Surely, Khrushchev thought, he would have the time he needed. For one thing, his mastery of foreign policy strengthened his grip on the levers of power at home. The onetime uneducated peasant boy now traveled the globe as a leading statesman of the post–World War II era, meeting and often outsmarting men like Tito and Mao, Adenauer and de Gaulle, Eisenhower and Kennedy, Churchill and Eden, Nehru and Nasser.

The toadies and the flatterers around Nikita Sergeyevich easily convinced him he was irreplaceable. No one else in the Kremlin carried the weight he did abroad in keeping the capitalist, Communist, and Third World troublemakers from getting out of hand. To a large extent, the security of the Soviet state depended on Khrushchev, or so they told him. It was a familiar pattern of ambitious younger men ingratiating themselves with a powerful older leader. Earlier, Nikita Sergeyevich himself had been one of the toadies, calling Stalin the indispensable man. Yet despite that experience, Khrushchev did not see through the flattery when he was on the receiving end.

Moscow's foreign community certainly believed Khrushchev to be solidly in charge. Embassy experts reported him in excellent health, and politically strong enough to get out in front of his Politburo and drag it toward meaningful economic reform. Henry Shapiro of United Press, the dean of foreign correspondents in Moscow with some thirty years of experience covering the Kremlin, had written earlier in the fall of 1964: "Seldom before has the mantle of supreme Soviet power rested more firmly and securely on the holders of one man than it does today on the former coal miner Nikita Sergeyevich Khrushchev. Confident of the loyalty of his subordinates . . ."

Such was the conventional wisdom of the day. And it was deliberately orchestrated by Kremlin disinformation specialists. How better to lull the leader to sleep and prepare for a Kremlin palace coup?

On the morning of October 12, 1964, when powerful gas rockets lifted the seven-ton *Voskhod* spacecraft into orbit, everything seemed normal. As always, Khrushchev's name and face were all over the state-controlled Soviet press. A huge color portrait of Nikita Sergeyevich, more than three stories high, stood on an upper balcony of the Moskva Hotel, looking down over the Kremlin and Red Square nearby. Khrushchev's image was literally dominating the center of Soviet power. No one could doubt he was still in charge. But was he?

The next day, Tuesday, October 13, was so bizarre that some people began to wonder. Suddenly, without explanation, the spacecraft returned to earth. The officially announced "long flight" had lasted only one day.

A new communiqué said the flight had gone according to plan. Nobody believed that. Even the cosmonauts themselves were surprised by the order to return to earth so soon. *Izvestia,* the Soviet government newspaper, proved that in a most extraordinary passage. The newspaper carried the text of the conversation between the cosmonaut pilot, Vladimir Komarov, and the anonymous "chief designer" running the ground control station at Baikonur. Komarov vigorously protested the decision to bring the *Voskhod* back, repeatedly seeking permission to continue the flight. Finally, the chief designer told him, paraphrasing *Hamlet,* "There are more things between heaven and earth, Horatio, than are dreamt of in your philosophy. Come down!"

Foreign correspondents chewed on that one, over and over again. Did it mean there was something technically wrong with the spacecraft? Had experts on the ground monitoring the cosmonauts' health found one of them ill? Or could it mean something involving Khrushchev himself? *Izvestia,* after all, was run by his son-in-law, Aleksei Adzhubei. Was the paper giving out a subliminal hint of a power struggle in the Kremlin? Indeed, if no one was in charge at the moment, that would be ample reason to bring the spacecraft back early. That sort of speculation was much too far-fetched to report—yet. But other curious developments were just beginning to make it seem plausible.

Among them was the strange experience of Gaston Palewski, France's minister for atomic energy. Palewski had been invited by Khrushchev to the dacha at Pitsunda at 11:00 A.M. on October 13, for talks, to be followed by lunch. They had plenty to discuss. Palewski was paving the way for a visit to the Soviet Union by President Charles de Gaulle, which the Kremlin saw as an opportunity to woo France away from NATO. Yet, despite the importance of the meeting, Khrushchev cut it back to the bare minimum, risking rude insult to the oversensitive French.

The Russians belatedly informed Palewski that his meeting with Khrushchev had been moved up to 9:00 A.M. Lunch was out, they explained, because Nikita Sergeyevich had to rush back to Moscow to greet the returning cosmonauts. The talks themselves were restricted to half an hour, an appalling discourtesy to an important foreign visitor. With translation, there was hardly time to get started. Furthermore, even within that short time, the Soviet leader left the room on more than one occasion to confer privately with his aides, offering apologies and the excuse that the *Voskhod* was about to land any minute. That was nonsense. In fact, the spacecraft did not return to earth until 10:57 A.M., nearly ninety minutes after the Palewski visit ended. Khrushchev had felt compelled to leave the room to discuss some other priority.

Still, despite the unusual behavior, Palewski received no direct hint that Khrushchev's leadership was in danger. Told that de Gaulle was in good health, Nikita Sergeyevich had replied to the French minister, "Yes, only death can wrest a statesman from his work." Clearly, Khrushchev expected to continue in power as long as he lived. Outwardly, he was still supremely confident with Palewski, his last foreign visitor. In fact, later that same day, Khrushchev would fly back to Moscow to fight for his political life.[6]

The next day, Wednesday, October 14, foreign correspondents in Moscow at last began to grasp the truth. We noticed long lines of official limousines arriving at the gray headquarters building of the Communist Party Central Committee near the Kremlin on Moscow's Staraya (Old) Square. Ominously, no Central Committee meeting had been announced, or even rumored, in the preceding week. A secret session there meant only one thing—a political crisis.

Incredibly, in 1964, Soviet leaders still acted like conspirators. After nearly half a century of Communist power, they remained so insecure that they continued to hide from their own people. Secrecy was an obsession. They raced around Moscow in special central traffic lanes, at twice the speed limit, in the backseats of black limousines, with white curtains drawn across rear windows so that no one could see who was in which car.

So afraid were they of assassination—and with reason—that their only public appearances came before select audiences rigorously screened by KGB security checks. They knew that in a country with no meaningful elections, the only real threats to their power and privilege were an assassin's bullet and the maneuvers of their colleagues. And of the two, Communist intrigues were by far the more threatening. As a result, the men who drew curtains even to conceal their routine trips around town grew increasingly careful as the risks rose. By definition, the greater the secrecy, the higher the political stakes. Any hurried, unannounced meeting of the Central Committee was a sure sign of an imminent political showdown.

In those days the Central Committee convened only twice a year or so, and only to discuss the most significant issues. The 169 voting members who assembled on October 14 included all the key Party, government, military, police, and regional leaders from all over the country. Their sessions, known as plenums, were always called to ratify important policy decisions taken earlier by the Party's highest authority, the eleven-member Politburo. Plenums met behind closed doors. No photographers were admitted; none of the debates were publicly released. Usually there would be a terse official announcement, giving only the date of the plenum, the main topic (for example, agriculture), and the keynote speaker, most likely Khrushchev.

This time even the plenum itself went unannounced. Almost certainly that meant it had been called to discuss changes in the top Kremlin leadership in the strictest secrecy. Either Khrushchev would remove the foot draggers in the Politburo who were slowing his latest reforms, or they would get him first. The initial signs were unmistakable. Khrushchev himself would be the loser.

Kremlinology is far from an exact science, but sometimes it provides clues that can have only one credible explanation. The next day, Thursday, October 15, was one of those times. That morning's official Soviet newspapers carried no photographs of Khrushchev, no quotation of his words, no mention of his name. One day after a secret Central Committee meeting probably called to discuss leadership changes, there was no mention of the most important man in the country in the state-controlled press.

Nor was that all. The president of Cuba, Osvaldo Dorticos, was in Moscow that day. He clearly expected to see Khrushchev. On arrival at the airport, Dorticos said he was looking forward to an exchange of views "with our dear friend Nikita Sergeyevich Khrushchev." Instead, the Cuban got a lunch in the Kremlin with all the members of the Politburo—or almost all. An official announcement listed every single member as having attended the lunch except Khrushchev and the ailing Frol Kozlov. No explanation was given for the top leader's absence.

Other signs, even more persuasive, pointed in the same direction. Messages of congratulations on the space triumph from the Communist Party leaders of Eastern Europe appeared in the Soviet press that Thursday. They were addressed "to the Central Committee" collectively, rather than to Khrushchev personally, as in the past. In fact, a check of the East European press, which carried the texts of the original messages, showed they had indeed been addressed to Khrushchev personally, as before. Russian censors had changed them in Moscow. There was no explanation. But by now, little explanation was needed.

Still, correspondents had to tread carefully. There had been no official confirmation of Khrushchev's removal, only Kremlinological tea leaves pointing in one unmistakable direction. Careful writing was essential. Only six months before, a correspondent for the West German news agency DPA had been expelled from Russia for reporting that Khrushchev was dead. Errors in stories about the Soviet leadership could be costly. That Thursday morning I wrote a low-key seven-paragraph story for the Associated Press, pointing out Khrushchev's mysterious absence from the Dorticos lunch and other indications that it was time to think the unthinkable.

That piece was quickly overtaken. Within hours, Victor Louis, a Soviet journalist with strong KGB connections, broke the real story to the world. Citing only anonymous Soviet sources, Louis reported in the *London Evening*

News that Khrushchev had been replaced by Brezhnev as Party leader and by Aleksei Kosygin as prime minister. Later that same day, East European embassies in Moscow, briefed by Soviet officials, told their correspondents the same thing. By nightfall, every foreign journalist in Moscow was reporting the leadership change. Still, there was no official Soviet announcement.

Moscow was misty that night. But a few minutes after 10:00 P.M., workmen were seen high up the front wall of the Moskva Hotel, opposite the Kremlin, removing the huge portrait of Nikita Sergeyevich. No further official confirmation was needed. The Khrushchev era was over.

Countless times throughout the night, the same operation was repeated. Portraits of Khrushchev came down from the walls of every Party or government office, court of law, factory, farm, school, hospital, army base, police station, and other public building in the world's largest state, a nation so vast that when the sun is setting on its West European border, a new day is already dawning on its East Asian border, eleven time zones and six thousand miles away. In that one night alone, tens of thousands of Khrushchev portraits came down and tens of thousands of Brezhnev and Kosygin portraits went up, in a tribute to the manpower and efficiency of the Soviet secret police, the KGB.

On Friday morning, October 16, two days after the event and one day after the rest of the world had been informed, the Kremlin finally announced the change to its own people. A brief communiqué in *Pravda*, the voice of the Communist Party, said that at a plenum of the Central Committee on October 14, Khrushchev had resigned his posts as Party leader and premier because of "advancing age and deteriorating health." It added that Brezhnev and Kosygin had been elected in his place. Photographs of the two new leaders, retouched to make them look younger, appeared on *Pravda*'s front page. All other Soviet newspapers carried identical coverage. There was nothing else.

There was not one word of thanks to the man who had ended Stalin's terror and led the country for more than a decade, and no word from the man himself or his successors. There was simply nothing. It was also the last time Khrushchev's name would appear in the Soviet press until his death. Henceforth, his ouster would be mentioned only obliquely as "the October plenum."

For months thereafter, Nikita Sergeyevich seemed to have disappeared from the face of the earth. Then it was learned he had been given a small dacha near Usovo, outside Moscow, a pension of $513 a month or roughly four times the average industrial wage of the day, two bodyguards, and a medium-sized official car, a Volga. Finally, on March 14, 1965, exactly five months to the day after his fall from power, Khrushchev appeared in the capital again for the first time as a private citizen. He came to vote in a parliamentary election, and he caused a minor sensation.

Nina Petrovna, Khrushchev's wife, had already been seen in Moscow sev-

eral times. She had taken a fifth-floor apartment on Starokonyushenny (Old Stable) Lane, next to the Canadian embassy, for shopping trips to Moscow. A source in the building tipped me that she had again come in to spend the night of March 13. There seemed to be a chance that Nikita Sergeyevich himself would appear the next day to vote. I got to the building at 6:00 A.M., just in case, and was not disappointed.

Khrushchev showed up at 9:50 in a chauffeur-driven black Volga, with a bodyguard next to him in the backseat. The former leader smiled and waved as he entered the building. Word soon spread that Nikita Sergeyevich was back. And by the time he reappeared from the building a half hour later with his wife, in order to go vote, a crowd of some seventy ordinary citizens had gathered outside. As soon as they saw him, the crowd broke into applause. It was the only spontaneous demonstration I ever saw in my first six years in the Soviet Union. All others were organized by Communist authorities.

Nikita Sergeyevich had tears in his eyes from the warm reception. I had time to shout out only one question—how did he feel? "Like a pensioner, okay," Khrushchev replied. Then he got back into the car and drove off to vote. His emotional ordeal was far from over. The car took him to 39 Herzen Street, two blocks from the Kremlin, where he had often voted as premier. This time, the only candidate on the ballot was the man who had succeeded him in that office, Kosygin.

Khrushchev climbed the stairs to the second floor and approached a low-ranking woman official seated at a desk. It was her job to check the identification papers of each voter before handing over the ballot.

She looked up at him—him—still the most famous face in the nation by far—and asked: "Name?"

"What's the matter?" Khrushchev replied. "Don't you trust me?"

"You know the rules," she snapped back, without a trace of a smile. The tone she used would have been more appropriate for addressing a village drunk.

Here was the man whose picture had appeared in almost every Soviet newspaper almost every day for eleven years. Here was the man who had made every major decision in the nation. Here was the man who used to fix elections just like this one by personally approving the one candidate allowed to run unopposed for each office. No matter. Like everyone else, even Nikita Khrushchev had to produce his identification papers on the demand of a bottom-level clerk. In the Soviet Union, the public humiliation of former leaders has no limits.

Khrushchev had no choice. He had to identify himself in order to vote for one of the men who had ousted him from power. Then he had to return to the countryside, to his enforced retirement, to live out his days under the watchful eyes of the KGB, with no chance to engage in any further political activity, to speak out in public, or even to answer his critics directly. They accused him of harebrained scheming and weakening the world Communist movement, but he could never reply with his side of the story, not in the U.S.S.R.

The former Soviet leader had already lost weight. His shirt collar, now two sizes too large, sagged around his neck. The old bounce was gone. Instead, he walked slowly, with a new stoop. Less than half a year into retirement, Nikita Sergeyevich's appearance had actually begun to suggest "advancing age and deteriorating health," the fabricated reasons for getting rid of him.

Khrushchev took his enforced retirement badly. At first he sat motionless in a chair for hours on end, unable to hold back the tears. "Grandpa is crying all the time," his young grandson told schoolmates. Later, however, he recovered some of his old vigor, defending his record in memoirs smuggled to the West. In the end, Nikita Sergeyevich knew he had made a great difference. "They were able to get rid of me simply by voting," he said with pride. "Stalin would have had them all arrested."[7]

There was ample justification for such pride. As a direct result of Khrushchev's efforts, the losers in Kremlin power struggles no longer got arrested and shot. Instead they retired on pensions generous in Soviet terms. Nikita Sergeyevich's own peaceful retirement confirmed that he had indeed ended the Stalinist terror, not only for his own era, but for his successors as well. Never again would the Soviet Union suffer another blood purge. Khrushchev's twilight years on pension thus became a living symbol of the historic sea change he had brought to Russia. In that sense, they were his crowning achievement.

2

Stalin's Legacy

I. THE KEY

For all its high drama, Nikita Khrushchev's humiliating forced retirement evoked little sympathy from his fellow countrymen. Some still hated him for carrying out Stalin's blood purges in the Ukraine long before becoming a reformer. Others resented his privileged treatment, continuing in retirement after his political disgrace, with a larger home and pension and a chauffeur-driven car that no average Russian would ever attain. Most of all, however, ordinary Soviet citizens rarely gave Khrushchev another thought, simply because they had more important things to worry about than a has-been who could no longer affect their lives.

The same week that Khrushchev fell from power, Communist China test-fired its first atomic bomb. From then on, the danger of a nuclear war with China got a lot more attention in the Soviet Union than the fate of the former Kremlin leader. Still, even that was not the worst problem. Far more worrying to most Russians was the continuing specter of Stalinism. Nuclear war with China was only a future possibility. Stalinism was still an everyday reality.

Khrushchev had ended the mass terror, but other instruments of Stalin's harsh rule remained in place, among them the KGB secret police and the Gulag prison camp system. From 1964 on it would be up to Khrushchev's successors to decide whether to push ahead toward further reform or backtrack toward more repression. No other issue was more important to Soviet citizens, and yet, for the next two decades, they would be powerless to influence the choice. Such was the awesome reach of Stalin's legacy. It would scar generations born after the dictator's death.

In the end, Stalinism stood out as the definitive factor for all seventy-four years of Soviet rule. After the 1917 Bolshevik Revolution, Stalin became the architect of every essential element in the Soviet system, from the command economy to the collectivization of agriculture to police state repression to relentless military buildup. Along the way, Stalin created the superpower that first subjugated Eastern Europe, then threatened the rest of the world with nuclear weapons. Long after he died, right up to the collapse of the U.S.S.R in 1991, Stalin was still defining the internal Kremlin power struggle. Mikhail Gorbachev was determined to do away with Stalin's legacy and his conservative opponents were committed to preserving it, both in the name of saving communism.

Thus Stalin was always the key to understanding the Soviet Union. His thirty-year reign became the single most important influence on all subsequent Soviet behavior. Among other things, the Stalinist legacy explained why Soviet leaders and their people often thought and acted differently from much of the rest of humanity. After all, no other country had lived directly under Stalin's rule. That unique Stalinist experience, and its significance down to the present day, needs to be examined in order to put all subsequent issues of Soviet history into the proper context.

The continuing leadership struggle in Moscow was a paramount part of the Stalinist legacy because in the Soviet Union the men at the top decided everything. Whether they led the country toward more Stalinism or less was the fundamental choice that determined every other policy decision. Khrushchev, for example, steered the nation through the first "de-Stalinization," the hallmark of his years in power and a trend abruptly halted after his fall. Khrushchev's removal was therefore a landmark in Soviet history, one reason this book starts with his fall.

Nevertheless, focusing on the leadership level cannot fully illuminate Stalin's definitive importance. That approach omits the other crucial aspect of his legacy—the suffering he imposed on the Soviet people. Indeed, Stalinism is often best explained by its innocent victims, such as my friend Alyosha Arens, rather than by the maneuvers of Soviet leaders. Only at the individual human level can the full extent of the Stalinist legacy begin to be understood.

II. ALYOSHA

Alyosha Arens never knew his father, but that was only the start of a lifelong Soviet tragedy.

By all accounts Alyosha's father, Jean Lvovich Arens, was an exceptional man. Brilliant and cultured, Jean Lvovich mastered foreign languages as effortlessly as he played the piano or charmed superiors in the Communist Party. His rapid climb in the service of the Soviet state seemed to have no limit. Stalin first sent him to Paris as a counselor in the Soviet embassy, then promoted him to a senior post in the foreign ministry in Moscow, then sent him abroad again, as Soviet consul general in New York. In America, Arens and his attractive young wife, Yelena Nikolayevna, lived the sort of fairy-tale life most Russians cannot imagine. They had a magnificent apartment, a generous expense account, and the finest clothes, and socialized with the lions of world capitalism. The black-tie life of caviar and champagne lasted until 1937, when Stalin ominously ordered Arens home for reassignment.

The purges were already well advanced, and friends urged the Russian diplomat to remain abroad. He would not hear of it. "They wouldn't dare touch me," Jean Lvovich told his anxious friends. "I know too much." Certain he was safe, and headed for higher things, Arens and his wife returned to Moscow. Like millions of other Russians who thought they understood Stalin, Jean Lvovich was wrong. Within a month of his return, the promising diplomat was fired. He had lived abroad too long, had gotten to know too many foreigners. Stalin no longer trusted him. At age forty-seven, Jean Lvovich no longer had a career. By then Yelena was already pregnant, and the jobless Arens had to live off savings, but compared to what was to come, that was a minor problem.

Alyosha was born in Moscow on June 3, 1937, his mother's thirty-fifth birthday. Jean Lvovich marked the double occasion by arriving at the hospital with a huge bouquet of red roses for his wife. It was the last joyous event of their life together.

The new father was arrested two months later, and was never seen by his family again. His wife, already devastated by his unexplained disappearance, suddenly, incredibly, found herself jailed as well. The Soviet secret police, with their infamous disregard for human suffering, separated Yelena from her infant son, although she was still breast-feeding the baby, and dragged her off to a basement cell in Moscow's Lubyanka prison, where they demanded she denounce her husband as an "enemy of the people." For three days they refused to let her sleep—or nurse her child. The pain in her breasts was excruciating. Still, Yelena never cracked, never signed or even said anything incriminating. So they let her go, and then her agony really began.

As the wife of an "enemy of the people," Yelena could no longer live in Moscow. Never mind that there had been no trial, not even a formal accusation. Arens was already regarded as a convicted criminal, and therefore by law his wife had to live at least 101 kilometers from the capital. So the young woman took her baby son and moved to a village near the city of Kalinin, just over the 101-kilometer limit. She made a living painting toy dolls, struggling to survive. Her only source of emotional support there was her neighbor and new friend Nadezhda Mandelstam, whose husband, the great Russian poet Osip Mandelstam, had also been arrested.[1] The two women consoled each other.

Both had been told the same thing, that the investigation of their husbands' cases was continuing, and that neither prisoner had the right to send or receive letters. There was nothing else—no word about their health, the place in which they were being held, nothing.

The two women did have one concession, however. Every few months they could send parcels of food and warm clothing to their husbands. They knew prisoners were held on starvation diets in freezing cells, so they sacrificed from their minuscule incomes to buy their men as much as possible. Then they rode the train to Moscow and went together to a reception room at the secret police headquarters in Lubyanka. Officers there unwrapped the parcels, checking each item to make sure no weapon or subversive literature was being smuggled in. Only then were the parcels accepted for forwarding to unspecified prison camps.

The difficult round-trip journey took a full day. Nonetheless, the two women made it together as often as they could between 1938 and 1941. They did not know that by 1939 both their husbands were already dead. The police at Lubyanka knew the truth, of course. But they continued the macabre charade for another two years. It allowed them to steal the food and clothing for themselves.

In 1941, the Nazis invaded the Soviet Union. Life for Yelena grew even harsher. Police evacuated her and Alyosha from the embattled Moscow region, giving them only an hour to pack. All their remaining valuables, including a typewriter and a radio, had to be left behind. They sat out the war far from the fighting, in a farm community on the edge of Siberia, so poor, Alyosha recalls, that they had to eat gruel mixed with grass to survive.

Yelena spoke fluent English, German, and French. She tried to make ends meet by giving foreign language lessons, but in the provinces there was little demand for such instruction. Yelena never earned enough to feed her family. Fortunately, Alyosha's uneducated grandmother also lived with them, and she saved the day by telling fortunes for the local peasant women anxious to know whether their menfolk would return from the war alive.

"Yes, your husband will return, but without a leg," Alyosha's grandmother would predict, for example, reading the cards. "Sometimes that would actually happen," he remembers. "Grandma was right often enough to become a local legend, and she earned the money that kept us alive."

After the war, Yelena brought the family back to Moscow, where they lived illegally, moving from friend to friend, one step ahead of the police. She repeatedly wrote authorities demanding news of her husband's fate, only to be told over and over again that he was alive and well but nothing more. Frustrated, Yelena appealed personally to Anastas Mikoyan, a member of Stalin's Politburo, whom she knew she had favorably impressed during his stay at the consulate in New York. "It's not the time to ask such things," Mikoyan wrote back in 1947. "Don't worry. Everything will work out well."

Alyosha believes Mikoyan was secretly in love with his mother and did actually help. Soon after receiving Mikoyan's letter, Yelena was summoned to a registry office. The major in charge there, in a sign of great respect, came out of his office to greet her, then handed over an official permit allowing her and her family to live in Moscow. "Only a telephone call from the

Kremlin could have arranged that," Alyosha says. He thinks it was Mikoyan's doing.

The help was crucial. Once allowed to reside in Moscow, Yelena could support her family by giving language lessons and continue to press her husband's case, although she made no progress for the next nine years. Then in 1956, a month after Nikita Khrushchev's secret speech denouncing Stalin's crimes, justice was finally done—Soviet-style. Yelena received a letter from the authorities saying her husband had been wrongly accused as an "enemy of the people" and was being rehabilitated posthumously.

She was offered a small pension in compensation, then equal to half the average monthly industrial wage. In fact, even that act of belated justice was a lie. The letter said Jean Lvovich had died of pneumonia in 1943. His wife refused to believe it, and continued to write officials, demanding more information.

Another six years went by. Finally, in 1962, twenty-five long years after her husband's arrest, Yelena got another official letter that for the first time told her some of the truth. It said Jean Lvovich had been convicted by a secret military tribunal on January 7, 1938, of spying for foreign intelligence services. The death sentence was carried out the same day by firing squad. Her husband confessed his guilt, the letter claimed, although it now conceded he had been innocent all along. "He must have been tortured into confessing," Alyosha says. Indeed, torture to produce confessions was all too common in 1938 at the height of the purges, but Alyosha has a special reason for his assumption. "If they were capable of inflicting atrocious pain on my mother at a time she was breast-feeding, you can imagine what they did to my father," he explains.

The official Soviet letter contained not one word of remorse for arresting an innocent man, or for his wrongful execution, or for telling his widow for the next two decades that her husband was still alive, or for first misinforming her that he had died of pneumonia five years after his execution.

Nor did the tragedy end there. "The rehabilitation changed nothing," Alyosha says. Yelena died without learning anything more about her husband's fate, and their son continued to suffer punishment for the crimes his father never committed. Even after the authorities conceded that Jean Lvovich had been wrongly accused and punished, Alyosha was still refused university admission. The reason, the authorities told him in classic Stalinist logic, was that his father had been listed as an "enemy of the people."

So instead of the diplomatic career he wanted, Alyosha went to work as a researcher for the *Great Soviet Encyclopedia*. His life's other work—his obsession, really—is finding out more about the father he never knew.

In 1993, at the age of fifty-six, bearded and a grandfather himself, Alyosha Arens hoped the relative freedom of the Yeltsin era would at last open the archives to the truth about his father. At the very least, he expected to be told where Jean Lvovich was buried. Alyosha always suspected his father's remains had been placed in a common grave, along with those of numerous other prisoners, but he had no idea where. Now at last he expected to find out. Alyosha was informed that the dossier on his father's case had been declassified. So he went to the former KGB secret police institute that keeps these archives and asked for the records on his father.

"They told me that if I could pay them in dollars, they would start searching," Alyosha says, "but they gave me no guarantee they would find anything." Alyosha didn't have the dollars to get them started. In the mid-1990s, in what is supposed to be an enlightened era in Russia, Alyosha Arens still cannot even lay flowers on his father's grave. No official will yet tell him where the man is buried.

Alyosha's story is tragic not because it is unusual, but, on the contrary, because it is all too typical. There are millions of stories very much like it, one behind each of the numbing statistics. Stalin routinely executed his innocent countrymen—from the best and brightest of the Soviet Union's generals, political figures, or intellectuals to ordinary farmers, workers, or housewives—without a shred of legality. To this day, the forced confessions produced at the show trials of his prosecutor, Andrei Vyshinsky, remain the definitive travesty of justice. And that was only the beginning. Most of Stalin's victims were either judged at closed trials, like Jean Lvovich, or shot with no trial at all.

Worst of all, and hardest to comprehend, are the numbers. Stalin deliberately murdered more of his own people than any other tyrant in history. Adolf Hitler's slaughter of six million Jews pales in comparison. Even Mao Zedong, who ruled a population five times the size of Stalin's, did not deliberately set out to exterminate as many of his own countrymen.

Eventually, the Soviet Union acknowledged officially that Stalin put to death "no fewer than twenty million" of his own people. Another twenty million Soviet citizens arrested during his reign of terror from 1929 to 1953 managed to survive the slave labor conditions of his prison camps, often with their health damaged and their lives ruined. The horrendous figures are only estimated minimums.[2] No one yet knows for sure how many innocent victims Stalin executed or imprisoned, for too many records have been falsified or lost. But even cautious guesses make the unprecedented scope of his crimes abundantly clear. When he died, preparing yet another blood purge, Stalin left his country as devastated as if he had turned nuclear weapons on his own people.

Nor can the psychological damage begin to be measured. The Soviet people lived in fear of the midnight knock on the door that led to prison and a bullet in the back of the head. One way or another, every Soviet family made Stalin's casualty lists. Even those rare people who never had a relative or close friend arrested carried psychological scars for the rest of their lives. Only in

Stalin's Russia, millions of husbands and wives never talked seriously with each other, so that if one was arrested and tortured, he or she could not incriminate the other.

The physical and psychological pain from Stalin's brutality are incalculable. The forty million or more direct victims killed or imprisoned during his repressions, like Jean Lvovich, suffered unspeakably in ways no statistics can measure. In addition, each left behind loved ones, like Alyosha Arens, whose own lives were painfully scarred by the same injustice, down to the present day.

Stalin's crimes were unprecedented in scope, but his motives thoroughly mundane. There is no mystery about why he escalated his war on his own people. Stalin first seized and consolidated supreme power in Russia by murdering his real and imagined political enemies. Then, increasingly fearful he would be killed in revenge, the dictator expanded his reign of terror to preempt that. Or, as Aleksandr Solzhenitsyn has written, "The more people he destroyed, the more he was oppressed by fear for his own life."[3]

Unfortunately for the Soviet Union and the empire it dominated, Stalin was as clever as he was murderous. His mastery of the state propaganda machine made him known and loved in his lifetime as "the Father of the Peoples," "the Wisest of Teachers," "the Genius of Geniuses," and so on ad nauseum. Stalin had no shame when it came to propagating lies about his godlike qualities. "Paper will put up with anything that is written on it," he once said.[4]

Behind the Kremlin walls, the adored Father of the People was a cold, calculating executioner. He would privately whip his secret police into a frenzy of bloodletting, approve years of their murderous work, then blame them publicly for an excess of zeal and have their chief shot, to the gratitude of his loving subjects. Next he would appoint a new chief of the secret police and start the cycle all over again.

Stalin's split personality, the murderer masked as saint, reached incredible heights of hypocrisy. "In the 1940s, in virtually every home in Moscow, you would find portraits of Stalin," the biologist Zhores Medvedev once told me. "Stalin was adored as a demigod and people were ready to die with his name on their lips." No successor ever won the same public trust or love. In Khrushchev's day as in Brezhnev's, in Gorbachev's day as in Yeltsin's, you could visit a hundred apartments in Moscow and not find one portrait of the leader. Meanwhile, in 1940, while Stalin was publicly adored, he was condemning ten men to miserable jail cells designed for only one or two prisoners, Medvedev said.

By the time ordinary Russians began to understand, it was too late. Stalin's control of all levers of power was complete. No one could stop the madness until the dictator himself died of natural causes. Russians knew any attempt to organize an opposition was hopeless. Their phones were tapped, their steps followed. Secret police agents posed as their neighbors.

Sonya, a Russian friend, once explained to me the common Soviet feeling of helplessness in the face of brutal repression. In the late 1930s, Sonya and her parents lived one floor down from her uncle in the same apartment building. The uncle worked for the secret police, then called the NKVD. One night the uncle came downstairs and arrested her father, his own brother, giving him only an extra five minutes of privacy to kiss his wife and children goodbye. Sonya never saw her father again. He died in Stalin's camps. Still, to this day, she is grateful to the uncle for the extra five minutes, rather than bitter at his treachery. "My uncle had no choice," she told me. "If he had refused to arrest his brother, he would have been shot. And someone else would have arrested my father anyway, with no time for farewells."

Such stories are worth remembering, particularly by those West Europeans who liked to say during the Cold War that Russians and Americans were very similar—the Soviet Union and the United States were both huge countries, both nuclear powers, both leaders of military blocs, both arrogant, and so on. In fact, despite such superficial similarities, Americans and Russians have totally different historical and psychological backgrounds, which make them think and act very differently in similar situations. What American would ever thank his uncle for sending his father to the death house? The truth is the United States does not even remotely resemble Russia, for one simple reason: it has never experienced anything like Stalinism.

III. PHARAOHS

Forty years after the dictator's death, Stalinism remains the central fact of the Soviet experience. As such, its origins, partial dismantling, and continued relevance in post-Communist Russia need further explanation, in order to put the entire Stalinist legacy in perspective. We will look at origins first.

Slaying the Stalinist dragon in Russia would have been easier if it had been some abhorrent exception to the traditional rule. Unfortunately it was nothing of the kind. On the contrary, one thousand years of Russian history show the Stalinist terror to be an extreme version of what passed for centuries as the natural order of things. Despotic tsars like Ivan the Terrible were capable of Stalinist cruelty. Only the lack of modern technical means limited their slaughter to thousands of people rather than millions. Even the relatively few reformers in tsarist days were totally ruthless, among them Peter the Great, who opened Russia to Western ideas and then had his son tortured to death.

The Bolshevik Revolution that swept communism to power in Russia in 1917 claimed to have created a brave new world. In fact, it changed nothing fundamental in Russia's age-old tradition of cruel repression. The tsarist secret police gave way to the Communist secret police. Individual citizens still had no freedom. The new ruling class, this time drawn from the workers and peasants rather than the aristocracy, still enjoyed privileged conditions on the earnings of the exploited masses. Under the commissars, as under the tsars, Russians lived through long eras of repression and short attempts at democratic reform. Up to now, reform in Russia has always faltered, and touched off a new age of repression.

Soviet ideologues and their Marxist soul mates in the West liked to think that Vladimir Ilyich Lenin could have ended all that. To them, Lenin was a visionary, determined to create a benevolent socialist state in Russia when he led his Bolsheviks to power in 1917. His new model was supposed to end the inequalities of capitalism, create new opportunities for the downtrodden masses, and serve as a beacon for the world to follow. They believe that had Lenin not died in 1924, when only fifty-three, he might have succeeded, but instead his successor, Stalin, corrupted and betrayed the revolution's ideals.

Their argument is nonsense. Lenin himself was ruthless, intolerant of opposing ideas, and determined to spill blood. His lifelong credo was to organize a conspiracy that would seize power by force, and those ends justified any means, however brutal. "An oppressed class, which does not learn to use arms, deserves to be treated as slaves," he said.[5] Like the tsars before him, Lenin planted the seeds for Stalin's harvest of terror.

It was Lenin who killed democracy in Russia, not Stalin. In the first and largely forgotten revolution of 1917, in February, progressives forced the last tsar, Nicholas II, to abdicate and hand over power to the first parliamentary democracy in Russian history. Aleksandr Kerensky, the new prime minister, then made two fatal mistakes. He kept the capital in St. Petersburg, the one city in the country where the opposition Bolsheviks could field a significant military force, in effect giving them the opportunity to take over the nation simply by seizing the capital. And he kept Russia in World War I, in the alliance with Britain and France against Germany, despite the certainties of defeat and starvation which that policy brought to Russia. Had Kerensky moved the capital to Moscow, blamed the war on the dethroned tsar, and sued for an early, separate peace, he might well have saved the world the nightmare of Communist power. Instead, he gave Lenin the opportunity of a lifetime.

The Bolshevik leader returned to St. Petersburg from his long exile abroad in April. Lenin arrived on a sealed train conveniently provided by the German enemy, in the hope that he would lighten their war burden. If Lenin could end the combat on their Russian or eastern front, then the Germans could throw all their forces against Britain, France, and America in the west. And that is precisely what happened. As soon as he returned, Lenin rallied public support by promising an immediate end to the war for Russia, land to the peasants, and bread for all.

Lenin struck all the right chords. In October, in the second and decisive revolution of 1917, his Bolsheviks seized the Winter Palace, the seat of government, forcing Kerensky to flee abroad.[6] Russia's initial experiment in democracy was over. As promised, Lenin surrendered to the Germans, taking

Russia out of World War I, but that alone did not buy peace. It took four years of civil war, from 1918 to 1922, for the Bolsheviks, now renamed Communists, to impose their will on the rest of the country and proclaim it the Soviet Union.

It was also Lenin, not Stalin, who began the terror. He did not wait long. In July 1918, the first year of Bolshevik power, Lenin sent the secret telegram from the Kremlin that sealed the fate of Russia's last tsar, Nicholas II, his wife, Alexandra, and their five children, all gunned down in the basement of the house in the Ural Mountains city of Ekaterinburg, where the Bolsheviks held them prisoner.

For seventy years, Soviet authorities protecting Lenin's reputation maintained the fiction that local officials in Ekaterinburg ordered the royal murder, without Lenin's knowledge. Finally in 1987, with Gorbachev's glasnost reforms well under way, Eduard Radzinsky, a leading Russian playwright, exploded that myth.

Radzinsky talked his way into secret state archives, claiming he wanted to research a new play about the Bolshevik Revolution. But once inside, he went instead for the documents that revealed the truth about the last tsar's death. He was the first outsider to read them. "Lenin himself decided the whole royal family had to be killed," Radzinsky told me in a 1990 interview in Moscow. "Lenin gave all the orders." Radzinsky later substantiated that claim in a best-selling book, *The Last Tsar*.

After the death of the tsar and his family, the bloodletting only got worse. Fanny Kaplan, a deranged young woman, shot at Lenin and wounded him, also in 1918. She was executed, and her act was used as the excuse to unleash the first terror wave in Soviet history, taking the lives of thousands of alleged enemies of the revolution. Lenin himself was responsible. Despite poor health, he would remain in charge of the government for the next six years.

In the end, Lenin had a rather low opinion of Stalin, finding him brutal and coarse. In a letter written in December 1922 to a Communist Party congress, Lenin proposed that Stalin be removed from the post of Party general secretary and replaced by someone with "a more considerate attitude toward the comrades, a less capricious temper," but this advice was rejected.[7] In any event, Lenin already had blood on his own hands.

Once again, it was Lenin who created the Soviet political system, not Stalin. "The single-party system and the limitations on democracy connected with it appeared under Lenin," the Russian historian Roy Medvedev told me during a Moscow interview in 1978. "They were elements of late Leninism."

In a word, far from corrupting or betraying Leninism, Stalin simply built on the foundations of terror and tyranny that Lenin laid down. The Soviet system that turned Russia into a superpower and threatened the rest of the world for much of the century was a joint creation of Lenin and Stalin.

Russians acknowledge that fact, as so many others, with a cruel joke. Hitler and Stalin meet in hell, each standing in a pool of blood. Hitler's pool comes up to his neck, Stalin's only to his waist.

"How come?" Hitler asks. "You killed millions more than I did, but there is less blood on you."

"Yes," Stalin admits, "but I am standing on Lenin's shoulders."

Once Lenin died, there was nothing inevitable about what followed. Various potential successors backed different policies. Leon Trotsky favored spreading world revolution as the top priority. Nikolai Bukharin saw relatively liberal economic policies as a key. There were many other views.

Stalin tolerated none of them. It was at this point, only seven years after the Bolshevik Revolution, that Stalin captured and redefined the Soviet system, permanently, in his own image. He alone among the key players had the ruthless cunning to eliminate physically all rivals and take over as head of both the Communist Party and the Soviet government. At the same time, the murderous hand had a clear head. Stalin alone understood the essential priorities of the day and the policies that could most convincingly be sold to the Party's ruling elite. Their support would be needed at the outset to confirm him as Lenin's successor. Ironically, it was Stalin, the foreigner, who knew best what Russia needed most.

He had been born Iosif Dzhugashvili, in the ancient kingdom of Georgia, which became a Soviet republic in 1921. In tsarist days, as a professional Marxist revolutionary, he had changed his name to Stalin—the man of steel. By the time Lenin died, he realized the most important thing was to make the Soviet Union as strong as steel, as quickly as possible.

Stalin knew Russia had always been weak. Over the centuries it had constantly been invaded from all sides—by the Mongols from the east, by the Turks and Persians from the south, and by Napoleon's French from the west, to name but a few—precisely because it had always been so weak. Stalin knew the young Soviet state had to strengthen itself at breakneck speed if it was to repel any future invasion and survive.

So he proposed a policy of "Socialism in One Country." Trotsky's world revolution would be put on hold until the U.S.S.R. was strong enough to support it. Bukharin's liberal economics would be quashed. Instead what was needed was total state control of the economy. Agriculture would be collectivized with unprecedented brutality. Rapid industrialization would be guaranteed by five-year plans, beginning in 1928, to dictate every production decision down to the last nut and bolt, with all resources allocated toward building a war machine, at the expense of consumer goods. The press, the arts, education, and science would slavishly follow Kremlin dictates, all to advance the cause. Even history would be rewritten. And above all, the secret police would be empowered to enforce everything.

Stalin sold "Socialism in One Country" to a Party congress in 1927, without hinting at his ominous hidden agenda. It was a decision the Russian elite would live to regret. Most of the party faithful who voted for the Stalinist line then would be liquidated later in his purges. The dictator had no regrets himself over the blood he spilled. To Stalin, the only important thing was that his single-minded strategy worked. He built the great power he wanted, in record time. Stalin's Soviet Union turned back Hitler's invasion and defeated a Nazi war machine that had been unstoppable. Then, when American forces rushed home after World War II, he seized Eastern Europe as a buffer zone against future attack.

By the time he died in 1953, Stalin had created the largest, strongest empire the world had ever known. It was a nuclear-armed colossus stretching from the Gulf of Finland in the west to the Pacific Ocean in the east, from the Arctic north to the desert sands of Central Asia in the south. It contained one-sixth of the land surface of the globe and one-tenth of the human race. The Roman Empire, at its height, would have been lost in it. The United States, China, and India, all added together, could not fill its space.

Stalin's body was embalmed alongside Lenin's in the mausoleum outside the Kremlin walls on Moscow's Red Square. Their joint resting place became the most hallowed shrine in the Communist world. They were modern-day pharaohs, to be honored forever.

IV. SPITTING ON THE MUSTACHE AND THE BALD ICON

The choice of a tomb as the landmark of communism was ironically appropriate. The system had been built on the corpses of the terror, in the process dooming itself, for no regime that bases its legitimacy solely on terror can survive indefinitely. With Stalin's death, the Soviet system began to unravel. Let us look at that process in some detail.

It was not a simple straight-line transition away from Stalinist repression. Along the way there was a bitter Kremlin struggle over how far to go and how fast to proceed, and a constant risk of backsliding to renewed dictatorship.

Nikita Khrushchev took the first essential step. He finally put a stop to Stalin's madness. Ending the terror was Khrushchev's greatest contribution, the key opening to reform in Communist Russia. Without the death threat from mass blood purges, dissent at last became possible, not only within the Kremlin's ruling Politburo, but also from everyone else.

Naturally, Nikita Sergeyevich never intended to encourage grassroots opposition. On the contrary, he kept the Gulag prison labor camps open to punish common troublemakers. His prime motive in publicly denouncing Stalin's crimes in 1956 and in ending the terror was to save himself and his colleagues in the Kremlin elite from another bloodbath. A second motive was to establish the legitimacy of his own leadership, but unintentionally, Khrushchev also accomplished something far more important. He began to remove the ordinary citizen's worst fears. Dissidents could at last "come out of the closet," as they called going public, now that political opposition no longer meant certain death. Dissent would rise as fear subsided. The process would take another thirty-five years to play out. It could be slowed, but never stopped again. Unintentionally, by ending the terror, by removing fear from the equation, Nikita Khrushchev had begun the long decline and fall of the Soviet empire.

The end of Stalin's terror made possible dissent in many forms. Political activists seeking to organize a democratic reform of Soviet society were a minuscule minority, although eventually an effective one. The far more common face of dissent was displayed by the mass of the population, more timidly at first, but ultimately no less effectively. To millions of Soviet people, the end of the terror meant they no longer had to pretend to believe in the official state ideology and could even begin to defy it openly. Religious worship was but one example.

Decades of repression failed to eradicate the religious faiths practiced in the U.S.S.R.–Christian, Muslim, Jewish. At the same time, Soviet Communists discredited themselves, rewriting and distorting the history books with each leadership change. The Soviet people were determined to find solace in religion, in the eternal truths that communism manifestly lacked. So they practiced their faiths secretly in Stalin's day, until it was safe to do so openly again after the tyrant died.

On its side, the Kremlin never dared close all the churches. That would only have driven religion underground and risked turning it into a political opposition. So instead, token churches were allowed to remain open, continually watched by the KGB, sometimes with the help of priests trained as informers. Through all the suffering, and probably because of it, the Soviet Union remained a profoundly religious country, where millions of people believed more in the God of their choice than in Communist ideology.

Ironically, cramped Soviet living conditions promoted the passing of religious faith from generation to generation. In the cities, most families lived in one room, with Grandma, parents, and children sleeping separately but hardly privately in curtained alcoves. On Sunday, their day off, young working parents wanted to be alone to make love. Grandma would take the toddlers out, to give them privacy. Invariably, she took the children to church.

Similarly, Soviet authorities could never suppress nationalism, although again not from a lack of trying, as we shall see.[8] In the end, religion and nationalism both proved stronger than communism. They survived and now prosper in each of the former Soviet republics where communism died.

More generally, along the entire ideological front, communism never won over the Soviet people. Stalin's repressions discredited it irreparably. His successors could never restore the faith. In the post-Stalin years, leaders cushioned by luxury–lavish country houses, curtained limousines, and caviar by the spoonful–could fool themselves into thinking the system was succeeding.

But the ordinary people knew better. For them the brutal facts of everyday life—arbitrary arrest, starvation diets, deadly pollution, three-generation families crowded into one-room apartments in the cities, outdoor toilets for most homes in the countryside, hospitals operating without anesthetics, endless lies in the newspapers, lives with little individual choice, and no real hope for the future—exposed communism as a sham of empty propaganda promises.

The vast majority of the Soviet people remained passive after Stalin died, unwilling to take risks themselves in pressing for change. Increasingly, however, they were becoming a nation of closet dissidents, waiting for a new leadership to show the way out of the Communist dead end.

Khrushchev understood perfectly well the dangers to the Communist system of letting de-Stalinization get out of hand. So he always tried to keep it a limited exercise. Khrushchev released political prisoners and rehabilitated the good names of Stalin's innocent victims—posthumously, of course. Nikita Sergeyevich no longer had political rivals shot. He even cut military budgets to invest more in the civilian economy, and he flirted briefly with relaxing censorship of the arts. Otherwise he made sure Stalinism continued long after the tyrant died. Under Khrushchev, the Communist Party maintained all its monopoly controls, backed by a repressive secret police.

Khrushchev even stopped short of destroying the Stalin myth entirely. Instead he only downgraded it. As part of this exercise, Khrushchev had Stalin's body removed from the mausoleum it had shared with Lenin. Where both had been honored equally before as the saints of communism, now only Lenin was preserved in the nation's holiest shrine. Stalin's remains were reburied just behind the mausoleum, in a place of honor near the Kremlin wall, next to Feliks Dzerzhinsky, the founder of the Soviet secret police, and a long pantheon of other Soviet heroes. A bust of Stalin's handsome mustached face, mounted on a pedestal, marks the spot. Most days, flowers can still be found on his grave. To this day, no one has fully consigned the Stalin legacy to the dustbin of history.

To Leonid Ilyich Brezhnev, even Khrushchev's limited de-Stalinization risked going too far. Under Brezhnev, the posthumous rehabilitation of Stalin's purge victims virtually ceased. There could be no clearer signal of a change in thinking at the top. In the Brezhnev years, Russians began fearing that a return to Stalinist repression, or re-Stalinization, was a real danger.

It never got that bad. There was no need to restore the mass terror. Brezhnev accomplished what he wanted simply by keeping the threat alive. His KGB secret police, the renamed successors of the Cheka, OGPU, and NKVD, remained above the law, with much of the power of their discredited predecessors. They were the living symbol of Brezhnev's repressive rule, the enforcement machinery he showed the nation he was keeping oiled and ready.

Arrest a few leading dissidents and sentence them to life-threatening conditions in the Gulag, and the rest of the population, still haunted by the Stalinist past, would get the message: toe the line or all is lost. Or so thought the mediocre minds in Brezhnev's Kremlin.

At the same time, other essential elements of Stalin's legacy would remain in place, among them the command economy, the relentless military buildup, the suppression of minority nationalities and individual rights, total control of the media and the arts, even a "Brezhnev Doctrine" to justify continued Soviet domination of Eastern Europe.

Taking yet another page from Stalin's lesson book, they determined to give their narrow repressions a firm legal base. During the second year of Brezhnev's eighteen-year rule, the criminal code was revised to punish "anti-Soviet activities." From then on, anyone who criticized the Soviet leaders or their policies or the system could be locked away in a labor camp or expelled from the country.

Never mind that the new laws did more to discredit the nation abroad than anything the dissidents said or wrote. These laws, regarded in the West as repulsive, served their purpose in Russia, effectively crushing dissent for two decades. The subsequent jailing of Anatoly Shcharansky and Yuri Orlov and the exile of Andrei Sakharov and Aleksandr Solzhenitsyn, to name but a handful of Russia's freest spirits, raised outcries in the West, but disrupted the small dissident movement. Brezhnev proved there was no essential need to re-Stalinize. Simply halting de-Stalinization produced the desired results—at least for a while.

The Soviet people never knew how far back Brezhnev was willing to go to save the system. Even leading intellectuals believed the worst of Stalinism could be revived. I once heard a vivid example of just how strong the specter of Stalinism—past, present and future—remained in the souls of his victims.

Lev Kopelev, the writer, told me the story on March 5, 1978, the twenty-fifth anniversary of Stalin's death. On that date, as they did every year, Kopelev and thirty other former inmates of Stalin's camps gathered in a Moscow apartment to mark the day that enabled their release. By tradition, each of them brought a sample of the food he had missed most while on a prison starvation diet—vodka, a wife's special borscht, apples, even the lowly potato. Also by tradition, they always exchanged little gifts, perhaps a paper model of a watchtower, wood carvings of camp guards, or a cardboard replica of a wheelbarrow or some other tool of forced labor.

The first toast always honored the comrades who had not survived the camps. Also by custom, the second-to-last toast was always raised to the thousands of political prisoners still in the Gulag then, the height of Brezhnev's rule. Finally, they would all stand for a last toast, observe a moment of silence remembering the horrors of Stalin's mass terror, and declare in unison, "Never again should anyone suffer our fate."

Kopelev himself, a huge, bearded bear of a man, believed that another Stalinist terror was indeed all too possible. "The Brezhnev generation won't conduct it," Kopelev told me, "not because they are humane, but because they want to save their asses. They can never forget Stalin, or the fact that once he began the terror no one could turn it off, and no one was safe. The real question is whether we can pass this knowledge to the younger generation with no firsthand experience under Stalin."

"The main prerequisite for mass terror," Kopelev explained, "is fanatical ideological belief. You can always find an executioner, but not the ideological fanatics to support him." Nonetheless, such extreme emotional zeal does exist in the Soviet Union, he said. Already in Brezhnev's day, Kopelev pointed to fanatic nationalists in outlying Soviet republics ready to take up swords against each other and the Russians who oppressed them.

His words were prophetic. By the 1990s, civil war was already the way of life in newly independent Georgia, Armenia, and Azerbaijan. Many of the twenty-five million ethnic Russians who still live there or in other former Soviet republics, from the Baltics to Central Asia, now as a resented minority, fear they could become victims of a new pogrom. The threat that a new nationalist leader on the fringe of the former Soviet empire can mount a terror of Stalinist proportions, possibly with access to nuclear weapons, is now taken very seriously indeed.

A new Stalin terrorizing Russia from the Kremlin cannot be ruled out either, although that is less likely. Thus one potential tragedy of the 1990s is that a new Stalin can emerge from almost anywhere in the former U.S.S.R., and create a nuclear Yugoslavia.

None of this minimizes the truly historic accomplishments of Mikhail Gorbachev and Boris Yeltsin. In a relatively short period, they have largely dismantled the Stalinist system. With great courage and brilliant political maneuvering, each in his own way moved farther and faster than almost anyone thought possible. Their changes look like miracles to anyone who lived in the Soviet Union only ten years ago:

- The Soviet Communist Party, which once exercised absolute control over all political, economic, and ideological levers of power, no longer exists.

- Minority nationalities have set up their own independent countries in former Soviet republics.

- Russia today has a multiparty system, competing candidates for office, and democratic elections.

- The privatization of factories, farms, businesses, and other former state property is the nation's biggest growth industry.

- The press and the arts are largely uncensored.
- The KGB is being tamed, and the military-industrial complex is converting to civilian production.

The list is far from complete. Change impacts every day on every life in countless ways. A rabbi can hold a religious service on the steps of the Russian parliament. A Russian can travel abroad, with his wife. Solzhenitsyn's *The Gulag Archipelago* is sold openly in Russian in Moscow. A Russian woman can buy a bra that actually fits. Stalin would not recognize the place.

Yet there is still a long way to go in the continuing transition from Communist dictatorship to a stable democratic state under the rule of law. Thoughtful Russians are the first to admit that the reforms are far from irreversible.

Among them is my friend Sasha Gorelik, a collector of rare books, who considers himself an optimist. "We never thought we would live without communism. Our children, perhaps, but not us," he told me in 1993. "Look at us now," Sasha continued with pride. "We can spit on the Mustache [Stalin] and the Bald Icon [Lenin]."

Nevertheless, Sasha's optimism is extremely limited. He also worries that there is still a danger of going back. "Until they take Lenin's body out of the mausoleum and bury him in the ground, he will continue to torment us," Sasha says.

V. NEVER AGAIN?

Of course, there are limits to going back. Once published in Russia, Solzhenitsyn cannot be unpublished. Nor would it be any easier to revive the totally discredited Communist ideology. Furthermore, in the day of the personal computer, the fax, and satellite communication, no dictator can again hold his countrymen in total ignorance behind an iron curtain, unable to communicate with or get help from the outside world.

Still, going only part of the way back is bad enough. Russia alone, with a population of 140 million people, and most of the land, resources, and nuclear weapons of the former U.S.S.R., is Europe's most formidable power by far. A new dictator seizing power in Russia, whatever his ideological bent, would be eminently qualified to revive the arms race and launch Cold War II.

One only has to think how much damage a relatively small-time dictator like Saddam Hussein has wrought on a regional level. A new tyrant in the Kremlin would command nuclear weapons and even oil wealth that Saddam does not. Any new dictator in Moscow could first impose his will on former Soviet republics, and then, with a reconstituted population base of some 300 million people, challenge vital Western interests globally. That danger will not fade quickly. The present power struggle in Russia between those who want to press ahead with reforms and those who want to turn the clock back is likely to continue for years.

In the most cynical scenario, the neo-Stalinists might be wiser to wait, let the West pour sufficient aid into Russia to revive the economy, and only then seize power to threaten those very benefactors again. These are the people who believe an idea attributed to Lenin, that "the capitalists will sell the rope to hang themselves."[9]

Millions of Russians, perhaps a majority of the country, would follow a new Stalin seizing power today. They would not want to, but they would say they had no other choice, that after all the reform talk under Gorbachev and Yeltsin, Russia had not fundamentally changed. They would do nothing to oppose a new dictatorship, arguing that they were powerless to stop it, that rebellion is as futile today as it was in Stalin's day or under the tsars. Once again, the ordinary Russian's awesome respect for authority would prevail. These attitudes, which helped create Stalinism in the first place, are still deeply ingrained today.

The great exception was supposed to be August 1991. That was when thirty thousand people surrounded Yeltsin's White House, the Russian parliament, prepared to defend it with their bodies against the tanks seeking to crush democratic reform in a coup d'état. It was a remarkable act of courage, and it worked. However, these people represented only one-third of 1 percent of the population of Moscow. The vast majority of the capital's residents remained at home, tucked safely in their beds, waiting out the crisis, resigned to following whichever side won. To them, dictatorship has been the natural order of things for a thousand years. If a new Stalin had emerged from the August 1991 coup, they would have passively accepted him as their immutable fate.

Today, with the economic promise of the Yeltsin reforms badly tarnished, there is no assurance that anything like thirty thousand people would risk their lives defending him against another coup attempt. At the same time there is absolute certainty that the majority of the Russian people would remain inert.

For proof of that, witness the behavior of the Russian masses in July 1993, year two of the Yeltsin revolution, when the government suddenly declared that all paper money printed before 1993 was no longer any good, and allowed each citizen to change only $35 worth for new bills. This move, designed to curb inflation, confiscated the life savings of millions of ordinary people. Imagine what the reaction would have been in London, Paris, or New York.

Incredibly, there was not one public protest in Moscow. Instead, people lamely lined up at the banks to change the pittance they had been granted. Fortunately for them, Yeltsin later revised the decision, but not from any public outcry. There was none. Once again the Russian people had shown their traditional passivity.

Millions of other Russians, mostly older and admittedly a minority, would rejoice if a new tyrant seized power. These people minimize Stalin's crimes and emphasize his achievements instead. They do so in order to avoid rejecting everything they were taught to believe in for most of their lives. Yes, Stalin made mistakes, they say, as if slaughtering millions of people were a clerical error, but he also turned the Soviet Union from a rural backwater into an industrial giant and a military superpower respected throughout the world, nothing like today's economic ruin with its hand out for Western aid. These people see democratic reform in Russia as a ticket to anarchy, and long for the iron fist of a new dictator to restore stability.

By the summer of 1993, they were gaining supporters, as more and more of their countrymen blamed the Yeltsin reforms for inflation running at 2,000 percent a year, for the fear they would be unable to afford food tomorrow. For these people the economic hardship far outweighed the new freedoms to say and read what they liked. The most constant refrain heard in Moscow from ordinary Russians was "Life was better under Brezhnev."

For still millions of others, mostly younger and another minority, there can be no going back, because there is now too much to lose. In the last decade of struggle they have won the right to demonstrate in the streets, to form opposition parties, to criticize their leaders, to vote for competing candidates, to read uncensored newspapers, to start private businesses, to play rock music, to emigrate, and to hope that their life will get better at home. Their new freedoms run the gamut from the sublime to the frivolous, from unhindered religious worship to topless beaches. They are not prepared to give all that up and let some new dictator turn the clock back. They would fight to retain democratic reforms and a market economy, even if that meant civil war in a country armed with nuclear weapons.

No one yet knows how or when Russia's continuing power struggle will be resolved. Only one thing is certain. Forty years after Stalin's death, his legacy remains *the* issue. Russia's future, well into the next century, will be decided primarily by one question—how much has really changed since Stalin?

Western journalists and scholars have focused up to now on what has changed. They were right to do so. The changes have been colossal. Russians themselves, however, have given equal thought to something just as important—what has not changed since Stalin's day. Understandably, having lived through the nightmare once, they are acutely sensitive to any danger it might return.

As so often before in the past, perceptions differ East and West. The West likes to think that since the collapse of communism in Russia, the transition to democracy and the market economy are assured. Such hopes have been encouraged by constant claims from Yeltsin spokesmen that his government is making democratic reform irreversible. For the most part, however, the Russian people know that is not yet true. Decision-makers in Western governments would do well to listen to them.

The true voice of Russia's anguished soul can be heard almost anywhere in the nation. I often heard it, but most memorably in 1992 on a visit to the Ural Mountains. One day, our helicopter touched down in a region of spectacular natural beauty, where the broad Chusovaya River meanders through hillsides covered in rich green pine and fir trees. Any normal country would have built a lodge there for people to admire the scenery. Stalin built a prison camp, part of his Gulag of slave labor that once interned five million people. The camp was rusted and falling apart. It had been abandoned for thirty years, but my Russian hosts, members of the memorial society formed to aid victims of Stalin's crimes, soon began arguing whether it could all happen again.

"Yes," said Volodya Vinichenko, a Russian writer. "If the economy collapses and a strong hand takes over, we can return to Stalinist repression."

"No," said Sasha Kalikh, a Russian journalist. "Everyone knows about the Gulag now. Every family lost a loved one. Just as the Germans cannot go back to Nazism, we cannot go back to Stalinism."

"But there is still a danger," insisted Volodya. "The authorities can tighten the vise again, little by little."

"We argue about this all the time," admitted Sasha.

So did most thinking Russians in the early 1990s. Deep down, they knew their nation could still turn back toward Stalinism—and soon.

In the balance sheet on Stalin's legacy, that danger has to be the bottom line. His crimes dwarf his considerable achievements. The cost in human life of his ruthless elimination of all potential opposition can never be justified, morally or politically. Nonetheless, something similar could well happen in Russia again. For that reason, all of Stalin's successors, from Khrushchev on, have judged largely on how far they were able to dismantle his repressive system and ensure that it could never be restored. Even today, as Yeltsin's fragile experiment in democracy hangs by a thread, Russians constantly express the hope that there can be no backsliding to the Stalinist past, then betray the very real fear that it can indeed happen again.

Similarly, the United States and its allies have been obsessed for the past half century by another aspect of the Stalinist legacy, the military threat to spread his repressive system globally. They fought the Cold War to contain communism, and now aid Yeltsin's Russia in the hope of preventing a Stalinist revival.

Since the collapse of communism in 1991, prospects have been more hopeful than ever that Stalinism in Russia can be buried for good. But that is far from a sure thing, especially with the 1990s democratic reforms foundering in corruption, crime, and economic chaos. The threat remains that a new dictator will again seize power in Moscow, win public support by promising to restore order, and then reimpose the policies of Stalinist repression at home and military adventurism abroad. Sadly, historical precedent suggests this gloomier outlook will long remain a danger. For most of the past thousand years, the forces of repression in Russia have been stronger than the forces for reform. It is likely to take at least one generation before that fundamental balance is reversed. In the following chapter, we will begin to see why.

3

The Permanent Power Struggle

I. IRON RULES

Josef Stalin's death opened a power struggle in Russia that continues to this day. The great dictator held all political, economic, and military decision-making authority in his hands. With his death, on March 5, 1953, all his formidable power was up for grabs. Ambitious potential successors have maneuvered ever since to secure as much of that authority as possible for themselves. The result has been a permanent battle for the top leadership, with no holds barred. No elections, no constitutional guarantees, have yet made a difference in any of the worst political crises in Moscow since the Stalin era. Ultimately, only the effective use of brute force has been decisive. No other aspect of the Stalinist legacy is more ominous for the future.

Even reformers like Khrushchev and Yeltsin had to resort to violence to seize the leadership or keep it. Khrushchev had his men rush into a Kremlin meeting, pistols drawn, to arrest Stalin's last secret police chief, Lavrenty Beria, and remove him from the 1953 succession struggle by execution. As extra insurance for that particular episode, Khrushchev had a revolver ready in his suit pocket in case Beria pulled a gun to resist. Incredibly, the leading statesmen of a nuclear superpower settled their political differences by nearly reenacting the shoot-out at the OK Corral.

Khrushchev later justified the extraordinary performance by claiming in his memoirs that if he had not acted early and decisively, Beria would have seized power and unleashed a new secret police terror. "I considered him a dangerous opportunist who would stop at nothing to obtain what he wanted." Khrushchev wrote.[1]

Forty years later, Yeltsin showed how little Russia had changed. Once again, brute force had to be used on political opponents, and then justified on the grounds that it was saving Russia from another vile dictatorship. This time Yeltsin claimed the only way he could put down an armed insurrection by his chief political rivals in October 1993 was to call out tanks to fire on them in the parliament building. Otherwise, he asserted, they would have turned the country toward fascism. Yeltsin was proving how far Russia must still go in order to establish a genuine democracy.

Since then, nothing fundamental has changed. Even after the fall of communism, well into the 1990s, democratic institutions are still too weak in Russia to rule out a return to dictatorship. That is what now makes the permanent power struggle the most ominous part of Stalin's legacy. Stalinist methods, the application of brute force, are still the key to Kremlin infighting, and as long as that remains true, the danger of renewed dictatorship will haunt Russia. Thus the Stalinist legacy still carries the seeds of its revival.

Of course, Stalin's terror is over, but its end only created a new threat of violence. Once the top man was no longer ordering the murder of all potential foes before they could rise up against him, an armed coup d'état against the leader became a significant threat. Thus instead of pacifying the country, the end of the Stalinist terror shifted the use of brute force in settling political disputes to a different level. The coup from below replaced the purge from above as the chief instrument of political violence.

No one should discount the momentous changes for the better, among them market economics and democratic elections. Nonetheless, a sinister undercurrent remains. Every Kremlin leader since Stalin has known that in his country the battle for political power always goes to the strongest, that oppositions are always forming and plotting, often secretly and often ready to use armed force, and that unless he keeps the military or the security police or preferably both on his side, he can be toppled at any moment. Both Gorbachev and Yeltsin learned to their sorrow that in Russia democratic elections are no guarantee against attempts to seize power by military force.

Western policy toward Russia has to begin with a recognition of one fundamental truth: the permanent struggle for power is as alive today in Moscow as it was the day Stalin died, and the rest of the world has a vital stake in the outcome. Whoever wins the leadership struggle in Russia, for whatever period of time, will play a critical role in either averting or fomenting nuclear war. Yet despite the stakes, Western influence on Kremlin political infighting has always been marginal.

One reason is as old as Russia itself. The nation has never been in the Western camp. Instead, as the world's largest Eurasian power, it always had a split personality. Appropriately, the symbol of tsarist Russia was a double-headed eagle. One head looked east to Asia, for centuries the model for traditional thinking and despotic rule. The other head looked west to Europe, the model for progressive reform. The heads may have looked both ways, but Russia's heart and soul were most often in the conservative East. Westerners seeking to liberalize Russia were always battling stronger currents of traditional influence from the East.

Periods when Russia's Westernizing reformers held the upper hand were relatively few and short. For most of its history, Russia was firmly anchored in the East. Its church and its politics were Orthodox and Byzantine, rather than Catholic and Western. Under the Communists, it created an East Bloc alternative to the capitalist West. Even today, Russia remains a profoundly Asian nation, far more comfortable with conservative Eastern traditions than with new Western ideas. An increasing cry heard under Yeltsin is that he puts too much faith in American notions of market economics and democratic politics that cannot be redesigned for Russia. The same malcontents claim the better model for Russia's transition from communism is the more austere version dictated by China.

Another reason for the weakness of Western influence in Moscow was the tendency of Western governments to handicap themselves by making avoidable policy mistakes. The West was particularly bad at reading Russian political tea leaves.

Winston Churchill called the Soviet Union "a riddle wrapped in a mystery, inside an enigma."[2] Admittedly, Moscow's obsession with secrecy made fathoming its intentions extremely difficult. Still, Western governments could always have done better. A clearer understanding of how Russia's permanent power struggle works would have helped enormously. It would have identified earlier the man most likely to take over the Kremlin next, and his most likely policies, and given the West a better chance to influence both.

That task was never the mission impossible Churchill described. Over the years, Russia's continuing power struggle displayed clear patterns. Given the rigidity of the Soviet system, these patterns became predictable, iron rules of behavior, confirmed over and over again. As such they threw up accurate signposts of coming change, but Western governments often failed to read the signs correctly.

This chapter will show how the West can improve on that record. It will do so by looking at Moscow's permanent power struggle in four different ways. First, the iron rules will be defined, from patterns that emerged in every leadership battle since Stalin's death. These rules will show where the West could have done better in predicting future Kremlin leaders and policies, and in influencing both—an exercise that remains valid in post-Communist Russia. Second, a view from below will be factored in, from an extraordinary Russian who lived through seventy-four years of Soviet history. His view of the permanent power struggle is very different from the one conveyed by Kremlin leaders, but no less essential to Western understanding. Third, the narrative will move from general principles to specific examples. It will return to Khrushchev's downfall, this time with the help of once-secret official documents, in a definitive case study of how a battle for the Soviet leadership was organized and won. Finally, a concrete example will be presented of how the West could have exploited the continuing Kremlin power struggle to help bring communism down decades earlier at no risk of nuclear war.

We begin with the iron rules set in 1953, when the West first demonstrated its appalling ignorance of how Kremlin infighting really works. With

Josef Stalin's death that year came the classic example of Western Kremlinology at its worst. The obvious first question was who would succeed him. Virtually everyone from journalists to academics to governments got the answer wrong. Georgi Malenkov, Stalin's designated heir, quickly assumed the dictator's two most important posts of Communist Party leader and prime minister. Official Soviet announcements listed the three key members of the new regime in order as Malenkov; the secret police chief, Lavrenty Beria; and the foreign minister, V. M. Molotov. So most Western experts forecast a power struggle involving these three, and then tapped Malenkov as the likely winner.

This time the CIA was more embarrassingly wrong than anyone else. A recently declassified CIA analysis dated March 12, 1953, one week after Stalin died, concluded that "no one can immediately threaten the dominant position of Malenkov." This CIA note, like other expert analyses of the day, did not even mention Nikita Khrushchev as a top contender. Yet only three days later, on March 15, 1953, Khrushchev took over Malenkov's job as Communist Party leader and became the most important man in the country. Perhaps never before had so important a CIA forecast been proved worthless so soon. The widely predicted Malenkov era lasted ten days. The totally unexpected Khrushchev era lasted eleven years.[3]

How could the CIA have been so wrong? Far more than the wisdom of hindsight is involved here. The experts of the day should have done better. Nikita Khrushchev was no unknown outsider. At the time he was fifty-eight years old and among the half-dozen top Soviet leaders. He belonged on any short list of potential successors. In fact, there was ample reason to make him the favorite, because when Stalin died, Khrushchev already held the second most important job in the nation.

To understand that, a brief look at the Soviet power structure is needed. Kremlin authority was divided between the Communist Party and the Soviet government. Both were important, as underscored by the fact that Stalin himself headed both—the Party as general secretary and the government as prime minister—but there was never any doubt that the Party was very much the senior partner in this arrangement and the government its obedient servant. The Party made all policy decisions. It gave out the marching orders. The government's job was to obey them and make sure all policy decisions got properly implemented. Stalin's supreme power came from his Party base, not the government side.

With all his titles and powers, Stalin had truly awesome responsibilities. There was no way he could keep watch on his key power base, the Party, by himself. So he relied on a loyal aide, a second secretary, to administer Party affairs, among them personnel assignments and promotions. Thus anointed by the supreme leader, the second secretary had enormous patronage powers and an inside track in any Kremlin succession struggle. Stalin himself had used the equivalent post as his springboard to succeed Lenin.

When Stalin died, the second secretary was Nikita Sergeyevich Khrushchev. For the CIA and other Kremlin watchers, that should have made him a top contender. Khrushchev wasted no time exploiting his advantage. Malenkov's claim to both the Party and government leadership rested on his position as Stalin's designated heir, and on the desire to show continuity in order to avoid public panic. However, Khrushchev easily turned that argument against him.

Stalin had too much power, Khrushchev contended, and should have no single successor. The dead tyrant's two key posts should be split and each go to the next in line. On the Party side that meant Khrushchev, already the second secretary. On the government side it meant Malenkov, who had been Stalin's deputy prime minister in the Council of Ministers. The other Politburo members agreed, since they all stood to gain more in a collective leadership than under one-man rule. So ten days after Stalin died, Khrushchev took over the key job as head of the Party and Malenkov was left with only the lesser post of prime minister.

That pattern became an iron rule of Kremlin succession politics. Every single Soviet leader since Khrushchev had been the Party second secretary immediately before taking over the top job. That was true of Leonid Brezhnev, Yuri Andropov, Konstantin Chernenko, and Mikhail Gorbachev. Speculation in the West about other rival contenders was always foolish. The various prime ministers, defense ministers, foreign ministers, and KGB chiefs were important players in policymaking, but none of them ever had much chance of going directly to the top.

The iron law created numerous opportunities for Western governments to spot the coming man in the Kremlin, seek to establish a relationship with him, and plan in advance how to deal with him. Unfortunately, all such opportunities were either squandered or ineffectively used. When Brezhnev became second secretary in July 1964, for example, it was a clear signal that he was the crown prince, the next man in charge. Yet the U.S. and other Western governments assumed wrongly that Khrushchev was in control for the long term and made little effort to cultivate his heir apparent.

Identifying future Kremlin leaders was always easier than forecasting their policies. But here again, the record since Stalin's death established its own probability laws. And once more, the key signposts first appeared in Khrushchev's rise to the top.

Two were virtual certainties. First, examining speeches or policies of future leaders on the way up was pointless. All rising Soviet leaders kept climbing only if they loyally toed the leadership line of the day. If they had any rebellious ideas on the way up, they kept them to themselves. Only when a leader finally took over the top job did he at last show what he was really made of, by invoking the second iron rule. In order to establish his own credibility as the new master of the Kremlin he would then denounce his predecessor and reverse his predecessor's policies.

Khrushchev set the most dramatic example in this pattern, which all subsequent Soviet leaders would follow. Nothing in Nikita Sergeyevich's background suggested that he would turn out to be a great reformer. On the contrary, Khrushchev was as loyal as any of Stalin's henchmen. Malenkov, who had a particularly subtle mind, and a handful of other trusted aides were permitted to argue with Stalin, but Khrushchev was pointedly not among them. Instead Khrushchev offered Stalin other assets, among them boundless energy, a gift for political intrigue, and remarkable ability as an agitator, transmitting the dictator's wishes to the working masses. Most of all, Nikita Sergeyevich offered total subservience. As Stalin's viceroy in the Ukraine, Khrushchev carried out the purges there, and he was rewarded for this service by promotion to senior Party ranks in Moscow. Thus the man who was to denounce Stalin for spilling so much blood had some of it on his own hands.

Even so, once Khrushchev reached the top, he could no longer keep silent. In a country with no meaningful elections, he had to find another way to establish his legitimacy as leader. In the end, there was only one effective way. Stalin's godlike myth had to be destroyed and his crimes revealed, so that his successor, Khrushchev, could be seen as the dragon slayer, leading the nation toward a progressive new era.

The result was Khrushchev's famous "secret speech" to the 20th Congress of the Soviet Communist Party on February 24, 1956. For the first time, the appalling extent of Stalin's murderous reign was admitted and denounced by a Soviet leader. "Stalin sanctioned the most brutal violation of Socialist legality, torture and oppression of innocent people," Khrushchev declared, criminal practices which "we must abolish decisively, once and for all."[4] The speech proved to be a historic turning point. Within months, five million political prisoners were released from the Gulag. The Stalinist terror was over. Political dissent and opposition became possible, and with them the promise of meaningful reforms.

The speech took enormous courage, and delicate balance. The country had to be de-Stalinized without overly offending those Stalinists still in the Kremlin leadership—like Malenkov, Molotov, and Lazar Kaganovich—capable of aligning to overthrow Khrushchev. Equally tricky, the speech had to destroy Stalin without damaging the credibility of the Communist Party that Stalin had headed for so long, or bringing into question the Party's continued monopoly powers to rule the country.

Khrushchev did so by stressing that Lenin had established legitimate Communist rule, which Stalin had corrupted and Khrushchev would now restore. At the same time, to placate hard-liners in the leadership, Khrushchev made clear that the repressive machinery would be dismantled slowly and far from completely. He did that by revealing Stalin's crimes against the Communist Party and to a lesser extent against the army, but he did nothing to denounce Stalin's crimes against the Soviet masses or against non-Communist intellectuals, for the very good reason that he intended to continue repressing them by keeping the Gulag open for business. The fine-tuning could hardly have been better.

The delicate balancing act worked in Russia, establishing Khrushchev's legitimacy as leader, at least for the time being. It was, however, far from a complete success. Internally, it failed to placate the hard-liners, who began to plot their revenge. Abroad, the speech was more of a disaster. The revelations of Stalin's crimes were a death blow to communism's appeal in left-wing Western intellectual circles.

In terms of the Kremlin's permanent power struggle, Khrushchev's secret speech firmly established a precedent every subsequent Soviet leader was to follow. Each in turn would establish his own legitimacy in office by discrediting his predecessor, despite the fact that on the way up he cheered for that same predecessor. Thus Leonid Brezhnev, who rose through the Party ranks as a Khrushchev protégé, toadying to his master and heaping praise on Khrushchev's often erratic reformist course, would later denounce Khrushchev as a harebrained schemer, halt all meaningful reform, and run a status quo regime for eighteen years. Thus Mikhail Gorbachev, who parlayed support for Brezhnev into becoming the youngest member of the Politburo, quickly turned on his patron when he took charge himself, denouncing Brezhnev for institutionalizing stagnation.[5]

To Western analysts, this signpost should have been clear from Khrushchev on. After all, that was not the first example. Stalin had done much the same thing earlier, downgrading Lenin to establish his own legitimacy and reversing Lenin's more liberal economic policies. By the time Khrushchev repeated the process in downgrading and reversing Stalin, the iron rule had been set. Khrushchev's successor, Brezhnev, would most likely be a conservative who would roll back reform. Brezhnev's eventual successor, Gorbachev, was virtually certain to be a reformer.

Western governments, however, failed to take advantage of these signals. Just as they refused to believe the Party second secretary would be the next man in charge, they also had little faith in predicting what his basic policy line would be. They were wrong.

Given the laws of probability established by every Soviet succession battle, there was reason to believe foreign governments could accurately forecast the basic policy thrust of the next Kremlin leader. There are, of course, no certainties in political life. Still, the probabilities were strong enough to justify drawing up a contingency plan when, for example, Gorbachev was named second secretary to the fatally ill transition leader Konstantin Chernenko. That meant, in all likelihood, that a reformist would be taking command in the Kremlin within months. It was the perfect time to think out a game plan exploring how the United States might help a new Soviet leader promote reform at home and lower tensions abroad. Instead, Ronald Reagan's administration wasted two years waiting for Gorbachev to take office, and then prove he was serious about reform, before establishing any meaningful dialogue with him. One can only wonder what opportunities were squandered.

With the collapse of the Soviet Union, the problem of predicting future Kremlin leaders and their policies has obviously changed. In some ways it got harder. For one thing, there was no longer a Communist Party second secretary to anoint as the coming man. In other ways, it got easier. Among the major new advantages in the more open Russian society was that Western ambassadors had better access to Kremlin leaders on the way up, and, with that, an improved opportunity to learn their views on key policy questions.

One illustration here makes the point. In the late 1970s, the able American ambassador to Moscow, Malcolm Toon, often met personally with Brezhnev. Nonetheless, the ambassador was not satisfied. Toon wanted to meet individually with each member of the Politburo to take the measure of all Brezhnev's potential successors. His requests for appointments with most of the others, however, were refused. "You see Brezhnev and that's good enough," the ambassador was told.[6] Among the Politburo members Toon was unable to get to know at the time was Mikhail Gorbachev. Today's ambassadors to Moscow have no such access problems. Furthermore, when they do get together, Russia's future leaders are now far freer to speak candidly to foreign envoys.

Nevertheless, despite the significant changes, it is still too early to reject the lessons from the Soviet past in predicting future Russian leaders and their policies. There are many reasons for this. One is that Kremlin power brokers are first of all Russians, before they are reformers, hard-liners, or anything else. Thus essentially Russian behavior patterns from Soviet rule still apply in the post-Communist era. Second, the transition from communism to democracy is far from complete, and therefore some probability rules from Soviet days still apply. Third and most important, Western governments continue to misread signals coming out of Moscow, indicating they still need to do a better job of absorbing the lessons of the past. For example, as with Khrushchev in 1964, they still underestimate the dangers of an armed coup d'état. As but one result of this tendency, the U.S. government was unpleasantly surprised by the August 1991 putsch against Gorbachev. Their lame excuse afterward, as a senior administration adviser on Soviet affairs told me, was this: "If Gorbachev himself didn't know what was coming, how could we?" In fact, unmistakable signs of a coup had been building for two years, and Gorbachev himself suspected what was coming, as we shall see.[7]

Another consistent Western mistake, held over from the Soviet period, has been to support the man in charge personally, by preferring to deal only with him, even after his power has peaked. Too often Western governments have been too slow in identifying new political forces emerging in Russia, on both the national and provincial levels, and in encouraging the more positive ones.

The United States and Britain got in trouble with that by limiting their backing to Gorbachev personally well into 1990, long after it was clear in Moscow that Yeltsin had seized the political initiative. At the time, British Prime Minister John Major went to Moscow and saw Gorbachev but not Yeltsin. In Washington, George Bush received Gorbachev at the White House but not Yeltsin. Thus when Yeltsin pushed Gorbachev into retirement in December 1991, both countries quickly had to play catch-up with him and smooth ruffled feathers. Both should have been building bridges to him far earlier.

More recently, Bill Clinton and other Western leaders have been repeating the same mistake, endorsing Yeltsin personally, while both his physical health and his political support have declined to dangerously weak levels. Clinton and the others would be better off supporting the principles of democratic reform and market economy in Russia. That backing would embrace both Yeltsin and the younger Russian political leaders in the wings who may soon do a better job of promoting reform than Yeltsin. Among them, Boris Nemtsov, governor of the Nizhni Novgorod region, is widely seen as one of the nation's brightest young hopes.[8] There are many others.

Yeltsin and the sixty-something-generation reformers are already largely discredited in Russia as yesterday's men. Nemtsov and the forty-something reformers are tomorrow's men. By limiting their endorsement to Yeltsin personally, Western leaders risk backing a faltering horse. Instead, they should be widening their support to reformers generally, and the more promising younger ones in particular, in order to help the progressive side ultimately defeat neo-Stalinist forces in Russia's continuing power struggle.

Personalities, of course, are only one key element in that battle. Policies are the other. Both keep changing, further complicating predictions. Fortunately, however, here again, the old Soviet behavior patterns are a useful guide, among them the iron rule in Soviet days that Kremlin leaders rise to the top preaching one gospel, only to shift gears and practice the opposite once in charge. Boris Yeltsin, the first leader of post-Communist Russia, may prove to be no exception.

Yeltsin rose to power on a reformist mandate. Nevertheless he could still roll back reforms and turn conservative, should that become the key to retaining power. His use of tanks against his parliamentary opponents in 1993 showed his willingness to reverse course in precisely that way. Through 1994, Yeltsin continued to back reform. If necessary, however, he is still capable of suspending elections, dissolving parliament, adopting emergency presidential rule by decree, and enforcing conservative policies. Boris Nikolayevich spent most of his life rising through Communist ranks, using whatever political expedient necessary to gain and hold power. Whether Yeltsin's current commitment to democracy and market economics is short-term tactical or long-term strategic remains to be seen. The jury is still out, one more reason for the West to support reform, the policy, rather than Yeltsin, the man.

If Yeltsin does not roll back on reform himself, then his successor as Kremlin leader is more likely to do so. That scenario needs to be considered far more seriously than Western governments have taken it so far. Admittedly, forecasting Yeltsin's successor is difficult. He could be any one of several contenders, and he could come to power either by election or by coup d'état. Still, the key point for Western governments to grasp is that whoever comes after Yeltsin, the old Soviet probability law is then likely to apply: the successor will reverse his predecessor's policy, this time the radical reform strategy.

That strategy was largely discredited by 1995. It was widely perceived throughout Russia as having brought the shock but not the therapy, of worsening rather than improving the economy. At the very least, Yeltsin's successor is likely to slow the reforms, to make the transition to the market economy more gradual and less painful. At worst, he could give up on democracy and market reforms, reimpose dictatorship, and again threaten aggression abroad.

Either way, some sort of rollback is likely after Yeltsin. In that case, America and the West clearly have a vital interest in backing those forces which would conduct a mere slowdown of reform rather than an outright abandonment. A temporary retreat can be reversed relatively soon in Russia's continuing power struggle. But if a new Kremlin dictatorship takes hold, the democratic option could die for decades. U.S. contingency planners should already be figuring out how to help limit any rollback, in order to keep the prospects of long-term democratic reform alive in Russia.

Needless to say, the possibility that a progressive will succeed Yeltsin cannot be counted out. The odds were against that as these lines were written, but odds can change. Thus contingency plans also need to be readied on how the United States could help a liberal successor to Yeltsin consolidate his position and strengthen reform.

The main point is that Western governments now have the potential to do a better job of influencing the Kremlin power struggle through an improved use of trade, aid, and other policy tools. We will discuss the wiser use of these tools in detail at the end of this book.[9] Suffice it to say here that Western governments have a vested interest in exerting democratic influence in Russia to its fuller new potential. The old iron rules of Moscow's continuing power struggle still provide guidance on what to expect, but, fortunately, they are now only the beginning. Today's more open Russian society gives a better fix on the intentions of the leading contenders to succeed Yeltsin, from reformists like Grigory Yavlinski, to moderates such as Prime Minister Viktor Chernomyrdin, to conservatives like Moscow Mayor Yuri Luzhkov, to reborn Communists like Gennady Zyuganov, to military strongmen like General Aleksandr Lebed to extremists like Vladimir Zhirinovsky. Much the same can be said about coming men at the next level down, among them

Yeltsin confidante and First Deputy Prime Minister Oleg Soskovets. Western governments no longer have the excuse that no one can fathom tomorrow's Kremlin leader or his moves. These days the range of Moscow's future options can be defined and influenced earlier.

This is not some academic exercise in political theory. Whether Moscow continues reform or returns to dictatorship matters to everyone on the planet. A new hard-line regime in the Kremlin, armed with nuclear weapons, could well renew the threat of Cold War and mass annihilation. After all, there is ample precedent from the Soviet past. Western statesmen have a duty to learn from that, and then do all they can to help keep Russia on the reform path. Anything less would be irresponsible.

II. THE WISDOM OF THE AGED

Analysis of Kremlin leadership behavior provides some valuable lessons from the Soviet past. That is far from the whole story, however. All too often, Russian leaders have been too corrupted by their own Communist backgrounds and privileged lives to give anything but a distorted account of history in their memoirs. For a more complete picture, one must also listen to their more humble countrymen. Often the views of thoughtful common citizens stand in stark contrast to the official leadership line. Both must be considered, if the West is to learn the reality of the Soviet past and its implications for the future.

Some of Russia's best-known former leaders still claim that communism brought the nation progress. They further contend that the long Kremlin power struggle to improve the system, or at least to save the better parts of it, was justified. Subscribers to this view include reformers like Gorbachev. Sometimes, as with conservatives like Yegor Ligachev, the implied subtext here is that a rollback toward dictatorship would not necessarily be so bad.

Less privileged Russians, particularly the more thoughtful ones, often disagree with both the Gorbachev and Ligachev sides of the Kremlin power struggle. They always had a more realistic view of the continued misery the system imposed on the population. Typically, thinking Russians wanted neither reform like Gorbachev nor rollback like Ligachev, but instead preferred to get rid of communism entirely. For most of Soviet history, however, ordinary Russians had no chance to press their views on their leaders. Thus the people with the biggest stake in the Kremlin power struggle had the smallest voice in its outcome. Today, as a consequence of that, thoughtful Russians usually have no sympathy for any Communist faction or leader. The message these Russians have for the Communists now is "A plague on all your houses."

I often heard this sentiment voiced, although never more effectively than by Aleksandr Kirillovich Cheburkov, a Russian whose life spanned the twentieth century. Cheburkov had seen it all, from Tsar Nicholas II to Boris Yeltsin. For much of his life, Aleksandr Kirillovich watched things get worse. "When I saw the tsar, he had four bodyguards, one in front and three behind," Cheburkov told me. "When I saw Stalin, two army divisions guarded him."

Cheburkov was one of the lucky ones. He was ninety years old and in good health when we last spoke in 1993. He was never arrested, and neither was any member of his immediate family. Still, even such a fortunate exception as Aleksandr Kirillovich suffered through Stalin's rule in other ways, narrowly escaping a death sentence during the terror. "They wanted to put a bullet in my head," he said. His life story is typical of the traumas ordinary people lived through during the century-long power struggle in Russia. It is a useful reminder that Kremlin politics was not only the clash of personal ambitions among the elite, but also the ultimate cause of generations of shattered lives among the population at large.

Aleksandr Kirillovich was a talented engineer. One day in 1938, the Soviet secret police went through the baggage of an Englishman returning to London and discovered in it the first page of a research paper by Cheburkov on ball-bearing technology. From then on he was a marked man. The KGB wanted him arrested and shot for passing state secrets to foreigners, but the manager at his factory saved him. The manager said Cheburkov's work was essential for the production of tanks and aircraft in any future war effort. "At the time, no one told me any of this," Aleksandr Kirillovich recalled. Still, he knew something was wrong. For years he was denied promotions and trips abroad.

Sixteen years later he finally learned what happened. It was then 1954 and Stalin was dead. The KGB called Cheburkov in, showed him the page confiscated from the Englishman, and asked, "Did you write this?" He admitted he had, and why not? His work on ball bearings had been published in the Soviet press in 1935, three years before the page was found in the Englishman's luggage, so no state secrecy had been breached. Furthermore, a copy of his paper had been lost in a move to a new office. Anyone could have torn off the first page and planted it on the Englishman. No charges were ever pressed, but his career was still ruined. He was suspected of treason, and that was enough to block all advancement.

Aleksandr Kirillovich survived the Stalin years by accepting his fate. The closest he ever got to a protest was at factory rallies in the 1930s praising Stalin. When it came time to applaud, he would put the middle finger of his right hand down, inside the palm, and then clap. No one else could see the small gesture of defiance. He appeared to be applauding normally.

In the late 1930s, Cheburkov and his wife often heard the sound of boots pounding up the staircase of their apartment building after midnight.

Boots meant the secret police, and the hour meant someone was about to be arrested. "First a neighbor on the right disappeared, then one on the left, then upstairs, and then downstairs," he explained. "We made plans on what to do if I was arrested. My wife and the children were to stay with relatives. We were prepared, but they never came for me." Still, Cheburkov said, the sound of boots on stairs at night has terrified him ever since.

Cheburkov retired in 1963. He found little improvement in the Khrushchev, Brezhnev, or even Gorbachev eras. The suspicions against him were never cleared. "The authorities harassed me all my life," he said. Similarly, Aleksandr Kirillovich believed the authorities harassed the nation throughout Soviet rule. "*Pravda* always wrote lies," he said. "The revolution was a lie." By that Cheburkov meant that the Bolshevik Revolution claimed to be helping the common people but in fact only tormented them. "We lived for seventy-four years in the inferno of communism," he said. "Only now is it possible to tell the truth, and we must, so this never happens again."

To Aleksandr Kirillovich, it all boiled down to truth and lies. "Communism was built on lies," he said. That was why it lasted so long. That also was why progress since Stalin's death was so disappointing. The only way to prevent a renewed dictatorship, therefore, was to tell the truth about the Soviet past, and only the Russian people were capable of that, not their former leaders. To Cheburkov, the truth was that nothing from the Communist past was worth saving, not even the elements that reformers like Gorbachev and Yeltsin tried to retain. There is no more important lesson for the West to draw from the long life of Aleksandr Kirillovich, spanning all of Soviet history.

Other Russians said much the same thing, although more politely. They called communism an "illusion" rather than a pack of lies. They began speaking out in Khrushchev's day when the leader described communism as an ideal society the Soviet Union was building, and would soon achieve. In one popular anecdote from that time, Khrushchev was quoted as saying, "Communism is on the horizon." The word "horizon" confused a peasant. So he went to his elderly village sage and asked, "What is the horizon?" The wise man responded, "The horizon is an imaginary line which keeps receding as you approach." The story proved entirely accurate. The Communist ideal would never get closer than the horizon.

History shows that Soviet leaders could never tell the truth about communism. Often they were brazen about suppressing it. Subscribers to the *Great Soviet Encyclopedia,* the nation's definitive historical source, regularly received official instructions to take the scissors to page so-and-so and physically remove the article on this or that newly disgraced Communist statesman, the latest victim of Stalin's purges. Not even post-Stalin Soviet historians were able to produce a full history of their Communist Party. Each time they made the attempt, they failed to finish the job before a new Kremlin leader took over with new orders to rewrite everything, to inflate his role and downgrade his predecessors. The only existing complete histories of the Soviet Communist Party were written by foreigners.

Soviet leaders were incapable of telling the truth about communism partly because that would have meant admitting the Stalinist command economy they had inherited was doomed to fail. In fact, the sooner they scrapped it entirely and put a more rational economic system in its place, the better off the country would be. But that was a truth they simply could not face. So they lied about communism's performance, to their own people and to the world, in everything from economic output to human rights, and then they lied again about its promise of a better future. Or, as Cheburkov put it, "Communism survived on lies."

Naturally, it was more complicated than that. The Soviet system could not survive on lies alone. It retained power by using many other weapons of state, among them the secret police, to suppress dissent. In this way, Communist leaders kept their system going long after it should have been pronounced clinically dead. They did so partly to maintain their privileged positions and partly in the hope that somehow the system could be reformed, improved, and ultimately saved. Here was the other main reason why communism lasted as long as it did. Unlike Cheburkov, Soviet officials believed their system was worth saving, if they could only figure out how. To some the answer was reform. To others the answer was to resist all reform. To understand that dynamic properly, one must return to leadership-level politics.

Nikita Khrushchev was the first to try to save communism through systemic change. From his day on, the Soviet Union's permanent power struggle focused largely on the battle over reform. In beginning that process, Khrushchev's experience set the precedent that would limit the prospects of reform under every subsequent Soviet leader, including Gorbachev, up to the collapse of communism in 1991. In the end, the system could not reform itself. Instead it would die trying. Because Khrushchev's experience was so fundamentally important in shaping the remainder of Soviet history, his precedent must now be examined in detail.

III. THE KHRUSHCHEV PRECEDENT

As the first great reformer in post-Stalin Russia, Nikita Khrushchev took on an extraordinarily difficult task. He was, in effect, one man against a powerful political machine. The man was the embodiment of reformist hopes. The machine was the Soviet Communist system and its hard-line defenders. Once the man began trying to change the system for its own good, the machine fought back, fearing that any change would weaken it irreparably. The conflict grew until there could be only one survivor, either the man or the machine. On two occasions, the defenders of the Communist system tried to get rid of Khrushchev. Their first attempted coup against him failed. It took years, and a new generation of plotters, before a second putsch finally brought him down. Nikita Sergeyvich's ability to survive the first coup, and to keep reform policies going for more than a decade in power, testified to his skills as a political infighter. But in the end, the machine proved stronger than the man. The Khrushchev precedent was clear to all his successors. Any Soviet leader who tried to reform the system risked being destroyed by it first.

The Khrushchev precedent was more than a warning. It also provided a manual on Kremlin political infighting. The two coup attempts against Nikita Sergeyevich were classic examples of why some plots fail and others succeed. Together they became a survival handbook for all future Soviet leaders, with chapter and verse on what to do to avoid Khrushchev's fate. As we shall see, these lessons would prove particularly important to Gorbachev.

The first lesson in the handbook was that new Soviet leaders have no state of grace, no hundred days of goodwill to establish themselves. Khrushchev himself proved that by stealing the Party leadership from Stalin's designated heir, Georgi Malenkov, only ten days after Stalin died. Khrushchev would have no state of grace either, as Malenkov immediately began plotting against him. Nikita Sergeyevich was thus in deep political trouble from the moment he took over the top Soviet leadership in 1953. Malenkov needed no further motive for personal revenge, but Khrushchev gave him one anyway, by putting Nikolai Bulganin in Malenkov's place as prime minister in 1955. Malenkov had now lost the nation's two most important posts, but he remained on the Politburo, with an influential voice in all policy debates, and he resolved to use it to bring down Nikita Sergeyevich once and for all. Khrushchev's "secret speech" of February 1956, denouncing Stalin and ending the terror, provided the opportunity. To Malenkov and the other Stalinist hard-liners still in the Politburo, the speech was a frontal attack on the Communist system, and the reformer who delivered it had to go.

In June 1957 they finally made their move. At a three-day Politburo meeting under heavy guard, Malenkov and Molotov demanded Khrushchev's removal. It had taken them a year to bring Khrushchev's divided opponents together in a plot to oust him. The main sin, his foes agreed, was that the secret speech had gone too far in exposing Stalin, and in the process, had weakened the Soviet Communist Party and the world Communist movement.

According to Khrushchev's biographer, the historian Roy Medvedev, the plotters were prepared to be lenient.[10] Khrushchev would be offered a lesser job if he agreed to resign the Party leadership. They considered making him minister of agriculture. They planned to arrest him if he refused. Molotov was to be the new Party leader. In all, seven Politburo members spoke against

Khrushchev, including all of Stalin's cronies—Malenkov, Molotov, Kaganovich, Bulganin, and Kliment Voroshilov. Only three spoke in Khrushchev's favor. In the formal vote, Khrushchev was removed from the Party leadership. In their arrogance, the members of the Politburo thought all they had to do was give the order and they would be obeyed. They had badly miscalculated.

Khrushchev refused to submit. Instead he demanded a meeting of the Central Committee, a larger body of senior officials. Strictly speaking, Party rules were on his side. One of the legal fictions of "Soviet democracy" was that the Central Committee, with some two hundred members from all over the country, was supposed to make the key policy decisions that would guide the work of the dozen or so Politburo members in Moscow. In reality, because of the Central Committee's unwieldy size and dispersed membership, there was no way it could control the Politburo. In actual fact, the process worked exactly the other way round. The small Politburo made the decisions in weekly meetings, then brought the large Central Committee in to rubber-stamp them two or three times a year. Nonetheless, there are moments when legal fictions can be useful. For Khrushchev this was one of them, particularly because he still had an assured majority in the Central Committee.

In the June 1957 political crisis, Khrushchev got the Central Committee plenum he demanded. He was able to convene it not because the Party rules said he should, but because the head of the armed forces, Marshal Georgi Zhukov, and the head of the KGB, General Ivan Serov, agreed to fly Central Committee members into Moscow and hold the meeting whether or not the Politburo approved. Here was the key to this and all subsequent Kremlin showdowns: might made right. In this case Khrushchev used the might of the armed security services to rig the decisive vote in his favor. It was a brilliant stroke by a masterful politician. This time, for once, a Politburo decision would be successfully defied.

The rest was child's play. At the plenum, Nikita Sergeyevich turned the tables on his opponents. The majority against Khrushchev in the Politburo was overturned by the majority for him in the Central Committee. Malenkov, Molotov, and their supporters were all fired, denounced ever after as the "anti-Party group." Khrushchev remained in power, stronger than ever. He soon took over Bulganin's job as prime minister and for the first time held both of Stalin's key titles as head of the Party and the government. He had also set the ground rules for all future showdowns in the continuing Soviet power struggle. Henceforth, no conspiracy would be based solely on a narrow majority in the Politburo. The backing of the full Central Committee also had to be assured. So did the support of the Army and the KGB. None of these lessons were lost on one of the chief beneficiaries of the June 1957 political crisis, a rising Khrushchev supporter at the closed-door meetings, who was rewarded afterward by promotion to the ruling Kremlin elite as a full member of the Politburo. His name was Leonid Brezhnev.

Khrushchev took the victory as an invitation to continue reform. Indeed, over the next seven years, he laid the basis for each of the revolutionary changes Mikhail Gorbachev was to champion two decades later. The similarities are truly uncanny. Gorbachev went considerably further, but in each area, from foreign policy to the economy, Mikhail Sergeyevich essentially started where the last great reformer, Nikita Sergeyevich, had left off.

There was nothing really new about Gorbachev's "new thinking" in Soviet foreign policy, for instance. Khrushchev had tried the same thing, and called it "peaceful coexistence." The basic idea was that the Soviet Union and the United States should move from nuclear confrontation and the arms race toward peaceful competition and even economic cooperation. Each side would have to prove its good intentions with concrete acts. Khrushchev did so in 1955 by withdrawing Soviet troops from Austria, where they had served as an occupation force since World War II. That set the precedent for Gorbachev, who proved his good faith in 1989 in much the same way, by withdrawing Soviet troops from Eastern Europe.

Khrushchev also set the example for Gorbachev's initiatives in arms control. The impetus was the 1962 Cuban missile crisis that brought the world to the brink of nuclear disaster. The first tangible step came with the signing in Moscow of the 1963 nuclear test ban agreement. Khrushchev and John F. Kennedy had intended to go substantially further, according to Fyodor Burlatsky, a Khrushchev aide.

"After the Cuban missile crisis, there was a unique opportunity to end the Cold War," Burlatsky told me in Moscow during a March 1993 interview. "Both sides understood nuclear war was impossible and there was no need to continue the arms race. Both sides already had enough nuclear weapons. Kennedy and Khrushchev exchanged letters after the Cuban crisis that began to consider an end to the nuclear arms race. The process was stopped tragically by the death of Kennedy and the political death of Khrushchev. It was a tragedy for Soviet-American relations. Both sides turned more conservative—[Lyndon] Johnson on the American side and Brezhnev on ours." A promising opportunity was lost for a generation, but a clear basis had been laid for Gorbachev to seize that concept twenty years later, and carry it through.

Gorbachev's policy of glasnost, or openness, also found its roots in the Khrushchev reforms. In 1962, Khrushchev allowed Aleksandr Solzhenitsyn to publish an anti-Stalinist novel, *One Day in the Life of Ivan Denisovich*, in the literary magazine *Novy Mir*. It caused a sensation after decades of heavy-handed censorship and became the seminal event in a brief burst of artistic creativity known as "the thaw." Khrushchev never intended, however, to abandon cultural controls. Instead his purpose was to permit publication of a work designed to discredit his political foes, the unbending Stalinist hard-liners in the Party bureaucracy still trying to block or slow his reforms. Gorbachev did much the same thing. Glasnost was not originally intended to create a genuinely free press. Instead it started as a vehicle to embarrass conservatives blocking Gorbachev's reforms. In the early Gorbachev years, the Soviet press was free to carry attacks on corruption by Gorbachev's foes in the bureaucracy, but it was not free to criticize Gorbachev himself.

Even perestroika, the Gorbachev restructuring of the economy, found its source in the Khrushchev reforms. Not that Nikita Sergeyevich had ever succeeded here. His economic reforms tended to be poorly thought out. Khrushchev energetically embarked on one proposed miracle cure after another. In agriculture, for example, it was better crop rotation one day, then increased use of chemical fertilizers the next. At the same time, there were continuous administrative shake-ups to improve production, among them the heresy of transferring more decision-making power from Moscow to regional councils. After each disappointment, Nikita Sergeyvich enthusiastically embarked on yet another approach, determined not to give up until he got it right.

Mikhail Sergeyevich started much the same way. Like Khrushchev, he believed the Communist system was basically sound, but had to be improved. Also like Khrushchev, he was willing to experiment until he found the right cure. The very name for his economic reform, "perestroika," restructuring, underscored his determination to rationalize the existing system rather than jettison it. His first effort was "acceleration," an attempt to improve the command economy by making it work faster. Gorbachev was to try several other approaches, including a limited use of free markets, but he never fully abandoned Communist economics. The main reason for his caution was again found in the Khrushchev experience. Khrushchev showed what happened when a reformist Soviet leader tried to move too far too fast.

By 1964, Khrushchev had done just that. He had moved too far in front of his Politburo, making decisions without consulting it, and, in the process, he was offending just about everyone who mattered in the Soviet hierarchy. He angered the armed forces by cutting their manpower nearly in half, to invest more in the civilian economy. He lost the KGB by a housecleaning that retired the agents of Stalin's blood purges.

Probably his biggest mistake was to antagonize the local Communist Party leaders, the backbone of the Central Committee and the very men who would ultimately decide his political fate. These men were the first secretaries of Communist Party local and regional organizations across the country. Khrushchev alienated them—permanently—by cutting their powers in half. In November 1962, he split their jobs in two, one to run a local Party organization on agriculture, and the other a separate but equal Party organization on industry. Thus the Party stalwart who once ran an entire region alone, much like a feudal baron, suddenly found himself reduced to half his former prestige, responsible only for agriculture or industry, and saddled with a rival of equal status running the other. Rarely has a single step by a national political leader done more to turn his key lieutenants against him. Khrushchev's idea was to improve the management of both agriculture and industry. Instead he earned the animosity of the men whose support he needed most. Brezhnev would soon correct that mistake.

By early 1964, Khrushchev had thus offended the same three power blocs that had saved him in 1957—the army, the KGB, and the Central Committee. He of all people should have known better. His enemies quickly seized the opportunity. By early 1964 they were actively conspiring to get rid of him.

Once again, the plot against Nikita Sergeyevich began at the top, in the Politburo. This time, its members were frustrated by Khrushchev's unilateral decisions and constant policy shake-ups, all of which, in their view, weakened the Communist system that gave them their powers. They also feared that he planned to replace them at a November 1964 Central Committee plenum with people from his personal entourage, including his son-in-law, Aleksei Adzhubei. They determined to depose Khrushchev first. They would prove the system stronger than the man trying to reform it. They knew they must act by October.

Who acted and how are at last generally known. Sources include authoritative reports in the Soviet press, personal accounts of key players in the drama, including Khrushchev's son, Sergei, and once–top-secret official documents only now becoming available. All agree the prime movers in the Politburo were Brezhnev, who would take over the Communist Party leadership, and Nikolai Podgorny, who would eventually become president or honorary head of state.

The plotters moved slowly, and with great caution. Pyotr Shelest, then the Communist Party leader in the Ukraine, claimed he was first approached privately by Brezhnev and Podgorny in March 1964 about joining the plot against Khrushchev.[11] "The masterminds were Brezhnev and Podgorny," Shelest told the *Moscow News* in a 1989 interview.[12]

Brezhnev and Podgorny made sure they would not be caught as Khrushchev's foes were in 1957. This time, before they confronted him, they would have both the Politburo and the Central Committee on their side. They would also secure the backing of both the KGB and the army. The KGB was never a problem. From the beginning, Party Secretary Aleksandr Shelepin, a former KGB chief, was a key member of the conspiracy. So was his successor as head of the KGB, Vladimir Semichastny. Defense Minister Rodion Malinovsky and the other armed forces chiefs were to be brought in later, once the plotters had all the political support they needed.

In a way, Khrushchev made it easy for them. In the first nine months of 1964 he spent more than four months—a total of 135 days—on trips in the

U.S.S.R. and abroad. The travel schedule made it hard for the leader to keep a proper eye on his political rear.

Meanwhile, Brezhnev, Podgorny, Shelepin, and the others covered their tracks well. Among other things, they toyed with Nikolai Ignatov, who hated Khrushchev for demoting him from the Politburo in 1961. In 1964, Ignatov was still chairman of the parliament in the Russian Federation, the largest Soviet republic. The job was honorary, holding no political authority. But it gave Ignatov a good excuse to travel around the country and meet with local and regional leaders. So the plotters put Ignatov on the road to rally support for their cause, discreetly, behind closed doors. Ignatov did so with gusto, thinking he would be awarded a big job in the new regime. He also gave the ringleaders deniability. If necessary, they could always claim his whispering about their coming coup was rubbish, the lies of a discredited has-been. In the end, Ignatov served them well, and they gave him nothing.

Sometimes the key plotters themselves seduced supporters, often on weekend hunting parties, or at vodka-laden dinners in dachas near the capital. According to Gennady Voronov, a Politburo member at the time, "the threads led to Zavidovo," a village seventy-five miles northwest of Moscow, "where Brezhnev would go hunting."[13] Brezhnev's lodge there was his favorite spot for inviting Politburo or Central Committee members and determining whether they would back the coup. "Brezhnev himself marked plus signs against names on a list of the Central Committee for those ready to support his struggle against Khrushchev, and he also marked some minus signs," Voronov said. "Everyone was given a personal working over. I was too, all night."

Similar soundings were taken by Brezhnev and Podgorny at dachas in the south. One crucial planning session, involving key members of the Politburo and the Central Committee, took place in September 1964, the month before the coup, during a hunting and fishing holiday near the Manych Lakes in southern Russia. Instead of hunting and fishing, the guests plotted against Khrushchev. Their host, Fyodor Kulakov, the Party leader of the region, would later be rewarded by Brezhnev with promotion to Moscow as the Party secretary in charge of agriculture.

Khrushchev flew off for a Black Sea vacation on September 30, leaving the plotters free to finalize their plans in Moscow. On October 12, the Politburo met in the Kremlin to put the plot into effect. The official record of that meeting is one of several still-classified documents obtained for this book. Document p163/II dated October 12, 1964, and stamped "Top Secret" said the Politburo had decided it was "urgent and necessary" to call Khrushchev back to Moscow. It also said the meeting instructed Brezhnev, Aleksei Kosygin, Ideology Secretary Mikhail Suslov, and Podgorny to phone Khrushchev and urge him to attend a new Politburo session on October 13. At the same time, the Politburo decided, "We think it expedient to summon to Moscow the members of the Central Committee." In contrast to 1957,

Khrushchev would have no chance to turn the tables on the plotters. This time, the fix was in.

According to Sergei Khrushchev, who was at his father's side at the time at the Black Sea dacha, Suslov actually made the call. The excuse was agricultural questions. At first the leader balked. "I'm on vacation," Khrushchev protested. "What could be so urgent?" But Suslov insisted. He told Khrushchev the Politburo would meet without him if he refused to attend.[14] Reluctantly, Nikita Sergeyevich then agreed to come.

Brezhnev should have made the call. As the senior man in the leadership next to Khrushchev and the nominal leader of the coming coup, it was his responsibility. A big, bushy-browed, gravel-voiced macho type, Brezhnev looked tough enough, a man's man who liked strong vodka, bear hunting, fast cars, and faster women. But according to several senior Communists in on the plot, Brezhnev clutched at the last minute and simply couldn't muster the courage to call Khrushchev himself. So Suslov, who never worried about scruples, did the dirty work.

Khrushchev was met at the airport in Moscow by only one man, KGB chief Semichastny. Normal protocol required the entire leadership to greet him. Nikita Sergeyevich could no longer have any doubts. The meeting was not about agriculture. It was about him.

At first, he tried to resist. There is no official stenographic record of the October 13 Politburo meeting available in the Party archives in Moscow. At least some of the remarks were apparently too rude to record. But sources close to the participants have given this account: Khrushchev refused to resign, denied all the allegations against him, and criticized his accusers.

Pyotr Shelest, the Ukrainian leader, attended that Politburo session, and he claims to be the only member to have kept a shorthand transcript of Khrushchev's self-defense. According to the Shelest transcript, Khrushchev complained he was accused of amassing too much personal power by combining the posts of Party leader and prime minister. Then he reminded his accusers bitterly, "But I, myself, did not seek this, you know. This question was decided collectively, and some of you, including Brezhnev, even insisted on it."[15]

Twenty top officials spoke against him. Only Mikoyan tried to soften the blow, saying Khrushchev should stay on in a lesser post. Here was Kremlin politics at its Byzantine best. In the downfall of Nikita Khrushchev, Anastas Mikoyan played at least a triple game, worth a brief review.

Mikoyan's first role was that of friend. Sergei Khrushchev had been tipped off to the coup by Vasily Galyukov, a bodyguard to Nikolai Ignatov, one of the plotters. Galyukov had accurately named Brezhnev, Podgorny, and Shelepin as the ringleaders. But when Sergei told the story to his father, Khrushchev refused to believe it. Instead, the Kremlin chief asked his friend Mikoyan to investigate.

At that point, Mikoyan assumed his second role, that of Judas. Mikoyan ordered Galyukov to repeat the story to him and had Sergei write it down as an official "protocol." Mikoyan listened to the bodyguard's warning but at the end said only that he considered Brezhnev, Podgorny, and Shelepin to be "honest Communists." Then Mikoyan instructed Sergei to add that positive evaluation of the Brezhnev group to the written record.[16] Mikoyan promised Sergei he would show the protocol to Khrushchev and discuss it with him. But according to Fyodor Burlatsky, an aide to Khrushchev, Mikoyan never showed the leader the protocol, not even on the plane back to Moscow to the meeting that deposed him. "Mikoyan betrayed Khrushchev," Burlatsky told me. Instead of giving the protocol to Khrushchev, Burlatsky said, Mikoyan gave it to Brezhnev as proof of his loyalty to the plotters.

Mikoyan's third role came at the showdown Politburo meeting on Khrushchev's fate, as the only speaker to defend the leader and propose he stay on in a lesser post. By sticking his head out alone like that, Mikoyan risked being fired as well. We shall never know whether Mikoyan did so out of courage, guilt, friendship, or calculation that he had paid his dues to Brezhnev and was therefore safe enough. Such are the secrets Soviet power brokers take to their graves. In any event, Mikoyan's one-man stand was rejected, without recrimination. No one else tried to save Nikita Sergeyevich. When the meeting adjourned for the night, Khrushchev decided further resistance was futile.

Another "top secret" document, no. p164/I, shows the Politburo meeting the next day, October 14, was relatively brief. It passed a resolution accusing Khrushchev of "violating the Leninist norms of collective leadership," of accumulating great power in his hands, of rudely ignoring the views of others, of committing "grave errors" of policy, and of "harebrained schemes" damaging the economy. The resolution further declared that "comrade Khrushchev is not capable of correcting the mistakes he has committed." Finally, it claimed to have satisfied Khrushchev's request to resign on grounds of "advancing age and deteriorating health."

The Central Committee was called in later the same day, October 14, to approve the change in leadership. Brezhnev ran the meeting as chairman. Suslov delivered the main speech, repeating the accusations heard in the Politburo and adding others. Among the new ones, according to Central Committee members who heard the speech, was the folly of risking nuclear war by putting Soviet missiles into Cuba. Suslov conveniently forgot to mention that he and other Politburo members had approved the move at the time.

Of all the men surrounding Khrushchev, Mikhail Andreyevich Suslov was perhaps the oddest. Tall, stooped, gray-haired, and painfully thin, he had a birdlike face and all the charm of a veteran pallbearer. From the 1950s to the

1980s, Suslov controlled ideological questions, but never once wrote as much as a single book, or even contributed one original thought to the theory of Marxism-Leninism. A dull bureaucrat at heart, Suslov contented himself with writing inane slogans for Soviet holidays like "Long live the unbreakable unity of the Party and the People." For a self-proclaimed intellectual, Suslov was remarkably slow and dull-witted. Typically, he alone among the Soviet leaders would observe the legal speed limit in Moscow of thirty-five miles an hour, instead of letting his driver hurtle down the special Kremlin central traffic lane at twice that speed. Again typical of Suslov, his speech denouncing Khrushchev was dull, repetitive, and largely unconvincing.

By far the most interesting aspect of Suslov's speech was that even the plotters themselves found it embarrassing in the extreme. They knew this collection of distorted charges would never stand the judgment of history. So they determined that the full text of Suslov's speech would never see the light of day. According to recently released official documents, the plenum decided the shorthand verbatim notes of Suslov's original text should be excluded from the Party archives. Only the abridged version of his speech, as edited by Brezhnev, Podgorny, and Suslov himself, survives. Among the passages cut out is the one about the Cuban missile crisis. In perhaps no other country would the top leaders themselves devote such effort to censoring the historical record.

Even what the censors left in now looks embarrassing. It shows a tightly managed script of manufactured joy. Once Suslov finished, Brezhnev called for a hand vote on Khrushchev's removal. He then announced the motion had been carried unanimously. According to the official record of the plenum, all Central Committee members then stood, and responded with "prolonged, stormy applause."

Next Podgorny took the chair. He asked for nominations for Party leader. The official transcript says that unnamed "voices from the floor" suggested Brezhnev. There were no other nominations. Another show of hands elected Brezhnev, unanimously, triggering another standing ovation of prolonged, stormy applause.

Brezhnev thanked the plenum, then asked for nominations for prime minister. "Voices," suggested Kosygin. Kosygin too was unopposed and elected unanimously. There was more stormy applause.

Then the plenum ended with shouts of "Long live our powerful Leninist Party, hurrah!" The formalities had taken only a few minutes. Kremlin power had passed to a new generation.

The plenum set the tone of the entire Brezhnev era. It had none of the fear and trembling of Stalin's day, none of the surprise or daring of Khrushchev's. By comparison, it was deadly dull. Leonid Ilyich liked that just fine. The plenum that had voted him into power was just what he wanted it to be. To use one of Brezhnev's favorite accolades, it was "businesslike."

IV. OPPORTUNITY KNOCKS

For Leonid Brezhnev, the road ahead was now clear. He would keep himself on top by risking no further reforms. Stability was Brezhnev's war cry. Simply ending Khrushchev's constant policy turns wasn't good enough. Instead Brezhnev worked very hard to maintain the old system until it atrophied. Policy hardly ever changed. As long as senior officials supported his status-quo approach, they held their jobs for life. When they died, their first deputies took over, again for life. Inevitably, the Brezhnev years turned into a gerontocracy, tired old men in their eighties running the same old system in the same old way for nearly two decades.

Russians now call the Brezhnev years "the period of stagnation." The description is misleading. Brezhnev did a lot worse than simply leave the economy in neutral. He saw salvation in raw military force. So Brezhnev conducted the biggest arms buildup in the history of the world. Under him, the U.S.S.R. grew from a junior member of the nuclear club, forced into a shameful backdown in the 1962 Cuban missile crisis, to the world's most heavily armed superpower, at parity with or ahead of the United States in key nuclear and conventional weapons. That awesome new muscle allowed the Kremlin to threaten Western interests globally.

The cost to Moscow was a military procurement program spiraling crazily out of control. Some 30 percent of GNP went to defense, robbing funds that should have gone into farms and consumer goods, roads, housing, schools, and health care, to name but a few needy areas. In rejecting reform, Brezhnev pandered to the worst Soviet instincts—feed the military and the hell with everything else. In the end, he did more damage to the Soviet system than the dissidents he jailed.

Workers outside the privileged defense sector were underpaid, with little prospect of improved living standards in their lifetimes. Not surprisingly, they underproduced. Absenteeism and alcoholism ran rampant. Cynical Soviet workers soon coined this description of their bargain with the state: "We pretend to work, and they pretend to pay us." It was a formula for disaster. Sure enough, Brezhnev's legacy was just that—a collapsing Third World economy, with nuclear missiles that no sane leader could fire.

It didn't have to be. The West, and particularly the United States, bears some responsibility for giving Brezhnev a free ride for so long. Once again, Washington misread the Kremlin's permanent power struggle. It thought, wrongly, that Brezhnev was in complete control, running a united leadership and a monolithic Party. Nothing could have been further from the truth. The real situation is worth recalling carefully. It is a classic example of the West's missing an opportunity to end the Soviet threat decades earlier.

Brezhnev was challenged at the outset of his rule by his own prime minister, Aleksei Kosygin, who understood that rational economic reform was overdue. An experienced industrial manager, Kosygin moved up the Party ranks in Leningrad, Russia's most sophisticated, Western-looking city. Intellectually, Kosygin was way above roughnecks like Brezhnev and Podgorny who had climbed through provincial Party ranks, running mining and farming regions in the Ukraine. When Charles de Gaulle visited Moscow in 1966 he met with Brezhnev, Kosygin, and Podgorny together. Later, the French president told aides Kosygin was "the smartest man in the room."

Aleksei Kosygin was smart enough to know exactly what needed doing. He championed the ideas of Yevsei Liberman, a Kharkov University economist, who proposed letting factory managers make more of their own decisions, based on local supply and demand. Instead of Moscow planners dictating the production of unwanted goods, rotting on store shelves and wasting millions, the factory managers themselves could decide to make the products that actually sold, in the colors, shapes, and sizes the public really wanted. It was, in short, a leap toward the market economy.

Unfortunately for Russia and the world, Liberman's ideas were rejected, mainly because Prime Minister Kosygin's backing was not enough. To be implemented, they also needed the Communist Party leader's support, and Brezhnev was opposed. The result was the postponement of reform for twenty years.

What the United States and other Western governments never understood at the time was that they had a chance to push this policy struggle Kosygin's way. And Kosygin's way led to meaningful economic change, opening Soviet society to Gorbachev-style political reform two decades earlier. Instead, the West missed the opportunity. This time, the key element was oil.

Oil was Leonid Brezhnev's savior. He was able to resist political liberalization in the Soviet Union because he was able to stop economic reform. And he was able to halt economic reform from the mid-1960s on only because of oil. In the Brezhnev years, oil and other energy exports brought in some $80 billion, the Soviet Union's largest earner of hard currency by far. In effect, oil paid for Brezhnev's mistakes. The domestic Soviet economy was stagnating, but oil earnings abroad allowed him to keep it going, along with the military buildup challenging the West. Ironically, it was the West that let him do this.

Western countries were buying Soviet oil throughout the Brezhnev years. A far wiser Western policy would have been a strict embargo on Soviet oil and gas. Turning off Brezhnev's oil earnings in the mid-1960s would have strengthened Kosygin's hand to push through economic reform. Indeed, at that stage, reform would have been Brezhnev's only option to put the economy right, because without oil earnings from the West he could no longer afford to keep the old system going. And once economic reform took hold, democratic political change would inevitably have followed, just as it did in the Gorbachev years.

This is not my own personal theory. The idea was first laid out to me in Moscow by Andrei Kortunov, one of Russia's leading experts on the United States. Kortunov then headed the foreign policy section of Moscow's USA Institute. I had asked him to give me a prime example of the West's missing an opportunity to push the Soviet Union toward reform decades earlier. The oil embargo in the early Brezhnev years was the example he gave. In short, a leading Soviet specialist on Cold War relations was convinced the idea would have worked.

One advantage of using a Western oil embargo to pressure Brezhnev toward reform was that Moscow had no way to fight back. The West was not dependent on any Soviet exports, so economic retaliation was out of the question. So was any military response. Moscow had just backed down over Cuba in 1962 and was still at least a decade away from closing the missile gap or seriously challenging the military superiority of the United States.

Admittedly, embargoes are not always effective. To work properly, any boycott of Soviet oil exports by the NATO allies and Japan would have required a very difficult policing operation. But this problem was not a key factor in the early Brezhnev years. Then and later, the West was favorably disposed to boycotts as a policy tool, against South Africa's apartheid, for instance.

The main reason a Western embargo on Soviet oil was not considered at the time was not feared retaliation and not difficulties in policing. The main reason, indeed the only reason, was that no one in Western governments had thought it through. No one correctly read the emerging split between Kosygin and Brezhnev, and how the West might exploit it to promote reform in Russia, two decades before Gorbachev, without a risk of nuclear war.

Perhaps never before had Western misunderstanding of the Kremlin's permanent power struggle been more damaging. This time, by failing to exploit its considerable leverage, the West allowed Brezhnev to keep the upper hand from 1964 until his death in 1982. Inside the U.S.S.R., the result would be an end to all reform from the top until then. Abroad it meant prolonging the Soviet nuclear threat for another two decades.

Throughout this book the reader will come across similar missed opportunities again and again. In each case the Soviet Union's relative economic, military, and foreign-policy weakness could have been more effectively exploited by the West to pressure an earlier collapse of communism. In each case, the main failing, the key reason why the West never properly seized its advantage, was an inadequate understanding of how the permanent Kremlin power struggle worked. That is the reason why the continuing Soviet leadership battle was explained in this early chapter. It should be kept in mind as subsequent Western mistakes are discussed.

Leonid Brezhnev was fortunate. He never had to face serious pressure from the West to reform the Soviet Union. But even Brezhnev, as we will see next, could not halt the pressure for change from his own determined countrymen. Although their rebellion from below was long and difficult, it eventually played a significant role in the collapse of the Soviet system. In the end, Brezhnev could not defeat reform. He could only delay it.

PART II

Leonid Ilyich Brezhnev

(1964–1982)

4

All That Jazz

It started like a spy thriller. The Russian said only to take Leningrad city bus number so-and-so and get off at the end of the line, just after dark. "Don't speak English," he warned the Americans.

They met at the appointed time and place in a heavy rain. The Russian hurried the Americans down a narrow street, then up to the second floor of what had been an aristocratic theater in tsarist times. Now its gilt-and-crystal chandeliers adorned a workers' club. And there, under a red banner saying "Forward Toward the Victory of Communism," began one of the weirder moments in people-to-people diplomacy. Perhaps for the first time ever in Leningrad, Soviet and American amateur jazz buffs sat down together for a jam session, with their favorite music their only common language. "A miracle," Volodya Petrov, a bearded young Russian engineer with a hot trumpet, said later. "I still don't believe it really happened."

For him and the other Russians, that jam session with the Americans in early 1965 capped years of struggle that most foreigners could not begin to understand.

Soviet authorities then still regarded jazz as bourgeois poison. They feared such decadent capitalist influences could lure the nation's youth away from the Communist path. And they were right. Indeed, that was part of the attraction. Millions of Soviet young people were only too ready to be seduced.

So the country's top art critic, Nikita Khrushchev, denounced jazz as "the kind of music that gives you a feeling of nausea and a pain in the stomach." He likened the sound to "a streetcar screeching to a halt." His Olympian disapproval officially gave jazz the status of forbidden fruit—and thus enormously increased young appetites to taste it.

Adam and Eve, the first pair tempted by forbidden fruit, had an easier time of it. They could eat the apple when God wasn't looking. In Moscow, Russian jazz aficionados had no apple, no tree, not even a seed. There were no Western jazz records or sheet music or technique books for sale. With jazz officially banned, there seemed to be no way to get started.

So Russia's jazz buffs learned the hard way. With remarkable zeal and ingenuity they planted their own seeds. Clandestinely, they listened to jazz programs on foreign shortwave radio networks like the Voice of America or the BBC. At first they recorded the music on x-ray film, later on tapes, playing them over and over again until the notes could be transcribed into sheet music. At last they could practice, and play their own jazz.

They were almost there. But technique was something else. Early Russian jazz sounded dreadful. To the first Moscow jazz combos, loud was nice, but deafening was really beautiful. They hadn't learned any better yet, although no one could blame them. After all, how can you learn technique when you only hear jazz loud enough to get through radio static, and never listen to the best in concert?

Unfortunately for them, détente and cultural exchanges were only starting. They wanted Dave Brubeck, Miles Davis, and the Modern Jazz Quartet. Instead the Russians brought in Benny Goodman in 1962 with the 1930s swing sound for the older folks, then went back to classical music.

Young Russian jazz musicians refused to be discouraged. They learned what they could from Goodman and waited impatiently for another opportunity, however imperfect. The next chance came when George Szell brought the Cleveland Symphony Orchestra to Leningrad's Philharmonic Hall in 1965.

Volodya Petrov and four friends seized it. On opening night, during the first intermission, they approached the percussion section of the Cleveland orchestra. In pidgin English and sign language they asked if the drummers or any of the other professional classical musicians were also amateur jazz buffs. Bingo. They got four Americans. Dick Weiner and Joe Adato played drums, Bob Matson jazz piano, and John Rautenberg the flute. All agreed to the hush-hush bus ride to the workers' club's jam session later in the week.

"The Russians were phenomenal," Weiner said afterward. "Any criticism of their playing is unfair. What they lack in technique they compensate for in enthusiasm and natural ability. There was no problem of amalgamation. It was as if we had always played together.

"Our jazz musicians could teach them a lot," he added. "We're only amateurs, but as it was they flipped with us."

Petrov was ecstatic. "What did it feel like?" I asked him after the jam session.

"Konyets sveta," he replied. "The end of the world."

He didn't know it then, but Petrov and other Russian jazz fanatics like him had started a revolution. Their younger generation simply refused to bend to the dictates of the state on one question important to them, musical taste. Over the years they would keep on playing jazz and demanding that it be given official approval until the authorities finally caved. First jazz would get the nod, and ultimately, incredibly, Russia would even become a country of rock and roll.

Significantly, the waves of political and economic reform which would eventually turn the Soviet Union toward democracy and capitalism over the next twenty-five years were not far behind the revolution in popular music. That is not to say one created the other. Jazz did not make Gorbachev. The determination of Russian young people to enjoy their own kind of music was only one thread in a huge tapestry.

Pressure for change rose in virtually all spheres of Soviet life, from the arts, to science, to education, to the marketplace and everywhere else. Examples are endless. In each case, stubborn Soviet citizens kept doing their thing their way until the authorities gave in and approved.

The same nonconformist artists whose abstract works were once smashed by KGB bulldozers at an illegal outdoor exhibit in a Moscow park now receive their own official one-man shows, at Russia's best museums. They defiantly kept on painting their way until the authorities changed.

Similarly, dissident writers kept on producing critical books, sometimes smuggled abroad, sometimes reproduced at home by *samizdat,* self-publishing on bad typewriter ribbons and worse carbon paper. They never changed. But the regime did. And eventually even Aleksandr Solzhenitsyn's bitterly anti-Soviet works were published in Russian and sold legally in the U.S.S.R.

Andrei Sakharov, the nation's greatest atomic scientist, turned dissident and became its conscience. Years of house arrest, forced feedings, and other KGB harassment sapped his health and shortened his life, but Sakharov never gave up his struggle for basic human rights in the U.S.S.R. Instead the authorities buckled, allowing Sakharov, in his final years, to become the most influential member of the Soviet parliament.

Sakharov was a rare exception. Most of those relentlessly insisting on change for the better were anonymous men and women, ordinary Soviet citizens, determined to do what they knew to be right, even at the risk of the Gulag. They started as a minuscule minority, scratching the fault lines of the Communist system, until they triggered the earthquake that brought it down.

Among them was the nameless Georgian entrepreneur. In the winter of 1965 he would leave sun-drenched Tbilisi in the south of the U.S.S.R., fly to snow-covered Moscow, and sell flowers in the subway there at huge profits, because shelves at state flower stores in the capital were bare then. He understood the laws of supply and demand better than the Kremlin leadership. It would take them another quarter century to see the light and move toward a rational market economy.

That pattern would be repeated infinitely. Khrushchev had opened a Pandora's box by ending the terror. Ordinary people could now push for change without fear of the death penalty, and they did, across the whole spectrum of Soviet life. Brezhnev never stopped them. All he did was delay reform.

Gorbachev gets the credit for at last permitting the inevitable changes. He deserves it, for his revolution from the top down took great skill and courage. But it is far from the whole story. For twenty-five years, people had been pushing from the ground up for a better life. By the time Gorbachev took power, they had provided a wave of pressure for him to ride. He would have accomplished nothing without them. Any thread to the mosaic makes the same point. Jazz, of course, was not the most important. But often, it was the most fun.

By the time Leonid Brezhnev took power in October 1964, jazz was a fact of Soviet life. Sure, it was still officially disapproved of. But determined young people played it anyway, in private in their homes, and, increasingly, in public in cafés. The Komsomol, the youth organization of the Soviet Communist Party, was worried. The Komsomol had a job to do—attract young people to a lifetime of service to the Party and the state. Yet the ban on jazz was turning young people off, and away from Komsomol membership. Threats no longer worked. Party leaders could hardly turn nuclear weapons on their own young people or condemn a whole generation to the Gulag for listening to jazz.

It was time for a new tactic, for admitting that if you cannot beat them, you join them. So, ludicrous as it may sound now, Komsomol leaders let themselves be talked into secretly putting jazz on trial, in April 1965. They had been looking for a fig leaf, a way of granting jazz official approval that somehow would not leave the Party looking naked in defeat. Young jazz lovers now gave them one.

The excuse was an international youth festival scheduled for Algiers later in the year. Moscow saw the festival as an opportunity to influence future Third World leaders. Komsomol bosses had to pick the Soviet delegation for Algiers with that goal in mind. As usual, they planned to include sports heroes and smashing girls, propagandists and KGB recruiters. But in one area of the festival's program, they knew Moscow was the odd man out. Other countries would send jazz groups. Russia, however, could not play that card, because jazz still lacked official Soviet approval. The situation was absurd. It made the Soviet Union look ridiculous in the eyes of the very same young people Moscow hoped to impress in Algiers.

Russia's young jazz lobby showed the Komsomol the best way out of that dilemma. Put jazz on trial, they said. Let us prove that you can sponsor our kind of music abroad and still not lose face at home. At last the bewildered Komsomol bosses, most of them over forty and hopelessly out of touch with the younger generation, agreed to listen. The result was one of the zanier trials in Soviet history.

Unlike Stalin's show trials of the 1930s, in which "enemies of the people" were made to confess in front of newsreel cameras, this tribunal was totally secret. It took place in a six-hundred-seat soundproof concert hall at Moscow's Hotel Yunost ("Youth"). Soviet newspapers never wrote a word about it. Invitation-only tickets went to musicians, pop singers, songwriters, Komsomol officials, and others with a stake in whether jazz got approved. Most Russians never knew it happened. Indeed, the trial was so secret that even the young organizers themselves never openly admitted what they were really doing.

On the surface, they had simply rounded up fifteen of Russia's best jazz groups to pick one for Algiers. It was a talent contest to solve a little foreign policy problem. But everyone knew the deeper meaning.

If all went well, jazz would get official Soviet approval for the first time. It didn't really matter who went to Algiers. Whichever Russian jazz group played there could only do so with the state's blessing. And that meant the music would at last be approved for everyone else. The real winners would be all Soviet jazz fans—millions of them.

The trial looked like anything but a jazz competition. There was no scruffy long hair, no drugs, no raucous noise-making, no torn jeans. Well-scrubbed young men arrived in crew cuts, white shirts, and ties, accompanied by girlfriends looking similarly prim and proper. I tried to sneak in. No luck. Foreign correspondents were no more welcome there than at closed Politburo meetings in the Kremlin. "This is a working session, not a concert," a Komsomol secretary huffed, as he firmly guided me out the door. "We are here to make political decisions."

Russia's young jazz fanatics knew exactly what they were up against. Komsomol bosses were typically humorless bureaucrats. That meant they were ignoramuses about jazz, easy to hoodwink, especially now with the Algiers problem.

The young Russians told them they were creating a new Soviet school of jazz. It had nothing to do with corrupting bourgeois Western influences, they insisted. Instead, they had composed unique new melodies from wholesome Russian folk themes. They gave their numbers Soviet-sounding names like "Lullaby for Svetlana" and "Five Steps in the Cosmos." Then they set those words to Dixieland tunes and other strains of typically American jazz.

Their ploy worked perfectly. The cretins on the Komsomol jury never made the connection. They didn't know—or didn't want to know—that the jazz buffs had simply set Russian words to American music. The Komsomol jury bought the Soviet-sounding titles, picked a group for Algiers, and gave jazz official approval.

The implications were mind-boggling. Russia's young generation, armed with nothing more than a determination to live their lives their way, had won their first Brezhnev-era battle with the monolithic Soviet state. They learned that if you push, you can win. Over the years, they would push again and again. The nation would never be the same.

Two years later, jazz blared out openly across the vast Soviet Union. Almost every organization capable of tapping feet formed yet another combo, among them medical students from the Ukrainian city of Lvov, scientists from a Siberian think tank in Novosibirsk, workers from the Far Eastern city of Khabarovsk. Three corporals and a private created the Little Star Quartet at their military base near Riga, capital of Soviet Latvia, and played jazz in their Red Army uniforms. Even the staid Moscow Conservatory, the nation's most prestigious university-level institute for classical music, introduced courses in jazz instrumentation. But the struggle was far from over.

Soviet jazz still played in not-so-splendid isolation. To come of age, it had to connect with the surrounding world. Young Russians still ached to see and hear Western groups, from Europe and most of all from the United States. By 1967 they were ready to escalate the war of nerves with the authorities to that level, by organizing the first international jazz festival ever held in the Soviet Union. Once again, mulish bureaucrats had to be convinced every step of the way.

No one said getting all the necessary approvals would be easy. And it wasn't. In the Soviet Union in 1967, you couldn't just rent a concert hall. The state controlled them all and could lock you out. Nor could you print up advertising leaflets. Again, the state ran all the presses. Nor could you invite foreign groups by phone or mail. The state tapped phones and stopped international mail whenever it liked. Yet somehow the young managed. The international jazz festival was set for Tallinn, the capital of Soviet Estonia, in May 1967.

Tallinn was a brilliant choice. No other Soviet city could match it as a window on the West. The Baltic Sea port city was only fifty miles across the Gulf of Finland from Helsinki, well within the range of Finnish television. More important, the similar Finnish and Estonian languages needed no translation. For a paltry sum, TV antennas in Tallinn could be rigged to capture Finnish television. In short, Tallinn pierced through the iron curtain. Ordinary Soviet citizens there could pick up Finnish television, and with it British, French, and even American programs in Finnish translation.

With that came Western ideas. The quaint little Estonian capital with its cobblestone streets and fairy-tale hilltop castle was, in Soviet terms, always a hotbed of radicalism. As it learned from the West, Tallinn became the first Soviet city where stores gift-wrapped packages, where ice cream came in flavors other than vanilla, where clothes, cafés, even discos looked Western. It was the right place for the first Soviet international jazz festival, just as twenty years later it would help trigger a Baltic independence movement leading to the collapse of the Soviet Union.

By the late 1960s, Moscow tolerated Estonian radicalism simply because it got good results. Shortsighted bureaucrats desperately needed some success, and Estonia worked as a model laboratory experiment for the rest of the U.S.S.R. At the time, they had no idea the process could ultimately unravel the whole Soviet State. To them, the Estonian experiment remained totally controlled, only somehow got better results.

Collective farmers were a good example. In Russia they would work only hard enough to fulfill state plans, or perhaps produce a slightly larger crop to earn a bonus. But in Estonia, that was only the beginning. In 1966 I visited an Estonian fish farm that used its extra catch to start and feed a thriving mink ranch, then turned its small boat repair shop into a huge furniture factory, all with official approval, at profits never foreseen by central planners, all at no cost to the state. As long as the Estonians met the fish quota, their Soviet masters were ready to let them expand into a conglomerate business improving the whole local economy.

The same tolerance pervaded the cultural scene. If the hardworking Estonians kept producing economically, they could have their international jazz festival. Naturally, there would be limits. Groups from Poland, Sweden, and even Britain got official invitations, to give the festival its international flavor. America, however, was something else, because of the Vietnam War.

Every day now, the Soviet press carried hate stories about barbaric U.S. warmongers dropping napalm on the peace-loving peasants of Vietnam. The Russians poured aid into Hanoi, not only to sink the Americans further into that quagmire, but also to outshine their archrivals for leadership in the Communist world, the Chinese.

Beijing couldn't match Moscow's generosity, so it played dirtier. At one point in 1967 the Chinese even stopped Soviet arms aid traveling by train overland across China to Vietnam, forcing the Russians into a longer, costlier, and more dangerous supply route on the open seas.

Kremlin leaders believed, rightly, that Beijing would stop at nothing to embarrass them in Hanoi, in order to increase Chinese influence there at Soviet expense. It was simply the wrong time for the Russians to be getting into bed with the Americans to consummate cultural relations. Any hint of that and China would gleefully point out Moscow's "hypocrisy" in consorting with the enemy. So even jazz had geopolitical fallout. As far as Soviet officials were concerned, the Estonians could have their international jazz festival, but without Americans participating.

"No way," the young Estonian organizers in Tallinn responded. How could you have an international jazz festival without the nation that invented jazz? To them it was like making apple pie without apples. One way or another, they determined, Americans would indeed play at their festival. Then they went whole hog and invited one of the wildest modern jazz groups then making its name on the American scene, the Charles Lloyd Quartet.

Charles himself looked like a black Leon Trotsky, complete with goatee beard, steel-rimmed glasses, and a thick head of hair combed skyward. He appeared on stage in a waistcoat and orange-and-black-stripped trousers, jumping up and down to the beat of the music he improvised on either the tenor sax or the flute, his hair flying. Keith Jarrett, later to outshine Lloyd as a solo artist, played piano then in the quartet, sometimes literally from the inside out, by stroking the interior strings instead of the ivory keys. Jack de Johnette on drums and Ron McClure, the only white member of the group, on bass followed Lloyd's moods with improvisations of their own. The Russians had never seen anything like them.

At age twenty-seven, Charles was then a rising jazz star, hungry to move higher fast. His quartet had won critical praise at the prestigious Antibes jazz festival in the South of France. Tallinn, he hoped, would add more international acclaim, much the way the Tchaikovsky Festival in Moscow had made the American classical pianist Van Cliburn a household name. So when the Estonians invited the quartet "to participate" in the first international jazz festival held in the Soviet Union, Charles grabbed the chance and agreed to pay his own way. Understandably he thought "participate" meant "play." He would soon regret having jumped to that conclusion.

Estonian festival organizers had chosen their words carefully, well aware that their Soviet masters would not let Americans play in the festival proper at Tallinn's six-thousand-seat sports palace. To them, "participate" meant give an informal workshop for Russian jazz buffs at some small schoolroom in town. They tried to explain that as Americans, the quartet was literally too hot to handle in the regular festival program. But Charles Lloyd was having none of that. He grew up in the Memphis ghetto, where he was constantly told what he couldn't do. The reason was always the same, the color of his skin. To Charles, Tallinn was Memphis all over again. "They won't let me play because I'm black," he declared.

I quoted Charles saying just that, in an Associated Press story sent around the world. Now the Soviets had another problem. Charles had made them look like racists. And, of course, racists they were. Most Russians thought blacks looked like monkeys and were better off living in trees.

Whatever they thought privately, however, Russians immediately turned indignant if foreigners publicly called them racist. On the contrary, they insisted, Soviet Communists always championed the downtrodden black victims of capitalism. So when Charles Lloyd accused them of racism, they were appalled, first because it damaged their international image, and second because in this specific case they believed his accusation totally unfair. To them, Charles was barred from playing in the festival because he was an American. Color had nothing to do with it.

It was as good an example as I ever saw of very different Soviet and American mind-sets clashing head on. Soviets and Americans come from such totally different planets that often they simply cannot understand each other at all. The gulf of misunderstanding between Charles Lloyd and the Soviet jazz festival overlords would now make that point increasingly clear.

The next day the Russians told Charles his quartet could indeed play in the festival hall, although in the afternoon rather than the evening. The Americans agreed. But when they arrived they found six thousand empty seats and one television camera ready to roll. It was glaringly obvious that Charles was being diddled. One quick splice job and the TV camera could make it look like his quartet had played the festival, when in fact it was still barred. Indignant, Charles and the others stalked out. "We are not going to be treated as second-class citizens," he told me. "They still won't let me play because I'm black."

I wrote a second AP piece about that. Predictably, the Soviets suffered further embarrassment. The young Estonian festival organizers were delighted. They thought their Soviet masters were now too humiliated to continue the fight. So they told Charles Lloyd his quartet could play that evening, the third night of the four-day festival. It never occurred to them that the Russians were still not ready to give up.

Charles and the others arrived at the sports palace that night. This time all six thousand seats were filled. Charles unpacked his sax and began to warm up backstage. Then at the last minute, the Soviets again said "nyet, you are not going on." Charles was outraged. "Now I won't play at this festival even if they beg me," he said. "Black men have pride too." I wrote a third story.

The next day, the Soviets literally begged him. Someone higher up in Moscow had decided enough was enough, phoned Tallinn, and told the festival chiefs to let Charles Lloyd play. He kept refusing. "You've insulted me," he explained. "I've had it with you."

Now the Soviets were desperate. Moscow had ordered them to put Charles Lloyd on, and he declined. They simply had to change his mind. But how? Then they thought of a way, in yet another total misunderstanding across the Soviet-American chasm. "If you agree to play tonight," they told Charles, "we'll get you a white girl to sleep with after the concert."

Their offer left Charles more insulted than ever. He was a distinguished young man who wore a tie and held a graduate degree from the University of Southern California. More important, he was a happily married man. Yet, instead of showing him respect, these Russians were transparently treating him as they saw him—as a savage in a loincloth. "What do they think I am, an animal?" he asked me.

Now I had a problem. For the next three hours I sat with Charles in my hotel room and tried to convince him he simply had to play that night. "Forget the bastards who insulted you," I told him. "The festival bosses are ciphers. The only people who matter are the jazz fans in the audience ready to kill to hear you play." I recapped their long struggle, from taping Western radio on x-ray film to the secret jam session with the Cleveland Orchestra to putting jazz on trial. "These kids started a revolution for you," I told him. "You owe them. You've got to play." In the end, I learned happily, I was preaching to the converted. Charles wanted his arm twisted.

They put Charles Lloyd on first for the closing night of the festival. They told him he had eight minutes. The quartet paid no attention. It had no sheet music. Charles improvised and the others followed. Then, as they picked up the response vibes from the clapping, stomping, yelling capacity crowd, they really took off. For twenty minutes, they were flying, the Soviet audience with them. When the quartet finally finished, it was rewarded with thunderous cheers and applause for another twenty minutes, in the greatest spontaneous outburst of affection for Americans I ever saw in the Soviet Union.

There was simply no way to stop the jubilant Soviet jazz fans. The master

of ceremonies tried. "Quiet down," he said. "Lots more acts are waiting."
They booed him off the stage. Five minutes later he came out again to admonish them: "Comrades, you are being childish." Again they booed him
off and continued applauding the Americans. Finally, even though Charles
had been the first act, they called an early intermission. Only then did the
crowd quiet down.

"It was beautiful," Charles said later as Russian fans besieged him for autographs. "I don't have the words. The music said it all."

Indeed, the music did say it all. And now there would be no stopping it.
Jazz had been only the first wave in the revolutionary defiance of Soviet
youth, the battle cry of the 1960s. By the early 1970s, another, far stronger
wave crashed onto Soviet shores and all but swept away the jazz craze. It was
called rock and roll. Once again, misguided Soviet authorities tried to hold
back the flood. Once again, they didn't have a chance.

Boris Grebenshchikov was fourteen years old when he decided rock music
would be his life. It took him another fifteen years to rise to the top of the
Soviet charts, and the climb still amazes him. Boris and his friends formed
a rock group simply because they wanted to play the music. They all held
odd jobs and played for fun. At first, it never occurred to them that they could
make money with their kind of music. But they did. Someone tape-recorded
a session, and they started selling the clandestine tapes in the Leningrad subway. Russian rock and roll was on its way.

The tapes led to underground concerts. Boris and his group made enough
money to buy Yamaha sound equipment from abroad, after a year of hassle. The deal was it had to be left at a Leningrad youth club for the use of
all. The first night some people who didn't know what they were doing
wrecked it. Then the Russians repaired it so crudely that it sounded like Soviet equipment.

Despite such frustrations, Boris persevered. By the time I met him in
Leningrad in 1987, his band, Aquarium, was the top rock group in the Soviet Union, and as such had been invited by Columbia Records to do a gig
in the United States with Bruce Springsteen and Sting, all with Kremlin blessings. Gorbachev had let rock music flourish in the U.S.S.R. to attract the support of the young for his perestroika changes. Boris Grebenshchikov, with
his shoulder-length blond hair tied in a ponytail, his faded jeans, and his T-shirt, was a national idol for Russian youth.

"Now we can fill any hall in the Soviet Union," Boris told me proudly.
"We're popular and the authorities need us. We can play when and where
we like." Everything he said was true. By 1987 his rock concerts guaranteed
sellout crowds in the nation's largest stadiums.

"But the most important thing is that we play what we want," Boris
stressed. "We play the same music we always did. We haven't changed at all.
The people in power had to change their thinking."

As a result, Leningrad had become one of the great rock music capitals of the world. Collectors took rock so seriously that it was easier to find an obscure group's 1960s tape there than in New York or Los Angeles. In Leningrad, all you had to do was dial a local telephone number to order virtually any rock and roll tape made anywhere at any time.

This was the same city where Stalin used to have poets, artists, and musicians shot. Older Russians never forgot that. Many feared the democratic revolution might soon collapse and a new dictator once again quash all artistic freedom. I asked Boris if he was afraid rock and roll might become the first victim of a return to authoritarian rule. But he was having none of that.

"They can shoot me tomorrow and I would die happy," Boris replied. "I got more than I bargained for. We made Russia a country of rock and roll. No one can take that away."

Boris Grebenshchikov has been right about a lot of things in his young life. He was right in his belief that if he determinedly kept playing his music his way, the authorities would eventually relent. He was right in showing what public pressure from the ground up can do, even in a police state. When he says rock and roll is in Russia to stay, he means that democracy may suffer temporary setbacks, but ultimately it will win out over dictatorship. His country and the world can only hope he is right once again.

5

Comrades

I. A HOUSE DIVIDED

Empires are always weakest at their edges. The Soviet empire, the largest in history, suffered greatly from that rule. No other empire ever had borders so long, so numerous, and so vulnerable. Every day, as the sun moved from east to west, it lit troubled Soviet frontiers with fifteen nations. Worse from Moscow's point of view, strained relations with every one of these neighbors either threatened war or had already caused one.

Worse still, this collection of past and potential enemies on Soviet borders included seven of the world's strongest global or regional powers, or their allies. First, starting in the Pacific, there was the United States, only fifty miles from Russia across the Bering Strait in Alaska. Then came the Soviet frontiers with Asia's two leading nations, China and Japan. Next was Pakistan, a U.S. ally, and Iran, a major player in the Middle East. Farther west, Soviet neighbors included Turkey on Europe's southern floor and Norway on its northern roof, both NATO members able to call on military help from the entire Atlantic alliance.

Adversaries on their frontiers were perceived in Moscow as one kind of threat capable of bringing down the Soviet system. Supposed friends raised other dangers. The four East European Communist nations on Soviet borders—Poland, Czechoslovakia, Hungary, and Romania—all posed threats of rebellion breaking up the empire. The Kremlin kept them in line by military occupation and economic subsidies. But ultimately that course too helped bankrupt the system.

Even the Soviet Union's four smallest neighbors strained Moscow's military and economic resources to the extreme, among them North Korea, in its Soviet-backed war on the South. Mongolia had to be run as a Soviet protectorate, in order to keep the Chinese out. Finland nearly fought off Russian invaders in World War II. Afghanistan eventually did.

Everywhere the pattern was the same. Russian aggression, beginning in tsarist days, and threats of more to come under Soviet leaders caused all the border problems. The Soviet empire was built on territory taken from neighbors, from Japan to China to Iran to Romania to Finland, to name but a few. Nonetheless, the bullies in the Kremlin saw themselves as the victims. Any demands by neighbors for the return of seized lands were regarded in Moscow as unwarranted anti-Soviet hostility. Any defensive measures taken by neighbors alarmed by Soviet militarism were just as invariably interpreted in Moscow as aggressive designs. To the worst-case theorists in the Kremlin, the Soviet Union was surrounded by revenge-seeking nations determined to recover lost territory in new wars that could break up the U.S.S.R. From Stalin's time on, that perceived threat was a top priority concern for all Soviet leaders.

They were almost paranoid about real and imagined dangers of hostile neighbors like China and even near neighbors like Germany combining to do them in. One far-fetched scenario that Brezhnev's contingency planners took very seriously indeed in the late 1960s, for instance, was capitalist West Germany and Communist China launching a two-front attack on the U.S.S.R., from Europe and Asia at the same time, each to regain territories lost in past wars.

Any analysis of the decline and fall of the Soviet empire has to start with the obsession about borders. Eventually many other factors played important roles, from dissent and economic weakness inside Russia to Western resolve abroad. Nonetheless, the rot began at the border, where Soviet leaders always knew it would. And building an impregnable defense, securing borders against military attack, would still not be enough to save them.

Even an iron curtain could not completely keep out ideas. Liberal reforms in Communist Eastern Europe or Islamic power in Central Asia were regarded as poisons that could seep across frontiers, stir up trouble inside the Soviet Union, and ultimately bring down the empire. Any such challenges had to be smashed at the outset. It is no accident that the only times Soviet troops invaded foreign soil since World War II were to put down precisely such challenges in three neighboring countries, all viewed in the Kremlin as strategic—Hungary, Czechoslovakia, and Afghanistan. No other foreign policy priority was ever deemed important enough to secure with invading Soviet troops.

Washington, by comparison, had a simpler outlook. It saw a two-dimensional world, with U.S.- and Soviet-led alliances competing for supremacy. Moscow had a much darker, more complex vision. It saw the Soviet Union standing alone against threats from just about everyone else, from declared foes to supposed friends. The world's three other leading nuclear powers allied in NATO—the United States, Britain, and France—were only the beginning.

In the Kremlin's view, the Soviet Union's Communist fraternity, from China to Eastern Europe, could be more trouble than capitalist adversaries. All too often, the comrades were anything but comradely. In the long run, the U.S.S.R.'s nominal Communist allies along its border would do more to bring down the empire than the Western democracies on the other side of the Cold War divide.

Moscow's response to all the perceived threats it faced was to build the most colossal military force in history, nuclear and conventional, beginning in Stalin's day and culminating in Brezhnev's. Soviet officials always insisted this was defensive, to hold the empire together, to defeat as many simultaneous threats as necessary and still crush an internal rebellion if need be.

Of course, the unprecedented military buildup also alarmed and threatened Western nations, among others, escalating the global arms race. But that was not the stated intention. The official Soviet goal was to protect its empire, under threat from all sides. Throughout the Brezhnev era, this line of argument got routinely repeated in Moscow as so patently obvious that no further justification was needed. On one such occasion, a Soviet government spokesman I was visiting explained Moscow's relentless military buildup by pointing to the map of the world on his office wall and saying, "The United States has peaceful borders with Canada and Mexico. The Soviet Union is entirely surrounded by hostile states."

For many years, China seemed to be the greatest single danger. Beijing challenged Moscow for leadership of the world Communist movement. The four-thousand-mile disputed border between the Soviet Union and China was a constant source of tension, and occasional firefights. Talks between the two Communist giants on territorial and ideological differences stalled for decades. Meanwhile, war jitters grew ominously. China outmanned the Soviet army conventionally. And when Beijing began to develop atomic weapons, the Kremlin nearly panicked into thinking the overall military balance would swing to China. According to reports I was shown privately by a U.S. Defense Intelligence Agency chief in Washington, Brezhnev's Politburo once considered a preemptive nuclear attack on China's atomic weapons facility at Lop Nor. But it dropped the idea when it realized the radioactive fallout could reach Japan. That risked bringing both Tokyo and its ally the United States into a war against the Soviet Union on China's side.

During the early Brezhnev years, the Chinese were the worst troublemakers in Moscow. At a demonstration I saw outside the American embassy in 1965, hundreds of rock-throwing Chinese students protesting the Vietnam War tried to smash their way into the building. Outnumbered Soviet police, required by diplomatic protocol to protect the embassy, called in reinforcements mounted on horseback. But the Chinese were ready for that. Some rolled marbles under the horses' feet to trip them into toppling their riders. Others brought down the horses by beating at their legs with wooden poles. The poles were just long enough to keep the Chinese students out of the range of Soviet mounted police uselessly swinging batons above them. In the end, the Chinese forced the Russians to call out the army to restore order in Moscow for the first time since the Bolshevik Revolution.

All Chinese students were then expelled from the Soviet Union, a shocking move. Never during the Cold War were American students as a group ordered to leave the U.S.S.R. But then again, American students never rioted in Moscow either. The unruly behavior by Chinese students was only one sign that Moscow often had more trouble with its Communist allies than its capitalist adversaries.

On their trip home, the expelled Chinese students managed to cause the Russians even more embarrassment. They walked onto planes home at a Moscow airport in perfect health. But many of them were then carried out of the same planes in Beijing heavily bandaged and on stretchers, complaining they had been victims of Soviet police brutality. When it came to attacking the Soviet Union, Chinese propagandists had no shame.

Chinese behavior on the Soviet border could be equally crude. At the frontier point for the Moscow-Beijing rail line in 1965, Chinese customs officers liked to show what they thought of Russia by dropping their trousers and pointing their bare bottoms toward the Soviet Union. Eventually Soviet customs officers brought out a portrait of Mao Zedong and placed it directly in front of the Chinese. Out of respect for their leader, the Chinese then felt compelled to turn around and pull their pants back up.

In Moscow, thoughtful Russians were not amused. Many feared war with China was a bigger danger than war with the United States. But they were looking the wrong way. The Achilles' heel of the Soviet Empire, the border region destined to do the most in bringing about the inevitable collapse, was always Eastern Europe.

Bad as the threat from China seemed to ordinary Russians, it still looked relatively manageable to Kremlin leaders. China was seen as too weak militarily to move much beyond the border region into the Russian heartland, let alone to defeat the Soviet state. The same could not be said, however, of the United States and its NATO allies. Soviet leaders understood that invasion from the West might indeed bring down the Soviet state, unless it could be stopped first in Eastern Europe, the likely line of approach. Thus holding Eastern Europe as a buffer zone against Western attack became the Soviet Union's top security priority throughout the Cold War.

Troop deployments proved the point. The Soviet Union kept nearly half a million men occupying Eastern Europe, and hundreds of thousands more nearby as potential reinforcements. In all, substantially more Soviet soldiers, planes, and tanks were kept ready for deployment in Eastern Europe than on the Chinese border, and with ample reason: China was the lesser threat.

Nor were long-term prospects with China necessarily all grim. At least communism had legitimacy in China. Under Mao's leadership, the Communists gained widespread public support, and eventually took power by winning a civil war. Whatever the subsequent problems between Moscow and Beijing, communism had a homegrown base in China, and, with that, grounds for an eventual rapprochement with the U.S.S.R.

Not so in Eastern Europe. Communism there had to be imposed by a foreign power, the Soviet Union, against the will of the local populations. After World War II, the Red Army remained in Eastern Europe, allowing Stalin to rearrange the political players there. In the end, East Germany, Poland, Hungary, Czechoslovakia, Bulgaria, and Romania—more than 100 million people in all—fell under Stalin's control. Only Tito's Yugoslavia retained genuine independence. Elsewhere in Eastern Europe a permanent Soviet occupation force would hold the region in the Communist bloc. Their numbers would remain massive because they had a double mission—to keep the West out, and to hold the East Europeans in.

The Sovietization of Eastern Europe was never very pretty. In an infamous example of the period, Jan Masaryk, a leader of Free Czechoslovakia, fell to his death from his office window shortly after a Communist coup in 1948. Whether he jumped or was pushed has never been made clear. From the beginning, East Europeans had ample reason to detest communism. The foreign power that had thrust it on them was more alien than most. Historically and culturally, the nations of Eastern Europe had far more in common with Western democracies than with Soviet Russia. For one thing, the profoundly religious Catholics of Eastern Europe could never accept Soviet atheism. Economically, their preferred trade routes were with the capitalist West, not the Communist East. Politically they were too well educated to accept the Communist straitjacket as passively as illiterate Russian peasants resigned to their fate.

East Europeans would resist the travesty of imposed communism for four decades, sometimes pathetically, as when they were reduced to throwing rocks at tanks. But they always regrouped, always maneuvered in new ways, always continued the struggle against enormous odds. For them the way out of communism was the road back to national dignity. They never gave up until they broke free—and broke up the Soviet empire in the process.

Eastern Europe did not operate in a vacuum, of course. Collectively, the Western allies contributed mightily to the collapse of Soviet power. For forty-two years they kept NATO strong, ahead in an arms race Moscow could never win, until the Soviet empire collapsed from its own internal contradictions. Western pressure was thus an essential element.

Despite the successful outcome, however, Western policy toward Eastern Europe was hardly covered with glory. On the contrary, the West as a whole and the United States in particular carry a heavy burden of responsibility for ever letting communism spread to Eastern Europe in the first place, and then allowing it to last there for four decades. Communist control over Eastern Europe through two generations was never inevitable. Instead it was one of the great avoidable tragedies of the twentieth century. To a large extent, the United States and the NATO allies let it happen.

The tragedy of Eastern Europe will be examined at length in the pages that follow. It is a leading example supporting one of the central arguments of this book, namely that the Soviet system was always doomed, and that wiser American statesmanship could have brought it down decades earlier, at no risk of nuclear war. The East European case study also shows that the main culprit behind this U.S. failing was neither Democratic nor Republican administrations in Washington, but rather a generally flawed American vision of both the unity of the Soviet leadership inside the Kremlin and its control of the entire world Communist movement, from the 1950s to the 1980s.

To put it in Marxist terminology, the way the Soviets themselves would immediately understand, the forces of history moved to Western advantage after World War II, but Western statesmen failed to seize opportunities over the ensuing decades. By the 1950s, even the world Communist movement was changing to the potential advantage of the West. It was becoming too diverse for the Soviets to keep together, let alone control. In Stalin's day, Moscow had dictated Communist policy globally, but by the time he died, Tito's Yugoslavia was already a rival model for Communist loyalty, and Mao's China another. In later years, the family feuds only got worse. Alexander Dubček offered yet another model in Czechoslovakia. Eventually even Eurocommunists in France, Italy, and Spain would provide still more alternative models. Once the world Communist movement split, no one could put Humpty-Dumpty together again. By the 1960s, the world movement was an enfeebled shadow of the monolith Stalin had created.

Through it all, the various fissures in the Communist world provided pressure points for the West to exploit. They were ripe for manipulation in the context of Russia's historic obsession with its own relative weakness, surrounded by adversaries on its borders. There was potential, for example, for the United States, Western Europe, and China, acting together, to discourage the Kremlin from sending tanks into Eastern Europe to crush reform. Wisely used, these pressures could well have won freedom for Hungary in 1956 and Czechoslovakia in 1968, without risking nuclear war, as we shall see. Instead, such options were not seriously pursued.

The United States and its allies never fully understood the extent of the divisions in the world Communist movement, or how they could be exploited to weaken the system earlier. It was a familiar shortcoming. In much the same way, the United States and its allies never fully understood the splits within the Kremlin leadership, or how the Soviet Union's internal power struggle could be manipulated to bring down communism earlier. Among the opportunities missed there, as we saw earlier, was that of strengthening Kosygin's reformist hand against the conservative Brezhnev. Not surprisingly, the Western response to the Soviet challenge abroad was often as inadequate as the Western response to Soviet internal policy.

Admittedly, the West faced difficult choices at each stage. Statesmen responsible for the decisions always claimed they had no alternative, that in the end they had to sacrifice the narrower interests of Eastern Europe for the broader cause of world peace. That was not always true, however. Far from it. A correct assessment of Western responsibility for the Communist calamity in Eastern Europe has to separate those occasions when there was no real alternative from those when better options existed but were never used. The historical record to be reviewed is long and bitter.

It began at Yalta, the tsarist summer resort on the Black Sea. Stalin, Churchill, and Franklin Roosevelt met there in February 1945, the eve of the Allied victory in World War II, to plan for the postwar world. The Allies had the Nazis in a fatal squeeze. The Russians were closing in from the East, the Americans and British from the West. The end was only a matter of time. At Yalta, Stalin made his naked bid for a free hand in Eastern Europe after the war. His Red Army troops had already driven the Germans back to within thirty miles of Berlin. In the process they had occupied Poland and most of Eastern Europe. The only way to stop him was for Roosevelt to keep American combat troops in Europe after the defeat of Nazi Germany, if need be to turn on their wartime allies, and push the Soviets back.

That was politically impossible. U.S. public opinion was demanding that Roosevelt "bring the boys home" as soon as Hitler was defeated. At Yalta, Roosevelt and Churchill really had no other choice. So they let Stalin have his way, extracting only the worthless promise that he would permit "free elections" in Eastern Europe. Stalin made sure the elections would be meaningless by refusing to let international observers monitor them. Thus Eastern Europe became a Soviet zone because the West had no stomach to stop Stalin by force.

There was the dilemma in a nutshell. Politically, practically, the West had no alternative but to let Stalin grab Eastern Europe. Morally, however, the West still had to accept responsibility for its decision to stand aside.

Yalta set a bad precedent. It established the conventional wisdom of Eastern Europe as a Soviet zone of influence where the West had no leverage. That myth outlived the reality. Situations changed, but the West never developed the will to challenge the Yalta precedent seriously. In later years the problem was no longer a lack of viable options. Instead it was one of priorities. Sadly for East European nations, they were not a top priority for the West when better opportunities arose to roll back Yalta.

In 1956, when Hungary rebelled against communism, the West was too distracted and divided by the Suez crisis unfolding at the same time to react effectively. Similarly, when Czechoslovakia tried to end Communist repression in 1968, the United States was embroiled in the Vietnam War and in a poor position to challenge Soviet claims in Eastern Europe at the same time.

Nevertheless, the West could have done better. No one seriously argues that either Hungary or Czechoslovakia was the moment to risk nuclear war. Still, unlike Yalta, both presented opportunities to force peaceful change for the better in Eastern Europe, partly by exploiting the growing splits within the world Communist movement. Instead the United States did worse than nothing.

Budapest was the classic example. In 1956, Hungary rebelled, and quit the Soviet-led Warsaw Pact alliance. John Foster Dulles, then the U.S. secretary of state, had encouraged the uprising with bellicose speeches calling for the iron curtain to be rolled back. But when the crunch came, with Budapest in revolt, Dulles proved all bark and no bite. Instead of pressuring Moscow to stay out of the crisis, he meekly informed the Soviet leadership that the United States would not seek to bring Hungary into the Western alliance.

State department records show that U.S. Ambassador Charles Bohlen delivered that message to the Kremlin on Dulles's instructions. It was another way of saying that Yalta lived, and that the United States still recognized Eastern Europe as the Soviet zone of influence, in effect, inviting Moscow to do what it pleased in Budapest. Khrushchev did so by sending in the tanks to crush the Hungarian rebellion. Dulles would have done better saying nothing. In fact, Dulles had a rare opportunity there to back his words with acts, and indeed roll back the iron curtain, short of war. The world was changing then. And there was adequate time for negotiation to keep the Soviet tanks from rolling.

In the first place, the Hungarian crisis built for three years before it exploded, from Stalin's death in March 1953 to the Budapest uprising in October 1956. Unfortunately, U.S. diplomacy was often behind the curve throughout this period, rushing to catch up to events rather than staying ahead of them. In the second place, numerous changes favored a negotiated settlement. For openers, Stalin's heirs were divided, obsessed by their own succession struggle in Moscow, anxious to avoid problems abroad, and therefore vulnerable to outside pressures.[1] They proved this in settling the Korean War, which had been impossible while Stalin lived, and in agreeing to Soviet troop withdrawals from Austria in 1955.

The Austrian example is particularly relevant. The Red Army's retreat from Vienna ended ten years of occupation since World War II and allowed Austria to became an independent, neutral nation. It was the result of a successful negotiation by the United States, Britain, and France with Stalin's successors in Moscow. One year later, there were ample reasons to believe the Russians could be pressed into similar Soviet troop withdrawals from Austria's neighbor Hungary to let that nation become neutral as well. Among them was Moscow's own view of Eastern Europe. Seen from the Kremlin,

Hungary was relatively expendable, never as vital to Soviet security interests as Poland or East Germany.

The key was always East Germany. As long as Germany remained divided, with the eastern half firmly in the Communist camp, the Germans would never dare attack Russia again, as they had in World War II, at a cost of more than twenty million Soviet lives. Therefore, Poland, which stood between the Soviet Union and East Germany, was also crucial. Only by keeping Poland in the bloc could Moscow maintain its hold on East Germany.

The other East European countries—Hungary, Czechoslovakia, Bulgaria, and Romania—expanded the buffer zone, the geographic insurance policy discouraging attack on the U.S.S.R. All were thus strategically important members of the Warsaw Pact, the Communist military alliance, but only two Warsaw Pact members, East Germany and Poland, were absolutely vital. That distinction was particularly important in Hungary's case. It meant that given enough pressure, Moscow could have been forced to let Budapest go.

When the Hungarian capital went up in rebellious flames on October 23, 1956, the divided Soviet leadership hesitated for eleven days, unable to decide between withdrawing its troops from Hungary or invading with more. China was urging Moscow against responding with force, a key restraining factor, since the Soviets wanted approval from the world Communist movement for any invasion. China thus added significantly to the pressure for a negotiated settlement.

Nor was that all. Yugoslavia, which had broken with Stalin in 1948, was talking about returning to the Soviet camp and was setting terms for a rapprochement. Moscow dearly wanted that, enough to make concessions. Among them, Belgrade could have insisted on no use of force in Hungary. The Yugoslavs, who had their own reasons for fearing Moscow's military might, would have been reassured if the Kremlin promised to keep its hands off Hungary. In the end, Belgrade did not play this card, a decision the Hungarians regarded as a betrayal. But for eleven days it was one of the many elements that could have been exploited by more effective American diplomacy.

The United States had a rare opportunity to change the face of Eastern Europe by pressing for a peaceful, negotiated solution to the Hungarian crisis. It could have done so from a position of strength. In 1956 the nuclear balance was so overwhelmingly in American favor that there was no way the Soviets could risk war. If challenged by the United States, they would have to back down, as they did six years later in the 1962 Cuban crisis. Most important, in 1956 there was no need for the United States to threaten nuclear war—or even to risk it.

Much could have been accomplished short of that. There was ample room to pressure the divided Soviet leadership with warnings against invading Hungary, carefully worded so they never specifically threatened to intervene with U.S. troops, but never completely ruled that out either. All that was needed was just enough ambiguity to give a shaky, divided Kremlin leadership pause.

There was also time to enlist the Yugoslavs in the cause, to back the Chinese call for moderation, to threaten to aid the Hungarian rebels. There was even room to revise the Yalta legacy, to warn that any Soviet invasion of Hungary would nullify Yalta and thereby strike at the legitimacy of Moscow's hold on Poland, East Germany, and the rest of the bloc. All these moves might well have convinced Moscow it had more to lose by invading Hungary than by staying out.

Unfortunately the United States did none of the above. It issued no warnings to Moscow, made no efforts to back Chinese demands for moderation, no attempt to enlist Yugoslavia in the cause, no threats to arm the Hungarian rebels, no noise about revising Yalta. There was, of course, no guarantee that such a diplomatic strategy would work, but it might have succeeded. And if it had, it could have led to the reform and demise of communism in Eastern Europe decades earlier.

However, the truth is that the United States was singularly unprepared. A prominent Hungarian analysis of the U.S. role at the time put it this way: "It has never occurred, not for a single moment, to the leaders of the United States to do anything tangible in support of or to rescue the Hungarian revolution. They have undeniably felt sympathy to it, but this sympathy never went beyond a few humanitarian gestures or statements. They had neither plans nor intentions to lend effective aid or to bind the hands of the Soviet Union."[2]

When the Hungarian rebellion erupted, the badly prepared U.S. government was unable to scramble and pull together an effective, immediate response, primarily for two reasons. First, President Eisenhower was running for a second term and the election was only two weeks away. He thought the last thing he needed then was another foreign controversy on top of the botched British-French-Israeli invasion of Suez. Eisenhower wasn't looking for a way to get involved in the Hungarian crisis, even though, properly handled, a strong stand there could have helped his reelection bid.

Second, Eisenhower's chief foreign policy adviser, Secretary of State John Foster Dulles, had long misread the situation. Dulles saw the Communist bloc and the Soviet leadership as monolithic. He was blind to the divisions inside the Kremlin and in the Communist world that could have been exploited on Hungary's behalf, by diplomatic pressure alone, without risking direct U.S. military involvement in the conflict.

This was not a partisan failing. It had nothing to do with Republicans and Democrats. Dulles, the Republican, failed to seize an opportunity to reshape Eastern Europe in 1956 during the long-building Hungarian crisis, because his vision of Soviet reality was skewed. The same flawed vision of a supposedly monolithic Soviet leadership would affect the Democratic administration of Lyndon Johnson a decade later, when it missed the opportunity to exploit the differences between Brezhnev and Kosygin and push Moscow into meaningful reform twenty years before Gorbachev. The failing was American. Presidents from both parties made the same mistakes, over and over again.

Sadly, their mistakes were clear at the time. This is not the wisdom of hindsight. After the Hungarian crisis of 1956, for instance, there was time for the West to rethink how it might do better the next time Eastern Europe exploded, as it inevitably would, but, in fact, the West did no better the next time.

By the Prague Spring of 1968, when Alexander Dubček's reforms introduced "socialism with a human face" in Czechoslovakia, the challenge was very different. Dubček deliberately left foreign policy alone. Unlike Hungary, he loyally stayed in the Warsaw Pact, to avoid provoking alarm in Moscow. Even his domestic reforms were relatively modest—press censorship ended and there were progressive economic changes, but in a further effort to reassure Moscow, the Czech Communist Party maintained its monopoly on power. There was no multiparty system in the Prague Spring reforms. Still, Brezhnev wouldn't buy even those deliberately restrained changes. To him the modest reforms in Prague were a frontal attack, imperiling the survival of world communism. So, as Khrushchev did in Hungary in 1956, Brezhnev sent in the tanks. Yet he did so only after making sure the United States would not intervene there, even indirectly.

During the Prague Spring, President Lyndon Johnson followed much the same flawed response strategy that Eisenhower used over Hungary in 1956. Once again, 1968 was an American presidential election year, a poor time for controversial foreign policy initiatives. Once again, America already had one quagmire abroad, this time the Vietnam War, and no stomach for a second crisis in Eastern Europe. Once again, a divided Soviet leadership hesitated over what to do, from April, when Dubček announced his controversial "Action Program" of reforms, to August, when the Kremlin finally decided to smash them with tanks. The long delay provided opportunities for U.S. diplomatic pressure that might well have stayed the Soviet hand. But once again, the United States waived any real chance to influence the course of events and persuade Moscow to stay out.

This time the evidence comes from Anatoly Dobrynin, the longtime Soviet ambassador to Washington. Dobrynin's job in 1968 was to sound out American leaders on how they would likely react to the crisis building in Prague, in particular whether Washington would give Dubček military aid. The Soviet envoy's assessment, preserved in official Kremlin archives, was obtained for this book.

"The question of direct U.S. military assistance to Dubček," Dobrynin reported to Moscow, "did not arise, either at the beginning or later." The Americans "recognized that Czechoslovakia belonged to the Soviet sphere of influence," he added. "The rather restrained reaction" of the American government to the developments in Czechoslovakia was explained by the fact that "U.S. policy and resources were tied up in Vietnam." The Johnson administration preferred not to jeopardize "the preparation of Soviet-American talks" on disarmament and other key issues and "would not yield to the temptation to give the Soviet Union several propaganda black eyes," the ambassador predicted.[3]

In fairness to Johnson, he was not alone. London, Paris, Bonn, and other allied capitals reacted much the same way. They preferred business as usual with Moscow, rather than any meaningful support to Dubček and the Prague reformers.

Once again the West had strong cards to play. The NATO allies could have demanded that Moscow stay out and issued warnings of dire consequences if the Soviets invaded, from trade sanctions to suspending arms control talks that Moscow needed more than the West. Once again there is no assurance such a diplomatic strategy would have worked, only that it carried no risk of escalating to nuclear war. Once again it is tragic that the West never even tried.

II. A HUMAN FACE

Czechoslovakia deserved better. The "socialism with a human face" that Dubček devised was just the sort of program Western democracies should have been supporting in every way they possibly could throughout Eastern Europe. It was the proper road ahead for the entire region, and one day even the Russians would admit that. In 1968, however, Czechoslovakia found itself virtually abandoned by the rest of the world, a nation of only fourteen million people standing alone against the Soviet superpower. Still, despite the odds, the Czechs refused to submit to Moscow's demands for a total rollback on reform, long after Russian tanks had occupied Prague. What they lacked in military muscle, they made up for in courage and brains.

Immediately after the August 20–21 invasion, Soviet KGB agents arrested Dubček and flew him to Moscow in chains. The independence of Czechoslovakia then depended on only one man, President Ludvík Svoboda, a former general decorated by the Russians for his bravery against the Nazis in World War II. Under the Czech constitution, the president alone had the right to name a new government. The Soviets, seeking at least the appearance of legality, were demanding that Svoboda install as Dubček's successors a regime of Czech traitors who had long collaborated with Moscow, but the president, whose last name means "freedom" in Russian, categorically refused. Svoboda said he would commit suicide first.

Then the white-haired old general flew to Moscow to confront the Soviet leadership face to face in the Kremlin. As an astonished Brezhnev looked on, Svoboda dramatically removed the Soviet medals from his uniform and flung them down on the conference table in disgust. His absolute refusal to accept a Soviet puppet government was his last word. Svoboda declared he would have nothing further to say until Dubček was released and restored to office in Prague. His demands were not negotiable.

In the end, this one unarmed but defiant old man accomplished what the United States and the entire NATO arsenal did not even dare try. Ludvík Svoboda forced the Brezhnev leadership to back down. Alexander Dubček was freed, and returned to office in Prague.

That was only the beginning. Dubček, of course, returned to a different country, now occupied by 600,000 troops from the Soviet-led Warsaw Pact. Czechoslovakia's neighbors and supposed friends—Poland, Hungary, Bulgaria, and East Germany—had joined in the invasion. Moscow was confident the huge occupation force on the ground would soon make Dubček shelve his reforms and then drive him from office. Again the Russians miscalculated.

Resistance in occupied Czechoslovakia continued to be nothing short of phenomenal. The beleaguered Dubček leadership still enjoyed broad public support, especially for the ingenious tactics it employed to stall retreat on reform.

The Soviet occupiers screamed, bullied, and threatened, to little avail. Dubček and the reformers carried on regardless. It took the Russians from their invasion of August 1968 to April of 1969 to get rid of Dubček and his reforms and finally force this small isolated country back into the mainstream Communist fold under the more conservative Gustav Husák. For most of these eight months, Dubček and his supporters were confident they could outmaneuver the Russians and keep the Prague Spring reforms alive. Had the United States and the Western allies given them even modest help, they might have made it.

I was privileged to work in Prague for the month of December 1968, the midpoint of Dubček's post-invasion resistance struggle. Czech confidence was still remarkably high. Virtually every measure the Soviet occupiers imposed by force to clamp down on reform was stood on its head by Dubček's people and used instead to promote continued reform.

Press censorship, brought back by Soviet demand, was just one example. Every morning the editors of all publications in Prague had to meet to receive their marching orders from the Soviet occupiers. Among other things they were told not to criticize Soviet policy, and they complied. But they really used the censorship meetings to coordinate the Czech resistance.

Every day they would agree on something all of them would carry to advance the Dubček cause. Perhaps it would be a report on a conference by students or workers or farmers called to support continued reform. All the editors would agree to treat that conference as the major news event of the day. The next day they would run a public opinion poll, as they did on December 17, 1968, showing that 91.2 percent of the people questioned preferred government policies before the Soviet invasion in August. And so it went, day after day.

For a journalist used to Brezhnev's Moscow, Dubček's Prague seemed wide open by comparison, even under the Soviet occupation. In Moscow, Communist Party Central Committee plenums were still top-secret affairs. In Prague, incredibly, members of Dubček's Central Committee called on Western correspondents in their offices in advance to tell them, accurately, what the next plenum would do. It was another way the Czechs fought Soviet pressure to roll back reform. By making their intentions public in the Western press, they hoped to forestall Soviet arm-twisting to change the script. I was given advance notice of a plenum that would reject a Soviet offer to withdraw occupation troops in return for Dubček's resignation. A few days later, the plenum met and indeed rejected that Soviet offer.

Even travel around Soviet-occupied Czechoslovakia was much freer for Western journalists than travel around the Soviet Union. One day my photographer and I rented an Avis car in Prague and drove twenty-five miles north to Milovice, the largest garrison of Soviet troops in the country. Along the road, four months after the invasion, there were still signs painted in Russian saying "U.S.S.R.–Aggressor" and "Invaders Go Home." No one tried to stop our car, despite the political implications of letting Western correspondents see such signs, let alone visit a military base. In Moscow at the time, one could not rent from Avis or any other Western car-rental firm. And certainly one could not drive off to the nearest military base without being stopped and turned back.

In Milovice, we found a small café, across the road from the base. It gave us a chance to share a few beers and some chat with off-duty Russian soldiers. These young draftees were on their first visit abroad, but Czechoslovakia was no pleasure trip for them. Their officers had told them NATO troops were threatening to take over the country, that Soviet forces had been sent in to prevent such aggression, and that the grateful Czechs would greet them as hero-liberators. Instead the Czechs had screamed at them the worst possible insult any Russian could hear. The Czechs had said they were just as bad as the Nazi invaders in World War II.

"Our officers lied to us," a Russian private admitted to me. But that wasn't the worst of it for him. He couldn't get over the Czech insults, which he regarded as totally unjustified. "We are not occupiers like the Germans," he said. "We live in the barracks and we don't bother anybody." His discomfort was typical. Morale among Soviet occupation troops was so bad that Moscow had to rotate in replacements. Often the new troops were from the

Soviet Union's Central Asian minorities—Uzbeks or Kazakhs—less sensitive to Czech taunts than European Russians.

At one point the scene in the café got nasty. A Soviet soldier named Vasily didn't believe I was an American. We had been speaking in Russian. To prove my nationality, I showed him my passport. He took a look, then decided not to give it back. I had to reach over and grab it from him. Fortunately, Vasily decided not to start a fight.

A young Czech soldier sitting alone at a table nearby watched all this without saying a word. When photographer Michel Laurent and I left the café, the Czech soldier did too, motioning us to follow him. Our new Czech friend explained to us that the base used to be the Czechoslovak army's main garrison for the defense of Prague. After August, the Czechs had moved out so the Soviet occupiers could move in. A few Czech soldiers had been left behind to do grunt work for the new tenants. Our friend was one of them. He now hated the Russians, and was willing to do anything to get back at them, even risk his life. He was about to prove it.

The Czech soldier took us into his barracks. He had a spare uniform that fit Michel, an absolutely fearless Frenchman, who a few years later would become the last photographer killed in the Vietnam War. In the Czech uniform, Michel was able to wander through the Soviet base at Milovice and take pictures of the Russian occupiers and their military equipment without being stopped. Had he stayed in civilian clothes, Michel never would have gotten past the first Soviet guard.

Even in the Czech uniform, Michel was taking a dreadful chance. By Soviet standards, he and our new Czech friend were conducting blatant espionage with every photo taken inside the base. For Michel, discovery would have meant confiscated film, arrest, detention, and eventual release. The young Czech soldier risked far worse. He would likely be executed by a Soviet firing squad, and he knew it. But he desperately wanted the outside world to get an accurate picture of what was really happening to his country, whatever the risk. Such was the courage and commitment of a young Czech soldier who never told me his name.

The contrast could hardly have been more stark. The Russian soldiers I met outside Prague were unmotivated and demoralized. My Czech army friend was spoiling for a fight and keen to sacrifice everything for his country. Had the United States and the West chosen to arm a Czech resistance, it might well have driven the Russians out, as Afghanistan eventually did. This time, however, it was not to be.

Czechoslovakia had to find subtler ways to resist. Among them was the refusal to buckle in fear under the pressure of an occupation. Instead the Czechs would carry on as best they could with a normal life far superior to anything their Soviet occupiers knew back home. Christmas 1968 in Prague was filled with this delicious irony. By comparison, Moscow did all the suffering.

Brightly colored Christmas lights dominated the Prague scene. There were none available in Moscow. Prague shoppers bought Western goods as presents for loved ones. In Moscow, there was not even any colored wrapping paper for holiday gifts, let alone items imported from the West. In Prague there was plenty of fresh meat, fish, vegetables, and fruit. In Moscow shoppers stood in long lines just to get bread, and often found little else in food stores. The irony was no surprise. The Soviet economy had long been bled dry to support the army now occupying Prague. The Czechs, with no great-power military ambition, could produce and enjoy consumer goods.

I had Christmas dinner with Czech friends. They included my translator, Iva, her scientist husband, Lubor, their son, Dan, then a university student, and Iva's mother. They lived in a comfortable three-bedroom apartment. In Moscow these three generations would have been squeezed together in only one room and shared a common kitchen and bathroom with three other families. For Christmas Iva got some French perfume and a nonstick frying pan. Neither was obtainable in Moscow.

Conversation around the dinner table was much more political and far more open than anything Russians would have dared with foreigners in Moscow. In those days most Russians were still too afraid to visit foreigners, let alone talk seriously with them.

Dan was particularly serious. Like other Prague students then, he criticized Dubček for telling the Czech army not to resist the Soviet invasion. Many older people thought that Dubček had been right to avoid unnecessary bloodshed, that any armed resistance by the far smaller Czech military would have been futile. But Dan was having none of that. "It's a matter of national dignity," he insisted. "The Poles would have fought back. We should have fought too." Once again, he was showing a potential for resistance that the West had chosen to ignore.

Lubor, his more urbane father, preferred to poke fun at the political situation. Czech anecdotes from the 1968 occupation were particularly telling.

"What is the safest country in the world?" Lubor asked. No one knew. "Israel," he replied, "because it is completely surrounded by enemies." The story got a big laugh from around the table. Czechoslovakia, of course, was surrounded by so-called friends—and had just been invaded by them.

Lubor then switched to domestic politics in this dialogue with himself: "Who was the prime minister of Czechoslovakia under Antonín Novotný, the former hard-line Communist leader?

"Answer: Oldrich Cernik.

"And who was prime minister of Czechoslovakia under Alexander Dubček?

"Answer: Oldrich Cernik.

"And who will be prime minister of Czechoslovakia when Dubček is removed and his reforms quashed?

"Answer: Oldrich Cernik.

"So, what's changed?

"Answer: Oldrich Cernik."

Iva was more optimistic about the prospects for meaningful political change. "The Soviets invaded and accomplished nothing," she said. "They haven't killed the reforms in four months and they won't."

I was apologetic to my hosts but much more pessimistic. Having recently finished a three-year assignment in Moscow, I was convinced the Russians were prepared to be ruthless in Czechoslovakia, to keep increasing the pressure until they had smashed the reforms.

So we made a bet. Iva said if she was right, if the Czechs succeeded in keeping the reforms, then she would invite my family to Czechoslovakia in one year's time, to go skiing in the Tatra Mountains. But if I was right, if the Soviets did nail the coffin on reform, then in a year we would invite Iva to visit London, where I then worked.

A year later, with the conservative Communist Gustav Husák firmly in power and the Dubček reforms long gone, we got a postcard from Iva. All it said was: "It's time to invite me to London."

We did and she came. At least under Husák's newly retightened noose, Czechs could still travel abroad more easily than Russians. But Iva was not the same. The bright optimist of a year earlier in Prague had become downcast and worried. She saw nothing good happening to her country in her lifetime. Sadly, we were now agreed. All of us, Iva's family and mine, wished that somehow things could have turned out the other way in 1968.

Some twenty-five years later, rummaging through newly opened official archives in Moscow, I made a startling discovery. Iva was almost right in her original optimism. The Dubček reforms might well have succeeded in 1968 and saved the country the next two decades of unnecessary suffering. Russian foreign ministry archives recently made available now show that the invasion of Czechoslovakia could have been avoided entirely, if only the Soviet embassy in Prague had accurately reported the situation there to the Kremlin leadership. It was that close a call.

Unfortunately, the embassy had little interest in accurate reporting. Instead it preferred to play politics. Ambassador Stepan Chervonenko and his staff in Prague, including the KGB, reported only what they thought their Kremlin masters wanted to hear. Their cables show they deliberately distorted the political situation in Czechoslovakia before the Soviet invasion, vastly inflating the conservative opposition to the Dubček reforms and totally ignoring the widespread public support for them. Soviet archives also establish that cables from the embassy in Prague were the major source of information the Kremlin leadership used in deciding how to respond.

By the summer of 1968, any accurate reading of the political temperature in Prague would have concluded Dubček had won the internal political struggle. Had the Soviet embassy been doing a proper job, it would have warned Moscow that Dubček now enjoyed overwhelming public support, which could be broken only by invasion and then months of subsequent repression by the occupying forces, all with still no guarantee of success.

In short, the embassy in Prague owed Moscow a proper assessment of the risks. And any sober analysis of those risks might well have made the Soviet leadership decide against military intervention. After all, Leonid Brezhnev was cautious to a fault. His Politburo waited months before deciding to invade Prague, carefully weighing all possible consequences. Any realistic assessment of the resistance a Soviet invasion faced would likely have tipped the Brezhnev leadership's decision the other way.

But the embassy served Brezhnev badly. Its one-sided reports quoted only Dubček's hard-line opponents and made them sound like the dominant voice in the country. The Dubček forces were dismissed as pro-capitalist plotters. The embassy also made it sound as if most Czechoslovaks were demanding Moscow's help to get rid of the Dubček regime. None of its assertions were true.

On June 1, for example, an embassy cable quoted a conservative member of the Czechoslovak Communist Party Central Committee, identified as only as F. Havlicek, as saying Dubček was preparing "a counterrevolutionary coup" against the Party, and that Moscow should intervene to stop him. Another embassy cable on June 6 quoted two other conservative Czech Communist officials as saying the Soviet Union "should fulfill its duty and use its troops" in Czechoslovakia.[4]

Distorted embassy reports on rising crime, food shortages, and strikes painted a further picture of chaos and a discontented public ready to welcome Soviet intervention to put things right again. Cables like this went out almost every day in the months just prior to the August invasion decision. In the end, Soviet leaders could be forgiven for believing ordinary Czechs were clamoring so hard for Moscow's "help" that the invasion would be almost risk-free. Their own embassy was deliberately lying to them.

Here was one of the great weaknesses of the Soviet Union, exposed for anyone to see. The system was so rigid that all subordinates had no choice but to toe the leadership line. As far as Eastern Europe was concerned, Kremlin leaders wanted to believe that communism had popular support there, that the only dangers arose from a treasonous minority, and that any Soviet crackdown on them would receive wide backing. It would take a very brave Soviet ambassador indeed to cable back to Moscow, "No, you are wrong, the anti-Communist movement in this country has overwhelming popular support."

Telling the Soviet leaders what they did not want to hear was a sure way for an ambassador to lose his job. Not surprisingly, he therefore preferred to send back reports that would please his masters, even if he knew them to be untrue. The result was an accumulation of data skewed to push the Kremlin leadership toward unwise foreign policy choices, in this case invading Prague.

How many other foreign policy mistakes the Russians made on the basis of deliberately inaccurate reporting from their own diplomats abroad is impossible to say. But clearly the overly rigid Soviet system must have produced many similar errors of leadership judgment based on faulty information input.

Stepan Chervonenko was not about to risk his career by telling Brezhnev the unpleasant truth. On the contrary, the Soviet envoy to Dubček's Prague had every personal interest in playing the system to advantage and reporting swelling demands for Soviet intervention. The one precedent for his position certainly looked promising. The Soviet ambassador to Hungary at the time of the 1956 invasion, none other than Yuri Andropov, had done very well indeed since calling in the tanks. By 1968, Andropov had already risen to be head of the KGB. Eventually he would succeed Brezhnev as the top Soviet leader. Ambassador Chervonenko might similarly benefit from an invasion of Czechoslovakia and be promoted to high office. So he advised Brezhnev to invade.

In the end, that solved nothing. Eastern Europe continued its drive to escape from communism through reform. Worse, the outside world was appalled by Czechoslovakia. No act of the Brezhnev years did more to discredit the Soviet Union abroad and raise fears of a Soviet military threat to world peace. Many in the West had wanted to believe that the Soviet Union had changed for the better since the 1956 invasion of Hungary. They had been proved wrong. After Czechoslovakia in 1968, the result was a renewed arms race that ultimately Moscow could not win.

Eventually, Brezhnev recognized his mistake. Czechoslovakia was the last time Soviet tanks would crush reform in Eastern Europe. Henceforth, Brezhnev understood, subtler ways would have to be found to accomplish the same thing. In 1981, when Lech Walesa's Solidarity movement threatened to bring down communism in Poland and beyond, Brezhnev agreed to the so-called internal solution. This time the Polish army conducted the crackdown. Soviet advisers provided communications, intelligence, and other essential backup assistance, but Moscow's role was relatively restrained. This time Soviet tanks didn't roll, because they didn't have to. Even the unimaginative Brezhnev could see there were other ways.

Chervonenko, the Soviet ambassador to Prague in 1968, would pay for his deceitful role by being passed over for promotion by a new generation of Soviet leaders. The new men would ultimately take a very different view of the invasion of Czechoslovakia. Among them was the Communist Party first secretary of the Stavropol region of southern Russia, who was allowed in 1969 to take one of his first trips abroad. One year after the invasion, this impressionable thirty-eight-year-old visited Prague for a firsthand look at the reforms that had been tried and smashed there. His name was Mikhail Gorbachev.

Twenty years later, in what must pass for poetic justice in the Communist world, Gorbachev was running the Soviet Union. He would decide that the arms race and maintaining Moscow's hold on Eastern Europe were bankrupting the Soviet system. So instead, he would pull out Soviet troops, let the East European nations chart their own futures, end the Cold War, and ask the West for aid.

Like other great innovators, however, Gorbachev had underestimated the downside risk. The Soviet withdrawal from Eastern Europe, he thought, would encourage a new generation of Dubčeks, leaders who would find ways to improve the Communist system there, and in the process create reform models that might work in Russia itself. But he was much too optimistic about a brighter Communist future.

Given the choice at last, the East Europeans had no interest in improving communism. Instead they moved to get rid of it entirely. With incredible speed, the Berlin wall came down in 1989, and with it, communism all across Eastern Europe. The nightmare scenario Khrushchev and Brezhnev had feared became reality. Eastern Europe was the crucible, the model of what would soon come to the Soviet Union itself. Russia's economic reformers had gotten their ideas largely from Eastern Europe. So had Russia's political dissidents. So had the nationalist movements in Soviet republics from the Baltics to the Ukraine to Central Asia, tearing the U.S.S.R apart. Within two years, all these forces would combine into the collapse of the Soviet Union itself. But all that was yet to come.

The year 1989, when Gorbachev let Eastern Europe go, was a time of great confidence. Anything seemed possible. In his commitment to reform, Mikhail Sergeyevich had gone to the Vatican and become the first Soviet leader to meet with a Roman Catholic pope. The pope he met was from Poland, a key influence in the rise of the Solidarity movement that had toppled communism there. Nor was that all. The same day Gorbachev made his peace with the Polish pope, he moved on to Milan and, in an extraordinary act of penance, admitted publicly that the 1968 invasion of Czechoslovakia had been a mistake.

And that was still not all. When communism fell in Czechoslovakia, Alexander Dubček was brought back from oblivion and elected president of the National Assembly in December 1989. In his new capacity, restored to political prominence, Dubček came to Moscow in May 1990 for a truly historic meeting with Gorbachev.

It seemed like a miracle. The great Czech reformer, once kidnapped to Moscow in chains, had lived long enough to return to the Kremlin in triumph and thank the great Russian reformer who had let Eastern Europe leave the Communist fold.

When Alexander Dubček left the Kremlin that day, he said of Mikhail Gorbachev: "I have just seen the human face of socialism." There was not a dry eye among the men and women who heard him say it. All were choked with emotion. No other man, no other words, could have said better what the Dubček-Gorbachev meeting of minds in the Kremlin really meant. The symbol of the Prague Spring and the new master of the Kremlin had fully agreed. A forty-year Communist tragedy was at long last over. Eastern Europe was finally free. There would be no going back.

6

Dissent Comes Out of
the Closet

I. THE MOVEMENT

In the Soviet Union, the writer had both artistic and political influence. So the Kremlin routinely bribed or threatened authors into becoming cheerleaders for the regime. Sometimes, however, all pressures failed, and a truly independent literary figure emerged, unafraid to tell the truth about communism's failings or to articulate the need for change. Such writers posed a special danger to a system that tolerated no opposition political parties, indeed no organized opposition of any kind. No other single individual in society had the writer's potential to mobilize the Soviet public against their leaders and demand that the evils of the past be eradicated. Aleksandr Solzhenitsyn, who long personified that role, understood it perfectly well. In his novel *The First Circle,* Solzhenitsyn had his hero, Innokenty, say as much, in these words: "For a country to have a great writer—don't be shocked, I'll whisper it—is like having another government."[1]

Solzhenitsyn's words proved prophetic. The Soviet dissident movement, the first serious opposition force in Russia since the Bolshevik Revolution, began with writers. They were not even great ones—critics today regard them as secondary literary figures. But no one denies their honesty and courage. Unable to publish in Russia works that criticized the Soviet system, they sent the manuscripts abroad simply in hopes of being read. Little did they realize at the time that they were starting a movement that would help end Communist rule.

Historians now have no difficulty pinpointing the birth of the modern Soviet dissident movement. It began in February 1966 with the trial of Andrei Sinyavsky and Yuli Daniel, two Russian writers who ridiculed the Communist regime in satires smuggled abroad and published under pen names. Both men were prominent enough in Moscow literary circles to have been pallbearers at the funeral of Boris Pasternak, the greatest Russian writer of the century. There could be no clearer proof of their status as free spirits.

Pasternak himself had defied the Soviet regime by publishing his epic novel, *Dr. Zhivago,* abroad. For that he had been hounded, denounced as a pig and a renegade, and forced to decline the 1958 Nobel Prize for Literature, but Pasternak was never jailed for his writings.

With the Sinyavsky-Daniel trial, Soviet repression of artistic dissent reached a new low. They were the first prominent Russian writers since Stalin's death in 1953 to be condemned to years of prison camp labor for their published views. It was a key signal that the new Brezhnev leadership intended to turn the clock back from Khrushchev's reforms toward Stalin's repressions. The sentences profoundly shocked the Soviet intelligentsia. Many feared worse Stalinist terror would soon be revived, but this time some of them determined to fight back. They created the Soviet dissident movement to prevent any further backsliding.

Thus were the battle lines drawn. Sinyavsky and Daniel were only a potential danger for the Kremlin, and a minor one at that, but the Brezhnev regime blew the immediate threat out of all reasonable proportion. Two writers with no effective way to break through official censorship to communicate with their own people, let alone mount a rebellion, were seen by the Kremlin as nothing less than a frontal challenge to Communist rule. Both the exaggeration of the threat and the brutal response of sentences to the Gulag proved to be colossal errors. They compounded the problem. Brezhnev's overkill reaction did far more to push thoughtful Russians into creating the Soviet dissident movement than anything either Sinyavsky or Daniel ever wrote. Once organized, the movement was never fully silenced. It would soon make human rights in the U.S.S.R. a *cause célèbre* worldwide. In only two decades, the dissident movement would become a major force leading to the decline and fall of the Soviet Empire, as important a contributing factor in its own way as the unworkable economy or rebellion in Eastern Europe. Now, with the wisdom of hindsight, one wonders how Brezhnev could have so dismally overreacted to books hardly anyone would have noticed if the Kremlin had simply ignored them.

Sinyavsky smuggled out through French friends, under the pen name Abram Tertz, a novel called *Lyubimov.* In it a humble bicycle mechanic with magical powers isolates his town from the rest of Russia by a sort of psychic curtain and wins support for his leadership by promising them everything from unlimited wealth to water that tastes like champagne. Sinyavsky's satire effectively exposed the emptiness of Soviet promises and performance.

Daniel, who wrote under the name Nikolai Arzhak, mocked the lawlessness of the Soviet regime with a story about "Public Murder Day," when the Kremlin allows its citizens to kill just about anyone they like, except high officials, of course.

Nobody in Russia or abroad paid much attention to either man's clandestine work. All that changed, however, when Soviet authorities put them on trial in a courtroom closed to the Western press, charged them with anti-

Soviet slander, and condemned Sinyavsky to seven years in the Gulag and Daniel to five. Then their books became world-famous.

The greatest living writers in the West rallied to their cause, among them Arthur Miller, Graham Greene, Günter Grass, and François Mauriac, in a propaganda disaster for the Kremlin. In the Soviet Union, the regime's favorite tame writer of the day, Mikhail Sholokhov, noted that in Stalin's time, Sinyavsky and Daniel would have been shot, "but now, if you please, people talk about the sentences being too harsh."[2] Needless to say, his defense of the sentences only made the Kremlin look worse in the West and added to fears in Russia of further backsliding toward a new terror.

In Moscow, a few young people stood in silent protest outside the trial. Fittingly, the courtroom was only yards from the stench of the city zoo. Foreign correspondents also waited outside the court for scraps of news on the proceedings. It was literally outside the Sinyavsky-Daniel trial that future Soviet dissidents made their first contacts with the foreign journalists who would soon publicize their names and views around the world. Among them was a tough, short, wiry young man named Andrei Amalrik, a historian who had already survived exile and forced labor in Siberia for his outspoken views.

Andrei was the first Soviet dissident I met. In 1966 we were both in our late twenties, recently married, fascinated by international politics and contemporary art. Andrei's Tatar wife, Gyusel, herself a talented artist, introduced me to the leading Russian nonconformist painters of the era, among them Oskar Rabin, Anatoly Zverev, and her own teacher, Vasily Sitnikov.

With so much in common we soon became good friends. Andrei took me to their tiny apartment off the Arbat in central Moscow, a rare treat. In those days foreigners almost never got invited home by Russians. The neighbors would talk; the KGB would interrogate.

Still, Amalrik was fearless. To him "inner freedom" was the essential prerequisite to freeing Soviet society. By inner freedom, he meant remaining true to his personal morality code. The authorities can arrest and punish you, "but they are powerless to deprive you of your moral values," he would say. To Andrei, being true to moral values meant a total refusal to bow to Soviet illegality or censorship, to speak the truth whatever the consequences, to fight for basic human rights, and in a very small way, to invite a foreigner home if he felt like it.

Andrei and Gyusel lived in one room with a wooden wardrobe I will never forget. Inside was a hanger with Andrei's only change of clothes—one other shirt and pair of trousers. It was another reflection of values. What little money he had, Andrei preferred to spend on books and art, not clothing.

Inside the wardrobe, glued to the back of the door, was an aging photograph clipped from *Pravda*. It showed Nikita Khrushchev and Mao Zedong, clasped together in a bear hug, grinning profusely. The caption read: "Long live the unbreakable friendship between the Soviet Union and the People's

Republic of China." By the time Amalrik showed it to me, the two Communist giants were already engaged in a bitter ideological dispute and occasional armed clashes along their four-thousand-mile border.

China was central to Andrei's thinking. In the essay that made him famous, "Will the U.S.S.R. Survive Until 1984?" he argued that economic stagnation and rebellions by minority nationalities would so weaken the Soviet empire that it would collapse after losing a war with China, before the year immortalized in George Orwell's novel.

Amalrik was wrong, of course, about the specifics. There was no war with China. But, in general, his vision was extraordinarily accurate. Economic stagnation, minority nationality unrest, and overall weakness would indeed produce the collapse of the Soviet empire, and only seven years after 1984. Tragically, Andrei did not live to see his prediction come true. Arrested, jailed, constantly harassed by the KGB, he unwillingly emigrated to France with Gyusel in 1976, and died soon afterward in an automobile accident. Fortunately, many others in the Soviet dissident movement were able to continue the struggle without him.

By 1968, only two years after the Sinyavsky-Daniel trial, they already had their own journal, the first uncensored publication in the Soviet Union. It was called *A Chronicle of Current Events.*

The first issue, dated April 1968, was a classic *samizdat,* or self-publishing operation. One copy handed to a typist armed with paper and carbons would become ten. Then each of those copies would multiply. After that, issues appeared every six weeks or so. Usually copies would find their way to specialists in the West in about two weeks. Eventually they would be quoted extensively in the world's leading newspapers.

Chronicle editors stayed anonymous at first. Their tone was calm and unemotional, the contents scrupulously accurate. Relentlessly, they reported on arrests and trials of dissidents, their mistreatment in the prison camps and mental hospitals, and the struggles of persecuted minority groups from Crimean Tatars to Ukrainians, Jews, Baptists, and many others. Reports came from all over the Soviet Union, even the Gulag. Hundreds of people were involved, from prominent scientists and intellectuals to ordinary workers, a minuscule fraction of the 280 million Soviet people, but enough to make a difference. No longer could Russians or foreigners say they didn't know about Soviet repression. From 1968 on, the *Chronicle* gave them chapter and verse, from the tiniest details of individual cases to a broad look at the whole continuing travesty.

That same year, 1968, the Soviet dissident movement went international. At noon on August 28, seven demonstrators sat down in Moscow's Red Square, outside the Kremlin, to protest the Soviet invasion of Czechoslovakia the week before. They unrolled banners which said, "Long Live Free and Independent Czechoslovakia," "Shame on the Occupiers," "Hands Off Czechoslovakia," and, most apt of all, "For Your Freedom and Ours."

Almost immediately, a whistle blew, and KGB plainclothesmen rushed at them. According to one of the demonstrators, the poet Natalya Gorbanevskaya,[3] they ran up shouting "They're all Jews," "Beat the anti-Soviets," and "Disperse, you scum."

The demonstrators sat quietly, making no attempt to resist. They were beaten and arrested. Among them were Yuli Daniel's wife, Larisa Bogoraz, and the physicist Pavel Litvinov, the grandson of Stalin's foreign minister Maxim Litvinov. Viktor Fainberg, a fine arts specialist, was beaten and bloodied until his teeth were knocked out. His face was so disfigured that Soviet authorities couldn't put him on trial in public. Instead they decided his participation in the demonstration was evidence of an unsound mind and confined him in a mental hospital.

The *Chronicle* dutifully followed the fate of the Red Square demonstrators until all were at last released. One typical entry, from 1969, covered Vadim Delone, a poet. It said: "Vadim Delone is now in a camp in Tyumen [western Siberia]. His poem 'A Ballad of Unbelief' was discovered during a search. For this poem, Delone was given ten days in the *shizo* [isolated in a punishment cell]." While there he tried to protect himself from the terrible cold one afternoon by climbing into his bunk. "For this violation of camp rules, Vadim Delone has been forbidden any parcels [food, mail, or clothing from home] or visits [from relatives] for half a year."[4]

Gorbanevskaya, the mother of two small children, was the only Red Square demonstrator not jailed. She immediately wrote an open letter published by leading newspapers in Europe and the United States. In it, Gorbanevskaya said the demonstration had been worthwhile, despite the arrests, if only to show the world how outraged thinking Russians were by the invasion of Prague and the official Soviet lies defending it. At the time, the Moscow press claimed Czechoslovak authorities had asked for Soviet help to put down an anti-Communist uprising inspired in the West, and that the grateful citizens of Prague had showered the invading Soviet troops with flowers to thank them for their "fraternal assistance."

Her words are worth repeating today to show the link they established between the Soviet dissident movement and the continuing anti-Communist rebellion in Eastern Europe. "My comrades and I are happy that we were able to take part in this demonstration," Gorbanevskaya wrote, "that we were able, if only for a moment, to interrupt the torrent of barefaced lies and the cowardly silence, to show that not all the citizens of our country are in agreement with the violence which is being used in the name of the Soviet people. We hope that the people of Czechoslovakia have learned, or will learn, about this. And the belief that the Czechs and the Slovaks, when thinking about the Soviet people, will think not only about the occupiers, but also of us, gives us strength and courage."[5]

Over time, the human rights struggles in Russia and Eastern Europe would indeed reinforce each other, with shared ideals and tactics, even with exchange visits and eventually with correspondence by fax. The strikes and mass demonstrations first staged by Poland's Solidarity would one day be echoed in the Soviet Union itself. Ultimately, those links would ensure that once the Berlin Wall fell, the collapse of communism in Russia would soon follow.

But first the struggle would take many years, and, most of all, much courage. Soviet dissidents knew only too well what lay in store for them. From Stalin's day on, people merely suspected of opposing the regime went to prison while their cases were investigated. Never mind that they had never been formally charged with anything or might be completely innocent. Never mind that the whole notion of political opposition as a crime is offensive to any civilized society. Suspects routinely got hauled off to jail cells they would be lucky to survive, in Khrushchev's day as in Brezhnev's. Admitted dissidents could expect only harsher treatment every step of the way.

The typical cell holding suspects was built in the nineteenth century. It lacked all amenities. That meant no toilet, just a bucket. It also meant appalling filth, rats, and no heat through bone-chilling winters. Suspects enduring all that were next refused sleep, subjected to starvation diets and brutal beatings, then denied medical care. Whatever tortures they suffered, suspects still had no right to contact relatives or lawyers during the investigation, which could last up to a year. Authorities rarely needed that long to force the confessions they wanted.

Conviction brought new cruelties, if not the death sentence then a living death. Prison camps provided an abundant supply of slave labor. In Siberia, when winter temperatures dropped to 40 degrees below zero, nails split when hit by a hammer blow, but Soviet prisoners kept on working anyway. They were expendable. In summer, Siberia turned into a swamp, infested with thick black clouds of mosquitoes. Prisoners worked then too. They worked that year-round hell outdoors, poorly clothed and fed, on construction sites stretching thousands of miles across Russia. Often they worked until they dropped. If they survived, their sentences could always be arbitrarily extended. There was no appeal, no justice. The jailers had all the rights, the prisoners none, until well into the Gorbachev reform era.

Punishment for political opposition was deliberately designed to be as cruel as possible to discourage further dissent. "It was based on the idea that the harder you squash the prisoner, the better you sleep," a senior Soviet police official once told me. That sinister policy was infinitely more subtle than it sounds at first. Not all political prisoners got squeezed to death. Enough made it out of the Gulag alive at the end of their sentences to spread the word across the country. Opposition to the Party line, they in effect warned, was fatal. "Don't even think about it."

For the most part, the Soviet regime's terror tactics against its own people worked as a deterrent. All opposition was ruthlessly stamped out in Stalin's time. After that, the great mass of the population stoically accepted every repression, convinced that any protest or demand for change was worse than useless. It was suicidal.

Against those monstrous odds, a tiny Soviet dissident movement began to emerge in the 1960s. Its numbers were pitifully small, literally a handful of men and women ready to stand up for what they believed was right, whatever the consequences. Most likely, they knew, that meant risking their health or their lives in the Gulag. And that made their courage even more remarkable. Most suffered arrest, prison, or expulsion from their homeland along the way. But their determination never broke. Armed only with their convictions, they unswervingly pursued their cause. It took them some twenty-five years. But in the end, they won. Their defiance beat the impossible odds. They forced their jailers to release them, and to change their country for the better.

The victory by the Soviet dissident movement ranks as one of the great achievements of the twentieth century. It is an object lesson for a cynical modern world of what only a few good people can accomplish. Their story is chronicled in the pages that follow by a reporter honored to have known many of them personally and to have watched their struggle develop on the ground in Moscow from the modest beginning to the ultimate success.

II. THE CONSCIENCE OF THE NATION

Soviet dissidents came from all walks of life. Some were writers able to articulate what their countrymen instinctively felt, ready to guide and to teach, Aleksandr Solzhenitsyn among them. Fated for repression, they continued to expose the Stalinist legacy and rally the forces of change that eventually swept away Soviet communism.

Other dissidents were scientists or technicians, often more narrowly focused on a single issue of human rights, such as the Soviet refusal to let the oppressed Jewish minority emigrate. Typical of them was Vladimir Slepak, a radio electronics engineer first denied permission to emigrate to Israel in 1970 on grounds that his job gave him access to Soviet state secrets. In true Catch-22 logic, the bearded Russian Jew was then fired from the very same job that held him hostage, for the disloyal act of trying to leave the U.S.S.R. Once fired, however, he could not leave the country anyway. The state said he still knew too many secrets.

Slepak had nowhere to turn. He could not work. He could not emigrate. Yet the longer he stayed idle, the greater the threat of arrest as a social parasite. The state, the nation's only employer, had made him unemployable. But the very same state could now arrest him, because not working was a crime under Soviet law. Like many other "refuseniks" thrown into this impossible situation, Slepak became a dissident, campaigning for the right of

Jews to emigrate. For nearly two decades, until he was finally allowed to leave for Israel in the Gorbachev era, Slepak suffered arrest, economic hardship, and long separations from his wife and sons. The worst was five years of forced exile in a remote Siberian village on the edge of Mongolia's Gobi Desert, so dusty that the windows of his shack could never be opened; the talkative Jewish intellectual's only company was illiterate Buddhist shepherds who hardly ever said a word to him.

The absurd humor of his fate helped keep him going, Slepak told me. "Where's the secrecy?" he once asked the KGB tormentors denying him emigration on the ground that he could betray the motherland if allowed to go abroad. "In my field of technology, we are fifteen years behind the Americans," Slepak reminded the KGB. "That's the secret," they replied.

Other dissidents were politicians-in-waiting. Among them was Vyacheslav Chornovil, a onetime Ukrainian nationalist who after independence from the Soviet Union would become a member of parliament and a candidate for president. Another, Sergei Kovalev, would one day be Russian President Boris Yeltsin's commissioner for human rights.

Soviet dissidents even came from the army, the most famous among them retired general Pyotr Grigorenko, whose incarceration in a mental hospital for promoting human rights stunned the civilized world. That Brezhnev-era practice of turning psychiatry on its head, as a punishment for the perfectly sane, did far more harm to communism's global reputation than any of the critics it silenced.

But in the end, one man did more than any other in carrying the Soviet dissident movement to its ultimate victory. Although he always stood alone, his single voice became a greater moral force than all the others combined. He exerted greater influence than the writers, Solzhenitsyn included. His championing of specific causes—from releasing political prisoners to safeguarding religious and ethnic minority rights to freer emigration and reuniting divided families—got more results than any of the experts in each field achieved. His program for Soviet reform ultimately won more acceptance than the views of any of the politicians-in-waiting. And no general did more to beat swords into plowshares than this inventor of the Soviet hydrogen bomb whose later struggle for nuclear arms reduction and human rights won him the 1975 Nobel Peace Prize. His name was Andrei Dmitrievich Sakharov.

Seldom in history has any one man held the moral authority at Sakharov's command. At his death, Andrei Dmitrievich was widely recognized across the Soviet Union as the conscience of the nation. Nearly a decade later, with most of the other Soviet dissidents largely forgotten, Sakharov was still universally praised by ordinary Russians as "a saint." Vitaly Korotich, editor of the influential Soviet weekly magazine *Ogonyok*, called him "one of the greatest men of this century."

That was no exaggeration, partly because Sakharov led two distinct lives, one as his nation's top scientist, the other as its leading dissident. In 1948, when only twenty-seven years old, the brilliant nuclear physicist joined the scientific team he led in developing the Soviet hydrogen bomb. He later worked with Igor Tamm, a Nobel Prize winner in physics, to turn atomic energy to peaceful purposes through controlled nuclear fusion. Sakharov had fame, respect, and all the privileges of the top Soviet elite, among them rare access to the best in housing, food, medicine, and foreign scientific journals, guaranteed for life. Lesser men would have turned inward to enjoy their good fortune, closing their eyes to the suffering around them. Andrei Dmitrievich could not. Instead, he chose to risk everything in the struggle for human rights. In 1962, Nikita Khrushchev warned him to forget politics and stick to science. The world is now a better place because Sakharov refused.

Andrei Dmitrievich made his fateful choice long before dissent in Eastern Europe became fashionable or even feasible. In Moscow in the 1960s, most people still lived in communal flats, sharing kitchens and bathrooms with three other families, where at least one of the neighbors reported to the KGB on all the others. There was no sure way to talk privately with one other person, let alone start a revolution.

Russians tried to shield their conversations from prying ears, human and electronic. They whispered confidences against the background noise of a running bath or a flushing toilet, or during walks in secluded woods outside town. But a KGB listening device planted secretly in the heel of a shoe could easily counter such primitive attempts to avoid surveillance. State security was so pervasive that no one could organize even the smallest protest demonstration without the KGB knowing in advance and positioned to bust it up in the opening moments.

One rare attempt in 1965 proved the point. The occasion was Constitution Day, December 5, an annual Soviet national holiday honoring Stalin's 1936 constitution, one of the most liberal in the world, but only on paper. Stalin's constitution guaranteed freedom of speech, assembly, press, and religion, and all the other liberties so manifestly missing from Soviet life. A small group of intellectuals making their debut as dissident activists, among them a young poet named Aleksandr Ginzburg, decided to exploit that hypocrisy in what they thought would be an acceptable way, to press for democratic change.

They gathered in Moscow's Pushkin Square on that holiday and unfurled banners saying nothing more offensive than "Support the Soviet Constitution." KGB plainclothesmen intervened within seconds to grab their slogans, beat them, and haul them off to jail. No unauthorized demonstration in Moscow was any more effective for the next twenty years.

Such was the climate facing Sakharov when he began his struggle for the principle that basic human rights should be inviolable, even in the Soviet Union. Denied access to state-controlled media in Russia, Sakharov used foreign correspondents in Moscow as his most effective channel. His interviews with us would be picked up by the Russian-language services of the Voice of

America, the BBC, and other Western stations, to be broadcast back into
the Soviet Union, where millions of "closet dissidents" too afraid to speak
out themselves would hang on to his every word, thinking that here at last
was a Russian who spoke the truth.

In Brezhnev's Russia, when Kremlin leaders preached détente, they could
no longer jam Russian-language broadcasts from the West. So in this round-
about way, Sakharov communicated with his own people. Andrei
Dmitrievich did so until he became an important political force, recognized
as such by both progressives and conservatives, but for different reasons. To
his admirers, Sakharov was worshiped as a national icon. To Communist
hard-liners, he was a Judas who had to be silenced before he harmed the state.

For a long time, however, Sakharov's international fame protected him.
Others were not so fortunate. The 1968 Soviet invasion of Prague marked a
low point in their long struggle. It made clear there would be no meaningful reforms in the Brezhnev era. And it signaled the start of yet another crackdown on human rights activists. Relentlessly, the Kremlin imprisoned scores
of Soviet dissidents, exiled them to Siberia, or, as with Solzhenitsyn, forced
them to leave the country. By the mid-1970s, Andrei Sakharov was the only
major critic of any international stature still free in Moscow to speak his mind,
a lonely voice in the wilderness. Then suddenly, the tide turned, breathing
new life into the dissident movement. The unlikely benefactor turned out
to be none other than Leonid Ilyich Brezhnev.

For thirty years, Soviet leaders had been seeking international recognition
of the territory seized by the Red Army in World War II, from Eastern Europe to the Kurile Islands off Japan. They feared, rightly, that until their
World War II borders were recognized by international law, the seized territories remained open to dispute. Finally, under Brezhnev, they offered the
West a palatable deal. In return for international recognition of its frontiers,
the Soviet Union promised to improve its performance in the field of human
rights. That basic trade-off was enshrined in the 1975 Helsinki Final Act,
signed by Brezhnev, U.S. President Gerald Ford, and other world leaders.

The Kremlin was convinced it had the best of the bargain. The recognition of borders, after all, was a tangible security enhancement for Moscow,
and the pledges on human rights were just pieces of paper. A delighted
Brezhnev ordered the full text of the Helsinki Final Act published in *Pravda*.
It turned out to be one his biggest mistakes.

At last, dissidents had a yardstick to measure Kremlin performance on
human rights. Among many other things, the Soviets had agreed at Helsinki
to allow their citizens freer emigration, religious worship, and access to foreign publications. There was Brezhnev's signature to prove it. No law prevented ordinary people from making sure the Soviet leader kept his word.
That opportunity breathed new life into Russia's human rights movement—
and a new generation of leadership.

Dissidents established the first Helsinki monitoring group in Moscow in

May 1976. Similar groups soon appeared in the Ukraine, Lithuania, Georgia, and Armenia. Together they compiled details on thousands of Soviet violations of the Helsinki human rights accords. Their evidence helped the United States and other Western governments insist the Soviets had to do better on human rights for détente to continue.

Sometimes the pressure campaign brought results, as when Brezhnev released political prisoners or let Jewish emigration rise. Sometimes the Kremlin rudely ignored it, with new repressions against dissidents. Sometimes Western leaders failed to keep up sufficient pressure on the human rights front. But whatever the Western mistakes, whatever the missed opportunities, the pressure never went away. Brezhnev had hoped to eliminate the human rights issue from East-West relations. Instead, he made it a permanent fixture. After Helsinki, pressure on the human rights front became a key element of every Soviet-American summit meeting. It would outlive Brezhnev and haunt his successors.

Helsinki monitoring groups were the brainchild of Yuri Orlov, a short, combative physicist with curly red hair, built like a bantamweight boxer. Orlov had become a dissident after Khrushchev's 1956 speech revealing Stalin's crimes. At a meeting in his Moscow physics institute that year, called to discuss the Khrushchev speech, Orlov raised some approving nods by arguing that Stalin was not the only one to blame, that other officials must have also been responsible and deserved to be punished. That brave, honest comment got him expelled from the Communist Party and fired from his job. Orlov moved to Yerevan, where he eventually won election to the Armenian Academy of Sciences, and continued to think about how dissent could be more effective. Twenty years later, back in Moscow, he found the answer when Brezhnev published the Helsinki Final Act.

It was tactically brilliant. Orlov combined in his Helsinki monitoring group the best of the Soviet dissident movement. There was at least one representative of each interest group, and some of the most respected human rights activists in the country were included. Among the founding members were Anatoly Shcharansky to focus on Jewish concerns, General Pyotr Grigorenko specializing in psychiatric abuse cases, Sakharov's wife, Elena Bonner, herself a formidable campaigner for human rights, and Aleksandr Ginzburg, who administered the Solzhenitsyn fund aiding Russian political prisoners. Their reports had the accuracy and impact of the old *Chronicle of Current Events*.

Naturally, it was too good to last. Yuri Orlov was still in his pajamas at 10:30 A.M. on January 4, 1977, when the doorbell to his ground-floor Moscow apartment sounded one long ring. Orlov made his living by tutoring privately late at night and rarely dressed before noon. The ring was unusual for Muscovites, he told me in what turned out to be the last interview before his arrest. "Only provincials and the police use the long bell," he said.

Sure enough, it was the police. They produced a search warrant and spent the next eleven hours confiscating documents Orlov had collected as head of the Helsinki monitoring group. Four plainclothesmen carried out the search, each with a pistol strapped to his hip. The only one who agreed to identify himself, Aleksandr Tikhonov, was a senior investigator from the Moscow prosecutor's office. At Orlov's insistence, Tikhonov wrote out an eleven-page protocol in pencil, listing 140 separate groups of confiscated items. Among them were papers detailing hundreds of cases of human rights violations, including the mistreatment of political prisoners, religious believers, and minority nationalities. Orlov and his wife, Irina, never took their eyes off the intruders, refusing to let them use the toilet for fear incriminating evidence would be planted there. The police took turns leaving the building to relieve themselves elsewhere.

Even before the search was completed in Orlov's case, number 46012/1876, on the Moscow prosecutor's books, Tass, the Soviet government news agency, published a report on its results. The report said evidence had been confiscated during the search tying Orlov, Ginzburg, and other members of the Helsinki group to the anti-Soviet émigré organization NTS. The search, of course, uncovered no such thing, and Orlov and the others denied any connection to NTS. Despite the clumsy timing and the unsubstantiated charges, the Tass report was clearly ominous. "It looks as if the authorities have now decided to stop our group at any price," Orlov told me. His grim forecast proved all too accurate.

In rapid succession, Ginzburg, Orlov, and Shcharansky were arrested in early 1977. Each was held in prison for more than a year of investigation, then sentenced in closed trials on absurd charges to long terms in the Gulag. Shcharansky, for example, was accused of treason, of working for the CIA through a cell headed by Aleksandr Lerner, another prominent Jewish dissident. Even the Soviet authorities didn't believe that, and proved it by never arresting Lerner.

Shcharansky was as brave as he was innocent. At his trial, given a final word, he addressed the Jewish people and his family with the hopeful words of a traditional prayer, that they would meet "next year in Jerusalem." Then he turned to the judges and added curtly, "To you I have nothing to say."

Courage was also the hallmark of Alek Ginzburg, a dissident for half his life and a key fixture at each stage of the human rights movement. In 1960, when still only a student, he was jailed for two years for one of the first *samizdat* publications, a collection of dissident poetry in typed carbon copies called *Syntax.* In 1965 he helped organize the abortive Constitution Day demonstration in Pushkin Square, the first public protest of the modern dissident movement. In 1967, Ginzburg published a "White Paper" record of the Sinyavsky-Daniel trial, yet another landmark in the dissident cause, and paid for it with five years in the Gulag for anti-Soviet activity. He married his wife, Arina, in a camp ceremony, with inmates picking wildflowers for her from beneath the barbed wire.

Ginzburg developed tuberculosis in the camps but never gave up the struggle for human rights, joining Orlov's Helsinki group as a founding member. His decision to administer the Solzhenitsyn fund, he knew, was certain to put him back behind bars before long. The money from the author's royalties went to the families of political prisoners in Russia, helping them to buy food and clothing for inmates and train tickets to visit the camps. But operating the fund clandestinely opened Ginzburg to a panoply of trumped-up criminal charges. He was accused of using Solzhenitsyn's fund to buy stolen icons and finance a life of sex orgies, heavy drinking, and tax evasion. For that, despite his frail health, he was sentenced to the Gulag for a third time, in July 1978, the same month as Shcharansky, this time to eight years at hard labor.

His wife, Arina, put up a brave front trying to maintain a "normal" life. Her husband had left their apartment on the night of February 3, 1977, to phone from a nearby call box, without saying goodbye. He never returned. KGB agents hauled him off a street corner. At the time, the Ginzburgs' two young sons were two and four years old. Arina told them their father was in a hospital. She never mentioned prison. Soon, even the older boy had trouble remembering their father.

After Alek's arrest, Arina's phone was cut off and her mail opened or stopped. She could not communicate with her husband. The KGB let her put a list in her own handwriting of the food items she could occasionally send in parcels to him. It was his only sign in prison that she was still alive. Arina eked out a living giving English lessons and worried that prison would kill her frail husband. Yet despite the many hardships, she never showed signs of any strain. On the many occasions I visited her, there was never a tear.

But even this defiant woman had limits. Arina finally saw her husband again at his trial, eighteen months after his arrest. The forty-year-old man who had left their home for the phone box was now white-haired, ashen-faced, and painfully thin. He looked sixty-five. "What have they done to him?" Arina gasped. Then, at last, even she broke down and cried uncontrollably.

Fortunately, Ginzburg survived. He was released in 1979 and flown to New York in an East-West prisoner exchange. Shcharansky and Orlov would be involved in similar swaps seven years later. They had not wanted to emigrate but were given no choice. Brezhnev's crackdown on political dissent in the late 1970s decimated Orlov's Helsinki movement. Once again, human rights activists were jailed, exiled to Siberia, or expelled from the country.[6] Only Sakharov and his wife, Elena Bonner, were spared. His world stature still protected them.

Like other Moscow correspondents in those days, I often made my way to Sakharov's two-room apartment on Moscow's garden ring road. The tall, stooped physicist would open the door himself, invariably dressed in a rumpled blue track suit and white tennis shoes. Together with Bonner, we would sit in the kitchen, sip tea, and discuss the latest outrage by the KGB. It could be new repressions against minority nationalities or religions, or more illegal searches, arrests, and detentions without trial, or a new refusal to ease emigration barriers or release political prisoners, all violations of the Universal Declaration of Human Rights signed by the Soviet Union.

The specifics of Sakharov's concern changed each time. There would be new names, new cases of human rights abuse. But the general theme never varied. He tirelessly argued that the United States government had ample leverage to push the Soviet Union into more acceptable behavior on both arms control and human rights. "The economic, military, and political power of the United States is incomparable with that of any other country," he told me in 1977, meaning the United States was far stronger than the Soviet Union. Because of that, Andrei Dmitrievich argued, the Soviets needed trade, technology transfer, and arms control with America much more than Washington needed them. Therefore, from its position of relative strength, America could insist that unless the Soviets improved their performance on human rights, they would not make the progress they wanted in all other fields, from trade to arms reduction. Sakharov further argued that such linkage was in the vital interest of the United States. "If the Soviet leaders cannot be trusted to live up to their obligations on human rights, then they cannot be trusted to honor their obligations on arms control agreements either," he told me.

That concept, constantly repeated in Sakharov interviews, eventually hit home. Jimmy Carter, on his election as president of the United States, made human rights the centerpiece of his foreign policy. In dealing with Moscow, Carter adopted the Sakharov linkage, deciding at the outset of his administration that Soviet progress on human rights would be the litmus test for moving forward on everything else, including arms control, whether Brezhnev liked it or not.

Brezhnev didn't like it, of course. He regarded Sakharov's advice to Washington as treason. But Brezhnev was afraid to silence the Nobel Peace Prize winner by Stalinist methods. Sakharov was too much of a test case of improved Soviet behavior, too important for the détente progress Brezhnev desperately wanted, for him to disappear mysteriously or face trumped-up charges at a new show trial.

So, at the beginning of the Carter administration, Sakharov occupied an unprecedentedly protected place as the leading Russian critic of Kremlin policy. Shortly after inauguration day, Jimmy Carter sent Andrei Sakharov a personal message of support in the human rights struggle. The Brezhnev regime regarded Carter's act as intolerable interference in Soviet internal affairs. But it curbed its anger and let Russia's most famous dissident receive the American president's letter. Nor was that all. Soviet authorities allowed Sakharov to go to the American embassy and collect Carter's message in person, in an official state car, a chauffeur-driven black Volga from the Academy of Sciences garage.

Brezhnev could afford to wait. The Soviet leader was confident that sooner or later the next American president, or perhaps Carter himself, would change course, realize that the essential choice in superpower relations was between confrontation and cooperation, that in reality the United States could not dictate Soviet human rights behavior, and that in the end, trade, arms control, and other détente measures would go forward anyway.

His cynical view was shared by many prominent American foreign affairs specialists, including some advising Jimmy Carter. Yes, these Americans agreed, human rights were important, and Soviet violations should be protested, but it would be wrong to let this issue alone foreclose opportunities for progress in even more important areas, like reducing the danger of nuclear war.

It took them nearly three years to convince Carter, but eventually they did. Arms control and the rest of the détente package would indeed go forward, despite continued Soviet abuses in the human rights field. By the time the SALT II treaty on nuclear arms limitation was signed in Vienna in 1979—and Carter kissed Brezhnev on the cheek at the end of the ceremony—the Gulag was no longer an overriding concern for the American president.

Nevertheless, in the years it took Carter to back away from his initial human rights stand, Sakharov enjoyed incredible room for maneuver inside the Soviet Union. The world's most powerful police state stood by helplessly as he publicly embarrassed it with constant demands for elementary justice and curbing of secret police illegality.

Admittedly, Sakharov's stature as a world figure made him unique. Alone among Soviet dissidents, his Moscow phone was not cut off. He would not be jailed. But those in the West who thought him untouchable were just plain wrong. The KGB did its best to break him, illegally searching his apartment, seizing his personal papers, and constantly pressuring him and his family to give up the struggle.

The KGB was never very subtle. In 1977, for example, Sakharov received none of the Christmas greetings sent to him from abroad. Instead he got only hate mail. One batch, posted anonymously in Norway, contained photographs of car crashes, dead bodies, and funerals, coupled with warnings that the Sakharovs could be beaten by street thugs or have unfortunate accidents. Andrei Dmitrievich never knew when his name would no longer protect him, when American support for the Soviet human rights movement would falter, when Soviet authorities would decide they would be better off with him silenced for good. But Sakharov refused to cave in, whatever the pressure.

Andrei Dmitrievich was a consummately gentle man, polite, aristocratic, with a soft voice and great patience. I saw him lose his temper only once, in a dramatic display of courage. It came at the end of the closed Moscow trial of his friend, the leading Jewish activist Anatoly Shcharansky, who was convicted in 1978 of treason and sentenced to thirteen years in the Gulag. Shcharansky's elderly mother, barred from seeing her son for the year since his arrest, barred again from the week-long trial, and now desperate to see him for perhaps the last time in her life, tried to enter the court, only to be brutally shoved aside by uniformed police. The old woman was left sobbing on the sidewalk, surrounded by a large crowd too afraid to raise even a single word of protest against police capable of arresting them on the spot for insulting Soviet authority. No one dared except Sakharov. Shaking and red-faced with anger, Andrei Dmitrievich shouted at the police, "You are not people, you are fascists. Hear me, a member of the Soviet Academy of Sciences, you are fascists."[7]

In those days, countless Soviets would bring evidence to Sakharov of human rights abuses. He did his best to substantiate them, never knowing when a KGB provocateur would slip in a false claim to discredit him. The strain was enormous, the caseload overwhelming, yet Andrei Dmitrievich gave each visitor his full attention and a sympathetic hearing. Once, when I came to see him, he asked why I looked worried. I told him my small daughter was ill. It was only the flu, and I soon forgot the incident. But Sakharov never did. After that, every time I called on him, despite the countless tales of far worse human suffering he received each day, Sakharov never failed to ask how my daughter was getting on.

Ultimately it was that level of personal concern which allowed Sakharov to save lives. Once he decided to intervene on behalf of a political prisoner or a would-be emigrant or some other victim of human rights abuse, Andrei Dmitrievich stayed the course until the authorities gave way. There is no way of telling how many lives Sakharov actually saved, but his support often made the critical difference, as it did with the Chudnovsky family, whom I had long tried to help.

The Chudnovskys were Jews from Kiev. Grigory, the younger son, had published his first mathematical treatise at age eleven, when the Soviet Academy of Science officially declared him a genius. His work, published abroad, gave him international recognition. But by the time I met him, "Grisha" was twenty-five and on his deathbed. He suffered from myasthenia gravis, a fatal wasting disease that kills by paralyzing the lungs. The one medical treatment that could save him was only available abroad. Relatives invited Grisha to Israel, but Soviet authorities refused to issue a visa, as they did for thousands of would-be Jewish emigrants. In Grisha's case, however, the refusal was tantamount to a death sentence. No reason was given. "We are not obliged to give you a reason," officials told the family. Grisha's older brother, David, himself a distinguished mathematician, thought the reason was "to discourage other Soviet Jews from even thinking of emigrating to Israel."

I wrote about Grisha's case in *Newsweek* in 1977. It began to get attention in the West, but nothing changed for the better. The family lived in Kiev, where at the time there were no resident U.S. diplomats or foreign correspondents. David had contacted me in Moscow, and the Kiev KGB wanted to persuade them never to try that again. One day the parents of Grisha and

David, both pensioners in poor health, were nearly beaten to death in Kiev by KGB thugs.

The story could have ended there, with all four Chudnovskys soon eliminated. It almost did. I tried to get other Moscow correspondents interested in the case, to no avail. It was hard for them to find the time to get away to Kiev, and besides, the story had already been told. So I took the case to Sakharov, and, fortunately, he got involved. Andrei Dmitrievich called a press conference in Moscow to denounce the treatment of both Grisha and his parents. This time the story got wide publicity. Sakharov's personal backing made the difference. Soon all four Chudnovskys were allowed to move to New York, where Grisha got treatment and David joined the faculty of Columbia University.

The man who made it possible could not go abroad himself. Sakharov would have liked to travel in the West, then return to Russia to resume the struggle. But Soviet authorities wouldn't let him. Andrei Dmitrievich found that out for sure when he applied to go to Oslo to receive the 1975 Nobel Peace Prize. Permission was refused because he was "an individual possessing knowledge of state secrets."[8]

His wife, Elena Bonner, went to Oslo instead. Soviet authorities could not stop her. She was already abroad at the time, in Italy for medical treatment. Bonner's presence abroad was yet another sign of the couple's privileged status among Soviet dissidents. None of the others were allowed to seek medical help in the West. Their privileges, however, had sharp limits. Sakharov himself could not be allowed out of the country, even to collect a Nobel Prize.

Denying Andrei Dmitrievich a foreign trip came as no surprise to anyone familiar with Soviet logic. The Kremlin could hardly refuse exit visas to thousands of low-level technicians on secrecy grounds and then let the father of the Soviet hydrogen bomb out of the country.

In the end, the Brezhnev regime went the other way. They decided to restrict Sakharov's movement within the Soviet Union itself, making him a virtual prisoner. In January 1980, shortly after Andrei Dmitrievich protested the Soviet invasion of Afghanistan, he was exiled to the industrial city of Gorky, closed to all foreigners because of secret defense installations there, and placed under house arrest.

The conscience of the nation was thus cut off from foreign visitors and effectively silenced. Jimmy Carter could no longer help. U.S.–Soviet relations were already poisoned by Afghanistan. Carter applied every sanction he could after that, including a boycott of the 1980 Moscow Olympics. He had no further reprisals available to push for Sakharov's release.

Some Soviet dissidents were disappointed. Often in the past they had criticized Carter for not being tough enough with Brezhnev. Now these people thought he had gone too far. The Olympic boycott, they believed, was a mistake. Without the U.S. team there, world interest in the Moscow Olympics paled. Had the Americans competed, a global television audience of a billion people or more would have watched. These dissidents thought that would have been the perfect occasion to unfurl banners in Moscow's Lenin Stadium saying, "Free Sakharov." They wanted to spoil Brezhnev's party in much the same way that an American black, Jesse Owens, outran the Nazi master race and ruined the 1936 Berlin Olympics for Hitler. Their campaign for Sakharov's release would now take longer.

Andrei Dmitrievich was silenced, but never forgotten. He protested with hunger strikes and suffered brutal forced feedings by the KGB, all duly reported to the West by his family. His health declined in Gorky, and his life was probably shortened by his treatment there, but if anything, Sakharov became an even greater international cause during his forced exile.

Human rights groups and government leaders around the world continued to demand his release. For most of the 1980s, Sakharov's detention was second only to the Afghan War in damaging the Soviet Union's global prestige and its relations with the democracies of the West.

Once again, by using all the subtlety of the boot to stamp out dissent, Soviet leaders had shot themselves in the foot. With Sakharov, their overreaction to his criticism only created larger problems. It was an old, consistent, and ultimately fatal flaw. From the very beginning, Moscow's handling of its minuscule dissident movement suffered from a counterproductive overkill. The barbaric suppression of dissent never killed it. On the contrary, the repressions only increased the demands for reform until they at last toppled the Soviet system.

The pattern repeated with Brezhnev's crackdown on the arts. Leading painters, writers, and other artists critical of the regime were pushed into leaving the country, among them Yuri Lyubimov, Russia's boldest theater director. At Moscow's 650-seat Taganka Theater, Lyubimov had managed in 1977 to adapt Mikhail Bulgakov's 1930s novel *The Master and Margarita* to the stage. In it, the devil appears in Stalin's Moscow, and eventually teaches doubting Soviets to find God. The message is clear: to reach salvation, one must first recognize the evil around one.

The play had a powerful impact. Russian audiences left the theater pondering the Stalinist evils still around them in Brezhnev's day. Elena Bonner, however, was not impressed. She used to scoff at Lyubimov; he provided a small escape valve for the Moscow intelligentsia and was of no real importance. His plays were never televised or filmed for the masses, she once told me. Instead, "They doled out the truth in small doses, never big enough to cause the regime any trouble." But Bonner was wrong. Even Lyubimov's small doses were too much. He too had to go.

The forced emigration of leading Soviet artists and writers was more than a brain drain. "It is a soul drain," the writer Vasily Aksyonov told me. But he was convinced the policy would fail. "We are a very big and talented country," Aksyonov explained. "If our literature wasn't destroyed by Stalin, it cannot be destroyed. Our cultural field is as vast as Siberia. Something will always grow there, however much hindered by permafrost." Aksyonov was talking about writers, but the same applied to dissidents. However deep the permafrost of repression, the dissident movement too would always grow again.

Soviet dissidents often appeared heroic to the outside world. But they were far from perfect, and often they hurt their own cause. Like every other group of human beings, the Soviet dissidents displayed familiar shortcomings. Some outright scoundrels were included in their midst. Among the worst was Zviad Gamsakhurdia, a leader of the Georgia Helsinki group, jailed for his human rights activities. Gamsakhurdia would later become the first freely elected president of Soviet Georgia, turn tyrant, conduct mass repressions of his own, and finally touch off the civil war that toppled him from power.

Even the most respected people in the Soviet dissident movement often made errors, but unlike Gamsakhurdia's, they were honest mistakes of judgment, typical human failings. Sakharov and Bonner, for example, once made a public statement blaming the KGB for a mysterious bomb planted on a Moscow subway train. They had no evidence for the charge, which was potentially libelous under Soviet law. The statement nearly got them arrested and did nothing to help their credibility.

Similarly, Solzhenitsyn could be a disappointment. I first met him for an interview in Zurich in 1974, just after his expulsion from the Soviet Union. The concerns he expressed then left a sour taste. His priorities seemed skewed to me. Solzhenitsyn was anxious about getting his archives, his wife, and his children out of Russia too—in that order. His biggest worry, by far, was the archives.

On another occasion, I saw Sakharov and General Grigorenko argue uselessly with each other at a Moscow press conference for Western journalists. The issue was the anniversary of the aborted Constitution Day demonstration in 1965 on Pushkin Square. Each year thereafter, dissidents had marked the December anniversary with a moment of silent protest on the square. Then Brezhnev changed the constitution and moved the holiday to October. Sakharov and Grigorenko disagreed over when the anniversary demonstration should henceforth be held, in December or October. It was an issue they could have settled privately, before the press arrived. Instead they harangued each other in front of the journalists, never agreeing, exposing the dissident movement as hopelessly split on minor details.

On the whole, however, Soviet dissidents were honorable, courageous, and remarkably effective people. Fired from work, then threatened with jail for being unemployed, these often top-notch scientists with doctorate degrees swallowed their pride and took any lowly job, whether night watchman or elevator operator, to keep going. Their phones would be tapped or cut off entirely. They would be followed, beaten, jailed, released, and warned to behave. Then somehow they would slip away to a meeting in the woods outside

Moscow and yet another typed broadsheet on human rights violations would appear and eventually get to Western hands.

They also brought out the best in Westerners determined to help them, not only governments, but also private citizens. The story of Mark Azbel was typical. Like so many other Jewish refuseniks, Azbel, a highly regarded physicist, lost his job after applying to emigrate to Israel. Early into the long wait for Soviet authorities to change their minds, Azbel decided he had better do something to keep himself and his refusenik colleagues on the cutting edge of knowledge in their specialities. So he invited some of the leading scientists in the West, including some Nobel Prize winners, to give seminars to qualified refuseniks like him in his small flat on the outskirts of Moscow.

Not only did his distinguished guests come, paying their own way for an expensive trip nearly halfway round the world, but they also refused to be intimidated by Soviet warnings that attending Azbel's seminar would be cause for immediate expulsion from the country and a permanent denial of future Soviet visas.

In some ways, Azbel's refuseniks got better treatment than the official Soviet scientific establishment from America's top scientists. In one such incident, Dr. Mario Grossi of the Harvard Smithsonian Center for Astrophysics brought to an Azbel seminar recently produced color slides from a U.S. Viking mission to Mars that had not yet been shown to the Soviet Academy of Sciences.

James Griffin, a University of Maryland specialist in nuclear physics, and himself a non-Jew, spoke for many when he told me why the Azbel seminar was important enough for busy Americans to make the time to help. "These are very exceptional and heroic people," Griffin said. "They have broken no laws in the Soviet Union. They spend their lives constructively in scientific research. They deserve the support of everyone who believes in freedom, especially intellectual freedom. If I were in their position, I would hope someone would try to help me."

In the end, Brezhnev never did more than weaken the Soviet dissident movement. He couldn't kill it. After each repressive wave, new human rights activists emerged to take up the cause, often aided by governments and private citizens in the West. No one could ever quash the demand for basic human freedoms, not even in the Soviet Union. Eventually, even the Kremlin would give up trying.

III. A DISSIDENT IN THE KREMLIN

It is tempting, but wrong, to think of the Soviet Union in simple black-and-white terms. It was full of greys. Just as there were scoundrels among the dissidents, so were there decent, courageous people in the ranks of the

Communist Party. They had joined for the usual reasons of personal ambition. The Party was the only accepted path to success. But the best of them sincerely believed that joining the Party would be the most effective way to improve Soviet society. They hoped that once they had their hands on the levers of power, they could do far more to promote reform than any of the dissidents howling in the wind outside. In 1985 they at last got their chance, when for the first time one of their number, Mikhail Sergeyevich Gorbachev, became general secretary.

In time, the new master of the Kremlin would become the country's biggest dissident. But at first, Mikhail Sergeyevich had trouble convincing Russia and the West that he was serious about reform. He soon accomplished that, however, in one brilliant stroke, releasing Sakharov from exile in Gorky and letting him return to Moscow to resume the human rights struggle.

That was only the beginning. In subsequent years, Gorbachev did nothing less than restructure the Soviet Union along the ideas first articulated by Andrei Sakharov. Gorbachev and his leading collaborators—Eduard Shevardnadze and Aleksandr Yakovlev—would take credit for developing glasnost and perestroika. They certainly deserved recognition for pushing them through, but the real inspiration belonged to Sakharov.

In 1975, in his book *My Country and the World,* Andrei Dmitrievich listed the specific reforms the Soviet Union desperately needed. His major proposals included:

- Privatizing state farms and industry
- A multiparty political system
- The right to strike
- Amnesty for political prisoners
- Laws guaranteeing freedom of opinion and freedom to circulate information
- Freedom to choose one's place of residence and employment
- Freedom to leave the country and return to it
- The banning of all Communist Party privileges and the granting of equal rights
- The right of Soviet republics to secede from the U.S.S.R.

Looking back now, Sakharov's vision is remarkable. Over time, Gorbachev would adopt every one of these nine recommendations. There is perhaps no better summary of what Mikhail Sergeyevich actually accomplished inside the Soviet Union.

Nor was that all. Gorbachev was to use Sakharov and the dissidents as his foot soldiers in the struggle against Party hard-liners who wished to hold back reform. Encouraged from the top, the dissidents could now take to the streets and at last demonstrate legally, in crowds of 300,000 or more. Across the vast nation, millions of like-minded citizens finally came out of the closet, now that it was safe to do so, to add their support.

Sakharov and other dissidents even won seats in the new Soviet parliament, chosen for the first time under Gorbachev by competitive elections, open to new political parties. No longer was that parliament to be a rubber stamp, with deputies who had run unopposed doing the Communist Party's bidding. It would henceforth have a will of its own. Gorbachev symbolized the change by selecting as the first speaker on the opening day of the new parliament the man who had done more than anyone else to bring about the change. He called on Sakharov.

Andrei Dmitrievich had every reason to be grateful to Gorbachev. The Soviet leader had freed him from exile, then freed him again to promote the political changes the human rights movement always wanted. But Sakharov never let that gratitude cloud his political judgment. Through it all, he remained true to his mission as the moral conscience of the nation.

When Gorbachev seemed to falter on reform, Sakharov was the first to raise alarm bells. When Gorbachev began to amass greater personal power, with constitutional changes to strengthen his presidency, ostensibly to push through more reform, Sakharov was the first to object that the result could be "extremely dangerous for the country." Power intended today for Gorbachev, Sakharov said in 1988 from his new parliamentary pulpit, "could be used by someone else tomorrow. And there is no guarantee he won't be a new Stalinist."

On December 14, 1989, Andrei Sakharov and Elena Bonner had dinner in their seventh-floor apartment. At about 9:00 P.M., Sakharov took out the trash, then excused himself and went downstairs. Since his return from Gorky, the Sakharovs had been given a second, smaller flat on the floor below, which Andrei Dmitrievich used as a study.[9] He told his wife he wanted to take a nap, then rework the speech he planned to give the next day in the Soviet parliament. He asked Bonner to wake him at 11:00 P.M. Andrei Dmitrievich was concerned about the next day's parliamentary debate and wanted to get his speech right. "Tomorrow will be a battle," Sakharov told his wife, then headed for the study. They were his last words. At 11:00, Bonner went downstairs to wake him as requested. She found Sakharov's key in the door and his body on the floor. At sixty-eight, he had died of an apparent heart attack.

No one man in this century had done more to advance the cause of peace and human rights. His passing was a loss for the entire world. The victory of the human rights movement in Russia and the nation's first moves toward genuine democracy were largely due to him.

Today, in Moscow, there is still no official monument to his memory.[10] None is necessary. Sakharov's legacy lives on in Russia, in a way no statue can capture, in the ideals of justice and freedom to which he dedicated his life. As long as Andrei Dmitrievich and his ideas are still remembered in Russia, there is real hope for its future.

7

Economic Madness

I. THE FACTS OF LIFE

The Soviet Union should have been an economic superpower. It was, after all, the world's largest nation, with more natural resources than any other country. Only the U.S.S.R. could rival both Saudi Arabia's oil reserves and South Africa's gold and diamond mines. Nor did Soviet economic potential consist only of vast mineral wealth. Its human resources, among them a highly educated population, had all the skills to create one of the richest, most advanced societies on earth. Its scientists, to mention but one example, sometimes outshone the best in the West, as when they orbited the first man in space, Yuri Gagarin. Despite such unprecedented assets, however, Josef Stalin and his successors managed to bankrupt the U.S.S.R. by imposing on it an unworkable economic system. No natural disaster in history ever took such a terrible financial toll. In the Soviet case, it had to be planned.

No single factor proved more critical in the decline and fall of the Soviet empire than the economic calamity Kremlin leaders built for themselves. Given sufficient economic strength, the Soviet Union might well have overcome rebellion in Eastern Europe, dissent inside the U.S.S.R., and all the other forces that eventually combined to bring it down. But no such cure was possible. Soviet leaders could never make their economic system work properly, whatever reforms they tried. In the end, this failure above all others doomed communism worldwide.

The major reasons for the collapse of the Soviet planned economy are generally known in the West. They include, among many others, gross bureaucratic incompetence, rampant corruption, and a relentless military buildup at the cost of everything else. But those cold words numb the reality they cover. To feel the absurdity of the Soviet economic system, to begin to understand why reforms could never work, one really had to live in the U.S.S.R., watching ordinary Russians trying to cope. Even the most routine transactions of everyday life, taken for granted in the West, quickly became

118

a nightmare in Moscow. An elementary comprehension of the fatally flawed Soviet economy has to start with that reality.

My Russian friend Ilya Zverev, for instance, told a story I could never forget. He had the bad luck to drop his eyeglasses on a Moscow street in 1965, breaking both lenses. Ilya went straight to the first optical shop he could find and tried to order two new lenses. But the woman behind the counter said she was only allowed to sell him one. "Two lenses are strictly forbidden," she explained. "Only one store in all of Moscow has this right."

Like most Soviet citizens, Ilya knew better than to ask why. Maybe there was a shortage, limiting sales to one lens per customer. Or maybe there was no reason, just a rule. So he asked the address of the one place that could help him. There was no other choice. Ilya couldn't see very well without glasses. And because the state had the monopoly in all businesses, only state shops could replace his broken lenses. He found the address with difficulty. Then the following conversation ensued:

"Is it true that you can sell two lenses here?" Ilya asked.

"Don't know," the surly salesgirl replied. "Let's see your glasses."

Ilya handed them over.

"Yes, it's true we can sell two lenses here, but not to you," the salesgirl declared.

"Why not?" Ilya wanted to know.

"We cannot accept your frames because they are in a soft case," the salesgirl explained, in a tone suggesting all this should be perfectly obvious, even to a complete moron. "According to the rules, they should be in a crush-proof case—to protect your glasses better, of course."

"Okay, then put my frames in a crush-proof case," Ilya suggested.

"We aren't given them, you know," the salesgirl snapped.

"Right, then let me buy a crush-proof case," Ilya said helpfully.

The moment of truth had arrived at last. The salesgirl shrugged, then delivered the knockout blow. "We only sell soft cases here," she announced.

This is not a piece of sadistic fiction from a Kafka novel. It is a true story from Moscow in the 1960s. Ilya eventually got his lenses fixed, one at a time. He was used to doing things the hard way. Getting virtually anything done in Russia usually became an obstacle course. Ilya often joked that the U.S.S.R was run by a "ministry of inconveniences," designed to make everyday life intolerable. He was wrong. If the Soviets had created such a ministry, it never would have worked so efficiently.

In fact, work in Soviet government offices themselves could be just as frustrating in its own way as Ilya's search for lenses. Take, for example, the scene at an office of twenty bureaucrats in the Ukrainian city of Kharkov, also in 1965. The mood: bored silence. The problem: no work.

An official yawns. "It wouldn't be a bad idea to have a nap," he says. More silence.

The supply expert draws flowers. The chief engineer draws female nudes.

The assistant manager draws little devils. A section chief draws circles and cubes. After all, they must look busy.

A clacking typewriter from the director's office interrupts the silence. The director, Comrade Nikitin, is filing another routine request for his office to get some work to do. It won't be answered.

Once this office, the regional department of light industry supply, handled a yearly volume of business worth millions. It lost that responsibility to another department in a recent bureaucratic reorganization. Now Comrade Nikitin still has the same staff, on the same pay, but no work, and no one has yet figured out what to do with them. Until they do, these people will still get paid. Soviet bureaucrats don't get fired; they stay on until they can be recycled into new state jobs. That helps Moscow boast that the Soviet Union has no unemployment problems. Meanwhile, the new office responsible for light industry doesn't have its act together yet, which is one reason why Ilya couldn't get his eyeglasses fixed without extra hassle. Light industry supply covers consumer goods like that.

Nikitin's office in Kharkov is no rare exception. On the contrary, it is typical. Similar offices all over the Ukraine—in Lvov, Donetsk, Kiev, and many other cities—now have no work because of the same reorganization. The Odessa office is a little different. There the staff doesn't bother doodling. Instead it goes to the beach. And the Ukraine is only one example. The same problem, no work in the local department of light industry supply, now exists in all fifteen republics of the Soviet Union. Thousands of bureaucrats are getting paid for doing nothing.

In the old days, under Nikita Khrushchev, these local offices were part of regional economic councils. In the bureaucratic vernacular, they were organized horizontally—that is, they served the supply needs of all the different industries across their region. But Leonid Brezhnev didn't like horizontal lines of organization. That gave regional bureaucrats too much independent authority. Brezhnev preferred vertical lines of command, with Moscow holding all the reins. So he scrapped the regional councils and replaced them with vertical lines of supply, all running downward from Moscow, where a separate government ministry now controlled each individual industry.

In the end, it didn't really matter very much whether the Kremlin used horizontal organization across a region or vertical organization down through an industry. Neither worked very well. Under Stalin's original vertical system, for instance, in which Moscow made all the decisions at the top, a dye maker in Kiev had no right to sell to his most obvious customer, the textile manufacturer across the road who needed dyes to color cloth. Instead, both had to get their buy and sell orders from different ministries in the Soviet capital. Inevitably, the separate ministries in Moscow, with no knowledge of local Kiev geography, had the dye maker sell to customers hundreds or even thousands of miles away, and had the textile manufacturer buy from equally distant suppliers, rather than take advantage of the most natural fit of all, the Kiev neighbor just across the road. It was hardly the most efficient, cost-effective system.

Khrushchev understood that. He created the horizontal lines of regional councils, able to deal across local streets, as a more rational alternative. But the bosses in Moscow didn't like the change. It curbed their powers. So they convinced Brezhnev that the Khrushchev reforms were responsible for the nation's continuing economic problems and got the old vertical system restored. Naturally, it didn't work any better the second time around. No one yet knows how much money or production was wasted by the various bureaucratic reorganizations.

Millions of ordinary Soviet citizens instinctively knew what the problem really was, far better than top Kremlin officials. They also knew how to put it right. The hopelessly inefficient state system of monopoly control over all economic activity had to make way for private enterprise. In the Soviet Union, however, that was not so simple. Yet another true story from the 1960s illustrates the point.

Workers at a plant in Leningrad making electric lightbulbs figured out a way of using the same tools and glass supplies to produce bottles of hair spray. The bottles were made in the factory. The hair spray they ginned up at home. That was no problem. Most Russians were amateur chemists. They got their training producing *samogon,* a moonshine they found eminently drinkable whenever the state raised vodka prices or slowed supplies.

The hair-spray boys were really on to something. At the time, the state planners in Moscow, who decided every item of production down to the last nail, had flooded the Leningrad market with lightbulbs, but had somehow neglected hair spray. It was a commercial disaster. Russian women have few luxuries, but one of them, which they absolutely refuse to do without, is going to the hairdresser. At the time, the favored style was a beehive hairdo, fixed in place by the liquid cement the Soviets called hair spray. The only trouble was, the hairdressers didn't have any.

So the entrepreneurs at the lightbulb factory decided to fix that. On their own time, they made the bottles and the hair spray, then sold it under the table to local hairdressers. Everyone was happy—the entrepreneurs, who made a fortune, the factory chiefs, who were bribed to look the other way, the hairdressers, who bought the spray to keep their businesses going, and their female clientele. It seemed like a great success story. But in the end all it did was underscore—yet again—the failures of the Soviet economic system.

The hair-spray entrepreneurs were stealing their supplies from the state. Inevitably, some informer at the lightbulb factory turned them in. They were tried and convicted of speculation and theft of state property. They got sent to the Gulag. It is not known whether they survived. Their hair-spray business certainly did not.

One could spend a lifetime compiling endless volumes of anecdotes about the absurdities of Soviet economic reality. But the above three examples will do. They show the essential facts of life in the Soviet economic system as it existed in the 1960s, summed up in three key points.

First, the system didn't work, as seen when poor Ilya tried to get his glasses fixed, or in millions of other frustrated daily transactions.

Second, Kremlin leaders invariably tried to fix the system by yet another futile bureaucratic reorganization, as seen in the Kharkov office with no work to do. They consistently tried to put order in the chaotic Soviet house by re-arranging the existing furniture, in this case the untenable command system of central planning. Never were they willing to admit the only real solution would be to throw this furniture out and start again with something better. Their ideological blinders wouldn't let them.

Third, ordinary Russians knew exactly what to do, as seen in the Leningrad lightbulb factory. They understood that only private initiative could make up for the failures of the state-planned economy. But tragically for them—and the country—the Kremlin would have none of that. In the capitalist world, entrepreneurs got rewarded by wealth. Their better ideas got turned into factories, increasing employment and benefiting the overall economy. In the Soviet Union, entrepreneurs were regarded as criminals. They were jailed or shot. Their better ideas benefited no one, and the economy suffered without them.

To be briefer still, the essential truth can be summed up in this one sentence: The Soviet centrally planned command economy was one of the great man-made disasters of all time, from top to bottom.

At the top, planners dictated all economic decisions for the nation, deliberately denying their own people adequate supplies of food, clothing, housing, and medicine so that more resources could be devoted to the military. Then what limited consumer goods they did allow the long-suffering Soviet citizen they usually planned in total ignorance of local conditions of supply and demand. As a result, the country too often produced the wrong goods in the wrong size or the wrong color or the wrong something or other, goods that no one wanted, to rot unsold on store shelves, while goods people really needed never got made. Or if they got made, they never got delivered, because of the chaotic distribution system that could inundate one town with matchboxes and forget to supply any matches at all to the neighboring city.

At the middle level, factory managers carried on regardless, playing the quantity game. They collected bonuses if they met or exceeded the often arbitrary numerical targets for their production imposed by Moscow planners, regardless of the quality of their output or whether it actually sold. Indeed, since all that mattered to them was the quantity churned out, factory bosses often sacrificed both quality and potential sales quite deliberately, in order to increase the raw production numbers, and with that their own bonuses.

Along the way they could pollute the local river or atmosphere to their heart's content, and largely ignore worker safety. Since raw production was all that mattered, the state would not let public health or safety get in the way. Factory managers could even forget about strikes, which were, of course, illegal. Trade unions were simply another arm of state discipline, ensuring that their men reported for work on time and sober. If not, the union could take away their residence permits to live in cities where food supplies were better and condemn them to lives of worse poverty in the countryside. So most workers toed the line.

Factory managers really had only one thing to worry about—the quantity of production. As a result, the little input they had each year at the beginning of the planning process focused on setting their quantitative production targets as low as possible. That way, it would be easier to beat the plan and collect bonuses.

This mind-set was pervasive, carrying over even to the world of sport. The great Soviet pole vault champion Sergei Bubka got promised a state bonus every time he broke a national record. No fool, Bubka would push the bar up only half as high as he thought he might go next, break the record twice instead of once, and collect two state bonuses rather than one.

In a way, he was stealing from the state. But that was only fair play. The state stole from the Soviet people every day. They gave them low-cost housing, low income taxes, and the illusion they were better off financially than most foreigners. But it was a cruel hoax. The key thing was that the state, the country's only employer, also set all salaries artificially low, far below Western standards and well below the value of the goods the Soviet workers produced. It was, in effect, a form of hidden tax. Instead of giving the Soviet worker the salary he deserved, the state paid low and pocketed the difference.

In a country of more than 200 million people, this was quite a piece of change. Soviet authorities, egalitarian to the core, made sure they stole from all the people. The state saved billions from pegging salaries artificially low, and then used the money to advantage many times over. For one thing, money taken in this way from workers' pay packets could go into arms buildups. For another, workers denied the disposable income they were entitled to could not increase demand for consumer goods as much as they would have liked. That let the state devote even more resources to the military sector.

At the bottom level, ordinary Soviet workers, white-collar and blue-, never really understood all this. But they sensed that somehow they were being diddled. And they determined they would get even. In their view, the state was "them" and the people "us." So whenever possible, the people stole from "them"—whether it was at a factory, farm, or office. Most never realized that in taking state property they were actually stealing from "us," the ordinary people, since, in a collective society, it is ultimately the people who own all state property.

The relative few who understood the nuances believed stealing from the state to be justified anyway. The bosses, after all, were stealing from the workers, pocketing part of their pay in order to finance privileged lifestyles of special stores, luxury cars, and country estates. It was, in short, a system where everyone was stealing from everyone else—hardly the way to run a railroad, let alone a great country. Yet somehow, all that was acceptable behavior under "the plan."

The bottom level showed its ugliest face in the shops. There the salesgirls got paid the same whether they sold anything or not. With no incentive to be pleasant, let alone actually work, they competed to see who could be nastiest to the customers.

The Soviet economic system was not always a top-to-bottom failure, of course. In the beginning of Stalin's rule, from the late 1920s to the early 1940s, his rigid command economy made eminent sense, as the U.S.S.R. surged ahead from a primitive agricultural backwater to a modern industrial society at breakneck speed. Only the iron fist could put order in Russia's chaotic house so quickly.

Once the U.S.S.R. was in the ranks of developed nations, however, the Soviet command system could no longer keep pace. Worse, it soon became counterproductive. In order to compete with the West at this stage, Soviet specialists in every field needed freedom to innovate, to put their knowledge to the best use, to make their own economic decisions on how research funds and other resources should be allocated. That was the proven path to further economic progress. But such individual freedom of choice for specialists would by definition exempt them from Party control, a concept the Communists found unthinkable. Communists always preferred total control, even if that meant sacrificing economic growth. In short, forced to choose between progress and control, the Communists chose control.

That basic choice allowed ignorant Communist Party bureaucrats to decide what the nation's best specialists could and could not do, hamstringing their work and damaging the economy. Among other things, Party overlords decided which projects specialists could undertake and on what terms. They also limited the funding granted to specialists, computer time, and access to Western scholarship to the point where relatively few Soviet economists, scientists, technicians, and other specialists ever lived up to their potential. In addition, Party loyalty rather than proven ability in a field of specialization determined promotion and success. In the end, the Soviet Communist Party educated some of the world's best scientists and technicians, with the potential to raise the economy to new heights, then largely wasted them for political reasons that made no sense at all.

The same held true at factories and farms. Party control remained the top priority there too, again at the expense of effectiveness. The farmer or the factory manager knew better what was needed locally to improve production—quantity and quality—but he had to bow to the uninformed dictates of party bureaucrats in Moscow, knowing full well the result would be worse.

At a stroke, the rigid Soviet planned system managed to strangle both the economy and science at the same time, falling farther and farther behind the West in every technological breakthrough from oil drilling and food processing to computers and microchips. By ruthlessly suppressing individual enterprise, the Soviet system embarked on an economic road to nowhere. The Party maintained its control, but only at the cost of presiding over perhaps the greatest waste of human resources in history. In the long run, the economic disaster that decision produced would finally break Party rule and destroy the Communist system it was designed to preserve.

II. A JOYLESS PARTY

I left the Soviet Union in 1967, early in Brezhnev's long reign, and returned only nine years later, in 1976, late in the Brezhnev era. There were many changes, not only superficial ones like more cars on city streets and more apartment houses in new suburbs, but also potentially significant ones, like eased barriers to contacts between Soviet citizens and foreigners.

On the economic basics, however, nothing had fundamentally changed. The system still didn't work any better, the bureaucratic reorganizations were still no help, and the refusal to shift from state planning toward private enterprise was still total. I soon began to understand that the system was doomed, that no reforms could save it. Never was that clearer to me than in October 1977, sixty years after the Bolshevik Revolution swept communism to power in Russia, when I visited Leningrad, the scene of that historic sea change, to measure the progress under Soviet rule since then.

Getting there was a revelation. I decided to go by car. In 1977, the main highway between the nation's two largest cities, Moscow and Leningrad, was still only two lanes wide, with no white line down the center and no lights at night. Trucks constantly broke down on this pothole-marred 430-mile route. It was well before the first winter snows, but I counted eighty-three trucks stopped for repairs on the side of the road during my trip, or roughly one every five miles.

At least this road was paved. Between lesser Soviet cities, dirt roads were common. Here was the Soviet superpower, fifteen years after the Cuban missile crisis, with roads straight out of the African bush. To be sure, the Soviet military was a privileged elite. But even they had to use the same battered economic infrastructure, the same inadequate roads, the same broken-down trucks as everyone else. In reality, the Soviet Union was a Third World country with nuclear missiles. Its economic base was much too weak to support a global military challenge.

Indeed, there was every reason to believe that Moscow's ability to threaten the world would now decline. The Soviets had built their military power largely by squeezing the civilian economy dry. Now, in the sixtieth year of Communist rule, there was not much left to squeeze.

Worse for the Kremlin, the neglect of the consumer sector was at last becoming a liability for the military too. Ordinary Russians, denied consumer goods and proper living space, had long refused to have more children. Most families stopped at one child. Hardly any went beyond two. So Moscow now faced an acute manpower shortage. There were simply not enough young men from the more highly educated European part of the country to fill the personnel needs of both the army and the civilian labor force. Something had to give, and whatever the solution, the armed forces were about to lose. Either they would not get as much uniformed personnel as they needed, or heavy industry would not get all the skilled labor it required to supply the army.

There was a surprising lesson here: even in a dictatorship like the Soviet Union, public opinion counts. Consumer goods could not be withheld indefinitely before the public began paying the leadership back. Now by simply refusing to have more children, the long-suffering Soviet people were denying their Kremlin masters the human resources needed to maintain imperial ambitions. It was just one more lethal flaw that had never occurred to Soviet planners.

Leningrad displayed that flaw and many others. The city which had given birth to the Communist revolution now provided ample evidence that the system was fatally flawed. The problems were simply too deep to be fixed. The ultimate collapse might well be postponed, but it could no longer be avoided. All it took to see that in 1977 was a visit of a few days. This was a joyless sixtieth-anniversary year. Leningrad had nothing to celebrate, and neither did the rest of the country. The Party was nearly over.

Andrei and Nina Smirnov, my Russian friends in Leningrad, lived in a modern one-room apartment overlooking the River Neva. On his engineer's salary, about the Soviet national average, they could afford to eat meat twice a week. Since the birth of their second child, six months before, the Smirnovs had qualified for a larger flat from the state. But they told me they would be kept on the waiting list for three to six years before they got one, because the housing shortage was still so acute. In the meantime, they made do with their double bed, a crib for their baby daughter, a chair that folded into a bed for their seven-year-old son, and a desk, bookcase, table, wardrobe, and piano, all crammed into one room fifteen feet long and ten feet wide. They were not complaining. After sixty years of Communist power the Smirnovs enjoyed living conditions that made them one of Leningrad's more privileged young families.

The view from their eighth-floor window was spectacular. Below them unfolded a panorama of eighteenth- and nineteenth-century palaces and mansions from the old tsarist capital, St. Petersburg, a hauntingly beautiful city on canals, sometimes called the Venice of the North.

"It's like living in a museum," Andrei said with a special Leningrad pride. The city's effort to maintain its architectural treasures had been truly heroic. More than 150,000 shells hit Leningrad during the nine-hundred-day Nazi siege of World War II, destroying a third of its living quarters. By the 1970s, the historic buildings had been largely restored, but the scars of war remained. Americans, who have never seen their country attacked, cannot imagine the suffering of a city like Leningrad, pounded by Nazi tanks for three years, its population forced to eat household pets to stay alive. The survivors of Leningrad's siege will never forget. Thus the special pride in seeing the city restored to its tsarist glories.

Still, they were left with a disastrous housing crunch that lasted for decades. Some 40 percent of the families in Leningrad's inner city still lived in communal apartments in 1977, more than thirty years after the end of the war. That meant three generations—usually grandmother, parents, and children—lived in one room, screening off alcoves for privacy at night, and sharing communal kitchen and bathroom facilities with three or more other families. The alternative for some was new one-, two-, or three-room apartments, each with private kitchen and bathroom, built on the outskirts of the city where there were fewer shops, fewer goods available, and poor public transport facilities. Many Leningraders still preferred to share communal flats in the center.

Not all of this housing shortage was Communist-made. Some could be legitimately blamed on the war, although the Soviet authorities exaggerated that element and underplayed their own role, like the planning decisions that put more money into Leningrad-area defense industries than into housing.

All these factors underscored the extraordinary good fortune of my friends the Smirnovs. They were not stuck an hour or more away in the poorly supplied suburbs. They lived in the center of town, and didn't share kitchen or bath with anyone. To them, the one cramped room was just fine. They knew they were lucky. Food supplies to the markets in central Leningrad, as to those in Moscow, were relatively good. People as far away as the Baltic republics of Latvia, Lithuania, and Estonia complained their homegrown farm produce was shipped off to Moscow and Leningrad, leaving them with shortages. All this had been brought home to Nina the previous summer while on holiday in the Black Sea port of Odessa when she tried to buy meat for the family dog. "People just laughed," she told me. "They didn't have meat for themselves, only sausages."

A look at the family budget for these lucky ones was instructive. Andrei made the ruble equivalent of $190 a month. Of that, $35 went to the rent and $25 for their son's piano lessons. That left $130 for everything else, or about $4 a day if spent entirely on food. Meat alone could cost more. Low-quality pork went for $4.70 a kilo. With winter approaching as I went shopping with Nina, tomatoes were selling at $2.75 a kilo, lettuce at $1.30 a head, and grapefruit at $1.90 a kilo when you could find any of them. At those prices it was a question of "either or" for most meals—either meat or vegetables; either fruit or vegetables—and the $4 a day was gone.

Of course, the Smirnovs couldn't afford to spend everything on food. That would have left nothing for clothing or anything else. So $4 a day on food was out of the question. Like most Russians, they got by on bread, potatoes, cabbage, and other cheap foodstuffs, largely starches and sweets, too often doing without fresh meat, fruits, and vegetables, at the expense of their figures, their health, and their life expectancy, among the lowest in the world.[1]

In almost any other country in 1977, the Smirnovs' cramped housing and poor diet would hardly have put them among the more fortunate. In Poland, for example, people would have started a revolution if the best they could hope for was meat twice a week. Soviet peoples were traditionally more patient, but even they would not wait forever for a better life.

Meanwhile the margin of error for the Kremlin was already painfully thin. There had been riots from time to time in various cities, when food suddenly ran out. Heretofore, the authorities had always stemmed such crises by rushing in extra supplies from better-stocked regions. Still, what if food riots suddenly broke out not in just one city but in four, or ten, or twenty, at the same time, and the problem became too big to resolve by simply shifting existing resources around? That was only one danger constantly threatening the Soviet economic system, even in a relatively favored city like Leningrad, even at the best of times.

The sixtieth anniversary of the Bolshevik Revolution in Leningrad was supposed to be the best of times. Extra food supplies were brought in for the celebration, but even then, Nina Smirnov, like other Soviet women, couldn't plan her evening meal before going out to shop. Trying to get items on a prepared list would mean looking all day and still not finding several items. Instead, Nina saw what was available on the day, then improvised. There were different stores for bread, fish, dairy products, and so on. At each one, she had to stand in three lines—one to see what was available, a second at the cash desk to prepay the exact total for what she intended to buy, and a third to receive her purchases. Nina counted on spending at least three hours a day just to shop for food.

Usually it took longer. Whenever a Russian saw a line forming outside a store, he or she rushed to get in it, before even knowing what was for sale.

A line was a certain sign that something new and rare had just arrived. When I was with Nina, wool-lined calf-high women's boots from Austria went on sale at Passage, the glass-roofed department store arcade on Nevsky Prospekt, Leningrad's main shopping thoroughfare. They were clearly of better quality than anything seen before in Russia. Within minutes, a line of four hundred women stretched back a block and a half. It turned out only one color was available, brown, only four sizes, 33 through 36, and no chance to try anything on.

Not even the price, about $120 or three weeks' pay, discouraged anyone. Most people saved not in state banks, which they distrusted, but at home, under the mattress. That way they could always go out shopping with a wad of cash, just in case they happened upon a special line. Our line was special. Every woman in it bought boots, if not for herself, then maybe for a friend or neighbor, to trade for some other treasure at the end of some other line, or for resale at a higher price. The boots sold out long before the end of the line got served.

Lines were a Soviet way of life. Often they were friendly as people met, chatted, and argued about life to pass the time, even fell in love and got engaged waiting in line, or fell out of love and decided to divorce, also while waiting in line. Sometimes they were nasty, shouting melees. Americans got a taste of it in the gas lines after the OPEC oil shocks. In the Soviet Union, there were those sorts of lines every day for just about everything.

The only real alternative to the lines was the black market. A second or parallel economy called *nalevo,* meaning literally "on the left," thrived in Leningrad, as everywhere else in the Soviet Union, and took several forms. One was the mutual back-scratching arrangement. A dentist and an auto parts store manager counted each other among their private, and therefore illegal, customers. Neither had to stand in line for the other's services.

Another was the Soviet version of the old-boy network. A secretary was hired more for her contacts than for her typing skills. A Russian woman office worker once pulled out four notebooks containing names and addresses and told me, "These are my yellow pages. It's a way of life here. You don't have to stand in line all day if you know the right people."

Other forms of the black market involved muscular gentlemen who got their supplies by making sure goods fell off the backs of state trucks. These and many other black market operations were tolerated as the only effective way to keep the Soviet economy going. Police sweeps now and then would score some points for law and order, but no Kremlin leadership could afford to crack down completely on the second economy, for fear that the first one would collapse with it.

There were some improvements in the Leningrad of 1977, compared with the city I had first visited in the 1960s. Earlier, only foreigners wore blue jeans there. By the 1970s, however, the locals got them from Poland. Foreigners were now distinguished more by the quality of their shoes or eyeglasses, less by their trousers. The old bolt-rattling, fume-spewing Russian city buses were gone. In their place were bright yellow modern Icarus buses from Hungary. In general, Leningrad, like most of Russia, was slowly progressing in material terms, and by 1977 had reached the living standards seen in Eastern Europe ten years earlier. Soviet Communists took credit for this "progress." They never tolerated the notion that progress would have been considerably faster under any other system.

Attitudes were changing too, although just as slowly as the improvements in living standards. "Thirty years ago, no one would talk to foreigners," Andrei Smirnov told me. "Twenty years ago I'd be sent to prison for talking with you. Ten years ago I'd still worry. Now I say what I like." That sounded good, but in his time scale, there was still a way to go. Smirnov asked that his real name not be published in the *Newsweek* piece I was doing for November 1977. Even in the late 1970s, officials, artists, and dissidents were normally the only Soviets ready to let foreign correspondents quote them by name. Others were still afraid. Ordinary people usually waited until the 1980s before taking that chance.[2]

Some things had not changed at all, however. Soviet authorities were still falsifying their own history as grossly as they were distorting their economy. And the falsification of history added further economic consequences. Any regime seen to be fabricating history—by the people who have actually lived through the period being distorted—is hardly going to be believed on economic promises either. Thus the more the Kremlin falsified history, the more the Soviet people lost faith in a Communist future. They worked shorter hours, less effectively, adding to the economic malaise.

Sometimes the distortion of history went to patently absurd lengths. In Leningrad museums on the sixtieth anniversary of the Bolshevik Revolution, in the countless displays honoring what the Soviets called "the most important event of the twentieth century," there was not one mention of the man whose role was second only to that of Lenin. Leon Trotsky, the military strategist of the revolutionary victory, was still an "unperson," blanked out of all official histories. Outmaneuvered by Stalin after Lenin's death, Trotsky was falsely accused of machinations against the Party, exiled, and murdered in Mexico in 1940 by Stalin's agents.

Thirty-seven years later, Soviet authorities were still incapable of telling the truth about him. They could admit neither Trotsky's essential contribution to the revolution nor Stalin's ruthless decision to assassinate him. Asked why there was no mention of Trotsky on the anniversary of the Bolshevik Revolution he helped lead, a Leningrad museum guide told me in 1977: "He betrayed the revolution. That is why we cannot put his name with the people who devoted their lives to the real deeds of the revolution." The answer was nonsense. Trotsky did not betray the revolution, Stalin did, by turning its egalitarian ideals into a totalitarian legacy. In 1977, Soviet authorities still feared that admitting Stalin's betrayal would discredit his heirs, themselves included. So they lied about Trotsky and had all officials under their control, down to lowly museum guides, repeat the same lies.

In Leningrad, the people had heard or read more than enough of these lies. They responded by turning off official propaganda of all kinds. As one result, the collected works of V. I. Lenin, reissued for the sixtieth anniversary year, stood unsold in the city's bookstores. The real heroes were the cultural giants of the city's past—Tchaikovsky, Pushkin, and Dostoevsky. Works by Pushkin and Dostoevsky were sold out of all Leningrad bookstores in October 1977. They could not be printed fast enough to keep up with demand.

Sixty years after the Bolshevik Revolution, eight years before Mikhail Gorbachev took power, it was already clear in Leningrad, and elsewhere across the country, that Soviet communism had failed. The economy was a disaster. Hardly anyone believed the leadership's claims of progress anymore, and without the Stalinist terror, public demands for a better life could not be denied indefinitely. The only real question was whether the Soviet system could be effectively reformed or would have to be scrapped altogether. The prospects for reform did not look too brilliant.

III. WASTING THE LAST BEST HOPE

Science could have made a vital difference, perhaps enough for economic reform to succeed. The Soviet Union had a great advantage here. Its scientists were among the world's best. Given a free hand, they might well have made the technological breakthroughs that could have first put their economy right, then given it the competitive lead in conquering world markets.

One shudders to think, for example, what might have happened if Moscow had produced the first cheap laptop computers for the mass market. At a stroke, that one invention could have compensated for all the inefficiencies in a Soviet bureaucracy still run on typewriters and the abacus. It could have earned billions in exports. And it could have made the Russian economy the strongest in the world. Nothing like that happened, of course. The great promise of Soviet science, the last best hope to save the Communist economic system, was wasted by Soviet authorities themselves.

For one bright moment in 1957, Kremlin leaders seemed to be on the way to an economic-technological miracle. When the Soviets launched *Sputnik*, the first man-made object orbited in space, they looked poised to take over this world and the planets beyond. Americans immediately had visions of Communists on the moon. Soviet science, technology, and education were all assumed to be light-years ahead of U.S. levels, but they were nothing of the kind. America had overrated Soviet capabilities. In reality, through a tremendous concentration of resources, Moscow had managed to put a 184-pound chunk of metal into earth orbit. In general, though, Soviet science remained appallingly backward. Achievements like *Sputnik* were islands of the spectacular in a sea of primitiveness. And sadly, Soviet science never progressed beyond that point.

Its scientists never got the free hand that could have saved the system. Instead they were shackled by their Communist masters. Triumphs like *Sputnik* showed only the promise that was there, but never fulfilled. Ironically, the *Sputnik* shock did more for America. Behind in the beginning of the space race, the United States was determined to catch up and win. Once America committed the resources, the outcome was never in doubt. The Soviets had the technology for the relatively simple beginnings, such as launching the first satellite, and then putting the first man into earth orbit, but they never developed the sophistication to put a man on the moon and bring him back safely.

Nor could they match American success in unmanned deep space probes, such as the Viking series to Mars, in terms of photographs, length of operation, or overall data collected. More important, the conquest of space eventually produced the computers and the other high-tech economic spin-offs that put America ahead of the Soviets for good, in every field of competition from the arms race to export sales. The gap would increase until Gorbachev conceded defeat and turned the Soviet Union toward the Western economic model.

As early as 1975, at the time of the first joint Soviet-American space mission, the Apollo-Soyuz coupling, the race to conquer space was already virtually over. The Soviet Soyuz satellite was relatively primitive and passive. The Apollo satellite, the more sophisticated American partner, was the active player. Soon after arriving in Russia, an Apollo technician took a look at the Soyuz, shook his head in disbelief, and said, "if they can get that thing up into space, we'll find them." And that is exactly what happened. This was no even show by two equal superpowers. At the time the Russians could do no more than launch the Soyuz satellite into orbit and bring it back. The Americans had the much tougher task of maneuvering the Apollo satellite through space into position alongside the Soyuz, and then arranging the linkup.

The best way to evaluate Soviet science and technology, however, was back on earth. Science was a privileged sector, all right, collecting the best and brightest of the Soviet intelligentsia, but it still suffered from the supply nightmare, like everything else in the Soviet Union. Amazingly, the planned society lacked a computerized inventory system. So in addition to the constant shortages, no one really knew where to turn for any missing item. The typical Soviet scientist had to scrounge for the most basic equipment before he could start work, perhaps a plug for the sink where he washed out his test tubes, or even the test tubes themselves. Chemists used to complain they often had to wait six weeks or more just to get hold of a common chemical reagent like hydrofluoric acid. Basic equipment the American scientist could always buy off the shelf, like a centrifuge or a spectrometer, was often simply not available to his Soviet counterpart. "Scientific equipment in this country is rationed like food in wartime," a Soviet researcher once told me.

Not surprisingly, many Russian scientists preferred to make their own equipment. Their ingenuity was impressive. They could put together one of almost anything, but, naturally, they could not provide the series production the country's scientific community needed. And much of the homemade equipment often looked slapdash to visiting American researchers and produced inferior results.

Importing was no solution either. The Soviets did buy scientific equipment from Germany, Japan, Britain, and even the United States. But if this machinery broke down, replacement parts could be an even bigger problem to import than the original apparatus. In one typical case, a chemistry experiment ground to a halt at the Novosibirsk scientific center in 1976 because of a chip in an imported microscope. The foreign manufacturer offered to fly in a representative the same week, hand-carrying the needed eyepiece replacement. Unfortunately, that was impossible. The Soviet scientists had to go through channels, requesting a special foreign currency budget allocation to get the needed part. The experiment was held up for months.

Soviet researchers often lacked the most basic timesaving devices. By the mid-1970s, virtually every American scientist had his own small hand calculator, but that was beyond the reach of nearly all his Soviet colleagues. The comparison only got worse when it came to computers. American scientists could make up programs, run them through, and count on answers the same day. A Soviet scientist in the 1970s would be lucky to have a computer at all in his institute. If he didn't, he might have to wait weeks until a friend at some other scientific center found the time to run a program through the computer there.

Nor could the conscientious Soviet researcher make up for lost time by working weekends. Most scientific institutes closed Friday night for the weekend, and all electricity in the labs was turned off until Monday morning. Arbitrarily, at the stroke of a pen, some Soviet bureaucrat who knew nothing about science had limited the research the nation could do by making it impossible to keep round-the-clock experiments going on weekends.

Worse still, there was no way a Russian scientist could ignore politics and just get on with his work, any more than any other Soviet citizen. Politics pervaded even the privileged scientific establishment, determining which institutes, projects, or people got funded and which didn't. The politicians picking the favorites often erred, as Stalin and Khrushchev did in backing the absurd theories of Trofim Lysenko, a charlatan who tried to prove that "a new Soviet man" and wondrous new agricultural products could be bred simply by making the appropriate environmental changes. In the end, all Lysenko succeeded in doing was to hold back legitimate Soviet genetic and biological research for decades.

Even when the leadership funded the right ideas, however, excessive political control continued to hamstring Soviet scientific progress. Attendance at regular political or ideological lectures was mandatory for every scientist in the land, taking invaluable time from his work. Scientists also had to interrupt their research for ten days to two weeks every year to help harvest crops. At least that was the theory. Practice depended on the normal level of Soviet efficiency. One year friends told me their Leningrad institute was closed down so the entire scientific staff could go off to the fields to pick potatoes. Then someone forgot to send the buses, so they never harvested crops either.

Most important of all, scientists had to curry favor constantly with the Communist officials who ran their labs and institutes. These were the people who decided on the staff cuts every five years or so, ordered by Moscow to keep down personnel growth in the scientific establishment. Oddly, in the Soviet scale of values, bureaucrats were hardly ever fired, but productive people like scientists often were. Decisions on whom to let go and whom to keep were invariably based on Party loyalty rather than scientific ability. The whole process encouraged the time-servers and herd-followers. Researchers with individual initiative or the guts to challenge establishment views, just the sort of people needed to make any progress, often got weeded out first, to the overall detriment of Soviet science. Those who survived, even the more talented ones, then had their potential deliberately reduced even further by Party controllers, through a lifetime of frustration.

By then they were used to it. The waste of their brains and talents began with a system of education that had stamped out illiteracy, but otherwise often ran counter to the goals of intellectual growth and economic progress. Soviet education limited by ideological blinkers what could be said, read, or even thought. Not only were whole subjects or points of view considered taboo, but also certain intellectual abilities were strongly discouraged, such as free, independent thinking. Instead, groupthink was enforced by rote. Among the many grave omissions of a Soviet higher education was any tradition of real debate.

I once attended a Moscow University debate which went like this: the first student speaker argued in favor of proposition A; then the second speaker argued for the same proposition; then the third speaker did the same. The winner was the student deemed to have presented the most effective argument in favor of the common proposition, or, if you will, the one acceptable political line. No opposing or negative arguments were allowed. In effect, Soviet students were being denied training in the normal cut-and-thrust of debate as commonly practiced abroad, and with it one of the more important tools for intellectual growth.

Soviet scientists started with the disadvantages of such flawed educations. Then came the shortages of supplies and the political hassles. And then, if they survived all that, their real troubles began. They would first be forced into overly narrow specializations, not permitted to know what the experts in adjacent fields of research were doing. Then they would be limited in access to Soviet research papers in their own fields, and even further restricted from foreign trips or contacts with specialists abroad. All these measures deprived Soviet scientists of the contacts, the cross-fertilization, essential for scientific progress, and often left them uselessly duplicating work they couldn't know others had already accomplished. But the authorities were ready to pay that price in the name of state security, for them the most important priority. In science, that meant making sure no one researcher knew too much or could do too much harm defecting to the West.

This logic could not have been more counterproductive. It limited the exposure of Soviet scientists to science, thereby ensuring they could never reach their potential. It guaranteed there was no way that Soviet scientists could make the technological breakthroughs that might have saved the Soviet economy. In the Soviet Union, the story was always the same. The state planners who set the priorities and the restrictions ensured the failures, from stagnant science to a collapsing economy.

Sometimes bureaucratic decisions were nothing short of criminal, as when the public health service was deliberately deprived of adequate funding in favor of the continuing military buildup. No expense was spared for the Politburo, of course. At the very top, Soviet medicine was world-class. Kremlin leaders had special hospitals able to conduct open-heart surgery or remove cancerous tumors with equipment as sophisticated and specialists as skilled as most in America. It was the ordinary people who suffered the low priority given to health care funding.

Even in Moscow, in the general surgery ward of the typical hospital, sixty men would have to share two working toilets. Their lavatory was rarely clean. No toilet paper was supplied. Patients were supposed to tear up sheets of newspapers like *Pravda*—and bring their own supply. In the provinces, conditions were far worse, often to the extent of lacking anesthetics for emergency operations. Once again, medicine was a story of islands of the spectacular, this time for Kremlin leaders only, in a sea of the primitive for everyone else. For the general workforce, the standards of Soviet medicine were appallingly low, one more crucial factor in the high rate of alcoholism and constantly poor level of economic output.

The reader may suspect anti-Soviet propaganda at work here, an American journalist slandering Moscow with false accusations repeated from hearsay evidence. But the reader should know that the example of medicine, like all others in this book, was taken from personal experience.

In 1977 my family spent a long weekend at Zavidovo, a beautiful riverside hotel and estate maintained by the Soviet government for foreigners resident in Moscow. Brezhnev had a hunting lodge nearby. Foreigners never saw that, but at least we had a chance to breathe the same clean air and enjoy the same glorious birch forests. On this particular weekend, my eight-year-old son cut the tip of his index finger off while playing with a jagged piece of metal. The finger was bleeding profusely, and the tip was hanging by a thread.

Emergency medical treatment was essential. Although we were only sixty miles from Moscow, and in an area frequented by the Brezhnev elite, medical facilities were primitive in the extreme. The ambulance turned out to be a pickup truck. The hospital in the nearest town was a log cabin. The doctor had no anesthetic. His instruments were not sterilized. He washed his hands, wiped them on a used towel, and went to work. A large woman nurse held my son very tightly. And the doctor sewed his fingertip back on. I can still hear the screams.

We were relatively lucky. At the U.S. embassy in Moscow the next day we got the resident American doctor to apply the proper anesthetic, tidy up the stitches, and make sure there would be no danger of infection later. Ordinary Soviets could not do that. They had no choice but to put up with the butchery that often passed for Soviet medicine, accepting the pain, the illness, and often the early death. That too was planned.

The public record is full of other examples of the failure of Soviet authorities to spend money to protect the health of the people. Chernobyl comes to mind. Sadly for the Soviet people, their country's public health disaster was not the invention of anti-Communist propagandists. It was all too true. And it was ultimately the responsibility of Soviet leaders themselves.

So was every other element of the economic madness that passed for normality in Soviet life. The most damning of them all was probably agriculture. Before the Bolsheviks seized power in 1917, Russia was an agricultural exporter, despite its harsh winter weather. That traditional success story never survived the Communist "improvements."

First came Stalin's brutal "collectivization" in the 1930s, when millions of peasants were slaughtered during the elimination of private farms across the Soviet Union, and millions more people died in the resultant famines. Then came the various futile experiments under Khrushchev and Brezhnev to rationalize an unworkable system, usually by some bureaucratic reorganization. None of this changed the stinging indictment that after sixty years of communism, the Soviet Union was incapable of feeding its own people. In 1978, for example, sixty-one years into Communist rule, the U.S.S.R. had to purchase $1.5 billion worth of corn and wheat from its ideological adversary, the United States, to keep the Soviet peoples from starvation.

Here is how the Soviet planned economy worked on agriculture: farmers got paid the same whether they loaded their trucks fully with produce or not. Often they didn't. The truck then went to the nearest railway station, where more problems arose. Because of the country's poor road system, most foodstuffs reached the distant cities by rail. But industrial goods had the priority on freight train shipments. So fresh food often rotted at the railhead, waiting for empty freight cars. Food that went out on trains in time often spoiled later in poor processing or storage plants. In the end, Soviet authorities themselves estimated that between the farm and the family dinner table, some 40 percent of the country's food supply got ruined by poor transport, processing, and storage facilities. Nowhere else was there a clearer monument to the wasteful inefficiency of the Soviet system.

The nation muddled on, but only by cheating on its ideological convictions. The savior was something called the private plot. Workers on state or collective farms had little incentive to produce more than what they could eat themselves. They got paid absurdly low wages. But after they finished their official chores, they had the right to work small private plots, where they could raise their own chickens, cows, fruits, and vegetables. The produce raised there could then be sold for their own profit, in farmers' markets. These private plots covered less than 3 percent of the arable land in the Soviet Union, but produced more than 30 percent of the country's food supply. The lesson was obvious. Collective farming was a failure; private farming worked.

Nonetheless, Soviet authorities refused to heed the lesson. They were committed to defending an ideology which taught that collectively shared economic assets were the path to Marxist Utopia, the proper way to overcome the evils of capitalism, which they saw as a society of the rich exploiting the poor. So they refused to expand their private farm sector. In the end they created a society where no one was rich, where the poor exploited the poor, and where nobody ate well. Even Kremlin banquets for visiting chiefs of state would be rich on starches and sweets, richer yet on vodka and champagne, but woefully poor on fresh vegetables and fruits.

It was not always thus, and did not eternally have to be. Yeliseyev was one reminder. In tsarist days, Yeliseyev was literally a food palace, a huge hall with crystal chandeliers where the customer could buy virtually any delicacy. But under Soviet rule it had been turned into the more proletarian-sounding State Food Store No. 1 on Moscow's Gorky Street, and sold little more than the same poor-quality sausage available in all other state shops.

Russians could only joke about the change. In one such anecdote, an old man walks into Yeliseyev and asks for black caviar. He is told there is none. Then he asks for fresh salmon. Same answer. Finally, he asks for quails. Again, there are none. So the old gentleman leaves empty-handed. Afterward, one salesgirl says to another: "Did you see how old that man was?"

"Yes," says the other salesgirl, "but what a memory!"

Indeed, the memory of the better life would never go away. The Soviet system, which failed to reproduce it, would collapse first.

IV. THE POLITBURO IN THE DARK

The key to Soviet economic survival was agriculture. If the Soviet economy was ever to be fixed, agriculture would have to be put right first. And if agriculture could not be fixed, if the Communists could not feed their own people after sixty years in power, then the system as a whole was also irreparable and would have to be discarded. In 1978, Leonid Brezhnev started the Soviet Union down this path of discovery, without even knowing it.

In July of that year, the Communist Party secretary in charge of agriculture, Fyodor Kulakov, suddenly died. Among the funeral orators in Red Square was a man with a red birthmark on his forehead. It was Mikhail Gorbachev's first speech in Red Square. Gorbachev had succeeded Kulakov as the Party leader in Stavropol, an important agricultural region. In November 1978, Brezhnev chose him to succeeded Kulakov again, this time in Moscow in a far more important job, as the Party secretary running agriculture for the entire Soviet Union.

The promotion also brought Gorbachev into the Party's inner sanctum, the Politburo. He was then forty-seven years old, fourteen years younger than the average age in that elite body, the first of his generation to make it into the top Soviet leadership. He would soon see, in the years ahead, that Soviet agriculture could not be successfully reformed. One day, he would have the opportunity to apply that lesson to the entire system. But he would have to wait.

Yuri Andropov, Brezhnev's immediate successor, knew what had to be done. In his previous job as head of the KGB secret police, Andropov learned just how low Soviet economic performance had sunk under Brezhnev. The KGB was the only Soviet government agency with the real figures on the nation's appalling economic crisis, not only in agriculture, but also in industry, transport, scientific research, and everything else. Andropov loyally reported the grim facts to Brezhnev, who then kept them to himself. In his secrecy-obsessed Kremlin, even other members of the Politburo did not know the full truth. Leonid Ilyich deliberately hid it, denying them the data needed to start charting appropriate remedies. Incredibly, Brezhnev kept his own Politburo in the dark so it could not blame him for the building economic disaster. In effect, he was securing his own position at the expense of the nation's economic well-being. Here at work once again was the old Communist penchant for control over efficiency, this time at the pinnacle of the Kremlin high command.

At least Brezhnev's immediate successor, Yuri Andropov, knew the bitter economic truth. Top-secret KGB analyses convinced him that Brezhnev had left the economy in ruins—and his heirs no choice other than to accept the political risks of change. Equally important, Andropov had what it took to push reform through. According to Soviet sources who worked closely with him in the Party and the KGB, including some who often disagreed with him, Andropov was brave, bright, talented, and ruthless. Unfortunately, Yuri Andropov never got the chance to show what he could do. Soon after taking over the leadership he was weakened by a debilitating illness, and he died after only fifteen months in office.

Fortunately, Andropov had groomed a worthy successor, Gorbachev. Like Andropov, Gorbachev understood that the Brezhnev legacy meant reform simply had to be risked again. Brezhnev's caution was now more dangerous than Khrushchev's boldness. Still, Brezhnev's aging cronies in the Politburo didn't see it that way—yet. They picked a Brezhnev clone, Konstantin Chernenko, for a last hurrah. Once again, Gorbachev would have to wait.

Chernenko soon proved to be too old and feeble to use the powers inherited from Andropov. For months on end, the Soviet people saw Chernenko only on television, on those rare occasions when he was well enough for aides to prop him up with a rehearsed, short script. Kremlin stage managers had rich experience with such theatrics. They had done the same for Brezhnev himself in his last years, and for Andropov in his last months. Nevertheless, I once got a rare chance to see how pitifully ill and confused Chernenko really was as the ostensible leader of the world's second superpower.

I had come to Moscow with the journalists accompanying French President François Mitterrand and attended the opening minutes of his official meeting in the Kremlin with Chernenko. By the time the white-haired Chernenko, age seventy-three, had walked the fifteen feet from the conference-room door to the negotiating table, he was already wheezing noisily and gasping for air, his chest heaving. Once seated, Chernenko was supposed to banter amiably about the weather, or something else of no consequence, while cameramen briefly photographed the scene. The real talks were to begin only when the journalists were shooed from the room. Instead of following this long-established routine, however, a clearly disoriented Chernenko began his solemn reading of a Soviet foreign policy statement meant only for Mitterrand's ears. Startled KGB security men hurriedly pushed the photographers and other journalists out early.

In the end, Gorbachev did not have to wait very long. Chernenko lasted only thirteen months. In the final weeks, while the terminally ill Chernenko lay dying, Gorbachev, as second secretary, was already chairing the weekly Politburo meetings on Thursday, Viktor Karpov, Moscow's chief disarmament negotiator at Geneva, told me privately. Mikhail Sergeyevich was ready for the top, or thought he was.

In fact, Gorbachev had not been properly informed about the task ahead.

Georgi Shakhnazarov, his closest political adviser, told me that Gorbachev had to wait until he took over the top job as general secretary of the Soviet Communist Party before he got his first look at the full KGB assessment of the impending economic disaster. Earlier access had been denied him, first as a Politburo member, then as second secretary and the clear heir apparent. Both Andropov and Chernenko, like Brezhnev before them, had kept their Politburo collegues in the dark. Even Mikhail Sergeyevich Gorbachev, one step from the pinnacle of Kremlin power, was ill prepared for the enormous economic challenge he would have to confront.

8

The Soviet Threat: The World's Largest Standing Army

I. HYPE

The Cold War was a war of illusions. In the end, no nuclear weapons exploded, just myths. Many of these illusions were deliberately manufactured by the political elite in Moscow and Washington. Each side exaggerated the threat from the other, for very different reasons. Those reasons are key elements in understanding why the Cold War lasted as long as it did.

Soviet leaders got enormous political mileage out of inflating the dangers of American attacks on their country or its allies. First they created the specter of "American imperialist aggression." Then they denounced it daily in their controlled press. Then they used it to justify the unprecedented military buildup they conducted in order to hold on to their expanded Communist empire by armed force. The Politburo knew perfectly well that internal opposition was always the greatest danger to continued Communist rule. But it could hardly admit that. So it invented an American threat to legitimize its need for the world's largest standing army as communism's security guarantee. At the same time, the Kremlin used the myth of an American menace to justify imposing decades of economic sacrifice on the Soviet people, in effect a permanent wartime effort. That funded the Kremlin's superpower ambitions.

American leaders rightly took the Soviet threat seriously. The U.S.S.R. ever since the 1940s had expanded Communist rule by military force, directly in Eastern Europe and by proxies in Vietnam, to name but two examples. Nuclear capability, and then essential strategic parity with the United States, only increased the Soviet Union's global aggressive potential. It would have been the height of folly for U.S. leaders to underrate the Soviet threat. Had they done so, much of the world might be Communist today. Fortunately, the Americans avoided this error. Unhappily, however, they then made the opposite mistake, overrating Moscow's ability to challenge the West, and, with that, they prolonged the Cold War.

Caution in the nuclear age is understandable, even commendable. But often, America's overblown view of Soviet power was a deliberate calculation rather than an honest mistake. In their own way, American leaders could be just as cynical as their Soviet counterparts in hyping the threat from the other side. For example, John Kennedy, one of America's more liberal Cold War presidents, rode to office on claims of a nuclear "missile gap" with Russia, then had to admit from the White House that the United States was not behind after all. Throughout the Cold War, Democrats and Republicans alike won congressional or presidential elections by standing tough against a magnified Soviet challenge. Anything less was considered being "soft on communism," a sure way to lose votes. Pentagon officials campaigning for steady budget increases gladly supplied the politicians with exaggerated Soviet threat assessments. The result of all this hype was to extend the arms race.

It also extended the Cold War, because hyping the Soviet threat had far more important consequences than simply winning elections or funding the military-industrial complex. The repeatedly stated American conventional wisdom that the Soviet Union was willing to start a nuclear war against the United States, perhaps with a preemptive first strike, took on a life of its own with enormous policy consequences. Among them was ceding Moscow an uncontested sphere of influence in Eastern Europe, and, often, a reluctance to confront Soviet expansionism in the Third World. In a word, the United States first hyped the Soviet threat, then became overly cautious in response, having persuaded itself that Moscow had a lead in the military balance. In fact, a more accurate assessment of the Soviet Union as by far the weaker superpower throughout the Cold War would have allowed the United States to confront and defeat the Communist challenge decades earlier. Such was the price of overrating the Soviet threat.

We now know from the historical record that the Soviets never came close to an offensive nuclear first strike against the United States. This remained true whatever the American provocation, including U.S. warplanes killing Soviet military personnel in bombing missions over North Vietnam, or U.S.-supplied weapons slaying Soviet soldiers in Afghanistan. That proven behavior pattern confirms that the United States had opportunities to pressure the Soviets more effectively in earlier Cold War crises, among them Hungary in 1956 and Czechoslovakia in 1968. In each of these cases, an accurate evaluation of Soviet intentions and capabilities could have led to a more forceful American stand, short of risking nuclear war, capable of accelerating the collapse of communism by many years. Instead, the U.S. missed the opportunities because of an exaggerated view of the Soviet threat.

Admittedly, the historical record provides the wisdom of hindsight. The lesson of Afghanistan in the 1980s could hardly have been applied in the case of Hungary thirty years earlier. Nonetheless, that is far from the whole story. At each stage of the Cold War, senior U.S. officials were well aware that the Soviet threat had been overblown. In both Hungary and Czechoslovakia, as we have seen, there were clear opportunities at the time for wiser, more effective U.S. diplomacy. In failing to seize these openings, the U.S. authorities of the day assumed a share of responsibility for letting the Cold War last as long as it did.

Harsh as that judgment sounds, it is true. Even American journalists in Moscow, without access to their government's secret intelligence reports, were well aware that the Soviet threat to the West had been hyped through most of the Cold War. Their conclusion had nothing to do with the Kremlin's constant claim of peaceful intentions. No one with any knowledge of history could believe such propaganda. Instead the realization that the threat had been hyped came from the evidence that journalists could see with their own eyes on the ground in Moscow. Here was a nation where telephones didn't work, which couldn't feed its people, which still relied on the abacus well into the computer age. In thousands of different ways, every foreign resident could see that the entire Soviet economy, including the privileged military sector, was in no position to risk war with the United States. In that sense, the Soviet threat to America was imaginary.

Thus did the argument come full circle. The Cold War and its nuclear stalemate were perilous enough. Soviet bullying of smaller nations always risked escalation to a wider East-West war. At the same time, any mistaken reading of radar screens could have touched off an unintended nuclear holocaust. There were many other all too real dangers, and no need to exaggerate them. But both Moscow and Washington did, throughout the Cold War, particularly in raising the menace of a nuclear first strike from the other side.

My own voyage of discovery into the world of Cold War hype came in the winter of 1977, on a drive through one of the prettiest parts of Moscow. My route took me southwest from the Kremlin, up into the Lenin Hills, along a broad, tree-lined avenue past lavish state villas where Soviet leaders once lived, among them Nikita Khrushchev. The road continued on past Moscow State University, a skyscraper in Stalinist wedding-cake architecture. Just before the university, I turned onto a small side road and stopped in front of a rectangular dirt mound, the size of an American football field, rising some fifteen feet above the ground. At the height of the Cold War, this huge mound was supposed to help the Soviet Union start—and win—a nuclear conflict with the United States.

When I made the trip, the mound was covered with snow and surrounded by a wood picket fence. A red lettered sign in Russian warned: "Forbidden zone, no trespassing." On the university side, there was a small concrete bunker with a steel door, apparently an entrance down into the mound. One uniformed guard sat in an adjacent glass booth. Perhaps two dozen green ventilating pipes sprouted like branchless trees from various spots on the mound. Experts in the West, armed with satellite photos, had recently identified this mound as the cover of a major bomb shelter capable of withstanding a nuclear attack. One of them, U.S. General George Keegan, said it was part of a massive Soviet civil defense program so superior that the U.S.S.R. could launch a nuclear war against the United States and survive.[1] It sounded as though Moscow had at last found a way to force a U.S. surrender to Soviet nuclear blackmail.

Such scare stories were not unusual during the Cold War. All it took was some respectable American figure saying the Soviets had developed some new weapon or defensive tactic to shift the military balance their way. Moscow would deny it, thereby only serving to give the story even more credibility in the West. Inevitably, the alarm would soon translate into higher U.S. defense spending to negate the latest perceived Soviet advantage. Just as inevitably, Moscow would respond with new countermeasures and the arms race would spiral higher. The only real beneficiaries in this escalating panic on both sides were the military-industrial complexes of both superpowers, which were getting ever more funding.

At the height of the Cold War, global military spending neared $450 billion a year. The United States and the Soviet Union together accounted for more than half of it. At the same time, development aid to Third World countries totaled only $20 billion. Experts estimated that malaria could be eradicated by using only one-thousandth of the total the world spent on arms.[2] Clearly the funds fueling the arms race might have been put to a better purpose, if it could have been proved that the military was exaggerating the threat.

That was never easy. Journalists and others with no security clearance had no way to investigate the truth of the various scare stories fueling the Cold War arms race. But civil defense was different. By definition, even a police state like the U.S.S.R. couldn't hide bomb shelters designed to be known to and used by the general public. So while in Moscow, I determined to find out if the Soviet Union's alleged strategic lead in civil defense was really true. The mound at the university was my first stop.

Experts from various Western embassies had already been there, and found it far less sinister than General Keegan did. They were convinced the mound was a covered reservoir, an emergency water supply for the university district. Their reasoning was simple, and persuasive. The ventilation pipes, they told me, were just the diameter needed to allow for air intake as the water levels of a reservoir receded, but nowhere near wide enough to provide filtered air for such a large bomb shelter. That was the common opinion of specialists from the British, French, German, and American embassies. None of them believed the mound was a bomb shelter.

Naturally, their opinion was not definitive. Keegan could have been wrong about the mound at the university, but right in general about the Soviet civil defense program. Yet again, military attachés based at various embassies in Moscow disagreed. Part of their job was to travel constantly around the Soviet Union. Naturally, they never got to secret military installations in special zones closed to foreigners. Nevertheless, they did get to all the major cities in the country where there would have to be bomb shelters to protect large segments of the population if the nation was to survive a nuclear war. None of them ever saw even one. They were convinced the Soviet leadership had such protection, and perhaps key military and industrial installations did too. But there was nothing for the general public, not as much as one sign on a wall in any major Soviet city saying "This way to the shelter."

The Moscow subway certainly had bomb shelter potential. It could have been an essential element in any really effective civil defense program for the population in the Soviet capital to survive a nuclear war. The subway system was able to hold one million of the city's eight million people. Stations were deep enough below ground and had the requisite blast doors. There was no evidence, however, that they had the air filtration systems needed to upgrade them from World War II bomb shelters or enable them to survive radiation from a nuclear attack. Without the subway there was simply nothing else in Moscow that could begin to do the job. Thus the only way the Soviet population could survive a nuclear strike would be to evacuate all the major target cities.

That was also to prove impossible. Evacuation can be tested on a small scale, say at the factory level. But there was no way the Soviets could test mass evacuation from entire cities. Any such exodus would immediately be picked up by U.S. satellites, trigger suspicion that Moscow was about to launch a preemptive nuclear first strike against the United States, and risk an American nuclear counterattack. For that reason, the Soviets never practiced a mass evacuation from big cities and could never be sure one would work.

The Russians themselves never believed their country had an effective civil defense program against nuclear attack. I asked dozens of Soviet friends, and none of them said they had ever been drilled on either going to a shelter or evacuating the city. One Russian I knew well suggested this procedure: "After the nuclear attack warning sounds, wrap yourself in a sheet and walk slowly to the nearest cemetery. Why slowly? So as not to panic others."

His cynicism was typical. Moscow University students, for instance, were never impressed with the civil defense course that told them to protect themselves from nuclear attack by digging a hole and covering it with leaves and tree branches. They called the course *grob*, a designation they derived from the first two letters of the Russian words for civil defense—*grazhdanskaya oborona*. They thought the shortened form was a particularly apt choice: *grob* means "coffin" in Russian.

In the end, the civil defense scare proved to be a red herring. The U.S. government never bought Keegan's "evidence." Fortunately, on this occasion, it chose to believe its embassy experts on the ground in Moscow, rather than the made-in-America myth of a Soviet civil defense system that could defeat the United States in a nuclear war. The decision saved billions of dollars that might well have been wasted constructing bomb shelters of questionable need and survivability in the United States. This time a Cold War scare story had a happy ending. But it is recounted here for another reason. The civil defense episode was a clear case, easily proved, of the Soviet military threat being blown out of all proportion. Unfortunately, during the Cold War, this happened far too often.

At the same time, however, it must still be remembered that all such hype was relative. It only meant that a problem had been exaggerated. It manifestly did not mean that there was no problem. The argument here is that the Soviet challenge was overblown, not that it didn't exist, or didn't deserve to be the U.S. government's top foreign and defense policy priority.

Of course the Soviet threat was deadly serious. Moscow proved in Eastern Europe after World War II that it was ready, willing, and able to impose its political-economic-ideological system on other nations by military force. In the decades that followed, that threat grew to global proportions and new levels of sophistication, not only in weapons but also in tactics, as in the use of Cuban surrogates to promote Soviet military expansionism in black Africa. The West was absolutely right to draw the line and contain the Soviet threat, if necessary by resorting to armed force.

Even a layman could see that the Soviets had created a formidable war machine. I once toured an army base outside Moscow with state-of-the-art training that was truly impressive. Infantrymen moved through a huge field as silhouettes representing enemy troops and tanks automatically popped up from 150 to 500 yards away. The advancing Soviet soldiers had from seven to thirty seconds to find and hit the targets, depending on distance and difficulty. All targets were controlled from a tower, and all shots were scored electronically. Years later I toured China and saw trainee infantrymen there aim rifles and yell belligerently, but never fire. The reason: Beijing couldn't afford the bullets.

Although the Soviets were often backward by Western standards, they were clearly way ahead of China and many other potential adversaries. That alone was ample reason not to underrate the Soviet threat, however primitive Soviet arms looked to Western eyes. The MiG-21 jet fighter was a good example. Its rivets were not flush, but it could fly combat missions against the best in the world. Granted, Moscow was least likely to risk a direct attack on America. Yet that never ruled out Soviet probes to test Western defense intentions in world trouble spots. There was always the danger that a Kremlin leader would try to distract his people from their economic misery at home by embarking on some military adventure abroad against vital Western interests. The "prudent man theory" required that the West adequately protect all those flash points from the Middle East oil fields to the emerging markets of Southeast Asia to Fidel Castro's backyard in Central America, among others, with conventional as well as nuclear weapons.

All that was bad enough, a tremendous challenge. There was no need to exaggerate the task. But exaggerate it we did, fearing that Soviet first strikes, conventional or nuclear, were a real threat to both the NATO allies and America itself. At the end of the Cold War the historical record demonstrated that the Soviets never dared risk anything of the kind. We can now at last see why.

The reasons start with the raw numbers. At the height of its military buildup, the Soviet Union boasted the world's largest standing armed forces by far, four million men, compared with three million in China and two million in the United States. By itself, that one statistic, underscoring overwhelming Soviet numerical superiority, was enough to give Western military strategists nightmares. Would the West one day decide it would rather be red than dead, refuse to escalate to a nuclear war that would destroy the world, and simply bow to an invasion by vastly superior Soviet conventional forces? That was only one doomsday scenario raised by the specter of the four-million-man Soviet military.

Yet on closer examination, even that horrendous specter turned out to be a straw man. It was almost irrelevant in assessing the dangers of an armed clash between the Soviet Union and the NATO alliance. In actual fact, there was no way the Kremlin could throw four million men into a war against the West.

For one thing, a quarter of the Soviet ground and tactical air forces were tied down defending their nation's four-thousand-mile border with a hostile Communist China. This force included forty military divisions, out of a total of 160 combat-ready divisions in the Soviet army. As far as the worst-case theorists in the Kremlin were concerned, these troops could not be moved West to fight NATO without inviting an attack from China and the unacceptable loss of huge tracts of the Soviet Union's Far East real estate. So they stayed deployed along the Chinese border throughout the Cold War.

For another thing, some thirty to forty military divisions, or nearly another quarter of the total, were tied down in Eastern Europe to insure that the Communist system would continue to rule that region. These were the troops used to suppress the rebellions in Hungary in 1956 and Czechoslovakia in 1968. Again, Kremlin planners could not count on deploying them farther West against NATO without leaving Eastern Europe exposed, this time to a successful armed revolution.

None of this even begins to take into account the number of Soviet troops that had to remain permanently deployed on the territory of the U.S.S.R., to prevent or crush uprisings by anti-Communists or by minority nationalities from the Baltics in the north to the Ukraine in the west, the Caucasus in the south, and Muslim Central Asia in the East. The number of divisions deployed for such duty on the home front was certainly significant. But for the purposes of this argument, they will be totally ignored. The essential point can be made without them, as follows:

Taken together, the Chinese border and Eastern Europe alone permanently used up nearly half the Soviet Union's active forces. That left Moscow, at most, little more than the other half, something over two million men, available for war against the West, a total outnumbered by the armed forces of the United States and the fifteen other NATO allies. Thus, far from holding a two-to-one manpower advantage, encouraging a conventional arms attack on the West, the Soviet Union was sure to be outgunned by NATO in any direct clash. In reality, Moscow therefore had every incentive to seek accommodation rather than confrontation.

Nonetheless, the Pentagon brass continued to beat this drum. Year after year, Congress was reminded that the Soviets maintained a dangerous conventional superiority in Europe and that bigger U.S. defense budgets were needed to right the balance. In the mid-1980s, for example, the Pentagon claimed the Soviet-led Warsaw Pact had a numerical advantage over NATO in battle tanks of better than two to one and in combat aircraft of better than three to one.

Their figures, as usual, were cooked. Among other things, they included tanks and aircraft from the Communist countries of Eastern Europe, which were by no means certain to join in any Soviet attack on the West. And they excluded factors like French fighter aircraft, which were technically outside NATO's command structure but were virtually certain to be deployed on the Western side in any European war. When all these elements were properly factored in, the East-West balance in tanks and tactical aircraft likely to used in a European war was closer to one to one.[3]

In short, the claimed overwhelming Soviet superiority in manpower and conventional weapons, when questioned seriously, turned out to be just plain wrong. Furthermore, even if the raw numbers had been right, they still would have proved nothing. Throughout its history, Russia and later the Soviet Union often fielded numerically stronger armed forces. Yet Moscow repeatedly learned that more quantity in manpower was no match for higher-quality foreign weapons. Thus Napoleon marched all the way to Moscow and occupied the Kremlin. Hitler's troops invaded a thousand miles to Stalingrad. In the end, both were defeated, but only at terrible cost to the defenders. The folly of relying on numerical superiority alone was etched forever on the Russian soul. As a result, no Soviet leader ever dared attack the West on the basis of larger numbers of soldiers, tanks, and planes.

More important, matching the quality of Western arms was always beyond the reach of Soviet leaders. At every stage of the arms race, conventional and nuclear, the Americans broke the ground for new-generation weapons, leaving the Soviets scrambling to catch up. The U.S. breakthroughs came in a long and impressive list, in conventional arms from the first aircraft carriers with global reach to the first "smart" weapons with electronic guidance systems for pinpoint accuracy, and in nuclear weapons from the first atomic bomb to the first hydrogen bomb, the first submarine-launched ballistic missiles, the first intercontinental ballistic missiles (ICBMs) and the first independently targeted multiple warhead (MIRVed) missiles, to name just a few.

Occasionally the Soviets produced a superior missile, tank, or plane in some category or other, but there was never any doubt that the overall quality balance overwhelmingly favored the United States. Proof came from the fact that no American commander ever wanted to change places and arsenals with his Soviet opposite number, despite all the talk of Moscow's numerical superiority. In every branch of service—army, navy, and air force—America's decisive advantages in quality held up throughout the Cold War.

Take the navy, as one way to establish this point. U.S. naval superiority made the difference in the 1962 Cuban missile crisis. John Kennedy's naval blockade of Cuba forced Khrushchev to back down and remove his missiles. After that, the Kremlin determined there would be no more humiliations at sea. It invested billions to turn the Soviet navy into a high-tech globe-girdling colossus, equal to or better than the U.S. fleet, but never got close to achieving that goal.

For starters, the Soviets maintained a conscript navy. Moscow took raw recruits off the farms and sent them to sea on equipment too sophisticated for them to master. The result was enormous problems in training, performance, and morale. The all-volunteer U.S. Navy, by contrast, relied on properly trained professional crews. Worse, even a top-priority program like the Soviet navy still suffered from the limited resources and shoddy workmanship of the civilian economy. On surface ships they could never match the size or quality of America's aircraft carriers, often the decisive factor in war. On submarines, and particularly nuclear-powered ones, they never managed to reduce high and therefore detectable noise levels. When the Soviets tested their Alpha class submarines in the spring of 1980 in the Norwegian Sea, the Americans heard the traces from as far away as Bermuda. Quieter, less detectable U.S. submarines remained superior. On the surface of the sea or under it, the Soviet navy was never a match for the Americans.

Worse still, the Soviet navy often proved to be a bigger threat to its own crews. Sloppy work habits, for example, led to dangerously high radiation levels in nuclear ships. Admiral Hyman Rickover, father of the U.S. nuclear navy, once toured the Soviet nuclear-powered icebreaker *Lenin* for half an hour. That brief visit exposed him to more radioactivity than half a lifetime on American nuclear submarines. The former navy secretary Ronald Lehman reported numerous fatal radiation leaks and other accidents on Soviet nuclear ships.[4] In Russia, reports of radiation leaks were so common that sailors even made sick jokes about it. Seamen used to say they could always tell a sailor from a nuclear ship because he glowed in the dark.

Nor was that all. The old Soviet mania of pursuing control at the expense of efficiency hampered the armed forces just as it did the civilian economy. Fortunately for the West, that mania considerably reduced the threat of war. In the navy, for example, only a small portion of the Soviet nuclear submarine fleet, around 10 percent, was ever at sea at any one time directly threatening the West. Any more would have exceeded Moscow's ability to ensure control of submarines far from Soviet bases. The Kremlin never developed the complex command system needed to maintain both a high degree of launch readiness and adequate safeguards against unauthorized use.[5] So it kept most of its submarine nuclear attack force stuck in home ports, effectively turned off.

That same caution also affected land-based nuclear missiles. The Soviets made it harder to fire them than the Americans did. At U.S. missile sites it took two air force crewmen acting together to do the job. In the Soviet Union, authority was further divided to avoid error. The responsibility for guarding nuclear stockpiles went not to the army but to the KGB security police. Often warheads under KGB guard were physically separated from the army missiles that would carry them. Four men were needed to fire a Soviet nuclear weapon. Two KGB servicemen armed the missile with a warhead and then two regular army soldiers launched it.

Outside Soviet territory, the precautions got even more complex. No nuclear warheads were stockpiled in any Soviet foreign bases, not even in Eastern Europe. Instead the warheads were kept in the U.S.S.R. for transfer to Eastern Europe only in a crisis or for occasional training exercises. The launch system first divided responsibility between the army and the KGB, and then divided it again by geographic region. How well this cumbersome procedure would work in war was never put to the test.

Nor, fortunately, was the technical proficiency of Soviet land-based ICBMs ever tested under wartime conditions. Here again there was ample reason to wonder how much might work how well on the day. In a nuclear showdown the lids would have to come off their silos, the missiles fire properly, and the warheads explode near targets. What percentage might fail one or more of those requirements was a favored guessing game among Western military attachés in Moscow. Most thought it would be high. "They need two rockets in case the first fails," a British military attaché in Moscow once told me.

Soviet leaders themselves had similar doubts, with reason. Khrushchev wrote in his memoirs that he was terrified on his first trip to the United States because he feared his Soviet-built airliner wouldn't make it nonstop across the Atlantic. The unproven reliability of Soviet ICBMs also gave him and his successors cause for concern. A retired colonel from the Soviet rocket forces told me, "Nuclear missiles often failed quality controls after production and had to be replaced by newly manufactured substitutes." He did not know the percentage, but conceded it was "unacceptably high."

Furthermore, Kremlin leaders knew if they attacked America, nuclear retaliation from the United States would likely destroy them, their Communist system, and most of their people. They well remembered the Nazi invasion of World War II that cost the Soviet Union an admitted twenty million dead and created a determination never again to suffer such horrors. Nuclear war with the United States, they understood, could cost them 200 million dead—or more.

Finally, their ideology taught them that history was on their side, moving away from capitalism toward Communism, that there was no need to rush into a confrontation with Washington and risk everything, because in time the world would inevitably move their way without war. In short, their incentive to launch a surprise attack on America was virtually nil.

They tried to say as much, to explain their awesome military power as purely defensive. In a typical speech in 1978, for example, Brezhnev declared: "The overall numerical strength of Soviet armed forces does not spell any 'military threat' to the West at all, although it is quite enough, if necessary, to deliver a retaliatory blow at the aggressor, no matter where he may be." In an interview the same year with a German newspaper, the Soviet leader went further and ruled out a preemptive nuclear attack. "The Soviet Union is not thinking of making a first strike," he said.[6]

Welcome as those words sounded, they were barely believable. Soviet military doctrine, written by the uniformed brass and approved for publication by the same Leonid Brezhnev, said just the opposite. They were all bellicose in tone and stressed instead the military offensive. When war starts, they said, you plunge ahead with a massive offensive based on superior numbers of men and weapons until you destroy the enemy's armed forces and civilian economic power. They never ruled out a first strike. Escalation to nuclear war was regarded as inevitable and winnable.

That very point is made in a typical passage from the classic work on Soviet military doctrine, the 1962 book *Military Strategy*, written by Marshal Vasily Sokolovsky, a former chief of the general staff, and fifteen senior officers. It declares that "a third world war will be a nuclear-missile war." Then it predicts: "This war will inevitably end with the victory of the progressive Communist social and economic system over the reactionary capitalist social and economic system, which is historically doomed to destruction."

Understandably, the Pentagon chose to discount Brezhnev's defensive claims and to believe instead the authors of the offensive Soviet military doctrine. The doctrine spelled out the Soviet threat that justified increasing U.S. military budgets in response. To be fair, the same Soviet armed forces could be used either offensively or defensively, and clearly the Pentagon had to take steps to contain any offensive threat.

Still, that was far from the whole story. Soviet military doctrine deserved to be largely discounted. It was written by uniformed military chiefs. Like all professional warriors, they considered their job to be to win battles. Inevitably they talked about certain victory and avoided any mention of insurmountable problems—like exactly how their nation was supposed to survive and win a nuclear war. In the United States, by contrast, military doctrine was often written by civilians, who, unlike professional soldiers, could worry in print about concepts like unacceptable damage and kill ratios in a nuclear exchange. If the military doctrines of the two superpowers were read side by side, it sounded like the Soviets were more willing to risk nuclear war. But that was largely because soldiers wrote the Soviet doctrine and civilian academics the American counterpart. In terms of actual policy, as history now shows, the Kremlin was no more ready to risk nuclear war than the White House.

The right way to analyze the Soviets' military intentions and capabilities was to look at what they actually did, rather than at the doctrines they wrote. The lesson could hardly be clearer. Since World War II, the Soviet army engaged in combat abroad only if it could literally drive to work across its own borders. Thus they invaded Hungary in 1956, Czechoslovakia in 1968, and Afghanistan in 1979, each time entering a nation on the Soviet frontier.

Even in Eastern Europe, they went no further. When Tito broke with Moscow in 1948, the Soviets never invaded to bring Yugoslavia back into the fold. There was one crucial reason: they shared no common border. To reach Yugoslavia over land, Soviet troops would first have to cross Hungary, Romania, or Bulgaria. Albania was the same story. It was the only European Communist country to side with China in the long, bitter ideological dispute between Moscow and Beijing. The Soviets, however, never seriously considered invading tiny Albania to put that right. Again, they had no common border. Albania was on the far side of Yugoslavia.

The pattern was no accident. Hungary and Czechoslovakia could be invaded to force their continued loyalty to Moscow, but Yugoslavia and Albania could not. Supply lines made the crucial difference. The Soviets were confident they could supply their troops across their frontiers into Hungary or Czechoslovakia. They were far less confident they could supply them properly at longer distances, even in countries of Eastern Europe with no common border, like Yugoslavia or Albania.

Farther afield, the problem only got worse. In Eastern Europe at least, Moscow could have supplied troops as far away as Yugoslavia or Albania by land. In Third World hot spots in the Middle East, Africa, or Latin America, Moscow would have to supply their forces by sea or air or both. And American superiority, both at sea and in the air, could have interdicted those supply lines, had the United States chosen to do so. As a result, the Soviets nibbled and probed. If there was no American response, they continued, with their own soldiers in Ethiopia, for example, or with Cuban surrogates in Angola. But if the United States replied with force, as in Berlin or in Cuba, they backed down.

Moscow's military threat to Western interests was always limited. It had no qualms about supporting Communists or "national liberation movements" on all continents. It supplied arms and military advisers to all sorts of scoundrels, among them Iraq's Saddam Hussein and Libya's Muammar Qaddafi. But throughout the Cold War, the Soviets always stopped short of any direct military confrontation with the West. If challenged, they pulled back. They had no other choice. Globally, despite essential nuclear parity, they were always in the weaker military position, and they knew it. Their numerical superiority was a myth. The West's qualitative lead was a reality. In any objective analysis, the superpower military balance strongly favored the West.

II. AT SEA

Any concrete case proves the West's superiority over and over again. Even personal ones underscore the point. A typical example was Yevgeny, or Zhenya for short, my Russian friend for thirty years, who served as a lieutenant in the Soviet navy. To protect his family, Zhenya asked that his last name not be used, but he never held back on the details that demonstrated the relative weakness of the Soviet military at every turn.

Zhenya was a top graduate of the Lvov Polytechnic Institute in 1950. Recruiting officers—"buyers," he calls them—told Zhenya he was wanted as a naval cadet. "There was no way to refuse," he recalls. "Once they tell you that your country demands your service, to say no means you don't like Soviet power and you end up in the Gulag." So, reluctantly, Zhenya agreed to train as a naval officer. Tens of thousands of other officers must have joined with the same enthusiasm.

Before he could get started, however, Zhenya had to fill out an official inquiry form containing thirty-two questions. Among them was this one: "Did your grandparents own property before the Bolshevik Revolution?" It was an ideological loyalty test two generations long. "If your grandparents were capitalist landowners, the Soviet navy wouldn't take you," Zhenya says. Other questions weeded out similar undesirables. How many qualified officers the Soviet military lost from such suspicions of ideological impurity is, of course, incalculable. So is the number who had to lie their way in.

Zhenya spent eighteen months at a Leningrad academy that trained the Soviet navy's top technical specialists. His field was electronics, and he was amazed to learn that none of the equipment used at this elite establishment was Soviet-made. When the Russians wanted the best for their best and brightest, they bought abroad, from West Germany, even from Sperry Rand in America. Then they put elaborate restrictions on who could use what, from complex guidance systems down to foreign-language books. Zhenya found Winston Churchill's *The Second World War* in the institute library, but never got permission to read it.

He soon learned that Soviet equipment was dangerously suspect. Zhenya's first training cruise, on a destroyer from Leningrad to Riga, traveled through sea-lanes that had never been properly cleared from the World War II Soviet mines planted a decade before. Over the years, cables broke and the deadly mines floated into what were supposed to be safe waters and killed the Soviets' own sailors. "There were several instances where Soviet navy ships went down because of this," Zhenya remembers.

Discipline was extraordinarily rigid. On shore leave, Soviet sailors were not allowed to get drunk. Instead they had to behave themselves at all times on land. Shore patrols, each consisting of a young officer and two sailors, made sure they did. If a Soviet sailor was drunk on shore, or his uniform was dirty or he failed to salute properly, he was arrested, sent to the brig, and released only in the custody of his commanding officer. The officer would then be reprimanded for failing to ensure proper behavior among his men, a permanent blot on the commander's record affecting chances for promotion or choice assignments. Invariably the officer took it out on the offending sailor by refusing him shore leave for the rest of his four-year tour of duty.

At most, only 30 percent of a ship's crew could go ashore at any one time during an active-duty cruise. Zhenya knew navy draftees who never got any such leave for all four years, even without violating the disciplinary code. It is not hard to imagine the effect of this unrelenting strictness on the morale of young men dragooned into years of military service.

Hazing was another problem. In the Soviet army, recruits from minority nationalities, from the Baltics or Central Asia, were often beaten mercilessly, sometimes fatally, by the young Russian toughs in their barracks. Eventually, under Gorbachev's glasnost, senior officers admitted as much. Zhenya never saw anything like that on the submarines where he eventually served. But the Soviet navy had its own unpleasant, if not fatal, hazing rituals. One involved misinforming new arrivals about how a submarine's toilet worked, so the poor victim would receive its contents in his face the first time he operated one.

After Leningrad, Zhenya was assigned to a Soviet submarine base at Balaklava on the Black Sea, near the site of the "Charge of the Light Brigade." For training, his unit used a World War II–vintage sub with a rusted hull that could dive no more than sixty or seventy-five feet in safety. On board there were always two KGB officers with tommy guns to enforce discipline.

On his first mission abroad, Zhenya's submarine was supposed to cruise Turkish waters across the Black Sea and film any U.S. naval vessel there. "Our ship was so frigging noisy that any sonar could hear us miles away," he recalls. "Our captain surfaced only once to film the Turkish shore so we could say we were there, praying all the time that no one would see us. Then we hid down below."

The captain and crew had ample reason to be scared. In those days Soviet subs had no low-frequency radio communication with their home base. When underwater they were cut off from the outside world, and on the surface, in Turkish waters illegally, they were sitting targets for superior U.S. forces. "We got out of there as soon as we possibly could, came home, and reported we never saw any American ships," Zhenya explained. It was hardly the performance of a naval force worthy of terrifying the rest of the world.

Soviet submarines rarely ventured out of their home ports, Zhenya recalls. Sailors spent most of their time onshore. The main reason, Zhenya says, was the cost of fuel and spare parts for sea duty. In Balaklava, and in the nearby port city of Sevastopol, Russians could tell with scientific precision how often submarines put to sea. Each sailor got a ration of special chocolate for every hour spent underwater. Invariably, that chocolate ended up in the hands of girls onshore. "From the amount of chocolate in port you could tell how many hours the submarines had spent at sea," Zhenya says. "And there was never very much chocolate around."

Submarine sea duty was no fun. Three men shared the same bunk in successive shifts. Each would spend four hours on duty, four hours on standby, and four hours asleep. By staggering these shifts, three men could use the same bunk, one at a time. On Soviet subs they shared the same sheets and slept in their clothing. Laundry was done once a week. Food was filling—mostly cabbage and potatoes. Nuclear subs were places for rapid promotion but were avoided like the plague, Zhenya says, for fear of radiation leaks. All too often, even Soviet conventional submarines were lost at sea, because of fatal accidents from faulty equipment. When subs went down for the last time, Soviet sailors broke the compass—where the needle was suspended in alcohol—for one last drink.

In 1953, Zhenya was assigned to the Urals, to a factory making new navigational equipment for the Soviet navy. While on that assignment, he visited Kapustin Yar, where the first Soviet missiles were made, modeled on the old German wartime V-2 rocket. They were fueled by a mixture of oxygen and spirit. Zhenya remembers seeing a scientific worker climbing a ladder propped up against a rocket to measure the fuel level inside. "It was that primitive," he notes. "And this was in 1953 when the whole world was scared of Russian potential."

Zhenya's factory was working on the first miniature computerized navigational system for Soviet submarines. He was the inspecting officer whose signature was needed to approve the device for production. It sounded like cushy duty, but the job existed in a dangerous web of typical Soviet intrigue. Before signing his approval, Zhenya wanted more tests, to be sure the new equipment performed well under sea pressure. "No way," the factory manager told him. His plant's work was a candidate for the Stalin prize of 1954, and with that, a considerable bonus. It was already November. There was no time to run more tests and still qualify for that year's honors. So the factory manager pressed Zhenya to approve the production first and test it later. His pressure, with threats and an offered bribe, was all too common in the Soviet system; managers were much more interested in the bonuses they could receive than in the officers and men whose lives depended on the quality of their production. It was one of the many reasons why the huge Soviet military machine was often third-rate. This time, however, Zhenya refused to play the game.

Then his captain called him in and ordered Zhenya to approve the new equipment, with no further tests. Zhenya said he would if the captain put the order in writing. There Zhenya had touched another fatal weakness in the Soviet system. No one wanted to take responsibility—with documentary evidence attached—for a possible future disaster. If the new navigational system proved faulty in an accident at sea, the captain who had ordered approval without testing would pay. In only a few words, a junior lieutenant like Zhenya had outmaneuvered a senior officer. The captain refused to sign. The tests were made, and the results revealed a fault in a coupling that would have proved fatal at sea. Production was delayed to correct the fault, at the cost of a Stalin prize, but this time the lives of Soviet servicemen were safeguarded. It was a victory for sanity all too rare in the Soviet system.

Zhenya also remembers a far more famous triumph for Moscow that was not what it seemed to the outside world. In 1960 the Soviets shot down an American U-2 reconnaissance plane spying on the U.S.S.R. and captured the pilot, Francis Gary Powers, for a later show trial. The incident was trumpeted around the world as an outstanding Soviet military success. The truth, however, was just the opposite, Zhenya said. The Russians had long tried and failed to shoot down the high-altitude U-2, an embarrassing failure that had enraged Stalin himself. Zhenya heard the story from frustrated Soviet air force pilots based at Saratov, southeast of Moscow, a front line of the capital's air defense.

According to their account, from 1950 on, U-2 spy planes flew from Turkey across Russia to Scandinavia on the November 7 anniversary of the Bolshevik Revolution, photographing Soviet military equipment on parade and even Stalin waving from the Lenin Mausoleum. Furious, the Soviet dictator ordered his air force to shoot down the intruders. They failed for years, because the American spy planes flew too high, too fast, and kept out of range.

"First Stalin, then Khrushchev fired the local air force commanders responsible," Zhenya quoted the Saratov pilots as telling him, and still the U-2s kept overflying Russia with impunity. In the end, it was nine years before the Soviet air force finally shot down such a plane, the one carrying Powers. That "success" highlighted a decade-long failure. Once again, an incident hailed as an example of Soviet military strength was in fact an indication of weakness.

III. HARDBALL

Zhenya's testimony, like other knowledgeable accounts, makes one fact stand out. From Stalin's time on, the power balance was overwhelmingly in favor of the West in any direct confrontation with the Soviet Union. It is instructive to retrace the history of the Cold War with that bottom line in mind. In any such exercise, the conclusion is inescapable that the United States had all the advantages to deal with the Soviet Union from a position of strength, but failed to use them to anything like their full potential. Washington could have played hardball more often in confronting Moscow over world trouble spots to force a Russian backdown, well short of risking nuclear war. With the military balance so clearly in the United States' favor, Soviet leaders were not about to let tensions escalate out of hand. When challenged directly, they would have to cave. They proved it in the Cuban missile crisis under the pressure of a U.S. naval blockade.

At other times, no actual deployment of U.S. military force would have been necessary to force a Soviet backdown. Just the application of diplomatic pressure, with the implied support of superior military strength, could have been enough. Unfortunately, the United States tended to play this card poorly. From the end of World War II, repeated opportunities arose for the United States to use diplomatic pressure alone to halt Soviet aggression, yet, according to official archives opened so far, we know of only one case where Washington actually did so.

It came in 1946 when Soviet forces occupied northern Iran. Teheran had been Moscow's ally in World War II, playing a key role in saving the Soviet Union from defeat by Hitler. Millions of tons of vital U.S. military aid to the Soviet war effort had crossed Iranian territory to the neighboring U.S.S.R. Now Stalin was showing his gratitude by trying to annex northern Iran.

Harry Truman was appalled. The president concluded that Stalin was again sending troops across Soviet borders to seize control of neighboring territory, as in the Baltics and Poland. Worse, Truman saw Stalin's move into Iran as the prelude to a seizure of Turkey and the strategic Black Sea straits to the Mediterranean, where he could then threaten Western Europe. This time, Truman decided to draw the line. He would insist on a Soviet withdrawal. At the time, the United States had a monopoly on the atomic bomb and was thus in an ideal position to play diplomatic hardball.

"Unless Russia is faced with an iron fist and strong language, another war is in the making," the president said in a memo to his secretary of state, James F. Byrnes. "Only one language do they understand. 'How many divisions have you?' I'm tired of babying the Soviets," Truman told Byrnes.[7]

The result was an ultimatum to Stalin that unless he began withdrawing from Iran within a week, the world's only atomic power would respond with military force. Stalin got the message and got out fast. According to Truman himself, it was nearly that crude.

"I had to send an ultimatum to the head of the Soviet Union to get out of Persia," Truman told a press conference in 1952. "They got out because we were in a position to meet a situation of that kind."[8] Truman later confirmed that account in his memoirs. "I told Byrnes to send a blunt message to Premier Stalin," he wrote.[9]

Some historians now doubt whether Truman's message to Stalin was actually an ultimatum or indeed all that blunt. One such academic, Herbert Druks, wrote that in a talk he had with Truman on August 1, 1962, the former president recalled having sent Stalin a note saying he expected the Soviets to withdraw all their forces from Iran. "He warned that unless their withdrawal did commence within a week's time and was completed within six, he would move the fleet as far as the Persian Gulf and he would send American troops back into Iran," Druks wrote.[10]

It matters little whether Truman's message to Stalin was blunt enough to be called an ultimatum. The effect was the same. Harry Truman, the man who had dropped the atomic bomb on Hiroshima and Nagasaki, had credibility with Stalin as a leader willing to use the ultimate weapon. Now here was the same Truman threatening to send the U.S. Army and Navy into Iran to confront the Soviet presence there, at the risk of war. Whatever Truman's initiative was called, an ultimatum or simply a note, it proved that strong diplomatic pressure alone could turn back Soviet aggression.

Once the Soviet Union also became a nuclear power, the situation obviously changed. Still, the Americans retained tremendous advantage in the overall military balance. That advantage should have been put to better use, within reason.

The acceptable limits were perfectly clear. For instance, during the Cold War, there was never an occasion when sending U.S. armed forces directly into combat on Soviet territory would have been justified. Any American president who went anywhere near that extreme would have been disowned by the European allies. But using the military in a peaceful way to defeat a Soviet challenge, as with the 1948 Berlin airlift, was quite another matter, appropriately applauded by the allies. There were other occasions when diplomatic pressure, reinforced by the Western advantage in the military balance, could have been exploited more effectively, including Hungary in 1956 and Czechoslovakia in 1968.

Contingency plans for nuclear war also developed clear limits, from the time the Russians produced their atomic bomb. As argued previously, America had little cause to fear a nuclear first strike from the Soviet side. But that was far from the only danger in the nuclear age. Pentagon war game specialists had to worry about many other scenarios. For example, what if some crisis somewhere escalated and the United States fired a first nuclear strike against the U.S.S.R? Could Moscow respond with nuclear weapons? And if yes, how much damage could they do?

These questions are not some far-fetched fiction from a Dr. Strangelove film. The Kennedy administration actually conducted this inquiry during the 1961 Berlin crisis. At the time, the United States had dominant nuclear superiority. The president was told by his advisers that American forces could knock out almost all of the Soviet Union's limited capacity for nuclear retaliation with one preemptive strike. The problem was the "almost."

Experts told President Kennedy that even if only a small portion of the Soviet second-strike capacity survived and retaliated, it could kill as many as fifteen million Americans. The president was stunned. There was no way he would risk that many U.S. lives. To him the vast superiority of the American nuclear arsenal had suddenly lost much of its meaning.[11] The odds of surviving a second strike only got worse as the Soviets moved to nuclear parity.

Clearly any direct American attack on the Soviet Union risked nuclear retaliation. In that case, Kremlin leaders would have no choice but to fire back. But was that the only case? What if the Americans, directly by themselves or indirectly by proxies, assaulted Soviet interests in the Third World, or even in allied Communist countries? Would that also risk escalation to nuclear war? No, the Pentagon reasoned correctly, because those interests were not vital to Soviet national survival.

So, for example, the United States sent conventional arms to Israel for use against the Soviet Union's Arab clients. Israeli pilots in American jets knocked out Soviet-built missiles on the ground in Syria, sometimes killing Russian military advisers as well. Moscow screamed, of course, loud and long, in bitter attacks on Washington in the controlled Soviet press. But there was never any question of the Russians' responding to this sort of provocation by risking nuclear war with the United States.

Indeed, in the more than forty years of the Cold War, there was never one case when Moscow seriously threatened nuclear retaliation for anything the United States actually did. This remained true after the Russians had achieved nuclear parity. It also remained true in the face of frontal military challenges by the United States to the Soviet Union as the leader of the Communist world. Two such examples stand out. U.S. troops fought a Soviet ally, Communist North Vietnam, and killed Soviet advisers during bombing raids there. And U.S. weapons helped Afghan rebels force the Soviet army into a humiliating retreat. Yet at no time in either of these long wars did Moscow dare threaten Washington with nuclear blackmail.

The lesson could hardly be clearer: Moscow would risk nuclear retaliation only if the Soviet Union itself, or a vital East European buffer state, came under direct American attack. The Russians said so themselves. The Brezhnev Doctrine warned American troops to stay out of Eastern Europe; Soviet military doctrine stressed that any attack on the U.S.S.R. would trigger a nuclear response. But other than that, the Americans could counter Soviet troublemaking around the globe without the risk of unleashing a nuclear war. In the late 1970s, to cite but two examples, U.S. air and sea power could have been used to halt the supplies that turned Ethiopia into a Soviet client, or Angola into a Marxist state.

In the end, no such hardball was necessary. The West "won" the Cold War during the 1989–91 collapse of communism without a shot fired in anger, or even the mildest diplomatic pressure. On the contrary, in the interest of maintaining his perception of stability, George Bush was desperately trying to support Mikhail Gorbachev's final efforts to hold the Soviet empire together. Bush's stand even included reluctance to back the independence demands of Latvia, Lithuania, and Estonia, officially recognized by the United States for the past forty years as legitimate, on grounds that that could weaken Gorbachev and his reforms. Far from pressuring the Soviet Union into collapse, the West in the end was trying to give it the kiss of life.

History now shows that the Soviet empire collapsed from its own internal contradictions, rather than from military pressure by the West. No war or even risk of war was involved. That suggests the conclusion that I have been stressing so strongly: tougher, wiser Western policy might well have accelerated the process and brought down communism much sooner, without igniting a suicidal war.

Had U.S. diplomacy challenged the Soviets more boldly in the fifties or sixties, communism could have collapsed decades earlier, sparing hundreds of millions of people years of suffering and deprivation, and saving the American taxpayer billions in defense spending. Instead the strongest military-economic power the world had ever seen held back, exaggerating the threat of a vastly inferior adversary. Future historians are likely to see this process as one of the great tragedies of the twentieth century.

For the United States, a hyped specter of nuclear annihilation sometimes became a convenient excuse for doing nothing. That was not always true, of course. America occasionally intervened at great cost in an effort to stop Communist expansionism, as in Korea and Vietnam. The convenient excuse applied mostly to Eastern Europe, the region that was, after all, the key to the Cold War, the geographic theater that marked both its beginning and its end.

Stalin's occupation of Eastern Europe started the Cold War. Eastern Europe's ultimately successful rebellion against communism led within only two years to the collapse of the Soviet Union and the end of the Cold War. America could have accelerated that process, perhaps by decades, with a wiser policy toward Eastern Europe. There was never a need to risk World War III by direct U.S. military intervention in Russia's strategic buffer zone. Low-key indirect action, a judicious blend of U.S. diplomatic, financial, and conventional arms aid in Eastern Europe, might well have altered the political landscape there far earlier. In that case, Moscow could not have responded by risking a superpower conflict any more than Washington did after 1962 in reacting to continued Soviet diplomatic, financial, and conventional-arms aid to Cuba. Properly calibrated, U.S. policy in Eastern Europe could have paid enormous dividends at low risk. Instead Washington preferred to exaggerate the dangers and do nothing. As a result, America missed its greatest opportunity to end the Cold War far sooner.

By exaggerating the Soviet threat, in Eastern Europe and elsewhere, America only prolonged it. In fact, the United States always could have done more to challenge Soviet aggression and abuse of human rights. We have already seen what one brave man like Russian dissident Andrei Sakharov or Czech President Ludvík Svoboda could do, defying the Kremlin, unarmed and standing alone. Surely it was possible for the United States to use its unmatched military and economic power more productively, in order to pressure Soviet leaders toward peace and democracy, at no more risk of war. But, sadly, the weaker Soviet Union often outmaneuvered the stronger United States by means of a more effective foreign policy, and such opportunities were lost.

There are several reasons for this. Most involve overrating the Soviet threat. All will be covered at length in a later chapter on foreign policy. For the moment, however, it is necessary to cite here only the most important factor, the primary reason the U.S. assessment of Soviet military potential was always overdone, namely this: the Kremlin never trusted its own armed forces.

Any political leadership that does not trust its own army is not going to risk World War III. That was why the West always had less cause to fear a Soviet attack, and why the West had more leverage to pressure Moscow without fear of military retaliation.

There is no question that Soviet leaders did not trust their own military. They proved that over and over again. They did so by using a separate security force, the KGB, to check constantly on the army, often to take on military missions too sensitive to be entrusted to the regular armed forces.

Thus the KGB rather than the army guarded nuclear warheads. The KGB rather than the army protected the national borders. The KGB infiltrated all units in the armed forces to guard against defections by men—or entire weapons systems like nuclear submarines—and to defend Kremlin leaders against military coups, and to make sure everyone down the military chain of command was doing his job properly. In perhaps no other country did political leaders spy so thoroughly and ominously on their own armed forces.

Josef Stalin so distrusted the political loyalty of his army commanders that he used his secret police to arrest and execute the cream of the officer class. That purge nearly cost him defeat in World War II. Stalin's successors stopped the bloodbath but otherwise kept the system. They too never trusted the army. The KGB continued spying on the military up to and after the collapse of the Soviet Union. To the conspirators in the continuing Kremlin power struggle, the main focus was always on the enemy within. Thus the KGB literally shackled the Soviet armed forces in ways the U.S. military never could.

To give but one example, cited by former senior KGB agent Peter Deriabin, when KGB officers spotted a security threat within a military unit but could not determine who was responsible, they could punish the commanding officer and disband the entire unit. Thus, after the crew of the destroyer *Storozhevoy* mutinied in the Baltic Sea in November 1975, the captain was shot, his officers jailed, the crew dispersed, and the ship's name changed.

In another example given by Deriabin, army training units had to turn in every emptied cartridge case from the firing range to make sure no ammunition had fallen into unauthorized hands. If a single round could not be accounted for, the commanding officer, his security officer, and others could be punished. KGB oversight extended to the most minute detail of military life.[12]

There was nothing exceptional about the KGB grip on the Red Army. Throughout the history of the Soviet Union, throughout its vast territory, no institution, no individual, was ever safe from the KGB. Ordinary citizens lived in fear of a security police empowered to arrest or even eliminate anyone, at any time, with impunity. Even top Kremlin leaders could never be sure the KGB agents protecting them would not one day join a coup against them. No other institution had a more profound influence on the Soviet way of life, not even the Communist Party.

KGB thinking was roughly as follows. No country wants to fight a two-front war. That only divides and weakens resources, limiting the chances of victory. The Soviet Union, however, always faced the danger of war on at least two fronts—one at home, and one or more abroad. The battle on the home front, keeping its own people in line and the Communist system in place, was always the top priority. It should not be forgotten that the Communists seized power in Russia by force in 1917, and for seventy-four years held on to it only by force, never by genuine elections. So the home-front war run by the KGB, with the support of regular army troops as necessary, was a constant struggle.

It was a struggle the KGB confidently expected to win, provided no major foreign war had to be fought at the same time. In the Kremlin view, the greatest threat to toppling Communist power in Russia always came from losing a war with the capitalist West. That conflict, therefore, was to be avoided at all costs. There could be no clearer bottom line. "All costs" meant that short of an attack on the U.S.S.R., the Kremlin leadership would not risk any military conflict with the stronger Western alliance.

Thus, for internal security reasons alone, the Soviet threat to the West was always overblown. The KGB was not about to let the Kremlin political leadership or the Red Army brass go off on any military adventure abroad that put the internal security of the Soviet state at risk.

This was not an idle threat. In the showdown of any Kremlin policy dispute, the KGB held the strongest hand. If necessary, as Soviet history amply proved, it could remove any military or political leader standing in its way. As a result, the KGB view of internal state security priorities was never seriously challenged in the post-Stalin years.

In effect, the KGB priority on Soviet internal security protected the West. The obsession with the home front, and the need to avoid a two-front war, meant all had to be quiet on the Western front. In effect, the emblem of the Soviet secret police, the sword and the shield of the U.S.S.R., was stood on its head by the KGB itself. Throughout the Cold War, the KGB pointed the sword of the Soviet threat at their own people first, and, in that process, shielded the West from Soviet attack. Such was the awesome power of the Soviet secret police. In the supreme irony of the Cold War era, the Soviet military threat menaced the Soviet peoples themselves far more than the Western allies.

9

The KGB: A Veto on
Russia's Future

I. ABOVE THE LAW

When Lavrenty Beria ran Stalin's secret police, he liked to refer to anyone hauled in for questioning as "the accused." One hapless victim actually worked up the courage to object. "I'm not the accused," he complained to Beria. "There has been no indictment. I'm only the suspect." With exaggerated patience, Beria escorted the poor creature over to the window of his office atop Lubyanka prison and pointed nine floors below to the ordinary citizens of Moscow walking around Dzerzhinsky Square outside. "Down there are the suspects," Beria explained. "Up here, you are the accused." Beria's secret police never had time for legal niceties. They were always a law unto themselves.

In the long Soviet nightmare, KGB excesses were unquestionably the worst recurring horrors. To the secret police, all Soviet citizens were suspected enemies of the state, from the humblest peasant to the highest government official or the most decorated army marshal. The KGB could accuse virtually any of them of any crime. Once accused, the victim then could be kidnapped, tortured, even killed by the secret police, without the slightest hint of legality, let alone a formal indictment or trial. In the Stalinist system of repression, there simply were no restraints on secret police powers. KGB agents could be as lawless as the Communist Party leader of the day let them be. Since Stalin's day, KGB power has been weakened, but never broken. Even today, ordinary Russians fear the repressive machinery lies dormant, but oiled and ready for a new dictator to restart at the turn of a screw.

When thoughtful Russians today talk of democracy or freedom, they speak first of all about the need to create "a law-based state." What they mean is the establishment of a legal system that would not permit the KGB, or a successor secret police of any other name, to break the law and arbitrarily spill blood, with full impunity, on the pretense of safeguarding state security. In the breathtaking pace and extent of Russian reform, including free competitive elections, a free and critical press, freedom of worship, and a free-enterprise economy, there is still no law-based state, still no effective curb on the KGB. To this day, the secret police could still be used by a new dictator to seize power, sweep away reforms, and return to the repressive past. The law-based state remains the ultimate litmus test of democracy in Russia, a noble, distant goal that may never be achieved.

Sadly, it was ever thus. The history of Russia is largely one of cruelty, repression, and illegality. Ivan the Terrible, the first grand duke of Muscovy to be crowned tsar, established Russia's first secret police, the Oprichnina, in 1565. The six thousand Oprichniki dressed in black and rode black horses. On their saddles they carried emblems of a dog's head and a broom. The emblem symbolized their mission: to sniff out treason and sweep it away. They did so with a vengeance, establishing a tradition of zeal in eradicating the enemies of the dictator, real and imagined, that continued to Stalin's day and beyond. The Oprichniki's victims included whole cities, among them Novgorod, whose citizens were massacred in 1570. Lacking modern weapons of mass destruction, the Oprichniki took five weeks to do the job.[1]

Stalin praised the Oprichniki's reign of terror. He hailed their "progressive role" in centralizing Russia's state power and in reducing opposition to the tsar among the Boyar aristocracy. But Stalin thought Ivan wasn't terrible enough. He criticized the tsar for wasting time at prayer that could have been more profitably spent liquidating more Boyars. It was a lapse of focus that Stalin himself determined not to repeat. In his day, Stalin would not be satisfied liquidating cities. The millions of people he slaughtered could fill whole nations.

Four centuries after Ivan the Terrible, ordinary Russians were all too painfully aware of how little their country had changed. The victims of Stalin's secret police in the 1930s, the NKVD, often called their jailers "Oprichniki" behind their backs.

Indeed, secret police repression is a constant of Russian history. It crossed the 1917 sea change of the Bolshevik Revolution with its powers and methods of operation largely intact. In tsarist days and Soviet, from Oprichnina to KGB, the biggest change in the feared and hated security police was literally in name only. Even the outstanding reformers, like Tsar Peter the Great, continued the secret police excesses. Tsar Peter, perhaps best known for opening Russia to the West, used his secret police, the Preobrazhentsy, to torture his own son.

In the 1800s, the tsarist secret police were renamed the Okhrana. As before, they continued to imprison, exile, and murder on their own authority, with no regard for the law. Under Communist power, they also had various names—from Cheka to NKVD, OGPU, and MGB, among others. Finally, from 1954 on through the collapse of Soviet power, they were known as the KGB. The initials stand for Komitet Gosudarstvennoy Bezopasnosti, meaning Committee for State Security. For the sake of simplicity, the secret police will be referred to throughout this book as the KGB.

As in all previous incarnations, the KGB was empowered to sniff out and sweep away treason, real and imagined, using whatever methods deemed necessary, with no regard for the law. Only this time there was one important difference. The KGB became the largest political police force and the largest foreign intelligence service in the world.[2] No longer would the secret police simply go after their own people. Now they had a global playing field.

The final name change of the security organs in the Soviet era—to KGB from 1954 on—was rich in symbolism. It was supposed to convey the message that since the death of Stalin and Beria the year before, the secret police had been fundamentally reformed forever. Like almost everything else about the KGB, that message was both true and false at the same time. It was true in the sense that Stalin's mass terror, which produced death totals on the scale of nuclear war, was indeed over at last. It was false in the sense that lawless KGB repression continued, albeit on a far smaller scale, still holding most of the population psychologically hostage, but henceforth by individual examples of arbitrary arrest or disappearance that could happen to any citizen at any time. In short, much of Stalin's secret police terror campaign lived on, but without the appalling number of victims.

Khrushchev's success in ending the worst of the Stalinist terror, while keeping the KGB's repressive powers largely intact, has already been recounted in detail earlier in this book. So has Brezhnev's use of those powers in ruthlessly crushing the dissident movement that arose during his era. Neither needs repeating here. Both are mentioned now only to introduce a fundamental truth about the last half century of Russian history, that ever since the death of Stalin, ever since his crimes were publicly exposed, no Kremlin leader has been willing or able to bring the instrument of those crimes, the KGB, under effective legal control. Not even Mikhail Gorbachev, despite his many truly historic reforms, made a proper start in this direction. Neither did Boris Yeltsin, well after the collapse of Soviet power. It is time to see why.

When Gorbachev took over as Kremlin leader, the KGB was a vast empire. It had 400,000 officers inside the Soviet Union, 200,000 border troops, and an army of informants. The KGB had little difficulty persuading almost anyone among the Soviet Union's 280 million citizens to do its bidding, at home or abroad. No Soviet, for example, could get a visa for a trip abroad without agreeing in advance to cooperate with the KGB during the trip and afterward, at the very least in supplying requested information. Within the U.S.S.R., it was no harder to pressure any Soviet into doing what the KGB asked, from spying on a neighbor to testifying falsely against a relative, or virtually anything else. The threat of arrest or worse was always there, but rarely needed. Usually it was enough for an agent to suggest that failure to help the secret police would mean loss of a job and no prospect of future work, or loss of a residence permit to live in a major city where food supplies were better, or, if that didn't work, the KGB could always hint at the danger of an unfortunate accident crossing a street.

No Soviet citizen was free from KGB surveillance, intimidation, or ruin, not even the general secretary of the Communist Party. The secret police proved that in the leading role they played removing Nikita Khrushchev from power. Not surprisingly, Gorbachev took that lesson to heart. Mikhail Sergeyevich also understood that he would need KGB support in the continuing Kremlin power struggle if he and his intended reforms were to survive. So, on taking office, Gorbachev refused to challenge the KGB's vast powers, or even begin to think seriously about trimming them. That attitude largely continued through his years in office, with a few timid exceptions.

Among them, one example of glasnost, or openness, stands out for just that sort of timidity. In December 1986, Soviet officials admitted for the first time that the KGB had massacred protesters in the southern Russian city of Novocherkassk in 1962, then covered up all evidence of their brutality. Under Gorbachev, the truth had finally come out, part of his campaign to establish credibility as a reformer and win public support. In the Soviet context it appeared as a sensational revelation, an all too rare moment of candor. Yet at the same time, the admission was safe enough, nothing like the kind of sweeping indictment of continuing KGB illegality that could have landed Gorbachev in serious political trouble. After all, this KGB travesty had occurred twenty-four years before, during the Khrushchev era. Thus when the truth became known, it sounded like ancient history—the Oprichniki sweep through Novgorod four hundred years before. "A whole town rebels and every trace is licked clean and hidden," Aleksandr Solzhenitsyn wrote about the Novocherkassk bloodbath.[3]

As this episode made abundantly clear, glasnost had severe limits. Exposures of KGB excesses would be highly selective. They would focus on the distant past. The closer the questions got to Gorbachev himself or to current KGB leaders or operations, the greater the certainty that the old coverups would continue.

That is precisely what happened. In April 1989, for instance, at the height of Gorbachev's liberal reforms, KGB special troops charged into a crowd of unarmed demonstrators in Tbilisi, the capital of Soviet Georgia, and, according to eyewitnesses, beat and hacked many of them to death, including several women. At the time, Gorbachev was in London, at the end of a foreign trip. He denied having anything to do with ordering KGB troops to rush the Tbilisi protestors, noting that he was abroad when the decision was made. But that explanation strained his credibility to the utmost. The Soviet leader had the capability of constant contact with the Kremlin on a secure phone line while he was traveling. "It is inconceivable that the head of state doesn't know the circumstances of the case," Yuri Vlasov, a member of the Soviet parliament, declared. "Otherwise, what kind of head of state is he?"

Almost certainly, a decision as important as the one to use force on civilians in Tbilisi was run by the top leader for approval. That is the way the Soviet system worked. Any evidence linking Gorbachev to the decision would then have been destroyed. That is also the way the Soviet system worked. Even without evidence, however, Gorbachev himself was still ultimately responsible. He had the power to curb the KGB and prevent it from conducting bloodbaths like Tbilisi. Instead, he chose not to do so.

Nonetheless, Gorbachev can perhaps be forgiven for never reforming the KGB. His accomplishments in ending the Cold War and in leading the Soviet Union toward democracy and the market economy have made him one of the great men of the century. What he accomplished in six years of power is truly extraordinary. Clearly, he could not do everything at once. Had Gorbachev lasted in power a decade or more, he might well have gotten around to curbing KGB illegality, but in the earlier phases he simply could not take it on. The only way Gorbachev could push through the momentous economic and political reforms he did was to keep the KGB on his side at the time.

In the beginning, the secret police were with him. The KGB understood perfectly well that the Brezhnev stagnation policies were no longer tenable, that the Soviet Union could not remain a superpower unless it underwent meaningful reform. Then the hard choices began—what specific reforms in what order, how far and how fast? Inevitably, those questions produced a new set of fundamental disagreements in the continuing Soviet power struggle, a new political landscape, and shifting alliances of convenience among Politburo members. In the end, the KGB leaders deserted Gorbachev, rallied his conservative opponents, and mounted a coup to remove him from office before he could begin to curb their powers.

During the Gorbachev era, despite glasnost and perestroika, the KGB remained a law unto itself. True, it was no longer Terror Inc., as in Stalin's day. Nor was it crushing all dissent, as under Brezhnev. On the contrary, political prisoners were leaving the Gulag. In many ways, during the Gorbachev era, the man running the Kremlin was doing more to dismantle the Communist system than the dissidents ever accomplished. Even senior KGB officers rejoiced that they could scale down the repulsive business of political witch-hunts at home and focus instead on what they regarded as the nobler calling of intelligence-gathering abroad. Yet none of that changed the essential point. The KGB was still above the law.

One fact confirms that assertion. There was still no parliamentary oversight on the KGB. This was not the same problem as in the West—far from it. Western lawmakers sometimes complained that their legislative control of intelligence services was insufficient, but their Soviet counterparts envied even those inadequate safeguards. For example, although the U.S. oversight system was hardly perfect, Congress could eventually expose and correct CIA abuses. In Moscow, there was no legal control at all. The KGB's budget, the number of its personnel, the names of its agents, and its methods of operation were still all entirely secret. No one had the right to probe KGB activities or correct abuses—not the Soviet parliament, not the government Council of Ministers, not the prime minister, not anyone. Wiser Russians always knew this. They always understood that if Gorbachev fell, a successor could return the KGB to the bad old days at a stroke.

They were, as usual, silent. During the heyday of Gorbachev's reforms, there was never any great public outcry to disband the KGB and destroy its illegal powers. Dissidents, of course, made those proposals, but they were an increasingly irrelevant voice in the wilderness. The country at large was thankful for Gorbachev's liberal changes, handed down from on high. There was no effective grassroots pressure from below to go further in curbing the KGB. To most Soviet citizens, KGB lawlessness was just a fact of life that they had no power to alter.

Yuri Vlasov was one notable exception. A bearded giant of a man, a former Olympic champion weight lifter, Vlasov spoke out with extraordinary courage in a speech to parliament, the Supreme Soviet, on May 31, 1989, at the height of the Gorbachev reforms. Vlasov himself was a beneficiary of those changes, having won a parliamentary seat in the first competitive elections under Communist rule in Russia. Unlike others in that new breed of Soviet legislator, Vlasov could not forget or forgive the sins of the past. His father had been arrested by the Soviet secret police in 1953 and never returned home. Yuri Vlasov feared that it could all happen again. He decided he had to speak out.

"The KGB is removed from the control of the people," Vlasov told parliament. "It is the most tightly closed, the most conspiratorial of all government institutions. . . . When coming in conflict with the KGB it is impossible to find the truth and dangerous to seek it."

Vlasov went on in a particularly damning indictment, "Even now people considered dangerous by the apparatus are threatened with seizure for supposed mental imbalance." The outside world thought Gorbachev had ended abuses like condemning dissidents to insane asylums, but here was a member of the Soviet parliament saying no, these horrors continue.

Then Vlasov got to the crucial point. "The democratic renewal in the country has not changed the position of the KGB in the political system. This agency exercises all-embracing control over society, over each individual."[4] In a word, as long as such KGB powers continued uncurbed, democracy in Russia hung by a thread.

Sadly, one brave voice is not enough. Vlasov's speech was taken as a sign of how far the country had come. It was now possible for a citizen to stand before parliament and denounce the KGB, without fear of reprisal. But his call to reform the secret police went unheeded. With no great public outcry echoing Vlasov's words, Gorbachev could afford to ignore them.

Boris Yeltsin was no friend of the KGB. He never forgave it for installing listening devices in his bedroom and his sauna, a Yeltsin aide told me in Moscow. At the time the KGB bugged Yeltsin's home, Gorbachev was in power, and Yeltsin was leading the radical reform opposition. When Yeltsin took power from Gorbachev, however, he too kept on the KGB. Eventually Yeltsin changed the name of the KGB yet again, and its top leadership, and brought the organization directly under presidential authority. But none of that changes the essential fact that four years into the Yeltsin revolution the secret police in the guise of a new KGB clone are still alive and well in Russia.

Indeed, the KGB's afterlife underscores a fundamental difference between Eastern Europe and Russia since the fall of the Berlin Wall. In almost all countries of Eastern Europe, the collapse of communism brought with it a disbanding of the secret police. Their files were opened, their offices closed, their powers curbed for good. In Russia, by contrast, it was business as usual for the KGB.[5]

The difference is no surprise. Poland, Hungary, and Czechoslovakia were always more Western-oriented. For them, the Communist dictatorship was an aberration that lasted four decades. For Russia, Communist repression was the natural order of things, the logical extension of tsarist repression in a thousand-year history of autocratic rule. Genuine democracy and rule of law were always fated to come more slowly to Russia than to Eastern Europe, if indeed they ever come at all.

Gorbachev and Yeltsin had no choice but to keep on the KGB, at least for the early years of power. Otherwise they could never build a democratic political base strong enough for them to dispose of the KGB later on. There is ample precedent for this view. No political leader has ever been able to survive in Russia—before, during, or after communism—without a secret police to spy on political rivals and warn of potential plots to remove him. In Gorbachev's day, on his behalf, the KGB spied on all members of the Politburo, their wives, and their wives' hairdressers, for starters, searching for hints of a coming coup d'état. The same KGB source in Moscow told me Yeltsin's secret police continue similar surveillance of today's potential political rivals and their inner circles.

It was never very difficult for the KGB chairman to ingratiate himself with a Kremlin leader. The chairman's first asset was credibility. His KGB always contained the nation's best analysts of raw intelligence, domestic and foreign. The KGB rather than the Soviet foreign ministry would have the most accurate estimate on the likely vote in the U.S. Senate on ratifying the next arms control treaty with Moscow. The KGB rather than the finance ministry or the State Plan, would have the most accurate picture of the Soviet economy at any given moment. Once such credibility was established, the KGB chief had no trouble inflating his own importance. All he needed to do was warn the Kremlin leader on the dangers of foreign espionage operations or domestic coup plots that the KGB, of course, would loyally and efficiently foil. Soon enough, Kremlin leaders came to rely on KGB chiefs.

Reliance was understandable. The mistake was to trust them. Both Gorbachev and Yeltsin learned to their sorrow that the same KGB chiefs they relied on as survival insurance could also turn traitor by joining plots against them. Herein lies the paradox that imperils Russian democracy to this day. No reform leader can survive in the Kremlin and carry out the transition to democracy without KGB support. But that vital support can turn against him at virtually any moment, and help bring back dictatorship in yet another palace coup. In this way it is ultimately the KGB that must choose between backing repression or reform. Its choice can be decisive. Thus even today, the KGB and its heirs have a veto on Russia's future.

That remains true because there has never been a serious attempt in Moscow to curb secret police powers. During the Soviet period, the KGB was said to be under the control of the Communist Party generally and its top leader personally. Nothing could be further from the truth. Ostensibly, it was under the Kremlin leader's command, a very different concept from control. At any moment, the KGB could choose to disobey a leader's commands. Thus, under both Khrushchev and Gorbachev, the KGB ignored the orders of its commander in chief and instead sided with coup plots against him. Command is not control.

After the collapse of communism, Boris Yeltsin fared no better. In the political crisis of October 1993, the KGB, still supposedly under the command of President Yeltsin, sat on its hands. Aleksandr Rutskoi, then Russia's vice president, and other anti-Yeltsin political leaders had taken refuge in the Russian White House, the parliament building, and were haranguing crowds to overthrow the president. At that point, the KGB's main job was to keep Yeltsin informed about what the Rutskoi opposition planned next. Incredibly, the KGB never told Yeltsin that Rutskoi's armed forces intended to attack Moscow's television center the next day as part of the attempt to seize power.

Of course the KGB knew. A secret police that gathered intelligence on every inane detail down to which Russians would come to dinner at my apartment the following week simply had to know about something as vital as an armed attack on the state's main television broadcasting center planned for the following day. They never told Yeltsin not because they didn't know, but because they wanted his rivals to defeat him. No other explanation is conceivable. They proved it again the night before this attempted coup, the crunch point of a national political crisis, when not one light burned at KGB headquarters. Instead the secret police, the agency primarily responsible for protecting the president, went home early. There could be no clearer sign of betrayal.

Fortunately for Yeltsin, this time the army agreed at the last moment to back him. Tanks attacked the parliament building and arrested his foes there. The president survived a close call. Predictably, soon afterward the KGB paid the price for choosing the wrong side. Yeltsin replaced its leaders and re-named and reorganized the agency yet again, this time to bring it under his direct presidential authority. Still, he would be wise to remember that command is not control. Anyone who thinks that Yeltsin now effectively controls the secret police must still believe in the tooth fairy.

So much for the top leader's keeping the KGB in line. The notion that the Communist Party collectively ever controlled the KGB was an even greater fiction. Suppose, for example, that at the height of Gorbachev's liberal reforms an honest Communist Party investigator sought to substantiate allegations that the KGB still tortured suspects during interrogation. He would soon discover that no outsider was permitted access to the KGB records or communications he would need to establish evidence.

Let's say our investigator refused to be discouraged by such general rules. He would not take *nyet* for an answer. Instead he would seek an exception and bend the rules. Here he would soon find out what Yuri Vlasov meant when he said that in conflicts with the KGB, "it is impossible to find the truth and dangerous to seek it." More than just KGB intimidation or threats of bodily harm was involved. Our investigator was now entering a perilous Catch-22 situation that could easily destroy his career.

In this case the truth was that the secret police had an independent chain of command, from the field agent up to the KGB chairman and ultimately to the general secretary of the Communist Party. The only way a Party "controller" like the investigator could break into that chain and look at the record was to get the personal permission of the top man, Gorbachev himself. Unfortunately for our intrepid controller, requesting such permission could be suicidal for his career.

Here's why. If the KGB was still torturing suspects, then Gorbachev himself could also be held responsible. The secret police, after all, were still operating under his command. Thus any request to Gorbachev for permission to look at the files implied that the general secretary himself was also under suspicion. Even the bravest Soviet investigator was not about to ask the Kremlin's top leader to investigate himself. Instead the probe would be quietly dropped. So much for Party control. It was always illusory. No outsiders, not even the Communist Party, controlled the KGB. That was why it was always a law unto itself.[6]

In any event, the KGB had all angles covered. Even if Gorbachev or another Soviet leader had given the go-ahead for a full-scale probe of the record, no one was ever likely to prove the KGB guilty of torturing suspects. It had hit upon effective and traceless substitutes decades ago. For men, the method was explained to me by a Russian friend whose father was arrested by the KGB in the 1950s. After three days behind bars, his father was taken to an interrogation room, where he was stripped naked and forced to sit on a block of ice. As soon as his testicles began to freeze, he told the KGB everything it wanted to know. The ice block did not leave a mark on him. In the decades since then, KGB cover-ups have only gotten more sophisticated and effective.

II. FOREIGN AFFAIRS

Long used to operating at will at home, the KGB also had no qualms about flaunting the law abroad. Some cases of KGB foul play on foreign soil are already infamous, among them the murder of Georgi Markov, an anti-Communist Bulgarian émigré. A stranger fatally stabbed Markov with a poisoned umbrella tip on London's Waterloo Bridge in September 1978. Both the poison used and the deadly umbrella were supplied by the KGB. This operation by the Bulgarian secret police had the personal approval and active support of Vladimir Kryuchkov, then head of foreign intelligence and later selected by Gorbachev as KGB chairman.[7]

This point is worth stressing. Mikhail Sergeyevich, the great reformer to the outside world, not only allowed the KGB to continue in the old lawless tradition but also chose a cold-blooded murderer to head it. In that way too, Gorbachev contributed to keeping the Soviet secret police above the law.

In other cases of foul play abroad, the KGB role is still suspected but unconfirmed. Among them is the attempt to assassinate Pope John Paul II in 1981. The motive was certainly there. The Polish pope had played a crucial role in the rise of Solidarity into a force threatening to bring down communism in Poland and elsewhere in Eastern Europe. The operational experience was also there. The plot against the pope was ostensibly run by Bulgarian agents, but, as in the Markov case, they normally did not undertake such sensitive missions without the approval of the KGB. All that is missing is the evidence. That too may emerge as former secret police archives in Eastern Europe become public in the years ahead.

The murder of political opponents abroad, while a subject of infamous publicity, was only a minor KGB sideline. The major foreign thrust of Soviet secret police work was, of course, intelligence-gathering. Just as the KGB regarded all Russians as suspects, it looked upon all foreigners as potential recruits. Every foreigner who applied for a visa to live and work in the Soviet Union, whether diplomat, businessman, journalist, or student, first went under the KGB microscope. A dossier would be established and judgments made on whether the applicant might be ideologically turned, bribed, threatened, sexually enticed, or otherwise coerced into working for Soviet intelligence, either in the U.S.S.R. or back in his home country. It was one reason the visa application process would take six weeks or more. Few resident foreigners in Russia were actually approached, only the most promising in KGB eyes.

Honey traps were a favored ploy. The KGB used attractive women "swallows" to seduce the foreigner, then produced the usual compromising photographs to blackmail him into working for Soviet intelligence. It didn't always work. Sometimes the victim committed suicide rather than betray his country, among them Colonel Louis Gribaud, a former French air attaché. Maurice Dejean, the French ambassador to Moscow from 1956 to 1964, was one of the higher-ranking victims of a KGB honey trap. Dejean was beaten up by the KGB officer posing as the outraged husband of the swallow sharing the ambassador's bed. Fortunately for the French, a KGB defector revealed the operation before serious KGB blackmail had begun. Charles de Gaulle summoned Dejean to Paris and fired him.[8]

The French embassy in Moscow had long been a security disaster. Before de Gaulle's official visit to the Soviet Union in 1965, French counterintelligence swept the embassy and removed bugs from the ambassador's office. The discovery of the bugs was never announced publicly. After all, Paris was anxious at the time to improve relations with the Russians. The French thought they had discreetly solved their embassy security problem. They didn't have a clue. At the time, all their confidential diplomatic cables were coded and sent to Paris by telex. The code man, embassy sources told me, had a Russian mistress. The French also used Soviet employees to collect confidential documents from various embassy offices and take them to the shredder, supposedly for destruction. Needless to say, the Russians took advantage of all such opportunities.

Years later, Paris still had not understood. In the 1970s the French foreign ministry shipped a new telex machine out to the embassy in Moscow on a Soviet freight train. Anxious to save funds, the French decided not to send a guard along. Sometime after the telex was installed at the embassy, the French discovered something that should have come as no surprise—the Russians had installed bugging devices on the telex during the unguarded shipment.

The French were hardly alone. Despite the KGB's well-deserved reputation for espionage on resident foreigners, most other embassies in Moscow also had security lapses over the years. The British suffered honey-trap and homosexual-entrapment plots. Even the Americans, more security-conscious than most, sometimes displayed incredible naiveté. In the 1980s, the United States chose to build a new embassy office block on low ground, between a Russian church steeple and a Soviet high-rise apartment house both crammed with listening devices. America also let Russian workers handle the construction. Before it was finished, the building was found to be riddled with bugs. The offices were never occupied. Subsequent debugging and reconstruction cost millions of dollars.

No one outside the KGB knows how many sexual or financial bribes, other coercion ploys, and electronic listening schemes actually worked. Only the failed plots, those eventually uncovered and admitted by Western counterintelligence, ever became public knowledge. One of the more spectacular surfaced in 1986 when two marine guards at the U.S. embassy in Moscow admitted giving KGB agents access to the building, where they could copy classified documents and install listening devices. One of the marines, Sergeant Clayton Lonetree, had been seduced by a Russian woman, Violetta Seina, a KGB plant working at the embassy. He was sentenced to thirty years in prison.

As a result of this case the embassy adopted draconian new security rules. All Soviet employees were dismissed. All American diplomats were forbidden to meet alone with Russians. They attended meetings in pairs and were required to file written reports after all such contacts. The full extent of the security damage from the Lonetree case was never made public. Nor is it clear that the measures taken later succeeded in closing embassy security leaks.

The only certainty is that the KGB and its successors continued their all-out espionage effort up through the collapse of communism and beyond. The unmasking in February 1994 of Aldrich Ames as a high-ranking Russian mole in the CIA is but one recent confirmation. According to the FBI, Moscow paid Ames more than $1.5 million over the years to sell out his colleagues, his agency and his country.

The Ames case raises a disturbing question. What in the end was more important in terms of national security, the failure to expose Ames earlier or the success in stopping him before he could do more damage? The same question could be asked of British double agent Kim Philby and all the other moles, defectors, and turncoats before him. Only senior officials with top security clearance in the affected intelligence agencies know the answers, and they are most unlikely to reveal them.

Similarly, there is no reliable way of estimating the overall damage of KGB penetration into Western intelligence agencies over the years. Clearly it was significant. Nonetheless, there is at least some indication that the Russians themselves were never satisfied with the results. Even some professionals thought the KGB should have done better. Among them was Oleg Kalugin, a former KGB major general in counterintelligence. "The KGB was always less effective planting moles abroad than the West liked to think, despite all the Philbys," Kalugin told me in Moscow. "We were always better controlling security within the Soviet Union."

Despite its formidable extralegal powers, the KGB's performance was far from perfect, at home and abroad. Like the CIA, MI6, and other intelligence services, the Soviet security police had some spectacular flops. Among them was the 1967 defection of Svetlana Stalin, the dictator's daughter, to the West. She had been allowed to leave Russia to attend the funeral in India of her third husband, an Indian Communist, and was expected to return to Moscow. Instead she fled to the United States. The defection proved to be an acute embarrassment to Moscow—the daughter literally running away from the system her father had created. Vladimir Semichastny, then the KGB chairman, took the fall for his secret police having let Svetlana slip through their fingers. The man who had played a crucial role in the ouster of Nikita Khrushchev was himself summarily dismissed. Under the Brezhnev-era practice, Semichastny was fired, then demoted into oblivion. He became a deputy prime minister of the Ukraine, with special responsibility for sports.

Probably the worst security lapse in Soviet history involved Colonel Oleg Penkovsky. An officer in Soviet military intelligence, the GRU, Penkovsky was recruited by the British and soon became the most important Western agent in Russia during the Cold War. Intelligence of the highest importance supplied by Penkovsky included more than five thousand exposures on a Minox camera over a period of eighteen months. Among the documents he secretly copied in this way were up-to-date surveys of Soviet ICBM accuracy and other capabilities down to defects in test firings. His reports kept twenty American and ten British analysts busy and eventually led to a major revision in NATO defensive strategy.[9]

Most important, Penkovsky's input was crucial in permitting a peaceful resolution to the Cuban missile crisis. Penkovsky photographed and passed to the West a top-secret document detailing stages of Soviet missile site construction. That information allowed U.S. intelligence to identify the Soviet ballistic missile bases under construction in Cuba. Armed with Penkovsky's proof positive, President Kennedy was then able to confront Khrushchev from a position of strength, before the Soviet missiles had actually been installed in Cuba and made operational. Without Penkovsky's advance word, the Soviet leader might well have succeeded in placing ballistic missiles ninety miles from the coast of Florida, holding the United States to nuclear blackmail and triggering an even more dangerous superpower confrontation.

Oleg Penkovsky may have saved the world from nuclear destruction, but only at the cost of his own life. During the Cuban missile crisis he took too many chances getting vital information to the West, thus leaving himself exposed. Penkovsky was soon discovered and arrested. The KGB never forgave him for its most embarrassing security lapse. He was tortured and shot in May 1963.

The Penkovsky case and other failures forced the KGB to review operations, to tighten security. Some policy changes were made as a result. But one basic tenet remained sacrosanct, unaltered to this day: unquestioned authority to operate above the law, abroad as well as at home.

III. MUSCLES AND BRAINS

Penkovsky is an extreme example. His death sentence is not. Virtually any Soviet citizen, even one not remotely connected with espionage, risked his life by defying the KGB, perhaps by simply refusing it requested information. In pressuring Soviets to "cooperate," the KGB routinely fabricated evidence against them for crimes they never committed, then shipped them off to life-threatening sentences in the Gulag if they protested. Such were the illegal powers of the Soviet secret police. Throughout the Cold War, only one category of people in the Soviet Union was relatively safe from such KGB excesses—foreigners who could be protected by their embassies. Americans, with better protection than most, rarely risked more than a one-way ticket home. In one of those Cold War ironies little known in the West, Americans resident in Moscow were usually safer than the average Soviet citizen.

The reason was simple. The United States could do little to protect Soviets from KGB abuse. It could, however, safeguard the individual rights of its own citizens in Moscow, and did so consistently under both Democratic and Republican presidents. However much the KGB would have liked to break American bones as well, the price was always too high. In the few cases where overzealous KGB agents jailed Americans on trumped-up charges—from Yale professor Frederick Barghoorn in the Kennedy era to journalist Nicholas Daniloff on Ronald Reagan's watch—the outcry from Washington was so swift, and the potential damage to superpower relations so great, that the Kremlin always intervened to send the American home before any further harm could come to him.

Usually, it never got that far. If any American journalist was expelled from Moscow, for example, then just as sure as night followed day, at least one Soviet correspondent would be forced to leave Washington. That left the Kremlin with the bigger problem, since Soviet journalists abroad were far more valuable government property than their American counterparts. Most Soviet foreign correspondents were doing double duty for the KGB, while the U.S. rarely used journalists as a CIA cover. Thus Moscow was the inevitable loser in tit-for-tat expulsions and was understandably loath to make the first move on this particular chessboard.[10]

For all these reasons, U.S. correspondents in Moscow were relatively safe. The KGB could never count on expelling us, let alone arresting or harming us. Without those cards to play, it was far harder for the Soviet secret police to intimidate or harass or influence us. Similar restraints curbed KGB pressures on businessmen and diplomats.

Some of these efforts are worth recounting here from personal experience, though not because foreigners had to be particularly brave in resisting KGB pressures. We never had much to fear. Instead a more detailed look at KGB operations is instructive because it shows that the Soviet secret police were not all muscle. They also had a brain, often a very subtle one. Indeed, that brain is the greatest asset today as hard-liners plot a return to dictatorship in Russia.

In the KGB, the muscle and brain worked in tandem. The muscle ran the first-level operations, like routine surveillance of all foreigners. The KGB had the capability to follow us, tap our phones, bug our apartments, whenever it liked. Any foreigner could be drugged, blackmailed, or otherwise compromised. For troublesome journalists there were special pressures. They could have their tires slashed for visiting dissidents. They could be denounced in the Soviet press by name, thereby scaring off their Russian sources for a while. Or they could be hauled into the foreign ministry and threatened with expulsion for anti-Soviet activities.

Most, however, refused to be intimidated, to color a story or pull critical punches. Instead they carried on their business as they would in any other country, attempting to report the story as fairly and completely as possible, whatever the consequences, and usually they finished their Moscow tours without real trouble. Somewhere along the way, however, the KGB was likely to shift gears. The brain would take over, and from then on its treatment of a correspondent would be anything but routine.

My own more subtle handling by the KGB began in 1966 during the trial of dissident writers Andrei Sinyavsky and Yuli Daniel, a major embarrassment in the West for the Soviet police state. All foreigners were barred from this closed tribunal. It soon became a *cause célèbre* in Western intellectual circles, proof that Stalinist thought control lived on in the Soviet Union. The KGB had to figure out a way to limit the growing damage. To my great surprise, their answer involved me.

Suddenly, at the height of the protests in the West, a Russian "journalist" I knew to be close to the KGB phoned and asked for a late-night meeting on a Moscow street corner. His purpose, it turned out, was to hand me a black-and-white photograph from inside the courtroom of Sinyavsky and Daniel standing in the dock.

"I can't use this," I told him.

"Why not?" he asked.

I probably should have known better, but I explained the problem to him anyway. In those days, anytime a Western journalist wanted to transmit a photograph abroad, he had to take it down to Moscow's central telegraph office. Naturally enough, the Soviets had control of the equipment there. Any picture they considered hostile, or even sensitive, they would simply refuse to send. "They'll never let this kind of thing out," I predicted.

"Don't worry," my contact replied. "For this photo, everything has been arranged." And indeed it had been—by the friendly KGB. The Russian at the central telegraph office transmitted it without any hassle to London, to my then-employer, the Associated Press, the world's largest news and photo agency. The picture soon appeared in hundreds of newspapers on all continents. It was, as they say in the trade, "a scoop," the only photo from inside the Sinyavsky-Daniel trial that ever reached the West.

It was also a carefully planned success for the KGB. The Soviet secret police wanted the photo out so the world could see that neither Sinyavsky nor Daniel showed any sign of mistreatment. Both defendants were pictured standing up straight, clean and healthy-looking, apparently well-fed. With the publication of this one photo, the KGB preempted accusations that the dissident writers had been tortured, thereby lowering the outcry in the West.

The KGB had sought out the AP to give the picture the widest possible exposure. As a scoop, it was an offer no journalist could turn down. And as an AP photo, even one clearly captioned as coming from Soviet sources, the picture had far more credibility than it would have had if it had appeared in *Pravda,* the Soviet daily justly renowned for photo doctoring. In short, I had been used in a smart and flawless KGB operation.

Despite its success, the KGB was not satisfied. Its agents soon tried to give themselves a second bounce from the same ploy. My Soviet "journalist" friend reappeared shortly thereafter with another proposition. "We did you a favor with the photo from the trial," he reminded me. "Now it's time for you to do us one." He wanted me to float a story about how Kremlin officials were upset by American policy toward the Soviet Union. I told him that if Soviet officials had something to tell Washington, they should say so themselves, but I would not carry their water. Thus ended a beautiful friendship. It would be twenty-six years before the KGB tapped me for another of its more subtle approaches.

In the meantime, the Soviet Union changed profoundly. By the time I returned to Moscow for my third tour as a correspondent, this time for *Newsweek* in 1988, KGB pressures on foreign correspondents were largely a thing of the past.[11] The Gorbachev reforms were a positive story, and the Soviets let us get on with telling it. Much else changed for foreign journalists. The AP and others got their own international photo-transmitting equipment. Print journalists filed to home offices by their own computer and satellite lines, rather than tapped Soviet phones or telexes. CNN broadcast in Russia, breaking the Soviet television monopoly.

In perhaps the most curious change of all, the KGB went into the public relations business, to improve its image. I will never forget the look on the face of my Russian driver, a KGB plant, when I told him to take me to 4 Dzerzhinsky Square, the Lubyanka building that served aboveground as KGB offices and belowground as prison cells. The driver couldn't believe I had been invited to a press conference there, the first time Western journalists ever set foot inside a building always strictly off-limits before. It was 1990, and the KGB, which previously never gave foreign journalists anything more than a "no comment," had just named its first official press spokesman. A few correspondents then took the trouble to phone him, on what seemed to be the minuscule chance that he would actually say something worth quoting. He surprised everyone. The KGB man not only spoke for the record, but also invited the callers to come on over. I was among them.

It was an eerie experience. A uniformed KGB officer inside the door at Lubyanka inspected my press card, then invited me to take an elevator up to a conference room on the third floor. There wasn't even a KGB escort. For a moment I considered getting off the lift on another floor and inspecting the building on my own. On reflection, however, that did not seem like a very bright idea. So I followed instructions, walking through a KGB museum honoring the heroics of past spies into a windowless, dark-wood-paneled theater, where the spokesman showed a film about how his agency was serving the people by combating black market crime.

"While preserving our professional principles," the spokesman quoted KGB chief Vladimir Kryuchkov as saying, "we shall give the public more information about our work." That promise turned out to be hollow. The professional principles Kryuchkov preserved included secrecy and lawlessness, as seen in the failed coup he led against Gorbachev in August 1991. The only information the KGB let out about its work was designed to make the long-feared agency look better in the public mind. Thus the film on combating crime.

Predictably, the KGB invitation to Lubyanka proved to be long on the symbolism of change and short on the substance. The most characteristic aspects of KGB operations, including their illegality, still changed most slowly, if at all. Among the other old constants still very much in play were the KGB's efforts to use brains rather than muscles in order to exploit foreign correspondents in ever more sophisticated ways.

In 1992, well into the Yeltsin era, I was again approached by a Russian journalist. He was another longtime contact, with a new KGB scheme that had yet another double bounce. This one was designed to improve the image of the spy agency and at the same time earn it $1 million or more.

I'll call my journalist friend "Anton." Over the years he had been an invaluable source, often tipping me, accurately, on coming changes in Kremlin policy, and on the names of rising political figures about to be appointed to high office. He was always so well plugged in that it seemed he must have a KGB connection. This time he no longer made any attempt to play coy. Instead Anton told me he had been a personal friend for thirty years of Yevgeny Primakov, then recently appointed to head the foreign espionage successor to the KGB. The new agency, the Russian Intelligence Service, had taken over the KGB's foreign espionage files. The incredible news Anton brought was that Primakov might be ready to sell some of the Soviet espionage secrets in these files for publication in the West.

Primakov, naturally could never admit to that. So a scheme was designed to give him deniability, then let him do precisely what he was denying. Anton's scheme involved creating a Russian-American joint venture, a quarterly magazine on Soviet espionage. The Russian partner would run the magazine. The American side would provide the seed money to get it started and keep it going. Primakov's agency would then arrange to leak hitherto secret KGB foreign intelligence files to the Russian editor of the magazine. That way, Primakov or his agency could never be accused of handing secrets to Americans.

What the Russian editor did later was his responsibility. The unwritten script of the deal called upon him to share the leaked intelligence files first with his American partners, as payment for putting up the seed money. Anton called it "the right of the first night." That meant the American partner got the first rights to translate and publish the Primakov files abroad, in magazine form in the United States, then resell the material to magazines and newspapers around the world, then resell it again as books marketed globally. Anton personally guaranteed the arrangement. He was to be the Russian editor of the new espionage magazine.

The whole deal, the Russians expected, would be worth at least $1 million. Profits would be split evenly by the Russian and American partners. Since none of this money would go directly to Primakov or his intelligence agency, they were assured deniability against charges that they were selling state secrets. But that is exactly what they would have been doing. The Russian joint venture magazine would simply be a front to launder money destined for Primakov and his KGB successors. Their motivation, Anton explained to me, was really that simple. "They want the money," he said.

I was supposed to find out if *Newsweek* or some other American publication might be interested. Two problems struck me from the outset. First, any American publication would have legitimate qualms about entering into a business arrangement serving at the end of the day to finance further operations of the KGB. Second, the deal was structured so that the Russian side had the right to select all the material to be used. That would allow Moscow to release only those case files reflecting greater glory on KGB espionage operations and to withhold anything that might go further than the Kremlin would like. In short, it was just another form of censorship. To give the deal any value, the American side would have to have direct access to the KGB files. I agreed to pursue the talks to see if that was possible.

The next step involved meetings with a longtime KGB professional I can identify only as "the colonel." Over the years, the colonel had been a KGB agent in London and other Western capitals. He was now working directly for Primakov.

Our meeting started well enough. The colonel explained that Russian intelligence "will insist on a thirty-year rule, as in Britain." That meant no KGB archives less than thirty years old would be made available. It sounded perfectly reasonable. No intelligence agency wants to make public documents that can reveal current operating procedures or the names of agents still active. Thus the minimum wait of thirty years. So far so good.

"So we can start in 1962?" I suggested.

"Correct," the colonel agreed.

"We'll want the archives on the 1962 Cuban missile crisis," I began.

"They are not available," he said.

"Why not?" I wanted to know.

"I am not obliged to give you the reason," he replied.

"What about the files on U-2 pilot Francis Gary Powers?"

"We don't have them," the colonel explained. "Military intelligence does."

"How about the American atomic spies Julius and Ethel Rosenberg?"

"We are not prepared to talk about that yet," the colonel said. "We cannot offend their children."

"Perhaps Kim Philby?"

"There are dozens of tomes on him," the colonel explained. "You cannot expect us to go through all those."

And so it went. One way or another he managed to reject every archive of major interest to any American partner, among them the KGB file on Kennedy assassin Lee Harvey Oswald's time spent in the Soviet Union. In addition, the colonel also made it clear that the American partners would never be able to get into the KGB archives themselves to look for what they might want. Instead, they would have to take what the Russian side offered. Needless to say, Primakov's people were not giving anything away. The material they selected included files on KGB hero spies of the 1930s, in the Spanish Civil War, or in Hitler's Germany, never before made public. These archives would reflect well on KGB prowess, but would be of far less public interest in the United States than my list of subjects already rejected.

Nor was that all. As our talks continued over several weeks, it also became clear that the Russians were using me for a stalking horse. They hoped my magazine would make an offer that could then be used in further auction-type bidding. What they really preferred, however, was to sell to an American book publisher, with no full-time representative on the ground in Moscow able to make knowledgeable demands or ask tough questions. And indeed, that's what happened. *Newsweek* never made an offer. The Russians eventually signed with Crown Publishing Group for a total reported in the U.S. press as approaching seven figures. At the time, the Russian side said the books covered by the deal would be based on KGB archives but would do nothing to compromise either the Russian Federation or its intelligence service. The editors at Crown are likely to find that the material they get has little meat on the bones.

Once again, the former KGB will enjoy a double bounce. It will be paid, handsomely, for giving away virtually nothing. Then it will be praised in the West for "revelations" about its past, a suggestion of honest new behavior, and an excellent cover for continuing in the old, secret, illegal ways.

Although my end of the negotiations failed, I got a rare insight into how the KGB operated. During our talks, the colonel eventually admitted a surprising reason why the American side could not get into the KGB foreign intelligence archives. "They are not computerized," he explained. "Many were put in boxes, locked away in storerooms, and never classified." In effect, he was conceding that even the KGB itself didn't know what they all contained. "We've brought in retired intelligence officers now to classify the files and put them on the computer," the colonel told me in 1992. "So far we are up to 1922." For once, the supposedly all-powerful KGB was admitting it had a long way to go to do the job right.

Unfortunately, it still has time to get its repressive act together once again. The conflict between Russia's reformers and neo-Stalinists continues under Boris Yeltsin, with the heirs of the KGB still capable of tipping the balance either way.

Signs of this ongoing struggle are everywhere in Russia. Perhaps nowhere in the country are they more ominous than in the city of Perm, and the nearby Gulag prison camps that bear its name, seven hundred miles southeast of Moscow in the Urals. In June 1992, I joined the first small group of foreign correspondents permitted to tour the dreaded Gulag system in the Perm region. We were allowed in to see the changes for the better. There were many. Inevitably, though, we also saw how much needs to be done before Russia can finally emerge from its Stalinist past.

No discussion of the KGB is complete without a closer look at its chief arm of repression, the Gulag system of prison camps. Today, that look is one of carefully staged ambiguity, of liberal reform and holdover repressions co-existing side by side, as if waiting for a decision from leaders in Moscow on which way to go. The Perm region, long the gateway to the Siberian prison camp chain, is a particularly good example of such ambiguity. Perm was always a leading barometer of the level of repression in Russia, past and present. It remains today a useful measuring rod for the dangers of renewed dictatorship in the years ahead.

The city of Perm itself is a study in ambiguity, symbolizing the struggle between reform and repression that has dominated Soviet history. On the same street there, less than a hundred yards apart, Russia's greatest ballet master, Sergei Diaghilev, was born, and the last tsar's brother, Prince Mikhail Romanov, was seized, to be executed without trial. The two events, commemorated to this day in Perm, remain a vivid reminder of how Russia's capacity for creative genius and its appalling brutality coexist side by side.

In Stalin's years, thousands of Russia's top intellectuals passed through Perm on their way to and from the camps. Those fortunate enough to survive forced labor in the Gulag had no right to return home to Moscow, Leningrad, or any other major city once released. In the eyes of Soviet authorities, the thought crimes they were convicted of committing, often without a shred of evidence, made them enemies of the state, undesirables to be kept far from the leading urban centers where they could do the most harm. Thus exiled, many of Russia's finest minds decided to settle in Perm. As one unintended result, the city blossomed from a provincial backwater into one of the outstanding cultural and university centers in Russia, renowned for its theaters, art, and scientific institutes. In a triumph of the human spirit, Perm showed that even Stalinist repression cannot extinguish intellectual or artistic genius.

Typically, Stalin soon recognized Perm's rising intellectual candlepower, then figured out a way to exploit it for his own purposes. He turned the city into a center for rocketry and other defense-related enterprises. During the Cold War, it thrived economically. The population swelled to 1.1 million. Finally, in 1990, with both the Gulag and secret defense industries winding down, it was opened for the first time to foreigners. Sadly, however, there is still no happy ending for Perm.

By 1992, the Perm Aeroengine factory, the city's largest employer and the nation's most important producer of aircraft engines, was nearing bankruptcy. Its largest customer, the state airline Aeroflot, "cannot pay its bills and cannot borrow money," Yuri Reshetnikov, the president of the engine maker, complained to me at the time. He had already laid off 10 percent of his workforce of thirty thousand, and more pink slips were coming.

His company's problems were typical of Russia's transition to the market economy. They made, he claimed, world-class engines for warplanes and civilian aircraft. Reshetnikov talked about hopes for privatization, and conversion from military to civilian production. But foreign investors were not coming in. And Russian banks were charging a ruinous 80 percent interest for essential development loans. Like other employers in the military-industrial complex, he admitted his firm was losing a battle for survival

In Perm, the result could already be seen. For the first time in decades, unemployed young people were leaving the city for the surrounding farms, willing to put up with outdoor plumbing because at least there was food. The seeds for a social explosion were clearly gathering. The neo-Stalinists and their friends in the KGB began to sense public disillusion with the uncertainty of reform and a desire to return to the stability of the past. Their day, it seemed to them, was coming.

Out in the Gulag, it sometimes seemed, the Stalinists had never let go. Our group was supposed to start the tour at a forest labor camp in the Ural Mountains, where inmates cut timber. We had permission from a senior official at the interior ministry in Moscow, General Valery Fyodorov, to visit there. So we took a helicopter 150 miles north of Perm to the village of Nyro, then a bus to a forest camp of two thousand inmates called SLON 2. But when we arrived, the camp commander, Colonel Anatoly Krutikov, refused to let us in. We asked why. "The camp is secret," he replied.

"Why secret?" we asked. This was 1992. Yeltsin had proclaimed a democracy. Did they have something to hide, like political prisoners or abused inmates? "The reason is secret," the colonel answered, in classic Stalinist logic. We never got in.

Fortunately, his counterparts at two prison camps, Perm 35 and Perm 10, were a different breed. They wanted publicity on how the Gulag had changed for the better. So they let us in, answered questions, and even gave us time alone with prisoners. Nothing could be less Stalinist.

Perm 35 was once the Gulag's most infamous camp for political prisoners. Beatings, hard labor, starvation diets, and isolation in freezing punishment cells were all routine there. A veritable who's who of Soviet dissidents did time at Perm 35. Survivors included Anatoly Shcharansky, Yuri Orlov, and the late Vladimir Bukovsky. Despite the terrible hardships, their struggle for basic human rights in Russia never faltered. Instead, Soviet authorities gave in first, let them go, and changed the country.

By the time I visited Perm 35 in 1992, officials claimed no political prisoners were held there anymore, only common criminals. Inmates still lived inside barbed-wire fences under the watchful eyes of armed soldiers in guard towers. But prisoners' heads were no longer shaved. They wore name tags instead of numbers. They ate meat or fish instead of watery gruel. There was even a guest house inside the prison walls where inmates would wear civilian clothes and sleep with their wives for one three-day period each year in return for good behavior. "We've become more civilized," the camp commander, Major Yuri Maksim, explained.

Down the road at Perm 10, it was much the same story. Prisoners there now got more food parcels and letters from home, more books, more visits, more privileges. Perm 10 even had a theater. Prisoners with electric guitars, literally a jailhouse rock band, were practicing when we arrived. In this respect, the Gulag now appeared freer than the whole country was thirty years before when Nikita Khrushchev banned rock music across the U.S.S.R.

Change for the better seemed to be enormous. Still, like much of Yeltsin's new more democratic Russia, both camps had the look of a Potemkin village, the peculiarly Russian showplace designed to make superficial or partial change look deeper and permanent. A tastier icing now covered the old inedible Stalinist cake. For one thing, fresh coats of green and white paint had spruced up the walls at both Perm 35 and Perm 10 just before our visit. For another, the prisoners claimed, when I finally got to talk to them alone, that nothing fundamentally important had changed at all.

Gennady Prudskov, a former soldier, was serving five years at Perm 35 for treason. The KGB officers who arrested him claimed he had tried to sell military secrets to Western embassies in Moscow. Prudskov admitted visiting the embassies, but said all he did there was apply for immigration visas. "Of course I am a political prisoner," Prudskov told me. "My only crime was that I tried to go abroad—legally." His story underscored a major question about today's Gulag. Russian officials insist there are no more political prisoners because all those jailed for criticizing the state have been released. Inmates say the state still sends political foes to the Gulag, although now under the cover of other criminal charges.

At Perm 10, a young man convicted of robbery, who identified himself only as Sergei, complained that guards still enforce draconian rules of discipline. Infractions can get the offender sent to a special punishment camp that Sergei called "the White Swan." He claimed many prisoners never return from there alive. "Prisoners are still sent to punishment cells where they are beaten, tortured, and sometimes killed," Sergei said. Camp officials denied his claims.

Prisoners, of course, are notorious liars. Unfortunately, so too are their Gulag jailers. In the Soviet Union, disinformation was always a high art form. So pinpointing the true picture in the Gulag today is difficult.

Still, some basic truths are beyond debate. One is that the KGB remains a formidable force, albeit under a different name, most recently the Federal Security Service. Another basic truth is that the KGB's chief disciplinary arm, the Gulag system of prison camps, remains in operation, although more humanely for now. Even in their present more benign form, however, neither the secret police nor the Gulag prison camp system have any place in a genuine democracy. Both are capable of returning to repression at a stroke, in order to support renewed dictatorship. There is still no law-based state to stop them. As long as that remains true, the successors to the KGB retain a veto on Russia's future. It is a veto that Western leaders must take very seriously indeed.

10

Détente as a One-Way Street

I. STRENGTH FROM WEAKNESS

The Kremlin Palace of Congresses is the only modern building in the citadel of Russian power. Built in the Khrushchev era, the mammoth six-story, white-marble-and-glass rectangle houses a cavernous meeting hall, modeled on United Nations decor, with six thousand plush red seats. For the last three decades of Soviet history, most major policy lines were announced there. Even a one-party state needs landmark celebrations to reinvigorate the faith, to reassert leadership. So the Soviet Communist Party held a congress there, approximately every five years, gathering together senior officials from across the land. Allied leaders from around the world dutifully attended as well. The highlight, trumpeted for weeks in advance by the controlled press, came in a speech by the Kremlin's top man, often lasting five hours or more, laying down the latest caveats of foreign and domestic policy to enraptured applause.

It was always an impressive show. Fidel Castro in olive drabs, Chinese in Mao suits, African Communists in colorful tribal robes, and the gray leaders of Eastern Europe joined with Soviet milkmaids, machinists, and marshals. Together they would express what the Moscow press always called the "unbreakable unity" of the world movement, or "unanimous support" for whatever the Kremlin's number one decided to say.

Such was the scene when Leonid Ilyich Brezhnev laid down the definitive foreign policy line of his eighteen-year rule. The occasion was the 25th Congress of the Soviet Communist Party, the date, February 24, 1976, the place, the Kremlin Palace of Congresses. As usual for such official events, its stage was decorated with a statue of Lenin and a huge red banner in white letters saying "Forward to the Victory of Communism." The scene had been prepared with meticulous care for a global television audience. It was designed to convey one bold message to every part of the planet: these were the people, this was the political system, that intended to take over the world.

187

Brezhnev was an appallingly boring speaker, reading his text stiffly in gravel-voiced monotone for hours on end, often putting the Party faithful to sleep. At the 1976 congress, however, Brezhnev actually said something unusually important, meriting the utmost attention. In a rare burst of candor, he was spelling out how communism would defeat democracy and capitalism, around the globe. "We make no secret of the fact that we see détente as the way to create more favorable conditions for socialist and Communist construction," Brezhnev told the congress. "Détente does not in the slightest abolish and cannot abolish or alter the laws of the class struggle."

The typically wooden Brezhnev phrases need some elaboration. They are built on code words familiar to the Communist camp but confusing to other mortals. By "détente" Brezhnev meant arms control, trade, and other peaceful moves to lessen tensions with the United States and the Western democracies. By "Communist construction," he meant building communism throughout the world, including areas of vital Western interest, if necessary by military force. Leonid Ilyich admitted no contradiction between these two totally contradictory policies.

There was no recognition by him that Communist expansion created Cold War tensions in the first place. On the contrary, Brezhnev saw the policies as two complementary, perfectly consistent elements in the same game plan. Détente was the most effective means, or, as he put it, "the way to create more favorable conditions" to expand communism. The West would be lulled into peaceful cooperation so that the Soviet side could better advance its continuing ambition of spreading communism worldwide.

In case anyone missed the message the first time around, Brezhnev repeated it by saying détente in no way altered the class struggle. For the Communists, the class struggle meant their battle to defeat capitalism around the world. In effect, Brezhnev was saying Communists would talk peace with the West while continuing class warfare up to the final victory of communism.

Later in the same speech, Brezhnev made clear that the class struggle would not stop at ideological debate, but, ominously, would still include military conflict. He was telling the comrades détente could save the world from nuclear war, but that still left Communists free to support conventional wars in the Third World. The military conflicts the Soviet leader approved were what he called "wars of national liberation" against the imperialists, his label for the Western democracies, and what he saw as their continuing neocolonial influence in the developing world.

Brezhnev said so in these words: "We are on the side of the forces of progress and the national liberation struggle. . . . The Soviet Union supports the legitimate aspirations of the young states in their determination to put an end to all imperialist exploitation."

There, in a nutshell, was the essence of Soviet foreign policy throughout the Cold War. Moscow would not choose between détente and class struggle. Instead, the Soviet Union would have it both ways. The men in the Kremlin would pursue peace, or armed struggle, or both at the same time, as it suited them.

In their eyes, détente was never intended to be an equal partnership with the West, a joint venture in moving the superpowers from nuclear confrontation to peaceful cooperation. On the contrary, to Soviet leaders, détente was always a one-way street, on which the traffic always moved their way, to meet their long-term goal of building communism.

That was the essence of the so-called Brezhnev Doctrine. In it, the West was warned to keep hands off Eastern Europe, an area of vital concern to Soviet security. Any Western intervention there, Moscow warned, would meet a resolute Soviet rebuff. Yet at the same time, the Kremlin felt free to expand Communist influence against Western interests on a global scale, either directly with Soviet troops or indirectly with allied or surrogate forces, throughout the Cold War. Thus the Kremlin backed North Korean and North Vietnamese aggression in Asia, intervened with its own troops in Afghanistan, and used surrogates to advance its interests in Africa, the Middle East, and Central America.

Soviet strategy was long-range, encouraged by the Marxist belief that the victory over capitalism was historically inevitable. Tactics involved constant probing of Western resolve, interspersed with temporary retreats when necessary. If challenged by a tough Western response, as in Berlin, Moscow would pull back, so there would be no escalation to the risk of nuclear war. If there was no serious Western response, Moscow would push further, as in Ethiopia or Angola. Stripped of ideological boilerplate, the Soviet attitude toward the West boiled down to this: what's mine is mine and what's yours is negotiable. Or again, as Brezhnev defined it in 1976, détente was a one-way street.

The arrogance of that stand is extraordinary. At the time, the Soviet Union was the weaker of the two superpowers by far. The global unity of the Communist movement and its unanimous support for Soviet policy, both loudly proclaimed at the 25th Party Congress in Moscow, were a total sham. In reality, both Brezhnev himself and the irreparably split world Communist system he claimed to lead were already dying from incurable illnesses. Nonetheless, here were the Soviets defining the terms of superpower relations to suit themselves. In effect, the weaker Russians were dictating the rules of the game to the stronger Americans. They were reversing the norms of power politics, standing logic on its head—and getting away with it.

Brezhnev himself was probably too dim to grasp the irony of it all. Never the brightest of men, Leonid Ilyich rose rapidly through Communist Party ranks because at the time, Stalin was constantly sending older, abler comrades to early graves. Brezhnev was a loyal Communist, a competent manager, a skillful bureaucratic infighter, a hard-drinking, tough-talking, back-slapping good old boy, just the sort Nikita Khrushchev would pick as a number two—good company, a trusted aide, but apparently not smart enough to pose a real political threat. Indeed, even after Leonid Ilyich took over the top Kremlin leadership, no informed Russian ever seriously regarded him as a major geopolitical strategic thinker.

Ordinary Russians were merciless in describing his reputedly low mental candlepower in endless jokes. Here is a typical example:

Brezhnev takes a break in talks with Indira Gandhi and tells aides he wants them to paint a red dot on his forehead just like hers.

"You cannot do that, Leonid Ilyich," a frustrated adviser explains. "In the first place, you have to be a Hindu. In the second, you must be a woman. Why on earth do you want a red dot on your forehead?"

"Simple," Brezhnev replies. "This morning in our talks, Indira kept tapping her forehead and saying, 'Leonid Ilyich, you have nothing up here.' "

Those stories were told during Brezhnev's days of better health. By the time Leonid Ilyich gave the 1976 keynote foreign policy address, his best days were long gone. His speech was already slurred, his walk a shuffle. Soon illness would almost totally incapacitate him. For long stretches of time he could work no more than one or two hours a day, and his attention span at any one time might be no longer than twenty minutes. Then for a while he would be better, could travel, speak in public, meet foreign statesmen, only to fall ill again. Aides propped him up and kept him going for another six years, largely because their jobs and privileges depended on his staying in office. Even at his best, however, Leonid Brezhnev was never the man to define the terms of superpower relations. That he continued to try, during his long illness, and often succeeded, is nothing short of mindboggling.

Brezhnev's importance cannot be minimized, despite his limited abilities and his long, debilitating illness. In the Soviet system, the top leader had to sign off on all important policy changes. As a result, no matter how brilliant the foreign policy experts in his government were, no matter how quickly and adroitly they might move to exploit international events to Kremlin advantage, they were powerless to act until Brezhnev approved. All too often that meant opportunities were missed and nothing got done, simply because Brezhnev was too ill even to read their recommendations, let alone think them through to approval. So for much of the Brezhnev era, as we shall see, Soviet foreign policy was totally inflexible, ultimately to the great disadvantage of the Soviet Union.

Strange as that sounds to a Western reader now, it was clear to correspondents, diplomats, and other foreigners in Moscow at the time. Let me cite only one example from personal experience. In May 1977 I went to see Yuri Zhukov, then the top foreign affairs commentator of the Soviet Communist Party newspaper *Pravda*. Zhukov was extremely well informed by senior officials. His articles always contained chapter and verse on the latest Kremlin thinking. I called on him rather naively expecting a serious exchange of ideas on current world affairs. Instead, the following conversation ensued:

"How do you evaluate the current state of Soviet-American relations?" I began.

"The peaceful foreign policy of the Soviet Union was laid down by Comrade Brezhnev at the 25th Congress of the Soviet Communist Party," Zhukov replied. "That policy has not changed. If there are any problems in our relations with the United States, it is the fault of the American side."

"Could you be more specific?" I asked, trying again to start something more useful. "After all, the 25th Congress was some time ago, and a lot has changed since then."

"Like what, for instance?" Zhukov wanted to know.

"Well, the United States has a new president, Jimmy Carter, who has placed a new emphasis on human rights as the centerpiece of his foreign policy. Perhaps you could comment on that," I suggested.

"I repeat," Zhukov responded. "The peaceful foreign policy of the Soviet Union was laid down by Comrade Brezhnev at the 25th Congress of the Soviet Communist Party. That policy has not changed. If there are any problems in our relations with the United States, it is the fault of the American side."

All other attempts to start a rational conversation got similar stock answers. In the Brezhnev era, this pompous, stubborn posturing typified Moscow's approach to foreign affairs. The Soviets awarded themselves the right to define the code of conduct for international relations, and then expected the rest of the world to sign on.

Such arrogance might have been justified in a nation of overwhelming economic, military, and political strength. The Soviet Union, however, was nothing of the kind. Its economy, the crucial base for any strong foreign policy, was anything but healthy. The Soviet military was untrusted by the Kremlin leadership. Communist power was maintained at home only by KGB repression. Even so, internal dissent was growing. Nor could Communist allies abroad make up for Soviet weakness at home. Democratic movements were rising in Eastern Europe. Fidel Castro was a loose cannon, China an ideological foe. World Communist unity was as big a myth as Soviet economic power. Nonetheless, Brezhnev hid the true extent of all these Soviet weaknesses, even from his Politburo colleagues, and carried on as if they didn't exist.[1]

In effect, Leonid Ilyich was attempting to dictate the terms of détente from his perch on a house of cards. Therein lies the supreme irony. In 1976, when Brezhnev publicly took this position of strength, the Soviet Union and much of the Communist world were only fifteen years from total collapse. These were not the people to dictate to the rest of mankind. They could not even save their own system.

At the time, of course, the rest of the world did not know the Soviet system would collapse so soon. That comes now with the wisdom of hindsight. Still, the ultimately fatal weaknesses of the Soviet Union in particular and the Communist movement in general were already apparent in the 1970s to Western specialists. In effect, the West knew enough at the time to call Brezhnev's bluff, but chose not to do so. Despite the double handicap of a dying leader and a dying system, the Soviet Union still managed to set the terms for superpower relations throughout much of the Cold War to Moscow's advantage.

It did so in many ways, but most came down to this: the weaker Soviet Union made the challenge, then left the stronger West in the inferior position of figuring out how to react. Examples are legion during the Cold War, but none better than Moscow's provocative decision to put nuclear missiles in Cuba, ninety miles off the American coast, in 1962, when the U.S. advantage over the U.S.S.R. in the strategic nuclear balance was more than seven to one.[2]

By any normal standard of international relations, the far stronger Western alliance could have and should have set the rules of superpower relations. At the very least there were always ample grounds for the West to insist that détente must be an equal, jointly managed two-way street. Indeed, such was the disparity in favor of the West in military, economic, and political power that real leverage existed to go much further, to push the Soviet system toward collapse decades earlier, without the risk of nuclear war, given wiser leadership on the American side.

None of this takes away from the fact that the overall American response to Moscow's challenge was correct. The containment policy designed by George Kennan nearly a half century ago to stop Soviet expansion globally stood up very well, holding the line until communism collapsed from its own internal contradictions. Nor can anyone argue that maintaining containment since the 1950s was ever easy. America and its allies paid a huge price, financing the military programs that kept the West ahead in the arms race throughout the Cold War. Furthermore, NATO allies held together for four decades despite a concerted Soviet effort to split them apart. The financial sacrifice, consistency of purpose, and loyalty of the allied effort is entirely praiseworthy.

That said, however, it is still perfectly valid to show where the American-led alliance could have done better and defeated communism sooner. The purpose of any such exercise is to highlight mistakes to be avoided in any future challenge to global survival, whether from Muslim fundamentalists armed with an Islamic bomb, a new Russian dictator with a finger on the old Soviet nuclear trigger, or some other threat to global survival from a totally unexpected quarter. Only by recognizing the errors of the past can the West be sure they won't be repeated in the years ahead. One Cold War lesson that needs to be learned now is how Moscow was able to shape superpower relations from a position of weakness for so long. Once that becomes clear it will be easier to see how the West could have responded more effectively. Two key factors are involved here—Soviet skill and American mistakes. We will examine the Soviet pluses first.

One was the extraordinary ability of the U.S.S.R.'s foreign policy establishment. Whatever the failings of the top Kremlin leadership—Stalin's tyranny, Khrushchev's erratic twists and turns, Brezhnev's mediocre mind— the professionals just below them responsible for formulating foreign policy and carrying it out were usually as good as or better than their counterparts anywhere in the world. They had to be. Only the brightest and the toughest managed to rise through the Soviet bureaucratic jungle to senior levels and stay there. By definition, veteran makers of Russian foreign policy had to be masters of detail, deception, and duplicity just to hold their jobs. For them, outmaneuvering foreign governments could be relatively easy, a welcome relief from the Soviet power game. No matter how weak a hand they were dealt in foreign affairs, they could and did play it from strength.

Soviet foreign policy professionals recognized early on one of the key fundamentals of international affairs. They understood that relative national strength often has no bearing on the outcome of foreign disputes, especially in the nuclear age. On the contrary, at the end of the day the crucial factor is not military or economic muscle at all, but which side has the wiser approach. Soviet statesmen tended to be cleverer than most. They understood that smarter tactics or strategy could outmaneuver a stronger adversary, and they developed that practice into a fine art. To cite but one example, Soviet negotiators managed to conclude nuclear arms limitation agreements with the United States containing enough loopholes so that Moscow could catch and sometimes surpass the U.S. lead in various missile systems.

There are many explanations for the Soviet ability to outwit a stronger America. Tradition plays one role. The Russian national "sport," for example, is chess. Where young Americans are trained in games of speed and strength, young Russians learn a mental game, essentially how to outfox an opponent several moves down the chessboard. There can be little doubt which sport produces shrewder policymakers later in life.

History plays another important role. Russia was always weak, always invaded by stronger neighbors from east and west. The country survived by its wits. In September 1812, when Napoleon led his Grand Army into Moscow and occupied the Kremlin, lesser nations would have bowed to the conqueror. Instead, the defeated Russian commander, Marshal Kutuzov, outsmarted the victors, setting the city aflame and evacuating the population. Napoleon found himself camping in a ruin, with winter fast approaching, food supplies running out, and the nominally defeated Russians refusing all overtures to discuss the terms of surrender. After five weeks, the baffled French emperor ordered a retreat. His troops stretched over a thin line all the way back to Poland, vulnerable to attack by a hostile Russian army and ill-equipped for the brutal winter. Napoleon himself survived, but he paid an awesome price. Of the 600,000 troops who entered Russia, 400,000 died of battle casualties, starvation, and exposure. Another 100,000 were taken prisoner. The Grand Army was reduced to a remnant, thus assuring Napoleon's ultimate defeat at Waterloo in 1815. Such was the power of a weak and beaten Russia.

That lesson was etched in Russian minds for all times. Played right, weakness could be turned to strength. Soviet officials constantly exploited it. Throughout the Cold War, first Khrushchev and then Brezhnev presented themselves to the West as embattled moderates, pushed by hard-line, neo-Stalinist rivals in the Kremlin to return to the bad old days. Their constant refrain was that any American military pressure on Moscow would only make matters worse. It would play into the hands of Russia's military-industrial complex, raise defense spending, and lead to a renewed hard-line dictatorship. For the most part, the West bought this line, that compromising with a self-proclaimed Kremlin moderate was preferable to bringing a new hawk to power in Moscow.

Particularly in Brezhnev's day, all this such pleading was nonsense. Leonid Ilyich was already pandering to the elite in the Soviet military-industrial complex, giving them all the budget increases they could handle in return for their political support. In the process, Brezhnev raised the Soviet Union from strategic inferiority to the United States to essential nuclear parity. As usual, he was having it both ways. He was telling the Americans, in effect, "Don't push me or the military threat will grow." Then he was turning around and making sure the military threat would grow.

One can only wonder what might have happened if the West had challenged Brezhnev's duplicity. The United States, after all, had other options. Among them, it could have given anti-Soviet forces in Eastern Europe both political encouragement and economic aid, in a bald attempt to hasten communism's demise. Predictably, Moscow would have protested that such provocative U.S. action only strengthened the position of the Soviet military-industrial complex and increased the dangers of war. That was the moment to call Brezhnev's bluff, by replying that his unprecedented military buildup was already strengthening the position of the Soviet military-industrial complex and increasing the dangers of war anyway. Moreover, the United States, as the far stronger party, then had room to seize the initiative and push even harder. Washington could have insisted that if the Soviet side wanted a genuine détente relationship between the superpowers, it would have to prove its peaceful intentions by concrete deeds, meaning a halt to the excessive Soviet military buildup, an end to adventurism in the Third World, and the granting of basic human rights in the U.S.S.R. as promised when Moscow signed the United Nations Charter.

All this is now only academic speculation, of course. No one can rewrite history and determine what might have been. Nonetheless, it should be clear that the West did have a margin of maneuver for making détente more of a two-way street, well short of risking World War III. Tactics, pressures, could have been fine-tuned to minimize dangers, maximize prospects. The essential point is that such an overall approach was never considered seriously.

Instead, the West preferred to be passive, letting Brezhnev set the rules for détente. Mistakenly, the United States viewed the continuing power struggle in the Kremlin as hawks versus doves. It was nothing of the kind. As Brezhnev knew perfectly well, there were no liberals in his Politburo, only hard-liners. Their relatively few foreign policy differences were over tactics, not over strategic goals like expanding Communist power worldwide. So Brezhnev was able to exploit U.S. misperceptions with a simple charade. Leonid Ilyich turned to the West and essentially said, "Help me, do it my way, or you will get someone worse." The West, uncritically, agreed to do just that. Once again Russia had turned weakness into strength.

The pattern continues to this day. Gorbachev in his time sounded the same refrain. He was the embattled reformer, fighting off the Stalinist Neanderthals. The West had to help him or democratic and market reform in Russia would fail, at the risk of a return to dictatorship in Moscow and the specter of Cold War II. Yeltsin in turn, took exactly the same line. This time there is far more truth to the claims than in Brezhnev's day: the reformers are genuine, the changes monumental, the determination of the hard-liners to turn the clock back very real. No one should equate Gorbachev or Yeltsin with Brezhnev. The point here is only that these very different leaders still used the same quintessentially Russian tactic of turning their weakness into strength.

The remarkable ability of the Soviet foreign policy establishment was only the beginning. A second major reason for Soviet success in managing the Cold War agenda was that Moscow's top people stayed in their jobs for decades, and got better as they went along. Andrei Gromyko served as a key player in Soviet-American relations for every Kremlin leader from Stalin to Gorbachev, first as ambassador to Washington, then as Soviet foreign minister for twenty-eight years. No other foreign minister anywhere in the world held the job so long. Anatoly Dobrynin was the Soviet ambassador to Washington for twenty-four years, until he was the longest-serving envoy in the American capital. Georgi Arbatov started Moscow's top academic think tank on relations with America, the USA Institute, in 1968 and still ran it twenty-seven years later.

These men were not necessarily brighter or abler than their American counterparts. They just had far longer experience in the jobs they held. Thus an American secretary of state in office for four years or less could not hope to approach Gromyko on an equal footing. The Soviet foreign minister, drawing on his unmatched wealth of personal experience, knew intimately every piece in the complex puzzle of Soviet-American relations. He had been back and forth so many times over all the key issues that he understood better than anyone where the Soviets had failed in the past and how they might do better next time, whatever the question. On the American side, by comparison, new secretaries of state had to start by reading up and then trying to reinvent the wheel.

Often the difficulty was compounded. Not only did the Americans insist on changing secretaries of state regularly, but they tended to pick outsiders, whether from academia (Henry Kissinger), charitable foundations (Dean Rusk), law (John Foster Dulles), business (George Shultz), Congress (Edmund Muskie), or the military (Alexander Haig)—from just about every field but the career diplomats with the most day-to-day inside official experience in foreign affairs. To no small extent, Moscow's ability to outmaneuver the West from a position of weakness during the Cold War came from the long continuity in office of top veteran diplomats like Andrei Gromyko and Anatoly Dobrynin.

Inevitably, that contributed to Moscow's arrogance. I remember calling on the Soviet embassy in Washington in late 1980 for an off-the-record chat with a senior official there. I asked him how Ambassador Dobrynin was looking forward to working with the newly elected American president, Ronald Reagan. The official explained that Dobrynin had dealt personally with every U.S. president since John Kennedy—Lyndon Johnson, Richard Nixon, Gerald Ford, and Jimmy Carter. Reagan was to be his sixth. "The ambassador is looking forward to working with the new president the way a kindergarten teacher looks forward to the first day of school," the Soviet official told me. Ambassadors are not supposed to look down on the heads of state they are accredited to as kindergarten tots. Still, the undiplomatic reply reflected typical Soviet arrogance. The Russians were the wise, experienced professionals. They would teach the new American president his ABCs, particularly one like Reagan, whose views they regarded as simplistic.

America too had its professional diplomats, of course. Those sent to Moscow as ambassador were the best of a very intelligent, talented breed. Invariably, they spoke fluent Russian, had studied Soviet affairs, and had served in the Moscow embassy at least once before on the way up the career ladder. They had all the experience and abilities the job required. It was my privilege to know five of them—Foy Kohler, Llewellyn Thompson, Walter Stoessel, Malcolm Toon, and Jack Matlock. All were fine public servants, but, unfortunately for the United States, that was not enough. America sent first-rate ambassadors to Moscow, then all too often ignored their advice or underused them.

Thompson, for example, warned Washington against making concessions to Moscow on the false expectation that the Soviets would then help the United States extricate itself from the Vietnam War. He turned out to be right, although no one at home was listening. The result, as we shall see, was one of America's great mistakes in the Cold War era.

Toon was particularly outspoken about being underused. During his time as ambassador to Moscow in the late 1970s, Washington preferred to do its

Soviet business locally through Dobrynin. The American reasoning went like this: Dobrynin spoke English, he was there, the U.S. government could talk to him directly. All this was quicker, easier, and preferable to sending cabled instructions to the American ambassador in Moscow, waiting for him to call on the Soviet government to carry them out, and then digesting a cabled reply. Toon, however, told me this was a grave mistake. As he saw it, Washington was putting itself at a considerable disadvantage. By dealing only through Dobrynin, the president and his secretary of state were hearing what the Soviet government wanted to tell them. At the same time, they could never be sure their own message was getting through to Moscow. They didn't know if Dobrynin passed on what they had actually told him or a doctored version of what the Soviet ambassador thought Brezhnev would like to hear. It was another way of making détente a one-way street.

Ambassador Toon argued that the only way the U.S. government could be sure its message was getting through to the Soviet leadership was to have him deliver it in Moscow to Gromyko or Brezhnev. That had another advantage. The Russian-speaking Toon could get more significance out of one raised eyebrow from Gromyko, responding silently to some point or other, in a few seconds than Secretary of State Cyrus Vance might get out of an hour's conversation with Dobrynin. Gromyko, after all, was a senior member of the ruling Soviet Politburo—a powerful decision-maker. Dobrynin was only an adviser. He had influence, but no power. By limiting their regular contacts to Dobrynin, the Americans were dealing with the Indians rather than the chiefs.

Toon's suggested remedy was that "we ought to be two-tracking." He meant the message traffic should go both through Dobrynin in Washington, as before, and also through the American ambassador in Moscow, to be certain it got delivered to the Kremlin leadership in the original meaning. That way, the channel of the détente dialogue would be a two-way street. Toon's proposal got nowhere, however. Washington preferred to deal only through Dobrynin. In the end, America handicapped itself, allowing the Russians to conduct détente business to their advantage, down to how communications between the two superpowers would be handled. It was just one more example of the weak leading the strong.

II. WEAKNESS FROM STRENGTH

Soviet diplomatic skill was only half the reason for Moscow's success in turning détente into a one-way street. American mistakes were the other half. The worst involved an essential U.S. misreading of the Soviet threat. American foreign policy errors continually flowed from that, in a pattern repeated over and over again.

The pattern emerged early in the Cold War, when Russia produced its first atomic bomb. At the time there was no way the Soviet Union could have risked using it against the United States without committing national suicide. Overwhelming U.S. military superiority then made it questionable whether a Soviet first strike could succeed, but it was an absolute certainty that American atomic retaliation would destroy the U.S.S.R. Nonetheless, the threat that the Soviets might start an atomic war was magnified out of all proportion. It became so distorted at the outset of the Cold War that decades later the U.S. had still not properly reassessed the dangers.

Initial reaction bordered on the irrational. American children in the 1950s had to practice hiding under their school desks in case Moscow launched a first-strike nuclear attack on the United States. Never mind that no Kremlin leader would dare press the button. Serious American adults, believing a Russian attack might be imminent, asked themselves if the United States should fight back or surrender to the Communists. "Would you rather be Red or dead?" became an American cliché. Senator Joseph McCarthy whipped up national hysteria about the global Communist conspiracy. Then a whole culture developed, from the film *Dr. Strangelove* to the novels *Fail-Safe* and *Seven Days in May*, suggesting that the biggest danger of a nuclear Armageddon was not the Soviet threat after all, but mad Americans misusing U.S. retaliatory capabilities.

The initial American overreaction led to serious policy consequences. Shorn of the emotionalism, the conventional wisdom of the day in the United States believed communism to be a unified military colossus, a world movement directed by orders from Moscow. Nothing could be further from the truth. Russia's appalling economic backwardness, the continuing power struggle in the Kremlin, the Soviet-Chinese split, and the breakaway movements in Eastern Europe, all well under way by the 1950s, would eventually expose the idea of global Communist unity and strength to be pure fiction.

Still, these signs were slow in developing. U.S. governments read them, unsure of the meaning. Were the splits in the Communist camp temporary or permanent, genuine or tactical? Prudence suggested preparing defenses against a maximum Communist threat. In the hysteria of the McCarthy era, that was the only politically viable option anyway. So Washington accepted the vision of Soviet power as a united global challenge. The perception was wrong.

Before turning to specific cases, it is important to see just how badly the American overview erred. The skewed vision of a united Communist world under direct orders from Moscow was wrong on both counts. The Communist movement was anything but united, and few besides Bulgaria slavishly followed Moscow's orders.

That led to two fundamental mistakes. First, it inflated the Soviet threat, at the same time underrating America's ability to respond. Second, it failed to see the most promising response option of them all, the divisions in the world Communist movement ripe for exploitation. A clear potential was there for manipulating these fault lines, for setting one faction against another until earthquakes split and destroyed the Communist movement. The United States, however, deterred by its exaggerated vision of Soviet power, was reluctant to get into this act.

Significantly, the Soviets showed no such reluctance, not even in the nuclear age. Throughout the Cold War, Moscow continually did its best to split the NATO alliance. Soviet leaders tried to set Europeans against Americans and Americans against Europeans on a wide range of political, economic, and military issues, from trade tensions to disputes over deploying U.S. intermediate-range nuclear missiles on European soil. They blatantly courted Charles de Gaulle to move France out of NATO's military wing. They supported ban-the-bomb marchers and unilateral disarmers from Britain to all corners of the continent. They alternately warmed up or cooled off, either with the Europeans or the Americans, trying to play one NATO ally against another.

In the end, they developed a no-lose policy that strained NATO ties no matter what happened. When Soviet-American relations were good, for example, Europeans worried that Moscow and Washington would build a condominium against Europe's interest. When Soviet-American relations were bad, Europeans worried that trigger-happy Americans might launch a war. Either way, Moscow profited by creating tensions within the Atlantic alliance.

All of it was nothing more than political mischief. Moscow understood perfectly well that this kind of manipulation could pay high political dividends at virtually no threat of escalation to war. NATO was not about to risk global nuclear annihilation just because the Kremlin meddled in alliance affairs. Once again, détente was proving to be a one-way street. If anything, opportunities for Western political mischief in the Communist alliance were even greater and the risk of escalating to serious conflict no higher. But the United States chose not to go that route. It left the field to the Soviets. The Americans preferred to believe Communist unity was a fact of life they could do nothing to change. That decision produced foreign policy mistakes that have harmed U.S. vital interests down to the present day, as the following case studies will make clear.

III. CHINA AND CUBA

China was the first, perhaps the most important, of America's fundamental foreign policy mistakes during the Cold War. In the late 1940s the U.S. government was backing the losing side in China's civil war, the nationalist dictator Chiang Kai-shek. John Service and other experienced American diplomats then in China accurately predicted that Mao Zedong would defeat Chiang and install a new kind of Communist regime in Beijing, independent of Stalin's control. The thrust of their reporting to Washington suggested that the United States move toward an accommodation with Mao, for two crucial reasons. First, it was important to improve ties with the winning side, and second, the United States could exploit the discord between Moscow and Beijing, which was growing even then. In the McCarthy-era atmosphere, however, when all Communists were regarded as Moscow's puppets, Service and others like him were disgraced as traitors for suggesting an approach toward Mao. Their advice was rejected. America chose instead to believe in the fiction of world Communist unity.

It was a costly error. Service turned out to be right. Had the United States recognized Mao after he took power in 1949, then helped establish him as a counterweight to Soviet expansion in Asia, the history of the last half century would have been very different. In that case, the Soviet-Chinese split would have dominated Asian politics from the early 1950s. The most serious danger of military conflict in the region would have been between the two Communist giants, China and the Soviet Union. Their mutual suspicion, in turn, would have prevented Moscow and Beijing from cooperating to push Communist expansion elsewhere in the region. There simply would not have been a joint Soviet-Chinese threat against American clients in Asia. With that, the Vietnam War, or at least the major rationale for involving U.S. forces in it, might well have been avoided.

Instead, the opportunity of 1949 was missed. It took the United States an additional thirty years to normalize relations with Mao and finally make Beijing an effective member of the global effort to contain Soviet expansion. Admittedly, there are many complex reasons why it took Washington so long, but none is more important than America's misguided belief in the myth of Communist unity.

This may look like hindsight, but it is not. The United States not only ignored the advice of its own diplomats on the ground in China in 1949, but also rejected the views of key allies when they soon reached similar conclusions. Britain and France, among others, saw the potential of playing the China card against Russia far earlier than Washington. Both established diplomatic relations with Mao's China long before the United States did. The Americans, handicapped by their flawed vision of Communist unity, were simply behind the curve at the time, as measured by the generally accepted international standards of the day.

Washington's error of judgment on Mao should not be minimized. His rise to power presented an unparalleled opportunity for the United States to weaken the world Communist movement and accelerate its demise decades earlier. Andrei Amalrik's apocalyptic prediction of Communist power collapsing in Russia before 1984, because of a losing war with China, might well have come true. It didn't even have to go to that extreme. Had the U.S.S.R. simply been forced to focus on a hostile China friendly to the United States, that alone would have immeasurably reduced the Soviet threat to the West for the last half century. Such was the room for maneuver the United States chose not to exploit.

Of course, it would have been difficult in 1949 to shift U.S. support from Chiang Kai-shek to Mao. America's anti-Communist mind-set of the day was against any such move. Still, this conventional wisdom could have been shown to be what it was—simplistic, ignorant of Soviet-Chinese differences, and wrong for America. Given the proper leadership, the United States had the option to change both public opinion and foreign policy. There was ample precedent for such a dramatic sea change. Throughout history, all great powers have reversed policy, turning yesterday's adversaries into today's allies, and vice versa. The United States is no exception. Its adversaries in World War II, Germany and Japan, became two of its key postwar allies. A vital U.S. partner in the alliance against Hitler, Stalin's Soviet Union, became America's long-term adversary after the war. All such policy changes are difficult and complex. They are possible, however, when policymakers have a clear vision of the national interest. Unfortunately, with China in 1949, U.S. vision got muddied.

Josef Stalin knew better. The Soviet dictator understood perfectly well that Mao was never Moscow's puppet and never would be. Stalin even had his doubts about the Chinese leader's ideological convictions, according to former Khrushchev adviser Fyodor Burlatsky. "When Stalin sent his first ambassador to China, he gave instructions to find out whether Mao was a Communist or what," Burlatsky told me. Apparently the United States was more confident about Mao's Communist credentials and loyalty to the world movement than Stalin himself.

The United States' mishandling of Mao established a pattern that was to repeat through the Cold War. The root cause, America's exaggerated view of Communist unity, led to many other missed opportunities over the years, but one such mistake stands out above all. It haunts the United States to this day. The Communist beachhead in Cuba, Washington's worst security nightmare in the Western hemisphere, was largely an American creation.

Fresh from his victory in the Cuban revolution, Fidel Castro turned first to the United States. He came to Washington in 1959 seeking recognition, trade, and aid. Dwight Eisenhower turned him down. The president was worried about Castro's Marxist background. To Eisenhower, that meant Castro was a Communist, and all Communists were essentially the same, agents of Moscow's global conspiracy.

Once again, America's mistaken belief in the myth of world Communist unity led to a major foreign policy mistake. The Eisenhower administration told Castro that if he wanted help from the United States, he should prove his democratic credentials by calling early national elections. "Why should I call elections?" Castro asked publicly at the time. "I am now the most popular man in Cuba by far. If I called an election tomorrow, I would win."[3] Castro thought Cuba didn't need elections. It needed trade and aid. If Washington would not supply them, there was only one other place to go. So Fidel Castro went to Moscow, but only after the Americans pushed him there.

The Russians certainly saw it that way. Georgi Korniyenko, the former Soviet first deputy foreign minister, told me so in a 1993 interview in Moscow. "I can confirm that for the Soviet side it looked like the Americans had made a big mistake pushing Castro toward us," Korniyenko said. "Our specialists had concluded that Castro was not a Communist. They were surprised by the American reaction. But Khrushchev was not unhappy about it. In 1961 while meeting Kennedy in Vienna, Khrushchev said that 'Castro isn't a Communist, but you will make him one.' Eventually, that proved to be true."

The implications of that statement are colossal. If America made Castro a Communist, then it was the United States that created both the Cuban missile crisis and the threat of Communist subversion in the Western hemisphere for the next thirty years. Such was the price to be paid for misreading Communist unity.

There can be little doubt that is precisely what the Americans did on Cuba. Khrushchev aide Burlatsky confirmed to me in a Moscow interview, also in 1993, Korniyenko's account of Castro. "The Americans made a big mistake with Castro," Burlatsky said. "Fidel was not a Marxist ideologue. He needed an economic partner for sugar and would have made an accommodation with Washington. Khrushchev had the feeling that from a Marxist-Leninist point of view, Castro was not a reliable revolutionary."

As with Mao, America's mishandling of Fidel Castro had grave long-term consequences for the United States. Had Eisenhower accommodated Castro with a sugar deal, Cuba would have been in the U.S. camp from 1959 on. The Soviet Union would have been deprived of its first and only important beachhead in Latin America. It would have lost the services of Cuban troops serving as Communist Gurkhas in Angola and other Third World trouble spots, doing some of Moscow's dirtiest work during the Cold War.

Admittedly, dealing with dictators is never easy for a democracy like the United States. Still, that is no excuse for the opportunities America wasted with Mao and Castro. Throughout the Cold War, the U.S. compromised on its principles and supported right-wing petty tyrants all over the world in the effort to halt the spread of communism. Pinochet in Chile, the shah of Iran, Mobutu in Zaire, and Marcos in the Philippines are but a few examples. Indeed, that policy is defensible. Where Washington went astray, however, was in its refusal to extend the same logic to cooperating with left-wing Communist dictators in an even better position to weaken the Soviet hand. Mao and Castro were not Moscow's puppets. They had their own agendas. With wiser American handling, either could have helped bury Soviet communism earlier.

IV. VIETNAM

Exaggerating Communist unity led to America's mistakes with Castro and Mao. Magnifying Moscow's ability to control or even influence other Communist nations proved to be an equally damaging U.S. error, and nowhere did that misjudgment prove more costly than in Vietnam.

Richard Nixon was elected president of the United States in 1968 largely because he claimed to have a "secret plan" to end the Vietnam War. In retirement, however, Nixon admitted no such plan existed before his election. Instead, his national security adviser and eventual secretary of state, Henry Kissinger, developed a strategy after Nixon took office for bringing the war to an end.

A key element of Kissinger's strategy was détente with the Soviet Union. One payoff of that policy was supposed to be Moscow's help in extricating the United States from Vietnam by pressuring Hanoi to the peace table. Kissinger pushed the Russians hard, but they never delivered. So his strategy failed, and, with it, the Nixon administration's effort to bring the Vietnam War to an early end. The strategy failed largely because Kissinger overestimated Moscow's control of the world Communist movement, in this case its ability to push North Vietnam toward peace. In reality, the Soviets had no such leverage in Hanoi.

After Nixon's reelection in 1972, he and Kissinger and, eventually, Gerald Ford did indeed end the Vietnam War. They did so by withdrawing U.S. combat troops on virtually the same terms that could have been obtained four years earlier. This delay, through Nixon's first term as president, cost 20,492 American lives in the continuing war and many times that figure in Vietnamese casualties. To a considerable extent, Kissinger's failed strategy was responsible.

Henry Kissinger was America's most overrated secretary of state, first of all by Kissinger himself. Future historians are unlikely to judge him as kindly as his own memories. Nowhere is he more vulnerable to criticism than in his handling of the Soviets in the endgame of the Vietnam War. To be fair to Kissinger, the original idea was Nixon's. In his 1968 presidential campaign, Nixon stressed that the Soviet Union "was the key" to settling the Vietnam conflict. At first Kissinger was skeptical, according to his biographer, Walter Isaacson, but later signed on enthusiastically to the notion that the road to peace with Hanoi ran through Moscow. Kissinger went that route by designing a policy known as "linkage."[4]

It was a typically complex, brilliant Kissinger concept. His various links between issues were all designed to push Moscow into pressing Hanoi toward peace. "We were determined to end the war in Vietnam and our overall relations with the Soviets depended on their help in settling that conflict," Kissinger wrote.[5] Linkage involved carrots and sticks. Carrots were rewards Moscow wanted, such as progress in trade or arms control talks with Washington. Sticks were pressures Moscow feared, such as the United States warming up to China at Soviet expense. Kissinger used both carrots and sticks to get Moscow's help in Hanoi.

As geopolitical strategic theory, it all made eminent sense. The practical reality was entirely different, however, as Kissinger himself eventually admitted. "On about ten occasions in 1969 in my monthly meetings with Dobrynin, I tried to enlist Soviet cooperation to end the war in Vietnam," Kissinger wrote in his memoirs. "Dobrynin was always evasive."[6] Despite all the carrots and sticks, however, as Kissinger himself later conceded, the Soviets "failed to exert a helpful pressure on the North Vietnamese."[7]

Significantly, nowhere in his lengthy memoirs does Kissinger get around to analyzing why the Soviets were never able to help out in Hanoi. The omission was no accident. It would have meant admitting his own emphasis on Moscow's influence had been misplaced. Indeed, as a historian himself, Henry Kissinger should have known better than to think the Soviets could push the North Vietnamese to an early peace.

Llewellyn Thompson, a two-time U.S. ambassador to Moscow, did know better. Thompson told me in 1967 there was no way the Soviets could pressure the North Vietnamese to the peace table before Hanoi was ready. Therefore any American effort to obtain Moscow's help with the North Vietnamese was wasted. Worse, any American concessions to the Soviets to enlist them in that cause were tantamount to giving away the store in a lost cause.

Thompson's reasoning was as follows. The North Vietnamese won their war against the French at Dien Bien Phu in 1954. Then they lost the peace at an international conference at Geneva in 1955. Under pressure from outside powers, Hanoi got less territory at the peace table than its forces had won on the battlefield. It was a mistake, the North Vietnamese decided, they would never make again. Not Moscow, not Beijing, no foreign power, would be able to push them to end the war with the Americans before they were ready, or press them to accept settlement terms they disliked. Thus asking Moscow to pressure Hanoi to peace was an exercise in futility.

In theory, Thompson conceded, Moscow did have leverage in Hanoi. The Soviets were major arms suppliers to the North Vietnamese. But in practice, there was little opportunity to play that card, because of the Soviet competition with China for leadership of the Communist world. Had the Russians threatened to withhold arms, for example, in an effort to push Hanoi toward peace, China would have crucified them for betraying the Communist cause, and then supplied the needed arms from Beijing. Once again, in Thompson's view, the bottom line held. Russian influence in Hanoi was sharply limited.

Ambassador Thompson turned out to be right. He relayed his thinking to Washington, correctly advising against pinning false hopes on Soviet help with the North Vietnamese. Henry Kissinger, who took office the following year, was among those who ignored Thompson's advice, and thereby prolonged the Vietnam War. Unfortunately, the consequences of that mistake went far beyond Vietnam. In the end, Kissinger's linkage policy helped Brezhnev turn détente into a one-way street to Moscow's advantage, and ultimately prolonged Communist power in Russia.

The key to Brezhnev's success was Moscow's ability to turn Kissinger's linkage policy against the United States. If the Americans wanted Soviet help in Hanoi, Brezhnev reasoned, then Washington would have to pay a price. Eventually, Kissinger himself recognized what was happening. In his memoirs, he cited an example where Moscow used leverage on Vietnam to push Washington into talks on strategic arms limitation on the schedule preferred by the Kremlin. "The Soviets," Kissinger wrote, "applied reverse linkage to us."[8]

Typically, however, the secretary minimized the damage his own policy caused. His reference to the problem of "reverse linkage" came in the context of a relatively minor issue, the timing of arms talks. In fact, the damage was far worse than Kissinger ever admitted. Brezhnev used reverse linkage across the spectrum of superpower relations, to enormous Soviet advantage, until the entire détente process was largely discredited. How that happened is worth examining.

In principle, détente was a good idea. The aim of lowering tensions between the superpowers and reducing the threat of nuclear war was certainly praiseworthy. The argument, however, was never over the intent, but rather on how to achieve it. Does each superpower make equal concessions to achieve mutual benefit? If not, which side gives up more or gains more? Needless to say, Leonid Brezhnev's version of détente made sure the balance heavily favored the Soviet side.

There was nothing subtle about it. Brezhnev never hid his intentions. He always claimed détente left Moscow free to conduct the biggest military buildup in world history, from humiliating inferiority to the United States at the time of the 1962 Cuban missile crisis to essential parity in little more than a decade. At the same time, Brezhnev's détente allowed Moscow to promote mischief in Third World trouble spots and to suppress human rights within the U.S.S.R. Brezhnev's way, however, was far from the only option. It did not have to be the version accepted by the United States.

On the contrary, Moscow needed détente more than Washington. The Soviets, as the weaker power, were always destined to get more benefit out of arms control, trade, and other détente agreements. That gave Henry

Kissinger, as architect of the Nixon-Ford era's foreign policy, leverage to extract a price from the Kremlin, and insist that détente become a genuinely equal, mutually beneficial process.

The principles of that approach were clear at the time. For example, in return for the détente benefits Moscow wanted, the United States could have demanded and won from the Soviet Union hard evidence of improved Soviet behavior on the world stage—such as curbing abuses in the arms buildup, Third World meddling, and human rights. Kissinger decided, however, not to go that route, not to pressure Moscow publicly on any of these counts. His priority was getting Soviet help in Hanoi to end the Vietnam War. So instead, Kissinger accepted the Brezhnev way to détente.

That decision, in the late 1960s and early 1970s, helped delay the collapse of Communist power in Russia by some twenty years. As we now know, by 1971, Brezhnev's economic policies were already bankrupting the U.S.S.R. The Kremlin was in no position then to challenge the United States or hold the world Communist movement together. Stronger U.S. pressure focusing world attention on Brezhnev's double game and demanding that he turn détente into a genuine two-way street could have forced profound internal change in the U.S.S.R. from Nixon's time in office, encouraging Gorbachev-era changes even then. Instead, by accepting Brezhnev's terms for détente, Kissinger inflated the Soviet leader's prestige at home, allowed him to extend the life of his nearly bankrupt regime and keep the lid on Soviet reform for another two decades.

V. AFGHANISTAN

America's mistakes in handling Mao, Castro, and the Vietnam peace negotiations were all caused by magnifying either the unity of the world Communist movement or Moscow's ability to direct it. The United States also made many other errors in response to the Soviet threat, difficult to pigeonhole in neat categories. One of them is examined in detail below because it kept escalating until the fallout was felt across the entire spectrum of superpower relations.

The problem looked relatively simple at first. In August 1979, the United States discovered the presence of a Soviet army brigade in Cuba. President Jimmy Carter wanted it out. Then Brezhnev sent Carter a message on the hot line, insisting the brigade was in Cuba for training purposes only, not combat, and was no threat to anyone. Brezhnev refused to withdraw it. Unhappy with that response, Carter sought at the very least further Soviet assurances that the brigade would not be reinforced, converted to combat, used elsewhere in the hemisphere, and so on. Cyrus Vance, his secretary of state, was told to negotiate a solution to this problem with the Soviet ambassador, Anatoly Dobrynin.

At the time, I was *Newsweek*'s chief diplomatic correspondent in Washington. A Vance aide who sat in on the talks with Dobrynin briefed me on them privately. According to him, Dobrynin kept insisting that Carter had Brezhnev's hot-line message on the brigade and that no further assurances were needed. Vance continued to press for a more positive response.

The talks dragged on for weeks. Soon the issue escalated into major political controversy in the United States. Eventually it turned U.S. public opinion against the SALT II treaty on nuclear arms limitation, which Carter and Brezhnev had signed in Vienna earlier in the year. Because of the mistrust touched off by the controversy over the Soviet brigade in Cuba, SALT II was never ratified by the U.S. Senate. Yet despite the importance of the issue, Vance's talks with Dobrynin were getting nowhere. Finally, Jimmy Carter lost patience. The White House announced the president would appear on nationwide television on October 1 and disclose America's response to the presence of the Soviet brigade in Cuba. The ambiguous wording suggested military action was a live option. At last, the Soviets changed their broken record to head off that possibility.

Dobrynin called on Vance with a new proposal. "The American side can interpret Brezhnev's assurances any way you like," the ambassador said. "And the Soviet side will not contradict you in public." Vance accepted. Carter went on television explaining that he had adequate assurances from Brezhnev, and that the Soviet brigade in Cuba was no longer a danger. The problem had been solved, the Carter administration thought, but, instead, it helped create a much bigger one.

Soviet leaders were delighted. They rightly viewed the settlement with Carter as a victory for the Kremlin. They got everything they wanted. Their brigade stayed in Cuba, they gave the Americans nothing, and the crisis was over. Brezhnev's arrogance only increased. He was more confident than ever that he could handle the Americans. Jimmy Carter, he decided, was a pushover. Only three months later, Brezhnev demonstrated his contempt for Carter, and his confidence that he could manage any adverse American reaction, by approving the Soviet invasion of Afghanistan.

When Carter protested the aggression, Brezhnev again showed his contempt by telling the president of the United States in effect to mind his own business. The Russian text of Brezhnev's December 29, 1979, letter to Carter, stamped "top secret," was obtained from Soviet archives for this book. It is remarkable for the lack of respect and diplomatic language normal in personal messages between world leaders. Instead Brezhnev bluntly told Carter the situation in Afghanistan "is solely the business of the U.S.S.R. and Afghanistan which are regulating their relations and obviously cannot allow any outside interference in them."

Needless to say, Carter's protests had fallen on deaf ears. Brezhnev had calculated correctly that an American president incapable of defending U.S. interests in a dispute as nearby as Cuba would be even less effective in a distant crisis like that in Afghanistan, literally on the Soviet doorstep. Indeed, the link between Brezhnev's success in outmaneuvering Carter on the Cuba brigade and his decision to invade Afghanistan is worth exploring further, because it demonstrates how one mistake in superpower relations can lead to a whole chain of serious consequences.

Afghanistan did not have to become a world problem. The Soviet Union enjoyed good relations with its Afghan neighbor until a revolution by local Marxists in Kabul overthrew the government in April 1978. Just how involved Moscow was in that coup d'état is still not completely clear, but in any event, from the coup on it was all downhill. The new left-wing Afghan leaders, weak and divided, fought powerful Muslim rebels and each other. Soon their regime was teetering on the brink of collapse.

The Soviet Politburo was not anxious to get more deeply involved. It suspected the new Kabul regime's Communist credentials, was wary of Western reaction, and feared getting into a Vietnam quagmire. Once-secret documents from Soviet archives now show that the Kremlin turned down fourteen separate requests from the Afghan Communist leadership to send in Soviet troops to save their regime. Then, in October 1979, Moscow began to change its mind.

That was the month Brezhnev outmaneuvered Carter on the Soviet brigade in Cuba. It was also the month a Soviet military delegation under General Ivan Pavlovsky, a deputy defense minister, returned from a fact-finding trip to Kabul with a recommendation that if the Kremlin wanted to save the pro-Communist regime in Afghanistan, it would have to intervene with Soviet troops. According to one Soviet account the first question asked in the Politburo was what the American reaction would be if Moscow intervened, and the answer was essentially "Don't worry, we can handle the Americans."

The Kremlin had just done exactly that over the Cuba brigade. No immediate decision was taken, however. The question was left in the hands of the "Afghan Troika" of three senior Politburo members—Defense Minister Dmitri Ustinov, KGB chief Yuri Andropov, and Foreign Minister Andrei Gromyko—for further evaluation.

Politburo documents until then show that all three consistently opposed intervening in Afghanistan with Soviet troops. Then, after October, something changed their minds, although exactly what their reasoning was has never been made clear officially. The Afghan Troika deliberated in strictest secrecy. No written record was taken of their consultations. Not even Georgi Korniyenko, Gromyko's longtime first deputy foreign minister, was told why his boss and the others in the troika changed their minds. All Korniyenko knows for sure is that after lunch on December 12, 1979, Gromyko,

Ustinov, and Andropov met with Brezhnev and Ideology Secretary Mikhail Suslov and agreed on the invasion. The full Politburo later agreed.

Korniyenko has made an educated guess, however, based on years of privileged conversations with Kremlin leaders and access to hundreds of secret documents. He thinks several factors were important. For example, Suslov and the ideologists saw a duty in propping up the pro-Communist regime in Kabul and a slap to Moscow's prestige throughout the world if such a regime on Soviet borders was allowed to fall. But Korniyenko thinks the crucial factor was something else. "The Soviet leadership gave great importance to the negative impact invading Afghanistan would have on our relations with the West," he explained to me, "and we had nothing much to lose there at the time."

By that Korniyenko meant that American reaction could be contained, as over the Cuba brigade, and if not, there was little more the United States could do then to harm vital Soviet interests. The SALT II treaty was already lost, so it could not be taken away in response to Afghanistan. Furthermore, NATO had just decided to install new U.S. intermediate-range nuclear missiles in Western Europe aimed at the U.S.S.R. In Moscow's view, no response to an Afghan invasion could hurt more. They were right. Jimmy Carter's toughest new reaction to the Soviet invasion of Afghanistan was his U.S. boycott of the 1980 Moscow Olympic Games.

VI. DEAD END

There is, of course, no way Carter's mishandling of the Soviet brigade in Cuba can be blamed for the invasion of Afghanistan. But clearly it was a prominent factor in Kremlin decision-making. One mistake by an American president had contributed to another much larger error by the leader of the Soviet Union.

Afghanistan turned out to be Leonid Brezhnev's biggest single foreign policy blunder. The war he launched there would last eight years and take thirteen thousand Soviet lives.[9] It drained an already collapsing Soviet economy, irreparably damaged the U.S.S.R.'s prestige throughout the world, and turned millions of once loyal Soviet citizens against the Kremlin. No other step in the Brezhnev years did more to weaken Communist power in Russia and hasten its eventual collapse.

Brezhnev's successors in the Kremlin would blame him for the Afghan debacle. He made the decision to invade Kabul. He focused on the short-term problem of managing American reaction rather than the long-term disaster of an unwinnable war. His arrogance convinced him Moscow could succeed in the quagmire of Afghanistan where the United States had failed in Vietnam. The real significance in the linkage between Carter's mistake on the Cuba brigade and Brezhnev's miscalculation on Afghanistan is one of scale.

Jimmy Carter's error was tactical. As a result he lost a battle in superpower relations. Brezhnev's mistake was strategic. It helped ensure that the Soviet Union would lose the Cold War. Ultimately, that difference in degree was all that mattered. Much the same can be said of the mistakes both superpowers made throughout the Cold War. The United States committed many errors in responding to the Soviet threat. Yet bad as they were, they often paled in comparison to the miscalculations on the Soviet side.

That thought is hardly comforting. No great power can assure its survival in the nuclear age by assuming the other side will always make the bigger mistakes. To improve security in the decades ahead, America will have to learn from the mistakes of both sides during the Cold War. One good place to start is with a better understanding of how the Cold War really ended.

It is not good enough to say the West won that struggle and the Soviets lost it. The real questions are why the Cold War ended the way it did, and whether the same outcome could have been produced decades earlier, at far less suffering around the world, and with no risk of nuclear war. The answers to those questions are already clear enough to draw the appropriate lessons for the future.

The West won the Cold War because for forty years the United States led the NATO alliance through a determined resistance to the Soviet threat. It was a long, hard slog. As Denis Healey, Britain's former defense secretary, once told me in London, "All the Red Army needed in 1945 to march across Western Europe to the Atlantic was boots." Had the United States abandoned West Europeans to their own defenses, had the allies not contributed sufficiently to the common cause, Western Europe could have fallen under Communist rule. At the same time, the NATO allies kept alive the alternate model of democratic, free-market societies that worked and progressed, for the Soviet-dominated peoples to see and envy. The Communists even built a wall in Berlin to keep their people from voting with their feet.

American leadership of NATO was a truly outstanding performance by presidents of both parties, from Truman to Reagan, and their foreign policy teams. They had the courage and the wisdom to ensure the survival of the United States and its allies through the hellishly dangerous and complex issues of superpower rivalry in the nuclear age. The overall U.S. policy cannot be faulted. It was right, and it worked in bringing the Soviet threat to an end. Nothing American leadership accomplished or could have accomplished in the last half century was more important.

Still, the rest of the U.S. record is less comforting. The United States also made enormous mistakes in responding to the Soviet threat, including those recounted here. None of them risked national survival, but all of them missed opportunities to end the Cold War earlier. None was more important than allowing Brezhnev to dictate the terms of the détente for eighteen years. Had the United States seized the initiative instead and set the détente rules for Brezhnev, Communism in Russia might not have survived the 1970s. There was no need to risk nuclear war. Only wiser diplomacy was needed. That was where America fell down. The United States could have done much better if, for example, it had only been listening to China. Unlike America, China saw through Brezhnev—at the time. China could have shown America how to respond far more effectively to the Soviet threat, but, unfortunately, Washington and Beijing were not even talking then, another missed opportunity.

As a military power, the Chinese were immeasurably weaker than the Soviet Union. The Russians were right across their border, a nuclear and conventionally armed colossus, and yet unlike the distant Americans, the Chinese never panicked at the Soviet threat. Indeed, proximity was the secret of their greater wisdom in handling the U.S.S.R. The Chinese had centuries of experience in dealing with a Russian neighbor. They knew far better than the Americans when to take Soviet threats seriously. The Chinese understood that Brezhnev's bluster was hollow, and, like the "paper tiger" they called him, the Soviet leader could not hurt them. In truth, the Chinese understood, the stronger Russians feared them. "The Soviets could get here in four days by tank or one day by air," a Chinese professor told me during a visit to Beijing in 1978. "If they weren't afraid of us they would have attacked us long ago."

The Soviets didn't attack because getting into China was the easy part. Getting out alive was the hard part. Even the entire heavily armed four-million-man Soviet military was no match for the Chinese population of 900 million people who would resist them. Then too, Soviet invaders would have to depend on supplies coming on a single-track railroad stretching four thousand miles along a border vulnerable to Chinese attack. In the Kremlin, an invasion of China by conventional forces looked like a suicide mission. Nuclear weapons were no answer either. If used on China, they would send deadly radioactive waste over Japan, risking military reprisals against the Soviet Union from Tokyo's American ally. In short, Moscow was not about to attack Beijing.

With little to fear, the Chinese adopted a particularly tough stance against the Soviets. If Moscow wanted better relations with Beijing, the Soviets would have to make the concessions China demanded. Until then, the Chinese would forgo trade and other cooperation with Russia. They would compete with the Soviets for influence in the Communist movement and the Third World. Meanwhile, there would be no limits on China's brutally anti-Soviet rhetoric. Compared to its own unbending posture, China saw U.S. policy toward the Soviet Union as weak, fearful, counterproductive, and totally inexplicable, given America's unsurpassed power.

"We sense a certain fear of the Russians in the West," Chinese Deputy Foreign Minister Wang Shu told me in Beijing in a 1978 interview. "It is useless to be merely afraid. Negotiating disarmament with them, supplying them with food grains and new technology, will not deter them from attacking you anyway. For a decade, the Soviet Union has preached détente and disarmament while it arms and prepares aggression. Has this been more to their advantage or yours?"

Wang's answer to his own question was that America would be better off learning from China's tougher approach. "You should remember that a strong China is in the interests of the United States and a strong America is in the interests of China. The Russian bear is a threat to us both."

Of course, the United States had even less to fear from the Soviets than China did, and even more opportunity to push Brezhnev toward concessions. China's long experience in dealing with its Russian neighbor could have provided wise counsel in Washington for any such effort. Unfortunately, however, the Americans were not even listening to the Chinese for thirty years. Had they been, they might have won the Cold War earlier.

The lessons from such foreign policy mistakes have to be drawn now. In future confrontations against stronger adversaries, the price of missing opportunities to take the initiative and right the balance could well be survival. With the Soviet Union, the United States and its allies were very fortunate indeed. In that confrontation they faced mediocre minds like Brezhnev, following policies that would sooner or later self-destruct. They could afford to waste opportunities, to sit back and wait. In the next global challenge that may not be possible.

Just how the United States might handle future threats, from Russia or anywhere else, is discussed in the final chapter of this book. That analysis is saved for last so that the policies of Gorbachev and Yeltsin can be factored in as well. For the moment, it is enough to consider Brezhnev's legacy here.

Leonid Ilyich died in blissful ignorance. He never learned the full extent of his folly. His insistence on détente as a one-way street, benefiting the Soviet Union at the expense of all other nations, eventually offended every other major power in the world, and pushed them all into strategic cooperation against his country, isolating it more than ever.

With Japan, Brezhnev wasted his best chance to build the Soviet Union into a leading economic power. His refusal to negotiate the return of Japan's Kurile Islands, seized by Russia during World War II, doomed any chance that Tokyo would provide the huge capital needed to develop Siberia's vast resources. No other Soviet asset had such economic potential. No country other than Japan had both the money and the proximity to do the job. Instead, Brezhnev drove Japan into normalizing relations with Communist China.

With China, Brezhnev could have halted the split that divided the world Communist movement into two camps. As the stronger power by far, it was up to the U.S.S.R. to make the first concessions. Stubbornly, Brezhnev refused to budge. China's hostility only increased as a result. Eventually Beijing normalized relations with both Japan and the United States. Their three-way anti-Soviet coalition tipped the power balance in Asia against Moscow to an unprecedented degree.

In Western Europe, Brezhnev called for peace and friendship. What he really wanted was Western trade, aid, and technology transfers and a split in NATO, while conducting inside the U.S.S.R. the biggest military buildup in history. Then he invaded Czechoslovakia, and even those on the far left in Britain, France, and Italy realized his double game.

With the United States, Brezhnev preached cooperation rather than confrontation. In practice he went right on supporting Communist uprisings around the world, threatening U.S. interests from Asia to the Middle East to Latin America. At the same time, none of the arms control agreements he negotiated with Washington put a stop to his relentless military buildup. As former U.S. defense secretary Harold Brown put it: "We build. They build. We stop. They build." Later rather than sooner, the United States also rejected Brezhnev's vision of détente as a one-way street.

No nation can attempt to bully the rest of the world forever. Eventually that policy reaches a dead end. The Soviet Union got there, literally, with the death of Leonid Brezhnev in 1982. By then Brezhnev had driven Japan, China, the United States, and Western Europe together in a global coalition against him. His military buildup had bankrupted his nation. But despite that enormous sacrifice, the balance of forces now lined up against the Soviet Union was stronger than ever.

Worse, the Communist hold on Eastern Europe and Russia itself was beginning to crumble. Brezhnev's immediate successors, fellow members of his ruling gerontocracy, were too old and ill even to begin addressing the colossal problems Brezhnev left behind. Neither Yuri Andropov nor Konstantin Chernenko lasted much more than a year in power. Both their reigns would be mere footnotes in Soviet history, the last hurrah of the old guard. Brezhnev's effective heir would be the youngest member of his Politburo, Mikhail Sergeyevich Gorbachev. And with his rise to the top Kremlin leadership, at the age of fifty-four, a revolution was well under way.

PART III

Mikhail Sergeyevich Gorbachev

(1985–1991)

11

Reform from the Top Down:
Perestroika (1985–88)

I. MAN OF THE DECADE

Mikhail Sergeyevich Gorbachev led his country from Communist dictatorship to democratic elections, and from Marxist central planning to a free-market economy. In the process, he brought the Cold War to a peaceful end. Gorbachev did it all in only six years. Before him, none of the world's foremost experts on the Soviet Union thought any of that was possible in this century.

Most Russians today, still suffering through a difficult transition, believe Gorbachev changed their nation for the worse. Most foreigners think he changed the world for the better. It may take decades before Mikhail Sergeyevich's place in history can be fully evaluated. Much will depend on whether democracy takes hold permanently in Russia, confirming Gorbachev's greatness, or whether dictatorship soon returns, leaving him diminished, as only a brief reformist exception to a thousand years of despotic rule. That choice, however, will be determined by his successors.

Thus it is not too soon to make a preliminary assessment of Gorbachev's own years in office, the legacy he left behind until now. There the record is already clear. It shows that despite numerous mistakes, some very human flaws, and nearly impossible odds against him, Mikhail Sergeyevich accomplished more than any other statesman in the world during the last half of the twentieth century. Just how Gorbachev achieved so much and why he failed to do even more is examined in the chapters that follow. It is an incredible story of exceptional resourcefulness, as Mikhail Sergeyevich continually rebounded from seeming defeat to devise yet another tactic that would give his reforms yet another chance of success.

The key to that *tour de force* lay in his personal character. Only someone with enormous inner strength, uncanny political instinct, and an extraordinary ability to learn could have raised himself from a country bumpkin to master of the Kremlin. The Gorbachev of today still reveals his remarkable rise from humble origins every time he speaks. His Russian is full of grammatical mistakes, and the accent of a provincial rube, which sophisticated Muscovites love to ridicule. His charm, energy, and intelligence overcame that handicap, however, as effortlessly as they did other obstacles in his way. Mikhail Sergeyevich had a wealth of natural gifts, and he used them all well, from early youth onward.

Like everyone else who grew up in Stalin's Russia, Gorbachev learned very early to keep his innermost thoughts to himself. As a student, and later as a young Communist official, Mikhail Sergeyevich enthusiastically supported the Kremlin line of the day. Any reservations, hesitations, or unconventional ideas he harbored remained private. He could not be blind to the horrors around him, but he knew overt dissent would be suicidal. Closet progressives like Gorbachev convinced themselves the best way to change the country for the better was to work inside the Party, where all the power lay, rather than to tilt uselessly at windmills outside it. So they kept quiet, worked their way up the career ladder, and waited for an opportunity to act. The right political timing, they knew, was crucial. At first their inner thoughts focused on correcting Stalin's worst perversions. Only later did they dare think of more fundamental change. Even when he took over as Soviet leader, Gorbachev had to mask the true extent of his reform intentions from his Politburo colleagues if he and his changes were to survive. Fortunately, by then he was ready. Mikhail Sergeyevich had been preparing for that ultimate act of political deception all his adult life.

A potential army of supporters had led similar double lives. These were not dissidents in the Sakharov mold, speaking out for democratic change. Instead they were Soviet officials, academics, editors, diplomats, and ordinary citizens, outwardly supporting the Kremlin line but inwardly thinking how to change it if a real opportunity ever arose. Although they were a small minority of the total population, they had enough intellectual influence to make a major difference. Individually, they kept the Khrushchev era's spark of reform alive through the long Brezhnev retrenchment, if only in their own minds, waiting for a progressive new leader to emerge. Many of them would eventually play significant roles in the administration of Mikhail Gorbachev, shaping and implementing his changes.

No small measure of Gorbachev's success stems from the fact that when he was at last ready to act, so were they. Eduard Shevardnadze, who helped Gorbachev devise his policy of perestroika ("restructuring"), and Aleksandr Yakovlev, the father of glasnost ("openness"), are but two that come to mind. There were hundreds of others who played key supporting roles around the country. Mikhail Sergeyevich was never a soloist. Eventually he would become a conductor, but until he did, the rest of the orchestra members each practiced separately.

Some of the future Gorbachev advisers could be relatively bold during the long waiting game. One of them, Abel Aganbegyan, headed a team of liberal economists at a research institute in the remote Siberian city of

Novosibirsk, where they were frustrated by demands from the Brezhnev regime to justify wrongheaded policies. The portly Aganbegyan would gather his young colleagues around the dinner table. Then, in a public toast quite brave for the early 1970s, he would say of the aged Kremlin leadership, "Comrades, we shall outlive them."

Gorbachev himself was not among the bolder ones. Instead, Mikhail Sergeyevich, with his superb sense of political timing, waited until challenging the system became safer. He could rightly be called a late bloomer in the reformist cause. At Moscow State University, for example, Gorbachev chose to study law. At the time, Stalin still ruled. Soviet law was a travesty of justice, epitomized by the Vyshinsky show trials. Young people like Gorbachev who chose law in those days were heading for a Party careerist track which required them to be anything but liberal. Genuine reformists went into fields like physics where there was less ideological control.

Nor was Gorbachev just another law student. Even then he was already active in the Komsomol, the Communist youth organization, and played an active role in getting students suspected of disloyalty to the Party expelled from the university. Later, as Soviet president leading the charge for perestroika, Mikhail Sergeyevich tried to improve his youthful reformist credentials. In November 1991 he received in the Kremlin the sculptor Ernst Neizvestny, a leading dissident in the Khrushchev years. The two men were about the same age, although they had led very different lives. Neizvestny explained why he had become a dissident. Then Gorbachev said to him, "I became a dissident in 1953, when I had my first doubts that things were right in our country."[1]

In truth, Gorbachev did nothing of the kind. Whatever he may have thought in 1953, the year of Stalin's death, Mikhail Sergeyevich certainly did not become a dissident. In those days, active or even suspected opponents of the regime still got shot. Far from becoming a dissident then, Gorbachev remained a convinced Party loyalist. It is perhaps no surprise that in later years, in his writings and in leaks through his aides, Gorbachev tried to revise history and turn himself into a lifelong reformist.

Still, the weight of the evidence points the other way. Zdenek Mlynar, a Czech Communist who roomed with Gorbachev in law school until 1955, says, "He, like everyone else at the time, was a Stalinist." In fact, Mikhail Sergeyevich was able to rise through Party ranks to the top precisely because no one could ever seriously question his loyalty. Never was there the slightest hint of dissent on his part. It is one of the ironies of communism that only the true believers last long enough to change the system. Or as Mlynar shrewdly put it, "In order to be a true reforming Communist, you have to have been a true Stalinist."[2]

Naturally, it was not that simple. Gorbachev's unquestioned loyalty to the Party line would be crucial in his later success. But so too was his double life, his willingness to listen to other opinions critical of the Communist dogma of the day, his ability to think them through for himself, and his determination to use them when the time was right. In sixteen years as a leading Party official in his native city of Stavropol, in southern Russia, Mikhail Sergeyevich did just that. He was one of the few provincial leaders receptive to critical ideas. Gorbachev managed the double life because he always knew where to draw the line. Whenever necessary he would shut off the channel to liberal thinking and play the Party loyalty card. Two examples make this clear—his law school roommate and his wife.

Zdenek Mlynar, Gorbachev's law school roommate, took the road to reform much earlier. By 1968, Mlynar was a secretary of the Czechoslovak Communist Party and a key ally of Alexander Dubček in the Prague Spring. He was also a reformist influence on Gorbachev. The two old friends had often discussed progressive ideas, long after law school. Mlynar made several visits to Russia. He last saw Gorbachev in Stavropol in 1967, when, he said, Mikhail Sergeyevich privately declared himself in favor of more independence for the Soviet Union's East European allies.[3]

Publicly, at the time, Gorbachev never deviated from the Kremlin line on Eastern Europe. That soon proved to be the wisest course for him. In August 1968, Brezhnev's tanks crushed Dubček's reforms. One year later, Gorbachev, as a loyal Brezhnev supporter, was included for the first time on an official Soviet delegation abroad. He went to Prague, saw for himself what Soviet tanks had done, then kept his inner feelings hidden. At the time, his old friend Mlynar still lived in the Czech capital, but, significantly, Gorbachev made no attempt to see him. Contact with one of the disgraced Dubček team would fail the Soviet loyalty test. Mikhail Sergeyevich's career priorities at the time would not permit that.

Instead, Gorbachev waited twenty years, until he took over the top Kremlin leadership himself, before he at last denounced the Soviet invasion of Prague and welcomed Dubček to Moscow as a reformist hero. In retrospect, the earlier hypocrisy now looks like the act of a consummate politician. Only Gorbachev's caution in Prague in 1969 allowed him to survive, reach the top, and courageously make amends in Moscow in 1989.

Like Mlynar, Gorbachev's wife, Raisa, was a positive influence on his intellectual growth. As a sociologist, with broad contacts in the academic world, she introduced her husband to some of the more progressive minds outside the sterile thinking of the Party. Again, as with Mlynar, the Gorbachev sponge soaked that in and stored it. Again, as with Mlynar, he knew when to bury the outside influence and focus instead on the ladder up the Party hierarchy.

Mikhail Sergeyevich was superb at flattering older men. He took his vacations at the side of Yuri Andropov. He praised Leonid Brezhnev's "moral strength," "philosophical skill," and "talent for leadership of the Leninist type." The subservience paid off. In May 1978, Gorbachev was brought to Moscow, put in charge of agriculture, and, at age forty-seven, made the only member of the Politburo under fifty. All he had to do then was work hard, avoid unnecessary risks, and let the clock tick. Seven years later, his moment finally came. Brezhnev, Andropov, and Chernenko were all dead. In the words of Aganbegyan's toast, Gorbachev had outlived them all. He was ready for the supreme test, the first contender of his generation for the top job of Communist Party general secretary.

Still, even though he was the likely "heir apparent," the succession struggle was never easy for Gorbachev. On the contrary, had Mikhail Sergeyevich not been a younger man in a hurry—and at the same time a master at political maneuver—he might never have become leader of the Soviet Union. Indeed, when the decisive moment came, Gorbachev was not the first choice of the aging Politburo majority.

Konstantin Chernenko died at 7:20 P.M. on March 10, 1985. Once again, the Brezhnev old guard had the power to choose his successor. Only the ten members then left on the ruling Politburo could make that decision. Of crucial importance, six of them—the clear majority—were men in their seventies and eighties, the last holdovers of the Brezhnev regime. They had the votes to choose one of their own as the Kremlin's next leader, just as they had done only thirteen months before when they selected Chernenko to succeed Yuri Andropov. This time, however, Gorbachev, the youngest Politburo member at age fifty-four, never gave them the chance.

For the final weeks of Chernenko's illness, Gorbachev had been chairing the Politburo's Thursday meetings as deputy leader. The number two role gave him a unique opportunity. The scheduling of Politburo meetings was his call. Gorbachev immediately seized that advantage, knowing he might never again have one as good. Only three hours after Chernenko died, at 10:30 P.M. the same evening, Mikhail Sergeyvich called the Politburo together in the Kremlin to decide on the succession. His speedy action made it impossible for three old-guard members to attend on time.

Vladimir Shcherbitsky, the Ukrainian leader, was traveling in the United States. Vitaly Vorotnikov, premier of the Russian Federation, was on a trip to Yugoslavia. Dinmukhamed Kunayev, the Party leader in Kazakhstan, was in his capital city, Alma-Ata, and could not reach Moscow until the following day. It is likely that all three of them would have voted against Gorbachev. Without them, the old-guard majority of six to four on the Politburo had suddenly become a minority of three to four. The new math made all the difference. The hurriedly called late-night Politburo meeting decided Gorbachev would take over, at a ceremonial session the following day. The outmaneuvered old Brezhnevites had no alternative but to make the best of it. They agreed to present a facade of unity to the world.

Thus orchestrated, the formalities at the Politburo meeting the next day, March 11, 1985, were harmonious. Only Gorbachev was nominated to succeed Chernenko. Then he was unanimously elected general secretary. The transcript of this meeting, once stamped "top secret" but now available in

Soviet archives, is quite revealing, despite the staged circumstances. Gorbachev's first words as general secretary to his Politburo comrades were these: "First of all I want to say the most important thing is that our Politburo meeting today is proceeding in a spirit of unity. We are living through a very complicated time of change. Our economy needs more dynamism. This dynamism needs our democracy. . . . without an atmosphere of mutual understanding in the Politburo nothing can be accomplished."[4] Those few words encapsulated the struggle that would last through the Gorbachev era. The Politburo "unity" Mikhail Sergeyevich stressed was a nonstarter. There was no way it could survive even his first day as leader.

Gorbachev was committed to economic and political reform. He told his comrades just that, up front, in his call for more economic dynamism and more democracy. Yet the old guard still held the Politburo majority, six votes out of ten on any key decision. They might not have been able to stop his assent to the Communist Party's top job, but they could still block or at least slow down every one of his proposed reforms. Worse for Mikhail Sergeyevich, if they decided he had gone too far, they could invoke the Khrushchev precedent and throw him out. There would be no unity in the Soviet leadership under Gorbachev. Instead there would be constant struggle.

Mikhail Sergeyevich had expected that. He knew what he had to do. He would learn from Khrushchev's mistakes. Khrushchev had been the first great Soviet reformer, Gorbachev would be the second. Only this time, Mikhail Sergeyevich would do a better job of protecting his political rear, and avoid Khrushchev's fate. Or at least he would try. That was a dangerous course, Gorbachev understood, but he felt compelled to launch reforms despite the risks. Fundamental change was essential, Mikhail Sergeyevich believed, if the U.S.S.R. was to survive as a global power.[5]

That meant an incredibly delicate balancing act. The reforms would have to be deep, broad, irreversible. They could not be the quick fixes that Khrushchev tried. At the same time, the Communist Party elite would have to be persuaded that the changes would strengthen the system rather than destroy it, and that in the end Party privileges would be preserved. The task was enormous, but no one else was better equipped to undertake it than Gorbachev.

He radiated energy and self-confidence. In one-on-one meetings, he was superb, with a concentrated eye contact that made a visitor feel like the most important person in the world for that moment. Gorbachev played many roles superbly well in selling himself and his policies. He could be alternately tough and charming; "A man with a nice smile and iron teeth," Gromyko said. In many ways, Mikhail Sergeyevich was a better actor than Ronald Reagan, while at the same time more intelligent and harder-working. Often Russians and foreigners came away from their first encounter with Gorbachev convinced that they had just met a giant of a man, so intoxicating was the aura of power he displayed. Later they would be surprised to learn he was actually only five feet ten inches tall.

Mikhail Sergeyevich firmly believed he could convince anyone of anything, given adequate time. Such were his powers of persuasion. Often he brought conservative Communist doubters around by reminding them that Brezhnev had reached a dead end, that reform was inevitable, and then asking: "If not me, who? If not now, when?"

Above all, Gorbachev was able to present himself as a defender of the faith. He constantly said he believed in communism, but that Brezhnev had proved the system had to change or die. Gorbachev insisted the only viable alternative was a third way between communism and capitalism, somehow blending the best of both. Instead of fighting democracy and market economics, the Communists should adopt and control them. Even the Brezhnev old guard conceded some change was necessary if the crumbling system was to survive. So they agreed to give Gorbachev a chance. Had he not been a dedicated Communist, however, a persuasive true believer, they never would have let him change anything.

Mikhail Sergeyevich himself had no illusions. He knew better than anyone that the conservative Politburo majority kept him on a short leash, limiting his room for maneuver. Gorbachev was no absolute ruler like Peter the Great, able to launch reform on his own. Unlike Tsar Peter, Gorbachev had to carry a hostile Politburo. That was only one factor ensuring his struggle would be long and difficult. Another was that when Gorbachev started, he had no long-term plan of specific steps in mind. All he had was a compass, and the conviction that the direction he must take was toward reform, no matter what the risks. "That is my destiny," he told his wife, Raisa, on the first evening he came home as general secretary. "We cannot continue living in the old way."[6]

Gorbachev might have made it easier on himself. Given good health, the new Soviet leader could expect to rule another twenty years by simply extending the Brezhnev pattern of stability, avoiding all risks of reform. True, the overall economy would continue to decline, but the Party elite were shielded from that by lavish housing, fully stocked stores, Western-level medical care, and many special privileges. The key to a long, rewarding, peaceful life at the top for Mikhail Sergeyevich was to change nothing at all. The Party faithful would have supported him, to safeguard their own considerable perks, and the KGB would have silenced any dissent. Instead, the new general secretary decided to risk everything, including the top Kremlin job he had finally won, by embarking on a struggle for fundamental reform. That choice alone is a sign of his greatness. So are his reasons for making it.

Anatoly Chernyayev, one of Gorbachev's two top political advisers, explained a key reason to me during a long interview in November 1991. He had first met Mikhail Sergeyevich in 1972, and had watched him closely ever since. Chernyayev worked in the Party's Central Committee building on Moscow's Staraya (Old) Square, where most of the key decisions affecting life in the Soviet provinces were made. He remembered seeing the young Gorbachev there on regular business trips from Stavropol. Like other provincial leaders, Mikhail Sergeyevich often had to call on senior officials at the center for help in the frontline effort to make communism work better in his region. Invariably, province chiefs like Gorbachev got little understanding in Moscow, let alone help.

"I would see him leaving the office of some high official," Chernyayev recalled. "He was always angry and dejected. When I asked him why, he replied, 'You come to this place, you talk to these officials, but they won't listen and you can't do anything.' From the very beginning, I thought this was an intensely moral man, who was angry because he felt enormous responsibility for the people." According to Chernyayev, when Gorbachev finally got the chance, he was determined to improve the system.

That account is, of course, self-serving. One of Chernyayev's jobs was to make his boss look good, and in that he always delivered. Nonetheless, his account contains some truth. One of the reasons Gorbachev often said that "we cannot go on like this" and insisted on reform was his long frustration, first in the provinces and then in Moscow, trying to get things done. Lesser men gave up attempting to improve the system. Gorbachev refused to quit.

Georgi Shakhnazarov, Gorbachev's other top political adviser, supplied another reason for the crucial decision to risk reform. According to him, Mikhail Sergeyevich saw no viable alternative. In a separate interview with me, Shakhnazarov claimed Gorbachev got his first look at the definitive KGB assessment of Soviet economic health only on becoming general secretary. Earlier, the full extent of the nation's economic malaise had been hidden from him, even as a Politburo member. According to Shakhnazarov, the top-secret economic report showed that Brezhnev's policies were bankrupting the nation, that unless it changed course and undertook fundamental economic reform the Soviet Union could not continue as a superpower into the twenty-first century. The risks of doing nothing could no longer be ignored.

Thus the difficult choice Gorbachev faced on taking over as Soviet leader boiled down to this: if he embarked on fundamental reform, he risked short-term political disaster for himself, the same fate as Khrushchev; if he did nothing, he risked long-term economic disaster for the nation. A lesser man would have taken the easier course of less personal risk and changed nothing. Gorbachev, in another sign of greatness, opted for the harder road.

Just how extraordinarily difficult that choice looked at the outset is worth recalling. In the first place, Gorbachev had no road map to follow. No leader of any country had successfully transformed a Stalinist command economy into a workable modern system. There was no precedent for the kind of change Mikhail Sergeyevich was undertaking, not even rough guidelines. Abroad, efforts to reform Communist economies, from Eastern Europe to China, were too new and unsure to serve as guides. At home in Russia, the only reform models were Khrushchev's and Kosygin's, and they helped only in a negative sense. Both showed that modest tinkering at the edges of the existing system was not good enough. This time, more fundamental change would be essential for any hope of success. But without a reliable road map available, either at home or from abroad, Mikhail Sergeyevich was flying blind.

In the second place, the task of reforming the Soviet system, as Gorbachev suspected even then, might prove to be politically impossible. Sooner or later he would have to challenge the conservative majority on the Politburo in order to push through meaningful reform. And rather than accept that, they still had the power to get rid of him instead. Khrushchev's fate could never be far from Gorbachev's mind.

In the third place, even modest reforms risked opening a Pandora's box, whetting public appetites for deeper and wider change until the process could no longer be controlled from the top by Gorbachev and his team, opening the way for their downfall. If the conservatives in the Politburo didn't do Mikhail Sergeyevich in, then the radicals and anti-Communists in society at large might do the job for them.

Finally, in the fourth place, any rational economic transformation requires a long-term strategy that can be published and held up as a yardstick to measure and coordinate progress. Yet that was something Gorbachev could not afford to do. It would tip off his political enemies in advance, allowing them to rally and defeat him. So instead, Mikhail Sergeyevich had to move by fits and starts, by sleight of hand and *faits accomplis,* which by definition would never produce the rational economic transformation needed. Gorbachev couldn't announce in advance how far he wanted to go down the reform road or the specific steps he had in mind to get there. Even his closest collaborators were kept in the dark. "I will go a very long way in reform," he told Chernyayev at the outset, "farther than even you can imagine."

At that point, not even Mikhail Sergeyevich himself understood where reform would take him. As Shakhnazarov told me, "None of the great reformers in history—not Peter the Great, not Franklin Roosevelt—none of them could foresee all the results of their actions." Like them, Gorbachev would go for reform only because he knew it to be the right course. Confident that his judgment was correct and his abilities would serve him well, the Soviet leader plunged ahead into an unknowable future.

Everyone recognized Mikhail Sergeyevich's abilities, even his critics.

Probably the most telling reproach came from General Dmitri Volkogonov, a historian and a Yeltsin adviser, who summed up Gorbachev's first five years of leadership this way: "A person who tries to accommodate everyone may, in the end, not accommodate anyone."[7] Volkogonov's phrase was both a compliment and an astute prediction.

Gorbachev did indeed try to accommodate almost everyone, and rightly so, at least at first. Only an extraordinary political operator like Mikhail Sergeyevich could have placated both Soviet reformers and their conservative opponents through years of controversy to produce the political miracle he did—a transition toward democracy and market economics in Russia without a civil war. Naturally no political leader can always satisfy all the competing forces swirling round him. Eventually, Gorbachev's attempts to accommodate everyone involved delaying or reversing too many key decisions. With each twist and turn, with every evasion of hard choices, Mikhail Sergeyevich lost key supporters, until, as Volkogonov had foreseen, the effort to placate all sides ultimately left Gorbachev without a sufficient power base and forced his resignation. That long process will be detailed in the chapters which follow. For the moment it is sufficient to note here that Gorbachev's constant attempts at accommodation turned him into a leader of disturbing contradictions.

Those contradictions start with his commitment to two mutually exclusive goals, strengthening communism and genuine reform. His long refusal to choose between them made each harder to achieve. Further contradictions arise in assessing Gorbachev's historic role. The reader will see Gorbachev hailed as a great man, then criticized for mistakes that brought down his presidency and destroyed the Soviet Union. Both assessments, I believe, are correct. This particular contradiction can be resolved by admitting that even the most outstanding leaders in history have very human faults which lead them to monumental errors.

Other contradictions remain more troubling. Among them, Gorbachev is seen now as a hero abroad and a traitor at home. Once again, both of these opposing assessments have merit. This time, however, they need to be examined more fully if the West is to understand better where today's Russia is heading.

Foreigners praise Gorbachev for ending the Cold War. There is little doubt that, as seen from abroad, his greatest successes were in foreign affairs. As one reflection of this, *Time* magazine proclaimed him "Man of the Decade" in its issue of January 1, 1990, an accolade it had never awarded to Winston Churchill, Franklin Roosevelt, or any of the other great men of the century. The trouble with such hero worship is that it minimizes the deep emotional resentment Russians themselves harbor toward Gorbachev and his reforms, and in so doing distorts the political realities on the ground in the former Soviet Union. Western governments would be well advised to pay more attention to these Russian views. They will help determine whether the Kremlin of tomorrow promotes democracy or dictatorship, peace or aggression.

Gorbachev's reform legacy is in deep political trouble in Russia because both conservatives and progressives there regard it as a betrayal, although for very different reasons. Conservatives say Mikhail Sergeyevich ended the Cold War by selling out to the West, among other things by allowing Germany to reunite in NATO. They blame his internal policies, such as his mishandling of minority nationality unrest, for the breakup of the U.S.S.R. They also blame Gorbachev for Westernizing their country and weakening it economically in the process, for turning their nation from a proud superpower into a charity case with a hand out for foreign aid. They say they would never vote him into another presidential term.

Progressives blame Gorbachev for not going far enough and fast enough down the path of radical reform. They say his continued commitment to communism crippled reform, weakening the chances for a successful transition to a free-market economy and a stable democracy. They say they would never vote for him either, even though they admit they have yet to find a candidate likely to do any better. Thus Gorbachev, the most successful reformer in Soviet history, left office with no solid base of political support, a fact that augurs poorly for the progressive side in the Kremlin power struggles ahead.

Such was the inherent weakness of the Gorbachev approach to reform—from the top down. He personally had to make all the key decisions, among them what to change, how far to go, and how fast. He personally had to make the judgment calls on where he could carry the Politburo and where he must defer to it. As the ultimate decision-maker, therefore, he would have to take the blame from all sides, for all the mistakes, disappointments, shortcomings. Never mind that no other mere mortal could have done any better in the same circumstances. At the end of his six-year rule, his country and the system that ran it were both falling apart. Inevitably, Gorbachev would be held accountable for that. However unfounded these criticisms strike a foreigner, they are nonetheless facts of life in Russia today, clearly indicating that Mikhail Sergeyevich, despite continued political ambition, is unlikely to be elected to the presidency again and get a second chance to salvage his reforms. Even his closest aides admit as much.

That was to be expected. The real surprise is that Gorbachev achieved as much as he did. At the very least, the legacy he left behind can be seen as a bottle, either half empty or half full. His successors will ultimately fill the bottle, establishing a stable long-term democracy in Russia, or empty it, returning the nation to dictatorship. The downside risk is nothing new. Despotism was always Russia's natural state. Gorbachev's great contribution was in establishing democracy, the rule of law, and market economics as genuine options in the former Soviet Union. Before him they simply didn't exist. The time has come to see in some detail how he managed to get that far—and why he could get no further.

II. ECONOMIC REFORM: FIXING AN AIRPLANE IN FLIGHT

Despite the enormous odds against him, Mikhail Sergeyevich got off to a fast and ambitious start. Only a month after taking over the Kremlin leadership he announced a bold new economic strategy at a Central Committee plenum in April 1985. Brezhnev's legacy had been "stagnation"—a gradual slowdown to zero growth. Gorbachev's initial answer was the Russian word *uskoreniye*, "acceleration."

On the quantitative or bean-counting level, acceleration was supposed to turn out more oil, steel, and everything else at a faster pace. On the qualitative level, acceleration called for faster growth through structural change, essentially a transition to more rational market mechanisms for financing, production, pricing, and trade. Taken together, the expected quantity and quality benefits of acceleration were supposed to double gross national income by the year 2000, according to official targets.

"We are going over from an authoritarian to a democratic economy, an economy governed by the people, with substantial involvement of the masses in economic management," summed up Abel Aganbegyan, by then Gorbachev's chief economic adviser. That was the intention of the new strategy. Gorbachev and his team of reformers articulated it well. Implementation in the years ahead, however, would prove to be a far tougher process.

Influential critics in official positions of responsibility found much to malign in the initial reforms, from all sides. Conservatives denounced them as too ambitious, encouraging unreasonable expectations, impossible to deliver, and thus discrediting reform. Progressives arrived at the same negative conclusion from the opposite direction. They called the changes not ambitious enough, a waste of the best opportunity to move immediately to more radical measures, a timid basket of half measures that could never work, thus discrediting reform. All the conflicting criticisms contained kernels of truth. Such was the first harvest of Gorbachev's initial perestroika campaign. Subsequent reforms would receive similar sniping from all sides.

Of all the diverse critics, only a half-dozen men really counted—the Brezhnev old guard, still the Politburo majority. They liked the general idea of faster growth. So they let Gorbachev launch acceleration. The fine print, however, was harder for them to accept, especially the moves to a free-market economy. That part they were determined to stop, and they had an army to help them.

The old guard's key weapon was the Soviet Union's most powerful special interest group, its twenty million bureaucrats. These were the officials who made the command economy run, down to planning the number of nuts and bolts the country would produce. In a free market, such decisions would be governed by laws of supply and demand. Most of the bureaucrats would not be needed. Thus they knew their jobs and privileges depended on derailing, or at least delaying, any transition from one system to another. No further motivation was needed for the bureaucracy to obstruct reform.

Just as important, the bureaucrats also had ample opportunity to sabotage Gorbachev's changes. They knew their obstructionism from the outset of perestroika could not get them fired in the foreseeable future. Any successful transition would still need them to keep the old command system running, while it gradually ran down over the years and gave way to the free-market alternative being constructed in its place. All this gave them the time, influence, and job security needed to emasculate the reform process before it ever took hold. In the end, this bureaucratic stranglehold on reform gave the hard-line majority on the Politburo a veto over Gorbachev and his progressive allies, a power they exercised with a vengeance.

In effect, Gorbachev's perestroika was an attempt to fix an airplane in flight. The damaged aircraft symbolized the Communist system. Aganbegyan and the reform economists drew up a good repair scheme for the plane. But it could never be implemented properly, because the flight crew on board, the conservative Politburo majority, could veto elements of the refit at any time. All the flight crew had to say was that certain fixes were too dangerous and risked crashing the plane. All too often, Gorbachev felt he must defer to their warnings. He claimed he had no choice but to delay or skip some planned repairs in order to conduct others. In the end, all that did was postpone the inevitable crash landing.

No economic adviser could stay that course. Aganbegyan would be the first of many to design a rational policy in economic terms, then see it emasculated by the political compromises Gorbachev felt compelled to make to keep reform going. The economic adviser, his game plan in ruins, would then leave the stage, giving way to another, who eventually came to a similar fate. Leonid Abalkin, Grigory Yavlinsky, and Stanislav Shatalin were but three of the economic gurus who devised workable economic models only to see them destroyed by Gorbachev's subsequent retreats.

The general secretary justified his tactical retreats on the ground that half a loaf was better than none. Indeed, slow progress was being made toward market economics, including the creation of private businesses, although nowhere near enough to assure the transition's ultimate success. Gorbachev's half-a-loaf rationale was typical of political leaders who don't fully understand the ramifications of sophisticated economic decision-making. His maneuvering would keep perestroika alive, all right, but in a disjointed, irrational, jerry-built way, far from the original comprehensive economic package that might have actually worked. Acceleration was only the first of many economic reform schemes to go awry. The Soviet intelligentsia had at first rejoiced over the prospect that perestroika would at last bring genuine economic improvement. Their euphoria soon faded.

III. POLITICAL REFORM: WIDENING THE INTERSECTION

To their credit, Gorbachev and his team understood perfectly well the linkage between economic and political reform. From the beginning, they realized a new political base would have to be constructed if perestroika economics were to have any chance of success. So all the while Gorbachev was compromising within the Kremlin leadership on economic strategy, tactically retreating one day to advance the next, he was also trying to recreate the Soviet political universe in a way more favorable to long-term reform. His political strategy had two crucial elements.

The first was democratization. Its intellectual origins came from an open letter to Brezhnev, written in 1970 by three leading dissidents—Andrei Sakharov, Roy Medvedev, and Valentin Turchin. Their letter compared Soviet society to traffic moving through an intersection. In Stalin's day, there were only few cars. Police easily controlled the flow. Then the stream of traffic continually grew until adding police or increasing fines was no longer the answer. "The only solution is to widen the intersection," the three dissidents suggested.

What they really meant was widen the decision-making process, bring in all elements of society, including non-Communists, to solve the nation's problems. In blunter political terms, their example of traffic cops no longer controlling the intersection symbolized a revolutionary idea—that Stalinist police-state tactics no longer worked in a modern society, that to grow and prosper, the state had to democratize.

That was precisely what Gorbachev did. To prove he was serious he allowed Sakharov to return from exile in Gorky to Moscow in 1986 and resume speaking out in public for democratic reforms. The gesture convinced the influential Soviet intelligentsia—writers, artists, scientists, filmmakers, and educators, among others—that Mikhail Sergeyevich meant what he said about reform. They rallied to his cause and took broad segments of public opinion with them. Gorbachev also released other political prisoners from the Gulag, encouraging them to speak out too.

As his reforms got more radical, Gorbachev widened the intersection further. He even let a small minority of non-Communists into parliament to play roles in making policy. But Mikhail Sergeyevich was no Russian Thomas

Jefferson, defending the rights of all mankind. Instead, Gorbachev used democratization as an effective, one-sided political tool, to rally progressive support, so it would weaken his conservative and bureaucratic opposition. Gorbachev's democratization always had its limits. In no way was it supposed to harm either him personally or Communist Party rule. Gorbachev's political reforms, like his economic and ideological changes, would prove far more limited than progressives had hoped. Such was the weakness of depending on reform from the top down. Still, that passivity had deep traditional roots in Russia. Additional time would be needed to weed out the rot, and to allow more meaningful reform from the bottom up to become possible.

IV. IDEOLOGICAL REFORM: GLASNOST

The second crucial element in Gorbachev's political strategy, glasnost, or openness, had exactly the same purpose as democratization. It was also designed as a weapon to be used against conservative opponents. Once again it gave the appearance of being more liberal than it was actually intended to be.

Under Gorbachev's glasnost, the Soviet press could at last criticize senior Communist officials. The change was intoxicating to ordinary Russians. Initially it looked like the end of the Party's ideological stranglehold over the media, but it soon proved to be a far cry from freedom of the press as known in the West. The new critical, investigative reporting in the Soviet media was sharply limited from the beginning. It attacked the conservative bureaucratic opponents to Gorbachev's reforms, perhaps for corruption or incompetence, but did not look into mistakes by Mikhail Sergeyevich or his allies.

In short, glasnost was completely one-sided. Gorbachev could be shameless in denying to everyone else the same sort of free expression he awarded to his own loyal followers. Among other things, this tendency revealed that Mikhail Sergeyevich had a surprisingly low tolerance for personal slights. Once he tried to fire a Soviet editor just for running a poll showing that the most popular figure in the nation was not Gorbachev but Andrei Sakharov.

Not surprisingly, given such sensitivity, one of the key limits of glasnost in the early years was the unwritten rule that exempted Gorbachev personally from even implied criticism. Another was that openness simply didn't apply if it would discredit the Gorbachev regime in general.

Chernobyl proved that. Gorbachev himself was involved in the cover-up after the nuclear accident there on April 26, 1986. The Soviet press did its best to minimize the health dangers at home and abroad, belatedly admitting the true extent of the disaster only when confronted with irrefutable foreign evidence. Gorbachev first stayed silent for eighteen days. Then he finally appeared on nationwide television on May 14 to claim the worst danger was over and the situation under control. He said nothing about the long-range health threat in the U.S.S.R. or the considerable fallout abroad, embarrassing admissions he had to make later. At the time, there was no criticism in the Soviet press about the way Gorbachev or his spokesmen handled the disaster. Glasnost this was not.

To be fair, glasnost was more than a Gorbachev political tool, to be used or abused as the Kremlin leader saw fit. It was also an effort to improve the Soviet image worldwide. With the exception of Chernobyl, it usually worked. Under glasnost, for instance, foreign correspondents in Moscow were no longer seen as the enemy, to be kept away from senior officials and told as little as possible. Such tactics were at last regarded as counterproductive, one reason the U.S.S.R. always got a bad press abroad. Instead, under Gorbachev, previously inaccessible officials now opened their doors to foreign correspondents, often speaking candidly, for the record. Some even answered questions by telephone. The foreign ministry put on press briefings with top officials from all government departments. All the changes were designed to get the new Kremlin line out more effectively and more positively. Foreign correspondents, the Gorbachev regime decided, could be useful in improving the Soviet image abroad. His aides talked enthusiastically to the foreign journalists, knowing that if they could be convinced the Gorbachev reforms were real, they would write and broadcast that message globally. Foreign readers, and foreign leaders, were more likely to believe foreign reporting than *Pravda*.

In the early Gorbachev years, it should be remembered, Ronald Reagan and other Western leaders were highly skeptical about Gorbachev's intentions. For the most part they adopted a "show me" attitude, leaving it up to the Soviet leader to convince them he was serious about reform. Glasnost was part of Gorbachev's response. He understood that if the outside world began regarding perestroika as a success, that would help make it so inside Russia as well.

In this sense, glasnost was just another Soviet global propaganda campaign, but a much more sophisticated and successful one than the crude Stalinist efforts of earlier decades. For journalists in Moscow, the changes were a welcomed improvement. No longer did we have to rely on quoting the controlled Soviet press, debriefing diplomats who had better access to Soviet officials, and hunting out the relatively few brave, knowledgeable Soviet sources who might actually tell a foreign correspondent something more than *Pravda*. Now we often had better access to senior officials than the diplomatic corps did. In my own case, during my first six years as a correspondent in Moscow, in the Khrushchev and Brezhnev eras, I was never once allowed to set foot inside the Central Committee building. Under Gorbachev, I often interviewed his closest advisers in their Central Committee offices.

Glasnost even turned bad news to advantage. In the old days, natural disasters like earthquakes would be covered up, in an effort, often unsuccessful, to hide Soviet difficulties at home and abroad. Under glasnost, all that changed. A devastating earthquake in Soviet Armenia was given wide publicity. Soviet authorities waived the usual travel restrictions, encouraging foreign correspondents to report the tragedy from the scene. Such openness paid off handsomely with a massive inflow of foreign aid.

In the end, despite the sophistication and the evident improvements, neither democratization nor glasnost saved Gorbachev. Eventually his conservative opponents learned how to turn them both against him. For example, hard-line KGB agents posing as liberal democrats got elected to national and local parliaments, then used their new legislative posts to combat reform. Similarly, conservative newspapers eventually co-opted glasnost to expose the failures of Mikhail Sergeyevich and the reformers. Nevertheless, in the early years, both glasnost and democratization helped Gorbachev launch economic perestroika, and keep it going.

V. BORIS IN WONDERLAND

It is worth recalling just how full of hope the early days of perestroika, democratization, and glasnost were in Moscow. At first the break with the past seemed enormous, the pace breathtaking, the scope bewildering. It would take some time for the disillusion to set in. Initially, the Gorbachev reforms were seen as a cause for celebration. Ordinary people gathered around the dinner table in 1986 to toast Mikhail Sergeyevich. Suddenly they had more freedom to say, do, read what they liked, even to travel abroad. In perhaps the supreme compliment, there were no nasty jokes about Gorbachev. The merciless anecdotes critical of Brezhnev or Khrushchev had run in the hundreds. Clearly Russians liked Mikhail Sergeyevich too much in the beginning to run him down the same way.

Among them were my friends Igor and Tanya Belyayev. They had been married for twenty years. As privileged members of the intelligentsia, each had traveled abroad, Tanya on scientific delegations, Igor as an interpreter, but always alone. As with other Soviet couples, each time one of them went abroad, the other had to stay behind as a hostage, to make sure the traveler would return. Finally, under Gorbachev, all that changed.

For the first time in their long marriage, Igor and Tanya went abroad together. They visited Warsaw in 1987. When they got there, Igor understood he was witnessing a most unusual role reversal. For once, the prospect for liberal change was greater in Russia than in Poland. The Soviet press, re-counting Gorbachev's revolution, was actually more exciting than the rela-tively dull Polish press. Poles, Igor discovered, were lining up in Warsaw to buy *Pravda,* the Soviet Communist Party daily. "For the first time in my life, I was proud of my country," Igor told me.

Soon enough, the heady optimism of perestroika's early days began to fade. The sharp limits on the reforms became clearer. Economic promise gave way to disappointment and further decline. Gorbachev's third way between communism and capitalism, presented as the cure for the nation's ills, was proving unworkable and instead making the economy sicker. The toasts stopped. The bitter jokes resumed. Mostly they began to describe perestroika as just another Kremlin sham of hollow talk that changed nothing impor-tant for ordinary people in terms of either freedom or prosperity. Under Gor-bachev, Soviets now had less to eat and could complain a bit more. Overall they thought themselves no better off.

In a typical example of these anecdotes, one dog tells another, "Perestroika has come to our yard."

"What does that mean?" the second dog asks.

"Nothing much," says the first dog. "My chain has become longer. The plate is smaller. But I can bark as much as I like."

To a great extent, Gorbachev had no one to blame but himself for the public's loss of faith in both him personally and his policies. Admittedly, the problems he took on were huge, perhaps unsolvable. Nonetheless, he had raised expectations. He had promised to raise living standards, then failed to deliver.

For one thing, Mikhail Sergeyevich made serious mistakes. The changes he produced, however well intended, were all too often poorly thought out and only made matters worse. His campaign against alcoholism, one of the first reforms in 1985, was a perfect example. The intention made good sense. Alcoholism was a major cause of the Soviet Union's relatively low life ex-pectancy. It also contributed mightily to lost production through absenteeism at the workplace. Gorbachev hoped to improve public health and national production output by fighting alcoholism. So he raised the prices of vodka and wine while lowering their availability.

Soviets, of course, did not stop drinking. They made their own substi-tute, *samogon,* often from liquids unfit for human consumption, like paint thinner, and public health only got worse. The state, meanwhile, the mo-nopoly producer of legitimate alcoholic beverages, lost substantial business. Soon some 10 percent of the government budget deficit leading the nation toward bankruptcy was due entirely to the state's lost liquor sales. In the end, everyone from local drunks to the country's leading economists saw Gor-bachev's anti-alcohol campaign as a damaging mistake. It was dropped, but his reputation continued to suffer from the episode.

In addition to mistakes on economic policy, Gorbachev also failed all too often in what was supposed to be his strongest suit, political maneuver. As the Brezhnev old guard died off, opportunities arose to replace them on the Politburo, or expand its size, or both, to increase the reformist votes at the summit of Soviet power. Here Mikhail Sergeyevich did not do well, because of the considerable political skills of his rivals in the Kremlin leadership. Every time Gorbachev tried to promote a progressive, his conservative opponents, still in the majority, insisted on bringing one or more of their own into the Politburo as well. Thus Mikhail Sergeyevich assured Politburo membership for a leading progressive, Aleksandr Yakovlev, but only at the cost of bringing on board the leading conservative candidate, Yegor Ligachev. The trade-offs were frustrating. They did nothing to bring Gorbachev nearer an assured Politburo majority for his reforms.

So the Soviet leader tried another tactic. If his reform effort was blocked by the Politburo on the national level, Gorbachev could lower the stakes and push it instead at the local level. His instrument for this exercise was Boris Nikolayevich Yeltsin, then the Communist Party leader for the city of Moscow and a candidate (nonvoting) member of the Politburo. Yeltsin was already the most radical reformer in the Kremlin leadership despite his relatively junior status; he was an outspoken advocate of more private enterprise, fewer Communist Party privileges, and other progressive causes. Yeltsin, Gorbachev decided, would be his stalking horse, pushing out ever farther the permissible limits of reform, in Moscow at first, but obviously setting precedents for the entire country as well.

Mikhail Sergeyevich placed himself between the radical Yeltsin and the conservative Ligachev. In any showdown, Gorbachev would have to side with Ligachev, who could speak with the voice of the Politburo majority. But short of that, Mikhail Sergeyevich could quietly encourage Yeltsin to push for still more reform.

There was one major problem with this game. Yeltsin eventually refused to play. He tried for a while. Then, after Ligachev continued to block his reform efforts in Moscow, Yeltsin wanted more support from Gorbachev, or, failing that, he wanted to quit. Instead, Gorbachev persuaded Yeltsin to continue the fight. At this point the two men reached a fatal misunderstanding. Yeltsin thought he had been promised more help from Gorbachev. Mikhail Sergeyevich thought Yeltsin had pledged to stick it out for the duration. Both assumptions turned out to be wrong. Each man felt betrayed by the other. The personal bitterness between them continues to this day.

The crunch came at a closed-door plenum of the Central Committee in October 1987. In a startling, unprecedented outburst, Yeltsin complained about "bullying reprimands" and "coercion" from the top Party leadership, particularly from "Comrade Ligachev," which he said were harming perestroika reforms. He also attacked Gorbachev for letting that happen. "There has been a noticeable increase in what I can only call adulation of the general secretary by certain full members of the Politburo,"

Yeltsin said, suggesting the conservative stroking and flattery was turning Gorbachev away from reform. "I consider this to be not permissible," Yeltsin said.

Such personal criticism of Party superiors was unacceptable. Yeltsin says he knew his Communist career was finished from the moment he opened his mouth. He had no illusions his speech could change the Party or produce more meaningful reform. He simply wanted to get out, as he said later in his memoirs, "guns blazing."[8] Before sitting down, Yeltsin resigned from both the Politburo and the Moscow Party leadership to begin a long, hard slog in the Soviet political wilderness.

He was far from finished, however. Even after giving up the Politburo seat and the Moscow leadership, Yeltsin remained a Communist Party member. Indeed, he still had his place on the powerful Central Committee. Boris Nikolayevich would never rise higher in the Party, but his continued membership in it would still protect him. From that point on, Yeltsin became, like Lewis Carroll's Alice, Boris in Wonderland, somewhere on the other side of everyday Soviet reality. He turned into a unique political maverick, a dangerous loose cannon, campaigning openly against the Party while still enjoying its benefits as a senior member.

The Communist old guard had let him off lightly. They allowed him to stay in Moscow, as a deputy minister for construction. Keeping a known critic like Yeltsin in the Party ranks, they thought, would help convince doubters that Soviet communism was becoming more democratic. In their old-school thinking, they also believed that once Yeltsin had been dropped from the Politburo elite, he was finished as a political threat. They had underestimated Boris Nikolayevich, and would live to regret it.

Eventually, Yeltsin would become the first political leader to rise to the top in the Kremlin by running against the Communist Party. Gorbachev's reforms would at last make possible competitive elections that anti-Communists could win. Yeltsin seized the opportunity, exploiting widespread public dissatisfaction with Gorbachev's changes by arguing they were not radical enough. In the process, Boris Nikolayevich turned Soviet politics upside down. He built grassroots support from the bottom up in order to defeat the Communists, who had always imposed their will from the top down. In a way, Yeltsin owed it all to Gorbachev. But there was no love lost between them. Their split became a Soviet political tragedy.

The damage was clear from the moment Yeltsin quit the Party leadership in October 1987. "This was the first conflict between the proponents of perestroika," Roy Medvedev told me at the time. "Gorbachev has been weakened by Yeltsin's departure." What he and others meant was that Gorbachev, the reformer, and Yeltsin, his more radical ally, had to stick together or the conservative opposition would profit from their disagreements and defeat perestroika. It was a theme often repeated by knowledgeable Russians in the years that followed. "I hope Gorbachev and Yeltsin will cooperate for the

The last Tsar, Nicholas II, the Empress Alexandra, their daughters *(from left)* the Grand Duchesses Maria, Tatyana, Olga, and Anastasia, and their son, the Crown Prince Aleksei (ITAR-TASS PHOTO FROM ROYAL ARCHIVES)

Vladimir Lenin in his Kremlin study, 1918
(ITAR-TASS)

Leon Trotsky in Siberian exile before 1917
(ITAR-TASS)

Idealized 1938 painting of Josef Stalin advising Lenin. The scene had to be faked by propagandists in a painting because no suitable photographs were available to show that Stalin was Lenin's natural heir. (ITAR-TASS)

Stalin holds a child to promote his image as "Father of the People," 1936. (ITAR-TASS)

Nikolai Bukharin in the 1920s (ITAR-TASS)

V. M. Molotov signs 1939 Nazi-Soviet Pact,
with Stalin in the background. (ITAR-TASS)

Stalin, Franklin Roosevelt, and Winston Churchill at Yalta, 1945 (ITAR-TASS)

Stalin in his coffin, March 1953. His legacy, the danger of reviving his
ruthless dictatorship, still haunts Russia. (ITAR-TASS)

Losers: Georgi Malenkov *(right)* and Lavrenty
Beria at Stalin's funeral. The early favorites to
succeed the dictator were soon outmaneuvered by Nikita Khrushchev. (ITAR-TASS)

The winner: The young Khrushchev
with Stalin, 1936 (ITAR-TASS)

Khrushchev in the cornfields, talking agricultural reform, 1964 (ITAR-TASS)

Khrushchev and his wife, Nina Petrovna, with their children and grandchildren, 1963. Son-in-law Aleksei Adzhubei, then *Izvestia* editor, is in back row left; son Sergei in back row right. (ITAR-TASS)

Khrushchev with the first Soviet Cosmonaut, Yuri Gagarin
(right), and the second, Gherman Titov, 1962 (ITAR-TASS)

Khrushchev, his wife, and Andrei Gromyko
with President Eisenhower at Blair House,
Washington, D.C., 1959 (ITAR-TASS)

Khrushchev with Fidel Castro in 1962, the
year of the Cuban missile crisis (ITAR-TASS)

Khrushchev with President Kennedy in Vienna, 1961 (ITAR-TASS)

Hungarian rebels on a captured Soviet tank during the
1956 uprising in Budapest (ITAR-TASS)

Betrayal. Leonid Brezhnev *(left)* praises Khrushchev on the leader's
seventieth birthday, April 1964. Six months later Brezhnev
led a coup to replace Khrushchev. (ITAR-TASS)

Brezhnev with Nixon
in the White House,
1973 (ITAR-TASS)

Kissinger with
Gromyko in the
Kremlin, 1972
(BORIS YURCHENKO)

Aleksei Kosygin
with Mao in
China, 1965
(ITAR-TASS)

The fit Brezhnev at his desk in the Kremlin, 1972 (ITAR-TASS)

The ill Brezhnev votes, 1974
(BORIS YURCHENKO)

Brezhnev with Jimmy Carter in Vienna, 1979
(ITAR-TASS)

The Gang of Four. A rare photo of the last four top Soviet leaders together in the same picture at a 1982 Kremlin reception. Brezhnev, Chernenko, and Andropov *(first, second, and fourth from left)*, with Gorbachev at far right. Others in the picture are Gromyko *(third from left)* and Moscow City Communist leader Viktor Grishin. (ITAR-TASS)

Soviet nuclear intercontinental missiles roll through Red Square, 1974, passing a sign that says in Russian, "All Power to the Soviets." (BORIS YURCHENKO)

Mikhail Gorbachev with François Mitterrand
in Paris, 1989 (ITAR-TASS)

Gorbachev with Reagan in the Kremlin (ITAR-TASS)

Style Wars. Raisa versus Nancy, with husbands in Moscow, 1988 (ITAR-TASS)

Star Wars. Gorbachev discussed disarmament with Reagan and
Vice President Bush in New York, 1988. (ITAR-TASS)

Gorbachev and Reagan at the 1985 fireside chat in Geneva that made the breakthrough toward nuclear arms accords (ITAR-TASS)

Andrei Sakharov as a deputy to the Soviet parliament (ITAR-TASS)

Aleksandr Solzhenitsyn
(ITAR-TASS)

The author with Richard Nixon
in the Kremlin, 1965

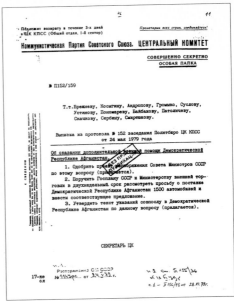

The official record of a 1979 Politburo meeting on Afghanistan. Stamped "Top Secret," it
is one of the dozens of formerly unavailable
documents obtained for this book.

The author with Gorbachev after a 1995 interview in Moscow

Boris Yeltsin on a tank in front of his besieged White House headquarters, defying the August 1991 hard-line Communist coup (ITAR-TASS)

Gorbachev and Yeltsin in September 1991, rivals for power, making no attempt to hide their hatred for each other (ITAR-TASS)

Yeltsin the tennis player, yesterday's man, no longer up to his game (ITAR-TASS)

good of the country," Georgi Arbatov later told me. Had they done so at the time, the early years of reform might well have been more successful. Instead, hopes of a Gorbachev-Yeltsin reconciliation proved to be wishful thinking.

VI. A TWO-HAT STRATEGY

By late 1987, some two and a half years into the Gorbachev revolution, the achievements of perestroika looked very shaky indeed. Cultural life was a good example. Soviet artists freely displayed in public the nudes, abstracts, and religious motifs that KGB bulldozers had once crushed, but no one knew how long it would last, or if a new wave of conservatism would again turn the clock back.

The theater was a good barometer of the new nervousness in the artistic community. It showed how increased freedom of expression could be more worrisome than the old system of Communist thought control. Under perestroika, plays were no longer censored by an official from the culture ministry who could get lines, scenes, or even entire scripts changed or banned. Anyone who thought that would lead to bolder performances, however, was soon disappointed. Once liberated from state censorship, the theater directors themselves had to take responsibility for what they staged. They had no idea how far they could go, for example, in criticizing the regime, with no censor around anymore to tell them. The new freedom was often so terrifying that the theater director censored himself, playing it safe by erring on the side of caution. In one of the ironies of the early perestroika years, the theater in Moscow was far less daring than it had been under Brezhnev, when theater directors constantly pushed censors to let them go further.

Gorbachev could have removed all the troubling ambiguity with one speech. All it would have taken was a strong signal that the time had come to cast off what remained of the Stalinist past. The fact that he never made that speech testifies eloquently to the continuing Kremlin power struggle. Even as general secretary, Mikhail Sergeyevich had to compromise with all Politburo factions, in order to keep his job. The result was continued ambiguity.

Probably the best example of this syndrome came on November 7, 1987, the seventieth anniversary of the Bolshevik Revolution. Gorbachev's three-hour speech was billed in advance as the most important of the year. It was supposed to tell the truth about past Soviet history, about the "blank spots" like Stalin's crimes, in order to increase credibility for future reforms. In fact, it did no such thing. Gorbachev offered no major new reforms. Nor did he clear up any of the important blank spots. The key test was Nikolai Bukharin, a Stalin rival who promoted economic policies resembling perestroika only to be denounced as an enemy of the people and executed in 1938. Gorbachev had been expected to rehabilitate Bukharin. Instead, in a compromise that satisfied no one, he said a new commission would study that question. Clearly both conservatives and progressives in the Politburo had whacked at his 101-page text until they reduced it to a directionless muddle.

In one of the understatements of the year, Andrei Sakharov said of Gorbachev's anniversary speech that "not everything satisfied me." Virtually every Soviet citizen could agree. As 1987 ended, none of them knew if reform would continue or collapse.

For most of the next year, the public mood continued to decline. Food supplies worsened, largely because of the shortcomings of the old Brezhnev system. Nonetheless, most people blamed Gorbachev for not improving agriculture sooner. My middle-aged friend Igor Belyayev was an exception. He cared more about intellectual freedom and still praised Mikhail Sergeyevich. "I can cope with the food supply situation in the country for the rest of my life, as long as I can read what I like, say what I like, go where I like, and see what I like," Igor told me.

His son, Dima, twenty-four, was more typical. The young man conceded that Gorbachev had improved some things, but thought the changes woefully inadequate. "Sure, my generation is lucky," Dima said. "We have it much better than the 1930s. But why compare with the worst? Why not compare with Americans my age? Why can't I have what they have?"

Outside Moscow, in the depths of provincial Russia, the criticism was much harsher. People there, struggling to survive, no longer believed in Gorbachev's unfulfilled promises of economic improvements. His meet-the-people walkabouts, once an exercise in public adoration for the great democratizer, were becoming nationally televised public relations disasters. On one such walkabout, in the Siberian city of Krasnoyarsk in September 1988, the following dialogue occurred:

Man: "There's nothing here. You cannot even have a wash where you want to."

Gorbachev: "And this is the region where there is the most water."

Woman: "Not hot water."

Second man: "It's probably the region where there are the most complaints."

Gorbachev: "Okay, comrades, I sense your mood."

The Soviet president had raised expectations with his talk of reform. He had brought some improvements, particularly in granting more individual freedom. The right to complain was but one example of this. Nonetheless, instead of thanking him for the progress so far, most Soviet citizens now focused instead on what needed doing. Sometimes the impact of Gorbachev's reforms was clearer to foreigners than to Russians themselves.

I saw that for the first time in late September 1988 when the Soviet government announced a press trip to Vladivostok. It was a historic breakthrough, the first time foreign correspondents would be allowed in there since

Stalin closed the great port and naval base on the Pacific to all but Soviet citizens. Even President Gerald Ford never got to see the city during his Vladivostok summit with Brezhnev in 1974. Their meetings were held in a guesthouse six miles out of town.

Competition for the twenty-five places on the press trip to Vladivostok was intense. Hundreds of correspondents from all over the world wanted to go. With luck, I managed to get a place on the list. Then that only led to a bigger problem. Suddenly, a plenum of the Central Committee was announced for the same time as the Vladivostok trip. As the only *Newsweek* correspondent then accredited in Moscow, I could not do both. But which would be the better story, the plenum or Vladivostok?

Plenums could either be political upheavals or deadly dull. In the secrecy-obsessed Kremlin, in Khrushchev's day, Brezhnev's, and into Gorbachev's, there was never any advance word of what a plenum might bring. Senior officials simply refused to talk about that, even privately. Vladivostok, on the other hand, was certain to be a fascinating trip. Still, could I really risk going and perhaps missing a key plenum?

The dilemma made yet another checking effort worth the trouble, however futile that might be. So I phoned a longtime Russian contact whose boss was a Central Committee member, explained the problem, and asked what I should do.

"Stay in Moscow," he replied, without hesitation.

"Why?" I asked.

"Because there are going to be changes at Politburo level," he told me, on the telephone no less. His candor in releasing what used to be forbidden information, over my tapped office telephone line, left me thunderstruck.

There could hardly be a clearer signal that the closed Kremlin political system was moving toward a more open process. Of course, it was still far from democratic, but at least more people outside the Central Committee elite were informed in advance of major change and allowed to speak about it. That trend could only be viewed as progress, even if most Russians still knew nothing about it. Needless to say, I decided to give up Vladivostok in order to stay in Moscow for the plenum, and I was not disappointed.

The September 1988 plenum turned out to be a milestone in Gorbachev's battle for perestroika. It was his first shake-up of the Kremlin leadership, a power play that substantially enhanced his stature. For Mikhail Sergeyevich, there were these major pluses:

- Andrei Gromyko and three other Brezhnev-era holdovers on the Politburo, who had all opposed reforms, were eased into retirement.

- Conservatives left on the ruling body were first weakened numerically by the forced retirement of the Brezhnev old guard, then weakened further when their job responsibilities were downgraded.

Ligachev, for example, long Gorbachev's leading conservative rival, lost his key power bases as the Politburo member responsible for both ideology and personnel questions. Instead he was downgraded to overseeing agriculture, traditionally a job for a more junior Politburo member. Viktor Chebrikov, another conservative influence, lost his power base as head of the KGB, but remained on the Politburo, downgraded into supervising legal affairs. As with Ligachev, his new post would cause Gorbachev less trouble. The new KGB chief, Vladimir Kryuchkov, was left off the Politburo, for the moment anyway, in a junior status less likely to harm Gorbachev.

• New members brought into the Politburo to fill vacancies were more progressive. Among them was Vadim Medvedev,[9] a leading Gorbachev supporter who took over the ideology portfolio from Ligachev, then announced the plenum results at a press briefing. A reporter asked him if the changes helped Gorbachev. Medvedev smiled and replied, "What do you think?"

• Last and perhaps most important, the plenum reshuffle left Gorbachev not only as general secretary of the Communist Party but also, for the first time, as president of the Soviet Union, the ceremonial head of state.[10] The presidency, as we shall soon see, would be crucial to Mikhail Sergeyevich's future strategy.

The September 1988 plenum was a milestone in another way. It also revealed a major new political tactic that Gorbachev would now follow. As public support for perestroika, and for Mikhail Sergeyevich personally, declined across the country, he would compensate by taking on increased political power for himself.

The presidency became the key first step in that direction. It was designed as a political insurance policy. Even the successful reshuffle at the plenum, weakening the conservative element, was not enough to safeguard Gorbachev's Communist Party position. To see why Mikhail Sergeyevich needed still more insurance, one first had to understand how the Politburo worked.

After the plenum, the new Politburo had twelve members. Many floated back and forth, sometimes voting with Gorbachev, sometimes joining the conservative opposition to vote against his stand, depending on the issue of the day. Despite all the changes, Mikhail Sergeyevich could still count on only four of the twelve Politburo votes on each and every issue—his own, Yakovlev's, Shevardnadze's, and Medvedev's. Getting Party approval for fundamental change would still be a struggle after all. So Gorbachev adopted a two-hat strategy. He would still wear his Party hat when that suited him. When it didn't, he could put on his presidential hat instead.

In the old days, the presidential hat was not worth wearing—only an honorary job, with no political power. The two jobs that counted most in the

Soviet system were the Party leader and the premier, or head of government. Stalin and Khrushchev had each taken on both these top positions. Later it was decided that making one man both Party boss and premier gave him too much power. So to avoid that, subsequent Party leaders were allowed to take on only the additional job of the ceremonial presidency.

Brezhnev, Andropov, and Chernenko each became president, but all ruled the country only through their post as Communist Party leader. Gorbachev determined to make the presidential hat worth wearing. Mikhail Sergeyevich officially became president on October 1, 1988, when the parliament, the Supreme Soviet, unanimously confirmed the earlier decision by the Party's Central Committee.[11] Only three weeks later, on October 23, Gorbachev proposed changes in the constitution and the election laws that would make the Soviet presidency a power in its own right for the first time. These changes, which he successfully rammed through, would revolutionize the nation's political system, and, it goes without saying, substantially increase Gorbachev's own authority.

Typically, it was all presented in the name of democratization. A new parliament, with a new name and new powers, would be elected more democratically. For the first time under Soviet communism, there would be competing candidates for most seats, and even non-Communists could run. The new election law would replace the discredited old system in which all candidates were nominated by the Communist Party and ran unopposed, their victory assured.

More important, the new parliament, to be called the Congress of People's Deputies, would have real legislative powers to propose, debate, and pass laws. It would no longer be a rubber-stamp assembly unanimously confirming every Politburo order. Most important, the new parliament would name a strong new executive president, with broader powers than those of the president of the United States, to run the country. Needless to say, the author of these proposals, Mikhail Sergeyevich Gorbachev, intended from the outset that he would be the first Soviet president with such enhanced powers. Constitutionally, he would have even more authority than Stalin ever held. It was a novel approach in the Soviet Union. Stalin held supreme power through terror. Gorbachev would now hold it through law.

With the stakes so high, Mikhail Sergeyevich was not about to risk defeat at the hands of the people in a direct election for the stronger executive presidency. Instead, the new president would be chosen indirectly in a vote by the new parliament. All Gorbachev had to do to ensure his own appointment as president was to manipulate various parliamentary factions into supporting him. Democracy this was not, but then democracy was not the aim.

The real intention was to make up for Gorbachev's declining support in the Communist Party and in the country at large by increasing his personal power through the new presidency and the new parliament. The main advantage for Gorbachev in this grand design was that he personally would run everything. From then on, if the conservatives on the Politburo blocked him, he could at last make an end run around them. The powerful new president, backed by the new parliament, could make perestroika irreversible whether the Party liked it or not.

Nor was that all. Even if the Politburo fired him and elected a new Party general secretary, Gorbachev would not be forced into retirement as Khrushchev had been. This time, Mikhail Sergeyevich could continue to rule the country as the executive president. It made little difference whether Gorbachev wore his party hat or his presidential hat. Either way, he would remain in charge.

With that scheme, for the first time, Gorbachev's political instinct began to fail him. His ambition had started to cloud his judgment. He was reaching for too much personal power. Western leaders had no objection. To them a stronger Gorbachev improved the long-range prospects of democratic reform. Inside the U.S.S.R., however, Gorbachev's power play looked very different indeed, more like an attempt to become a modern-day tsar. Critics from all sides began to think he needed to be stopped.

Sakharov spoke out for the progressives. Gorbachev's proposed changes, he said, would give the new executive president almost unlimited powers to issue decrees between parliamentary sessions. Although those powers were intended for the reformer Gorbachev, Sakharov told me at the time, "tomorrow it could be someone else. And there is no guarantee he won't be a neo-Stalinist."

Soviet hard-liners were also alarmed, although for different reasons. They saw Gorbachev taking on sufficient new power to make perestroika reforms irreversible. They began to think he might indeed destroy the Soviet system. So they determined not to let him. They could not stop him from becoming the Soviet Union's first executive president, but they could make sure he was the last, by bringing him down in a coup d'état. None of Gorbachev's insurance policies protected him against that. The Soviet power struggle was entering a new and ultimately decisive phase.

VII. THE SORCERER'S APPRENTICE

Gorbachev's sensitive political antennae quickly picked up the danger signals. He knew the time left for him to make perestroika work was growing short. In one unusually gloomy prognosis, in December 1988, Mikhail Sergeyevich told the Politburo he probably had only a year and a half left, to June 1990. In fact, he was overly pessimistic. The long-feared coup against him did not come until two and a half years later, in August 1991. Still, despite the timing error, Mikhail Sergeyevich knew what he was up against. Unless perestroika succeeded—and soon—he would have to go.

Reading his prediction in the once-secret Politburo transcript is chilling, even now. The session took place on December 27, 1988. According to the verbatim text made available in official Soviet archives, Mikhail Sergeyevich told the Politburo he was well aware Soviet people were saying perestroika was failing, that it had brought no tangible economic benefits, that the Kremlin leadership was divided and "leading the nation toward chaos." Ominously, Gorbachev then added, "The future of today's leadership is said to be on the skids. If one is talking straight, then one hears that Gorbachev is living on borrowed time. I am given a year, a year and a half, isn't that so, Vladimir Aleksandrovich?"

Gorbachev's question was addressed to Vladimir Aleksandrovich Kryuchkov, the KGB chairman.[12] In August 1991, he would lead the failed coup against Gorbachev. It was thus uncanny that Gorbachev chose to ask Kryuchkov point-blank about the growing opposition and how much time he had left. The KGB chief's answer, in the light of subsequent events, was a transparent evasion. To the question "I am given a year, a year and a half, isn't that so, Vladimir Aleksandrovich?" Kryuchkov replied, "People say all sorts of things." Mikhail Sergeyevich was not pacified. "You don't want to commit yourself," he told Kryuchkov, "but that is so."

Gorbachev's astute premonition about his personal destiny was only one sign that his time at the top was running out. His reforms were increasingly seen across the country as having weakened the Soviet system since 1985 in four key areas—democratization, economic performance, unrest by minority nationalities, and foreign policy. By the end of 1988, alarm bells from all four signaled that Mikhail Sergeyevich was already in deep trouble. All four were to be crucial elements in the political struggle that continued through the remainder of Gorbachev's rule. Each of the four will be examined in subsequent chapters, beginning with democratization, the newest factor.

For the first time in Soviet history, thanks to Gorbachev's democratization, ordinary people had started to play a major role in shaping their own destiny. Instead of the Communist leadership controlling all reform from the top down, public opinion was beginning to influence the course of events from the bottom up. The countervailing force of democratization would now grow, beginning with the election to the new parliament in March 1989, until it became the single most important factor in the fate of both Gorbachev himself and perestroika. From the sorcerer whose magic invented democratization, Gorbachev would become the sorcerer's apprentice, unable to sweep it under control again. No one can hope to understand the Gorbachev era without first appreciating the sea change that his democratization brought.

12

Reform from the Bottom Up:
Democratization (1989–90)

I. BRAVE NEW WORLD

The word "democracy" in the Soviet lexicon was always a perverse abuse of language. Soviet leaders worked hard at creating the appearance of democracy, while at the same time continuing the totalitarian reality of their tsarist predecessors. This charade was another sign of communism's relative weakness. Russia's tsars, more confident of their legitimacy, never needed to stage public endorsements of their private decisions. The Communists, however, were always less secure, if only because they could not claim to rule by divine right. Unlike the tsars, Soviet leaders from Stalin on felt compelled to show they had public approval.

Free elections would not do, as that risked a vote against communism. So the "democracy" the Soviets designed involved only dubious staged spectacles of broad support from the masses. In effect, the Soviet people were mobilized to say yes to whatever their leaders wanted. The approval could come in parades with thousands of marchers carrying slogans written by the regime. Or it could come in parliamentary elections, in which the Kremlin permitted only its handpicked candidates to run unopposed for each seat in the national legislature. All such yes votes were hailed by the propaganda machine as "outstanding examples of Soviet democracy."

From such hypocritical origins, Gorbachev conducted the first genuine democratization in Soviet history. He changed the reality, not just the appearance. Under Mikhail Sergeyevich's reforms, two or more candidates could compete for the same post, beginning with the March 1989 election to the new Soviet parliament. The winner could be a candidate who had never joined the Communist Party, even an anti-Communist. Thus, for the first time, Soviet citizens could vote no to the demands of their Communist leadership. At last, they had a real choice. They could vote against the regime by sending a critic of communism to parliament. They could say no to economic deprivation, no to Party privileges, no to KGB repression. Furthermore, for the first time, they could now demonstrate against the regime, in cities across the Soviet Union, in crowds numbering in the tens of thousands, to make sure their vote of no got a wide public hearing.

Nonetheless, right from the beginning, Gorbachev imposed sharp limits on all such democratic change. His reforms would give communism a more humane face, all right, but they would definitely not allow Soviet voters to jettison Communist rule. Even under Mikhail Sergeyevich, the old Soviet commitment to democratic appearance still counted more than the first substantive realities.

Gorbachev designed democratization with narrow aims in mind. His goals were to strengthen perestroika and his own power at the expense of his conservative opponents, nothing more democratic than that. In the new contested elections for parliament, for example, some progressive newcomers would defeat old hard-liners. Some anti-Communists would win seats. They could help the reform cause, but, in the end, all such independents would be only individual minority voices, because no official opposition parties were yet allowed. Mikhail Sergeyevich still manipulated election rules to guarantee a solid Communist majority in the new parliament. In that way, he assured the Politburo, Communists would retain control. It would no longer be total monopoly control, but an overwhelming majority was still effective control.

In fact, Mikhail Sergeyevich had no choice but to limit democratization from the start. Otherwise the Politburo would never have approved his changes. There was nothing very subtle about this trade-off. Under Gorbachev's election law, one hundred seats in the new parliament were awarded to Communist Party candidates. As in the past, they could run unopposed to certain victory. Naturally, the hundred places went to the party elite. Mikhail Sergeyevich thus assured himself, conservative leader Yegor Ligachev, the rest of the Politburo, and most senior Central Committee members reserved seats in the new parliament.[1] Only lesser mortals would have to compete in contested votes. By such crude maneuvers, Gorbachev and his Politburo thought they would continue to control democratization.

It was a fundamental error. Once given the power to say no, the Soviet people would no longer be satisfied with partial reform granted from the top down. They would press to extend the limited franchise Gorbachev had given them until pressure from the bottom up became the dominant political force in Russia. Ultimately that force would break up the U.S.S.R. Short of a military coup d'état in Moscow, a civil war across Russia, or another Stalinist wave of mass repression—all thought to be unlikely in 1989—the public right to say no could not be limited or taken away again.

Gorbachev had raised the stakes higher than he had imagined. His "third way," an attempt to adopt democracy under Communist control, would prove impossible to implement. Instead it would show that once communism embarks on genuine reform, there is no going back. With its first timid steps at democratization, the Soviet system was doomed.

The democratization designed for the March 1989 parliamentary election opened a Pandora's box, by only a crack. The Soviet leader sat on the lid. He thought he could control the forces below. Instead they eventually blew him away. I was privileged to witness that process in Moscow, from the start, as democratic forces seized the political momentum in Russia, against enormous odds, from what had been one of the most repressive police states in history. It is comforting to remember today, when post-Communist Russia risks backsliding toward totalitarianism, that the courage and ingenuity of the nation's democratic movement should not be underestimated.

I first realized that in early 1989, attending a meeting called to nominate candidates from Moscow district number 21 for the new Soviet parliament. It was a classic example of how Gorbachev's democratization really worked at the grassroots level. That was where hard-line Communist apparatchiks tried to make meaningless all the democratic reform Mikhail Sergeyevich handed down from on high. It was also where the newly enfranchised democratic movements would strike back, often with remarkable success.

The nominating session for Moscow district 21 took place in a citadel of Communist power, the auditorium of the Party newspaper, *Pravda*. Those chosen at this meeting would get on the ballot and run in the March election. The favorite of two hundred reform delegates, selected earlier in democratic votes at workplaces, was Vitaly Korotich, a hero of the progressive movement. His liberal magazine, *Ogonyok* ("Little Flame"), championed perestroika. Conservative Communist Party managers were determined to stop him, however. They packed the hall with four hundred loyalists, appointed illegally as "additional delegates," with instructions to keep Korotich off the ballot. Their transparent maneuver stole the majority from the legitimately elected delegates, but when reformers tried to object, the chairman of the meeting turned off their microphones. The reformers, ready for anything, brought out a battery-powered bullhorn. "This is not democratization," the man with the bullhorn screamed over mounting bedlam. "Don't take us for idiots."

The chairman still refused to give them the floor. Korotich stalked out of the meeting in disgust, but not out of the campaign. Eventually he was nominated for parliament by a district in the Ukrainian city of Kharkov, and won the seat. Despite their strong-arm tactics, the Communist old guard had failed to stop him. Such was the brave new world opened up by Gorbachev's democratization. It was only the first of many examples I saw of reformers pushing harder from the ground up than the Kremlin had thought possible.

Later on in the March 1989 campaign, I went to see Boris Yeltsin make his political comeback, in a further illustration of the same trend. The former Moscow Communist leader was then running for the new parliament by campaigning against the Party. He told a rally of two thousand people in a Moscow theater that it was time to do away with the perks of the Communist elite. "The ruble of a janitor should be worth the same as the ruble of a Party leader," Boris Nikolayevich said to cheers and rhythmic applause.

Yeltsin was a magnificent campaigner, a formidable figure with a huge frame and a deep authoritative voice. He spoke slowly, gesturing emphatically with his powerful fists. The audience hung on every word. Boris Nikolayevich was grateful that fallen Communists like himself, and even non-Communists like Sakharov, could now run for parliament as individuals. Nevertheless, Yeltsin complained that the Gorbachev democratic reforms had still gone nowhere near far enough. Yeltsin demanded that opposition parties be allowed to organize legally, knowing full well that Gorbachev's conservative Politburo could never permit that. In so doing, Boris Nikolayevich was attacking the most sacred principle of Communist rule, its one-party monopoly on power. "It is time to open the question of a multiparty system to wider discussion," Yeltsin declared. The audience responded with a standing ovation.

Soviet citizens had never seen anything like it. For the first time their elections were not fixed in advance. For the first time the public was eagerly attending rallies. For the first time candidates were saying largely what they liked—in public. Some even attacked Communist Party leaders by name. At one rally a candidate said there would not be genuine democracy until Gorbachev himself ran for the presidency, by direct popular vote, against an opposition candidate. That would not happen this time because Gorbachev would not risk losing. At another rally, a speaker attacked Yegor Ligachev, the Politburo's leading conservative, and declared, "Ligachev should resign." That wouldn't happen either. No matter. Perhaps the most important point about this unprecedented Soviet election was that nothing at all actually had to happen. In a nation where political critics used to be shot or jailed, just plain critical talk, by itself, was a revolution.

Of course, in March 1989, Soviet elections had little in common with democracy as practiced in the West. Reserving one hundred seats for top Communists was only one step in Gorbachev's elaborate plan to guarantee a solid Communist victory. In addition, the Party manipulated the nominating process for all other parliamentary seats. Either it fixed nominating meetings at the outset against reform candidates, like Korotich, or a subsequent review commission later found "irregularities" sufficient to remove unwanted nominees from the ballot.

Independent-minded celebrities like Yeltsin or Sakharov were too famous to treat so brazenly without discrediting the entire election, at home and abroad. So the Communists let them run, although only under constant harassment. Apparatchiks continually sabotaged their campaigns, trying to drown them in red tape and dirty tricks. One favorite tactic was to switch the permitted site of an independent candidate's speech to a new location at the last minute, so that his supporters could not get there in time.

Less-known Party opponents fared even worse. Outside of Moscow, especially in other Soviet republics where no foreigners monitored the campaign, more violent totalitarian tactics often prevailed. In the Ukraine, protesters accused hard-line Communist Party leader Vladimir Shcherbitsky of rigging the election to ensure seats for his cronies. A crowd of forty thousand people gathered in the Western Ukrainian city of Lvov on March 12 to object, chanting, "Boycott the elections." Club-wielding police broke up their demonstration. "Police were vicious, beating people," said Stephan Khmara, one of the protesters.

These various Communist maneuvers produced the intended election results. Some prominent progressives like Yeltsin, Sakharov, and Korotich overcame all obstacles to win seats, but 80 percent of the members elected to the new Parliament were mainstream Communists. Thus the vast majority of the new legislature were still subject to Party discipline, still likely to vote the way their superiors demanded, or so it seemed then.

"It's just the Communist apparat playing games," Nina Belyayeva, a progressive lawyer, concluded at the time. "Actually they leave us worse off than we were. Before, we could argue that we had no democracy at all. But now the authorities can say, 'Look, you have elections. What are you complaining about?' " With hindsight, we now know she was wrong. Even with their huge Communist majority in the new parliament, the apparat could no longer control the game. The reformers had won far more than they realized at first.

In fact, the March 1989 parliamentary elections were a political watershed. Much more than idle talk and empty public rallies was involved. Despite all Gorbachev's limitations, despite all the Communist apparat's heavy-handed tactics, these elections marked nothing less than the beginning of the multiparty political system in the U.S.S.R., which would doom Communist rule. They did so because, quite unintentionally, Gorbachev let these elections risk losing the key to totalitarian power in the Soviet Union. Just how a Communist leader could set up his own Party for its ultimate fall, without knowing it at the time, needs a fuller explanation.

The key to Soviet totalitarian power was always the one-party state. That principle was enshrined in the constitution of the U.S.S.R. as Article 6, giving the Communist Party the "leading role" in Soviet life, meaning monopoly powers to run the country. Communists understood that any weakening of Article 6, any move toward a multiparty system, would be fatal to them. They knew that once given the opportunity to vote against communism and for opposition parties instead, the Soviet people would certainly do so. In the worst case, they feared such opposition could grow until communism was defeated and dumped into the dustbin of history. In short, any tampering with the Party's "leading role" in Article 6 was considered heresy by the Communist faithful.

That was the reason Gorbachev permitted individual independents to run in the 1989 parliamentary elections, but not opposition parties. He thought his decision was playing it safe, that Article 6 would be as strong after the election as before. Once again, Mikhail Sergeyevich had badly overestimated his ability to control events. He had focused on only one outcome of the campaign, his need to produce the largest possible Communist head count in the new Parliament. Yet in so doing, he had overlooked other consequences which would soon haunt him.

In the first place, elections are not only about people and parties. They are also about issues, and the relatively free speech in this campaign radically changed the issues at the top of the Soviet political agenda in a way Gorbachev had not foreseen. For the first time, the Communist Party's leading role at last became a major national political issue, openly debated by millions across the country. Yeltsin and other progressives constantly used the campaign to call for the repeal of Article 6. It was their way of demanding that opposition parties be legalized. Suddenly, the issue of a multiparty system, a key to any genuine democratic reform, was thrust front and center into the Soviet national consciousness.

In the second place, the seeds for that multiparty system had just been planted. Gorbachev's reforms had earlier permitted new grassroots political groups to organize on the local level, free from Communist Party control. These new grassroots organizations ran the gamut from pressure groups like environmentalists to trade associations and various clubs. They were part of Gorbachev's attempt to widen the intersection, to bring new segments of society into the political process. These groups were supposed to provide independent support for the Communists, and they did, although often without great enthusiasm.

Originally, their room for maneuver was small. They could not become opposition parties, as Article 6 still made that taboo. So instead they called themselves informal movements or societies, or any other label that avoided the name of party. Then they played politics on the local level, probing how far they might go.

The March 1989 parliamentary elections were a godsend for them. Suddenly, these grassroots groups could do what genuine independent parties do. They could support candidates of their choice for office in their district—perhaps a liberal young Communist, or even an independent—whether the old-line local Communist bosses liked it or not. With that, they made themselves the opposition political parties of the future. Despite being political newcomers, the grassroots groups did extremely well in the 1989 elections. Many helped elect candidates who, as new members of parliament, would push for constitutional change on issues like Article 6.

The new political forces did so well partly because they gave the progressive wing of the Communist Party a campaign advantage. Since the new grassroots groups were legal public organizations, Communists were free to join them. Many of the more liberal ones did so, or enlisted their support. Thus for the first time, young, promising, progressive Communists had an independent political base from which to challenge the older, more conservative Communists nominated by the Party for parliamentary seats. Simply put, if two or more Communists could run for the same seat, why not make one of them a young reformer? Let the official Party organization nominate old warhorses as usual. But now, a young Communist reformer could also run in the same district, with the support of the new grassroots organizations, and actually win. Ambitious newcomers quickly seized the opportunity.

Among them was Anatoly Sobchak, then an unknown young law professor from Leningrad University who had joined the Communist Party to back Gorbachev's perestroika reforms. Sobchak made his political debut by winning a parliamentary seat in 1989, backed by the new grassroots movements. In a campaign startling for the Soviet Union, the young professor called for genuine democratic rights by invoking Martin Luther King and declaring, "I too have a dream." His brilliance in televised parliamentary debates soon gained him national prominence. Sobchak later became mayor of St. Petersburg and one of the leading progressive politicians in Russia.

By the same token, old hard-line Communists often did poorly in the election to the new parliament. They lacked campaign experience, having never needed to compete for seats in past elections. Furthermore, they now entered the fray as damaged goods. The public blamed them for economic hardships, intolerable environmental pollution, KGB repression, privileged lifestyles, and much more. The old Party hacks were relatively easy targets for younger, more liberal Communists who called for meaningful reform and an end to Party perks. Thus in many districts, where a Party establishment figure stood against a Communist newcomer with grassroots backing, the competitive elections favored the younger candidate and turned into a generational sea change. Failure could be costly for the old guard. The most prominent loser in March 1989 among the hard-line Communists was Yuri Solovyov, first secretary of the Leningrad region and a candidate member of the Politburo. His rejection by the voters in the parliamentary election enabled Gorbachev to retire him from both his high Party jobs.

In the end, the overwhelming Communist majority in the new Parliament was less important than the composition of that majority. The more progressive young Sobchaks elected and the more conservative older Solovyovs defeated, the stronger the position of reform within Communist ranks. For the first time, the new grassroots parties in waiting had changed the mix. Reform Communists were still a minority, but their numbers had significantly increased.

As the architect of this election, Gorbachev was far from unhappy with that result—at first. Then he soon changed his mind as new deputies started marching farther and faster down the radical track than he thought wise. Moreover, these stronger new reform voices would now have to be heard. The clamor they raised on key issues, such as changing the one-party system enshrined in Article 6, would resound far beyond the halls of parliament.

Debates there would be televised nationally. Reform Communists like Sobchak tended to be the most articulate, effective speakers. The conservative Communist majority in the parliament might not like what they said, but often the country at large did.

It would take months to sort out the real political significance of the elections. What eventually emerged was something Gorbachev and the Politburo had not foreseen. Non-Communists like Sakharov, fallen Communists like Yeltsin, progressive Communists like Sobchak, and the liberal historian Yuri Afanasyev joined together in a radical bloc called the Interregional Group. At times they commanded hundreds of votes in the new parliament, more than any other faction except the mainstream Communists. They could not be an opposition political party. That was still illegal, but by calling themselves a parliamentary group instead, an informal alliance of independent members, they could be an effective legislative opposition anyway, pushing Gorbachev to more radical reform than he had intended.

Their pressure to scrap Article 6 and create a multiparty system became relentless. In this they had strong support from both the new grassroots organizations and large segments of society as a whole. Had the March 1989 parliamentary elections done nothing else, had they simply started the process toward a multiparty system that would soon break the Communist monopoly on power, they would have been a major milestone.

But in fact, these elections did a great deal more. They also fueled the nationalist movement that would soon break up the U.S.S.R. In Russia, the new grassroots forces had helped the more liberal Communists. In most other Soviet republics, however, these opposition parties in all but name would give new legitimacy to the struggle for independence. The Baltic states of Latvia, Lithuania, and Estonia led the way. Grassroots groups there became known as popular fronts, a transparent name for independence parties. The idea soon spread across the U.S.S.R., with republics from the Ukraine to Central Asia creating their own popular fronts.

In March 1989 these popular fronts supported Communists from their republics in the election to the new Soviet parliament. Often the Communists they backed were really separatists at heart. Some were both Communists and members of their popular front organizations. Once elected, these new deputies would use the Soviet parliament as an effective new platform to push for independence for their republics from the U.S.S.R.

This platform turned out to be far more than just a place for public speeches. Before long, it also became a coordinating center for nationalist rebellions. As legitimate new parliamentarians, the separatist deputies from various republics had every right to meet one another and coordinate strategy. As a direct result, popular fronts soon began helping each other push for self-rule. Their cooperation was to make their individual campaigns more effective.

Nor was that all. The popular fronts were happy to be represented in the

Soviet parliament. Still, they knew that all of them added together controlled only a small minority of the votes there. Indeed, they believed, that was why Gorbachev had let them into the new parliament in the first place. In so doing, however, Mikhail Sergeyevich had again been looking in the wrong direction. This time the Soviet leader had made one of his biggest mistakes.

The battle for independence would not be won in the Soviet parliament, where separatists were a minuscule minority. The battle for independence would be won at home in the various republics, from Latvia to the Ukraine to Armenia, where the separatists had a growing majority. These two political arenas, one in Moscow relatively safe for Gorbachev, the other in the republics highly dangerous for him, were linked in a way the Soviet leader had not properly foreseen. Having let popular fronts organize for the Soviet parliamentary elections that meant very little, Gorbachev could hardly bar them from organizing for elections inside their home republics that meant a great deal more. Once up and running, the popular fronts naturally focused on what counted most for them, mobilizing their own people for the independence struggle. They would build at home until they could challenge and defeat the Communists in elections to run their own republics. Then they would lead their Soviet-occupied homelands to independence.

Here was the real significance of Gorbachev's miscalculation. The Soviet leader thought he could contain nationalism in much the same way he expected to manage democratization. He failed at both for much the same reason. Mikhail Sergeyevich still believed reform could be imposed from the top down, in limited, controlled doses. Instead, it would begin to explode, from the bottom up. Ultimately, the March 1989 parliamentary elections left behind a fateful legacy. They gave birth to the multiparty system that would doom Communist power, and they encouraged the wave of nationalism that would break up the Soviet Union.

None of that was yet clear at the time. The decisive battles which would determine the fate of perestroika lay ahead. They could still go either way. Gorbachev would continue to show remarkable resilience. After each mistake, after every defeat, he would bounce back, breathing new life into perestroika for a time, in ways that would only create larger problems ahead. The cycle would be repeated again and again. Eventually it proved that reform Communism was an impossible goal, beyond the abilities of even an extraordinary leader like Mikhail Sergeyevich to achieve. In the end, there would be either communism or reform, not both. The evidence for that case, however, was still far from complete.

Gorbachev had no intention in 1989 of dooming either communism or the Soviet state. Instead he expected the new parliament would help him strengthen both, by approving new perestroika measures, over the objections of his Party's conservative old guard. Indeed, the Kremlin leader had every reason to believe he would succeed. The parliament was Mikhail Sergeyevich's idea, his creation, and he intended it to be his servant as well. Appropriately, the first major task of the new deputies was to elect Gorbachev, running unopposed, as the country's first executive president, with broad new powers to push for controlled reform. Mikhail Sergeyevich ordered the coronation process to be televised nationally so that all citizens could see him assume his enhanced status.

Such was the mentality of all Soviet leaders, even Gorbachev. They had spent lifetimes orchestrating public meetings in advance. This time, however, Mikhail Sergeyevich was in for a surprise. The parliament he had created, the Congress of People's Deputies, was not about to follow any preordained script. Gorbachev would ascend to the presidency, all right, but the final climb was an unexpected obstacle course that augured poorly for the fate of perestroika.

The Congress met for the first time in May. It convened in the same mammoth Kremlin hall where Brezhnev routinely got unanimous yes votes from the Party faithful for anything he wanted. The atmosphere could hardly have been more different when the new Congress opened there, with Gorbachev in the chair. This time, even the right of the most powerful man in the country to run the first meeting of the parliament he had personally created would be thrown open to rowdy questioning.

From the opening minutes, the Congress erupted into a bedlam of shouted objections. The initial outburst was a technical one. According to the rules, the chairman of the election commission, Vladimir Orlov, should have presided at the first session. When Gorbachev took the chair instead, it was the first chance for progressive deputies to show their independence by screaming he was out of order. The Soviet leader took it with good grace. "Do you want to overthrow me? Do you think I am not democratic enough?" Gorbachev asked with a smile.

"Maybe we should vote," Mikhail Sergeyevich decided before anyone could answer. Predictably, an overwhelming majority of the 2,250 deputies, by a show of hands, voted for him to chair the session. That was exactly the image Gorbachev had wanted to convey. He was strong enough to permit more democratic criticism, but at decision time, he still had the votes to get his way. After that, however, Gorbachev's intended coronation began to go awry.

Once he became the only nominee for the new executive presidency, Mikhail Sergeyevich had to submit to questioning over his qualifications. Deputies subjected him to a two-hour grilling, unprecedented for a reigning Kremlin leader. Questions tended to be offensive. Should he have a country dacha financed by the state? Shouldn't he give up the Communist Party leadership if he wanted to take over the presidency? Why were perestroika reforms so slow, the food shortages in the shops so bad? Some deputies didn't even bother with questions, preferring simply to hurl insults at Gorbachev. "You are unable to avoid the influence of flattery and that of your wife," one lawmaker declared.

Marju Lauriston, a deputy from independence-minded Estonia with a gift for going straight to the jugular, raised the toughest question of the day, the use of Soviet troops to put down recent nationalist demonstrations in Georgia and Armenia. "Tell us, please," she asked Gorbachev, "is it right to use the army for punitive operations against its own people?"

Mikhail Sergeyevich did his best to answer them all. To Lauriston, he replied, "We are still learning all the mechanisms of democracy." On the economic front, he admitted "major failures." Only once did the Soviet leader lose his composure under the torrent of accusations in the form of questions. "Don't think that Gorbachev can't see," he told the deputies. "He sees everything." His transparent attempt at intimidation, the thinly veiled threat that awkward questioners would pay politically later on, had no effect at all. With the Stalinist terror long gone, deputies could now defy a Kremlin leader. They would not be put off by mere words. So they continued their humiliating cross-examination.

A Soviet national television audience watched spellbound. Never before had they seen a reigning Kremlin leader subjected to offensive questioning or forced into embarrassing admissions of inadequacy. With each such blow, Gorbachev lost stature in their eyes. All their lives the Soviet people had only seen Kremlin leaders with awesome powers that no mere parliamentary deputy would dare challenge. Now, on television, they saw a Soviet leader who could be defied repeatedly, by opponents who would not be punished for such impertinence. They also saw a Kremlin chief confronted with questions for which he had no adequate answers. Before, Gorbachev had always seemed to them to be energetic and in control. Now, for the first time, he appeared weak and inadequate.

When the grilling finished, Gorbachev was duly elected Soviet president. The vote was 2,123 in favor, 87 against, with 11 abstentions. Inside the hall he had won. Outside, on the country's TV screens, his public image had been substantially diminished, if not irreparably damaged. His intended coronation was a public relations disaster. The lesson to the Soviet people could not have been clearer. If deputies could challenge Gorbachev with impunity, then so could they, each in his own way. It was a telling moment.

The popular army which Gorbachev had expected to enlist in support of perestroika reforms now turned against him. The manifold grievances felt by typical Soviet citizens far outweighed any benefits they recognized from Mikhail Sergeyevich's rule. The right to read Solzhenitsyn meant very little if they couldn't get enough to eat. Most people had seen their living standards decline under Gorbachev's perestroika. The reasons for that will shortly be examined in detail. Suffice it to say here that economic decline produced even bigger problems. For one thing, it fueled nationalism. Had minority nationalities been better fed in the Soviet Union, their incentive to wage independence struggles might well have collapsed. Soon Gorbachev's controversial foreign policy added to the mix of grievances. The half million Soviet troops brought home from Eastern Europe with no place to live contributed both to the economic malaise and to the danger of a social explosion. All these grievances found their outlets in public demonstrations, thanks to Gorbachev's democratization. Thus, for the first time, the four key ingredients that would determine the outcome of the battle over perestroika—economic decline, rising nationalism, foreign policy controversies, and democratization—had all come together in a potentially fatal mix for Gorbachev.

II. ECONOMIC FAILURE: GOD CRIES

Nowhere was the outlook now grimmer than on the economic front. By 1989, four years into Gorbachev's rule, his economic reforms were failing. Unless that could soon be reversed, political reform would be finished as well. For that reason we now need to interrupt the story of political democratization for an economic reality check.

If ever there was a time for effective Western economic help, early 1989 was the moment. It might have made a difference. Unfortunately, among Mikhail Sergeyevich's admirers in the West, the more influential Soviet specialists in government and the academic community failed to see the Soviet economic situation was so grave.[2] They knew the stakes were high, that hopes for democratic change in the U.S.S.R. and for a more peaceful international climate both depended to a large extent on the success of perestroika's economic reforms. Still, their judgment was clouded. They overrated Gorbachev's political strength. The United States government, among others, was thus ill prepared when Mikhail Sergeyevich ran out of time and his power collapsed.

Newsweek was the first American publication to sound the alarm, with a comprehensive report on the economic failure of the Gorbachev years. I wrote it from Moscow in March 1989. "Why His Reforms Don't Work," the headline on the *Newsweek* cover read. Professor Stephen Cohen of Princeton dismissed that judgment as "premature." In fact, it was quite accurate, even then. Cohen and other pro-Gorbachev Soviet specialists in the West were behind the curve. They would have served both Mikhail Sergeyevich and their own governments better had they pointed out the problems in time. That way the West might have done more sooner to help Gorbachev's reforms succeed. Instead, valuable time was wasted.

George Bush, for example, the newly elected president of the United States, spent his first six months in office, to June 1989, conducting a leisurely review of policy toward the Soviet Union. As vice president for eight years, Bush had been well briefed on U.S.–Soviet relations. Nevertheless he ordered the review to separate his administration from that of his predecessor, Ronald

Reagan. In Moscow, senior officials, including top Gorbachev aides, suspected more sinister motives. They thought the policy review was a delaying tactic to pressure Gorbachev into concessions on arms control and other superpower negotiations. At precisely the time when Gorbachev's reforms were seen in Moscow to be failing, when Western help could have made a difference, the Bush administration appeared to the Kremlin to be making unnecessary waves.

Later rather than sooner, Bush decided to help Gorbachev and the reforms. By then, however, much time had been lost. Admittedly, earlier Western help for perestroika may not have been politically feasible or economically effective, given the manifold difficulties involved, but we will never know that now. All we know for sure is that the Western help eventually provided turned out to be too little, too late.

On the crucial issue of economic performance, Gorbachev was in desperate trouble from early 1989 on. Unless he could make early and substantial progress in fixing that, his battle for perestroika reforms would be lost. Despite such desperate stakes, the Soviet leader entered 1989 with little hope that the West would help or that the U.S.S.R. itself could straighten out the economic decline. His New Year's message to the Soviet people was unusually downbeat. After reviewing the reform effort to date, Gorbachev admitted, "The results cannot satisfy us."

He had no choice but to admit the obvious. His own government's official account of the past year's economic performance was a chronicle of failure—missed plan targets in agriculture, industry, consumer goods, investment, and overall growth. "The economic reform is still not working at full capacity, and the national economy has still not mastered the necessary acceleration," the government report said, four years into Perestroika. It was a damning indictment.

The Soviet people didn't need government reports to confirm the economic failure so far. Their living standards, never very high in Western terms, were getting worse. Shortages in food, housing, and virtually all consumer goods continued to grow. Increasingly, they blamed perestroika for the mess, with good reason. Gorbachev had wanted to revitalize the stagnating Brezhnev economy. His answer was to free factories and farms from excessive bureaucratic control so they could respond better to free-market laws of supply and demand. Only so far, his transition from the command economy to the market economy had produced the worst of both worlds, a disruptive mix of only marginally freer enterprise and only slightly looser central control. It had neither the stability of the now crumbling old system nor the promised improvements of the still all too fragile new one. The result by early 1989 was fewer goods on the shelves and longer lines outside the shops.

"There's nothing in the stores now," Sasha Cheburkov, a young Russian doctor, told me at the time. "The supply situation has never been worse." Thus discouraged, he soon emigrated to the United States. Sasha was not alone. The brain drain he represented ran in the thousands. Gorbachev's reforms had permitted freer emigration. Among those taking advantage of this new opportunity, mainly because of the bleak economic outlook at home, were some of the country's best and brightest young people. It was yet another blow to the first Soviet leader to let them leave.

For the vast majority of Soviet citizens who stayed behind, the economy was also crucial. If the decline continued, it risked provoking mass public protests, now permitted by democratization. These rallies could turn violent, and could be used as a pretext by Gorbachev's conservative opponents to bring him down and roll back reform. Thus economic failure was now the frontline issue, likely to decide the fate of the entire reform effort. As such it needs to be examined in some detail. Only in that way can the enormousness of Gorbachev's task become clear.

Four years into the Gorbachev era, every key sector of the Soviet economy was sending the same signal. It was this: reform has failed so far, and the original target dates for success in a year or two are much too optimistic. Leonid Abalkin, one of Gorbachev's top advisers, admitted that "it will probably take one or two generations" to turn the economy around. That was particularly bad news for the Soviet leader. No politician could count on generations at the top. Meanwhile, everywhere the experts looked they found evidence to justify Abalkin's pessimism.

In industry, for example, even the best success stories attributed to the Gorbachev reforms were nowhere near good enough. Mikhail Bocharov, one of those early successes, showed me why that was true during a visit to his factory in early 1989.

Bocharov made a dazzling first impression. He sat in his office under portraits of Karl Marx and Friedrich Engels, explaining how capitalist methods were now saving his Butova building materials combine outside Moscow. His plant was one of the first in the country to adopt successfully to self-financing, a crucial element of the Gorbachev reforms. He reeled off the details with obvious delight. On January 1, 1988, Bocharov offered shares in the business to his 450 workers. He promised them 6 percent interest on their investments, roughly twice what they could get in state savings banks. Then he used their money as capital to modernize production of bricks and other building materials. In the first year, profits soared from zero to $1.4 million. Part of that, Bocharov said, would now go into a sports club, covered tennis court, and sauna for the staff. It all sounded too good to be true.

Sure enough, the bad news became obvious once I insisted on leaving Bocharov's showcase office to tour the real world of his factory. The production line was hopelessly outdated, barely automated to 1920 standards in the West. A relatively small input in modernization capital had produced the first year's big jump in profits. In the baking of bricks, for instance, only one low investment, a small new device to regulate oven temperatures automatically, had made all the difference. To remain profitable now, however, and to make the plant a long-term success, Bocharov had to undertake full-scale modernization. For that he needed large bank loans he could not finance, or huge state subsidies he had no hope of getting. Furthermore, there was no way he could ease the financial squeeze by his own management decisions. Despite Gorbachev's reforms, central planners still largely determined production, marketing, pricing, and supply questions. "We still need more freedom from central authorities here," Bocharov admitted. His year-old experiment in self-financing was already in serious trouble. So much for the model success story. Worse for Gorbachev, few other plants in the country could claim even that much progress.

In agriculture, the outlook was no better. The fundamental problem there was the proven failure of the state-run collective farm system.[3] Private farming had to be reestablished if the Soviet Union was to feed itself properly. China, in fact, recognized this as the key to overhauling the Communist economic system. With one billion mouths to feed, the Chinese had no other choice but to start their reforms with agriculture. They converted successfully from communal to family farms, their method of agricultural privatization, thus increasing food supplies substantially. Only with that essential triumph in hand, and the public support it generated, did they then embark on reforming other economic sectors.

Many Western specialists believe Gorbachev's Soviet Union should have taken the same road to reform and started with agriculture. By focusing first on the farms, Mikhail Sergeyevich could have concentrated his resources on the economic sector that most needed fixing. Any success in improved food supplies would have done more to widen and deepen his public support than any other single step he could have possibly taken in the early years of perestroika. Furthermore, Gorbachev was uniquely equipped to start with farm policy. He knew the issue inside out as the former Party secretary in charge of agriculture. Still, economic logic and personal experience were not the overriding factors here. The sad truth is there was no way Gorbachev could have started perestroika by converting to private farming.

For one thing, the Soviet Union was not China. Soviets suffered from subsistence-level diets, but there was no serious threat of Chinese-scale mass starvation. Unlike Beijing, therefore, Moscow was not obliged to start reforms on the farm. More important, as a world superpower, unlike China, the U.S.S.R. had long deliberately held down all consumer sectors of the economy, including agriculture, to remain in the arms race with the United States. Gorbachev could now shift those priorities only at his peril. Effective agriculture reform would need not only privatization, but also huge investments in transport, storage, and food-processing facilities. And financial resources on the scale required could come only from the military-industrial complex. If he had launched perestroika with agriculture, Mikhail Sergeyevich would have had to sacrifice arms for farms, but in that case, the conservative majority on the Politburo would never have let him get started. They would have thrown him out first.

Finally, collectivized agriculture was still a major principle of Soviet ideological faith. No new Kremlin chief could start off by turning that upside down in a rush to private farming. Inevitably, therefore, the perestroika reforms on agriculture were much too timid. Gorbachev compromised between collective and private farming. He offered collective farmers fifty-year leases so they could work state land privately, as their own. Once again his compromise was doomed to fail.

There were many reasons for this. First, most Soviet farmers already had assured incomes from collective or state farms and additional revenue from small private plots. They had little incentive to take on a new risk of profit or loss by investing in a lease. Second, leases were good only for their lifetime and could not be passed on to their children. Third, local officials were not compelled to mount propaganda campaigns to sell the leasehold idea, which meant no one had to take it very seriously. And fourth, local farmers had no faith that the leasehold law would last any longer than other perestroika changes which had been loudly proclaimed as new laws one day only to be rescinded the next.

The second reason alone was enough to condemn the leasing plan. "Nobody will believe there is real private ownership of farmland until people are allowed to leave leases to their heirs," liberal economist Nikolai Shmelev predicted. He was right. Gorbachev's leasehold experiments got little support and changed nothing. By 1989, four years into his reforms, agriculture was still a disaster area. In winter, tractors were still left to rust in snow-covered fields because there were no sheds to house them in. A third of the country's livestock was still lost each year because of poor veterinary care. Food was rationed in eight of the fifteen Soviet republics.

Agriculture was also typical of Gorbachev's overall performance on reform. On the farm he had tried for a third way, his leasehold idea, a middle road between collective and private farming, only to get lost in unworkable compromise. Similarly, in his broader economic reform, Mikhail Sergeyevich was seeking a middle road between the command and free-market systems. There too he got lost in failure. Once again, on political reform, his answer was a third way between democracy and Communist control. Predictably, all his compromises proved unworkable there as well. In truth there was no viable third way in any of these areas. Communism and capitalism would mix no better than oil and water. Sooner or later, Gorbachev would have to choose between them. His compromise third way was a road to nowhere, creating more problems than solutions.

Nowhere was that clearer than with the cooperatives, the small private businesses created under Gorbachev's reforms. They were the thin wedge of capitalism, tolerated to make the Communist economy work better. Where the state fell down, they would fill gaps, from shoemaking to dentistry to restaurants, usually with higher-quality service. In May 1988, a new law permitting entrepreneurs to set up co-ops for profit touched off an explosion. By the start of 1989 there were 77,000 co-ops in the Soviet Union employing 1.5 million people. Unfortunately, the early success created more controversy than joy. The co-ops soon became a political football in the continuing battle over reform.

Part of the trouble was culture shock. For decades in the Soviet Union, "capitalism" had been a dirty word. Perfectly normal business practice in the West was criminal behavior in Russia. Now suddenly, the Soviet people were supposed to forget all that and think just the opposite, that capitalist activity was actually quite good. It proved to be a difficult adjustment.

In the Soviet command economy, for example, there had been no middlemen. Indeed, that had been one of its major weaknesses. Middlemen provide an essential service in any rational economy, bringing suppliers and customers together. In the Soviet Union, however, all middlemen were outlawed as capitalist speculators. If the country's only permitted supplier, the state, did not reach its customers, the public, because of bureaucratic ineptitude in the distribution system, well, too bad. No middleman, no private individual, had the right to do anything about it.

The shortage-plagued economy was an invitation to try, of course, but relatively few dared to take on the risks involved. Any middleman who bought anything from the state at a low price, sold it to the public at a higher price, and took the difference as a profit for this service could be branded as a criminal speculator, to be jailed, or even shot. Those ground rules had been clear for decades. Then suddenly Gorbachev had waived the rules. Middlemen were no longer speculators. They were legitimate businessmen. They could buy low from state suppliers and sell high to the public, pocketing the profit as legal cooperative businesses. The law could be changed at a stroke of the president's pen, but old public attitudes would be much slower to adjust.

To most Soviet citizens, the new co-ops were at least price-gougers, if not outright criminals. Many suspected it was usually the former criminal speculators and black marketeers who now became the legal cooperative businessmen, because they were the only ones with experience in taking risks for profit. Others still thought that whatever the background of the new entrepreneurs, there was still something dirty about private trading.

The culture shock led to public outrage and government rollback. Before the end of 1988, the same Gorbachev who had created the co-ops earlier in the year started approving new laws to restrict them. First the government barred co-ops from many businesses, including book publishing and medical supplies. Then it imposed controls on prices. Then Gorbachev signed a decree raising taxes on co-op revenue from a maximum 5 percent to an obligatory 35 percent. "It's the revenge of the bureaucrats," Arkady Zaitsev, a young co-op manager, said. "This decision was just taken by officials. There was no public discussion, certainly not among cooperatives. They are breaking down what has just been created." Worse, Gorbachev's rollback was defeating his original purpose. The climate of uncertainty he created—the permissions one day, the restrictions the next—would discourage entrepreneurs from taking the risks and launching the private firms Gorbachev wanted.

In some ways the state was doing too much to control co-ops. In other ways it was not doing nearly enough. The worst failure was inadequate protection, and with that, the Soviet Mafia was born. The first symptoms appeared in 1988, as soon as the new private businesses started making big money. In one early example, the manager of a new, privately run Moscow restaurant received a typed letter from a Mafia-style criminal gang. "Your cooperative is located in the district served by our organization," the letter said. "You must pay us an annual tax of 300 rubles [then $489]" for protection. "In case you don't pay," it warned, "your windows will be smashed and your tax increased to 400 rubles [$652]."

Refusing to be intimidated, the manager worked with police, who caught two culprits red-handed at the payoff meeting. Then, even though the crooks confessed, police had to let them go. The reason: Soviet law on extortion still covered only state firms, not the new private businesses recently legalized. Their release was a fitting omen for the years ahead. The once-feared Soviet police state would be no match for the coming criminal challenge.

The Mafia would quickly become one of the Soviet Union's major growth industries, exceeding all expectations. It would diversify into every economic activity, including the illegal sale abroad of Soviet nuclear weapons technology. Its protection demands would soar from hundreds of dollars to millions for a single enterprise. Its bribes would buy the services of senior government officials. Its enforcers would escalate from breaking windows to hired killings and street shoot-outs in broad daylight. Mafia excesses and corruption would soon become a key political issue in Gorbachev's Soviet Union, and would only get worse after the collapse of communism.

Many Russians still blame the Mafia menace on Gorbachev. They think his reforms created it. That is not quite fair, but not completely false either. Criminal gangs in the Soviet empire traced their origins back to tsarist days, often on ethnic or tribal lines. Gorbachev's reforms, and particularly the co-ops, did not create the gangs, but rather a new climate of opportunity, which the criminals soon exploited. Mikhail Sergeyevich then compounded the problem by failing to meet the Mafia challenge. In most Soviet minds, crime and private business were always related. At the very least, Soviets thought the criminals' success marred the progress of legitimate private business. At worst they were convinced no private business could succeed without Mafia links. Those attitudes would help discredit Gorbachev's reforms for the rest of his rule, one more sign that perestroika was failing.

The Gorbachev reforms had brought declines in industry and agriculture and a rise in crime. There was only one major economic sector which held fairly steady through perestroika, where nothing much changed: the military. And that too was part of the problem.

In the shortage-racked Soviet economy, the military remained a privileged zone of relative plenty. It could still count on the best personnel, the best supplies, the top-priority deliveries. According to Western estimates it still swallowed some 30 percent of Soviet GNP every year, impoverishing other economic sectors in the process and further endangering Gorbachev's perestroika. Never was the privileged position of the military more obvious than in December 1988 when a disastrous earthquake leveled the Armenian city of Leninakan. The Soviet government rushed in cranes to lift up slabs of concrete from collapsed apartment houses, but the search for survivors soon ground to a halt. Local authorities could provide no more fuel to run the cranes. Fortunately, they knew where to turn. In the Soviet Union there was always one privileged economic sector that never suffered from shortages—the military. Sure enough, the Soviet army commander in the Leninakan region had abundant fuel. He provided the needed gas. The cranes began to dig again for earthquake survivors. Lives were saved.

Gorbachev's failing perestroika also needed an infusion of energy from the military. This time emergency short-term measures would no longer do. Large, long-term defense budget cuts were necessary to transfer enough resources into the civilian economy to save reform. Yet despite the need, Gorbachev never really got started. He talked a lot about converting defense plants to civilian production, but in 1989, with only modest cuts ordered in military spending, his conversion program hardly got off the ground.

With that, all the leading economic indicators pointed in the same bleak direction by early 1989. Perestroika was failing, and there was little realistic prospect that reforms could recover. The Soviet people were losing faith. They began to think reform would never improve their lives. Jokes turned even more bitter. In one such anecdote from the late 1980s, showing what Soviet citizens thought of their own plight, Ronald Reagan, Margaret Thatcher, and Gorbachev appear before God.

Reagan asks, "When will the American people be happy?" God replies, "In one hundred and fifty years." Reagan cries and says, "I won't live that long."

Then Thatcher asks, "When will the British people be happy?" God answers, "In one hundred years." Thatcher cries and says, "I won't live that long."

Finally, Gorbachev asks, "When will the Soviet people be happy?" This time God cries and says, "I won't live that long."

Such was the depth of Soviet pessimism by early 1989. Gorbachev had begun to lose his way. From then on his political authority would decline with the economy. Foreign policy successes could no longer save him. Nationality unrest would increasingly hurt him. Democratization would make his troubles all the more obvious.

Boris Yeltsin was among the first to appreciate the gravity of Gorbachev's position. On June 1, 1989, in an interview with me, Yeltsin said: "The situation in the country is extremely alarming. Anti-perestroika forces are consolidating and becoming more active. Corruption and criminality are growing. Social equality is declining and poverty rising. The faith of the people in the results of perestroika is collapsing."

Yeltsin's views all proved to be correct. The situation was indeed getting out of hand. But the real significance of that interview was what it said about how fast Gorbachev's perilous position would unravel. In the end, the speed must have surprised even Yeltsin. In June 1989, when Yeltsin agreed to this interview, he did not even have an office. He had just been elected to the new parliament and no office space had yet been allocated to him. So he agreed to meet me on a park bench outside the Kremlin wall. During the interview, it began to rain. Yeltsin and I then stood under a tree. He held an umbrella for the two of us while I took notes. The next time I interviewed Boris Yeltsin was in December 1991, inside an opulent Kremlin reception room, on the day he arranged to take Gorbachev's place as the country's top leader. The speed of Yeltsin's rise was phenomenal. In only two and a half years, the man who had no office at all would move into the highest office in the land.

Gorbachev also understood the gravity of the situation in mid-1989. He saw no reason to give up, however, because despite the manifest problems, he now had more power to resolve them than ever before. He was both the leader of the Communist Party and the nation's first executive president. He had the political initiative and the skill to play the Party against the new parliament he had created as an alternative. He would soon add to those powers. One way or another, Mikhail Sergeyevich believed, he would still steer perestroika through all the dangers and make the reforms irreversible. His optimism was still infectious. Indeed, at the time, it looked like he still might be right.

III. HOLIDAYS FROM HELL

The Soviet president was always toughest in adversity. Gorbachev proved that once again at a Central Committee plenum in September 1989. When it was over, his political position at the head of the Communist Party had been immeasurably strengthened. For the first time since he became general secretary in March 1985, Mikhail Sergeyevich could now count on a Politburo majority. As before, when his program was in trouble, when his popularity was sinking, Gorbachev compensated by adding to his own power.

At the September 1989 plenum, Gorbachev retired three conservative opponents on the Politburo, including the last of the Brezhnev holdovers, Ukrainian Party leader Vladimir Shcherbitsky. As usual, he paid a price. This time, he was obliged to elevate another conservative, KGB chief Vladimir Kryuchkov, to full Politburo membership. It was ultimately a fateful move. In August 1991, Kryuchkov would lead a coup d'état against Gorbachev. In September 1989, however, despite his conservative views, Kryuchkov was widely seen as the president's man. He had leaped straight into full Politburo membership without serving the normal apprenticeship, often lasting several years, as a nonvoting or candidate member. At the time, usually well-informed Communist Party sources in Moscow explained Kryuchkov's rapid rise this way: the KGB chief had effectively given Gorbachev advance warning of various maneuvers by Ligachev and other hard-line opponents. Immediate promotion to full voting status on the Politburo was the KGB chief's reward, they said, for services rendered to the president by a loyal supporter.

The September 1989 reshuffle involved both retirements and replacements. When it was over, the Politburo had eleven members. Of them, Soviet sources and Western diplomats agreed, Gorbachev could now count on a majority of six votes. Thus, for the first time, the Communist Party's most powerful body would be under his control. Party hard-liners could not legally fire him, the way they had gotten rid of Khrushchev. His new invulnerability would let him push perestroika reforms even more effectively. Or so he thought.

The reality in the country was very different. That same month, September 1989, the Soviet weekly magazine *Ogonyok* published excerpts from a new novel by Aleksandr Kabakov called *The Defector*. It began this way:

> It is 1992, winter in Moscow after a coup d'état. A burst of machine-gun fire is heard in the area of Maslovka Street. The first extraordinary constituent assembly of the Russian Union of Democratic Parties is beginning its work in the Kremlin. . . . The president of the preparatory committee is a general, entering the Kremlin not on a white horse, but on a white tank.
>
> There is hunger in the country. Moscow is under martial law. Groups of different forces, including armed nationalists, are committing outrages. In the evening, citizens do not go out without a Kalashnikov [automatic rifle]. Our days, the blessed times of shortages of delicacies and difficulties with vodka, are recalled as a paradise. Now everything is different. There is the thunder of an explosion somewhere in front of me. I fasten a bayonet to my machine gun. There are cruel checks by the National Security Commission. There is hatred, black ruin in the streets. Blood has become a part of everyday life. . . .

The novel caused a sensation. Its fiction reflected truth, its vision of the near future an all too likely outgrowth of the potentially calamitous present. The specter it raised of military coup, civil war, and national chaos would remain high in the national consciousness for the rest of Gorbachev's rule.

Gorbachev himself was not blind to these dangers. In a September 1989 speech he acknowledged "voices predicting imminent chaos, and speculation about the threat of a coup, or even civil war." That was no exaggeration. From then on, those threats only got worse. By January 1990, East Germany, Czechoslovakia, Bulgaria, and Romania had all turned against communism. Nicolae Ceauşescu, the longtime Romanian Communist leader, had been toppled in a coup, then executed along with his wife. Inside the Soviet Union, the Lithuanian Communist Party made independence its official policy, and communal clashes in Armenia and Azerbaijan escalated toward civil war. The dangers of rebellion, coup, and civil war were no longer the stuff of popular novels. They were now the reality of East European and Soviet communism.

Mikhail Sergeyevich responded with the boldest stroke of his rule. He knew now that given the dangers around him, going back or standing still would solve nothing. Only a more radical leap forward could save perestroika. It was time to bet everything on one throw of the dice. He would gamble on genuine democratization. The Soviet Communist Party's monopoly on power, its seventy-two years of one-party rule, would have to go. Article 6 of the constitution would at last be changed. A multiparty system would be installed, and would save the perestroika reforms. Such was the plan Gorbachev now imposed on his incredulous Communist Party.

Until now, Communists had stuck with him, not only because Communists traditionally played follow the leader, but also because they believed his key reform goal was to improve and strengthen the Party. Communists simply could not believe that their leader would deliberately set out to weaken or risk destroying their own Party. Gorbachev was about to prove them wrong. At a Central Committee plenum in February 1990, he would get rid of Article 6 and make the Party drop its monopoly on power.

Mikhail Sergeyevich had two main reasons for acting when he did. First, since the previous September, he had had a working majority on the Politburo. He could get what he wanted from the Party, but how long that situation would last was anyone's guess. Second, the multiparty system now had broad public support. On February 4, on the eve of the fatal plenum, more than 100,000 people, at the time the largest unofficial demonstration in Moscow in Soviet history, marched to the Kremlin walls to demand an end to one-party rule.

The huge demonstration had a deliciously appropriate historic parallel. In February 1917, a popular revolution had overthrown the tsar and turned Russia into a democracy. But the triumph of that uprising, known as the

February Revolution, was short-lived. In the second revolution of that year, in October 1917, Lenin's Bolsheviks seized power and imposed a Communist dictatorship. Now, in February 1990, Russians were marching again to restore democracy. "Long live the peaceful revolution of February 1990 that is now under way," the liberal historian and parliamentary deputy Yuri Afanasyev shouted in an address to the demonstrators.

At the February 1990 plenum, Gorbachev and other progressives insisted Article 6 and the one-party state had to go, or the winds of change already swirling through Eastern Europe would sweep them away anyway. Mikhail Sergeyevich confidently predicted that if they embraced genuine reform, the Communists would earn their power through free, competitive elections. Or as Foreign Minister Eduard Shevardnadze told the plenum, "A Party possessing vital capacity does not need a monopoly on power." Other Central Committee members used darker arguments. "If we don't change here ourselves, we could end up like Romania," one warned.

The shift to a multiparty system was only the beginning. It would be tested in future elections for the first time against newly legal opposition parties. No one could yet predict how that might pan out. The Communists might win or lose at the ballot box in the years ahead. But Gorbachev was not satisfied with future change. He wanted immediate changes in the present power structure. The Soviet leader was out for blood.

So he also rammed through the same plenum another political change, this one with immediate effect. From now on, the key political decisions in the country would be made not by the Party Politburo but by the president and his cabinet. As Aleksandr Yakovlev put it at the time, "The president and his cabinet will have full powers of government in this country. It is a major step away from the administrative command model of socialism, toward a new democratic society."

Nor was that all. Sources close to Gorbachev said the Soviet leader planned one more key step. He would have the new parliament amend the constitution so the president would henceforth be directly elected by the people. Mikhail Sergeyevich himself would then run, in 1994, for a second five-year term. Only this time, instead of being appointed by the rigged Communist majority in parliament, as in 1989, he would have the legitimacy of a public vote of confidence. By then, the Gorbachev camp hoped, the economic reforms would be working, and a grateful public would give Mikhail Sergeyevich a vote of thanks.

At that stage, Politburo power would be history. Instead of the Politburo, the president, his cabinet, and the parliament would run policy. Instead of the Politburo, the public at large would choose the nation's leader by democratic vote. All the Politburo could do then would be to run what was left of the Communist Party in its uphill battle to survive competitive elections on local, regional, and national levels.

There could be no clearer declaration of war by Gorbachev against his own Communist Party. All the old ambiguities of a compromise "third way" were finally gone. Gorbachev had at last chosen. He had selected reform over communism. Furthermore, he held the initiative. Mikhail Sergeyevich secured approval from the February 1990 plenum for all the changes he wanted. He would push next to make those reforms irreversible. Despite his early advantages. however, Gorbachev had not yet won. The conservative Party faithful were in no mood to accept permanent defeat. They would regroup, and fight another day.

Ligachev made that clear at the plenum. "I am against turning our Party into a shapeless organization, a political club," he said. Then Ligachev warned ominously, "The most valuable thing in our life is the confidence of the Soviet people in a socialist future. Now we are losing much of that." He and others decided Gorbachev had gone too far. They would strike back.

The long struggle for power in the Kremlin would continue. Gorbachev had simply reorganized the battle lines. In one way, Mikhail Sergeyevich had done the conservatives a favor. His abandonment of Article 6 had made him a traitor in the eyes of the Party rank and file. They could no longer have any illusions. Ligachev and the other conservatives were at last free to campaign openly against Gorbachev within the Party, to bring him down and reverse his reforms.

The February 1990 plenum did not solve Gorbachev's long-term problems. Instead, it raised the stakes and hastened the day of ultimate decision. Hard-line Communists were not the only ones dissatisfied with the plenum. For all its admitted progress, radical reformers were still not happy either, Yeltsin among them. "I still find Gorbachev trying to write his proposals with his right hand and his left hand—always compromising," Yeltsin said.

Radicals like Yeltsin had little confidence in Gorbachev's belated commitment to genuine democracy. To be sure, he was now favoring reform over communism, but, they suspected, he could always turn back the other way if that proved a better expedient to retain power. The main trouble with Gorbachev, they argued, was that he continued to impose reform from the top down. Welcome as the February plenum decisions were, reform from the top down was no longer good enough. What Gorbachev gave one day, he could take away the next. Furthermore, the compromises Gorbachev handed down from on high were often unworkable or even counterproductive. The radicals knew that for reform to succeed, it must now come from the bottom up. Increasingly, public opinion was siding with them.

Gorbachev still occupied the political center between Ligachev's conservatives and Yeltsin's radicals. It was the Soviet leader's favorite middle ground. From there he could maneuver, compromise, and keep holding the key strings. His political base in the center, however, was now beginning to evaporate. From now on the two extremes, the radical reformers and the conservative hard-liners, would grow at the expense of Gorbachev's middle ground. In the end, for all his new powers, for all his success at the February plenum, 1990 was not a good year for Mikhail Sergeyevich. On the contrary, it was the year opposition on both sides of him gained crucial strength and began to squeeze him out. Moreover, those troubles were on public display, on the two most important Soviet holidays of the year, May Day and November 7. For Gorbachev, both occasions this year would look like holidays designed in hell.

Traditionally, May Day, the international labor day that Moscow celebrated on May 1, was a mass exercise in hail to the Kremlin chief. Tens of thousands of Soviet citizens dutifully marched through Red Square, carrying portraits of the *vozhd*, the top Soviet leader, and slogans singing his praises. Bands played, flags waved, red balloons soared skyward. The leader and his fellow Politburo members stood atop Lenin's tomb, inundated with flowers from a grateful public, smiling and waving back to acknowledge the continuing cheers from the masses parading through the square. The script had always been the same, whether Stalin, Khrushchev, Brezhnev, or Gorbachev was the leader waving back. In May 1990, however, Moscow's radical reformers changed it beyond recognition.

"Communists exploit the workers," said one of the first banners paraded past Gorbachev and his Politburo on May Day 1990. "Down with the Cult of Lenin," said a second. A third, directed personally at Gorbachev, declared, "Freedom for Lithuania: Shame on the Imperialist President." For the first time ever, Soviet citizens by the thousands marched through Red Square, attacking the Communist Party, its ideology, and its leaders, literally under the noses of the Kremlin elite. Stalin had had Russians shot for less. Brezhnev had sent them to labor camps. All Gorbachev and his Politburo could do was turn their backs on the critical onslaught and walk grim-faced off the reviewing stand. Their departure triggered a final, unprecedented insult. "Resign, resign," the marchers chanted at the departing Soviet leadership.

"This is now a country pregnant with revolution," remarked a West European ambassador watching in Red Square. A Russian marcher was more specific. To him the time for reform communism was over. Now, he said, the time had come for reform without communism. "The people want to get rid of communism," he declared.

On November 7, 1990, the anniversary of the 1917 Bolshevik Revolution, Gorbachev returned to Red Square for another parade and an even worse holiday shock. Aleksandr Shomov, an unemployed factory worker from Leningrad, managed to smuggle a sawed-off shotgun into Red Square under his raincoat. How he did so, past twenty thousand KGB agents on duty there, remains a mystery to this day. Every person allowed onto the square to watch the parade had to have a personal invitation. And before he was allowed in, he had to get by at least five security men who checked both the invitation and his identity papers again and again.

When Gorbachev appeared on Lenin's Tomb, Shomov took out the shotgun and aimed it at him. Miraculously, an alert uniformed policeman, who just happened to be standing nearby, saw the move and immediately grabbed the weapon before Shomov could release the trigger. During the struggle, two shots fired harmlessly into the air echoed across the cavernous square. Shomov was wrestled to the ground, then bundled off under arrest by the KGB, charged as a terrorist, and declared to be mentally unbalanced. The disturbing incident raised far more questions than it answered. Many Russians believed the first known assassination attempt against Gorbachev could never have happened without the cooperation of anti-perestroika KGB agents who had let the gunman into the square.

Whatever the truth of that, a clear pattern had now been established. Holidays were a bad time for Gorbachev. Radical reformers had attacked him on May Day. A disgruntled worker tried to kill him on November 7. So far, only the summer holidays had been spared. That would change the following year, during Gorbachev's August vacation on the Black Sea, with the hardline coup that seized power from him. Bad as the holidays were for Gorbachev in 1990, they would only get worse in 1991.

IV. BUCKING THE SYSTEM

Despite the danger signals to Gorbachev personally, 1990 would still be remembered most of all as the year of democratization. It was the year the Communist monopoly on power gave way to a democratic multiparty system. It was the year unofficial mass demonstrations of 100,000 or more became routine. It was the year May Day marchers for the first time told the Soviet leadership what they really thought. And it was the year that democratization reached down from the national to the regional and local levels.

In March 1990, a year after Gorbachev's new Soviet parliament was elected, the people again went to the polls, this time for regional and local assemblies. I decided to measure the extent of the new democratization in Moscow, where my old friend Igor Belyayev was running for the city council.

For many years, Igor had been an important measuring rod for me of what the real Russia was like. With Igor, I could forget the absurd claims from Soviet officials and their controlled press about progress across the country. Igor would show me what ordinary Russians were up against in their everyday lives, from food shortages to bureaucratic nightmares to a cruel absence of adequate medical care. He was never a dissident. Instead he was always a patriotic citizen who believed Russians must first recognize the shortcomings of their system, then work to correct them. At first I thought he was naive, embarking on an impossible task. No individual Soviet citizen, I believed, could do anything effective to buck the system. Igor was to prove me wrong in a remarkable way.

In the late 1970s, Igor lost his job at a scientific publishing house where he translated Japanese technical documents into Russian. His employer had been ordered to reduce the staff. Instead of doing so legally, however, on the basis of seniority and ability, the boss decided on a basis of Party loyalty. Igor, as a nonmember of the Party, was first to be let go. The dismissal was illegal, Igor insisted. He determined to fight it with a lawsuit. I told him he was being foolish, that the Party controlled the courts and no one could expect justice there. But Igor disagreed. He hired a lawyer to file suit. Then the lawyer proved to be incompetent. So Igor argued his own case in court. Surprisingly, he won. The court ordered the publishing house to give Igor back his job. He had proven that even in Brezhnev's day, a determined Soviet citizen could demand and win justice. Thus encouraged in his struggle to improve the system, Igor was a natural to enter local politics under Gorbachev's democratization.

Igor was fifty-two in 1990 when he decided to run for the Moscow city council. He had never entered politics before, but that was an advantage. In his district of ten thousand voters, he was the only one of seven candidates who had never been a member of the Communist Party. As such, he had Yeltsin's endorsement for the seat, and a good chance of winning, if he could only tell his constituents who he was and what program for change he was running on.

At first that looked impossible. For all of Gorbachev's reforms, the Communists still held all the cards. They could make sure that by election day, practically no one had heard of Igor Belyayev. It was a real eye-opener on the progress of Gorbachev's democratization. For starters, there was no way Igor could advertise in the newspapers or on radio or television. The Communists still controlled them. Similarly, there was no way he could rent a hall for a speech. The Communists still controlled all buildings. There was also no way he could get leaflets printed. The Communists still controlled the presses too. Just about all he could do was get volunteers to stick up handwritten notices in public places. His opponents, of course, would have them immediately torn down.

Igor spent his campaign talking to groups of no more than twenty people in apartment compounds. As election day neared, practically no one in the district knew who he was. At that point I became his unofficial political adviser, probably the only American involved in the Soviet local elections. The fact that that was even possible showed democratization was at least making some progress.

We designed a new campaign tactic. Igor wrote out a campaign flyer on one page of paper. It said he was the only non-Communist running in the district and that he had Yeltsin's endorsement, and then it summarized his key campaign proposals. Among other things, he would work to get rid of the Communist Party elite's special stores, hospitals, and other privileges. And he would throw Party bureaucrats out of central Moscow offices to convert that space into housing for the poor. I then arranged to get his flyer duplicated on a small Xerox machine common in those days only to Western offices in Moscow. We decided on three thousand copies, because that was roughly the number of apartments in Igor's district. In effect we could reach ten thousand voters through three thousand flats.

Each apartment had a mailbox in the lobby of its building. Mail was placed in the box through a slot, and from then on it was safe. Only apartment residents had the keys to open their own mailbox. It was the one sure way to get Igor's message to his voters. Volunteers distributed the flyers to the mailboxes, and they proved to be extraordinarily successful. Igor was one of the few to win an absolute majority on the first ballot. In most other districts, the two leading candidates were required to enter a decisive second ballot.

"We have democratization in this country, but not democracy," Igor said in his campaign. Now, with a seat on the Moscow city council, he had a chance to help put that right.

In 1990, the more progressive grassroots forces had seized the reform initiative from Gorbachev. At last democracy from the ground up was alive and well in the Soviet Union. Once up and running, these grassroots forces would not let go. Although they were still a minority, there seemed to be no limit to what they might achieve. Even if Gorbachev himself faltered, they were now determined to carry the torch through and make democratic reform irreversible.

13

From Reform to Rebellion: Nationalism

I. THE SPARK

Josef Stalin had no respect for the Vatican as a political force in Europe. The Soviet dictator cynically dismissed it with a phrase that went down in history. "The pope," Stalin asked, "how many divisions has he?"

With the election of Poland's John Paul II in 1978, the first pope from Communist Eastern Europe, Stalin's phrase came back to haunt his successors in the Kremlin. This pope indeed had divisions, not the troops Stalin meant, but ordinary citizens, fifty million Roman Catholics in Eastern Europe, including thirty million in Poland, and over four million in the Soviet Union itself. More than any of his predecessors, the first Polish pope knew how to mobilize the faithful in Eastern Europe by touching their hearts and minds.

By simply visiting Warsaw for the first time as pope, in June 1979, John Paul II sanctified rebellion against Communist rule in Eastern Europe as an act of faith. Eventually, this crusade would no longer be pacified by Gorbachev-era reforms or crushed by Stalinist repressions. Instead it would unite religion and nationalism to destroy the Soviet empire.

In Poland, the pope's visit inspired the Solidarity movement, which in only a decade would free that nation from communism. Across the Polish border in Soviet Lithuania, the impact of John Paul's visit to Warsaw was ultimately even more profound. There it marked the start of a struggle for independence, first in Lithuania and the Baltic states, that would spread across the U.S.S.R. and break the Soviet Union into fifteen independent nations. The moral force of this pope would change the political map of Europe. Even the Soviet army would be helpless to stop him.

Lithuania had never lost faith. Decades of Stalinist repression in the tiny Baltic nation had closed churches, barred religious training for children, infiltrated the priesthood with KGB agents. So the faith survived the Stalin years underground, with catacomb churches, priests, and bishops sanctioned by Rome. By June 1979, the worst repressions were long over. Traditional churches operated again, although far fewer than before Communist rule.

Religious life had returned to Lithuania much more rapidly than in Russia. By the late 1970s, Lithuanians were free again to marry in church, to decorate their homes with crosses or portraits of Jesus. John Paul II had even named a new cardinal for Lithuania "in his heart" *(in pectore),* a device used in Eastern Europe when a public announcement would threaten the new cardinal's life. In Lithuania, the pope's visit to nearby Poland had been eagerly awaited. It was seen as confirmation that the still troubled religious rebirth in the Soviet Union would continue to strengthen.

The weekend John Paul II arrived in Poland, the Roman Catholic faithful in neighboring Lithuania bought their local Communist Party newspaper by the thousands. As expected, there was not a word about the papal visit in the paper. Few Lithuanian Catholics bothered to look. They needed the newspapers for another purpose. Many of their churches had no pews, only bare floors. They laid the Communist newspapers on the floor before they knelt down and gave thanks for what seemed like a miracle. The first pope to visit Eastern Europe was praying for them.

In southwestern Lithuania, close enough to the border to receive Polish television, Soviet Catholics actually saw the Pope's arrival in Warsaw and his mass on Victory Square there. The following day, in one such Lithuanian border community, Kybartai, Father Sigitas Tamkevicius told the Sunday congregation in his Holy Eucharist Church, "I hope you all saw on television how the Polish people welcomed the pope. They too have had Communist power for more than thirty years, and yet the Polish people are believers."

In Vilnius, the Lithuanian capital, Soviet Catholics were able to follow the pope's visit only on Polish radio. That too was enough to pack Sunday services to overflowing. For each mass, the thousand or more believers of all ages were jammed together so tightly from the altar to well outside the church entrance that often less than half had room to kneel. At the Dominican Catholic Church in Vilnius, the priest declared in his Sunday sermon, "The Polish-Lithuanian people rejoice that Pope John Paul II is now in Warsaw." People of all ages sobbed openly. "We are crying tears of joy," a white-haired woman of seventy told me.[1]

She said her first name was Yadviga, and that she had rarely cried, despite a lifetime of suffering. Yadviga had served four years in one of Stalin's Siberian labor camps "because I am a believer." Her husband had died in another camp, and her two sons had perished in World War II during the Nazi blockade of Leningrad. Since the war, she had lived alone in Vilnius for nearly thirty-five years. "Yesterday when I heard on the radio that the pope had arrived in Poland, I walked around my apartment and cried for joy," she said. "Perhaps now, finally, we will have freedom to practice our faith."

Many others voiced similar hopes. A Lithuanian priest, Father Alfonsas

Svarinksus, a sixteen-year veteran of Stalin's camps, told me: "Psychologically, morally, the visit of Pope John Paul II to Poland has significance for all of Eastern Europe. The pope knows very well our conditions, our struggle against godless authorities. Morally, his visit can only help our struggle."

Indeed, it did just that. Over the years, Catholic Lithuania would spearhead the independence struggle in the Soviet Union, repeatedly taking the first daring steps for other more cautious republics to follow. Thus the Communist Party of Lithuania would be the first to break away from the Soviet Communist Party, the Lithuanian Republic the first to declare its independence from the Soviet Union. Lithuania would be the spark for the entire independence movement in the U.S.S.R. And that was no accident.

On the contrary, it was a historical inevitability, part of a pattern that would have to start in Eastern Europe. There was never any doubt that the collapse of the Soviet empire would begin in the East European countries forced into the Communist orbit after World War II. They were the most advanced areas of the Soviet bloc, the most independent-minded, the most vulnerable to Western influence, and the closest geographically to the West. Furthermore, when the crunch came, they would be a strategic loss, not a fatal one. The Soviet Union could survive on its own, as a formidable nuclear superpower, even without its East European buffer zone.

Similarly, when the Soviet Union itself began to unravel, there was no doubt it would start on the Baltic fringe. The three Baltic states were the most advanced Soviet republics economically, with the best chance of becoming viable independent nations. They were the most independent-minded, the most vulnerable to Western influence, the closest geographically to the West.

Within the Soviet Union, they mirrored the same conditions that the Eastern European satellites did across the border. Moreover, as the closest Soviet republics to Eastern Europe, they were most likely to be affected by the independence movement there. In addition, they had another advantage. They were small. Taken together, the Baltic states accounted for only 3 percent of the Soviet population. Again, as in the case of Eastern Europe, they would be a strategic loss, but the Soviet Union could survive without them too.

Nor was there ever much doubt that of the three, Lithuania would lead the way. Alone among the Baltic states, Lithuanians were still an overwhelming majority in their own country, some 80 percent of the population in 1979. Elsewhere in the Baltics, immigration by Russians and other Soviet nationalities had cut the native majority down substantially. In Latvia in 1979, only 53 percent of the population were Latvian. In Estonia that same year, 64 percent were Estonian. Those less favorable population mixes led to more cautious policies. Lithuania, with its large ethnic majority and strong Catholic heritage, would ignite the Soviet independence movement.

Although Lithuania proved to be the spark, the Ukraine would play the crucial role in the eventual breakup of the U.S.S.R. That too was inevitable.

The Ukraine was the largest Soviet republic except for Russia, a territory the size of France with a population of fifty million people, or 16 percent of the U.S.S.R. total. The Ukraine was also the Soviet Union's most important agricultural and industrial producer after Russia, accounting for a quarter of the U.S.S.R.'s food supply and nearly a third of its industrial output. As such, the Ukraine was absolutely indispensable to the Soviet economy. "If Lithuania leaves, there will still be a Soviet Union," Maksim Strikha, a Ukrainian nationalist, once told me. "But if the Ukraine leaves, the Soviet Union will fall apart."

Fortunately for Moscow, the Ukraine was in no hurry to leave. The republic was really two nations, split on geographic lines. In the east, around Kiev, the Russian language, the Russian Orthodox Church, and the large Russian minority population predominated. Those in the east favored continued union with the U.S.S.R. In the west, however, around Lvov, public sentiment was exactly the opposite. There the Ukrainian language, the Catholic Church, and the Ukrainian majority population prevailed. Those in the west pressed for independence. It would take years for the Ukraine to decide which way to go.

At first, the pro-Moscow eastern Ukraine dominated the republic. When Lithuania started the independence struggle, the Ukraine seemed firmly in Moscow's control, but, slowly, the balance shifted. After the Chernobyl nuclear accident poisoned much of the Ukraine in 1986, anti-Soviet sentiment soared. The Kremlin's clumsy attempts to cover up the damage led to widespread mistrust of continued Soviet rule. Oles Honchar, a Ukrainian writer, explained, "When officials from Moscow visit the Ukraine, they bring their own bread and their own tea—and then they tell us there is no danger of radioactivity here."

Later, as the Soviet economy declined, even Russians in the east thought they would be better off in an independent Ukraine. During the Gorbachev years, the separatist western Ukraine would gradually take the upper hand. Its final victory, in a 1991 independence referendum, forced the collapse of the Soviet state.

The long struggle for independence, which Lithuania began and the Ukraine finished, was the last of the three great battles that doomed Soviet communism. The first two, over economic and political reforms (Chapters 11–12), broke the Communist Party's monopoly powers. That made possible the third and final battle, over independence for Soviet minority nationalities. The third battle raised the stakes from reform to rebellion. From then on the fate of Gorbachev's perestroika was no longer the issue. Instead the issue became the survival of the Soviet state.

The turning point came in 1989. By then, Gorbachev's restructuring had given the non-Russian republics more economic autonomy. His democratization had let them start moving from economic to political freedom. Independence movements, in the form of popular fronts, were either already operating successfully, as in the Baltics, or about to, as almost everywhere else.

In September 1989 the most important of them all made its debut. The popular front of the Ukraine, known as Rukh, held a founding congress in Kiev. I attended, and found all the essential elements for success were already firmly in place—economic reform, political reform, the blessings of the church, mass support, and internal unity. A brief word on each is in order.

Rukh would build on economic reform. "We want to move from a free-market economy to a free Ukraine," economist Vladimir Chernak told the congress.

Rukh had already built on political reform. The Ukrainian Communist Party had been weakened in March by Gorbachev's new competitive elections. Several key leaders lost bids for seats in the new Soviet parliament in Moscow. The Ukrainian Communists were then further weakened in the summer by another result of Gorbachev's more liberal policies, a crippling strike by coal miners. Any attempt to strangle Rukh at its birth would have led to more strikes and more Communist losses at the polls. So Ukrainian nationalists held Rukh's founding congress free of KGB harassment.

Rukh immediately got the influential support of the church. "God gave us Rukh to lead us out of the house of bondage, into the promised land," Father Nikolai Negoguz told the congress.

Rukh was a political powerhouse from day one, with 280,000 active members at birth.

And Rukh was united, with one clear goal—independence. The founding congress heard speeches which would have been banned only a few months before.

Economist Mikhailo Schveik complained that Moscow's central planners ran 95 percent of Ukrainian industry and took out 90 percent of the profits. "There is no precedent for that, not even from colonial Africa," Schveik said. Rukh's answer would be freedom from Soviet colonial rule. Levko Lukyanenko, a lawyer who had served twenty-six years in Communist prison camps for his separatist views, made that abundantly clear in a keynote speech to the founding congress. "The principal goal of our movement must be to leave the Soviet Union," he declared. The 1,109 delegates rose to their feet in response, cheered, and waved the blue-and-yellow flag of the independent Ukraine.

They would no longer be denied the nationhood that had once been theirs. Ukrainians had been struggling since the fourteenth century to restore their independence. Whatever the men in the Kremlin said in the months and years ahead, Rukh would now press on, until it won a majority in the Ukrainian parliament, and from there, at long long last, realized the ancient dream of independence once again. The poet Ivan Drach, named the president of Rukh by the founding congress, said it all. "If there is no nation," Drach concluded, "there is no reason to live."

One nation's victory, of course, is often another nation's defeat. In achieving its own independence, the Ukraine would force the breakup of the Soviet Union. It did so as the spearhead of a minority nationality rebellion that could no longer be controlled from the Kremlin. That rebellion was highly complex. The Ukraine was only the largest, single most important element in the independence movement, but far from the only one, and even the independence movement itself was just one of the pressures that minority nationalities exerted to make their rebellion succeed.

Had independence been the only problem, the Kremlin might have coped. In the explosive world of Soviet nationality politics, however, that was just the first of many intricately related challenges. To understand why the U.S.S.R. unraveled, a closer examination of the nationality problem as a whole is needed.

II. MISSION IMPOSSIBLE

The Soviet Union was a nation of 280 million people. Russians accounted for half the population. More than a hundred different minority nationalities made up the rest. Resulting ethnic problems were both simpler and more complex than those raw figures suggest. They were simpler because the twenty-two largest nationalities made up 98 percent of the total population. Thus only the larger players really counted. And of them, only fifteen of the largest nationalities had their own republics within the Soviet Union.

The Russians, with half the Soviet population, had their own republic, called the Russian Federation. The Ukrainians, with 16 percent of the population, also had their own republic. So did each of the five largest Muslim nations of Central Asia, which together accounted for roughly 20 percent of the Soviet population. Even the three Baltic peoples, with a total of only 3 percent of the Soviet population, each had their own republics too. After that, most of the other minority nationalities in the Soviet Union were not only too small to have their own republics, but also too small to cause serious political trouble, even within republics.

The nationality problems were more complex because some sixty million Soviet people lived outside their national republics, among them Russians in Kazakhstan, Ukrainians in Latvia, and Armenians in Azerbaijan. Thus suppression of all Soviet minorities by the Russians was only one level of problems. Another level often had nothing to do with Russians but could be even more serious. It involved an ethnic majority in a particular region suppressing a minority there, as, for example, when Muslim Azerbaijan conducted a pogrom against its Christian Armenian minority.

Even Russians themselves were a potential minority problem. Some twenty-five million Russians lived outside Russia in other Soviet republics.

Often they had been encouraged to move in order to help enforce Soviet rule over various ethnic minorities. Independence would make these Russians a vulnerable minority, subject to reprisals for decades of repressive Soviet rule, from the Baltics to Central Asia. Their potential plight was just one more incentive for the Kremlin to hold the Soviet Union together.

In fact, the problem was so complex that even the term the Soviets used, "the nationality question," did not begin to cover it. This was not one question to be resolved with one answer. It was six very different problems, with no ready solutions, roughly as follows:

1. *Independence Movements.* For the most part, these were anticolonial in nature, as whole nations, conquered by tsarist Russian or Soviet troops and occupied ever since, sought to restore their freedom. Examples include the Baltics, the Ukraine, Georgia, Armenia, and the various Muslim nations of Central Asia.

The convenient "colonial" image did not entirely fit. In the Soviet Union, there were complexities within complexities. "The Estonian people do not have a colonial mentality," parliamentary deputy Marju Lauriston once explained in an interview with me. "They do not feel themselves inferior to the metropolitan power, nor do they feel they ought to ape the culture or the manners of Russia." Soviet republics were colonies, all right, but not colonies in the traditional sense of French or British holdings in Africa. In such nuances lay the beginnings of understanding Soviet nationality problems.

2. *Ethnic Conflicts.* These involved disputes within the U.S.S.R. between minority nationalities, for example over land two nationalities claimed. Unlike the independence movements, in which minority peoples rose up against Russian rule from Moscow, the ethnic conflicts pitted minority peoples against each other. The worst of them, the conflict between Armenia and Azerbaijan over the disputed territory of Nagorno Karabakh, turned into a long civil war. There were many others.

Although Moscow had no direct role in fomenting such ethnic conflicts, these disputes put the Kremlin in a no-win situation. Either it intervened to restore order, at the risk that Soviet troops would then become targets for continued military operations from both sides, or the Soviet government stayed out, at the risk that it would look weak and only encourage more ethnic conflicts elsewhere.

Ethnic conflicts were not always between republics, as with Armenia and Azerbaijan. Sometimes they flared within republics, as between the Uzbek majority and the Meskhetian Turkish minority in the Central Asian republic of Uzbekistan. A 1989 brawl over the price of strawberries in a market there, for example, touched off two weeks of violence in which at least sixty-seven people were killed, hundreds of others injured, and eleven thousand evacuated as refugees.

At times, these ethnic conflicts scattered across the Soviet Union looked more dangerous than the independence movements themselves.

3. *Divided Peoples.* Russian and Soviet expansion divided countries and peoples. The Soviet Republic of Moldavia consisted of land and people taken from Romania. Soviet Azerbaijan was half a country; the other half was in Iran. Other parts of the Soviet Union were made up of land and people seized earlier from the Chinese, Persian, and Ottoman empires. The losers never fully abandoned hopes of retaking their land and reuniting their peoples. They thus added an international dimension to Soviet minority nationality problems.

That international dimension then took on many different forms. It was one major element in the Soviet-Chinese dispute. It helped create the threat of Muslim fundamentalism expanding into the Soviet Union from Iran and Afghanistan. It was also a cause of capitalist influence from Turkey reaching into Soviet Central Asia. It was even a source of friction between Communist Romania and the U.S.S.R. Nevertheless, most of all, the tensions over divided peoples added significantly to Soviet nationality problems.

4. *Displaced Peoples.* As part of his obsession with security, Stalin uprooted whole peoples from sensitive areas in the Soviet Union and resettled them far away where they could do less harm. Among them were 238,000 Tatars deported by Stalin in 1944 from their traditional homeland in the Crimean Peninsula, one of European Russia's strategically vulnerable border areas, on the absurd charges that this entire ethnic minority had collaborated with Nazi Germany. The Tatars were transplanted to Central Asia and the Urals, deep inside the U.S.S.R. Decades later, a decree restored their constitutional rights but not their property. The Tatars were still demanding a return to their former land.

Needless to say, the non-Tatar local populations in the Crimea who had taken over these properties and worked them for decades were loath to give them up. Thus the only way to resolve a past injustice would be to create a new one. The restoration of one minority nationality's land would require taking that territory from another. The solution of such problems would require the wisdom of Solomon, a faculty never associated with the Soviet leadership.

Many other ethnic minorities suffered mass deportations and similar fates, among them ethnic Germans.

5. *Disadvantaged Peoples.* These were people dissatisfied with their status as ethnic minorities within republics, among them the Abkhazians in Georgia and the Chechens in Russia. In Soviet logic, their populations were too

small to rate their own republics. Nonetheless, they were ready to fight for their own separate mini-states. In the Gorbachev era they were already another serious potential source of political instability and armed conflict. In the post-Soviet period, rebellions in Abkhazia and Chechnya would trigger civil wars in Georgia and Russia.

6. *Russian Nationalism.* Russia contained half the Soviet population, two-thirds of its territory, and most of its natural resources. Yet the Russian people never saw their dominant position reach its potential in terms of higher living standards for them. Instead, much of Russia's wealth went into subsidizing poorer Soviet republics and the Soviet army that held the empire together.

For decades, most Russians were convinced that was their duty. Then the birth of the minority nationality independence movements began to change their minds. At first Russians thought republics seeking to break away from the Soviet Union were ungrateful for Moscow's past subsidies. On reflection, however, they decided, why not let the ingrates go? If the Soviet Union broke apart, Russia too would be better off as an independent state. Then its wealth could stay home and subsidize Russia. In time, Boris Yeltsin would exploit this change in thinking, ride it to the presidency of Russia, and ultimately ensure that he and Russia would replace Gorbachev and Soviet power. Such was the potential of only one aspect of the Soviet nationality question.

Each of the six different nationality problems weakened the Soviet government, compounding the problem of controlling the independence movements when the crunch came. Worse for Gorbachev, this problem had only grown more ominous over time.

In Stalin's day, resolving Soviet nationality problems had been relatively simple. Ethnic conflicts were exploited by a Kremlin policy of divide and rule. Nationalist pretensions were awarded meaningless concessions, such as seats in a powerless Soviet parliament. State ideology downplayed national differences. It claimed the Soviet peoples were united, and would work together for the benefit of all. And when such methods failed, there was always the iron fist. Stalin never hesitated in his ruthless crushing of minority nationality dissent. Fear of ethnic genocide proved very effective.

Gorbachev had no such option. Without Stalinist terror, there was no quick fix to Soviet nationality problems. These challenges would have been extraordinarily difficult for any reformist Soviet leader to resolve. Mikhail Sergeyevich then made them even harder. His policies soon turned them from difficult into impossible. Gorbachev was singularly ill equipped to deal with minority nationality problems. Among top Soviet leaders, he alone had never worked outside Russia during his climb to the pinnacle of power. That would turn out to be a crucial omission in his preparation for the Kremlin leadership.

Each of his predecessors had held responsibilities on the way up in at least one of the outlying republics, learning firsthand how to manage minority nationality unrest. Khrushchev had been Stalin's viceroy in the Ukraine. Brezhnev first ran an important industrial region of the Ukraine, and later headed Kazakhstan. They knew what to do once the terror was over. They would enact measures that gave the appearance of more autonomy for minority nationalities, but in fact did nothing to weaken the reality of Soviet controls. One of Khrushchev's subtler strokes in that direction involved the appointment of police chiefs in minority nationality communities. The top job in the police department of major Soviet cities outside of Russia often went to someone from the predominant local nationality—an Uzbek in Tashkent, an Azeri in Baku, a Georgian in Tbilisi, and so on. Still, the number two would always be a Russian, and the Russian would run the police department. So much for appearance. So much for reality.

Nothing in Gorbachev's background prepared him to carry on that practice. When it came to nationality questions, Mikhail Sergeyevich did not fully understand either the appearance or the reality. He put too much faith in appearances, among them the ideological fiction that communism would do away with nationality differences by rallying all Soviet peoples to work together for a better tomorrow, for the benefit of all. Worse, Gorbachev totally underestimated the reality. He had no idea of the depth of anti-Soviet feeling among minority nationalities in the republics, much of it raw hatred for Russian occupiers. He had never worked there, and was in for an unhappy surprise.[2]

Gorbachev got his first close look at the minority nationality problem on a trip to Lithuania in January 1990. It was his initial visit as Soviet leader to the Baltic republics, the hotbed of the independence movement, and it came very late in the struggle. He might have accomplished more had he come earlier. The timing reflected Mikhail Sergeyevich's priorities. He had waited five years to visit the Baltics because he had underestimated the problem there. When he finally came to Lithuania, Gorbachev was still underestimating it. Mikhail Sergeyevich arrived in Vilnius, the Lithuanian capital, as the great communicator, as a conciliator. He would be reasonable. He would offer Lithuanians more local autonomy within the Soviet Union. Problems could be talked out. Things would improve. Or so he expected.

He had not understood it was already too late for conciliation by dialogue. The Berlin Wall was down. Eastern Europe was breaking away from the Soviet empire, inspiring the Baltics to do the same thing. Lithuanians would no longer be satisfied by negotiations with Moscow on further reform. They wanted out of the U.S.S.R. "The Czechs and the East Germans did more in a month of freedom than the Soviet Union did in five years of perestroika," Vilnius editor Algimantas Cekoulis told me.

The day Gorbachev arrived in Vilnius, 300,000 people gathered in Cathedral Square to send him a message. They came from all over Lithuania. Those who couldn't get into the square climbed trees, sat on rooftops, or filled nearby streets. They waved yellow-green-and-red independence flags. They carried signs reading "Red Army Go Home." And they chanted, "Freedom, Freedom." Then, lighting candles against chill winds and a dark, drizzly sky, they heard Vytautas Landsbergis, the leader of the independence movement Sajudis, declare: "Let us be silent, with one thought and one wish. We are a free people. We will create a free Lithuania." Fifteen minutes later, as cathedral bells broke the silence, the crowd joined hands, swayed from side to side, and sang the Lithuanian national anthem, with a tearful dignity befitting the rebirth of a nation.

Gorbachev was not in Cathedral Square for that ceremony. But he got the message anyway, during a Vilnius walkabout the next day. His appeals for dialogue were falling on deaf ears. The Soviet leader tried to establish his sincerity by getting personal. Nationality problems have to be resolved, Mikhail Sergeyevich said. "My own fate is at stake." Then he tried to be reassuring. "Nothing will be decided without you," Gorbachev said. "We will decide everything together." The crowd, however, would have none of it. "People must decide their own fate," a man in the crowd shouted back. And there it was. The leader of the Soviet Union was debating his own people—and losing.

Mikhail Sergeyevich did no better with the Lithuanian Communist Party leadership. He could no longer convince them to do his bidding either. It was a trap of his own making. The reasons for their unyielding opposition were the result of his own reforms.

Gorbachev's glasnost had totally discredited the Lithuanian Communist Party. It had allowed their nationalist rivals to publish the truth about the past. The grim record showed in embarrassing detail how Lithuanian Communists had collaborated with the Kremlin, and therefore shared responsibility for Stalinist repressions in the republic. In this way, glasnost had already cost Lithuanian Communists their reputation. Further damage lay ahead. Gorbachev's democratization, his new contested elections, were about to cost Lithuanian Communists their power. The Communists knew that Sajudis, the independence party, would likely beat them in the upcoming elections for the Lithuanian parliament, form the next government in the republic, and lead it out of the Soviet Union.

As far as the Lithuanian Communists were concerned, Gorbachev's reforms had nearly killed them politically. Only desperate measures would allow their party to survive. Among them, they would have to defy Gorbachev and distance themselves from the Communist leadership in Moscow. They began doing that a month before his visit to Vilnius. In December 1989, in a last-ditch effort to restore their credibility, the Lithuanian Communists withdrew from the Soviet Communist Party and declared themselves an independent political force. They did so, as Lithuanian Politburo member Vladimir Berezov told me, as the only way to prevent their political extinction. "We were not just trying to win the parliamentary elections," he said. "We had to prepare for defeat. We had to ensure that if we lost, we could continue to exist afterward, and function as a healthy opposition." Such was the measure of desperation. From that point on, they were determined to continue defying Gorbachev as the only viable way ahead.

Lithuanian Communists now saw themselves as no longer under the control of the Soviet Communist Party. Their nation was still part of the U.S.S.R., but their party was independent. At a stroke, instead of being a brake on the republic's independence movement, the Lithuanian Communist Party could now get out in front and help lead the way. Naturally, it was an unprecedented challenge that Moscow could not tolerate. If the Communist Party in one republic could withdraw from the Soviet Communist Party, why not others? And if the Party unraveled, so too would the Soviet state. With the stakes so high, tensions between Moscow and Vilnius escalated immediately into a dangerous new game of brinkmanship.

Lithuania's Communists declared themselves an independent party on December 20, 1989. The next day, a furious Gorbachev telephoned Algirdas Brazauskas, the Lithuanian Communist leader, and demanded that the decision be reversed. Brazauskas refused. His party's declaration of independence had been taken by democratic vote at a special congress, he explained. It could not be reversed on Kremlin orders. Gorbachev, now even angrier, insisted on reversal. "I have the means to stop you," Gorbachev warned. "I can remove you if necessary." But Brazauskas refused to be bullied. "You cannot remove me," he said. "I am the leader of an independent party."

The source of that episode was Bronius Genzelius, then a member of the Lithuanian Communist Party Politburo. He was in the room when Gorbachev called, and personally heard the conversation. Genzelius later related it to me. His willingness to do so was another sign of how far Lithuania had come. In Moscow, Soviet Politburo members rarely spoke with foreign correspondents and never told them anything about internal Communist Party problems. In Vilnius the situation had been much the same, but all that changed radically from 1989 on. After that, Lithuanian Politburo members regularly saw foreign correspondents and spoke candidly about the most sensitive issues, including talks with Soviet leaders. Journalists could often learn more from them than from Moscow about what was going on inside the Kremlin. Lithuania's top Communists were now acting very much like Alexander Dubček's aides in the Prague Spring. It looked like they might share the same fate.

Gorbachev was under heavy conservative pressure to force the Lithuanian Communists back into line, by sending tanks to Vilnius if necessary. Significantly, however, even at the height of his anger, Mikhail Sergeyevich resisted all such hard-line pressures. "I won't have blood on my hands," he said. Instead, the Soviet leader decided, he would do everything in his power to resolve the issue by negotiation first. The result was his January 1990 visit to Vilnius.

Before his arrival, Gorbachev changed his attitude toward Brazauskas. Instead of making further bullying demands to reverse the Lithuanian Communists' independence decision, Mikhail Sergeyevich would now press them to compromise it by delay. He began pushing the Lithuanian Communists in this direction a week before setting foot in Vilnius. Among other things, this pressure campaign included an old Kremlin favorite, the weakness card. Aleksandr Yakovlev, Gorbachev's closest ally on the Soviet Politburo, played it in a phone call to Brazauskas early in the New Year. Lithuanian Communists had to delay their departure from the Soviet Party, Yakovlev said, or Gorbachev might be replaced by a Kremlin hard-liner who would be much worse in the long run for Lithuania. "Clouds are gathering over Gorbachev's head," Yakovlev said. "His fate to a considerable degree will depend on the stand of the Lithuanian Communist Party."

The pleading did no better than the bullying. Gorbachev left Vilnius empty-handed. His January visit accomplished nothing. Even with the Lithuanian Communists, it was now too late for talk. They could not delay their break from the Soviet Communist Party and remain a viable political force in Lithuania. Besides, they were no longer afraid of anything.

"At some point we could experience a Soviet invasion," Lithuanian Politburo member Romualdo Ozolas explained to me. But he was convinced that any decision to send tanks on Vilnius would sound the death knell for all Gorbachev reforms. The command economy would return, no more workable than before. Inevitably it would first bankrupt, then break up the U.S.S.R. "Then we would get our independence that way," Ozolas said. Most of the Lithuanian Communist leadership agreed with him. One way or the other, they believed, independence was assured. Their fear gone, they could not be forced to compromise. With that, Soviet rule in Lithuania was doomed. Independence was no longer a question of if, but when.

Much the same principle applied throughout the Communist world, whatever the country. Once the fear was gone, the system could not last. Tiny Lithuania would win its independence from the Soviet colossus. A Baltic ministate with a population of only 3.6 million people and no nuclear weapons would successfully defy the Soviet Union, a nuclear superpower with 280 million people and the world's largest standing army. The loss of fear was the essential precondition for victory.

It was not the only factor, of course. Many other elements played key roles. Among them, Lithuania was convinced of the justice of its cause; its people had never abandoned their goal of restored independence; Eastern Europe's success in breaking away from Communism was profoundly encouraging. Most of all, from long experience, Lithuanians knew how to exploit the weaknesses of their giant Soviet neighbor to win independence and then assure their survival as a separate state. In all this they had much to teach the Western powers, including the United States, about how and when to stand tough against the global Soviet threat.

Mikhail Gorbachev's mission to Lithuania in 1990 was a political disaster, a classic case of too little too late. Now, with the wisdom of hindsight, it is hard to see how an intelligent, capable, and powerful leader like Gorbachev could have let that happen, how he could have neglected for so long and then mishandled so badly an issue like minority nationality unrest, so important to the fate of the Soviet Union. The answer to that question exposes fatal weaknesses in Mikhail Sergeyevich himself, in his perestroika policies, and indeed in any serious attempt to reform communism.

In fairness, Gorbachev can hardly be blamed alone. Too many of his advisers were like him. They too had spent their careers in Russia and had no firsthand knowledge of nationality problems in the republics. They too came to high office without having thought out any detailed new approach to solving ethnic tensions. Their lack of experience in the field of minority nationality questions and their lack of attention to it matched Gorbachev's. So they did not prepare him properly. In the early days, when it could have made a difference, there was no one on Gorbachev's team to warn him of the coming explosion. That too was his fault, but only partly. He had picked his advisers, but then they let him down.

Mikhail Sergeyevich was not even thinking seriously about minority nationality problems when he launched perestroika. That was to prove to be one of his gravest errors. His reforms were intended to improve economic performance, his own personal authority, and ultimately the power of the U.S.S.R. Nonetheless their unintended result was to strengthen the rebellion by minority nationalities until it destroyed the Soviet Union. In the process, without intending to do so, without fully understanding the implications, Gorbachev reversed the appearance and the reality in minority nationality questions. He made Soviet control the appearance, and minority nationality power the reality. Each of his major reforms contributed to that role reversal. They were not designed to do that, of course, but each of his reforms created major opportunities for minority nationalities to exploit in their struggle for independence.

The list of Gorbachev policies that proved to be unintended godsends to the independence movement is long and impressive. It contains all five major initiatives of his rule, as follows:

1. *Economic Reform.* Perestroika was supposed to break the stranglehold of Moscow's central planners, by promoting private enterprise and local decision-making. Individual factory managers and private businessmen benefited enormously, but so did governments in non-Russian republics. They got new economic autonomy, which they gratefully seized. Then they refused to stop there. They went further than Gorbachev intended, using that economic autonomy as a stepping-stone to political independence. More power

to run their local economies was by definition already additional political power. Soon places like the Baltics were making the economic reforms work better than Russia. Anxious to demonstrate perestroika as a success, Gorbachev gave them even more economic room for maneuver, still minimizing the political implications involved.

2. *Glasnost.* Gorbachev increased press freedoms in order to expose corrupt bureaucrats who were blocking reform. He also allowed the truth to be told about embarrassing blank spots in Soviet history, previously covered up, in order to increase public confidence in the honesty of his leadership. The independence movements quickly turned both weapons against him. They used their freer press to attack Soviet rule. And telling the truth about Soviet history allowed them to stir up nationalist passions by exposing Moscow's past treachery, such as the 1939 Nazi-Soviet nonaggression pact. By signing that deal with Hitler, dividing much of Eastern Europe between them, Stalin was able to seize the then-independent Baltic states and incorporate them into the U.S.S.R., literally at gunpoint. His Red Army troops occupied the Baltics to ensure their "request" to join the Soviet Union. In 1989, thanks to glasnost, the Baltic press was giving huge publicity to the fiftieth anniversary of the pact, triggering mass anti-Soviet protest rallies. Gorbachev had not intended anything like that either.

3. *Democratization.* Contested elections to the Soviet parliament were designed to widen the participation of the public in the decision-making process and generate new support for the Gorbachev reforms. Separatist movements then exploited them for very different goals—to form opposition parties, defeat the Communists, take control of republic governments, and declare independence.

4. *The Rule of Law.* Gorbachev trimmed the illegal powers of the KGB and increased individual human rights as an incentive to his people to work harder, especially in the private sector, and make reform a success. These limits on KGB repression also produced unintended results, among them increased daring by national independence movements to defy the Kremlin.

5. *Travel.* Gorbachev finally removed the iron curtain. He eased foreign travel restrictions so that most ordinary Soviets could at last go abroad. Mikhail Sergeyevich understood, as did his Kremlin predecessors, that freer travel would not mean a permanent mass exodus. Most Soviets just wanted to see the outside world and then return home. For Stalin, Khrushchev, and Brezhnev, that was precisely the problem. They did not want their people traveling abroad, comparing for the first time their system against democracy and capitalism, collecting new ideas, and then coming back to apply them in the U.S.S.R. Gorbachev, on the contrary, yearned for that. He wanted his people to go abroad, acquire new skills and better ideas, then come home and put them to work.

Mikhail Sergeyevich was right to permit travel, although once again, he had overlooked the impact on the minority nationality independence movements. The freer travel let them contact émigrés abroad for funds and other support. Freer travel meant freer information flow, about the suppression of human rights in the republics, to mention only one area. All that became effective ammunition for lobbies in the West, pressing their governments to back independence movements, starting with the Baltics.

Taken together, Gorbachev's unintended gifts to the national independence movements underscored the impossibility of reforming communism. They proved that no one could alter any one part of the Soviet system without affecting other parts as well. No matter how well intended any leader's specific reforms might be, they were also certain to bring about unexpected changes he could not control.

Nowhere was that more true than in loosening the screws of Stalinist repression. Without coercion, control of minority nationality unrest was impossible. More broadly, without coercion, there was no practical way that public support for communism could be maintained. Once any leader started down that road, once any leader removed the coercion that gave communism its monopoly on power, the system was heading toward extinction. Reform could not stop at improving or humanizing communism. That would never be enough. Once controls were loosened, reform would keep on increasing demands for more and more reform. Given the choice, East Europeans rejected reform communism, preferring instead to end Communist rule in their countries. Soon Soviet republics, even Russia, would make the same choice.

There was no middle way. Either reform would be halted by force, or it would start a process that eventually could only kill communism. And over time, smashing reform with tanks would become increasingly difficult. Once censorship was lifted and authors like Solzhenitsyn were published, even the Red Army couldn't unpublish him or snuff out his ideas. Once people began owning property, making money, running their own businesses and lives, they would not give that up without a fight. Russians themselves used to describe the difficulties of rolling back reform with an old cliché—the impossibility of putting toothpaste back into the tube. Once any Communist country seriously started down the reform road by restraining coercion, the odds were there would be no going back.

No sector of Soviet society was free from this syndrome. As repression gave way to glasnost and democratization, not even the Red Army could resist the winds of change within its ranks. Soon these changes would substantially weaken Soviet military power. But still, there was no going back.

Rytis proved the point. The nineteen-year-old Lithuanian draftee deserted from his Soviet army unit near Moscow in January 1990. When I met him he was still too scared to give his last name. His face was covered with frostbite, cuts, and bruises. Russians in his outfit had beaten him unconscious, Rytis said. Then they left him outside their barracks in subfreezing weather all night. They had singled him out for abuse because of his Baltic nationality, calling him "Nazi" or "Fascist." They forced him to go out at night and buy vodka. If he refused, or failed to bring back a bottle, "They beat me and beat me," Rytis explained, until "I couldn't handle it anymore." The last time he went out, Rytis kept running. He vowed he would never go back to the army. "If I had stayed, I would not have come out alive," he said.

His story was all too common. Draftees from Soviet minority nationalities, like Rytis, were often subject to beatings, sexual abuse, even murder. The army used to hush up such outrages. But under glasnost, that was no longer possible. Reports of ill treatment started off in letters to parents and ended up in the local press duly confirmed by competent authorities. They ran the gamut of human depravity. One young man, castrated in an army hazing, later committed suicide. Another was forced at gunpoint to perform acts of oral sex. Others were burned or beaten to death.

Publicity in such cases fueled waves of draft dodging and desertions by young men from minority nationalities. As a result of democratization, by 1989, youths had demonstrated against compulsory military service in six of the fifteen Soviet republics. "Anti-army manifestations, and I say this with bitterness, have become more frequent," admitted General Dmitri Yazov, the Soviet defense minister. Recognizing the problems did Yazov little good. He was powerless to stop them from growing even worse. Eventually the embittered Yazov turned against Gorbachev, for this reason among many others, and helped lead the abortive August 1991 coup against him.

The Soviet military had always relied on coercion. The draft meant they could dragoon young men from non-Russian republics into the army, much like an occupying power in its colonies. Since minority nationalities made up 50 percent of the Soviet population, they also constituted roughly half of the military intake each year. Without them, the manpower of the Red Army, the enforcer that kept the Soviet empire together, would soon lose half its conscript strength. Gorbachev's reforms were directly responsible for this massive loss of recruits. Thanks to democratization, minority nationality youths were able to demonstrate against serving in what they called the "Soviet occupation army." Worse, the army had no legal way to step in and stop the rot.

Both draft dodging and desertion were against the law in the Soviet Union, of course. Unfortunately for the army, it was up to local authorities to enforce these laws. And in republics already agitating for independence, local authorities were not willing to enforce desertion and draft-dodging laws against their own people.

Evading service in the Soviet army soon became routine. By October 1989, Azerbaijan was refusing to send conscripts to the Soviet army. Later that same year, Armenian officials were complaining of "numerous instances

of murder, persecution, and beating of servicemen of the Armenian nationality." Local officials said more than fifteen hundred Georgians and more
than a thousand Latvians, Lithuanians, and Estonians refused induction in
1989. Mothers in the Baltics were marching against conscription.

The army did its best to deny the brutality charges. It claimed to suppress
violent hazing. It said desertions had nothing to do with ethnic differences,
but resulted rather from the pampered upbringing of modern Soviet youths.
Again, under the Gorbachev reforms, it was too late to get away with such
transparent falsehoods. In Vilnius, the Institute of Sociology, Philosophy, and
Law documented the horrible truth. It asked two thousand university students about their service in the Soviet army. In response, 95 percent said soldiers had been beaten, 50 percent said there had been at least one suicide,
and 20 percent reported at least one murder in their units.

As usual, Lithuania led the independence movements across the
U.S.S.R., this time to dangerous new ground on the military front. By January 1990, a commission of the Lithuanian parliament started excusing Soviet army deserters from further military service on medical or other legal
grounds. Sajudis, the independence party, pushed a new law in the Lithuanian parliament to give young men the right to choose whether or not they
wanted to serve in the Soviet army. Women's groups refused to wait for that.
They arranged a massive sit-down on railroad tracks in March to protest the
next intake of draftees into the Soviet army. "This is not a Baltic cause," a
spokeswoman for the organizers said. "It is a national cause." Other republics
got the message quickly. They too cut down their flow of conscripts. Once
coercion had been lifted, not even the Red Army could stop reforms striking directly at its power. Their ultimate recourse was to seize power by a
military coup, but that raised new dangers, and would long prove too risky
to try.

The army held back primarily because it was divided. Like every other
segment of Soviet society, the military was split between enemies and advocates of perestroika. The top brass, leading lives of privilege, shielded from
the shortages and other failures of the command economy, usually favored
the old system. Younger officers in junior and middle grades, forced to live
in conditions of everyday reality, were far more inclined to favor reform. In
any coup scenario to remove Gorbachev and stop reform, the top brass could
never be sure its subordinates would support them across the Soviet Union.
And that kind of total support would be essential. It would be relatively simple to send a column of tanks into the Kremlin to take over the seat of power
there, but holding the countryside would be an entirely different proposition. Unless the top brass were assured of support throughout the ranks, a
coup in Moscow could touch off civil war across the Soviet Union.

A military coup against Gorbachev would be the last resort. Before that,
all other options had to be exhausted. High among them was using the army
to put down nationalist unrest. The military brass didn't like that either. They

preferred to stay out of domestic politics. No officer wants to order his troops to shoot their own people. Still, as long as Gorbachev was commander in chief, if he gave the order, they had to comply. And Mikhail Sergeyevich, despite his reformist zeal, was still prepared to use military force to preserve the Soviet Union from internal rebellion. By 1989, he faced challenges to Soviet authority across the U.S.S.R. The only question was which powder keg would explode first.

III. BLOODBATH

The answer turned out to be Azerbaijan. The popular front there stirred up ethnic passions from the war with Armenia over disputed Nagorno Karabakh. They blamed Soviet authorities for letting that conflict get started and then escalate out of control. Muslim rebels in Soviet Azerbaijan also wanted to reunite with the rest of the Azeri nation across the border in Iran. Most of all, they wanted out of the U.S.S.R., and were losing patience. It was late January 1990. Gorbachev had just come back from Vilnius. Events were now moving so fast in the independence movement that the Soviet leader hardly had time to catch his breath between crises.

In January 1990, Azeris in the capital, Baku, launched a pogrom against the Armenian minority there. The communal violence quickly turned into an Azeri armed rebellion against Soviet authority. "What is going on here can be called civil war," said Major General Yuri Kosolapov, the Soviet army commander in the region. Worse for Moscow, the rebels were only days away from winning it. The popular front had more public support than the Azeri Communist regime. It rapidly took over key buildings in the capital, then began declaring whole areas of the republic independent.

Gorbachev decided to draw the line. Azerbaijan would be the place where he used Soviet military power to crush minority nationality rebellion. It would serve as a lesson for independence movements throughout the U.S.S.R.: their defiance would no longer be tolerated. The decision was no surprise, but it proved harder to implement than Mikhail Sergeyevich had expected. When he mobilized reservists for the Baku crisis, there was a public outcry. Soviet television showed a Russian woman in Stavropol, Gorbachev's provincial political base, shouting angrily, "I won't give my son for this." Gone were the days when a Kremlin leader could automatically order Russian reservists to risk their lives putting down armed rebellions in the provinces. Democratization had now weakened that option. Gorbachev had to retreat, promising he would use only regular army troops to restore order in Azerbaijan. He sent in eleven thousand of them. After that, the situation only deteriorated further.

Soviet soldiers attacked after midnight on Friday, January 19, 1990. The first target was Baku, in quieter times an exotic jewel of a city, a graceful crescent of shoreline on the deep blue Caspian Sea, a meeting point of old and new, a teeming Muslim old town of narrow streets, mosques, and minarets contrasting with the broad avenues and drab concrete apartment blocks typical of newer Soviet cities. Baku was a place where diners still ate succulent shashlik while seated on oriental carpets, as merchants had done for centuries, only in recent years they looked out on modern oil rigs in the bay promising new wealth. All that was now to become a war zone. As Soviet troops approached the first roadblocks set up by rebellious Azeris in the broader streets of central Baku, they first fired into the air, then into the crowd. Some in the crowd shot back. Then army tanks crashed through barricades, firing at buses that blocked their way and crushing vehicles with people still in them, survivors of the carnage claimed later. By midday Saturday the onslaught had succeeded. "The center of Baku is now controlled by the army," the rebel popular front admitted. The fighting had claimed at least 129 lives in the capital alone.

The slaughter extended into the countryside, where resistance was often fierce. Azeris already well armed for the struggle against Armenia now turned their weapons on Soviet "peacekeepers," vowing to continue a guerrilla war. Grisly photographs of civilians crushed by Soviet tanks in Baku inspired the resistance. "If Gorbachev wants a second Afghanistan," said Ekhtibar Mamedov, a popular front leader, "he will get it in Azerbaijan."

His warning had more bark than bite, however. Soviet troops, taking advantage of their greater numbers and heavier weapons, soon wiped out the resistance and restored order in the countryside. This time, no reliable official death toll was reported. Foreign correspondents were barred from the war zone and never learned the true extent of the casualties, but unquestionably they were heavy on both sides, given the thousands of Soviet troops deployed and the level of armed resistance. In January 1990, Azerbaijan demonstrated the terrible cost of using troops to put down minority nationality unrest. It showed that the toll of dead and wounded in any such action was likely to be intolerably high.

The crackdown in Azerbaijan also underscored the high risk to Moscow of escalating armed resistance by independence forces. The Kremlin now had to consider the strong possibility that sending in the tanks might be counterproductive, triggering an even stronger rebellion, perhaps lasting for years. That had not happened in Baku this time, but it could happen in another republic next time. The Soviet government was not about to risk another endless war on the heels of the decade-long stalemate in Afghanistan. So the bloodbath in Baku gave the Kremlin pause. It would think long and hard before committing troops to put down nationality unrest again.

Lithuania was the first to benefit. One month after the crackdown in Baku, in February 1990, the Lithuanian independence movement Sajudis won a majority of seats in a parliamentary election. Communist power in the republic had been defeated. Given a free choice for the first time since Stalin seized the Baltics a half century before, the people of Lithuania had voted against Soviet communism and for national independence. The situation was unprecedented, fraught with new dangers for Soviet power. For the first time, a Soviet republic was now legally in the hands of a minority nationality. For the first time in Soviet history, the opposition in a republic had become not just a recognized party, but the legitimate government there. Moscow's immediate reaction, in the face of all these dangers, was to do nothing at all. The tanks did not roll. It was too soon after Baku. Instead, Gorbachev decided to watch and wait.

He did not have to wait long. The new parliament convened in Vilnius for the first time on March 11, 1990. The same day it declared, "Lithuania is once again an independent State." It also elected Sajudis leader Vytautas Landsbergis, a militant anti-Communist, the first president of that new state.

Gorbachev refused to recognize Lithuania's declaration of independence. He immediately called it invalid. Then he gave the Lithuanians just three days to withdraw their decision and again pledge allegiance to the U.S.S.R. The Soviet leader refused to negotiate. He only negotiated with foreign countries, Gorbachev said, and Lithuania was still a Soviet republic. As further pressure, Gorbachev ordered a hundred tanks into Vilnius to strengthen Soviet forces already there. His implied threat could hardly be clearer. The Kremlin leader was giving the Lithuanians three days to comply with his demands. If they didn't, he would order tanks to smash the rebellious Lithuanian parliament and crush independence.

Landsbergis called Gorbachev's bluff. The former Vilnius music teacher proved to be no pushover. He refused to be intimidated and instead took the offensive. First Landsbergis denounced the threat. "Once again, the Soviet Union is unable to release its prey," he said. "The specter of Stalin is stalking the Kremlin." Then the Lithuanian independence leader appealed to the outside world for recognition and support. "Lithuania returns to the world family of independent, democratic nations, and hopes for their kind assistance," Landsbergis said in a broadcast over Vilnius radio. "An important sign of political and moral support would be the international recognition of the new government of Lithuania." It was a masterful performance. The musician had struck all the right chords, not out of foolhardy courage, but rather out of a confident calculation that Soviet tanks would not yet roll.

Independent Lithuania's new leaders had interpreted Soviet thinking correctly. It was still too soon after the bloodbath in Baku, only two months earlier, to use tanks again, especially in Lithuania. The Baltics had always been a special case. They had far more support in the West than any other Soviet republics. An attack on any one of them would have more serious international repercussions than the crackdown in Azerbaijan. That too helped Landsbergis defy Gorbachev.

The United States government had never officially recognized Stalin's brutal takeover in the Baltics, or subsequent Soviet authority there, as legal. Alone among the Soviet republics, the three Baltic states were always regarded by Washington as still sovereign. Latvian, Lithuanian, and Estonian émigrés were allowed to maintain diplomatic missions in Washington. Similarly, Britain and others in Western Europe had also long seen the Baltics as a special case. America and its allies could not regard the Lithuanian crisis as a Soviet internal affair. After fifty years, Baltic independence was still a concern to them. They made that immediately clear. George Bush and other Western leaders pressed Gorbachev to solve the Lithuanian crisis peacefully.

Gorbachev understood he could not invade Lithuania without turning the West against him. That would risk the détente cooperation Mikhail Sergeyevich needed to keep his reforms going. Without continued trade and arms control agreements with the West, without a substantial lowering of East-West tension, there was no way Gorbachev could justify shifting resources from the military to the civilian economy, and that sort of shift was still crucial to the success of perestroika. Thus the Soviet leader would have to pressure Lithuania in other ways, so that he could continue business as usual with the West. The Lithuanian problem was already bad enough. He would not make it worse by turning the West against him and thereby threatening everything he had accomplished so far. Landsbergis had rightly seen through his threats.

Gorbachev found a face-saving way out. He would still refuse to negotiate with Lithuanians, but he would discuss things with them. The three-day deadline passed and the discussions started. Mikhail Sergeyevich made them as tough as they could possibly be. In no way were they simply negotiations by another name. They were the sort of discussions conducted between the hangman and the condemned.

The Soviet leader had read the West correctly. Gorbachev knew Western governments would not tolerate a Soviet invasion of Lithuania, but he also knew they were unlikely to act against him if he simply applied economic pressure. The worst he could expect then would be verbal protests. Mikhail Sergeyevich would go that route. He would squeeze the defiance out of Lithuania by economic pressure, forcing it back into the Soviet fold that way, as a lesson to other independence-minded Soviet republics. "Let Lithuania be the first to swallow the bitter pill of independence," he privately told aides.

IV. ENDGAME

The Soviet Union certainly had the economic leverage to force a Lithuanian surrender. The small Baltic republic lacked its own energy resources. Lithuania had long depended on the U.S.S.R. for all its oil and gas, all at subsidized prices, simply to keep the economy running. That alone gave

Moscow ample means of applying economic pressure. "If they want to be independent, then real life will begin," said Vladimir Miloserdov of the Soviet state planning committee. He meant Vilnius would no longer be able to buy cheap Soviet oil and gas. Instead it would have to buy fuel at higher world market prices it could not afford.

This move was only the opening shock. Stalin's sophisticated economic strategy for discouraging independence and holding the Soviet Union together still applied. In that system, each republic was forced into a few narrow economic specialities, and thus left totally dependent on trade with other Soviet republics in order to survive. "Every one of our enterprises gets at least a hundred different little products from somewhere in the Soviet Union," a Lithuanian industrialist commented. "If we don't get these components, we will have to overhaul our entire production."

That was exactly what Gorbachev had in mind. He imposed an economic blockade on Lithuania, expecting misery to increase until its people rose up in favor of rejoining the Soviet Union. Even conservatives in the Politburo agreed that was the way to go. "Tanks will not help in this matter," said Yegor Ligachev.

I went to Vilnius in April 1990 to check on the results of the blockade after the first two weeks. To my surprise, there was no sign there of the economic deprivation the Politburo had expected the blockade to produce. Instead the city appeared to be no different from before, still prosperous by Soviet standards. Traffic was normal, despite the halt of Soviet gas and oil supplies. Shops were full of goods, lines short. There was no hoarding.

The Lithuanian people remained defiant, in spite of the Soviet measures. Jonas, thirty-three, lost his job because of the embargo, but thought the sacrifice worthwhile. "We have to go on fighting the blockade for as long as we can," he said. Some Lithuanians even joked that nothing had changed. Algis, thirty-six, a truck driver, contended that the chronic shortages of Soviet economic mismanagement had always forced economic hardship on the republic anyway. He claimed to see no difference from the blockade. "We've had a blockade in Lithuania for fifty years," he said. "I was born in a blockade. It's all I've ever known."

Lithuanians could afford to be defiant. They had always thought the blockade would fail. For one thing, cheap fuel was still available in the neighboring Soviet republic of Belorussia. Despite Moscow's embargo, there were still no effective controls on borders between Soviet republics. For Lithuanian motorists the blockade meant only the inconvenience of a quick trip to Belorussia to fill up the car, or tanking up from a fuel truck that had made the journey for them. Other improvising took care of everything else.

Gorbachev had raised the stakes by cutting off Soviet rail traffic to Lithuania. So Vilnius switched its freight traffic to trucks. As a result of Gorbachev's reforms, private barter deals were now possible between various regions of the U.S.S.R., outside the state-planned economy. Barter trade by truck saved

Lithuania. Ironically, Gorbachev's blockade failed because of his own reforms.

Lithuania was one of the few Soviet republics with surplus meat and dairy products. Not only could the republic feed itself, but it could also trade in excess food. Lithuania survived the blockade by bartering meat, milk, butter, eggs, and cheese for essential supplies from other areas of the U.S.S.R. that were desperately short of food. Lithuanian trucks took meat as far away as the Tyumen oil fields of western Siberia, and brought back oil. "The only way Moscow can really enforce the blockade is by closing Lithuania's borders with other Soviet republics, but that would only underscore our independence," Carla Groudis, a Landsbergis aide, told me.

The lesson Lithuania taught the rest of the Soviet Union was the opposite of the one Gorbachev had intended. Vilnius showed that independence was viable. Tanks would not roll. Economic blockade would not work. As Lithuania moved successfully to consolidate independence, other republics moved toward declaring theirs. The independence of the other Baltic states was only a matter of time, for these republics had long been linked in the same struggle. In August 1989, more than one million people formed a human chain stretching 370 miles from Tallinn, the Estonian capital, through Riga, Latvia, to Vilnius, Lithuania. First, they held hands. Then each in turn repeated one word to the next person until it had traveled the length of the chain. That word was "freedom."

With Lithuania free, from March 1990, the other Baltic states would not be denied. Nor would the independence movements in other Soviet republics. Popular fronts in all of them drew inspiration from the Lithuanian example. They too would be independent. The only question was when.

Gorbachev entered 1991 not knowing it would be the last year of his rule. He also began 1991 not knowing his battle to contain minority nationalist rebellion was already lost. The Soviet leader was still optimistic. He still believed he would make perestroika a success and his reforms irreversible. He had some grounds for that assurance. His foreign policy, as we shall see in the next chapter, was a major plus. Western governments were now increasingly helping him.

Nonetheless, his fate, and that of the Soviet state, had already been sealed by 1990. He would not last long, and neither would the Soviet Union. The destinies of Gorbachev personally and the Soviet state he headed were now intertwined. The crunch for both would come within days. In the same week of August 1991, a hard-line Communist coup toppled Gorbachev from power and the Ukraine declared its independence from the U.S.S.R. The timing was no coincidence. The disarray from the coup in Moscow made it the perfect moment for the Ukraine to act.

The world focused on the coup. It virtually ignored the Ukraine decision, but in the long run, Ukrainian independence was far more important. Today, the August 1991 coup is largely forgotten. It failed to stop either Gorbachev or the reforms. It resolved nothing. Gorbachev himself returned to power, albeit briefly. Four months later he was replaced by Yeltsin, who continued the struggle for reform. The coup had failed.

The Ukraine's declaration of independence, by contrast, was a success. Unlike the coup, it was never reversed. Instead, it accelerated the collapse of Soviet power, as we shall see. Ukrainian independence was, in fact, a key last step in forcing both Gorbachev's resignation and the breakup of the Soviet state. It thus accomplished far more than the August military coup. In the final test of wills in Soviet history, a peaceful, democratic independence movement proved stronger than the largest army on earth.

14

Foreign Surprises: Détente as a
Two-Way Street

I. GORBACHEV'S FINEST HOUR

No patriotic American is supposed to forget December 7, 1941. That was the day Japan bombed Pearl Harbor in a surprise attack and brought the United States into World War II. Nearly half a century later, another December 7 again marked a historic turning point, this time for peace. Although few Americans remember anything special about December 7, 1988, it was ultimately more important to U.S. and global survival than Pearl Harbor. That was the day Mikhail Sergeyevich Gorbachev delivered the most significant of his diplomatic surprises, launching the process that would end the Cold War, the arms race, and four decades of nuclear nightmare.

Gorbachev's speech to the United Nations General Assembly on December 7, 1988, would be his greatest triumph on the world stage. Even now, years later, it remains an astonishing performance. With one speech, Mikhail Sergeyevich reversed the Soviet global image from the primary threat of war to the leading initiator of peace. He did so by revolutionizing Soviet foreign policy. And he pulled it off in terms that convinced Communists, the Western allies, and Third World neutrals alike to take him seriously. No statesman before or since has used the UN platform more effectively for a series of major policy initiatives.

First, Gorbachev discarded the trump card of the Stalinist approach to the world, the threat and use of armed aggression. "Force and the threat of force can no longer be, and should not be, instruments of foreign policy," Mikhail Sergeyevich declared. Then he denounced the arms race as unwinnable, saying: "The stepping up of force does not make any single nation all-powerful." Next, instead of aggression and the arms race, the Soviet leader called for "a new world order," based on "freedom of choice." To underscore that point, Gorbachev made it into an absolute must. "Freedom of choice is a universal principle to which there should be no exceptions," Mikhail Sergeyevich said.

Finally, to prove he meant business, Gorbachev moved from stirring words to unprecedented deeds. "The Soviet Union has made a decision on reducing its armed forces," he announced, by half a million men over the next two years. The reductions would remove fifty thousand men and five thousand tanks from Eastern Europe alone. Furthermore, all the "reductions will be made on a unilateral basis," Gorbachev promised, meaning they would not be dependent on the West's making similar cuts.

Veteran diplomats at the United Nations had never expected to hear an offer like that in their lifetime, least of all from the Soviet Union. The size of the cuts was staggering, the offer to make it unilateral almost inconceivable. Suddenly, the Cold War order was changing, more rapidly than anyone had thought imaginable. This was an opportunity too good to pass up. Around the world, various political interests seized it, in very different ways.

East European opposition movements took Gorbachev's UN speech as an invitation to reject communism. If freedom of choice was to be a universal principle, with no exceptions, that meant their nations could now determine their own futures. Withdrawal of Soviet troops and tanks, the ultimate enforcers of Communist rule on their soil, made Gorbachev's offer an invitation they could not refuse. Dissidents in Hungary and Poland each entered a power-sharing process that eventually dethroned their Communist parties, and when Moscow offered no resistance, East Germany and Czechoslovakia followed suit. The Brezhnev Doctrine, by which the Kremlin justified holding Eastern Europe by force, had been repealed. It would be replaced, joked Soviet foreign ministry spokesman Gennady Gerasimov, by the "Sinatra Doctrine," with former satellite states now free to do things "their way." By November 1989, less than a year after Gorbachev's UN speech, the Berlin Wall was down and Eastern Europe's headlong rush out of the Communist bloc was unstoppable. The cause and effect could not be clearer. The speech had produced the rush.

In the United States and Western Europe, Gorbachev's UN speech finally convinced the doubters that this Soviet leader was a genuine peacemaker. For three years the Reagan administration and like-minded officials in Europe had dismissed his "New Thinking" as empty propaganda. But no skeptic could pin that label on a unilateral offer to cut half a million troops. Furthermore, Gorbachev's address to the General Assembly gained additional credence in NATO because it enunciated a promising new military doctrine. No longer were the Soviets seeking weapons superiority, or even parity with the West. Instead, Mikhail Sergeyevich said, "we will maintain our country's defense capability on a level of reasonable and reliable sufficiency, so that no one should find themselves tempted to infringe upon the security of the U.S.S.R. and its allies." With that Gorbachev had also struck at the Pentagon's rationale for ever larger defense budgets. If Moscow was no longer seeking military superiority, then Washington could also let up on the arms race.

The Soviet leader left "reasonable and reliable sufficiency" undefined, but NATO was not in a position to ask for more. Every nation has the right to defend itself. And Gorbachev was now saying the Soviet Union could do that at parity with the United States or even less. His new doctrine was thus the essential opening to effective arms control. In less than three years of further negotiation, it would make possible the treaties on nuclear and conventional weapons that would at last end the Cold War arms race.

It is well worth remembering at this point that the Cold War started over two issues—the Soviet occupation of Eastern Europe and the nuclear arms race. With only one speech to the United Nations, Gorbachev had set in motion a process that would resolve them both. He could have been satisfied with that, but there was still a great deal more. In his UN address, Gorbachev had also spoken of "a new world order," a phrase U.S. President George Bush would adopt as his own four years later. Both leaders eventually had the same ideas in mind, a framework for a more peaceful post–Cold War world. But the vision belonged to Gorbachev, and remarkably so, because he spelled it out in a 1988 speech, long before anyone could be sure the Cold War would ever end.

In Gorbachev's new world order, the Kremlin would no longer stir up tensions in Third World trouble spots. Instead it would work with the United States, the West, and the United Nations to resolve them. True to his word, Mikhail Sergeyevich in the following years would contribute to settling regional conflicts from Cambodia to Angola to the Middle East and Central America. The practice continues to this day, with Russia joining in Western efforts to restore peace in former Yugoslavia rather than fanning the flames of war. Once again, this process too owed its start to Gorbachev's extraordinary vision. Thus one speech had fundamentally changed the global playing field, not only for the Warsaw Pact nations of Eastern Europe but also for NATO and the Third World as well.

Finally, in the contemporary era of government-managed media events, Gorbachev's UN speech may never be surpassed as a triumph of televised image-making. At a stroke, he had turned the reputation of the Soviet Union from warmonger to peacemaker, and he did so at the United Nations, the site of one of Moscow's more lasting Cold War embarrassments. No longer would the Soviet image at the UN be the ruffian Nikita Khrushchev, disrupting the General Assembly by banging his shoe on a desk. Henceforth, it would be Gorbachev's innovative statesmanship applauded by the entire world.

The Soviet leader's "handlers" were delighted with the performance. "The postwar period is almost over," Nikolai Shishlin, Gorbachev's senior media adviser, told me after the speech. "The Cold War is dying." And although every word of the text was approved in advance by the Politburo, a leading progressive member of that body, Aleksandr Yakovlev, was still awestruck that Gorbachev had pulled it off. "If three years ago someone had told me we would be doing this today, I wouldn't have believed it," Yakovlev said.[1]

Gorbachev never got to savor his own triumph. He spent only forty-six hours in New York, because on the day of his UN speech, a disastrous earthquake struck Soviet Armenia. The worst-hit city, Leninakan, turned into a dust-shrouded wasteland filled with the dying and the dead, as block after block of nine-story apartment houses collapsed on occupants. First estimates reported 40,000 dead from the quake and 500,000 homeless, a tragedy worse in human terms than the Chernobyl disaster of 1986. Gorbachev had no choice but to cut his New York trip short, rush home, and head the relief efforts. A visit to Leninakan to inspect the damage left him deeply moved. He looked exhausted, overcome with grief.

It was a telling omen for the entire Gorbachev era. This time the triumph of the UN speech was marred by the tragedy of the Armenian earthquake. Ultimately, his foreign policy overall would have much the same effect—triumph abroad, disaster at home. In the West, Gorbachev's foreign affairs initiatives made him a hero. Among other actions, he pulled out of Afghanistan, cut Eastern Europe loose, let Germany reunite in NATO, led the way to verifiable arms control treaties on nuclear and conventional weapons, and ended the Soviet military threat. At home, however, each of these steps made him into a villain in the eyes of the military-industrial complex, Party hardliners, and millions of ordinary citizens. To them, Gorbachev's compromises—in giving up Soviet-held territory and reducing Soviet weapons and troops—were treason, and the benefits of less international tension, more Western trade, and eventually even aid were simply not worth the price. Gorbachev's mastery of foreign affairs, his principal asset abroad, became a liability at home and contributed to his downfall.

Such is the destiny all revolutionaries risk. The forces of change they themselves unleash can in the end do them in. As a great revolutionary, well read in history, Gorbachev knew the dangers. Yet still he plunged ahead. He had started a genuine revolution within the Soviet Union, and that process had unavoidable foreign policy consequences. There was no way Gorbachev could end Stalinist policies at home and keep them going abroad. Inevitably his domestic reforms would revolutionize Soviet foreign policy as well. Moreover, that logic was never a burden for Mikhail Sergeyevich. Indeed, he saw a significant advantage in extending his revolution from domestic to international affairs.

Gorbachev had long understood that Soviet foreign policy was a cause of the U.S.S.R.'s domestic problems. The cost of challenging U.S. military power in order to pressure the world from a position of strength was bankrupting the Soviet economy. Gorbachev knew that to remedy this he would have to make foreign policy part of the solution. The withdrawal from Eastern Europe and the end of the arms race would provide economic benefits that could finance his domestic reforms. In sum, the success of perestroika would depend in part on an abrupt change in foreign policy. Mikhail Sergeyevich decided to take the risks abroad to reap the benefits at home.

He tried to convince the doubters in the Soviet elite that there was no other viable option. Among his key arguments was that the preferred policy of the past, Brezhnev's unprecedented military buildup, had proved counterproductive, despite the huge economic sacrifice involved. Rather than making the Soviet Union more secure, the Brezhnev buildup had done just the opposite. It had driven the United States, Western Europe, Japan, and China together into a worldwide coalition against a commonly perceived Soviet threat. After the buildup and the enormous financial sacrifice, the U.S.S.R. was less secure, for two reasons: its economy, the backbone of any defense, had been weakened, and its potential adversaries had been strengthened by unity of purpose.

That is what Gorbachev meant when he told the United Nations that "a one-sided emphasis on military force, in the final analysis, weakens other components of national security." The Kremlin could no longer afford to suppress Eastern Europe. Politically the cost was too high because it alarmed the West, and economically the cost was too high because the money just wasn't there.

Moscow's attempts to spread communism farther afield, to promote "national liberation movements" in the Third World, made even less sense. Often such operations involved impoverished nations of no strategic value, drained Soviet resources, and only added to Western resolve to resist Kremlin expansionism. Once again, they frequently proved counterproductive.

Gorbachev's reversal of this Brezhnev foreign policy legacy was astonishingly bold. He would withdraw Soviet troops from Afghanistan and Eastern Europe to prove the U.S.S.R. no longer threatened anyone. Then he would go further. Instead of confronting potential adversaries, from the United States to Europe to China, he would cooperate with them, by turning détente into a two-way street, of benefit to both sides. Instead of provoking conflict by supporting national liberation movements, he would pressure Third World clients into settling regional problems. Instead of blocking arms control, he offered the concessions that would make verifiable, mutually beneficial treaties possible.

All these steps would lower international tensions, and, with that, Gorbachev could concentrate on domestic reform. The economic benefits were truly formidable. In the first place, Mikhail Sergeyevich could now divert resources from the bloated Soviet military to the crumbling civilian economy. In time, the reduced international tensions would pay further dividends, among them trade possibilities blocked throughout the Cold War, such as Russian access to Western computer and other technology needed to make the reforms work. Eventually the lower tensions abroad would even open up aid from former adversaries. Financial help for Moscow to keep the Gorbachev reforms going became the top agenda item at the annual meeting of the Group of Seven, the capitalist world's most advanced nations.[2] Now, instead of the ruinously wasteful Cold War arms race, Western trade, and even aid, would actually help Soviet economic recovery. By challenging the West,

Brezhnev had bankrupted communism. By cooperating with the West, Gorbachev would save communism, or so he believed.

Gorbachev's thinking had been formed by an elite in Soviet government and academic circles who were convinced that past policies had failed and there was now no alternative to risking fundamental change. Among them was Vyacheslav Dashichev, a senior scholar at Moscow's Institute of International Economic and Political Studies. In a 1989 interview with me, Dashichev explained the basis for Gorbachev's new thinking. "For forty years we spent more than twenty percent of our GNP for military purposes," Dashichev said. "We developed our military sector and neglected our civilian sector. We thought we were increasing our defense against the West by maintaining our dominance over Eastern Europe. But all that was based on a false understanding of our real national interest, on the ideologization of foreign policy. We now understand that our real national interest is in devoting our resources to investment in the domestic economy. Giving up our dominance over Eastern Europe does not undermine our strategic position. On the contrary, it frees us from confrontation with the West."

His words contained all the key points of Gorbachev's new thinking: that reliance on military force was wrong, that the West would not attack, that reliance on an ideology which divided the world and closed off the Communist half was also wrong, and therefore the U.S.S.R.'s top-priority interest was to open up, cooperate with the West, and rebuild its home economy. Gorbachev summed it all up in his UN speech. "Today, the preservation of any kind of 'closed societies' is barely possible," he said.

The Soviet leader could not conduct such a change, of course, without a brutal internal policy battle. Yakovlev's awestruck remark at the UN, about not believing it possible three years earlier, attested to that. The time frame was deliberate. It had taken Gorbachev three years, from the day he took over the Soviet leadership in 1985, to win approval for the foreign policy reversals in his 1988 UN speech. On taking office, Mikhail Sergeyevich first had to face down Brezhnev-era hard-liners in the higher reaches of the armed forces, the Party, the KGB, and the government, who opposed increased cooperation with the West for a multitude of reasons. Hard-liners shared several long-held beliefs:

- Increased Soviet military power automatically enhanced Soviet security.

- Greater Soviet influence in the Third World supporting national liberation movements tipped the global balance Moscow's way.

- East-West trade gave the West leverage and made the U.S.S.R. vulnerable, as, for example, when embargoes on grain and technology were used as reprisals for the Soviet invasion of Afghanistan.

- Détente measures, such as an end to jamming foreign shortwave radio broadcasts, allowed Western political and cultural influences to penetrate the U.S.S.R., on everything from human rights to rock music, undermining Soviet values and with that state security.

By the time Gorbachev took over in 1985, however, these hard-liners were losing influence. Over the next three years, Mikhail Sergeyevich was able to convince a majority of Politburo members that the Soviet Union had become weaker, and the West stronger, largely because of Brezhnev's stubborn refusal for eighteen years to consider meaningful reform. Reluctantly, a Politburo majority agreed to give Gorbachev a chance to show what new thinking in foreign policy could do. They did so mainly because evidence of the Soviet Union's weakened economic and security status at last discredited the Brezhnev line. Thus in foreign policy, as in the home economy, Brezhnev's errors fathered Gorbachev's reforms.

Politburo approval, however, was hardly a blanket endorsement. The conservative majority on the Kremlin's ruling body was determined to keep Gorbachev on a short leash on foreign policy as well as domestic. Once again, the general secretary's room for maneuver would be sharply limited. His first hurdle, getting the foreign policy reversal past the extremist hard-line opposition, had been relatively easy. The more difficult part for Gorbachev would now be to get his proposed policy changes past relatively moderate conservatives in the top leadership, men like Yegor Ligachev. These people were intelligent, experienced, competent. They understood some changes were needed after Brezhnev. In general they approved reforms they thought would strengthen the Soviet system, and rejected those they feared would wreck it. Their relatively open-minded, reasoned approach made them a far more effective brake on Gorbachev than the die-hard extremists who opposed virtually all reform on principle.

To cite but one example from the beginning of the Gorbachev years, Ligachev was in favor of more economic cooperation with the West, but not at any price. He explained that in his memoirs in these words: "Quite a few politicians in the West make economic aid to our country conditional on a series of demands, including the introduction of an unregulated market, and private ownership of the means of production. There are those among them who simply hope to turn the Soviet Union into a raw-materials appendage of the West. . . . This politicized approach is a mistake. The socialist Soviet Union for decades was considered one of the most reliable business partners in the world—it paid its bills on time. Western firms have gained a great deal by doing business with us. The important thing is that in relations among states, mutual benefit, not political and ideological considerations, should be the cornerstone."[3]

The passage is Ligachev at his best—reasonably flexible, entirely pragmatic, but adamantly tough about defending the Soviet system. He is telling the

West, "Take us as we are, and trade with us for mutual benefit. But don't try to make us capitalists." He sees Western demands for a free market and private ownership as transparent attempts to weaken the U.S.S.R. and turn it into an economic colony of the West. To that, he firmly says, "No sale."

Because of the caution of moderate conservatives like Ligachev, it took three years of political maneuvering for Gorbachev to get Politburo approval for his 1988 UN speech. Tactics included reshuffling of personnel, shifting alliances, persuasion, arm-twisting. When it was over, Mikhail Sergeyevich still had to tone down the text. Conservatives like Ligachev forced him to include such lines as "We are not giving up our convictions, philosophy, or traditions." In other words, in spite of Gorbachev's commitment to "free choice," the U.S.S.R. was not abandoning communism. The Ligachev faction chose to interpret "freedom of choice" in Eastern Europe as the right to select separate roads to Communist reform. They were flexible enough to see Hungary and other countries as laboratories where reforms potentially useful in the U.S.S.R. could be tested or proved. But they were not sending Eastern Europe their blessings to leave the Communist movement.

To make that clear, the conservatives insisted on phasing Soviet troop withdrawals from Eastern Europe over time. They also limited the numbers of the initial retreat, so that, if necessary, it could be reversed. Gorbachev's UN speech promised to withdraw over the first two years only 50,000 of the 400,000 Soviet troops then in Eastern Europe. It was a significant number, enough to make the point that Moscow was relaxing controls, but the far larger number of Soviet troops remaining in Eastern Europe was supposed to signal Kremlin determination to draw the line of permitted reform well short of abandoning the Communist system. That was a message the Communist leadership of Eastern Europe understood and appreciated. The remaining Soviet troops would help them keep power, they believed. But that was old thinking, a Brezhnev-era mind-set. Under Gorbachev's new thinking, the Communist Party leaders in Eastern Europe were no longer the only players in the game.

Growing opposition movements in East Europe now had significant political weight, and they chose to interpret Gorbachev's UN speech the other way. To them, the minority of Soviet troops to be withdrawn voluntarily was far more important than the majority that would stay. Continued occupation had not stopped them before and would not now. The new element for them was the unprecedented withdrawal. They saw it as an encouragement, to keep pushing reform even harder until all Soviet troops were forced to leave.

Gorbachev's UN speech produced consequences that went much further, much faster than his Politburo colleagues intended or even he had expected— to the collapse of communism in Eastern Europe within a year. From then on, moderate conservatives like Ligachev would rein him in more sharply. Never again would Mikhail Sergeyevich be able to take such giant strides on the world stage. His room for maneuver narrowed. Domestic political pressures stopped him from going as far as he might have liked in foreign affairs.

With Tokyo, for instance, he could not cut the one deal that might have ultimately turned the Soviet economy around. The makings of the trade-off were clear. Moscow would have to give back the Kurile Islands seized from Japan at the end of World War II, and, in return, Japan would then provide the massive investment needed to bring billions of dollars in Siberia's untapped resources to market. Gorbachev could not consummate that deal, however, largely because giving back the Kuriles would have set the precedent for changing the rest of the Soviet Union's disputed postwar borders, from China to Iran to Romania to the Baltics. To conservatives in the Soviet leadership, the prospects of development aid from Japan were not worth the risk of insecure Soviet borders everywhere else. So they said *nyet* to a compromise on the Kuriles, and thus deprived Gorbachev of what would have been a great foreign economic success.

II. ON THE ROAD

For six years I watched Gorbachev chart a foreign policy on unfamiliar seas, maneuvering brilliantly between what he hoped to accomplish and what his Kremlin colleagues would let him do. I followed him from Moscow to the United Nations and Cuba, to London, Paris, Berlin, and Rome, to Beijing and Tokyo, reporting on his progress. I covered his summits with Ronald Reagan in Geneva and New York, and with George Bush in Malta, Washington, Helsinki, and Moscow. Sometimes he failed, often he succeeded. In the end, he did more to change the world for the better than any political leader has a right to expect.

Gorbachev began in Paris, on his first trip to the West as Soviet leader, in October 1985. There he offered for the first time to negotiate a 50 percent reduction in offensive strategic nuclear missiles. Years later this offer would form the basis of the Strategic Arms Reduction Treaty (START), but at the time, no Western leaders took him seriously. His Paris offer was dismissed as part of a charm offensive, more propaganda than substance, and as a transparent ploy to get the United States to drop its Star Wars program for a space-based defense that Moscow could not hope to match. It was all of these things, but it was also a serious opening bid. Here was a different kind of Soviet leader, with a new strategy worth careful examination.

Mikhail Sergeyevich underscored this point at every opportunity. At a joint press conference with François Mitterrand, under the ornate crystal chandeliers of the Elysée Palace, a French reporter asked Gorbachev if Sakharov, then in increasingly frail health, would be released from house arrest in Gorky. The standard Brezhnev-era reply was a rude lecture on how

Soviet internal affairs were no foreigner's business. Gorbachev, however, changed the script. The Sakharov question, he said, "is being considered by the competent authorities in the context of reuniting divided families." That more positive response was a hint of things to come. Sakharov was soon released and reunited with his family in Moscow, a shrewd move which enhanced Gorbachev's stature in the West. If the new Soviet leader could be trusted on human rights, why not on nuclear arms?

That would come next. Gorbachev finally met Ronald Reagan in Geneva in November 1985. Mikhail Sergeyevich had a history of impressing and then manipulating older men, beginning with Leonid Brezhnev. He was sure he could do much the same with Reagan. I watched as they first made contact. The U.S. president waited outside the door of an American villa to greet his Soviet visitor. On arrival, Gorbachev took the first of many initiatives. He strode up a short flight of stairs, firmly grabbed Reagan's hand, and looked him straight in the eye, with a supremely confident smile. The new Soviet leader had made the opening move. It was his way of saying he was in charge of the relationship.

The first photo opportunity with Reagan would have been enough. It represented Gorbachev's personal entry into the elite world of superpower summitry. For the readers of newspapers around the planet, and most important for those living inside the U.S.S.R., that picture conveyed exactly the image the new Soviet leader wanted. He was now the accepted equal of the U.S. president. Thus, from the opening moment, the Geneva summit was a political plus for Mikhail Sergeyevich.

From there it only got better. The two leaders met six times during the Geneva summit for more than five hours in all, including a memorable fireside chat in a pool house with only interpreters present. In the end, Ronald Reagan decided Gorbachev was sincere about reform, that perestroika had substance, not only style. That was the great significance of the Geneva summit. From then on, Reagan would negotiate seriously with Gorbachev on arms control and other key superpower issues. Like Margaret Thatcher, Reagan decided he could do business with Gorbachev.

It took a while, but the new working relationship between Reagan and Gorbachev led directly to a historic breakthrough in arms control. In December 1987 the two sides agreed to remove their intermediate-range nuclear weapons from Europe by signing the so-called INF treaty. Previous Soviet-American arms deals only limited the growth of nuclear arsenals. INF for the first time went significantly further, actually reducing existing stockpiles and even eliminating certain weapons categories. Gorbachev's flexibility made it happen. The key concessions came from him.

All the concessions took courage and leadership, but Gorbachev delivered. He agreed to a treaty that eliminated more Soviet than American missiles, and with that gave away a Moscow plus in the military balance. He also deferred to allied NATO concerns, reversed Soviet policy, and agreed that

British and French nuclear stockpiles would not have to be cut at all. Most important, he dropped Moscow's objection to on-site inspections within the U.S.S.R. to safeguard against cheating. With each concession, Gorbachev had to beat back objections from conservatives in the Soviet establishment. In so doing, Mikhail Sergeyevich was signaling to the world that in the continuing Kremlin power struggle, he had the upper hand, at least for the time being.

Gorbachev thus proved by concrete acts that his words about new thinking were serious. When he promised a changed foreign policy, he delivered. Eventually the INF treaty would lead to far more important arms reductions, including reductions in long-range nuclear weapons under the START agreement, but its more immediate effect was to convince skeptics in the West that Gorbachev's peacemaking was for real. By the time Mikhail Sergeyevich made his UN speech in December 1988, his credentials had been established. The entire world was now taking him seriously, and that encouraged the Soviet leader to go even further in his series of diplomatic surprises.

In foreign affairs as in domestic, 1989 would be the memorable year for Gorbachev. The same year that proved to be the turning point for the worse for Gorbachev's economic and political reforms at home, the same year that saw Eastern Europe break away and minority nationalities launch their rebellion within the U.S.S.R., turned out to be the year of Gorbachev's greatest personal diplomacy abroad. Over the course of 1989, Mikhail Sergeyevich pulled Soviet troops out of Afghanistan, then visited Havana, London, Bonn, Beijing, Rome, the Vatican, and Malta for a summit with George Bush, all to promote his new world order, with considerable success. The timing of his whirlwind activity on the world stage was no accident, and its accomplishments were sorely needed. The Soviet leader's economic and political reforms were in deep trouble at home. By seizing the peace initiative abroad, by basking in triumphant welcomes from grateful publics around the world, Gorbachev hoped he would improve his sagging reputation in the U.S.S.R. and give a new boost to perestroika reforms.

Mikhail Sergeyevich began the yearlong diplomatic offensive by resolving the Soviet Union's worst immediate foreign policy problem, Afghanistan. It was another sign of his greatness as a world leader. People sometimes forget that the main function of a leader is to lead, a point that should be obvious, but often is not. On all too many occasions, leaders of nations do everything but lead. They wait for opinion polls to show them the way to go, or they delegate responsibility to cabinet ministers or parliaments, or they defer tough decisions in the hope that over time problems will go away. Gorbachev himself was not immune to such criticism. His tactics could appear indecisive, shifting first one way, then another. His speeches often rambled inconclusively. But on the big strategic questions he was not afraid to take the lead, however controversial his course might be. Part of his greatness came from a willingness to make the tough calls and take the responsibility.

Afghanistan was a case in point. It was no easier for a Soviet leader to admit defeat and pull out of Afghanistan than it was for a U.S. president to write off the Vietnam War as a lost cause. That unwelcome task fell to Gorbachev.

By then, the Vietnam comparison was obvious to the entire world. If anything, the treatment of Soviet veterans returning from Afghanistan, dead or alive, was even more callous than the reception America's Vietnam vets got when they came home. Among them, Sergeant Yuri Shevchenko, killed in action in Afghanistan in 1986, returned to his village in the Soviet Ukraine in a zinc coffin. His tombstone, provided by the state, listed only his name, date of birth, and date of death. His father, Anatoly, was outraged. "One might think he died in a drunken brawl," the father complained. "Why can't it be inscribed that he was doing his international duty in Afghanistan? What are we ashamed of?" Anatoly tried to put that right by placing an obituary on his son in the local newspaper. "It just isn't done," a Communist Party official told him. "Your son isn't the first to be killed. What are we supposed to do, write in the newspaper about every one?"

Those who came home alive—wounded or healthy—got no more sympathetic treatment. One former soldier who had lost both legs in the Afghan War applied for a transfer to a ground-floor apartment. His request was turned down by a local bureaucrat. Another, told that his service in Afghanistan entitled him to priority university admission, missed the opportunity because the discharge papers needed for the application arrived four weeks late. Yet another soldier, wounded in action and having trouble regaining his health in civilian life, went for medical help, but the doctor said he could do nothing and refused even the courtesy of hearing him out. "I didn't send you to Afghanistan," the doctor said.

Afghanistan, of course, was not Vietnam. The differences between those wars were often more important than the similarities. Among them, there was no antiwar movement in the Soviet Union, no mass demonstrations against Afghanistan, no burning of draft cards. Gorbachev was under no great public pressure to end the war. He could have let the quagmire drag on. Instead, he had the courage to say enough and end the war, on terms a less confident Soviet leader would have been loath to accept.

In fact, the U.S.S.R. had been seeking an honorable withdrawal from Afghanistan since 1982. Talks under United Nations auspices in Geneva sought a suitable fig leaf. During the Brezhnev, Andropov, and Chernenko regimes, none could be found. Moscow pushed a variety of formulas to guarantee that the pro-Communist regime in Kabul would remain in power after a Soviet withdrawal, among them various election formulas and curbs on new arms supplies, all designed to prolong the rule of the Kremlin's Afghan clients. Without such favorable withdrawal terms, the Soviets said, their 110,000 troops would stay. The anti-Communist Afghan rebels refused all such terms, so the war dragged on.

By 1988 it had lasted eight years. The Soviet Union's officially admitted casualties included 13,310 dead, 35,478 wounded, and 311 missing in action.[4] Still, there was no military solution in sight. The only way Gorbachev could stop the carnage was to withdraw. He knew he would have to pay a heavy price. There would be no fig leaf to cover the Soviet humiliation. The Red Army would simply have to pack up and go home, leaving the Afghan Communists to take their chances. But Gorbachev had foreseen that even an unconditional withdrawal would have its financial and diplomatic rewards. While the war lasted, there would be little prospect he could cut military spending or that his various peace initiatives elsewhere would be taken seriously. By ending the Afghan War, he could reverse that prospect overnight. With Afghanistan settled, even on unfavorable terms, the Soviet leader could move on to more important long-term matters, like ending the nuclear arms race with the United States. And funds no longer wasted in Afghanistan could be invested in economic reform.

Three years into his rule, Mikhail Sergeyevich decided he was strong enough to take the political risks of unconditional withdrawal from Afghanistan. He announced Soviet troops would start pulling out in May 1988, and the last would leave Afghanistan by February 1989. He got nothing in return to help his Afghan clients prolong their rule after the Soviet withdrawal, no guarantees they would stay in government, no curbs on arms supplies to their opponents. So Gorbachev made the best of it. He blamed Afghanistan on Brezhnev. The decision to invade had been a mistake, Mikhail Sergeyevich declared. At the time, that argument played well in Moscow, just as blaming Brezhnev's stagnation for the nation's economic mess was also largely accepted by the Soviet public. Gorbachev also explained away the long, unwinnable conflict. That, he said, was due to the arming of the Mujahedin rebels by the United States.

Internationally, Gorbachev raised his own prestige by keeping his word. The promised Soviet troop withdrawals from Afghanistan began on schedule in May 1988, a factor that gave credibility to his pledge at the United Nations, in December of the same year, to start pulling Soviet troops out of Eastern Europe as well. The only major question left was whether Gorbachev's Afghan client, President Najibullah, would survive the Soviet withdrawal. I went to Kabul in February 1989, just before the last Russian tanks left, to find out. Najibullah himself insisted all was well. He told a press conference at his presidential palace, "We are in control." Then halfway through that session with reporters, the electricity failed and the lights went out. It took ten minutes to get them back on. The episode was hardly a promising omen. If the Afghan government couldn't even keep the electricity going in the president's palace, it seemed unlikely it could keep running the country.

Nevertheless, Lieutenant General Boris Gromov, the Soviet commander in Afghanistan, insisted the Afghan government would survive. "The Afghan military has been considerably strengthened," Gromov said, and he turned out to be right. Moscow's aid and training proved sufficient. The war continued after the Soviets left, of course. There could be no stopping it. The conflict had left deep scars, a million Afghani people dead and five million refugees, but the Mujahedin guerrillas, so adept at harassing Soviet troops in the field or interdicting convoys, were ill prepared to capture a capital city. Kabul would remain in government hands.

The Soviet clients there would not suffer the fate of America's Saigon allies, who lost power soon after U.S. troops left Vietnam. Najibullah's Communist regime would last another three years.[5] Gorbachev won his gamble. The Soviet Union pulled out of Afghanistan with no concessions from the international community, and still made sure its pro-Communist allies stayed in power.

I rode out of Afghanistan on a Soviet tank. It was part of the last Red Army convoy to leave the country. We crossed the border on the last day of the withdrawal, February 15, 1989, just ahead of the commander, General Gromov. It turned out to be an emotional trip. The Afghan war veterans on my Soviet tank began to relax when they were thirty miles from home. From there on, the two-lane road crossed desert flatland all the way to the Soviet border. There was no place for Mujahedin ambushers to hide. If they tried to attack, Russian helicopter gunships providing air cover would have blown them away. There was no longer any danger, so my Soviet hosts started talking over the roar of the tank treads. "I've been waiting for this moment for eighteen months in Afghanistan," said the commander of my tank, Lieutenant Aleksandr Korotkin, puffing on an unfiltered Russian cigarette. "Not everyone managed to make it, you know."

Far from it. Lieutenant Sasha Morozov, commander of an armored personnel carrier in our convoy, recalled the horror of the war from his first day in the country. On August 10, 1986, his group was waiting at the Kabul airport, unarmed, for transfer to a provincial center, when ambushers attacked. "The Mujahedin opened fire at us with mortars," Morozov said. "A shell exploded twenty yards from me. Many were killed and wounded, including my best friend. He was standing six feet away and had only just arrived in Afghanistan."

Morozov also remembered the fear, particularly of being taken prisoner by the rebels. "There are many terrible stories," he explained. "The Mujahedin cut off ears, poke out eyes, mutilate bodies. I don't want to say any more because it's too upsetting. But they are very cruel." Other Russian soldiers were not so shy about details. They were full of atrocity stories, about Afghan rebels cutting the penises off live Soviet prisoners, of slitting the skin around the waist and pulling it up like a shirt. No doubt the Mujahedin thought the Soviet invasion cruel, and any means justified to repel it.

Still others in our convoy spoke of the pride that comes mainly from courage proved in battle. A captain who identified himself during a rest stop only by his first name, Konstantin, said, "We defended the city of Kabul.

Our tank fired five hundred shells and we hit the target four hundred and sixty times."

Even those soldiers who never saw combat said they had matured in Afghanistan. "I came as a kid," recalled twenty-year-old private Vitaly Shagayev. "All I cared about was sports and rock music. Now I am going home as an adult, thinking about getting married and starting a family."

Yet permeating all of these emotions was a distinct feeling of deception, a sense that the Soviet invasion, that all the sacrifice, had been a ghastly mistake. Captain Arkady Anonich was brutally frank. "The decision to enter Afghanistan was ill-considered," he said. "Another way should have been found to solve the problem."

That night the convoy halted near the Afghan town of Hayratan, just across the Amu Darya River from the Soviet city of Termez. A soldier got out his guitar and began singing of the "hot time" he expected across the border when he returned to his homeland. He would not be disappointed. The next day our convoy of Afghan veterans crossed the steel "friendship bridge" and crawled into Termez to a hero's welcome back in the U.S.S.R. They were showered with flowers, and the traditional Russian welcome gift of bread and salt. They also got tears, kisses, speeches, a brass band, and, at long, long last, a chance to send telegrams home to loved ones unseen for more than a year.

For the Soviet Union, the war in Afghanistan was finally over. For Mikhail Gorbachev, there were now fresh opportunities to push his new world order. Withdrawal from Afghanistan removed the largest single obstacle to improved relations with the United States. Now Gorbachev took aim on the longest-standing one, Cuba. The Soviet leader would visit Havana, from April 2 to April 5 1989, to start removing Cold War tensions from Central America.

Fidel Castro had already made it clear that perestroika reforms were not for him. Instead, he would carry on with his long dictatorship in Havana. "The Soviets apply Soviet formulas to their problems, and we try to find Cuban solutions to Cuban problems," Castro said. Despite such resistance, however, Gorbachev had ample leverage to push the reluctant Castro toward change. At the time, Moscow was still pouring more than $5 billion in economic aid into Havana every year. Without Soviet help, Cuba faced economic disaster. There was no reason why the Cuban tail should wag the Russian bear. On the contrary, if Castro wanted continued Soviet aid, he would have to play ball Moscow's way. As further evidence of that, Castro's troops were no longer needed as the Gurkhas of Africa, backing Communist expansion there. On the contrary, Gorbachev was trying to end those conflicts. Angola was being settled, and the Cuban troops there sent home. That in turn would give Moscow another excuse to cut aid to Havana.

On the surface, Gorbachev's trip to Havana was all sweetness and light. Cuba was Moscow's most important client state outside Europe. The Soviet leader was visiting no other Latin American nation, underscoring Cuba's pre-eminent position in the region in the Kremlin's view. Havana loved Gorby. A million flag-waving Cubans cheered him all the way from the airport to the city. The two leaders seemed to be getting along well, beginning with bear hugs at the airport.

"I almost never comb my hair," Castro told Gorbachev shortly after the Kremlin chief's arrival. "But today I told myself, millions of people watching television will see you meet Gorbachev, so even I combed my hair."

"Fidel, that's not exactly true," Gorbachev replied. "You were impecca-ble when you came to Moscow two years ago."

Still, once he got down to substance, Gorbachev pulled no punches. To show he meant business, the Soviet leader even went public on the crucial point during a major speech to the Cuban National Assembly. "We are cat-egorically opposed to any theories or doctrines that seek to justify the export of revolution," Gorbachev said. Instead, he called for "peace and security in the region." Then he added this key sentence: "One of the principal condi-tions for that is the cessation of military supplies to Central America from any quarter." Diplomatically, Mikhail Sergeyevich had mentioned neither Castro nor Cuba by name, but his meaning was clear—that the days of Cuba exporting revolution, with Moscow picking up the tab, were over. As in An-gola, as in Afghanistan, the U.S.S.R. now wanted to settle regional disputes in Central America politically.

Privately, Gorbachev went even further, a senior Soviet foreign ministry official told me in Havana. "The Soviet Union will stop arming Cuba and Nicaragua if the United States stops arming the other countries of the re-gion," he said. Gorbachev had made that clear to Castro and to the new Bush administration in Washington. With Reagan, the Soviet leader had pro-posed that both superpowers cut arms supplies to Central America. Now he was going further with Bush, urging that they both stop arms supplies alto-gether.

His proposal fell far short of a specific solution to such key Central Amer-ican problems as Nicaragua and El Salvador, but this was still the early days. Gorbachev could not always do it all himself, with unilateral Soviet moves, as in Afghanistan. "He cannot forever be pulling rabbits out of the hat," said Soviet foreign ministry spokesman Gennady Gerasimov. "Maybe it's time for someone else to make initiatives." In time, Washington would indeed engage in a more serious give-and-take with Moscow on Central American disputes, but it was Gorbachev's initiative that made a settlement possible by the end of the Bush administration. The Soviet leader had taken the key first step by deciding that Moscow would no longer supply the funds and arms to foment Communist revolution in the region. Over a relatively short time, negotiators of goodwill would settle the rest. Then even Cuba could no longer prevent Soviet-American détente from becoming a genuine two-way street.

On the way home from Havana, Gorbachev stopped in London to consolidate his good working relationship with Margaret Thatcher. She would be his insurance policy in case the new American president, George Bush, continued to resist détente advances. Gorbachev was beginning to lose patience with Bush. The new U.S. president was not saying no to Gorbachev. He was saying later. As noted earlier, Bush had embarked on a broad foreign policy review from his inauguration in January 1989. In April, that review was still continuing and Gorbachev's proposals were still in the "pending" tray at the White House. The Soviets, including Gorbachev, began to suspect sinister motives for the delay. They thought Bush to be well up on all aspects of foreign affairs from his years as director of the CIA and vice president. They suspected the long policy review was a ploy designed to pressure them into concessions on arms control and other superpower issues.

In London, Gorbachev instructed his spokesman to tell reporters that "any attempt to pressure us with artificial delay is bound to fail." The American pause to study was understandable, the spokesman explained, as long as it didn't drag on too long. "We don't want the pause to become an interval," he said. "The main point is not to lose momentum with prolonged reviews of foreign policy or other obstacles." Soviet impatience was expressed in London in public and in private. In a speech at London's Guildhall, Gorbachev said, "The question of a fifty percent reduction in Soviet and U.S. strategic offensive arms continues to be on the top of the agenda of our relations with the United States." Then, in a pointed invitation to Bush to get moving, Mikhail Sergeyevich stressed that the Soviet side was waiting for him. "We are ready to resume negotiations at any time," Gorbachev said.

In private talks with Thatcher, the Soviet leader pushed the same themes—the Bush review was dragging on, time was wasting, the American motives for delay were suspect in Moscow's eyes. Gorbachev knew that Thatcher, as America's closest ally in Europe, would report his concerns to Washington. That might help bring the Bush policy review to an early conclusion.

Moscow still preferred to focus détente on the Soviet-American track, and wanted to achieve movement there first. But if that effort stalled, Gorbachev would then move détente down a second or alternate track, this one of improved Soviet–West European relations. He spent most of his three hours of talks with Thatcher detailing for her the progress of his perestroika reforms in the U.S.S.R. and exploring how Soviet–West European cooperation might take the initiative on arms control, the Middle East, and other key regional problems if the Bush policy review were to drag on. The British prime minister could help on this second track as well. Indeed, so could leaders in Paris, Bonn, and Rome. Gorbachev's visits there had much the same purpose.

By April 1989, Mikhail Sergeyevich had done his best to improve relations on the Soviet Union's western flank. Ambitious arms control proposals were on the table, regional problems from Afghanistan to Angola to Central America were either settled or making progress, offers of friendship and dialogue were out to leaders in the United States and Western Europe.

The western flank, however, was only half of Gorbachev's foreign policy problem, and not always the most troubling half. The Soviet leader had to secure his eastern flank as well. The long, dangerous dispute with China had to be settled too. Only when the U.S.S.R. had détente going with former adversaries in both the West and the East could Gorbachev successfully divert sufficient resources from the military to the civilian economy and give his perestroika reforms a real chance for success. So in May 1989, he flew to Beijing to normalize relations with China.

The last Soviet-Chinese summit had begun on a deliberately sour note. In September 1959, Nikita Khrushchev tried to give Mao Zedong a bear hug on arrival in Beijing, but Mao stepped backward, eluding the Soviet leader's embrace and offering only a cold handshake in greeting. It was the beginning of an estrangement that was to last thirty years, through ideological and territorial disputes, punctuated by sporadic armed clashes along the four-thousand-mile border. Gorbachev was determined to relegate all such difficulties to the past. As a first step in that direction he would make sure the next summit began as an exercise in exaggerated courtesy.

Since the last summit had been held in Beijing, the next one, according to diplomatic protocol, should have been held in Moscow. However, Deng Xiaoping, already eighty-four and in frail health, could no longer travel, so the younger Gorbachev, then fifty-eight, waived protocol "in a Chinese manner, out of respect for Deng's age," and agreed to come to him, an aide to the Soviet president explained. In fact, Gorbachev did more than that. He came to Beijing bowing to Chinese conditions. As the stronger by far of the two Communist powers, it was always up to the Soviet Union to make the first compromises on the way to normalization. The dispute lasted three decades because the Chinese stubbornly insisted on Soviet concessions and the Russians just as stubbornly refused to budge. Gorbachev was finally able to break the deadlock only because the concessions China demanded as preconditions for normalization all helped on the Soviet Union's western flank as well.

China demanded the removal of three obstacles before it would normalize relations with the U.S.S.R. Gorbachev delivered on all three, not entirely, but enough to satisfy Beijing and, at the same time, the West. The first was a Soviet withdrawal from Afghanistan. That he had completed in February. The second was a reduction of Soviet troops on the Chinese border, a concession that was included in the cuts announced in the December 1988 UN speech. The third was the removal of Vietnamese occupation troops from Cambodia. There Moscow was pressing Hanoi to withdraw, and, for the moment, that was enough for the Chinese leaders. As far as they were concerned, Gorbachev had caved in to their demands. He could come to Beijing to normalize relations. "This summit proves that the foreign policy adopted by the

Chinese government was the correct one," Xu Kui, director of the Institute of Soviet Studies in Beijing, told me in an interview. In sum, that policy was a total refusal to make any compromises, until Moscow gave in to all of China's demands—and it worked. It was one more example of what the Chinese could teach the Americans on how to handle the Russians.

On their side, leading Soviet experts on China were convinced the price Gorbachev paid in meeting Beijing's demands was well worth the achievement of a normalization. "Complete restoration of relations with China is a very important victory of perestroika," Mikhail Titarenko, director of the Far East Institute in Moscow, told me. It becalmed the U.S.S.R.'s long-threatened eastern flank.

The normalization of relations between the Soviet Union and China was also a major plus for the rest of the world. For one thing, it defused the risk of nuclear war between them, to the benefit of everyone else on the planet. For another, this time Soviet-Chinese cooperation would not be aimed against the United States and the capitalist West. This would not be a return to the Soviet-Chinese alliance of the 1950s. Instead, this would be an exercise in reducing friction along the fiercely armed frontier, so that both China and Russia would have more resources for economic reform at home. This would normalize relations so that both countries could learn more from each other's attempts to reform the Communist system.

Best of all for the West, the two leading Communist countries were now focused on an area in which capitalist countries had consistently outperformed them both—economic development. The West could now help them both convert from military to economic priorities with the appropriate trade and aid policies. In short, thanks to the Soviet-Chinese rapprochement, the West had important new leverage to keep them both on a more peaceful track.

I went to China in April 1989, before Gorbachev's arrival, for a look at the very different attempt there to reform communism. The two leading Communist nations had approached reform problems from opposite directions. China first loosened economic restrictions, while keeping political controls very much in place. The Soviet Union, on the contrary, first loosened political restrictions, through glasnost and democratization, while largely maintaining centralized economic controls. The results of these opposite approaches were fascinating. It had been ten years since I had last visited China. In the interim, living standards there had risen far faster than in the Soviet Union. The reason was simple. Deng had done far more than Gorbachev in the field of economic reform.

Examples were everywhere, among them:

- Chinese food markets had higher-quality fruits and vegetables, in greater quantities, and with more choice. Chinese stock markets were up and running; their Soviet counterparts were still organizing.

• In the South China village of Luo Fang, private farmers in coolie hats got on their bicycles, crossed a barbed-wire frontier checkpoint, sold their produce in Hong Kong, and returned home richer. With the proceeds they built three-story houses with Japanese air-conditioning and French VSOP brandy in the bar. No Soviet farmers were so free or so rich.

• In eight years, Shenzhen had turned from a sleepy Chinese village on the Hong Kong border into a modern city of 600,000 people, with dozens of skyscraper office blocks, several Western luxury hotels, and even a golf course. As one of China's five "special economic zones"—exceptional restricted areas where capitalism was allowed to run free—Shenzhen offered foreigners tax breaks and other incentives to invest, including cheap labor for manufacturing plants. By 1990 the zone was earning $2 billion a year in exports. The U.S.S.R. had not even begun to create anything like China's special economic zones.

• In Moscow, personal computers were still so rare that a $2,000 model bought in the West fetched $60,000 on the Soviet black market. In Beijing, in a ten-block stretch dubbed "Silicon Valley," computers sold at close to normal price levels in the West. Chinese scientists and businessmen borrowed from banks and set up private firms there to market high-tech electronic gear, often with foreign components. One Beijing store, called Stones, offered Chinese shoppers on the premises a selection of eight thousand spare parts for computers and electronic equipment, an absolutely mind-boggling choice for a visitor from Moscow. In the Soviet capital the shortage of spare parts was still so acute that often the only way to repair a broken computer was to cannibalize another one or replace it entirely.

China, of course, still had its economic problems. Inflation rose as the economy shifted from central planning to private enterprise. Often Chinese citizens could not afford to buy the new goods now available in the shops because they didn't have the money. In the U.S.S.R., the problem was just the opposite. Soviet citizens had money, but there were no goods in the shops. They were forced to save because there was nothing to buy. Overall, however, the Chinese benefited far more than the Soviets from economic reform, especially in improved food supplies, but ultimately, China fell down on the political side.

There was no way the Chinese leadership could permit more economic freedom, and still hold back political freedom, without risking an explosion. It began to build while I was in Beijing in April 1989. At one student demonstration I attended, someone had nailed a black shoe to a tree on the campus of Beijing Teachers University. "A policeman used this shoe to kick students, so we took it from him," a sign underneath said. Nearby, crowds of young people were meeting to denounce the nation's political leaders and plan more protest marches. "Deng Xiaoping has become too autocratic," one of the campus organizers told them. "Deng is unable to accept democracy."

Students and workers who agreed with him would no longer be denied political freedom. Some 100,000 of them took their demands to Tiananmen Square in a peaceful demonstration, determined to stay until the leadership gave them a hearing. Instead martial law was declared, and the army brutally cleared the square by force on June 3–4, leaving an estimated seven thousand dead and ten thousand injured. Some ten thousand protesters were arrested, and 31 of them were tried and executed. The regime would tolerate no dissent. It would maintain Communist political control even at the expense of slaughtering its own people.

In the end, the Chinese did no better than Gorbachev in their attempt to reform communism. Coming at the problem from different approaches, China and the Soviet Union each learned that it was impossible to have both reform and communism. Ultimately a choice had to be made. Gorbachev eventually chose reform at the expense of communism. The Chinese chose communism at the expense of reform. They had each proved the same case: communism cannot be effectively reformed.

The Russian writer Vladimir Bukovsky put it very well. Communism cannot be reformed, he said, "no matter how cautious the reformers, and how gradual the reforms." The reason, he explained, is that reform inevitably puts intolerable pressure for change on the Communist system, until its leaders can no longer stand the strain. Then they have only one choice. "Either they crack down or they break down," Bukovsky said.[6] This time, China cracked down. The Soviet Union would eventually break down, but it was not yet there.

Gorbachev returned from China in May 1989 still confident he could make reform communism succeed. Normalized relations with China would now help, he thought. The Soviet leader had been in Beijing during the buildup of demonstrations in the hundreds of thousands. Aides said he had been impressed by the numbers and by the friendly, peaceful nature of the protests. But, they insisted, Mikhail Sergeyevich had no concern on returning home that he too might face such protests on the streets of Moscow. Their reason was simple and persuasive. Gorbachev's political reforms had already moved a long way toward democracy. "There was a general feeling that the Chinese students were demanding steps which we had already taken," one official in Gorbachev's delegation to China told me privately after returning to Moscow. Later, after Tiananmen Square, Gorbachev was more convinced than ever that he had nothing to learn from China's alternative model for reforming communism. Instead, Mikhail Sergeyevich believed that the fundamental difference in his perestroika approach—the greater political freedom allowed—would make it more successful.

III. NO EXCEPTIONS

Gorbachev continued his policies unchanged. Among them he maintained the principle that every Communist country had a free choice to determine its own future. The U.S.S.R. would no longer hold other countries back by force. Nowhere would that prove more important than in divided Germany. A brief historical look shows why.

Communist East Germany could never survive in a free competition with capitalist West Germany. When the best and the brightest got fed up with the East, they went to Berlin, the Cold War dividing line, and crossed to the West. By 1961, some two million East Germans had escaped communism that way. Never was there a clearer example of people voting with their feet.

There was only one way to stop the exodus: by force. The East Germans put up the Berlin Wall in 1961, with Nikita Khrushchev's blessing. It was not very subtle, but it worked. The escapes slowed to a trickle, and most Germans never expected to see reunification in their lifetime. They thought the Soviet Union, which had lost an admitted twenty million dead in the Nazi invasion of World War II, would never allow it. At the time, they were right.

Under Brezhnev, the U.S.S.R. was determined to keep Germany divided, too weak to attack Russia ever again. Almost every night in Brezhnev's Russia, television carried documentary films from World War II, claiming that West Germany was still seeking revenge for eastern land lost by the Nazis, and would stop at nothing to take it back. The message to the Soviet people was clear: they had to maintain constant vigilance against a very real German threat to unite and attack Russia again. The message was repeated so often, etched so deeply in the Soviet consciousness, that it became as unquestioned a fixture of patriotism as love of country.

In the Brezhnev era, Soviets believed German reunification could never happen. Then, suddenly, incredibly, Gorbachev changed all that. He made German reunification a real possibility. No longer was the Soviet leader talking about divided Europe or divided Germany. Instead he spoke about a "Common European House" where nations of East and West—Britain, France, the U.S.S.R., and all the others—worked together to solve common problems on everything from national security to trade to environmental pollution. It was supposed to be a long-term vision, but it held promise for Germany, whenever it might apply. If all the European nations came together in a common house, they would, in the process, reunite Germany.

Furthermore, if the Germans themselves wanted to speed the process along, Moscow would not stand in the way. Aleksandr Yakovlev, Gorbachev's closest confidant on the Politburo, signaled this changed Soviet attitude in a private talk with the West German ambassador to Moscow in January 1989. "The Soviet Union did not build the Berlin Wall and we are not responsible for maintaining it," Yakovlev told the ambassador, according to a German aide who briefed me. In other words, the East Germans had built the Berlin Wall. They alone could decide if and when to take it down. Moscow would not intervene with troops to keep Germany divided. And with that, thanks to Gorbachev, German reunification at last became feasible.

West Germany certainly saw Yakovlev's hint that way and soon arranged to give Gorbachev public credit for it. Mikhail Sergeyvich received a hero's welcome to Bonn on a visit June 12–15, 1989. "Gorby! Gorby!" the huge crowds screamed in delight at every glimpse of him. It was the most enthusiastic reception any foreign leader had received since John F. Kennedy's mission to West Berlin in 1963. But whereas Kennedy had promised Berliners U.S. support in Cold War confrontation, Gorbachev told West Germans something they wanted to hear even more. "We are destined to live in a new period, a period of peace," he said. The message sent West Germans into a state of public ecstasy one Bonn official described as a "Gorbasm."

With Moscow keeping its hands off, East Germany could no longer hold back the tide of change. Events now moved with breakneck speed. Erich Honecker, the longtime hard-line Communist leader there, resigned in October 1989. The Berlin Wall came down only a month later, in November 1989, allowing divided Germany to reunite, realizing what had seemed to be an impossible dream for nearly half a century. Less than a year later, Gorbachev approved the final act in this astonishing drama. In July 1990, the Soviet leader dropped objections to a reunited Germany in NATO. By that momentous decision, the former Communist East Germany, once a pillar of the Soviet-led Warsaw Pact, would switch sides and join the Western alliance instead.

In return, West German Chancellor Helmut Kohl agreed that Soviet troops could remain in East Germany for another four years. Kohl also promised Moscow $10 billion in economic aid. In the end, Gorbachev decided, German aid and friendship would be a bigger help to perestroika than continued tension over Berlin. At home, it was his most controversial foreign policy decision of all. At the time, Ligachev and other Soviet conservatives denounced the trade-off as a sellout, but were then powerless to stop it. Gorbachev and Shevardnadze had persuaded a thin Politburo majority to go along.

Years later, in a 1995 interview in Moscow, Anatoly Dobrynin, the longtime Soviet ambassador to Washington, told me that Germany was Gorbachev's biggest foreign policy mistake. "Gorbachev could have made unification of Germany contingent upon including the Soviet Union in a new European security system," Dobrynin said, such as an expanded NATO.

But instead, Dobrynin complained, "the West told Gorbachev Germany should be united first, and we'll talk about a common European house later—and he believed them. Gorbachev had the cards but he played the hand badly." Despite such misgivings, however, the deal was done. Only a year and a half after Gorbachev's landmark UN speech, what had long seemed the toughest of all the Cold War issues—the reunification of Germany—had been swiftly resolved.

The UN speech had provided the key. It is worth recalling the words again. "Freedom of choice is a universal principle to which there should be no exception," Gorbachev had told the world body in December 1988. German reunification in NATO proved once again that he meant what he said. It is hard to think of a tougher foreign policy concession for any Soviet leader to make than to let East Germany join the Western alliance. But that was the East Germans' free choice. Gorbachev was true to his word. There would be no exceptions.

He proved it yet again, visiting the Vatican on December 1, 1989. The Polish pope and the Catholic Church had been instrumental in fomenting the independence movement now tearing the Soviet Union apart. But that had been another free choice. The religious revival in the U.S.S.R. would not be crushed by force either. Again, there would be no exceptions. Besides, it was now too late for that. Repressing religious expression again in the U.S.S.R. would only make the nationality problem worse—and set back the broader perestroika reforms at the same time. Another important syndrome was at work here. Once a Communist state embarks on any reform, in this case more religious freedom, it becomes increasingly difficult with time to reverse course. So Gorbachev decided to make a virtue of necessity. Religion could be an important force of support for perestroika. He would encourage that. He would let religious practice flourish in the U.S.S.R. He would be the first Soviet leader to visit the pope and normalize relations with the Vatican.

Gorbachev and John Paul II had much in common. The Russian leader and the Polish pope were both of Slavic origin. Both had lived under communism and worked to reform it. They conversed privately in Russian, without interpreters, and quickly came to a meeting of minds. Gorbachev assured the pope that the Ukrainian Catholic Church would soon be legalized, and he invited the Holy Father to visit the U.S.S.R. In return, the pope blessed the Communist party general secretary's program of perestroika, a gesture Gorbachev's advance men had requested.

As I watched their ceremonial encounter in the Vatican, I could hardly believe my eyes. Of all Gorbachev's foreign surprises, this one seemed to me the most astonishing. It was logical to expect one day that a Soviet leader might improve relations with the United States, with China, even with Germany. Statesmen are often pragmatists, able to see fundamental policy change as something very much in their national interest. But communism was a secular religion, with its own self-proclaimed monopoly on truth, an implacable foe of everything the Roman Catholic Church stood for. In its own way, the Vatican was just as uncompromising. Rapprochement between the Kremlin and the pope always seemed to me to be the least likely of the many historic changes Gorbachev might produce. And yet, there it was. The words of reconciliation they exchanged struck me as particularly significant.

"The Holy See follows with great interest the process of renewal which you set in motion in the Soviet Union," the pope told Gorbachev. "It wishes you success and declares itself ready to support every initiative that will better protect and integrate the rights and duties of individuals and peoples, so that peace may be ensured in Europe and the world."

"We have changed our attitude on some matters, such as religion, which admittedly we used to treat in a simplistic manner," Gorbachev replied. "Now we not only proceed from the assumption that no one should interfere in matters of the individual's conscience, we also say that the moral values that religion embodied for centuries can help in the work of renewal of our country, too. In fact, this is already happening."

The same day that he received the pope's blessing, December 1, 1989, Gorbachev flew to Milan. There he admitted publicly for the first time that the 1968 Soviet invasion of Czechoslovakia had been a mistake. That night the Soviet leader moved on to Malta for his first summit with George Bush.

The long American policy review was over. Gorbachev's withdrawal from Afghanistan, his normalization with China and the Vatican, his resolution of the German question, his positive impressions on Thatcher and other allied leaders, and his diplomatic contacts with American officials had all convinced the Bush administration to take the Soviet leader's proposed new world order very seriously indeed. They would now work with him to conclude ambitious arms control agreements and settle virtually all the outstanding East-West issues. On December 2, 1989, Bush and Gorbachev held a joint press conference in Malta, a first for a superpower summit. They agreed the Cold War was virtually over. Bush said the world was on the "threshold of a brand-new era of Soviet-American relations." Indeed it was. He and Gorbachev would increase cooperation until they at last signed the START treaty in Moscow in September 1991. Its main provision was a 50 percent cut in strategic nuclear weapons, first proposed by Gorbachev in Paris in 1985.

The Malta summit finally provided the political will for successful endgame negotiations on START. It was also a fitting end to 1989, a year of remarkable diplomatic triumphs for Gorbachev. In only twelve months since the UN speech, the Soviet leader had settled his Afghan, Chinese, and German problems and established a good working relationship with the new president of the United States.

Never again would Mikhail Sergeyevich enjoy such a diplomatic high. His accomplishments abroad would win him the Nobel Peace Prize for 1990, but by then foreign successes could no longer help him politically at home. "Pity it wasn't the Nobel Prize for Economics," his own spokesman, Gennady Gerasimov, quipped. True enough, progress on the economic front at home would have done a lot more for Mikhail Sergeyevich politically than all the hero worship he was getting abroad. Here was one of the more tragic contradictions Gorbachev faced. He needed to undertake foreign policy changes in order to give his domestic reforms a chance, but in the end even those historic changes would not save the revolution he was conducting at home. In fact, from now on they would harm it.

Gorbachev's foreign policy was now making his domestic economic problems considerably worse. For one thing, progress during the year with the West on reducing conventional armed forces had raised the stakes. Gorbachev was now committed to bringing home the remaining 400,000 Soviet troops from Eastern Europe, with no place to put them and their families. The half-finished barracks and tent cities provided were at best interim solutions. These people would have to be permanently resettled. They would place added strain on an already severe housing shortage, and there were insufficient funds to retrain them properly for jobs in the civilian economy.

Moreover, at the same time, there was no Western economic payoff to ease the pain. Gorbachev's improved relations with the West had not brought in anywhere near enough aid to begin making a difference. There would be no Marshall Plan for the Soviet Union. Nor could there be. The problems were too enormous, the funds available to help too small. The Bonn government, for example, planned to give over $100 billion in aid to bring former Communist East Germany up to Western standards. Such was the inevitable obligation of reunification. The Soviet Union, far larger and more backward than East Germany, needed many times that amount of help, but unlike Bonn helping its new eastern provinces, the West had no similar obligation to aid the U.S.S.R. on the same scale. In addition, Western governments decided, rightly in my view, that Gorbachev's Soviet Union, in its troubled transition toward democracy and a market economy, was still far too unstable, both economically and politically, for aid to be used effectively. The best the Group of Seven, the West's most industrially advanced nations, could do was talk about providing some $6 billion in aid to Moscow, a small fraction of the need. Corporate investors in the West also saw the Soviet Union as a sure way to lose funds, and stayed away.

Furthermore, Gorbachev's foreign policy decisions had added substantially to his political problems at home. His conservative opponents now had a whole litany to attack him on, among them a humiliating retreat from Afghanistan, a sellout on Eastern Europe and united Germany, and unwarranted concessions on agreements with the West for reducing nuclear and conventional arms. They would add these grievances to charges that his reforms had weakened the economy and spawned a minority nationality rebellion threatening to break up the U.S.S.R. They made that strong case publicly, using glasnost to attack him through new conservative press organs.

It soon became apparent in the West that Gorbachev's diplomatic triumphs abroad had hurt him at home. There was, however, little the West could do to help. Significantly more economic aid was not an option, for reasons already discussed. The West continued to back Gorbachev with verbal political support, and Western governments also tried to help by not exploiting Gorbachev's many domestic problems, for example by not encouraging the independence rebellion in the Baltics. Soon, however, Western support began to look marginal. Gorbachev's own fate and that of his perestroika reforms would from now on be decided primarily by the continuing Soviet internal power struggle. There would be worse to come. In time, Gorbachev's weaker position at home would make it harder to pull off diplomatic successes abroad.

Mikhail Sergeyevich still kept trying, although by 1991 the magic was gone. He was no longer the miracle worker on the world stage. Gorbachev attempted to push Saddam Hussein into a voluntary withdrawal from Kuwait and a political settlement that could have avoided the Gulf War, but his initiative failed in January 1991, and operation Desert Storm began. In April 1991, Gorbachev went to Tokyo, but failed to make any progress on the Kurile Islands dispute. Mikhail Sergeyevich now had less negotiating room because of his political weakness at home. Politburo conservatives were more easily tying his hands. That in turn discouraged Japanese investment in Siberia. The timing was wrong. Gorbachev would have been better off cutting a deal on the Kuriles earlier. Now his trip to Tokyo was a dead loss. Some Japanese government officials and businessmen were saying that if the Kuriles dispute was resolved, they would have to invent another excuse for turning down the economic and political risks of investing in the U.S.S.R.

By spring 1991, Mikhail Sergeyevich was running out of time in the continuing Kremlin power struggle. His political opponents, his economic difficulties, and the national independence movements were all now stronger than ever before. His biggest trump card, his past successes on the world stage, could no longer be effectively played. With that gone, the Soviet leader began a slide from which he could not recover, as we shall see in the following chapters. It is sufficient to note here that Gorbachev soon lost power, but he did not fail, because even after his retirement and the collapse of the Soviet Union, his democratic reforms at home and his peace initiatives abroad continue in place as testimonies to his extraordinary vision.

Those who see Mikhail Sergeyevich only as a brilliant short-term tactician with no long-term strategy are mistaken. So are those who think the results he produced were mostly unintended. Gorbachev did have a long-term vision. He made it clear way before his downfall, and he largely succeeded. That vision was spelled out to me in May 1990, more than eighteen months before Mikhail Sergeyevich resigned, by one of his top policy advisers, Georgi Shakhnazarov. "His main idea is to integrate the Soviet Union into the international system, as a modern, democratic state," Shakhnazarov said. "If this experiment proves successful, it will be his victory."

Shakhnazarov chose every word with great care. "Integration" meant the U.S.S.R. had to give up military force as its chosen instrument of foreign policy, threatening the rest of the world. Integration also required the Soviet Union to end the isolation behind the iron curtain which for decades had kept it backward. "Modern" meant acceptance of market economy concepts. "Democratic" meant such institutions as a multiparty system and contested elections.

The experiment that Shakhnazarov defined as the litmus test of the Gorbachev era did indeed succeed. Mikhail Sergeyevich integrated his country into the international system as a modern, democratic state. It was his victory, and it was a historic victory, of global importance, valid to this day. In the terms of his own vision, Mikhail Sergeyevich was a great success.

His victory was not complete, of course. The vision defined by Shakhnazarov applied to "the Soviet Union." Those words too were used deliberately, to make clear that Gorbachev meant to keep the U.S.S.R. together. Mikhail Sergeyevich himself later admitted to me in an interview that he regarded the breakup of the Soviet Union as his greatest failure.[7] Even so, he still managed to achieve a large part of his strategic vision. The U.S.S.R. as a whole did not integrate into the international community. But Russia, the Ukraine, the Baltic states, and other component parts of the former Soviet Union did indeed integrate as Gorbachev had wanted.

Instead, Gorbachev's greatest failure was one that neither he nor his loyal aides would ever admit at the time—his inability to make Communist power and democratic reform coexist. That proved to be an impossible task. He tried to have it both ways for most of the nearly seven years he ruled. Only near the end did he understand that he would have to choose, and he made the right decision. Gorbachev chose reform over communism, but by then it was too late to save either the Soviet state or his own presidency.

Nonetheless, democratic and market reforms live on in post-Communist Russia, testifying to Gorbachev's greatness as a historic figure. The world at large rejoices, perhaps prematurely. Moscow reserves judgment. The battle for Russia's soul continues. If Boris Yeltsin and his successors have the strength and wisdom to build on what Gorbachev left behind, their country and the world will benefit enormously. Mikhail Sergeyevich provided an opportunity for world leaders to begin the twenty-first century as a time of greater peace and prosperity. If that happens, the success will be largely his. If not, the failure will be theirs.

15

Countdown to a Coup (1990–91)

I. A TALE OF TWO LEADERS

A s president of the Soviet Union, Mikhail Gorbachev lived in a country dacha some ten miles west of Moscow. A high green wooden fence, with a red-and-white "no entry" sign, sealed off the property from prying eyes. Inside, an asphalt driveway led through pine and birch trees to a large two-story mansion in mustard-colored stucco and white trim, with stained-wood window frames and a forest-green roof. The driveway, lit by white electric lanterns, circled in front of the main entrance, dominated by four white columns and a second-floor balcony. A wind vane on the roof marked the year of construction, 1956. At the back, a large marble terrace looked out over a gentle slope, down to the Moscow River, meandering through peaceful grass fields. Furnishings, from crystal chandeliers to marble fireplaces, stressed opulence. Every care was taken to assure the comfort of the president and his demanding wife, Raisa.

On Thursday, December 26, 1991, Gorbachev still lived at the dacha, although he had resigned as Soviet president the day before. This was supposed to be a particularly civilized transfer of power, a leisurely departure from the trappings of high office. In fact, that first morning of his retirement, Mikhail Sergeyevich still had his presidential police escort cars in front, behind, and on the side of his black Zil limousine, roaring down a special VIP center lane, helping him cut the thirty-minute trip to the Kremlin in half. All those temporary holdover privileges had been arranged with his successor, Russian President Boris Yeltsin. As Gorbachev understood it, they had even agreed that Mikhail Sergeyevich could keep his palatial third-floor office in the Kremlin a few more days, to Monday, December 30, so he could hold previously scheduled meetings and clean out his desk. He was in for a rude shock.

When Gorbachev arrived at the Kremlin on December 26 he found the brass nameplate outside his office had been changed during the night to read "Yeltsin, B. N.," and indeed Boris Nikolayevich had been sitting at Gorbachev's former desk since 8:30 A.M. Yeltsin aides denied there had been any deal about keeping the nation's most prestigious office another few days. Thus humiliated, Gorbachev had no choice but to walk down the hall to the more modest office of his last chief of staff, Grigory Revenko, for a previously scheduled meeting with Japanese visitors. The personal belongings of the Soviet Union's first, last, and only executive president had been cleared out of his office and desk for him.

Still, that indignity was the only blemish on a historic transfer of political power, a change which marked, among other things, the collapse of the Soviet empire and the first time in Russia's thousand-year history that a freely elected leader took over the Kremlin. Remarkably, in a country renowned for ruthless, bloodthirsty political struggle, this leadership change took place entirely peacefully, despite the enormous stakes involved.

No one was killed, not a shot was fired in anger or a weapon raised. No one was even disgraced, or forced to live out his days in political obscurity under house arrest, like Nikita Khrushchev. This time Gorbachev drew up a list of what he wanted, including pension, cars, housing, and an academic institute from which he could continue to speak out freely on world affairs, and Yeltsin approved everything on the list. The disputed timing of Yeltsin's taking over Gorbachev's desk, an incident known only to the staffs of both leaders and a few journalists, paled in comparison to what they had accomplished. Two men who intensely disliked and mistrusted each other had pulled off a bloodless, civilized transfer of power from dictatorship to democratic rule in the world's most heavily armed state.

By then, of course, it was Yeltsin's victory. Gorbachev had not intended to leave office that way. He had expected to be the one to carry perestroika reforms through. Instead he had been forced to resign, and turn over that responsibility to a political rival who only eighteen months before had been a relatively minor player in the Soviet political spectrum.

The final phase of Gorbachev's reform battle was an extraordinary political drama. It involved not only the continuing struggle for power in the Kremlin but also the fate of the first serious attempt to end the arms race and the Cold War. It nearly resulted in the rollback toward Stalinism intended by the plotters of the August 1991 coup. Above all it was a drama that produced a remarkable reversal of roles for Gorbachev and Yeltsin in the eighteen months between June 1990 and December 1991. At the end of that period, Yeltsin would be running the country and Gorbachev would be only a minor political influence, rather than the other way around. Yet both would emerge honorably from that reversal of roles. To Gorbachev would go the credit for successfully dismantling the repressive Soviet system. To Yeltsin would go the opportunity of building a democratic structure in its place. The last eighteen months of Soviet history is largely a tale of two leaders, Gorbachev and Yeltsin. It is recounted in the pages that follow.

Up to the final moment, the turning over of the Kremlin's most prestigious office, the two leaders didn't make it easy on each other. Had they co-operated more fully, Gorbachev and Yeltsin might well have given democratic reform a more solid base than it enjoys in Russia today. Instead, they fought each other most of the way.

The final eighteen-month struggle between Yeltsin and Gorbachev revealed the inner strengths of both men. Gorbachev emerged as the innovator who got reform started as a cautious but promising enterprise, Yeltsin as the bolder pragmatist who then seized the initiative and pushed the reforms further and faster than their author had intended. In their struggle, the two men engaged in a complex match of political chess. Yeltsin won, primarily because he was better than Gorbachev at looking three or four moves down the chessboard. Mikhail Sergeyevich made spectacular moves, often not knowing their consequences. Boris Nikolayevich figured out first where Gorbachev's moves would lead, then used those moves against him. Yeltsin's brilliant opening gambit was the first of many that illustrate this strategy. He made it by using the Russian parliament, once a powerless laughingstock of Soviet politics, to become the second most powerful leader in the U.S.S.R., only a few short chess moves away from eclipsing Gorbachev.

In some ways, Russia had been as much of a Soviet colony as Estonia or Armenia. The Russian Federation was the largest and richest of the fifteen Soviet republics making up the U.S.S.R. But like all the others, Russia's government was a sop to regional pride, with no independent power. Its role was blind obedience to the Soviet Politburo. True, Russia had its own government and parliament, with its own separate headquarters in Moscow, the marble "White House" a mile from the Kremlin. All that, however, was for show. The only job of the White House was to ratify for Russia the decisions taken earlier by the Soviet government and the Soviet parliament in the Kremlin. To make sure of that, the Soviet Politburo appointed one of its members to run the Russian government, and the Soviet Communist Party controlled the members of the Russian parliament, telling them how to vote. It was all a very cozy arrangement. The Soviet constitution had in fact given all the republics, including Russia, considerable autonomy, on paper. But in practice they did what the Kremlin told them. Then Gorbachev changed everything.

Mikhail Sergeyevich thought the draconian central control interfered with economic potential. So he gave the republics real autonomy in an effort to make his perestroika reforms work. Republics got more economic decision-making power. They also got the right to hold contested elections in order to increase political support for the reforms. As we saw earlier, one unintended result was to fuel a nationalist rebellion in republics from the Baltics to the Ukraine to Central Asia that were unsatisfied with the limited autonomy Gorbachev offered. They would push instead for full independence. Similarly, under Yeltsin's leadership, Russia would do much the same thing, and this soon gave Yeltsin his chance to turn Russia into a rival base of legitimate political power. Gorbachev had not properly looked several moves down the chessboard, leaving Yeltsin in a position to exploit this weakness.

In June 1990, Yeltsin was elected chairman of the Russian parliament. It is important to remember that this was another indirect election where the people had no choice. Only the newly elected members of parliament had the right to vote for their chairman. It was, however, a new parliament, formed by competitive elections, with new blood and new ideas. Yeltsin was the natural candidate of reformist forces there. He also won votes from Russia's Communist deputies by demanding that from now on Russia should have the right to make its own political and economic decisions, instead of continuing to bow to the dictates of Gorbachev's Soviet regime.

Yeltsin gambled that many Communist deputies would put the interests of Russia ahead of those of the Party and vote for him, rather than for any of the preferred Kremlin candidates backed by Gorbachev and the Soviet machine. He was right. Russia had no independence movement such as the Baltics had, but it had Boris Yeltsin, hitting similar themes. Enough Communist deputies broke Party discipline and voted for Yeltsin to make him the president of the Russian Parliament. Yeltsin had defied Gorbachev and won. The victory would be particularly costly for Gorbachev.

Under Yeltsin's leadership, the Russian parliament would no longer be a tame rubber-stamp body. It would now take the lead in pushing Gorbachev toward further, faster reform. It would take the powers that in the past had only been on paper and turn them into reality. It would pass laws for Russia at odds with Soviet law, and say they applied to the two-thirds of the U.S.S.R.'s territory that fell within Russia. Among other things, these laws would try to ensure that taxes collected in Russia would go to the Russian government rather than to Soviet authorities. Naturally, the Kremlin fought back, insisting its laws took precedence. The result was a constitutional crisis, a "war of laws" between Yeltsin's Russian government and Gorbachev's Soviet regime. Suddenly Yeltsin himself, as the elected president of the Russian parliament, had as much legitimacy as Gorbachev, elected president of the U.S.S.R. by the Soviet parliament. At a stroke, Yeltsin had transformed himself from a minor parliamentary deputy to nearly the equal of Gorbachev. Incredibly, the country now had two presidents. From then on, the momentum would favor Yeltsin until he eclipsed Gorbachev.

In July 1990, Yeltsin resigned from the Soviet Communist Party. As the most prominent non-Communist official in the U.S.S.R., he was now the undisputed leader of democratic forces across the nation. "Every day the number of Russian democrats will grow," Boris Nikolayevich predicted at the time. "That's why I am looking at life with optimism and hope." Battle lines were also drawn in one other fundamental way. Yeltsin became the de facto leader of the movement to decentralize power from the Soviet government in Moscow to authorities in the various republics. In this process an odd assortment of republic leaders gravitated to Yeltsin's side. They ranged from corrupt feudal lords in Central Asia, determined to retain old privileges, to democratic separatists in the Baltics, resolved to achieve new independence. All thought their differing goals could best be advanced by a shift of power from Moscow to the republics. So they backed Yeltsin's campaign to decentralize, raising the specter that the U.S.S.R. would soon break apart.

No longer was it simply Gorbachev versus Yeltsin, or one path to reform versus another. Their struggle had now widened to incorporate such broader historical forces as Communists versus Democrats and unionists versus separatists. The stakes were now far higher. The battle between Gorbachev and Yeltsin could now decide whether Communist power and the Soviet state would survive. Communist hard-liners were determined not to leave it up to Yeltsin and the republic leaders. One way or another, they would have to bring down Yeltsin, but first they would handle Gorbachev, still the top man in the country, the key player to control.

Since Gorbachev's decision in February 1990 to give up the Party's monopoly on power, the Communist hard-liners no longer trusted him. They would keep him out front as president, to calm Western fears of a rollback to Stalinism, but inside the Kremlin, they would restrict his room for maneuver and push him into more conservative policies. If he objected, they would throw him out. Gorbachev, they reasoned, would prefer to keep power, and would bend to their demands.

This tougher attitude by hard-liners was strengthened by the retirement of Yegor Ligachev at a Party congress in July. Long Gorbachev's leading conservative rival, Ligachev had been a moderate conservative in a radical time. He had tried to rein in Gorbachev, to slow reforms, to protect the Party's interest, all by Politburo rules. But Mikhail Sergeyevich had outmaneuvered him by going around the Politburo and creating the new executive presidency. Ligachev's successors as conservative leaders, among them KGB chief Vladmir Kryuchkov, were hard-liners who regarded the Ligachev approach as ineffective. The new hard-liners were more interested in their own power, less committed to cautious reform. They would be more willing to remove Gorbachev by a military coup, if it came to that. Naturally, though, they hid their intentions, working to unite their forces while waiting for the right moment to act.

At first, with Ligachev gone, Gorbachev thought he still had the advantage. The conservative opposition had yet to unite behind any one new leader. On the progressive side, Yeltsin was a problem, but was still in the inferior position. Mikhail Sergeyevich placed himself in the political center, between the Communist hard-liners and Yeltsin's radical reformers. Gorbachev expected to play the role of the essential man in the middle. He would turn one way, then another, extracting concessions from each side, and would still run the country. But it didn't work out that way. Each time Gorbachev shifted tactically between the conservatives and the radicals he lost support. His backers despaired at the continuing shifts and deserted him to join one side or the other. The center, Gorbachev's base of support, was collapsing.

I saw that by visiting the office of a senior Communist Party official at the time. He was a former Gorbachev supporter, with six telephones on his desk, a telling sign of rank in Moscow. They used to ring constantly, with orders from the Politburo. But since February 1990, when the Party's monopoly on power ended, they had turned silent. The official was bitter. "Gorbachev is now a one-man show," he told me. "The president and a few personal advisers make all the decisions. Until they do, everything stops." I asked him for an example of botched decisions. "Show me one example where something is working right these days," he replied. Increasingly, thousands of key Gorbachev supporters agreed.

Political tensions were so bad that coup jitters broke into the open by September 1990. Two paratroop regiments flown to a military airfield near Moscow on September 10 raised the alarm. "Military coup in the U.S.S.R.?" headlined the weekly *Moscow News*. Bungling military spokesmen claimed the paratroop regiments had flown in for parade practice. If so, Soviet newspapers asked, then why were they wearing combat gear and bulletproof vests? More likely, they were involved in coup practice. "Allegations that the military are plotting a coup are senseless and groundless," Defense Minister Dmitri Yazov said then. No one was reassured. "A counterrevolution by neo-Stalinists under the slogan of saving socialism cannot be excluded," the government newspaper *Izvestia* warned. The words were prophetic. Less than a year later, the same Yazov helped lead a coup against Gorbachev.

By October 1990, Gorbachev understood that he would have to shift political ground, that he could no longer rule from the center. The Soviet president would have to join either the Communist conservatives or Yeltsin's radicals. The key issue was a plan by his latest top economic adviser, Stanislav Shatalin, to rush to a free-market economy in five hundred days.[1] Among the controversial provisions were privatization of farmland and a shift of economic policy decision-making power from the Soviet government in Moscow to the republics. Such radical measures were necessary, Shatalin argued, because "the economy is already on the brink of bankruptcy."

The crunch had finally come. The Shatalin plan would have destroyed all remnants of the Communist command economy and replaced them with a capitalist free market. Either Gorbachev approved the Shatalin plan, joined Yeltsin's reformers, and killed communism, or he sided with the Communist hard-liners, rejected Shatalin, and turned his back on meaningful reform. Mikhail Sergeyevich could no longer compromise, dither, or delay. Trying to chart a workable "third way" between communism and capitalism was as impossible as becoming half pregnant. With the Shatalin plan on the table, Gorbachev had only two options left: communism or reform.

The Party power barons certainly saw it that way. They could not live with the Shatalin plan. It meant the end of their centralized control, their bloated budgets, and their dictatorial powers. So they went to Gorbachev and warned him that if he approved the Shatalin reforms he was through as the leader of the country. The Gorbachev aides who told me this said the pressure then came from the same people who tried to depose Gorbachev ten months later in the August 1991 coup—KGB chief Vladimir Kryuchkov, Prime Minister Valentin Pavlov, Interior Minister Boris Pugo, Defense Minister Dmitri Yazov, and Oleg Baklanov, the Politburo member in charge of the military-industrial complex, among others.

In October 1990, Mikhail Sergeyevich caved in to their pressure. He rejected the Shatalin plan and shifted his policies to the conservative camp. As he saw it then, he had no choice. Gorbachev no longer had enough centrist support to resist the hard-liners, and he could not turn to Yeltsin's radicals for help because they no longer trusted him. Later Mikhail Sergeyevich would claim that his shift to the conservative side had been temporary, tactical, designed for reversal at the first good opportunity, but the hard-liners didn't see it that way. They had pushed Gorbachev, and he had given way. They decided to continue pushing, to keep him in their pocket, permanently.

October 1990 turned out to be the beginning of the end for Gorbachev. To his more conservative opponents in the leadership, the Shatalin plan was less important as a specific blueprint for a transition to market economics and much more important as a frontal attack on the Communist system as a whole. They were not about to let it become a long-term Gorbachev project, to be revised, renamed, and reborn at a later date, whenever that suited Mikhail Sergeyevich's shifting tactics. To them, the Shatalin plan would be the last attempt at meaningful reform of the Soviet Communist system. They understood that the final choice was communism or reform, and they were determined that reform would be the loser.

From this point on, Gorbachev was a virtual prisoner of hard-line Communists in the top Soviet leadership. In their view, the three key pillars supporting Communist power—the Party's total control over ideology, the economy, and politics—were all beginning to crumble because of Gorbachev's reforms, and unless all three pillars were maintained, communism would collapse. Hard-liners were now determined that Mikhail Sergeyevich would not go farther down the reform road. Instead, he would have to reverse course or they would replace him. In the view of Soviet hard-liners, Gorbachev had threatened to destroy the three pillars in these ways:

- His glasnost ended the Communist monopoly on ideology by letting other voices be heard, even those discrediting the Party.

- His contested elections broke the Communist monopoly on political power.

- His encouragement of private businesses and farms ended the Communist monopoly on the economy.

Admittedly, the Communists were still the dominant power in the land, still the biggest single influence by far, in all three fields. Ideologically, they made sure that glasnost kept press freedom sharply limited. In politics, the infant opposition parties could not hope to win a vote in the Soviet parlia-ment. They were too small and divided. In economics, the tiny private sec-tor barely dented the powers of the state planners. But Russia's Communists always preferred complete control to sharing power, even if their slice was by far the biggest. They feared, rightly, that once they gave up their monopoly hold, the trickle of opposition permitted would inevitably build to a flood and eventually drown them.

They didn't have to look very far for compelling evidence. Poland's Sol-idarity grew from a local shipyard strike committee to a national government in less than a decade. Independence movements in the Soviet Baltic states threatened to replace Communists there in even less time. Demands for more independence, democracy, and private enterprise were already mushroom-ing throughout the U.S.S.R. Kremlin hard-liners understood perfectly well that despite all the reforms, the power balance was still heavily on their side. Indeed, that was one reason they were determined to stop Gorbachev at that point, before the dangers got completely out of hand.

By December 1990, only two months after the Shatalin plan was dropped, Gorbachev's closest collaborator in the leadership, Foreign Minister Eduard Shevardnadze, could no longer stand the conservative dominance. She-vardnadze had helped Gorbachev formulate perestroika at home and end the Cold War abroad. Now he saw all that in danger. To him, Gorbachev was clearly under the thumb of reactionary forces plotting to roll back reform and return to the Stalinist past. A dramatic gesture was necessary. In a speech to the Soviet parliament that shocked Gorbachev, the nation, and the world, Eduard Shevardnadze abruptly resigned to "protest against the advance of dictatorship" in the U.S.S.R.[2]

Shevardnadze's dramatic warning went unheeded, however. Right-wing forces continued to push Gorbachev their way. The results turned bloody the very next month. In January 1991, Soviet paratroopers and tanks attacked the television tower in Vilnius, Lithuania, to silence the voice of indepen-dence there. Unarmed civilians defended the broadcasting center with their bodies. Tanks rolled over them. The post-midnight carnage, immortalized in Baltic history as "Bloody Sunday," killed thirteen civilians and injured 120.

Gorbachev's explanation was a public relations disaster. The Soviet president regretted the loss of life. "We did not want and do not want this," he said, but then Gorbachev went on to deny any personal responsibility, claiming that the Soviet commander in Vilnius took the decision to attack and only informed him afterward. If this was true, the commander would have to be punished. Under Soviet law, any officer ordering an attack without the prior approval of the president risked treason charges. But this time there would be no treason charges, no disciplinary action at all. In fact, Gorbachev himself defended the officers involved. He said they had acted properly under the circumstances, thus contradicting himself. According to Mikhail Sergeyevich, the killing was wrong, but he wasn't responsible and neither was the army. It was another way of saying the bloodshed was all very unfortunate, but no one was responsible. Even the simplest Soviet citizen could see that the president's explanation made no sense at all.

More sophisticated Soviets were outraged. Many believed that either Gorbachev was lying when he denied authorizing the attack or he had lost control of his army and was no longer an effective president. Of the two explanations, the lie seemed more likely. As Latvian Vice President Dainis Ivanis put it, "Either Gorbachev is lying, which I believe, or he is not in control of the situation, and I don't believe that."

In fact, the situation was even worse than Ivanis imagined. Gorbachev was both shading the truth and losing control. The Soviet president had earlier given his Baltic commanders permission to use force in restoring order in their region. He had also left them the discretion to decide when it was necessary to apply force. He had given the commanders that authority during a meeting in the Kremlin. According to a source in the room at the time, Gorbachev told the commanders, "If the situation gets out of control you can move in to establish order." The Soviet president also said, "I don't want any casualties." But the commanders left the room with the understanding that they could decide when and how to apply force, without first checking with Mikhail Sergeyevich.

Thus when Gorbachev claimed he was informed of the Vilnius attack only after the event, that was hardly the entire truth. Since he had given the commander there blanket authority in advance to use force, he could not have been surprised when the attack came. The responsibility for the bloodshed was very much on his hands. In fact, that was one purpose of the exercise. The hard-line forces who designed the attack on Vilnius "wanted to bloody the president's hands, to cut his connections to the progressives and force him to move to the right," a Gorbachev aide told me. Thus not only was Gorbachev bending the truth, but he was also losing control.

Boris Yeltsin went straight for the jugular. He called the attack in Vilnius "the beginning of a mighty offensive against democracy. The president is under very heavy pressure from conservative forces, and he doesn't have the courage to withstand it," Yeltsin asserted. His point was that if Gorbachev could be pushed into a military clampdown in Lithuania, he could be further manipulated to roll back reform by military means in Russia as well. The argument was by no means far-fetched. Valentin Varennikov, the Soviet general in charge of ground forces, led the attack on Vilnius in January. He would also run the military side of the coup against Gorbachev in August. Vilnius was a dress rehearsal for Moscow.

Several of Gorbachev's progressive advisers resigned immediately after Vilnius. Among them were Shatalin and the other senior economic adviser, Nikolai Petrakov. "After Bloody Sunday in Vilnius, is there much left of what we so often heard from the president about humane socialism and new thinking?" they said in a joint statement. "There is almost nothing left." In Moscow, 300,000 people protested the Vilnius bloodbath and demanded that Gorbachev resign.

He would not, of course. Instead, he remained under conservative influence and struck out at Yeltsin. In March 1991, Gorbachev tried to strong-arm the Russian parliament into dumping Yeltsin as their president. He ordered Soviet troops to surround the meeting site to increase the pressure. Yeltsin responded with a radio appeal for public support. In response, more than 100,000 Muscovites took to the streets to protest the military pressure on Yeltsin, defying a Gorbachev ban on demonstrations. I watched as the huge crowd of unarmed civilians marched up to within inches of the troops carrying riot shields and batons. Another bloody clash seemed inevitable. This time, however, Gorbachev backed down and called off the troops, but not before they had practiced taking the television tower and other strategic points in the capital. This time the dress rehearsal for the coming coup took place in Moscow.

Gorbachev emerged from the episode badly weakened. He had tried to get rid of Yeltsin—and failed. He had tried to impose a ban on demonstrations in Moscow—and failed. He had similarly failed to ban strikes. Coal miners continued to defy him by refusing to work until they got better pay and conditions, raising the specter of fuel shortages in the harsh Russian winter ahead. In the end, Yeltsin, not Gorbachev, got the miners back to work. At the time, public opinion polls gave Yeltsin a 59 percent approval rating, Gorbachev only 13 percent, largely because most people then still wanted radical reform. Gorbachev had not only moved right to roll back reform, he had also lost authority to impose his will and was increasingly being challenged by his own people. Boris Yeltsin was now the key player. His ability to see farther down the chessboard than anyone else made the crucial difference. Never was that demonstrated more clearly than in March 1991.

That same month, Gorbachev scheduled an unprecedented nationwide referendum. For the first time, a Soviet leader put a major policy question to his people for their vote to decide. The question Gorbachev chose was whether the Soviet Union should remain intact. A yes vote was to be his way of showing the nation and the world that the U.S.S.R. was being held together by popular will rather than force of arms. It looked like a brilliant tactical move. The idea of "union" was still popular with a majority of Soviet citizens, despite the breakaway mood in small republics like the Baltics, and putting the question to the people to decide helped restore Gorbachev's democratic image. The Soviet president invested all his prestige in the referendum, campaigned hard for it, and won 70 percent approval to keep the U.S.S.R. together.

Yeltsin tacked a second referendum question onto the same ballot in Russia. His question was whether the people should directly elect the president of Russia. His initiative, piggybacking on Gorbachev's ballot, showed short-term tactical brilliance, a play for equal status. If Gorbachev could have a referendum, then so could Yeltsin. But in addition to that, it also had more long-term potential. As usual, Yeltsin was thinking several moves down the chessboard. If his referendum question won, Yeltsin planned to run and win. Then as the president of Russia, directly elected by the people, he would have more legitimacy than Gorbachev, who had never risked popular election and instead had been named Soviet president only by the orchestrated vote of a tame parliament. Yeltsin invested all his prestige in the second referendum question, campaigned hard, and also won a 70 percent approval for direct presidential elections in Russia.

Within weeks it was abundantly clear who had made the smarter referendum call. Gorbachev's initiative was rendered virtually meaningless. He had public approval for continued "union," but what kind of union was left undefined. Yeltsin and two other key republic leaders, Leonid Kravchuk of the Ukraine and Nursultan Nazarbayev of Kazakhstan, set out to define "union" their way.

The three ringleaders had formidable political clout. Yeltsin's Russia had a population of 140 million people and most of the Soviet Union's mineral wealth. Kravchuk's Ukraine, with 50 million people, was the largest Soviet industrial and agricultural producer outside Russia. Nazarbayev's Kazakhstan led 60 million people in five Central Asian republics. Together, they represented 250 million of the Soviet Union's 280 million people. Their pressure could be overwhelming.

By April 1991, only a month after the referendum, they had forced Gorbachev to negotiate a new Union Treaty. The idea was to shift decision-making power from the Soviet government in Moscow to the fifteen constituent republics. Gorbachev could have his continued union, but the central government in Moscow would end up a weakened coordinating body. The republics would call the shots. In effect, the republic leaders had given up on Gorbachev. They regarded him as a prisoner of Communist hard-liners. So they seized the reform initiative from him. Their model for the new Soviet Union would make Gorbachev, the hard-liners, and all the other Kremlin players increasingly irrelevant, as power shifted to the republics.

Negotiations over the terms of the new Union Treaty continued for months between Gorbachev and the leaders of the fifteen Soviet republics. These talks dominated the Soviet political agenda and forced Gorbachev to turn away from the conservatives, back once again toward the reform path. In so doing, they led directly to the hard-line frustration that produced the August 1991 coup.

Through the months of talks on the Union Treaty, Gorbachev's March referendum victory proved no help to him at all. It was quickly forgotten. Yeltsin's referendum win, by contrast, proved crucially important. During the Union Treaty negotiations, Boris Yeltsin became the first freely elected president of Russia. His new legitimacy helped swing the treaty terms in favor of the republics. Thus did Yeltsin prove after the next several moves on the chessboard that his referendum call was by far the smarter one.

Kremlin hard-liners watched in dismay as Gorbachev shifted course once again, this time turning away from them and toward Yeltsin and the republic leaders. The conservative opposition now decided they had to act. They made their first move against the Soviet president in June 1991. Refreshingly, it was legal this time. As in October 1990, when they forced Gorbachev to drop the Shatalin plan, the prime movers were once again KGB chief Kryuchkov, Defense Minister Yazov, Interior Minister Pugo, Prime Minister Pavlov, and Oleg Baklanov, chief of the military-industrial complex. This time they proposed that the Soviet parliament withdraw some of Gorbachev's presidential powers and transfer them to the prime minister.

Their intended parliamentary coup had some promise. Conservative deputies likely to lose their seats in elections Gorbachev was expected to call the following year rallied to Prime Minister Pavlov. They hoped that a shift of power to him would delay the elections and keep them in office. "This is the first public challenge to the president's authority by members of his own team," a Gorbachev aide told me. "We are taking it very seriously."

I watched the spectacle from the press gallery. The gang of five—Kryuchkov, Pavlov, Yazov, Baklanov, and Pugo—were all parliamentary deputies. With the exception of Pavlov, occupying a seat in front reserved for the prime minister, the other four sat in a row at the back, conferring together frequently during the debate. Gorbachev confronted them with a bravado performance. He denied that his reforms and his seeking Western aid had been mistakes. Trimming his powers, he argued, would only delay needed measures and hurt the economy even more. "You sit there, completely detached from reality," Gorbachev said, pointing his index finger at the plotters, then pounding the dais with his fist for emphasis. "We have reached the stage where delay is equal to death." His performance stunned and confused his critics. They took soundings, realized they didn't have the strength, and withdrew the motion before it came to a vote. After the session a triumphant Gorbachev left the chamber to meet the press, surrounded by the gang of five. They looked embarrassed. Gorbachev was laughing. "The coup is over," he announced.

It was a rotten joke. Rarely had Gorbachev been so wrong. The plotters would simply move the playing field. They had failed in parliament, but they would continue to prepare a coup. Next time they would send tanks into the streets.

Incredibly, Gorbachev kept them on. He had appointed them all to office. They had turned against him, but still he did not fire them. Gorbachev aides offered only one lame excuse. The Soviet president was afraid any replacements would now be even worse. Indeed, there was some reason for that fear. Gorbachev had earlier removed Prime Minister Nikolai Ryzhkov and KGB chief Viktor Chebrikov for getting in his way. Their replacements, Pavlov and Kryuchkov, had only turned out to be more conservative, more obstructionist. The same pattern held for the others in the gang of five. And there was a danger that new replacements could be worse still, even more reactionary.

However, that explanation was never fully satisfactory. Many Russians believe to this day that Gorbachev kept the gang of five in office because essentially he was on their side of the political struggle against Yeltsin's radical reformers. How he got there is a matter of some dispute. Some think Gorbachev sided with hard-liners out of personal conviction. Others think he was forced to do so because by then he was under their political control. Either way, these Russians believe, Gorbachev showed his true colors by refusing to fire the gang of five. In that alone, they say, he bears major responsibility for the August coup that soon followed.

II. GORBACHEV BECOMES THE QUEEN

The drama was now moving rapidly into its final act. The momentum belonged to Yeltsin. In June 1991 he had become president of Russia, the country's first democratically elected leader after ten centuries of autocratic rule. Boris Nikolayevich won more than 60 percent of the popular vote, against five other candidates. Unlike Gorbachev, he was now legitimized, directly elected by the people, with a broad mandate for change. His spectacular victory, Yeltsin said, was nothing less than "the rebirth of Russia."

Russia was not yet an independent nation, but was well on its way. The largest Soviet republic by far now had half the U.S.S.R.'s population, two-thirds of its territory, and most of its mineral resources, managed by a government with strong popular support, determined to defend Russia's national interests to the end. The victory was more than Yeltsin's. It was Russia's. And it belonged mostly to the forces struggling to sweep away Soviet communism. In the same election, reformers Gavriil Popov and Anatoly Sobchak were named mayors of the nation's two largest cities, Moscow and Leningrad. In Leningrad, 55 percent of the residents added a final humiliation to

Communist pride. In a slap at the Soviet Union's founding father, they decided their city should no longer be named after Lenin. Instead they voted to return to its former name as the tsarist capital, St. Petersburg.

The progressives gained the most in this election, but Yeltsin had made sure his support was broader than that. He wanted the widest possible mandate, and he assured it with a shrewd choice for a running mate. Yeltsin, the radical reformer, had chosen as his vice presidential candidate General Aleksandr Rutskoi, an Afghan war hero with appeal to more conservative voters.[3] That way progressives and conservatives alike could find common ground in their missionary zeal to remake Russia a great country. In that, they had the blessing of Aleksei II, patriarch of the Russian Orthodox Church, who endorsed Yeltsin during the campaign as "the man capable of saving Russia." Boris Nikolayevich himself, baptized as a child but later indoctrinated as an atheist, also spoke in religious terms. "I have firm faith that Russia will become alive again," he said after the election victory.

The focus on Russia would be the key to all further Yeltsin strategy. As the elected president of Russia, Boris Nikolayevich was now where he wanted to be. He had no desire to replace Gorbachev as Soviet president. Instead, he would work to weaken the Soviet presidency to the advantage of Russia's. Ruslan Khasbulatov, then first deputy chairman of the Russian parliament, put it this way in an interview with me in June 1991: "I don't think Yeltsin wants to stand at the head of the U.S.S.R. He wants to be the head of an independent country." At the time, however, not even Khasbulatov believed that could happen by the end of the year.

In fact, on the heels of the election victory, the Yeltsin people sounded much too self-confident for their own good. They made no effort to hide their plans to seize decision-making power from Gorbachev. And their ambition knew virtually no limits. They were not talking about simply taking the power to run the Russian economy. They wanted authority over everything, including defense and foreign affairs. They even took pains to explain there would be no coup involved. All powers would be transferred legally, gradually, beginning with the new Union Treaty still under negotiation. Gorbachev would remain a figurehead president, with his Soviet government emasculated, reduced to a weak coordinating body. Real power would pass to the republics.

To show they meant business, Yeltsin aides made clear that the transfer of power would have to include Yeltsin's effective control over the Soviet army and its nuclear weapons, most of which were on Russian soil. In this scenario, they said, the Soviet army could still remain loyal to Gorbachev. Their model was Britain. British troops, they noted, swear allegiance to the queen, but take their orders from the elected prime minister. "In our country," a Yeltsin adviser told me, "Gorbachev becomes the queen." He meant there was no need to take the Soviet presidency from Gorbachev. Instead, the priority would be to take the powers of that office away from him and transfer them to Yeltsin, the popularly elected Russian president. In effect, Gorbachev would then become the queen, a ceremonial head of state.

Now, with the benefit of hindsight, none of this strategy sounds preposterous, but, at the time, it was outrageous. Gorbachev was in power, the Soviet Union very much intact, the Communist Party still in control of most levers of power. Yet here were Yeltsin's upstarts claiming the right to grab it all for themselves. No such prize could be secured without a fight. Indeed, the fight was coming, and soon. Communist hard-liners were appalled by the Yeltsin game plan. If Gorbachev proved incapable of defusing the Yeltsin challenge, they would get rid of him, and do the job themselves.

Gorbachev thought he still had cards to play. In July 1991 he went off to London, invited to attend the annual economic summit of the world's seven richest industrial nations—the United States, Britain, France, Germany, Italy, Japan, and Canada, the Group of Seven (G7). It was a major boost in prestige to be the first Soviet leader invited into this formerly exclusive Western club, and given a place of honor. Thanks to Gorbachev and perestroika, Western aid to the U.S.S.R. was now the key policy question on the G7 agenda. Mikhail Sergeyevich understood the G7 support would be long on talk and short on cash. So to encourage his new Western partners to dig more deeply into their pockets, he made them an offer he thought they couldn't refuse. It was to be the last of the Soviet president's great foreign policy initiatives.

Gorbachev made his once unthinkable offer in a confidential paper distributed to G7 leaders. He proposed selling a stake in the Soviet defense industry to the West. His paper, a copy of which I obtained in London, suggested that Western companies participate in a $30 to $40 billion program to convert Soviet defense plants to civilian production. In return for business expertise and capital, Western firms would gain access to elite Soviet defense factories and research centers. Gorbachev was prepared to sweeten the deal even further, encouraging Western participation through tax incentives and favorable licensing treatment. But it was the open access to once-secret Soviet defense plants that provided the real shock. "Unjustified secrecy was a serious impediment" to foreign investment in the past, the Gorbachev paper said. "The Soviet side would provide for foreigners a regime of openness."

Nyet, the Soviet Union's top military brass said to themselves. They would not agree to any deal that would emasculate their awesome firepower by destroying their industrial base. Nor would they allow Western spies to snoop through their arsenals. The whole idea was inconceivable to them. Soviet defense plants had been so secret that workers there were even forbidden to divulge locations. The only address they were allowed to give relatives or friends wishing to contact them was a post office box number. Now, suddenly, Gorbachev was proposing to give foreigners the run of such places.

The military brass determined to stop him. The more reactionary of them decided he had to go. In London, in July 1991, Mikhail Sergeyevich had just waved a red flag in front of a raging bull. His days were numbered. The question of a coup was no longer if, but when. The answer would come the very next month.

16

The Death of Communism

I. CHECKMATE

August turned out to be the fateful month in the decline and fall of the Soviet empire. On August 20, 1968, Soviet tanks invaded Czechoslovakia to crush Alexander Dubček's Prague Spring. Reform was threatening communism. Brezhnev's Kremlin cracked down, saving communism by crushing reform. Twenty-three years later, virtually to the day, Soviet tanks returned to the streets of a national capital, on August 19, 1991, once again to save communism by crushing reform. This time they rolled on their own home ground, Moscow. The anniversary of the Czech invasion provided delicious irony for a historic occasion. Much had changed since Prague. This time, Boris Yeltsin stood on a tank, rallied democratic forces, and defied the Kremlin hard-liners. This time a Soviet crackdown would have meant slaughtering Soviet people. So instead the hard-liners backed down. The result was the exact opposite of Prague. This time, reform was saved, and communism defeated, once and for all.

It was no surprise that August 19, 1991, proved to be the showdown day in the long-building Soviet crisis. That was the last day before Gorbachev planned to sign the new Union Treaty negotiated with Yeltsin and the leaders of other republics. The treaty would have shifted substantial powers from the center to the republics. Among other things, the treaty would have allowed the Baltic states to move quickly to full independence. More generally, it would have sounded the death knell for centralized Soviet control. To Kremlin hard-liners, that was totally unacceptable, just like the Shatalin plan of October 1990, for much the same reasons. The same men, the gang of five, were involved. This time they determined to stop the treaty, if necessary by seizing power themselves. They knew they must act before August 20.

The prime mover was KGB chief Vladimir Kryuchkov. On August 6, after Gorbachev and his family had left for a vacation at Foros, in the Crimea, Kryuchkov called in two senior aides and ordered them to prepare for an

imminent coup. Their first step was to be a memorandum detailing a cata-
strophic economic situation in the country. The memo would then be used
to justify a declaration of national emergency. With that, the Communist
hard-liners could prevent the signing of the Union Treaty and take power
themselves.

The KGB, however, could not do the job alone. Kryuchkov knew the military would also have to agree to a state of emergency, or the coup would
never get off the ground. Defense Minister Yazov was already on board, but
one man is not a whole army. Kryuchkov wanted more insurance, some defense ministry input on the expert level to help devise the game plan. So he
asked a top general to join a secret KGB study team on justifying a state of
emergency. Kryuchkov's choice was General Pavel Grachev, a Soviet deputy
defense minister, and it illustrated a major difficulty for the coup plotters.
They had to bring in senior people in order to assure the plot's success, yet
each time their circle widened, the danger increased of defections and security leaks. Grachev, as it turned out, was willing to study the declaration of
a national emergency with Kryuchkov's working group, but when the crunch
came, he refused to join their coup plot. Instead Grachev sent a security de-
tachment to Yeltsin's side. Boris Nikolayevich later rewarded Grachev's loyalty by making him Russian defense minister.[1]

First reports from Kryuchkov's working group were discouraging. They
told him declaring a state of emergency would be a complex undertaking
which risked touching off "widespread disorders" throughout the country.
The phrase was a euphemism for deep divisions within the military and other
power blocks, between those for and against reform. At worst, a declaration
of national emergency in such a situation could lead to civil war. "But after
the Union Treaty is signed it will be too late," Kryuchkov replied. For him,
it was now or never, despite the risks.

On August 17, Kryuchkov convened a meeting of the plotters at a KGB
safe house southwest of Moscow. Key players attending included Defense
Minister Yazov, Prime Minister Pavlov, and Politburo member Oleg Baklanov, chief of the military-industrial complex. The only member of the gang
of five missing was Interior Minister Boris Pugo, still on vacation in the south,
but on his way back to take part in the conspiracy. This time the plotters
were joined by the Judas in the drama, Valery Boldin, Gorbachev's chief of
staff. They were convinced they had isolated Mikhail Sergeyevich, for the
members of the group represented all the key power bases, including the military, the KGB, the Party, the government, even the Soviet president's personal staff. Anatoly Lukyanov, the chairman of the Soviet parliament, was
with them. So was Vice President Gennady Yanayev, a nonentity Gorbachev
had deliberately selected for this post to avoid any challenge to presidential
power.

The plotters would name Yanayev as Gorbachev's successor as soon as
they seized power, in order to give their conspiracy the appearance of legal-

ity. According to the Soviet constitution then in effect, the vice president was supposed to succeed when the president died or was disabled by illness, and in this plot scenario Gorbachev would be described as too ill to continue. Nonetheless, Yanayev was a poor choice. He had been a trade union leader and Communist time server, a cipher in the Soviet bureaucracy, a dim-witted weakling and drunkard. When named vice president, he had replied publicly to a question about his health by smirking and saying his wife was satisfied that he was "performing my marital duties quite well." The cretinous reply had stunned the nation. Russians expected more dignity from their leaders. Yanayev was simply not up to fronting for the coup leaders as Gorbachev's successor. But if they wanted a fig leaf of legality, they had no alternative. It had to be Vice President Yanayev.

During the meeting which Kryuchkov organized at the KGB safe house on August 17, the plotters decided to send a delegation to Gorbachev in Foros the next day. They would give him an ultimatum: agree to a state of emergency or resign. They expected he would agree. Gorbachev had given in to their pressure in October 1990, when they forced him to drop Shatalin's plan for a five-hundred-day rush to a market economy. This time, the Union Treaty was about to do the same thing, transfer power from the center to the republics. The hard-liners expected Gorbachev would once more side with them to save his job. Or so most of them testified later to prosecutors investigating the coup.

According to some of these testimonies, Gorbachev's role was expected to be that of willing victim. They claimed the Soviet president had cynically agreed in advance to declare a state of emergency if the hard-liners pushed him to it. In other words, they contended that Gorbachev himself was in on the plot. Once again, getting at the truth in the Soviet Union was like peeling an onion, layer after layer of tearful frustration, leaving a very bad smell. This time the layers peeled back in a series of disturbing claims and counterclaims ending in total confusion, as follows.

First, Gorbachev went on vacation and said he would sign the new Union Treaty when he got back. Second, leading Soviet newspapers said he didn't really mean it. According to their unconfirmed accounts, Gorbachev did not want to sign the treaty because it had been forced on him by Yeltsin and the other republic leaders. Third, the coup plotters pictured Gorbachev as changing his mind not once but twice on this issue. According to their accounts, the president was willing to throw out the Union Treaty and declare a state of emergency if hard-liners made it look as though they were forcing him into it, but, at the last minute, he changed his mind, for his own reasons, and refused to go along with them. From their jail cells they vowed they would testify at their trial that Gorbachev was in on the plot, as a key element of their intended defense. Fourth, Gorbachev denied the double-dealing and called his accusers liars. He declared emphatically that he had had no role in either planning or carrying out the plot.

At this stage only the pending trial of the coup leaders offered any way of getting at the truth. Then suddenly that last chance collapsed. The plotters were pardoned and released from jail, on the initiative of conservatives in the Russian parliament. There would be no trial and no new revelations from the plotters, nor would Gorbachev be obliged to testify and face cross-examination in a court of law. As a result, the whole truth of the August 1991 coup will never be known.[2]

Nonetheless, despite all the confusion and conflicting claims, enough is already clear to make a preliminary assessment. It shows that Gorbachev himself was partly responsible for the coup. He appointed the plotters to office and kept them there, despite warnings from Shevardnadze and others about them. Gorbachev also encouraged the conspirators to believe they could pressure him their way. But all that proves is poor judgment. Gorbachev was probably not part of the plot, however. The events beginning on August 18 establish that rather convincingly.

Gorbachev's vacation retreat outdid Khrushchev's, a three-story mansion filled with marble and gold, an indoor pool, and an escalator to the Black Sea below. On August 18, at 4:50 P.M., the Soviet president was working on his speech for the Union Treaty signing when unexpected visitors arrived. The delegation from the plotters included his chief of staff, Boldin; Politburo member Baklanov; and General Varennikov, chief of the ground forces. The conversation, reconstructed for prosecutors by the participants and later published in the Russian press, went like this:

"Who sent you?" Mikhail Sergeyevich asked.

"The committee," one of them replied. He meant the State Committee for the State of Emergency, the name the plotters had coined for themselves, a mouthful abbreviated to the Russian letters GKChP.

"Who appointed such a committee?" Gorbachev demanded. "I didn't."

Varennikov said it didn't matter. He delivered the ultimatum: support the state of emergency declaration or resign.

Gorbachev refused to declare the state of emergency. "You are nothing but adventurists and traitors, and you will pay for this," he told them. "Only those who want to commit suicide can now suggest a totalitarian regime in the country. You are pushing it to civil war."

The president reminded them that the Union Treaty was to be signed in two days.

"There will be no signing," Baklanov said.

Then the emissaries demanded that the president resign.

"You'll never live that long," Gorbachev snapped.

"Mikhail Sergeyevich, we demand nothing from you," Baklanov said. "You'll be here. We'll do all the dirty work for you."[3]

The president's objections were now irrelevant, as far as the plotters were concerned. He could no longer stop them. Gorbachev's refusal to declare the state of emergency was no problem. Neither was his refusal to resign. The plotters would now hold him at Foros under house arrest, unable to communicate with the outside world, and then explain publicly that he was too ill to continue as president. Then they would declare the state of emergency. That is what Baklanov meant when he said nothing was expected from Gorbachev, that the GKChP would do all the dirty work for him. Thus was the president pushed aside by a coalition of KGB, army, and other hard-line leaders Gorbachev was powerless to stop.

There was nothing more to discuss. The visitors turned to leave. "You are all going to meet defeat," Gorbachev told them defiantly as they filed out. It was not the performance of a man in on the plot. He had refused to play their game, and they had taken all power from him.

From there it only got worse. Gorbachev and his family were confined to their villa. Their own security men had turned against them. Their phone lines were cut. They feared for their lives. The president's wife, Raisa, suffered a nervous breakdown and has yet to recover fully. Gorbachev was not playacting. His opposition to the coup was real.

The plotters also meant business. They took the nuclear "football" from Gorbachev, the box containing the Soviet Union's nuclear trigger, one of the more disturbing incidents of the coup. He was no longer commander in chief. The "football" went to Defense Minister Yazov.

Whether Yazov could have fired Soviet nuclear weapons after that is by no means clear. Yevgeny Velikhov, a top Gorbachev science adviser, told me probably not. He said the "football" was not simply a box of communications equipment that could be handed off to someone else. Gorbachev also had special codes, known only to him and the chief of the Soviet rocket forces, which had to be used in order to launch a nuclear strike. Yazov would have had to arrange similar codes with the rocket forces chief before he could activate the communications equipment in the "football." Even if that had been possible, there were other technical factors, which Velikhov refused to disclose, that led him to believe the coup plotters could not have pressed the nuclear button. But Velikhov, a vice president of the Academy of Sciences, admitted that even he could not be completely sure that there was no danger of unauthorized access to the nuclear trigger. "There has never been enough public discussion on this question," he told me. "It is still top secret."

Russians who still believe Gorbachev was in on the plot say the telephone is the key. If the Soviet president still had effective two-way phone communication during the coup and didn't use it to call George Bush and other Western leaders, that would prove he was part of the conspiracy and wanted the state of emergency to succeed. Some say the phones in the house at Foros were cut but the one in the car still worked. They wonder why Mikhail Sergeyevich didn't go to the garage and try the car phone. If he had tried, however, it would have been useless. The car line went through an operator, and operators were instructed not to connect calls to or from Gorbachev.

Soon after the coup was announced on August 19, President Leonid Kravchuk of the Ukraine tried several times to get through to Gorbachev to see if he was all right. But each time, "The operator said in a very nice voice, 'Mikhail Sergeyevich is not to be disturbed,' " Kravchuk told journalists in Kiev. The Ukrainian president was not about to be put off by an operator. The Crimea, where Gorbachev was staying, was part of the Ukraine. The Soviet president was his guest, and therefore his responsibility. Kravchuk told the chief of the Crimean KGB to get through to Gorbachev. "But Soviet troops stopped him and warned, 'Don't interfere,' " Kravchuk said. "Our Ukrainian KGB was completely ignored."

Kravchuk's experience, typical of many, suggested Gorbachev really was cut off. Other Russians maintained that is impossible, because the Soviet president still had top-secret communication lines connected to the nuclear football. However, those who made this argument were unaware that the football had been taken from him. Thus did much of the theory that Mikhail Sergeyevich was in on the plot begin to unravel.

On Monday morning, August 19, tanks rolled onto the streets of Moscow. The declaration of the state of emergency was broadcast. The coup was on. A Tass bulletin said Vice President Yanayev had taken over for an ill Gorbachev under Article 127, Clause 7 of the Soviet constitution. In their arrogance, the plotters thought a massive show of force would be enough to cow the population into submission. They followed the old Khrushchev scenario, a coup while the leader was vacationing at the Black Sea. They thought it would work just as smoothly as 1964. All they showed was how out of touch they were with the realities of 1990s.

For one thing, they no longer had blanket control of all sources of information and communication. Soviet state television played Tchaikovsky's music, but CNN was also available now in Moscow, free on a trial run, in English, of course. Russians didn't have to understand the words. The pictures said it all. They saw resistance to the coup develop around the Russian White House. Tens of thousands would join Yeltsin's stand there, ready to defend against tanks with their bodies. The fax was another new development the putschists had ignored. Russians used faxes to communicate with each other and to get information and support from abroad. The fax proved to be a major resistance weapon.

The plotters had drawn up a list of seventy top officials to be arrested, starting with Yeltsin. On the eve of the coup, an elite KGB unit called the "alpha arrest team" moved into the woods outside Yeltsin's dacha at Arkhangelskoye in the Moscow suburbs, but the order to arrest him never came. Inside the dacha, the phones and the fax were never cut. Yeltsin and his team spent the morning organizing the resistance. At 9:00 A.M., Boris Nikolayevich left the dacha to take personal command at the White House. As he got into his car, his daughter Lena said, "Papa, everything now depends on you."

Incredibly, no one stopped his entourage on the drive into town. Anyone who has ever read newspaper accounts of a successful coup d'état knows that the essential elements include arresting political opponents, closing the airport, seizing the radio/TV tower, and cutting phone lines. Yet the leaders of the August 1991 coup in Moscow, all highly trained professionals well aware of coup essentials, did none of the above. There is only one acceptable explanation for their lapses: they deliberately decided against the traditional coup scenario.

"Kryuchkov was attempting to harness events so the coup would indeed be bloodless," Yeltsin later explained. "He canceled the planned arrests, although the machinery had been in place for them. . . . He quickly saw that such a roundup would produce a sharp backlash of resistance leading to the possibility of excessive force and bloodshed. Second, such arrests would be too harsh a transition from the Gorbachev thaw. The new leadership would not only be subject to numerous international sanctions but relations could also likely break off altogether. For a country like ours, with numerous interests in various corners of the globe, this would be extremely painful. Kryuchkov, clever intelligence apparatchik that he was, was thinking pragmatically."[4]

In the first instance, Kryuchkov hoped intimidation would be enough to make the coup succeed, without the arrests and other traditional elements. The tanks would make a show of force. Yanayev would assume the presidency and then the old Soviet Union would resume business as usual. The KGB chief had not expected an organized resistance. Indeed, on the first day, it looked as if the coup might succeed. Reformers were intimidated. Many thought their arrest imminent. On the phone that day, a Shevardnadze aide said to a Western reporter, "Goodbye for the last time," as if expecting to be a victim of some new Stalinist repression because of his reformist record. There was little doubt the hard-liners had the upper hand. The Communist Party supported the coup. So did Vladimir Zhirinovsky, who would soon lead a nationalist revival in Russia. Millions of ordinary Soviet citizens agreed Gorbachev had failed, and deserved to go. Tens of millions passively accepted their fate. But not everyone. This time, the forces of reform refused to cave in under pressure.

The coup plotters "made a big mistake," Yeltsin said in a later interview, "when they didn't shoot me in the morning."[5] They would not get a second chance. The Russian president arrived at the White House at 10:00 A.M. to organize what was to become the second Russian revolution. There had been nothing like it since the Bolsheviks seized power in 1917 and brought communism to power in Russia. First Yeltsin broadcast to the nation from a makeshift radio station inside the White House. He condemned the coup as "reactionary" and "unconstitutional." Then Russian Vice President Aleksandr Rutskoi, in a second broadcast, spoke as a general and an Afghan war hero, "calling on my brother officers, soldiers, and sailors not to act against our own people."

At noon, Yeltsin climbed on a T-52 tank outside the White House. There was a only a small crowd of Russians then, but enough reporters and photographers to capture that one image as the enduring symbol of the revolution to come. "Citizens of Russia," Yeltsin said, "give an appropriate rebuff to the putschists and demand a return of the country to normal constitutional development." All decisions and decrees of the GKChP were illegal, Yeltsin said. They should be opposed by a general strike and civil disobedience. Yeltsin knew he was breaking the coup leaders' version of martial law, but he also knew that that would force Kryuchkov and the other hard-liners to rethink their strategy. Intimidation and a show of military force would no longer be enough. Now the plotters would actually have to use military force to smash Yeltsin's resistance. It was a daring gamble that the putschists would not be willing to fire on their own people, although Yeltsin and his supporters feared they might well do so.

Hurriedly, the Russian president and his military advisers began reinforcing their defense of the White House. In the streets of Moscow, ordinary citizens rallied to Yeltsin's appeals. Their old fear of the army was gone. Instead, people were talking to the troops calmly and affectionately, as members of their own families, urging them to switch sides and join Yeltsin. Women gave them food and flowers. Young girls flirted with them. Civilian youths argued the Yeltsin cause. I saw one grandmother lean on a tank and tell the lieutenant in command, "Sonny, you can't shoot your own mothers and sisters, can you?"

Defections from the military began to occur in growing numbers, and not only in Moscow. In Leningrad, Mayor Sobchak talked the military commander, General Viktor Samsonov, into defying Yazov and keeping his soldiers from enforcing the coup there. Yazov had other options. He called Kronstadt, the naval base on Kotlin Island, eighteen miles west of Leningrad, where tens of thousands of sailors were stationed. In 1917, support from Kronstadt sailors had played an important role in the success of the Bolshevik Revolution. This time, Yazov wanted them armed and deployed in the streets of Leningrad in support of the coup, but Captain Aleksandr Melnikov, the base commander, disobeyed. Instead, Melnikov went on the base radio and broadcast to Leningrad, urging citizens there to support Yeltsin's resistance. He then offered Kronstadt, an impregnable island fortress, as a base for Mayor Sobchak and the city council to take refuge, in absolute safety, and work to oppose the coup.

It was a remarkable performance by the young naval officer. Melnikov was forty-three years old, with a brilliant naval career ahead of him. He was already running one of the country's most important bases and could confidently expect to become one of its top admirals before long. Yet he risked all that to defy his defense minister's order and obey his conscience instead. Melnikov was a remarkable man. His generation of forty-somethings was a very different breed from the sixty-something Yazovs and Kryuchkovs running the coup. Among other things, Melnikov and his generation put much more emphasis on individual initiative and responsibility. His generation also welcomed ideas outside the Party line. When the coup was announced, Melnikov told me during a later interview in Kronstadt, he called in the local Russian Orthodox priest for advice. Then he decided, "I could not personally give the order to fire on our own people." So he defied Yazov's order and sided with Yeltsin's resistance. Other commanders, in Moscow and around the country, would make similar decisions. Even if the coup had succeeded in the capital, it would have taken a civil war to bring the rest of the country along.

The talk with Melnikov left a profound impression on me. In 1991, Russia really was changing. I could go to Kronstadt, a military base once closed to all foreigners. And there I could meet a Soviet military commander who took advice from a priest on the most important decision of his career. The Melnikov generation would prove to be the country's best hope in the Yeltsin years ahead. But first it would help save reform from the hard-line coup.

In Moscow, the public mood changed profoundly on the first day of the putsch when some of the plotters held a televised press conference. It was an unmitigated disaster for the would-be successors to Gorbachev. All their weaknesses were displayed for the world to see. The State Committee for the State of Emergency was divided. Kryuchkov, the operational ringleader but by no means the boss, was not even there. Neither was Yazov. Divisions within the committee had so far prevented agreement on a concrete program. Beyond the seizure of power and the determination to turn the clock back on reform, they had no plan on how far to retreat or how fast; they had no specific program for running the nation. Worst of all, their nominal leader, Yanayev, was a pitiful wreck. He appeared half drunk, no match for the non-Communist journalists appalled at the seizure of power. Tatyana Malkina, a twenty-four-year-old reporter for the country's most respected independent daily, *Nezavisimaya Gazeta*, cut through all the nonsense about a state of emergency and an alleged Gorbachev illness forcing the vice president to take over. "Tell me, please," she asked Yanayev, "do you realize you have carried out a state coup?" The vice president's hands shook uncontrollably. He had no coherent answer. The GKChP claim to power was shown to be farcical.

Yazov watched the spectacle from his office in the defense ministry, with his wife, Emma. "What have you joined?" she asked him, incredulous. "You always laughed at them. Call Gorbachev and call off the coup." But he couldn't do that. Instead General Dmitri Yazov had to explain to his wife that all phone lines to Gorbachev had been cut.

Meanwhile, Yeltsin seized the momentum. The Russian president was barricaded in a building impossible to defend. Any determined military attack could have destroyed his White House and all those defending it within fifteen minutes. Yet from this position of extreme vulnerability, Yeltsin was demanding nothing less than the capitulation of the coup leaders and the restoration of Gorbachev, the personification of constitutional rule.

By late evening on Tuesday, August 20, that bravado had paid off. More than thirty thousand people had flocked to the White House, risking their lives to defend it. They ringed the building in rows eight deep, locked arms, and prepared to stop tanks with their bodies. In all there were over 100,000 people in the streets near the White House, defying a curfew in order to support the resistance. Like much of the coup, the curfew was a bad joke. There were no police in the streets to enforce it. Interior Minister Boris Pugo, who ran the uniformed police, was a leading coup conspirator, but his ministry was far from totally on board. Worse for the plotters, the military was badly split. Yevgeny Shaposhnikov, the air force commander, threatened an airborne attack on the Kremlin if the putschists sent tanks against the White House.

George Bush and other Western leaders strongly backed Yeltsin's demand for the restoration of Gorbachev's constitutional regime. In Washington, Deputy Secretary of State Lawrence Eagleburger told Soviet Ambassador Viktor Komplektov, "You should know that from the president on down, we're outraged." The United States, Eagleburger said, was not ready to see reform die in the Soviet Union. America did not want another Cold War, but it would have nothing to do with an illegal regime like the GKChP. While it held power, there would be no question of U.S. aid. Here at last the United States government was unambiguously warning Soviet hard-liners that they had gone too far and would have to back off or suffer the consequences in terms of a costly deterioration in relations with America. This time, Washington would not be put off by Soviet complaints about unwarranted interference in Moscow's internal affairs or by Soviet threats of escalating tensions. This time the United States rightly brushed aside all such arguments and clearly insisted that any rollback toward Stalinism would not be tolerated. Finally, the Americans, as the far stronger party, were setting the rules for superpower relations, as they could have been doing all along.

This warning, it should be recalled, was directed at the leaders of the Soviet armed forces, KGB, and Communist Party then in effective control of the country. They were powerful, experienced men, long players in the Kremlin leadership, no brash newcomers. And still the United States did not hesitate. This time, the tough U.S. stand contributed to the collapse of the coup. One can only wonder what might have happened if Washington had taken similarly tough stands against Soviet hard-liners years or even decades earlier.

The coup was nearly finished. Unfortunately, it would not be bloodless. In Moscow on the night of August 20, three young men challenged tanks and were crushed under them. They became martyrs. The spot where they died was closed off to traffic for months. Their public funeral was an incredible first for the notoriously anti-Semitic Soviet Union. One of the young victims had been Jewish, so in his honor, a rabbi chanted prayers in

Hebrew. The ceremony took place near Red Square and was attended by Gorbachev and 100,000 people. Never in my lifetime did I expect to see a rabbi and a Soviet Communist leader participating in a religious service in the shadow of the Kremlin wall.

On the third day, Wednesday, August 21, the coup collapsed. The plotters were not willing to slaughter thousands of their own people. They had to give up. Yanayev and Pavlov were ill, Pugo despondent and soon dead, officially listed as a suicide. At a meeting that morning of the defense ministry collegium, the policymaking body of the military brass, top commanders demanded that Yazov withdraw from the coup junta. The defense minister refused. "I cannot make a decision one day and reverse it the next," he said. Instead, Yazov rose and left the room.

Varennikov, the ground forces commander and another key coup leader, then took over the meeting, issuing the orders to withdraw troops from the streets. Kryuchkov called the White House and spoke with Yeltsin's chief aide, Gennady Burbulis. The Yeltsin team had been working nonstop for seventy-two hours. "It's okay," Kryuchkov reported. "You can go to sleep." The coup was over.

Gorbachev flew back to Moscow to a different country. In personal terms, Yeltsin was the hero of the hour. For the first time, his stature had now eclipsed Gorbachev's, although Mikhail Sergeyevich did not yet understand that. At a press conference on Thursday, August 22, Gorbachev described his Foros ordeal, as if he were once again the undisputed leader of the nation. His public gratitude to Yeltsin was minimal. That was his first mistake, but not the last.

In policy terms, the Communist Party was in disgrace. It had supported the coup, only to be defeated by Yeltsin's democratic forces. Yet Gorbachev failed to grasp that as well. He reiterated his commitment to the Party's "renewal." Even now, after the putsch, Mikhail Sergeyevich was still not ready to sacrifice the Party for the sake of reform. He had just shown himself to be hopelessly out of touch with the new mood of the country.

After the press conference, when the TV cameras stopped rolling, Gorbachev stayed around to talk with journalists. A Soviet reporter asked him if he planned to award Yeltsin a "Hero of the Soviet Union" medal for defeating the coup. "What for?" Mikhail Sergeyevich shot back. "We all work"— as if risking one's life facing down tanks was a normal day's work. Gorbachev was really angry. "We don't work for this," he added with a scowl, dismissively brushing his hand against the breast of his suit jacket. The reference was to Brezhnev, who had worn three gold hero medals on his suit. Gorbachev, who wore no such decorations, was reminding his listeners he had stopped the hero business. It was one of the rare times Mikhail Sergeyevich lost his temper in public. He really hated Yeltsin, was not about to make him an official state hero, and had not yet realized his long struggle with Boris Nikolayevich was lost.

It took one more day for Gorbachev to acknowledge publicly that Yeltsin had indeed eclipsed him during the coup. On Friday, August 23, Mikhail Sergeyevich appeared at the Russian parliament, and Yeltsin humiliated him, before a national television audience. The Russian president, towering above Gorbachev, handed him a document and demanded that he read it aloud. The document Yeltsin handed over was a transcript of a meeting in which two government ministers appointed by Gorbachev had expressed their support for the coup. Mikhail Sergeyevich asked Yeltsin what he was doing. They had not discussed this matter between them. Yeltsin was relentless. "Read it now," he commanded. Meekly, Gorbachev complied. The nation understood. Yeltsin was now in charge.

On Saturday, August 24, the end of the momentous coup week, Gorbachev resigned as general secretary and dissolved the Soviet Communist Party. The same day, the Ukraine declared its independence from the U.S.S.R. Gorbachev was still Soviet president, but he no longer had the Party to support him, and the Soviet Union he ran was falling apart. The army and the KGB had long held the country together by force. Now both had been disgraced by the coup. They could no longer prevent the collapse of the U.S.S.R. Without them, there was little left to keep the Soviet Union together. "There were only three other factors," former Yeltsin adviser Grigory Yavlinsky told me at the time, "ideology, the enemy threat, and the economy. Now the first two are gone and the third is going." He was right. Ideology had been a key factor. But with the collapse of the Communist Party, it was gone. The enemy factor disappeared with the end of the Cold War.

Economic ties were still important. Republics were mutually dependent on one another. Most relied on Russian fuel. Russia needed food, among other things, from various republics. But independent nations could maintain the same economic rationale, cooperating voluntarily with each other. They no longer needed Soviet bureaucrats in Moscow to run things for them. Indeed, the republics were now moving in that direction. As Yavlinsky noted, the economic rationale for keeping the Soviet Union together, the only one left, was rapidly disappearing.

The Union Treaty that had precipitated the coup was not the answer. Although ready for signing August 20, it was put up for renegotiation after the putsch. Gorbachev had hoped it would still hold the U.S.S.R. together, even if that now meant further concessions to the republics, but they were not interested. They wanted out. The Baltics representatives were the first to leave the talks at Gorbachev's Novo-Ogaryovo dacha on the revamped Union Treaty, and others soon followed.

The next decisive step was up to the Ukraine. It scheduled a referendum for December 1 to confirm the declaration of independence in August by the Ukrainian parliament. In effect, the Ukraine referendum was a vote on the fate of the Soviet Union. If the largest, richest non-Russian republic left the union, the rest of the U.S.S.R. could no longer hold together.

Approval was a foregone conclusion. At the time, Kiev radio already called its reports from Moscow "news from abroad." I spent a week in the Ukraine before the ballot and found hardly anyone in favor of staying in the U.S.S.R. The views of Vitaly Karpenko, editor of the afternoon daily newspaper *Vecherniy Kiev*, were typical. "The former Soviet Union is absolutely bankrupt," he said. "We can overcome our crisis only if we are independent."

President Kravchuk told me in an interview he was "confident the West will provide us with recognition and direct assistance." Kravchuk also said he expected an accommodation with Yeltsin that would avoid any trade war between Russia and an independent Ukraine. Gorbachev and the Soviet government seemed almost irrelevant in his calculations. The referendum was approved by an overwhelming majority, more than 80 percent. "The Soviet Union has disintegrated," Kravchuk said after the vote. He was almost right.

One further nail had to be driven into the coffin. Yeltsin, Kravchuk, and President Stanislav Shushkevich of Belarus[6] met secretly at the Belovezhsky Nature Reserve in Belarus, near Minsk, under a soft snowfall. Their three Slavic republics—Russia, the Ukraine, and Belarus—had long provided the leadership of the U.S.S.R. Now they would take the lead in burying the Soviet Union. The Ukraine's independence had provided the impetus for their final act, only one week later. On December 8, the three Slavic leaders signed the "Belovezhsky Treaty." It was, in effect, a radical alternative to Gorbachev's proposed Union Treaty, doing just the opposite.

In the key provision, the three Slavic leaders agreed to do away entirely with the central Soviet government. Their three republics would become independent, but they would continue to cooperate as one political, economic, and military region. Other Soviet republics could join them if they wished, in what would become known as the Commonwealth of Independent States. In the end, all but the Baltics did so. With the signing of the Belovezhsky agreement, Yeltsin said, "the Soviet Union ceased to exist."

This agreement is still denounced today as a "silent coup" by Yeltsin's political enemies, those who want to restore the Soviet Union. And indeed, they have a point. But Belovezhsky was fundamentally different from the August 1991 hard-line coup, in that it was entirely legal. When confronted with the reality of the Belovezhsky Treaty, Gorbachev had no choice but to resign. He could no longer be president of a country that no longer existed.

By luck I managed to see Yeltsin in his Kremlin office on the crucial day. He had long agreed to a December 24 interview with four journalists, including me, and suddenly that timing had become exquisite. Immediately after finishing with us, Yeltsin was going to see Gorbachev to arrange the transfer of power.

Our interview began two hours before the session with Gorbachev, but Yeltsin clearly felt he had already taken over. With supreme confidence, Boris Nikolayevich picked up a pencil during the interview and drew us a diagram of how he planned to reorganize the Soviet military under Russian commanders he would name. Yeltsin was particularly blunt in explaining where Gorbachev had gone wrong: "He wanted to combine things that cannot be combined—to marry a hedgehog and a grass snake—communism and a market economy, public property ownership and private property ownership, the multiparty system and the Communist Party with its monopoly on power. But these things are incompatible."

We asked Yeltsin if we could stay and talk to him again after the fateful meeting with Gorbachev. He agreed, but when he returned he sent an aide instead to fill us in. The aide said that when Yeltsin got back he told his staff, "It's over." The two leaders had agreed the Soviet government would cease to exist by the end of the year. Its powers would be transferred to Yeltsin's Russian government. Gorbachev would resign on Christmas Day.

"That's the last time I will have to go to see him," Yeltsin told his staff.

"You mean that from now on, Gorbachev will have to come see you?" an aide asked.

"What for?" Yeltsin replied. "Well, maybe to pick up his pension."

Once again, the mutual animosity between the two leaders was all too clear. Yeltsin had no use for Gorbachev. There was no intention of employing Gorbachev, or even listening to his advice, in Boris Yeltsin's future plans.

Gorbachev, however, had already earned a place in history as one of the twentieth century's great men. Each of the major reforms he ushered in was nothing short of miraculous at the time. He broke the Communist Party monopoly on political, economic, and ideological control by permitting contested elections, private enterprise, and an independent press; he let Communist East European countries go their own way and allowed Germany to reunite in NATO; he ended the quagmire in Afghanistan by withdrawing Soviet troops without any concessions in return; he let ethnic minorities form national independence movements from the Baltics to Central Asia; he ended censorship of the arts and permitted religious freedom.

These had been heresies before, sufficient reasons by themselves to depose a reformist leader. In 1985, when Gorbachev took over, had anyone thought to ask twenty Western experts how many of these things a new Kremlin leader might accomplish, twenty out of twenty would have said none.

Of course, he failed in the end, but what he accomplished before that is far more important. Again, had anyone thought to ask these same twenty experts what had to be done when Gorbachev took over in 1985, most would have answered something like this: "There are two essential tasks. First, the unworkable Soviet system must be dismantled. Second, a rational alternative must be put in its place. And of the two, the first job will be by far the hardest. Any serious reformer would inevitably risk being axed, just like Khrushchev, long before he could reform the system."

Gorbachev managed to accomplish that seemingly impossible task, not the way he intended, but effectively nonetheless. Therein lies his greatness. The second task, that of building a rational alternative to the Soviet system, would now fall to Yeltsin. As we shall see, that too would often seem impossible. The problems he faced and the responsibilities he shouldered were colossal. As his daughter said on the day of the August coup, "Papa, everything now depends on you."

Mikhail Sergeyevich Gorbachev resigned on Christmas Day, December 25, 1991. Thirty-three minutes later, the red Soviet flag with the Communist hammer and sickle came down from the Kremlin walls. In its place flew the red-white-and-blue flag of reborn Russia. All that remained from the Communist era that had shaken the world for most of the century was the Lenin Mausoleum on Moscow's Red Square. Fittingly, the most enduring symbol of Soviet communism was a tomb.

Only by the ruthless use of deadly force did the Communists seize and maintain power in their own country and expand their influence abroad. There was no way their repressive ideology and their bankrupt economic model could compete with the Western democracies for the hearts and minds of ordinary people, let alone keep pace in the arms race. In the end, Soviet communism had to reform or die. After the failed August coup, it had no choice but to die. It was buried with its founder in the cold red marble of Lenin's tomb.

On the afternoon of December 26, 1991, one day after his resignation, Gorbachev appeared at a farewell reception hosted by his last press secretary, Andrei Grachev, at the Oktyabrskaya Hotel, to say goodbye to a small group of Russian and foreign journalists. I was among them. The hotel had once been the exclusive preserve of the Communist Party Central Committee but, in a sign of the times, had begun catering to big-spending foreign tourists. Gorbachev was in top form at his farewell—relaxed, composed, generous. "A great task fell to my lot, and it was accomplished," he said over a glass of champagne. "Others will come who will perhaps do a better job. I wish them success, not failure." In the end, Mikhail Sergeyevich chose to be noble. There could be no more graceful exit.

II. POSTSCRIPT

Years later, I had a chance to meet privately with Gorbachev and ask him to reflect on his leadership. It was January 1995, ten years after he began perestroika and three years after he resigned. Mikhail Sergeyevich had thus profited from ample time to think over the record. He had also just returned from a two-week vacation and was in robust health. We met in the Moscow office of his academic think tank, the Gorbachev Foundation, from which he continues to comment on world affairs. The ninety-minute conversation provided an opportunity to pose the kind of questions journalists never got to ask Soviet leaders in power. Some of Gorbachev's answers clarified the historic issues running through this book, and are therefore reproduced below at length.

"When you started perestroika," I asked, "did the example of Nikita Khrushchev's fate weigh heavily on your mind? And, if not, what made you confident you could both conduct reform and keep power?"

"Yes, I did think about the fate of Khrushchev—and the example of the Kosygin reforms," Mikhail Sergeyevich began in reply. The reference to Kosygin in the same breath was significant. Khrushchev had shown that a top leader could be deposed if he pushed reform too far too fast. But Kosygin, a former prime minister and arguably the second most important man in the Kremlin in his day, had shown that a Soviet reformer got nowhere unless he held the top post of Party general secretary. Gorbachev had chosen to draw lessons from both, not just Khrushchev. "These two examples convinced me that if reforms in this country were to emerge from the totalitarian regime, they could begin only from above—from the very very top," Gorbachev went on. In short, despite the risks of the Khrushchev precedent, Mikhail Sergeyevich had decided he had no choice but to lead the reform effort himself.

Gorbachev then explained that through 1985 and 1986 he felt the Communist Party establishment, the *nomenklatura,* put the brakes on his intended reforms, and that from January 1987 on, he was determined to reduce the Party's powers to thwart him. That determination led Gorbachev to usher in competitive elections, a stronger parliament, and a stronger executive presidency.[7]

"The central questions were democracy and political reform," Gorbachev said, "the use of a separation of powers to push the Party out of authority, so that it would not have day-to-day controlling functions, so that it would be a normal political force. We wanted the political reform to lead to free elections, and to open the way to new, fresh forces. Otherwise, if we did not do that, I felt that Khrushchev's fate was in store for me.

"And the fact that I was right was shown in 1991, when the *nomenklatura* tried a coup," Mikhail Sergeyevich continued. "Of course, Khrushchev's experience was important to me. I still hold a high opinion of him, even though he was a man of his time and remained a prisoner of ideology. Nonetheless, he tried to introduce something new. His great merit is that he took the first steps against the totalitarian regime, against Stalinism."

In reporting from Moscow through the Gorbachev years, and in preparing this book, I had always assumed the Khrushchev precedent must have been a major concern for Gorbachev and a leading influence on his political strategy. Many other analysts disagreed. To them, Khrushchev was ancient history, with little relevance to the changed world of the Gorbachev years. Now Mikhail Sergeyevich himself had confirmed my assumption, by acknowledging his fear that "Khrushchev's fate" was in store for him unless he could "push the Party out of authority." Here was a rare case of a Kremlinological assumption being confirmed years later by the Soviet leader concerned. It was enough to encourage the hope that speculation in this book about Russia's future may prove to be just as accurate.

During the same interview, I also asked Gorbachev what he felt was his greatest single mistake in power and his greatest source of satisfaction.

"I'll begin with the achievement," he replied, "because it's closer to my heart. Through perestroika, I and those who supported me brought this country freedom. That's the most important thing. No matter what happens, in the long run, historically, that will yield fruit.

"My greatest source of regret is that I did not preserve the Union," he admitted, meaning the U.S.S.R. "My basic premise was that we needed reform to create a union of really sovereign states, but that, at the same time, we needed to preserve the country. Here the [1991] coup plotters played a role, and, also, the Russian leaders [Yeltsin].

"The Russian leaders made a strategic mistake, assuming that by ridding itself of the other republics, Russia could develop more quickly, first of all carry out reforms faster, and also take control of the natural resources, most of which are on its territory. They figured that in three to five years, Russia would be a prosperous country. But now three years have already gone by and I'm afraid those hopes have all been crushed."

Despite this miscalculation, the Russian leaders "still had an advantage" in 1991, Mikhail Sergyeyevich explained. By then, "most citizens felt that Gorbachev had been trying to reform the country for five years and there had not been much progress in living standards, while Yeltsin promised to do everything very quickly. . . . Gorbachev was an obstacle to faster reform, so the Russian leaders needed a way to push Gorbachev out." The device they used to get rid of him, Mikhail Sergyeyevich said, was to break up the U.S.S.R. "That's why I failed to preserve the Union.

"Everything else is details," he said. "I could have done this differently or that differently. In some cases I may have waited too long, in others I may have moved too fast, like a general who runs ahead of his army. All that is true, but none of it was irreparable. The breakup of the Union, however, was very serious, a real blow to society and to reform in general."

It was a telling analysis. Gorbachev blames himself for letting the U.S.S.R. break up, but Yeltsin even more for making it happen. Historians are likely to agree.

PART IV

Boris Nikolayevich Yeltsin

(1991–1995)

17

The Battle for Russia's Soul
(1992–93)

I. INTO THE WILDERNESS

Communism was an age of certainty. Everything had to be planned. People had no freedom and were generally poor, but at least they rarely had to worry about making enough money to feed their families. For all its other failings, the Soviet state kept prices, rents, and taxes low enough for just about everyone to get by. Although life under communism was hard, often boring, it was at least predictable. Tomorrow would be very much like today. With the fall of communism, however, all that changed. Now people were free from the state-planned straitjacket, but often less secure. They had a chance to become rich—or to starve. Nothing was certain anymore, least of all the future. Indeed, the fundamental fact in the new post-Communist Russia was that no one knew which way the country would turn, or when. People knew only that the political struggle to shape the nation's destiny continued, with no agreed rules, no holds barred. The jury was still out on whether an election, a coup, or even a civil war would be decisive.

When Boris Yeltsin stood on a tank to turn back the August 1991 coup, Russians knew what they did not want. They were against a return to Stalinist tyranny. Enough of them risked their lives taking that stand to bring down communism, but there was little agreement on what to build in its place. The defeat of communism did not assure the birth of a stable democracy. Instead, it began a new battle for Russia's soul. Democracy was one possibility. Benevolent, reformist dictatorship was a second. Nationalist or even fascist despotism was a third.

Thinking Russians quickly understood that the transition from communism to whatever eventually replaced it would be hard, uncertain, and, above all, long. In 1992 they began likening their plight to that of the ancient Jews who fled Pharaoh's Egypt, crossed the Red Sea, and wandered in the wilderness for forty years. "Why forty years?" Russians asked in a story often repeated at the time. "Because they had to wait for a new generation of leaders to show the way to the promised land."

361

In that context, Boris Yeltsin is already yesterday's man. As a Communist apparatchik most of his adult life, now in his sixties and in poor health, Yeltsin can only start the transition from communism. What will come after him is hazardous to predict, but even a hard-liner might be transitory too. So far conservatives have no coherent answers to the nation's economic problems either. If the early Israelite comparison holds true, Russia's next long-term course is unlikely to be charted for decades, not perhaps until someone now in his twenties, who came of age in the Gorbachev era and carries none of the earlier Communist baggage, leads a new generation to power.

However, forecasts in Russia have a poor track record. Thirty years ago when Leonid Brezhnev assumed the Kremlin leadership, he was widely seen by Western experts as a short-term transition figure. In fact, he lasted eighteen years. There is no guarantee Russians will wander in the wilderness until a new generation comes along. Hard-liners can move the tanks anytime.

In its own interests, the West would be wise to show patience and prudence. There will be no quick economic fix in Russia, even with far more aid than the West has been willing to offer to date. And without economic progress, democracy in Russia will remain weak. Yeltsin may recover from his heart attacks sufficiently to continue to deliver on arms control and other East-West cooperation, but that is no guarantee his successor won't turn Russia again into an aggressive nuclear superpower. Given the uncertainties, it would be foolish for NATO to run down allied defenses. Policy toward Moscow has to be based on a hardheaded assessment of reality on the ground in Russia, not on pious Western hopes for progress there. This chapter and the following one attempt to bring home to the reader, as accurately as possible, that new Russian reality.

Fortunately, understanding Russia is not the problem it was in Churchill's day, when the secrecy-obsessed Kremlin even falsified its own maps to confuse foreigners. Diplomats, journalists, and businessmen can now visit the entire country, even once top-secret military labs or bases, and meet regularly with responsible officials ready to answer any questions. If Western governments misread Russia today, they have only themselves to blame. The way ahead to understanding the new Russia is now abundantly clear. All it takes, as a first essential step, is getting out of Moscow.

The capital no longer runs the country with an iron fist, so now pretends to know more than it actually does. The national government hypes its accomplishments and prospects. The opposition complains, but offers no credible alternative vision. The national press, freer to criticize although less knowledgeable than in Communist days, confuses rather than clarifies. As a result of all this, the public mood swings erratically in Moscow. One day Yeltsin's reforms seem to be working, making democracy and the market economy irreversible in Russia. The next day their failure is seen as inevitable, likely to bring on renewed dictatorship. These contradictory perceptions make grassroots soundings in the provinces more important than ever.

Often, the farther one gets from the capital, the clearer the real Russia becomes, the more focused its future prospects. In the heartland, Russian towns and villages sometimes seem entirely untouched by Gorbachev or Yeltsin reforms. Or, if they have been, people say the changes have mostly made things worse. Such criticism from the heartland must be taken very seriously indeed. For the ultimate fate of Yeltsin's radical reforms is most likely to be decided by how well they actually work in the Russian countryside, rather than by the spurious claims of success made in the capital. No Russian facing economic ruin in the provinces is going to believe Kremlin leaders claiming progress, or vote for them, or oppose a hard-line coup that removes them from power.

I found that to be true early in Yeltsin's rule, on a trip to Siberian oil fields in November 1992. Winter in Siberia brings its own special reality dose. Oil workers said that when temperatures drop below minus forty degrees, machinery stops and pipelines burst. Spit freezes before it hits the ground. Yet work has to continue in those conditions. Oil was Russia's biggest export earner, bringing in $13 billion in 1991. Moscow had to improve on that to finance the economic reforms underpinning Yeltsin's democratic revolution. It had the potential. Russia boasts some of the world's largest untapped oil reserves, on a Saudi Arabian scale, much of them in Siberia. To a large extent, Yeltsin's ambitious reforms hinged on bringing in that oil. I went to Siberia for a firsthand look at how they were doing.

It took two days, two jet planes, and a helicopter to get from Moscow to Drilling Station No. 159 in the Kammenoye oil field of western Siberia. A towering rig planted in deep snow prospected for oil a mile and a third below the surface. This was supposed to be one of the nation's top-priority economic projects, but it looked more like a battered wreck. The 1970-vintage equipment broke down constantly. The Siberian oil workers, brought in for weeklong work shifts, had to live in rusted metal sheds with no toilets or running water. Worst of all, the glass windows of the sheds had been broken for over a year and were still not properly repaired. The makeshift cardboard or plastic patches did little to keep out the Arctic cold. "We have the oil but not the money," drilling master Nikolai Pershin explained bitterly.

His workers were convinced that corrupt Russian officials in the new era of capitalist reform were lining their pockets with oil earnings that should have been invested in improving field conditions. "Someone up high is raking in money on oil, but we workers never see it," a twenty-nine-year-old driller named Vasily groused. "I can't even afford a decent pair of winter boots." He and others agreed pay and working conditions had been better under Brezhnev's communism.

Almost everything was wrong here—unhappy workers, underfunded operations, poor results. There was no way Russian crews like this one were going to bring in the new oil riches needed to finance Yeltsin's reforms and get the national economy back on its feet. Nor was there even a hint of budget help to improve that prospect anytime soon. Nor was foreign expertise going to make a difference in the foreseeable future. At the time, a Canadian firm had spent $10 million bringing in the latest equipment to drill test wells in the region. But Russian bureaucratic infighting over who had the authority to supervise the Canadian project—the national oil ministry, or the regional or the local government authorities—delayed the operation. After three months of wrangling there was still no permission to start test drilling. Disgusted, the Canadians cut their losses and went home. Their new equipment never got a chance to show how it could help.

Sadly, the Siberian example was all too typical. Yeltsin's intended radical reforms were in real trouble in the countryside, where they were counted on most to produce desperately needed results. The bitter truth was that reform needed to show improved economic results soon, in order to establish a stable democracy, but there were too many cards from the holdover Soviet deck stacked against any early economic improvement, among them corruption, bureaucratic red tape, inertia, and ignorance. And if economic reform failed, democracy in Russia would almost certainly perish with it. Such were the conclusions likely to be drawn from virtually any trip to the Russian countryside in Yeltsin's first year. It was an omen to be taken seriously. Over the Yeltsin years conditions would get worse rather than better. Odds began to build against the success of his democratic experiment.

Still, the outlook was not entirely bleak. Russia was not an economic basket case. It was not Bangladesh, not some Third World pauper dependent on a Western handout to avoid mass starvation. On the contrary, Russia was potentially one of the richest countries in the world, with vast wealth in oil, natural gas, gold, diamonds, and many other valuable natural resources. It was one of the world's largest producers of steel and other essential commodities. It had a well-educated elite. And yet, despite all those advantages, Russia's economy was still on the edge of collapse, not because of any inherent weakness, but simply because it had been appallingly mismanaged over the past seventy-four years by the Communist economic system.

To give but one illustration, the Russian economy Boris Yeltsin inherited was in a state of supply chaos. Moscow in 1992 was the only capital in the world where people lined up on street corners to buy burned out lightbulbs. The reason was simple. No new ones were then available in the shops. If a lightbulb blew at home, the only way to replace it was to steal one from the office. To hide the theft at the office, a burned-out bulb had to be inserted in place of the working one removed. Thus the demand for dead lightbulbs.

In the Russian economy, distorted by communism for most of the century, conversion to a more rational market system would be impossible overnight, or even in a few years. Businessmen, bankers, and economists had to be reeducated. Laws had to be approved to create and protect markets and to combat organized crime. Companies and investments had to be established and prove themselves. Proper distribution systems had to be created. Decades would be needed. And no politician—not Boris Yeltsin nor anyone else—could count on decades in office to do the job.

There was the rub. Conservative forces waited in the wings, ready to seize on economic failure to drive the nation back toward dictatorship. Yeltsin's reformers risked having too little time to do too big a job. Still, they refused to be discouraged. Russian reformers had been given a chance most thought would never come in their lifetimes. The death of communism had at last made genuine democratic and market reforms possible. They were determined to use the opportunity to the fullest extent possible. They thought big, admitted the struggle would be long and hard, then forged ahead. But from the very beginning, they underestimated the task.

This first became evident to me when I visited the newly renamed St. Petersburg in 1991 in the final months of Soviet power. I went to see Mayor Anatoly Sobchak at his office in the Mariinsky Palace, where many Russian tsars had made history, including Aleksandr II, who signed there the proclamation that freed the serfs in 1861, allowing Russia to rise to the ranks of Europe's industrial powers. Now Sobchak was determined to free his people from the shackles of Communist economic failure. As he saw it, the city that gave birth to Soviet communism in 1917 would lead the return to capitalism. "We are no longer Leningrad," he said. "St. Petersburg will rise again in all its greatness."

Perhaps never before had the city's future looked brighter. St. Petersburg was the heart of the Soviet Union's military-industrial complex, with 20 percent of the national research and development budget. With the fall of the U.S.S.R., that asset was to be converted to high-tech civilian production, a Silicon Valley of Russia. Also, with the loss of the Soviet Union's Black Sea ports to the newly independent Ukraine, St. Petersburg was now, once again, Russia's largest port, its leading window on the West, as it had been in the days of its founder, Tsar Peter the Great.

The city planned to expand the port into a major center of East-West trade. St. Petersburg would become an economic free zone, luring foreign investors by lifting currency restrictions and offering cheap labor. The resultant economic boom would finance restoration of the most beautiful palaces north of Paris and revive the cultural standing of the city that gave the world Pushkin, Dostoevsky, and Tchaikovsky. "In ten years this city will be one of the largest financial and cultural capitals in Europe," Sobchak told me. Such was the vision of Russia's radical reformers.

The reality was something else. Never since the nine-hundred-day Nazi blockade in World War II had the city suffered as much as it did in 1991, the year the Soviet Union collapsed. St. Petersburg's pothole-filled streets reminded the visitor of rural Siberia. Drinking water came out of the tap the color of tea. Sugar, butter, meat, and eggs were rationed, and bread was in short supply. City officials admitted they could not get through the winter without Western aid. Germany offered 100,000 tons of potatoes in that cause, if St. Petersburg could provide the transport. In desperation, the mayor's office called the only available resource, the navy, which had to send a battleship to pick up the potatoes in order to keep the city afloat in the winter ahead.

On a small scale, reforms were beginning to work. Nadezhda Druganova, twenty-four, was one of the early success stories. In April 1991, she and friends from a puppet theater scraped together the cash to buy a city toy shop bankrupted by state supply shortages. Nadezhda and her friends made their own unique, high-quality stuffed toys. Most were imaginary animals, like the one with bulging frog's eyes, antennae for ears, and a rabbit's tail. The irresistibly cuddly toys were her only ads. Mothers saw them held by toddlers, asked where to buy them, and crossed the city to her shop. Sales rose from the ruble equivalent of $36,000 in May to $300,000 in September. Nadezhda saw herself soon becoming a capitalist millionaire. "I want to buy two more shops," she told me. The city was also benefiting. It sold 160 shops like Nadezhda's to private entrepreneurs in 1991 for more than $5 million, and stood to make millions more from taxes on their increasing profits.

On a larger scale, however, the outlook was grim. The huge state-owned Arsenal factory in St. Petersburg was a good example. It first made cannons for the Russian navy, and later became a contractor for space-age rockets. Now it was supposed to be converting from defense to civilian production. Technically, it was doing well. The gas cooling equipment the plant produced for the Soviet space shuttle *Buryan* was converted into a breakthrough in commercial refrigerating units. The problem was finance. Factory director Vyacheslav Petrov explained that they needed a loan of $8 million to retool production lines in order to produce sales of over $100 million in the new refrigeration units. He applied for the money to three government ministries and four state committees, all without reply. "If I don't hear soon, I am going to turn our cannons on the bureaucrats," Petrov said. "That's a joke," he added. He didn't look like he was kidding.

Private financing was not an alternative yet. It was just getting started. The St. Petersburg Stock Exchange, founded in 1990, met Tuesdays and Thursdays in a former exhibition hall. The hundred or so brokers, mostly tieless young men in jeans and leather jackets, would bid for shares or commodity contracts. They had learned their craft from the only available Russian-language books in local libraries—pre-1917 texts, hardly the cutting edge of modern finance. It was only one indication of how far Russia had to go in building a market economy.

On balance, my 1991 visit to St. Petersburg showed, the city's hopes would likely be crushed by the hugeness of the task ahead. Sure enough, three years later, Sobchak's grandiose plans for the rebirth of St. Petersburg had still not gotten off the ground. A few big foreign companies invested in the area, among them Gillette and Unilever, but their trickle is far from the flood Sobchak anticipated. Political instability, inflation, and Mafia violence have been discouraging factors. But the major curb on foreign investment is the lack of legal protection and a stable tax system. For that, Mayor Sobchak needed help from the national government, particularly new laws to reduce the tax burden on foreign companies, protect their patents, and fight the economic crimes ushered in by market reforms. Similarly, the mayor needed national government help to fund port expansion and defense conversion. The Russian parliament, however, had a conservative majority opposed to the kind of reforms Sobchak had in mind. It denied St. Petersburg the legislative help the city needed.

Some well-informed officials foresaw long ago that the mayor's ambitious plans would falter. "You cannot build capitalism in just one city," Anatoly Chubais, then Sobchak's economic adviser, and the architect of the city's groundbreaking privatization program, told me in 1991. Chubais was right—and lucky. He would soon get the chance to prove his point. There was no way capitalism could be built in one city alone. If it was ever to work properly, it had to be tried across the entire country.

Boris Yeltsin understood that perfectly well. The Russian president also realized that if capitalism was to work across the nation as a whole it would have to be built on the sort of privatization effort that Chubais had successfully launched in St. Petersburg, by encouraging shops like Nadezhda's toy store. This pioneering city experiment would now be a model for the nation, and Yeltsin would pick Chubais to run it. The president soon called Chubais to Moscow, made him a deputy prime minister, and put him in charge of the program to privatize all of Russia's state-owned business. For a reform economist, there was no more important job in the nation, an absolutely crucial task in the Russian power struggle after the fall of communism.

That struggle has been described in many different ways. Some commentators saw it as a battle between president and parliament. Others called it a fight between reformers and conservatives. Still others viewed it as a contest between democracy and totalitarianism, or as a drive by the smaller restructured Communist Party of Russia, now in opposition, to regain power. It was all those things, but the most important struggle was almost never mentioned: the clash between the advocates of public and private ownership of property. From 1992 on, the nature of property was the key issue that would determine the outcome of all other power struggles in Russia. In Gorbachev's day, the key question had been communism or reform. In Yeltsin's it was public or private property.

Property covered everything above or under the soil, from housing to industry, agriculture, and the nation's vast mineral wealth. In Russian terms, a shift to private ownership of property—a breaking up of state monopolies into the hands of individuals—involved transferring decision-making power from a dictatorial state to free people. The more decision-making power in private hands, the better the chance of strengthening both political democracy and the market economy. The more decision-making power remaining in the hands of conservative state officials, the greater the threat of a return to political dictatorship and the command economy. Yeltsin and the reformers understood that. They intentionally focused the economic reform effort on privatization. And, indeed, the sell-off of former state property soon became their most popular measure. Each citizen received free of charge a privatization voucher worth the ruble equivalent of $15. Vouchers could be exchanged for shares in former state companies, or they could be traded like shares themselves—bought, sold, or held in the hope their value would increase.

Workers could band together, buy their formerly state-run shops or factories, and turn them into private businesses. Similarly, tenants who had rented from the state could now buy and privatize their apartments. In short, private property, banned under the Soviet regime, had suddenly become a fact of life in the new Russia. Any citizen could now become a property owner. Polls showed the idea to be so popular that at first not even the Communists dared campaign against it.

Privatization brought a second, equally important political benefit to Yeltsin's camp. It not only generated public support for his reformers, but also destroyed a major power base of their conservative opponents, namely publicly owned property. Conservatives in the new Russia were mostly privileged holdovers from Soviet days. Some were bureaucrats in government ministries running every industry in the country from milk to steel, others regional barons in charge of vast sections of the nation, still others managers of huge state factories or farms. All of them drew their power from the public ownership of property. If farms and factories and housing were all to be privatized, their power base would be gone, and their jobs and privileges with it. For these bureaucrats, the battle against privatization was a struggle for survival. And in that battle they had one great advantage. Together with other conservative forces like the military, the nationalists, and the Communists, they controlled a majority in the new Russian parliament. The conservatives were determined to defeat privatization in parliament with new laws delaying, weakening, and eventually killing it.

Thus were the battle lines drawn. The property issue was seen by all sides as the key in the struggle between president and parliament in the first instance, and ultimately between the forces of totalitarian control and democratic reform. As the minister in charge of privatization, Anatoly Chubais was the man in the hottest seat in government. He was racing against time, determined to privatize as much as he could as quickly as he could, to make reform irreversible by later parliamentary action or military coup.

The conservative opposition was just as committed to stopping him before he got there. "The political fight over privatization has become the crucial one," Chubais told me in Moscow in a March 1993 interview. This tall, thin, soft-spoken redhead had become the key yardstick for measuring the prospects of the Yeltsin reforms. While he remained in office pushing privatization, the reforms had a chance. If the conservatives forced Yeltsin to get rid of him and halt privatization, the reforms were as good as finished.[1]

II. CRIME PAYS

The fight over privatization was indeed the critical one. It would determine the success of the economic reforms, which in turn would seal the fate of political reform. With so much at stake, I decided in 1993 to take a closer look at the privatization effort, which was off to a promising although troubled start. Nowhere was that clearer than in Nizhni Novgorod, a city of 1.5 million people commanding Volga River trade routes. Its young, progressive administration, run by Governor Boris Nemtsov, gave Nizhni Novgorod and the surrounding region Russia's largest and most successful privatization program. Nemtsov was elected governor in 1991 when only thirty-two years old. In little over a year, he had privatized some 40 percent of the area's enterprises. He was also the first governor in Russia to auction farmland to private owners. His success as a reformer, his movie-star dark good looks, and the brains that earned him a Ph.D. in physics had turned Nemtsov into the most talked-about young political leader in the country. Many, including Boris Yeltsin, spoke of him as a possible future president of Russia. I decided to take the 250-mile trip east from Moscow to meet Nemtsov and see how well the showcase privatization example was really doing.

Nemtsov was an extraordinary young man. Under Communist rule, well before the Gorbachev reforms, when the city was still called Gorky, he was the only would-be politician with the courage and foresight to befriend and learn from the most famous political exile under house arrest there, Andrei Sakharov. Later, in August 1991, Nemtsov stood at Yeltsin's side defending the Moscow White House. Since then, he had pioneered privatization, with help from resident Western advisers, as the best defense against backsliding toward totalitarian rule.

Nemtsov was also a refreshing change from the older Russian officials lobbying for huge outlays of U.S. financial aid. "It would be better for America to organize aggressive technical assistance than to send Russia billions of dollars," he told me. Nemtsov had in mind expert advisers sent from the United States at government expense to start a private banking system, improve management skills, and create small businesses in Russia. "This kind of thing is not very expensive for the United States and will yield better results in only a few years," he said. Also unlike his older, corrupted political counterparts elsewhere, Nemtsov continued to live modestly. The governor and his wife and daughter resided in only a two-room apartment, a factor that helped him retain voter support. Despite his strong leadership and enlightened views, however, privatization did not live up to its advance billing in the Nizhni Novgorod showcase in March 1993.

Igor Kanashkin's cheese shop, which was supposed to be one of the great success stories, turned out to be the first disappointment. After a year of private management, his shop outsold the state cheese store down the road by eight to one, but Kanashkin was not a happy man. The state took 70 percent of his income in taxes, he complained. Worse, local officials, even in a reformist city like Nizhni Novgorod, still demanded bribes to let delivery trucks get anywhere near his door. Worse still, Kanashkin only managed to lease his shop from the city for five years, rather than buy it outright. Technically that qualified as privatization, but it sounded a lot better than it was. Although Kanashkin got to keep any profits from the sale of cheese, the city would get the big money from his success, not him. That was because the city could reclaim the shop after five years and sell it at auction to the highest bidder, probably for ten times what Kanashkin had paid for the lease. By then he would be looking for other work, Kanashkin said, because there was no way he could raise enough money to buy the shop himself when the lease was up. "They call us private owners, but we're not," Kanashkin told me bitterly.

Vitaly Yanover's short-haul trucking firm was the second disappointment. Yanover and his workers actually bought full ownership of their business, not just a lease. That change was one of Nemtsov's more recent improvements, but it led only to new problems. Six months after Yanover privatized the business, the city had second thoughts. It had previously run the trucking firm, and had built a number of assets with city funds, among them a small swimming pool and rest house for the drivers. Belatedly, city officials decided they should not have included these assets in the privatization sale. So, at a stroke, they took them back, expropriating them for city use again, without paying the private trucking firm a kopeck in return. They were showing, once again, that Soviet management habits die hard.

The new Russia, however, was already a very different place. Now businessmen at last had recourse against the old Soviet bureaucratic ways. At the time, Yanover was on vacation in Israel, something he could not have done in Soviet days. His workers phoned him there, something they could not have done from the U.S.S.R. Yanover immediately telephoned Alan Bigman, an American adviser to Nemtsov, who got the governor to reverse the city's decision. The swimming pool and rest house remained in the private company's hands. "Bigman saved us," Yanover told me in an interview. "He convinced Nemtsov that letting us keep our assets would encourage privatization." Incredibly, a Russian businessman could now fix a problem by phoning the

American adviser to a Russian political leader. Clearly remarkable changes were taking place. But at the same time, Yanover's story also showed how far the privatization effort had to go to become irreversible.

Continued harassment from bureaucrats was only one problem Russia's new private businesses had to face. Cash flow was another. Because of cash flow problems, Yanover's trucking firm risked bankruptcy. Thanks to Russia's disastrous economy, his clients already owed him more than $50,000 in unpaid bills. To keep operating, Yanover took a one-year bank loan for twice that amount. He got what passed for sweetheart terms in Russia, since his private company was a founding member of one of the region's new private cooperative banks. They charged him only 80 percent interest instead of the usual 130 percent. Those exorbitant interest rates were only part of the horrendous financial bind squeezing new private firms like Yanover's.

What happens, I asked Yanover, if clients still cannot pay when the loan runs out? "We'll maneuver," he replied, meaning he would try to dream up something. "The main thing is that as private owners we make the decisions, not the state. There can be no going back." He and others certainly hope that is true, but they will need more than blind faith to make privatization survive in Russia.

At the time, Chubais was boasting in Moscow that he had already privatized sixty thousand firms across Russia. There were no figures, however, on how many of these were simply short-term leases, like Kanashkin's, or on the brink of financial disaster, like Yanover's. The struggle over privatization was a long way from being won.

Aleksandr Lavrov, the privatization chief for Nizhni Novgorod, provided the third disappointment. In December 1992, he said, city officials were privatizing twenty-five firms a week. Four months later they were down to half that rate. The city wouldn't make its target of privatizing 60 percent of its small shops by the end of 1993, he told me. "The reason is the situation in the country," Lavrov said. "The opposition is getting too strong." By opposition, he meant conservative forces in the Russian parliament in Moscow, anxious to shut down the shift from public to private property. Rampant corruption across Russia played into their hands. Bent officials were making huge illegal profits from privatization, threatening to discredit the program irreparably in the public eye and hastening the day when the conservative parliament could quash it.

In Moscow, former Communist officials were largely to blame. They changed hats, became "democrats," and continued to steal from their own people. Naturally, their methods had been revised. In Communist days they stole by underpaying workers, in order to finance privileges for themselves. Now as capitalists they stole public buildings for their own profit. To these predators, the transition to private enterprise proved to be a godsend. For the first time, their larceny was taking in big bucks.

Unlike Hitler's Nazis, Soviet Communist senior officials never paid for their crimes against their own people—for the murders carried out by their secret police, or even for their thefts. The reason was simple. The Nazis paid only because they lost a war and the victors imposed the Nuremberg trials on them. But Soviet Communists were not defeated in war. No foreign power could impose trials on them and convict them as war criminals. And former Soviet Communists were not about to put themselves on trial. Instead they preferred to declare themselves democrats or capitalists. They continued to run the nation as the most experienced officials available, and they kept on thieving, only now for much bigger profits.

One common scam worked this way. Officials formed private companies, bought hundreds of former state buildings at rock-bottom prices, resold them at huge profits, and banked the gains abroad. They bribed the bureaucrats who sold low with all-expense-paid trips to the West, or high-paying jobs in their firms that required no work, or just plain cash. One of the richest men in Moscow in 1993 was said to be E. I. Bystrov, a former aide to Gorbachev turned property wheeler-dealer. Bystrov reportedly still had four special Kremlin telephone lines on his desk for his real estate dealing. "The democrats are more corrupt than the Communists," Denis Molchanov, an investigative reporter for the respected weekly *Literaturnaya Gazeta,* said.

Molchanov showed me evidence to back his claim. One document, signed by the former liberal mayor Gavriil Popov when he was still chairman of the Moscow city council, awarded a $2 billion redevelopment contract for hotels, office blocks, and a shopping mall in central Moscow to a Russian-French joint venture of which Popov conveniently served on the board of directors. His conflict of interest was so blatant, even for Moscow, that officials quashed the deal. In the end, however, Molchanov failed to make the case that the democrats were now more corrupt than the Communists, for the simple reason that they were often the same people. Yesterday's corrupt Communists were today's corrupt democrats.

The cast of characters may have been the same, but politically, corruption was now helping the conservative side of the power struggle, thanks to a very cozy arrangement. First, former Communists engaged in corrupt business practices. Then other former Communists, now conservative members of parliament, blamed the problem not on their former Party colleagues but on Yeltsin's reforms. In the resultant publicity generated by newspapers like Molchanov's, the general public was convinced that corruption was indeed worse since the reforms began, and that the reforms were therefore to blame.

The real problem was not the reforms themselves, but rather the lack of a legal framework to make sure the players in the new economic climate would act responsibly. In the absence of enforceable laws, unscrupulous officials and businessmen could exploit the reforms more or less as they wished, in order to line their own pockets—with complete impunity. The first major lesson of capitalism Russian-style was simply that crime pays. Yeltsin's Russia was rapidly becoming a twentieth-century Yukon, a lawless rush for private wealth. The ugliest face of socialism had been replaced by the ugliest face of capitalism.

Crime and corruption had been problems in Russia before, of course. Many people still blamed Gorbachev's reforms for creating the Russian Mafia. Under Yeltsin's more radical changes, however, both the Mafia and official corruption rapidly expanded. The Russian Mafia became a nationwide menace, with global reach in a wide variety of criminal activities from drug and arms dealing to art theft. Official corruption was so widespread that by 1993 the accepted bribe just to get in to see a government minister was $10,000.

Far more money was leaving the country illegally than coming in from Western aid.[2] Much of it was the ill-gotten gains of corrupt officials who preferred to keep them in the safety of foreign accounts. A friend who runs a private investment bank in Geneva, which demands a minimum of $1 million to open an account, told me the majority of his new clients were now Russians.

In Nizhni Novgorod, Nemtsov attempted to free his privatization from such corruption. State properties were auctioned off in public to the highest bidder, to prevent corrupt officials from fixing deals in private. But that only created another problem. Soon prices soared so high that only criminal syndicates, the Russian Mafia, could afford to buy at property auctions. "The scale of the process makes some corruption inevitable," Chubais told me. In Russia that scale meant thousands of people handling millions of dollars in property deals, with no legal framework in place to check wrongdoing.

Not surprisingly, Al Capone ethics soon riddled the Russian capital, and privatization was only one angle. Extortion and protection rackets also flourished. When all else failed, hired killers could be employed to eliminate troublemakers or competitors. According to Molchanov's newspaper, some sixty professionals in Moscow offered such services by early 1993 for minimum fees of $5,000, satisfaction guaranteed within twenty-four hours. Drive-by shootings soon came to Russia. By 1994, the murder rate in Moscow topped New York's. Not all the new democratic officials or capitalist businessmen were corrupt, of course. Far from it. But enough enriched themselves illegally to make official corruption and criminal Mafia ties a major scandal of the Yeltsin era.

Indeed, official corruption may have been exaggerated in the public mind for political reasons. In Communist days, political scores were settled on ideological grounds. Rivals were removed on charges of ideological deviation. But in the democratic Yeltsin era, that would no longer do. A new basis for political infighting had to be found, and it didn't take long. Yeltsin's top aides and his leading political rivals began smearing each other with charges of corruption and Mafia links. Whatever the truth of these accusations, the mud stuck. Suddenly official corruption had become a major public concern in Russia.

Conservatives at last had the issue they had been waiting for. Now they eagerly exploited public anxiety over rising corruption and crime, claiming them to be the inevitable result of Yeltsin's privatization and other reforms. No one longed to return to Stalinist tyranny. But the milder Brezhnev police state began to look better in retrospect to Russian public opinion. A little over a year into Boris Yeltsin's revolution, capitalist criminality was seriously tarnishing the image of reform and Yeltsin's reformers themselves. Progressives admitted as much. "Just as a fish begins to rot from the head down, so the fight against corruption must start at the very top," said Yeltsin's former finance minister Boris Fyodorov, a leading liberal. By the "very top" he meant Yeltsin's inner circle in the Kremlin, which either had to root out corruption or take responsibility for letting it flourish.

III. SHOCK WITHOUT THERAPY

Corruption was bad enough, but it was far from the only issue giving Yeltsin's reforms a bad name. If anything, economic performance was an even worse problem. Yeltsin had begun 1992 with enormous political capital. He had stopped the August 1991 coup, defeated Soviet communism, and created a new, more democratic Russia by the end of 1991. The stage was set to fulfill his greatest ambition. He could now embark on radical economic reform, unhindered by the former Communist controls. Unfortunately for him, within a year much of that political capital had been frittered away by a disastrous economic record. Yeltsin had gone for a speedy transition to a market economy. He promised his radical reforms would begin to show economic improvement in less than a year, then failed to deliver and lost credibility. Both Yeltsin and his reforms have been in deep political trouble ever since.

The key economic decision leading to Yeltsin's continuing political troubles was the freeing of prices. Under the Soviet system, prices had been set by the state, often artificially low, significantly less than the cost of production on key items like meat and other food products. Government subsidies making up the difference were bankrupting the state. The irrational price system had been a major cause of the long Soviet economic decline. A transition to a market economy inevitably meant freeing prices so they could rise to market levels, according to supply and demand. Everyone knew prices had to go up. The only question was how fast. One option, "shock therapy," was to free prices immediately. Another was to lift price controls more gradually, a less painful course but potentially less effective. Yegor Gaidar, Yeltsin's radical acting prime minister, and his Western advisers persuaded him to go with shock therapy.

In his 1992 New Year's address to the nation, Yeltsin said things would have to get worse before they got better. Under shock therapy, prices would be freed from January 2, he said, and they would rise. But the higher prices would encourage increased production, filling the shops and ending the Russian disease of long lines outside nearly empty stores. "Within six to eight months," the Russian president promised, prices would stabilize at lower levels and the economy would begin to recover. "We should not give in to feelings of defeat," he said. "What has been defeated is not Russia but the Communist idea, the experiment that was thrust upon our people." Yeltsin asked his people to trust him. There was no alternative to radical reform, he said, to return Russia to economic health. The phrase no one forgot was Yeltsin's promise that economic recovery would begin "within six to eight months."

That was the theory. The reality was something else. On January 2, 1992, the sign at the supermarket on Moscow's Kalinin Prospekt read, "Happy New Year." Shoppers took it as a sick joke. The store had reopened for the first time after the holidays with prices raised to market levels. Bread prices had soared 400 percent, flour 1,100 percent, and sour cream 2,000 percent. I took some informal soundings outside the store, and virtually all Russians I spoke with were outraged.

"We used to go shopping with one ten-ruble note," said Yuri, a worker. "Now we need a suitcase full of them."

"The new prices are a crime," said Anna, a pensioner.

"We ate better during the war," complained Nina, a chemist.

Worst of all, Yeltsin's prediction of lower, stabilized prices in six to eight months soon stood out as hopelessly wrong. Instead, inflation topped 1,900 percent in 1992 and climbed another 900 percent in 1993, according to official figures.

Russia was changing at a dizzying pace, and most people thought the changes were for the worse. Before there had been almost nothing in the shops, and endless lines outside. Now stores were full and there were no lines outside, because few could afford the prices. When there had been nothing to buy, people piled up savings. With runaway inflation, their life savings quickly vanished.

Not everyone suffered. A new entrepreneurial class emerged, often younger people more willing to take risks, and soon numbered in the tens of thousands across the country. Some of them sold consumer goods privately from sidewalk kiosks. Others started private companies. Either way, they tended to get rich quick. A nation that had been uniformly poor by Western standards suddenly displayed vast disparities of extreme wealth and extreme poverty. The most successful of the new entrepreneurs bought foreign cars, designer clothes, even villas in the West, while the average Russian could barely feed his family.

The new disparities in wealth were only one problem. Worse for the country's prospects, the reforms were killing Russian science, one of its few real hopes for long-term economic progress and salvation. Freed at last from Soviet controls, Russia's scientific labs now had opportunities to produce new products, win export markets, and put the economy right. Instead the reforms were breaking up the labs. The reason was a new scale of economic values.

The backbone of Russian science had long been highly skilled laboratory research teams. In Soviet days they were elite state employees with relatively high salaries and privileges. But under the Yeltsin reforms they became a poor underclass. They no longer got the defense contracts that had largely funded them in the past. And their state pay soon fell hopelessly behind incomes in the new private sector. A middle-aged physicist with a Ph.D. on state salary now made ten or even twenty times less than his eighteen-year-old son who traded consumer goods from a street kiosk in one of the private markets. Not surprisingly, one of the major results of the new values and new pay scales brought in by the Yeltsin reforms was an alarming breakup of the nation's scientific laboratory teams.

The older scientists soon retired on pension. Middle-level specialists now free to emigrate to the West and command higher salaries did so, in a damaging brain drain. Younger lab specialists often quit to earn far more money as street traders. Within the first two years of Yeltsin's rule, many of the nation's scientific research teams dissolved. Nor were they likely to be replaced anytime soon. Bright young people avoided university training as pointless and chose instead to become street traders, the quick road to new riches. Russia soon risked losing much of the next generation of trained scientific specialists it desperately needed.

Meanwhile the less enterprising and the disadvantaged suffered most of all. Their average state salaries barely kept pace with rising prices. Pensions bought only one two-pound sausage a month. Senior citizens survived only with help from relatives and friends. There was no mass starvation, but neither was there the beginning of the promised recovery. In their daily struggle to survive, Russians had largely lost faith in Yeltsin and his reforms. At the same time, they also lost faith in the help America and the West could provide. Capitalism, after all, was the West's system. Russia tried it—and things only got worse. "They tried to put an American suit on Russia and it didn't fit," said Gennady Zyuganov, head of the Russian Communist Party.

Part of the problem was unrealistic expectations. Russians anticipated far more Western aid than they got. They had hoped for a miraculous foreign bailout. But their prayers went unanswered. "They thought we were going to send a convoy of Brinks trucks into the Kremlin," Robert Strauss, then the U.S. ambassador, told reporters. In fact, there was no way the United

States and its allies could provide the scope of aid needed, as we have seen.[3] Russia needed more than $100 billion worth of financial aid, and the best the West could talk about was $6 billion. Perhaps the most valuable aid the West could provide was expert advice on building a market economy. Russia would have to finance most of the cost itself.

Unfortunately, Western advice, much of it American, was not always all that good either. Shock therapy was a case in point. It had been successful in Poland, so the Western advisers urged it on Moscow, but Russia was not simply a larger Poland, where the same reforms could be expected to work. It was fundamentally different. For one thing, "the aggregate spending on defense in this country devours 25–30 percent of GNP," said independent Russian economist Vasily Selyunin. Poland did not have to worry about a military procurement system gone mad. Furthermore, when the Solidarity government in Poland launched shock therapy, it enjoyed greater public support than Yeltsin's did in Russia. Nor did Poland have the explosive mix of more than a hundred minority nationalities threatening ethnic strife in Russia.

To be fair, however, there is no way of knowing whether a more gradual transition to market prices would have worked any better in Russia. The slower option, tried in the Ukraine, produced disastrous inflation there too. Indeed, Russia's economy was so badly damaged by communism that virtually any cure would have inevitably been extremely long and painful. But none of that is relevant now. The point is that shock therapy was applied. As far as most Russians are concerned, the pain it produced discredited Yeltsin's policy of radical reform devised in the West. All they felt was the shock, never the therapy.

IV. A POLITICAL SEA CHANGE

At the end of his first year as president of the new democratic Russia, Yeltsin was fast losing his political credibility. Instead of enjoying his promised economic recovery, Russians still suffered increasing economic misery. Corruption scandals further tarnished his reforms. As the president's personal standing declined, the political advantage shifted to his more conservative rivals running the Russian parliament. They proved that in December 1992 when the parliament forced the resignation of Prime Minister Yegor Gaidar, thirty-six, the young architect of shock therapy and symbol of radical economic reform. Yeltsin replaced him as premier with Viktor Chernomyrdin, then fifty-four, a holdover oil minister from Soviet days, who favored more cautious policies.

The new prime minister was a compromise acceptable to the hard-liners. Chernomyrdin would slow reform but not reverse it. There was no doubt the conservatives would now move to finish the job. Their next target would be Yeltsin himself. "I am concerned about the danger of a radical nationalist and Communist takeover," Gaidar told me in an interview in February 1993. He was right to worry. A month later, hard-liners in parliament made their first attempt to impeach Yeltsin. They withdrew their motion at the last minute after counting noses and finding themselves only forty votes short of the 691 needed to impeach. But the political battle between president and parliament was only warming up, and it had a familiar ring, recalling Gorbachev's final year in office. Once again, hard-liners had tried first to weaken a reformist president by parliamentary means. When that failed, the likelihood only increased that another attempted armed coup was on the way.

For the next six months the struggle got increasingly tense. The parliament accused Yeltsin of exceeding his authority and violating the constitution by taking major policy initiatives without consulting them. The president countered by saying both the parliament, elected in 1990 under Soviet rule, and the constitution, written under Brezhnev in 1978, no longer had any legitimacy. Thus, Yeltsin claimed, in refusing to adopt the laws he wanted, deputies were illegally obstructing reform. With the political process thus paralyzed, there was no hope of new measures to improve the economy.

Yeltsin finally provoked the crisis that would prove decisive. On September 21, 1993, he dissolved the parliament and announced he would rule by decree until new legislative elections in December. Conservative deputies defied him by blockading themselves in the White House, claiming they were now Russia's only legitimate government. Like everything else in the new Russia, even symbols were changing at a breakneck pace. The White House, the same building that had symbolized democratic resistance to the hard-line coup in 1991, became the headquarters of an antidemocratic coup attempt only two years later.

Yeltsin himself seemed to be changing just as rapidly. The champion of Russian democracy was now leading the nation from the Kremlin, and showing little tolerance for his hard-line political foes holed up in the parliament to which they had been freely elected. He ordered their electricity and water supplies cut in an effort to force them out of the building and end their defiance. Still they refused to budge. Their leaders, parliamentary speaker Ruslan Khasbulatov and Vice President Aleksandr Rutskoi, both former senior Yeltsin aides, were now his opponents, in yet another dramatic role reversal. They had stocked the White House with weapons and mercenaries and were well prepared for a showdown. President Yeltsin was not. "We were not preparing for war," he admitted later. The reason, Yeltsin aides told me, was a betrayal by the security services.

The Yeltsin team had no accurate account of the activities inside the White House, no fix on the number of armed men in that building or the extent of their weaponry. Both the security ministry, the successor to the KGB, and the interior ministry, responsible for the uniformed police, had failed to report such essentials to Yeltsin's Kremlin. It was the first indication that the security services would sit on the sidelines and let the president fend for himself in the coming crisis. It was far from the last.

On Sunday, October 3, Rutskoi and Khasbulatov made their move. They sent an armed force to seize Moscow's main broadcasting center, the TV tower at Ostankino, and call for an uprising to overthrow Yeltsin. To get there, busloads of armed men had to cross the city in broad daylight. No police or KGB security troops made any attempt to stop them on the way. "The reason was clear," the Yeltsin aide told me. "Senior officials in both the interior ministry and the former KGB were sitting on the fence, waiting to see which side would win the struggle."

The attack caught the Yeltsin team totally by surprise. Not one senior presidential aide was on standby duty that Sunday afternoon in the Kremlin. Belatedly they hurried in, but it was hours before they coordinated an effective response. The nationwide evening TV news carried horrendous pictures of the continuing battle outside the Ostankino TV tower, with heavy gunfire streaking across the night sky. Eventually special "alpha" forces loyal to Yeltsin beat back the attack, but the White House command center, headquarters of the hard-line opposition, was still functioning. Rumors spread that Rutskoi and Khasbulatov were now rallying fresh troops for an attack on the Kremlin.

Inside the Kremlin walls, Yeltsin put in a phone call to Defense Minister Pavel Grachev. With the KGB and the police on the sidelines, the military was his last chance. The president asked for army support, but General Grachev stalled. The defense minister had repeatedly insisted in public that the armed forces would remain outside any domestic political struggle. Also, Grachev was not sure of his troops. Before making any commitment to Yeltsin, he had to be absolutely certain the armed forces would support the president. The caution was justified. In the August 1991 coup, Defense Minister Yazov had assumed he could carry the high command with him, but in fact the air force chief of staff and other key uniformed chiefs had refused to go along. Grachev would not make the same mistake. So he called a meeting of the collegium, the defense ministry's top brass, to consider Yeltsin's request. The meeting ran through most of the night.

The delay unsettled the Yeltsin team. "Fear turned to panic," recalled Sergei Parkhomenko, a Russian political reporter covering the Kremlin. Another Russian journalist there described the scene as "pandemonium." Yeltsin called Grachev several times. The president finally came to the defense ministry well after midnight that fateful Sunday, to appeal personally to the entire collegium for army support. Again, Yeltsin was told to wait. It was already 3:00 A.M. Once he left, Grachev polled the room. Only when all the other collegium members had spoken in support of the president did the defense minister himself sign on.

Soon Yeltsin phoned once more. This time the president was no longer asking. As commander in chief he was ordering armored troops to be brought into Moscow to recapture the White House and put down the rebellion. "I give you the appropriate orders. I take full responsibility for it," Yeltsin said.

"I understand," Grachev replied. The decision to use the army for a political battle was the president's, not his. And the collegium had approved.

At long last, the defense minister delivered the army, but even then, Grachev was taking no chances. According to Russian intelligence sources, the tanks that fired on the White House on Monday, October 4, were driven only by loyal officers. The high command was unwilling to risk using the usual conscript tankmen in such a politically sensitive operation.[4]

The television pictures were unforgettable: Russian tanks firing on their own parliament; flames and black smoke billowing from its upper floors; Rutskoi and Khasbulatov humbled and disarmed, led off to prison. The army had turned the tide, in bloody fighting that left at least two hundred people dead. This time, at the last possible minute, it had intervened to save Yeltsin's reformist regime. The immediate reaction in Russia's progressive circles was one of profound relief. "The fact that the president and the democratic forces have won is a true miracle," said Father Gleb Yakunin, a Russian Orthodox priest and a leading progressive in the disbanded parliament. "Russia narrowly escaped fascist rule," agreed *Izvestia* commentator Otto Latsis.

Turning tanks on parliament is hardly democracy. Nonetheless, the United States and other Western governments approved. They accepted Yeltsin's rationale—that a parliament elected under communism, working under a Communist-era constitution, had first obstructed democracy, then tried to overthrow it by armed force, leaving the democratically elected Russian president no choice but to respond by crushing the armed challenge with tanks. Bill Clinton and other Western leaders continued their personal support for Yeltsin as the only hope for consolidating democratic rule in Russia. Once again, the West was behind the curve on the developing political reality in Moscow. Every element in Yeltsin's rationale should have been seriously questioned.

First, the Russian parliament had been elected in 1990, when Soviet power was already in sharp decline and Communists had to compete for seats. It was no less legitimate than Yeltsin himself, elected president of Russia in 1991, under precisely the same conditions of declining Soviet power. Or, put the other way around, the Russian parliament was no more a Communist puppet than President Yeltsin. Second, the constitution of 1978 had already been amended so many times as to be unrecognizable. The charge that it still imposed Brezhnev-era conditions was hard to defend. Third, in the long showdown between September 21 and October 3, Yeltsin made no serious attempt to negotiate a settlement with Khasbulatov and Rutskoi. On the contrary, his government scuttled the one promising effort to settle the crisis peacefully.

This story, entirely unknown in the West, was later told to me by Vyacheslav Novikov, former chairman of the Krasnoyarsk regional parliament in Siberia. Novikov was one of the officials involved in planning the only peacemaking effort with any chance of success. He gave the following account.

On September 26, the governors of Russia's eighty-eight regions planned to meet in St. Petersburg to issue a call for immediate national legislative and presidential elections. Their appeal was to be offered as the only balanced political initiative with a chance of resolving the crisis. In that scenario, both Yeltsin's presidency and Khasbulatov's parliament would have been required to seek a new mandate from the people, instead of sending their armed forces to shoot it out in the streets of Moscow. This initiative, carrying the weight of all regional leaders across the country, might well have averted the October bloodbath. But Yeltsin's prime minister, Viktor Chernomyrdin, sent the governors telegrams ordering them to boycott the September 26 meeting in St. Petersburg and stay home. All but three of them did. The only compromise idea with any prospect of success was thus doomed by the action of Yeltsin's government. "The president wanted this showdown," Novikov told me.

Boris Yeltsin had now come full circle. The hero of August 1991, who stood unarmed on a tank outside the White House to face down a coup and save democratic reform in Russia, had become the trigger-happy heavy of October 1993. This time Yeltsin had ordered tanks to fire on the same building in order to destroy his parliamentary opposition. In so doing, many Russians believed, the president had turned his back on meaningful reform and crushed his nation's hopes for genuine democratic rule. That judgment may yet prove too harsh. But there is no doubt that October 1993 marked a watershed in Yeltsin's fragile experiment in democracy. From then on, the Russian president turned authoritarian, ruling by decree. Little meaningful opposition from parliament or other democratic institutions could be expected in the foreseeable future. Reform was not necessarily dead, but it now depended almost entirely on presidential orders.

It was time for the West to express serious concern about Yeltsin's performance and attempt to influence him back on the democratic path. Instead the Clinton administration and others continued to give him blank-check support. In effect, Boris Nikolayevich could do almost anything he liked, call it transition to democracy, and not have to worry about losing Western backing.

There may have been something inherently Russian in Yeltsin's transformation from radical reformer to authoritarian ruler. Like Gorbachev before him, Yeltsin moved right when his reforms generated enough political trouble to risk bringing him down. But whereas Gorbachev allowed himself to become a temporary prisoner of more conservative forces in the Kremlin leadership, Yeltsin was out front leading the authoritarian charge, and going farther to the right than Gorbachev ever dared.

In short order, Boris Yeltsin used tanks to dissolve his parliament, arrested their leaders, and rounded up some ninety thousand other suspected opponents in a two-week emergency crackdown. Then he drafted a new constitution that increased the president's powers and reduced parliament's. Yeltsin also disbanded the constitutional court that had opposed him in the past and trimmed the powers of regional governments to defy him. Press criticism was blunted by threats to cut off government subsidies of paper supplies. Political opponents were told to tone down criticism of Yeltsin or face investigation by state prosecutors on corruption charges. Democratic pluralism this was not. "The October 1993 tragedy has deprived us of the chance to build a civilized society on the principles of separation of powers and laws," said Valery Zorkin, former chairman of the constitutional court and onetime presidential hopeful. "The overriding task now is to make sure that authoritarianism is not transformed into tyranny."

Parliamentary elections in December 1993 showed that keeping tyranny at bay would not be easy. Yeltsin had expected parties favoring further democratic reform would win a majority in the new legislature, to be called the State Duma. He confidently predicted this to Western visitors, including French Foreign Minister Alain Juppé in November.[5] To put it crudely, having used tanks to wipe out the previously hostile parliament, the Russian president now expected to put its replacement legislature in his pocket. But Yeltsin's confidence was totally misplaced. He lost the parliamentary election he had expected to win.

Instead, hard-line forces won the election. In preferring them, Russian voters had shown they were fed up with the president and with his political allies, the ineffective, squabbling reformist parties in parliament. The public now blamed Yeltsin and his reformist allies for the nation's continuing economic plight and were putting more faith in his hard-line rivals. The conservative nationalist and pro-Communist opposition took 43 percent of the seats in the new parliament, while the president's allies, the democratic reformers, won only 34 percent. Centrists and independents took the rest. For the first time in the post-Soviet era, the political momentum had swung from Yeltsin's reformers to their conservative opposition, reflecting a major shift in voter preferences. Subsequent reports of election irregularities would do nothing to change the result.

Worse for the president and his progressive supporters, there was now every indication this conservative trend would continue to strengthen. Russian political analysts predicted that in the presidential elections scheduled for June 1996, Yeltsin or a democratic successor would likely lose to a more conservative rival. Two years into Yeltsin's democratic experiment, his hard-line opposition was now poised to return to power in a free election. A political sea change had swept the country.

It was time for a preliminary assessment of the Yeltsin years. The bottom line made grim reading. Yeltsin had embarked on the radical reform he promised. Unlike Gorbachev, he was no longer hampered by the need to justify all changes in Communist terms. Indeed, Yeltsin could and did conduct fundamental reform unhampered by Communist controls. But still, his reforms were already in deep trouble because of opposition from an entrenched bureaucracy and an inherently conservative society slow to adopt to new realities. And the new entrepreneurial class, the first to profit from the Yeltsin reforms, was in fact discrediting them. In sum, Yeltsin's reform struggle was proving that even without communism in the way, fundamental reform in Russia would still be a herculean task.

Boris Yeltsin's reforms, largely discredited by economic hardship and rampant corruption, already hung by a thread. Now his conservative opponents, committed to roll back reform, had exploited widespread public dissatisfaction, seized the political initiative from him, and become, entirely legally, a government-in-waiting. Such was the reality on the ground in Russia in December 1993, exactly two years after the collapse of Soviet communism. In the West, government leaders continued to voice pious hopes that reform in Russia was on its irreversible way to stable democracy and a working market economy. Increasingly that began to look like a vision that would never come closer than the horizon.

18

The Waiting Game (1994–95)

I. JITTERS

In any Kremlin leadership struggle the three so-called power ministries—the army, the KGB, and the uniformed police—play decisive roles. In the October 1993 showdown between president and parliament, two of them, the KGB and the police, betrayed Yeltsin, and the third, the army, came on board only at the last moment. It was not the sort of record to instill confidence in the stability of Yeltsin's troubled democratic experiment. Worse for the president, he entered 1994 with two strikes against him. His economic reforms were failing and his conservative opponents had seized the political momentum from him in their December 1993 parliamentary election victory. They were now primed to take over the country, either in the next presidential election or by a coup, with every chance of support from the power ministries. Thus began a test of nerves, from 1994 on, likely to decide the next phase of the continuing Kremlin leadership struggle.

Boris Nikolayevich made the best of a bad moment. He claimed victory from a referendum, held at the same time as the December 1993 parliamentary election, in which voters approved Yeltsin's new constitution. That let the president downplay his embarrassing loss in the parliamentary ballot. What Yeltsin liked best about the new constitution was its stronger presidency, permitting the chief executive to ignore parliament and rule by decree. Boris Nikolayevich had created such enhanced powers for his own personal advantage.

However, the new constitution was a double-edged sword. While it was designed to help Yeltsin, his conservative foes decided that it would suit them too. Rather than futilely oppose Boris Nikolayevich from a weakened legislature, they devised a subtler strategy. They would play a waiting game. Simply by waiting, they expected to gain in public esteem as the economy declined further and the nation increasingly blamed Yeltsin's reformers for their plight. That would allow the conservatives to win the strengthened presidency for themselves in elections promised for June 1996, and they could then use its new constitutional powers to reverse democratic reforms. They knew Yeltsin might try to deprive them of their predicted presidential victory by canceling the 1996 ballot, as some of his advisers suggested. But that would only outrage the public. In that case, conservatives could seize power in a coup, this time with wide public support. One way or another, conservatives believed, the stronger presidency would soon be theirs.

Meanwhile they had ample opportunity for political mischief. In February 1994, the new conservative-led parliament arranged a pardon and release from prison for the ringleaders of both the August 1991 coup against Gorbachev and the October 1993 uprising against Yeltsin. The hard-liners thus set free were described as patriots who had defended their country's best interests. One of them, former vice president Aleksandr Rutskoi, left his jail cell to become a candidate for president. A charismatic speaker and a popular Afghan war hero, Rutskoi set out on a campaign that could rally the widespread discontent across the country to his side.

For Yeltsin's embattled reformers, it was a time of deadly serious challenge. His key advisers read the December 1993 election results as a political rebuff, shifting the advantage to his hard-line opponents. They urged the president to respond by stealing the opposition's thunder, tapping into the new conservative public mood, slowing reform, and becoming more authoritarian himself. "Popular democracy is not an option in Russia right now," Andranik Migranyan, a Yeltsin adviser, told me in January 1994. The president, who had earlier come to much the same conclusion himself, followed their advice. It was, in fact, a classic behavior pattern of Russian leaders through Gorbachev—when worried, become more authoritarian. And Boris Nikolayevich had plenty to be worried about. Those jitters would dominate his last years in power, especially his fear of losing the crucial support of all three power ministries.

The army quickly became the main beneficiary of such worries. In October 1993, only an eleventh-hour decision by Defense Minister Grachev saved Yeltsin. In the next political crisis, the army might stay neutral and let the president go under, or even back his more conservative rivals. The military thus emerged from the October 1993 crisis as a big winner, the acknowledged kingmaker of Kremlin politics. To keep the army happy, Yeltsin would have to give it more funds and more say. In future policy disputes with the foreign ministry, the army would now have more leeway for footdragging in implementing disarmament agreements or for intervening in former Soviet republics from the Baltics to the Ukraine to Central Asia. Even if he pandered to the military, Yeltsin could still not be sure of its support. "Grachev is a loose cannon," a Russian intelligence source told me in 1994. "Yeltsin doesn't control him."

In assessing Yeltsin's potential problems with the military, Grachev was only the tip of the iceberg. The defense minister could always be replaced, but any successor would still have trouble keeping the army's increasingly powerful regional commanders in line, among them key supporters of a renewed dictatorship.

By early 1995, the fastest-rising political star in Russia was General Aleksandr Lebed, the outspoken commander of the 14th Army, based in the Trans-Dniestr region of Moldova. Lebed gained national fame by saying the country needed a military dictator like Chile's Pinochet, and by describing Yeltsin as a "minus." Indeed, the Pinochet model had wide appeal in Russia, a formula promising law and order from iron-fist rule, while at the same time stimulating economic growth. "What's wrong with a military dictator?" Lebed liked to ask. "In all of its history, Russia has prospered under the strictest control. Consider Ivan the Terrible, Peter the Great, or Stalin." In June 1995, Lebed resigned from the army to explore a political career. By July, only eleven months before the presidential election scheduled for June 1996, he was already the front-runner, with one poll showing him likely to get 38 percent of the vote, against only 8 percent for Yeltsin.[1]

The former KGB was another chronic headache, causing more jitters for the Yeltsin team. In less than four years since the fall of the Soviet Union, Yeltsin had to reorganize the KGB four times, in successive attempts to bring the secret police under presidential control. In the first go-around he renamed it the Russian Security Ministry, and put a longtime aide, Viktor Barannikov, in charge. Barannikov had shared saunas, drinking bouts, and confidences with the Russian president for so long that he was known in the Moscow intelligence community as "Yeltsin's right-hand glass." Despite that history, however, Barannikov sided with Rutskoi in subsequent political maneuvering and was fired by Yeltsin in July 1993 for "disloyalty to the president."

Next Yeltsin brought in Nikolai Golushko, a KGB veteran, to restore the agency's professionalism and reliability. But Golushko kept the secret police on the sidelines in the October 1993 showdown. Incredibly, on the night of October 3, midway through the worst political crisis of Yeltsin's rule, no lights were burning in the security ministry headquarters. Golushko had kept the former KGB off the case. He was sacked soon afterward.

In the third incarnation, the agency became the Federal Counterintelligence Service under Sergei Stepashin, irreverently known as "the fireman" because in Soviet days he wrote his graduate school thesis on "the role of party cells in extinguishing fires." Stepashin was not talking symbols for political fires. He literally meant rounding up the Party faithful in bucket brigades to put out real fires.

To reduce the threat of the KGB as a Kremlin coup supporter, Yeltsin divided its functions into several separate agencies—foreign espionage in one, border guards in a second, and so on. The big winner in this bureaucratic upheaval was Major General Aleksandr Korzhakov, Yeltsin's longtime chief bodyguard, who took charge of a new, expanded "Personal Security Service of the President," an elite force of four thousand men. In one of the major results of this reorganization, Korzhakov's bodyguards rather than Stepashin's former KGB now kept tabs on Yeltsin's political foes. In another, Stepashin, as the nominal head of the nation's security service, had to report to Yeltsin through the bodyguard Korzhakov, a key sign of where the real power lay on security issues.[2] Korzhakov's influence would grow until he was widely seen as a power behind Yeltsin's throne. Many of the president's more authoritarian decisions were later attributed in part to Korzhakov's hard-line influence, among them the invasion of Chechnya in December 1994 to crush an independence movement. "Korzhakov's presidential guard has become more important than the former KGB," Oleg Kalugin, a former KGB general, told me.

Only four years earlier, Korzhakov had been just another KGB major. By late 1994, however, senior Russian officials were accusing him of taking actions that went far beyond the security brief of his former KGB bosses. They charged that Korzhakov had tapped Prime Minister Viktor Chernomyrdin's phone, meddled in his personnel appointments, and even given the head of the Russian government written advice on economic policy. The bugging of senior officials was said to be particularly widespread. "We're not talking about tapping one minister's phone," Vladimir Kvasov, Chernomyrdin's former chief of staff, stressed. "We're talking about bugging across the board."

Naturally, the bodyguard denied he was a modern Rasputin manipulating a Tsar Yeltsin. "I've never engaged in politics," he told the newspaper *Argumenty i Fakty.*[3] In a way, he was right. Korzhakov had no base of political power independent of Yeltsin's patronage. His only clout came from influencing the president, or as the loyal servant doing Yeltsin's bidding. Without Yeltsin, Korzhakov was nothing. With Yeltsin, however, he was becoming a major political force, despite the denials.

In addition to dividing the KGB's functions, Yeltsin also sharply reduced its manpower. The key element of the organization, the security police, was cut in half. Russian intelligence sources said the KGB had 140,000 agents at the collapse of the Soviet Union. This number was nearly halved to 75,000 by late 1994. But despite the manpower cuts and the bureaucratic reorganizations, the former KGB remained a formidable force, more than three times the combined total of U.S. counterintelligence agents from the CIA and FBI. And whatever it was called, whatever its size, the KGB had changed little. "Go into any office of the new counterintelligence service in 1994," Oleg Kalugin told me, "and you still see statues of Vladimir Lenin and Feliks Dzerzhinsky, the founders of the Bolshevik state and its first secret police, the Chekists. These are not superficial symbols. In their heart of hearts today's agents are still Bolshevik and Chekist."

Given that mind-set, even a reduced and reorganized KGB could still play a key role in any new conservative plot to oust Yeltsin and kill democratic reform. A fourth reorganization proved necessary. The Chechnya war and the botched attempt to rescue fifteen hundred hostages held by Chechen gunmen in a hospital in the southern Russian city of Budyonnovsk in June 1995 provided the occasion. KGB and interior ministry troops first rushed the hospital, touching off a bloodbath that solved nothing, then had to let the gunmen go to save the remaining hostages.

Yeltsin fired Stepashin for his role in this debacle. The new head of the KGB, now called the Federal Security Service, was Mikhail Barsukov, former head of the Kremlin palace guards and a close political ally of Yeltsin's chief bodyguard, Korzhakov. Many Russian commentators saw Korzhakov's hand pulling the strings on this appointment, one more sign of the bodyguard's outsized influence, but the move also carried serious risks. Barsukov, the new head of the renamed security service, was widely regarded as a Yeltsin loyalist, an outsider brought in to discipline KGB professionals still in the senior ranks. The appointment could backfire, however, by angering these powerful secret police veterans into joining a new coup plot against the president. After four reorganizations of the former KGB, Yeltsin's security in office was still far from assured.

The interior ministry was yet another security worry for Yeltsin. Its uniformed police also betrayed the president in October 1993. Viktor Yerin, the interior minister, was loyal, "a good soldier who took Yeltsin's orders," but a poor general, detractors said, "with only half a brain" and little clout in his own ministry. His number two, Deputy Minister Andrei Dunayev, ran the place and kept the police on the sidelines in the October 1993 showdown. In the end, Dunayev was arrested with Rutskoi and Khasbulatov. That disloyalty made the Yeltsin team nervous about counting on the uniformed police as well. Yerin was eventually fired for his role in the Budyonnovsk hostage debacle, but whether his replacement, Anatoly Kulikov, would prove more effective, or loyal to Yeltsin, was far from clear. In a word, the loyalty of all three power ministries remained questionable.

Outwardly, the Yeltsin team tried to give the appearance that all was well. The president and his chief aides projected an image of supreme confidence in their ability to remain in office and determine the pace and extent of reform. Yet privately they rightly remained worried about their hold on power. As one sign of these continuing jitters, they began to act tougher abroad, in the hope of strengthening their grip at home.

II. DIPLOMATIC ARROGANCE

The prospect for a stable Western-style democracy in Russia was only one key question that went unanswered. Another was whether post-Soviet Russia could be a strategic partner of the West in assuring what George Bush called a peaceful "new world order." With time, the odds began building against that too.

Once again, in Russian foreign policy as well as in domestic politics, the October 1993 crisis proved to be the turning point. Shortly after Bill Clinton endorsed Yeltsin's decision to send tanks against his parliament, the Russian president and the foreign minister, Andrei Kozyrev, concluded they could do virtually anything they wanted in foreign policy and still keep this U.S. administration's economic and political support, Andrei Kortunov, a Yeltsin adviser, told me. Among the things they had in mind were peacekeeping in former Soviet republics and taking stands against the Washington view on foreign policy issues from Bosnia to Iraq.

There were limits, of course, but the Yeltsin team concluded there were only a few ways they could lose Clinton's backing, Kortunov explained, among them invading to reincorporate the Baltic states in Russia, cheating on arms control deals, or arresting American businessmen in Moscow and seizing their property. Yeltsin had no intention of doing anything like that. Those limits aside, there was plenty of scope for a newly assertive Russian foreign policy, which the United States and its Western allies might not always like, but in reality could do little to stop.

With the hard-line victory in the December 1993 parliamentary elections, a more assertive Russian foreign policy also became a domestic political necessity for Yeltsin. The ultranationalist Vladimir Zhirinovsky had shown the way by winning an astounding 25 percent of the vote for his aggressive views, among them outrageous demands to restore imperial Russia's borders, annex Alaska, invade Turkey, and repartition Poland. Over time, Zhirinovsky might well prove himself to be a political clown, and burn out before becoming a serious presidential contender. But he had clearly touched a chord in this election. A more muscular foreign policy was a vote-getter. Yeltsin was not about to leave this field to the extremists. He would steal their thunder by becoming more assertive himself.

Yeltsin's Russia would no longer lamely follow America's foreign policy lead. It would now insist on being treated as an independent great power, with its own vital interests to protect, even at the risk of what Yeltsin called a "cold peace," meaning frostier relations with the United States. Among other things, Russia would now demand the right to set the terms under which the former East European Communist states could move closer to NATO. Moscow would take a share in the UN peacekeeping role in the former Yugoslavia, including the unprecedented deployment of Russian troops on the ground there. Not even Stalin had dared station his soldiers on Yugoslav soil. In Bosnia, Russia would back its fellow Slavs, the Serbs, and often veto the air strikes the United States proposed in response to Serb aggression. In Iraq, the Russians would oppose U.S. efforts to continue UN sanctions against Saddam Hussein.

Viewed from abroad, the arrogance of Russia's newly assertive foreign policy was astonishing. Here was a nation still largely dependent on aid from the United States and the West. And yet the client was telling the donors how business should be done around the world. Arrogance in Russian foreign policy was nothing new, of course. Brezhnev showed it for years by dictating the terms of détente from a position of weakness.[4] The arrogance of Yeltsin-era foreign policy was but one more sign of how little eternal Russia ever changes.

Yeltsin's newly assertive stand began in Russia's "near abroad," the former Soviet republics, now newly independent countries. Moscow established a new military presence there, for various reasons. In Armenia, Azerbaijan, and Georgia, it was to halt civil wars. In Tajikistan it was to guard the frontier against encroachment by Muslim fundamentalists from Afghanistan. To many in the West, however, these reasons sounded like pretexts, a way to establish military beachheads which could eventually be used to force these former Soviet republics back under Russian rule. But if Western governments complained, Moscow replied curtly that they had no right to protest.

Russia's argument was essentially this: "If the West won't send troops under UN auspices to keep the peace in our region, then you cannot object if we do the job ourselves." It was another way of saying there would be no Western restraints on Russian military activity in former Soviet republics. Nor was Russia's arrogance limited to former Soviet territory. Yeltsin and Kozyrev wanted their say everywhere. As Aleksei Pushkov, deputy editor of the weekly *Moscow News*, put it, "Russia is a truly Eurasian superpower, with considerable opportunity to influence the situation in nearby regions, including the Balkans, the Middle East, and the Korean peninsula."

Moscow's assertive new foreign policy was found to be tolerable in far-off America. But it rang alarm bells in neighboring countries with centuries of experience living next to an expansionist Russia, among them Turkey, which shares a thousand-mile border with the former Soviet Union. To the Turks, Russia's new muscle-flexing in the near abroad carried a new threat to them.

Turkish Prime Minister Tansu Ciller went to Moscow and put her concerns to Yeltsin with great skill. She gave the Russian president a history lesson. When the Ottoman Empire collapsed, she said, the successor state, modern Turkey, defined its borders publicly. Ethnic Turks living outside those borders, from Central Asia to Bosnia, would be citizens of those countries, no longer under the protection of the Turkish army. The announcement reassured Turkey's neighbors and helped keep peace. With the breakup of the Soviet empire, Prime Minister Ciller suggested, Russia should now do the same thing. It should publicly define its borders and say the twenty-five million ethnic Russians living beyond them in former Soviet republics would no longer be protected by the Russian army. That would similarly reassure neighbors and help keep the peace. Yeltsin, however, would do no such thing. Under pressure from Zhirinovsky and other hard-liners, he may still have to intervene militarily to protect ethnic Russians, from the Baltics to Ukraine to Kazakhstan, risking new regional wars.

Turkish Deputy Foreign Minister Ozdem Sanberk accompanied Ciller to Moscow, sat in on her talks with Yeltsin, and told me about them when I interviewed him in Ankara in April 1994. Sanberk was concerned that Yeltsin's more assertive foreign policy could lead him or a more hard-line Kremlin successor into rebuilding the Soviet empire and again threatening Turkey, a NATO member, now on the front line. Sanberk pointed to Russian troops now nearly surrounding Turkey from Bosnia to Armenia and Azerbaijan. The United States, he said, was blind to this new threat of Russian expansionism. Washington no longer feared a nuclear attack from Moscow on American cities, so it was giving Yeltsin a blank check in his border regions.

The Turks were angry. They had the second-largest army in NATO and had deployed it to support the U.S. effort against Saddam Hussein in the Gulf War. But now, when Turkey was troubled by a newly assertive Russia on its borders, the United States didn't seem to care. In the Turkish view, both America's global leadership and the future of NATO were put at risk by this shortsighted U.S. stand. Sanberk showed me a letter he had written to U.S. Deputy Secretary of State Strobe Talbott, raising Turkey's concern. "The West must distinguish between supporting democracy in Russia and supporting new Russian imperial designs," Sanberk told me.

Indeed, a new Russian empire already appeared to be taking shape. Less than three years after the U.S.S.R. broke up into fifteen independent nations, the pendulum was swinging back the other way. Most of those former Soviet republics were now economic basket cases dependent on Russian aid. Five of them—Georgia, Armenia, Azerbaijan, Moldova, and Tajikistan—needed Russian troops to keep the peace on their soil. In July 1994, Ukraine[5] and Belarus elected new presidents who campaigned for a new union with Russia. Only the three Baltic states wanted neither Russian aid nor soldiers. Otherwise, a rush "back to the U.S.S.R.," a new superpower under the Russian boot, seemed well under way. It was far from a sure thing, however, for a surprising reason. Yeltsin himself had strong reservations.

"Russia is the main obstacle to the restoration of the Soviet Union," Yeltsin adviser Andranik Migranyan told me. The reason was simple, he and other presidential aides explained. Moscow cannot afford it. Already, they claimed, Russia spends 20 percent of its GNP subsidizing former Soviet republics in the Commonwealth of Independent States, the loose confederation that replaced the U.S.S.R. A formal union would make Russia even more of a donor, forced to provide cheap energy and other subsidies to poorer republics at levels impossible for Moscow to finance. "Reintegration of the former U.S.S.R. runs contrary to the economic interests of Russia," said Emil Pain, a Yeltsin economic adviser.

Worse, it would imperil Yeltsin's economic reforms. The more backward former Soviet republics are not ready for transition to a market economy. Searching for common economic policies with them would inevitably slow down Yeltsin's reforms in Russia. "The choice now is between reform and reintegration of the U.S.S.R.," said analyst Andrei Kortunov. "Russia cannot have both at the same time."

For Yeltsin, the choice was tougher still. If he said yes to reintegration, he risked economic disaster. If he said no, he risked political disaster. His conservative opponents, including Zhirinovsky, favored restoring the U.S.S.R. borders as a way of returning to superpower status. They would be only too happy to point to Yeltsin as "the obstacle" to reintegrating the Soviet Union, a concept increasingly popular with voters. Not surprisingly, Yeltsin was hedging his bets toward some kind of workable compromise. He withdrew Russian troops from the Baltics, as promised. But he was still negotiating closer cooperation with Ukraine, Belarus, and other republics, although probably short of another formal union.

His conservative opponents had no such qualms. For them there was no contradiction between political and economic aims. They knew perfectly well that incorporating former Soviet republics into Russia would doom economic reform. Indeed, that was one strong reason why they wanted to restore the former U.S.S.R. Should they take power, they would dial back on economic reform and expand Russia to former Soviet borders.

The significance for the West of any renewed Russian empire would be great. Clearly a more belligerent, nuclear-armed Russia, with its land stretching to Soviet borders and its population doubled to nearly 300 million people, could constitute a significant new threat. If Russia expands, much would depend on how it does so. Marriage and rape can both lead to childbirth, but the difference in the process is important. If Russia expands by voluntary cooperation with former Soviet republics, the West can hardly object. But if Russia absorbs them by military force, the result could well be Cold War II.

Short of that, many other issues could also spoil prospects of a new Russian strategic partnership with the West. Among them would be confirmed cases of Russia selling nuclear weapons technology to a terrorism sponsor like Iran or Libya. The Yeltsin government claims to have taken measures to prevent that, but the effectiveness of its controls are often suspect. Further nuclear accidents in Chernobyl-type reactors, still on-line and still unsafe, could similarly poison relations with the West. Yeltsin also faces foreign policy challenges that have nothing to do with America or the West, but are nonetheless quite dangerous for global peace. China is among the more serious.

For decades, Soviet-Chinese friction along their contested border threatened to escalate to nuclear war. The collapse of Soviet communism in 1991 buried the ideological strains. But ideology was always a fig leaf covering the more important territorial dispute. The battle over these conflicting land claims continues to this day, raising a new threat of war between two of the most heavily armed nations in the world.

Mao Zedong once claimed Russia had illegally seized 1.5 million square kilometers of Chinese land in tsarist days, from the Pacific to Central Asia, through unequal treaties. Now, Russian specialists claim, Mao's heirs in Beijing are trying to get it back through long-term illegal Chinese immigration to resource-rich Siberia. "There is a deliberate Chinese policy of economic and ethnic expansion in Russia," Vladimir Myasnikov, deputy director of Moscow's Far East Institute, told me in a July 1994 interview.

Russian officials say the latest problems with China started as a result of their post-Communist reforms. Border posts were reduced on the previously sealed frontier, inviting illegal Chinese immigration. Other Chinese bribed their way past corrupt Russian border guards. Still others came to Russia legally as tourists, businessmen, or workers, or on family visits, then stayed illegally. The numbers are staggering. Myasnikov and others estimated there were one million illegal Chinese in Siberia in 1993, two million a year later. "There are thirty million people in Siberia and more than one billion in China," Valery Zubov, governor of the Krasnoyarsk region of eastern Siberia, explained to me. "If only three percent of the Chinese people come to our country, Russians will be a minority in Siberia and you would be interviewing a Chinese governor here."

In Siberia's Pacific coast region, Russian officials say, the new Chinese presence is clearest. There are seven million Russians on their side of the Amur River border and 100 million Chinese on the other side. In Khabarovsk, a Pacific-rim Russian city of half a million people, there are now more than fifty thousand Chinese merchants alone. Some 20 percent of the private land bought in Khabarovsk is said to be in Chinese hands. Across the border in China, businesses are offered a five-year tax holiday if they agree to construct shops and factories in Russia, one clear sign that the expansion policy has official blessing from Beijing.

China denies any strategic plan to take back lost territory by sending its people into Siberia. But the Russian parliament gives such denials little credence. Russian deputies want to appoint more border guards and a new immigration service that would check Chinese residents and deport the illegals, although so far lack of funds prevents such steps. That may leave it up to the Cossacks, the Russian roughnecks who settled Siberia in the seventeenth century and now see their land and jobs being taken by Chinese. Any move against the sizable Chinese community in Siberia, either by Russian police or Cossack vigilantes, would likely be resisted in escalating violence. From there it is only one step back to the armed clashes along border rivers that marked the Soviet Union's final decades.

The Russian-Chinese dispute is only one of many foreign dangers smoldering beneath the surface of the political waiting game in Moscow. None of these threats is getting the attention it deserves in the Kremlin. All sides in Russia's continuing power struggle are now focusing instead on a 1996 presidential election that may never come. Until that leadership question is next resolved, either by ballot or by armed coup, foreign policy will continue to be exploited by all sides to score domestic political points.

At worst, this could lead to shortsighted saber-rattling and foreign military adventurism. Even at best, Russian foreign policy over the near term is likely to be inconsistent. In that sense, sadly, Russia is not yet a reliable partner for the West in any effort to construct a lasting new world order.

III. DESPAIR, APATHY, AND CYNICISM

Boris Yeltsin faced a daunting array of economic, political, and diplomatic problems. Yet through it all, he maintained an Olympian calm, a confidence that somehow Russia's future would turn out just fine. "There will be no return to communism in our country," the president told a news conference in June 1994. Yes, he admitted, in the new Russia there would be a smaller Communist Party, a minority Communist faction in parliament, "but their influence is rather insignificant, and it won't grow." Similarly, he has predicted, the Russia that fought Hitler's fascism in World War II is not about to accept Zhirinovsky's fascism now. "I am an optimist," Yeltsin said in a 1994 interview with *Newsweek*. "I believe that, no matter what, reforms cannot and will not be reversed, no matter who crows like a rooster to prove the opposite."[6]

He could hardly be expected to say anything else. But beneath the bold words there was little in Russia's post-Communist performance to justify such optimism. By early 1995, most Russians regarded Yeltsin's record—and prospects—with a mixture of despair, apathy, and cynicism.

To be sure, Yeltsin's government often claims progress. By July 1, 1994, when the first phase of privatization ended, some 85,000 small firms across the country, 71 percent of Russia's small businesses, had been put in private hands. It was a genuine achievement, worth trumpeting. But this first phase was also the easy part. The crucial part comes next in phase two, when thousands of large state factories are to be privatized. The bankrupt ones will no longer be kept afloat by state subsidies and instead will be allowed to collapse, at a cost of hundreds of thousands of jobs. The pain from that, when added to the previous pain of sky-high free-market prices, could well touch off a social explosion that sinks Yeltsin and the reformers for good.

In August 1994, Yeltsin's government announced it had brought inflation down to only 4 percent a month. It neglected to mention that a major reason for this "success" was several months of pay withheld from millions of state employees because of a cash-flow crisis. That meant the much-touted lower inflation rates could be short-lived. In order to meet demands for back pay long overdue, and to avoid threats of crippling strikes, the government faced heavy pressure to print money and send inflation soaring again.

In Moscow, Yeltsin's reverent aides were telling him his three years of reform were working. But in Krasnoyarsk, an industrial city of one million people in eastern Siberia, four time zones from the Russian capital, the reality looked very different indeed. In the summer of 1994 I went to take a look. Once again the old principle was proving its value—the farther one got from Moscow, the truer a picture one got of Russia.

Blunt Siberians told me the Yeltsin regime was a disaster. They said his inflationary reforms had wiped out personal savings, bankrupted regional governments and industries, created mass unemployment, fueled unprecedented corruption. Polls showed local people now blamed Yeltsin more than the former Communist regime for stealing the wealth of their region's natural resources and deepening their economic misery. Lyudmila Vinskaya, a Krasnoyarsk journalist, said her grandfather had warned her that would happen. "Why are you so happy about getting rid of the Communists?" he asked. "They had full stomachs. Now you'll get the hungry ones."

Siberia was always the key to Russia's economic recovery. The vast region holds more than half the nation's raw materials and export earning potential. It was long exploited by Moscow. Kremlin regimes pocketed the lion's share of profits from Siberian exports instead of investing them in the region. Yeltsin's reforms were supposed to change all that, leaving more tax revenue, export profits, and control over resources in the region. Instead, local officials complained, the Yeltsin regime's broken promises have left Siberia with less tax revenue, profits, and control than before. "No one expects anything good from the central authorities anymore," Yevgeny Dobryansky, deputy governor of the Krasnoyarsk region, said in an interview with me.

Krasnoyarsk displayed the huge disparities of wealth now typical of Russia. One of the new breed of entrepreneurs, Sergei Biryukov, thirty-seven, greeted visitors to his ten-room apartment dressed in a bathrobe. That way he could invite them to join him in his sauna or indoor pool. Biryukov made his money borrowing from Russian banks at 40 percent interest when the inflation rate was 120 percent. The difference allowed him to repay the loan with devalued rubles at a huge profit. Then he bought technology from the local defense industry and built a thriving satellite communications business. "I live better in Krasnoyarsk than I could in New York," he told me. He knows. He's been there.

On the other end of the scale, the poor suffer worse than in Communist days. Krasnoyarsk officials said they would collect only 45 percent of their expected tax revenues in 1994 because of various economic upheavals blamed on the Yeltsin reforms. There was no longer a social safety net for the poor. "We can't even put out the fires," Olga Felde, the regional welfare chief, said. Such extreme disparities of wealth and poverty are social dangers in any country, but perhaps nowhere more than in Russia, where public attitudes are often very different from those in the rest of the world.

An old Russian fable provides a good example. The fable involves two peasants who live on neighboring plots of land. One peasant owns a goat; his neighbor does not. One day an angel of mercy comes down from heaven and speaks to the peasant who has no goat. The angel offers him one wish, anything he wants. The peasant makes up his mind immediately. "Please kill my neighbor's goat," he says. Such jealousy has broad political implications in today's Russia. Millions of poor would be only too happy to see a new regime sweep away the reforms that have let a few of their neighbors amass great wealth. In effect, they too would be saying, "Please kill my neighbor's goat."

Meanwhile they have no faith that Yeltsin's reform government will be able to provide a better life for them. They are mad at the new rich who have done so well, and mad at the government for making them even worse off. In Krasnoyarsk, the anger at the government had its positive aspects. Ordinary people there now understood at last that they would have to rely on themselves; the state would not provide. Unemployed people stayed alive by raising vegetables in kitchen gardens or trading clothing in street markets, and factories taxed at over 80 percent hid money from the state by not banking it. These, however, were survival tactics, not solutions.

Eventually the new self-reliance could move from economics to politics, with citizens' committees forming and pushing the government toward more effective reform. But this has not happened yet. On the contrary, people in Krasnoyarsk—and increasingly across Russia—were turned off to politics. They no longer demonstrated or listened to speeches. Voter turnout had hit new lows. To a large extent, the activism of the Gorbachev years appeared to be finished. Russians were returning to their traditional passivity. And with that came opportunities for a new dictator to seize power while no one was paying attention.

For the first time since the start of the Gorbachev era, the fight had gone out of those Russians who once put such hope in reform. Now they spoke mostly of bitter disappointment. Among them was Alyosha Arens in Moscow, who lost his father in Stalin's purges. Alyosha had spent three nights risking his life defending Yeltsin's White House against the August 1991 coup. Three years later he told me: "Now I ask myself why I bothered."

My friend Igor Belyayev left politics in disgust, when his Moscow city council was dissolved by Yeltsin after the October 1993 crisis. In three years as a deputy, Igor said, he had not once been able to help a constituent get better housing or right any injustice. "The city council turned out to have a majority of former Communists and KGB agents who campaigned as 'democrats' but who voted as conservatives once they were elected," Igor said. "True reformers were a voice in the wilderness." He went into business, and has no plans to return to politics.

The Russian intelligentsia was reassessing values. To them, capitalism and Western models were the big failures. Academician Joseph Golodarsky, a physicist, recalled that for decades, Soviet propaganda insisted communism was bliss and capitalism a disaster. Now, in the post-Communist era, he told me, Russians have learned that "everything we heard about communism was false and everything we heard about capitalism was true."

Vadim Mezhuyev, a history professor, agreed. "Our intellectuals mistakenly thought the question was socialism or capitalism," he said. "The real question for the years ahead is Russia with its traditions or a new road on a Western model." For him and others, the most likely choice would be Russia with its traditions—meaning renewed authoritarianism.

Of all the intellectuals, however, Aleksandr Solzhenitsyn probably said it best. The great writer returned to live in Russia in 1994, after nearly twenty years of exile in the United States. He crossed the country from the Pacific coast to Moscow, talking to people from all walks of life. Then in a report to the Russian parliament, he said: "Our people are discouraged. They are ashamed of their own impotence, but they no longer believe that the reforms undertaken by the government will serve their interests. . . . Those people who have not succumbed to despair have fallen into apathy."[7]

The implications of Solzhenitsyn's words could hardly be more frightening. He now sees the ordinary Russian people as discouraged, despairing, and apathetic, with no faith any longer in democratic reform or market economics. They would welcome a new dictator who promised to smash crime and corruption and restore economic stability. It is not that simple, of course. Reform still has strong support in Russia, particularly among the younger generations, the intelligentsia, and the "Westernizers" in their old struggle with conservative "Slavophiles." The battle is far from over. But the public mood in late 1994 was clearly disappointed with the reform record so far. The hard-liners sensed a new opportunity. The momentum was moving their way.

Even the new rich, the prime beneficiaries of the Yeltsin reforms, were already thinking out how they too could support a renewed dictatorship. They would prefer continued reform. But if necessary, they decided, they could accommodate another autocrat in the Kremlin without losing their new wealth. To the general public's apathy and despair, the elite were thus adding a cynicism that further imperiled Russia's fragile experiment in democracy.

Tatyana proved that to me. She was a tall, slender, striking brunette in her thirties, dressed as smartly as if she had just stepped off the pages of an Italian fashion magazine. She spoke impeccable French and English. At first glance there was nothing Russian about her. But she was Russian to the core.

Tatyana was a child of the *nomenklatura,* the most privileged level of Soviet officialdom. Her father had been one of the Soviet Union's most famous Cold War ambassadors.[8] So she had grown up in Western Europe. The fall of communism had not hurt her a bit. Along with her husband, a prominent Soviet foreign trade official, she started a private import-export business. In three years she and her husband built a successful conglomerate, as capitalists. They traveled to Paris several times a year, first-class of course. We met at a dinner hosted by one of her wealthy clients, at a world symbol of bourgeois opulence, the Hotel Ritz.

In her second life as a mink-clad capitalist, Tatyana was no more worried than she had been in her first life as a privileged Communist. She looked to Russia's future with supreme confidence. "A new authoritarian regime would not necessarily be bad," she told me. "They would reestablish law and order. But they won't reimpose communism. And they cannot stop private business without ruining the economy. So we don't have to worry. As long as we can continue our company, as long as we can travel abroad, we will be all right." She had it all figured out. She would be fine too in her third life, if need be, under a new Russian dictatorship. To make sure of that, Tatyana and her husband had ample funds safely stashed in the West.

Suddenly Tatyana reminded me of Oldrich Cernik, the prime minister of Czechoslovakia before, during, and after the Dubček reforms. The Cerniks of the Communist world, the ruling elite, are great survivors. In Russia, there are thousands of them, just like Tatyana. They were, are, and will be Russia's elite. They have the education, the experience, the power, and the personal contacts. They ran the country in Communist days. Nothing has stopped them since. Should a nationalist dictatorship come to Russia next, the same people could put on yet another hat and continue as the ruling elite. They need not risk their lives or even their positions opposing a return to authoritarianism.

It is hard to see who will fight against a return to the iron fist after Yeltsin goes. Most of Russia's ordinary people probably won't. And neither will the elite. At this stage, the forces of genuine reform appear too weak numerically and too divided to swing the nation the other way, at least for the short term.

IV. FUTURE WATCH

Yeltsin may already be on the way out. The Chechen war he launched on December 11, 1994, could ultimately prove to be the third and fatal strike against him. In addition to his appalling economic record and his loss of political momentum to the hard-liners, Boris Nikolayevich had now been humiliated by his brutal and bungled suppression of a minority nationality revolt in the southern Russian province of Chechnya. The Russian military brass, which had expected to capture Grozny, the Chechen capital, in two days, took more than a month, at a cost of more Russian lives than the nine years of war in Afghanistan.[9] Chechen rebels then regrouped in the mountains, vowing to continue a guerrilla war—and terrorism in Russia—for years to come.

By January 1995, the president's approval rating in opinion polls was down to 14 percent, an all-time low. As with Gorbachev before him, Yeltsin's mishandling of economic, political, and minority nationality questions threatened to destroy his presidency. And like Gorbachev, Yeltsin had responded to his collapsing public support by increasing his own authoritarian powers. The differences here were largely one of degree. Both changed constitutions and parliaments to make stronger presidencies, but only Yeltsin did so with tanks. Both tried to quash minority nationalist dissent, but Gorbachev's bloodletting in Lithuania paled in comparison to Yeltsin's slaughter in Chechnya.

In the end, Chechnya was likely to be the biggest single factor in the collapse of Yeltsin's reformist reputation, and perhaps his presidency. For more than a century, wars have been the determining factor leading directly to the most historic changes in Russia. Thus the Crimean War broke serfdom. The Russo-Japanese War brought on the Russian revolution of 1905. World War I enabled the Bolsheviks to establish Communist power in 1917. World War II made the Soviet Union a superpower. The Afghan War discredited Brezhnev and allowed Gorbachev to launch his perestroika reforms. The Chechen war in turn could usher in an equally important change, perhaps the end of post-Communist democratic reform in Russia.

Former prime minister Yegor Gaidar, leader of the nation's main reformist political party, "Russia's Choice," called Chechnya a "massive military crime" and said his democrats would no longer support Yeltsin for reelection. "Chechnya appears to have permanently ended the alliance between Yeltsin and the democrats," said Michael McFaul, an analyst with the Carnegie Foundation's Moscow office. That split could only enhance the chances that a hard-liner would succeed Yeltsin, either by election or in a coup. Meanwhile, Yeltsin himself had clearly turned authoritarian. The Chechen war largely discredited what was left of his legacy as a democrat, suggesting that if he won reelection, he would use his second term to roll back his own reforms.

Three television images now encapsulated the Yeltsin era. In the first, Boris Nikolayevich stood on a tank to defeat the August 1991 hard-line coup and save democratic reform in Russia. In the second, Russian tanks fired on their own parliament in October 1993. Yeltsin claimed he ordered that assault to save democracy. But this time many of his admirers at home and abroad began to doubt his sincerity. In the third image televised around the world, Russian planes and artillery pounded civilian targets in Grozny, day after day. No national leader could authorize such an attack against one of his own cities and convince anyone that it was all done in the name of preserving democracy. In the course of those three television images, Boris Yeltsin had turned from the hero of democratic reform to the embodiment of renewed autocratic rule. Rarely has there been a clearer wake-up call.

For the most part, however, Western leaders chose to ignore it. They tempered their criticism of Chechnya and continued to support Yeltsin as the best hope for continued democratic reform in Russia. It was a decision they may soon regret. Hard evidence of Yeltsin's shift from democracy to autocracy had been building for more than a year. The pattern was too strong, too long, to be dismissed as a temporary tactical shift. Boris Nikolayevich was no longer the democratic solution for Russia. Instead he had become a leading part of its autocratic problem. More than ever, the West should have been supporting reform, the policy, rather than Yeltsin, the man.

Incredibly, bureaucratic rule has actually prospered in what is supposed to be Yeltsin's "democracy." When communism collapsed, Russian bureaucrats at first looked like an endangered species. The loss of half the Soviet population, the fading out of Communist controls, and the privatization of state industry should have meant less work, fewer jobs, and less power for Russian bureaucrats. But it did not work out that way. Yeltsin kept the bureaucracy going, then began increasing its powers and numbers again, as a way of securing his own authority. By 1995, Yeltsin presided over a system of power largely controlled by the man at the top, a system which, in bureaucratic terms, often resembled its Communist predecessor.

A prime example of this trend was the president's swollen personal staff, a cast of hundreds, created by Yeltsin to keep all government cabinet departments in line. For instance, the cultural department of the presidential staff supervised the government's ministry of culture, restoring the practice of Soviet days when the cultural department of the Communist Party's Central Committee effectively ran the government ministry of culture. In much the same way, Yeltsin's expanded presidential staff also replaced the old Central Committee in supervising all other government ministries. In short, Yeltsin re-created the old bureaucratic structure, without the Communist ideology. Fittingly, his presidential staff was now headquartered in the very same Staraya Square offices once occupied by the old Central Committee.

The parallels didn't stop there. Yeltsin's security council, the top leaders who approved the Chechnya invasion, was widely regarded by Russian commentators as a new Politburo. And, as we have already seen, the new Yeltsin constitution emasculated parliament. The bloated Yeltsin staff was the final blow, a private bureaucracy at the service of the Russian president, larger in numbers and influence than the personal staff of former Soviet leaders. Gorbachev was among the first to point that out.

"Today in Russia the apparatus is bigger than it was in the Soviet Union,"

Gorbachev told me in a January 1995 interview in Moscow. "This means the president is not betting on democratic processes and institutions, but on the bureaucracy. Yeltsin has completely discarded his mask of a democrat." For Gorbachev, Yeltsin was nothing but an "opportunist" who rode a democratic wave to power and then kept it as autocratically as the tsars and commissars before him.

By that logic, Yeltsin could well decide to remain in office by canceling the June 1996 presidential election, if opinion polls continue to show he is likely to lose. Boris Nikolayevich himself denied any such intention, but two of his aides told me in January 1996 on my last reporting trip to Moscow for this book that the possibility had been discussed by senior members of the presidential staff. According to these sources, a state of national emergency could be declared, because of Chechen terrorism or some other pretext, and the election postponed. No decision had been taken yet, these aides said, because several factors had to be measured first, including the likely reaction from the West, Russia's provincial governors, opposition political parties, and the power ministries.

Like Yeltsin's insiders, Russian political commentators were obsessed by the prospect of presidential elections. They speculated endlessly on a broad range of questions, among them: Would Yeltsin's health hold long enough for him to run a strenuous campaign? Could he win? If not, would Yeltsin seek to postpone or cancel the election? If so, on what pretext? Could he cancel the election and survive in office or would a coup bring him down? Assuming the election was held, who had the best chance of beating Yeltsin? Did any other "reformer" have any chance at all? If Yeltsin did not run, or if he ran and lost, would the next Russian president inevitably be a hard-liner—that is more authoritarian at home and aggressive abroad than Yeltsin? Could a Communist revival under Zyuganov be stopped?

Predictions and assessments changed constantly. With so many variables at play, no one could make an accurate forecast six months in advance, before the lists closed and the campaigns actually started. This was no longer the rigid Soviet system with a second secretary waiting in the wings as the only clear heir apparent to the Communist leadership. Instead, political forecasters in Moscow now had to factor in numerous unknowns, somewhat like their American counterparts. In the United States, before the campaigns started with the first primary in New Hampshire, no one could be sure who would win the 1996 presidential race either, but in Russia the outlook was even more complicated. For one thing, American analysts have never had to contend with the very real possibility that the election could be canceled.

After Russia's version of a primary, the December 1995 parliamentary election, the outlook was very grim indeed. Zyuganov's reborn Communists did best, polling 21 percent of the vote and winning a third of the 450 seats in the new parliament, the State Duma. That result made Zyuganov a leading contender to succeed Yeltsin and raised the specter of Communists returning to power in Russia, by election no less. Such a scenario, however, was far from certain. The legislative election was more a protest vote against Yeltsin and the economic pain of his reforms than a groundswell for a return to Communist rule. Zyuganov himself recognized as much. He called the parliamentary election "a no confidence vote in the government."

Outwardly, Yeltsin continued to display supreme confidence. "We have no reason to worry or assess the elections as a tragedy," he said. "I'm sure the majority of Russians don't stand for communism." Yeltsin was at least partly right. The results were not tragic. The Communists fell well short of the 70 percent of the Duma seats they would need in order to roll back reform by amending the constitution. In fact, they were by no means assured of a 51 percent simple majority in the new parliament, even with help from smaller allied parties. For 51 percent, they would need support from Zhirinovsky's nationalists, an unlikely prospect, and even if they got it, the potential for parliamentary obstruction was sharply limited by Yeltsin's constitution, which had shifted most powers to the presidency.

Nonetheless, Yeltsin was being overly sanguine. While far from tragic, the parliamentary election results certainly suggested sobering implications for the presidential ballot in June. Zhirinovsky's party, with some 11 percent of the vote and 50 parliamentary seats, finished second, making him and Zyuganov the two leading candidates. With six months to go, Russians faced the potential Hobson's choice for president between the fascist-sounding Zhirinovsky and the Communist Zyuganov.

Zhirinovsky, largely discredited as a political clown, remained a player due to continued support from disadvantaged Russians, especially in the provinces, where resentment of the Yeltsin reforms was highest. Zyuganov benefited from the same syndrome. Whether he was sincere about a new kind of communism that embraced private property and free markets, or whether he would revert to the Soviet system if given the chance, remained an open question.

All other leading presidential candidates did relatively poorly in the parliamentary elections, among them the moderate prime minister, Chernomyrdin, the reform economist Yavlinsky, and the military favorite, General Lebed. That could change radically in the next six months as any of them could retake the lead, but the danger remained that Zhirinovsky and Zyuganov could emerge from the large field in the first round of the presidential election as the two top vote getters and then face each other in the decisive second round.

Yeltsin was still a key factor. The president, sixty-five years old and hospitalized twice for heart attacks in 1995, decided to run for a second term if his health held. For one thing, the Communists had threatened to prosecute him for corruption and treason in the breakup of the Soviet Union, and thus remaining in office could be his best way of staying out of prison. For another, Yeltsin suddenly had new opportunities, All other progressive politicians had shown weakness in the parliamentary balloting. "Yeltsin only stands to gain," said Nikolai Petrov, a Russian political analyst. "He now emerges as the only guarantor of democratic reform." As a candidate, Yeltsin could tell the nation the choice was between moving ahead with him through an admittedly painful transition to a better life or back to the dark ages with Zyuganov or Zhirinovsky.

The trouble with that, Western diplomats in Moscow said, was that if Yeltsin's health forced him to drop out of the running, or if strikes by miners and others against his economic management got out of hand, or if he ran and lost, the choice could still be Zhirinovsky or Zyuganov.

Furthermore, even a Yeltsin victory was not necessarily good for the West anymore. Immediately after the December 1995 parliamentary results, which showed the Russian electorate favored more conservative policies at home and abroad, Yeltsin was among the first to get the message. The president took pains to show he was turning more conservative himself, in order to enhance his reelection prospects in June, both by slowing reform at home to ease the economic pain and by a more anti-Western foreign policy.

His first moves in a more conservative direction came with key personnel changes. Yeltsin forced the resignation of his pro-Western foreign minister, Andrei Kozyrev, and replaced him with an old Communist hard-liner, foreign intelligence chief Yevgeny Primakov, who favored more stress on Russian national interests even at the risk of renewed East-West tensions. Similarly, the president removed from office Anatoly Chubais, the driving force behind privatization of state industry, and Sergei Kovalev, his outspokenly liberal adviser on human rights. Both departures were devastating blows to the progressive cause. Chubais had long been the litmus test for continuing economic reform, and Kovalev the symbol of hopes for further democratization. At the same time, Yeltsin approved a military assault against hostage-taking Chechen rebels, resulting in another bloodbath, this time in the southern Russian province of Dagestan. Taken together, these moves all gave the same signal—the new Yeltsin would be significantly more authoritarian than ever before in his presidency, at least for the near term. In the months ahead there would be less economic reform, less protection of human rights at home, more risk of military expansionism abroad.

What remained unclear to world leaders was whether Yeltsin's latest harder-line posturing was short-term election tactics or a long-term strategy likely to carry through a second presidential term. Most had not given up on him. Czech president Vaclav Havel spoke for many foreign leaders when he said, "Boris Yeltsin, despite a tendency to govern in a very authoritarian manner, is really trying to reform Russia."[10] Indeed, enlightened dictatorship was in principle a valid way to conduct reform in Russian conditions. The trouble with that theory, however, was that almost nowhere in the world have dictatorships ever been very enlightened in practice.

In fact, Russia now appeared to be approaching more of an historic

watershed than simply a presidential election. One way or another, the reform era Gorbachev launched in 1985 seemed to be drawing to a close—either by the election of a Communist, an extreme nationalist, a militarist, or
a more authoritarian Yeltsin as president, or through weak health preventing Yeltsin from turning back toward reform in a second term, or through a
pro-Yeltsin coup such as postponed elections, or through an anti-Yeltsin
coup by hard-line extremists, or by the backlash to a coup from either side.

There was little cause for optimism over the near term. The best that could
be said about Russia in January 1996 was that the next presidential election
would prove to be the wrong test for the country's long-term course. Neither an early ballot for the national political leadership nor a seizure of
power by coup d'état in the near future was likely to answer definitely the
key question of whether Russia will become a stable democracy or return to
prolonged dictatorship. Should presidential elections be held on schedule,
any relatively moderate winner would still be vulnerable to a hard-line coup.
Should conservatives come to power, through an election or a putsch, they
might not last long either. These conservatives, the late historian Dmitri
Volkoganov noted, "have nothing in their souls except food coupons and
long lines." In other words, should a new dictatorship fail to resolve the nation's economic problems, it could have to give way again soon to more democratic forces.

The real test in Russia is neither the short-term election timetable nor the
threat of an early coup. Instead it is the long-term transition of the nation
from communism toward democratic rule. That transition is nothing less
than the world's most important political work in progress, and could well
take a generation or two to play out.

Already, the preliminary assessment is encouraging. Four years after the
collapse of the Soviet Union, the transition has made significant progress
against extraordinarily difficult odds, indeed more progress than Russia or
the world could have expected. Among the many pluses are the new freedoms of speech and association, freedoms to acquire capital, to own property, to travel abroad and return. By late 1995, even the long economic
decline was said to be bottoming out, and perhaps about to start a recovery
phase. Against all that, the many minuses included the anger of the poor,
struggling to survive without a proper social safety net, the fragility of democratic institutions, and the widespread belief that capitalism equals corruption and criminality.

Over the long term, one factor above all was likely to determine which
way Russia turns: the creation of a law-based state—a legal system that guarantees equal rights for all citizens, a workable tax collection system, and stable political institutions no longer vulnerable to military-backed coups. No
such law-based state has yet been created in Russia, and indeed none could
be in only four years. But a promising start has been made in that direction,
with the collapse of the Communist dictatorship and the beginnings of

democratic rule. Should the trend continue and a genuine law-based state emerge in Russia early in the next century, democratic reform will at last be irreversible. If not, Russia is likely to enter a long new era of repression at home and aggression abroad.

Either way, Boris Yeltsin will be seen by then as a historic figure, even though Chechnya tarnished his image. As Russia's first democratically elected president, as its first post-Communist reformer, he faced an awesome challenge which his apologists will argue he could surmount only by turning more autocratic. They will also say there was no way he could be expected to do the whole job himself or do it with entirely clean hands, any more than Nikita Khrushchev, the first great reformer of the Communist era, could have completely reformed that system by himself or retired with hands unsoiled by Stalinism.

They may be right. What Khrushchev started had to wait for Gorbachev to complete. Similarly, what Gorbachev and Yeltsin started a future leader may yet complete, perhaps after another long conservative interlude of power. If so, Boris Yeltsin, the architect who laid the democratic foundation for a post-Communist Russia, will deserve much of the credit.

Even Gorbachev remains optimistic in the long run. "Yeltsin has gotten lost," Mikhail Sergeyevich told me in January 1995. "His regime is sliding toward totalitarianism." But Gorbachev called it a "temporary setback" on the road to further reform. In the longer term, the former Soviet president stressed, "I can say unambiguously that a revenge of fundamentalist forces will not take place. There will be no return to the past. This is a well-educated society. It has tasted freedom and glasnost and openness, and the ability to vote. This means too much. No one can turn the clock back." Sooner or later, Mikhail Sergeyevich believes, Russian voters will return genuine reformers to power.

The trouble with such Gorbachev optimism is that it has so often been wrong. In November 1991, for example, he was confidently predicting that Ukraine would vote to remain in the U.S.S.R. and allow him to hold the Soviet Union together, when in fact, only weeks later, Ukraine overwhelmingly approved by more than 80 percent a referendum on independence that finally broke up the U.S.S.R.

Sadly, the only safe long-term prediction about Russia is that the Kremlin power struggle will continue, probably well into the next century. The split between reformers and conservatives fueling this struggle runs through all sections of society, including the army and the former KGB. The battle between them could well go on for decades before Russia turns definitively one way or the other.

In one of the more optimistic long-term scenarios, a stable democracy and market economy do indeed take hold. A well-educated new entrepreneurial class develops Russia's vast natural resources and low labor costs into a booming economic success. Moscow becomes a major force in world trade and a new global threat—this time to beat America and the West at their own capitalist game by winning away a large share of competitive markets. Thirty years from now, Americans could be worrying more about Russia's economic domination than its military capability.

In one of the more pessimistic long-range scenarios, a new dictator takes power, expands Russia to former Soviet borders, and renews the arms race, the Cold War, and the nuclear nightmare. Russian disputes with neighboring countries from Eastern Europe to the Middle East to China raise new threats of global conflict.

There are many other possibilities. Among them, the current battle for Russia's soul continues indecisively for many years, with neither the forces of reform nor their conservative rivals able to establish either a secure political regime or a genuine economic recovery. The tension raises a constant threat of armed conflict between them, the specter of civil war in a nuclear power, and with that a permanent source of dangerous instability in world affairs.

Whatever happens, Russia is certain to pose a serious challenge to the world in the years ahead. Western leaders have no more vital interest than to channel that challenge toward peaceful economic competition and away from military confrontation. Yeltsin had his faults, but his regime was at least listening to the West, providing the democratic camp with a rare chance to influence Kremlin behavior. Future historians will not forgive Western leaders for missing this window of opportunity. If Russia closes itself off in another aggressive dictatorship, there may never again be as promising a chance to build a peaceful world. The time has come to look at what precisely the West can and should do to meet the new Russian challenge.

19

What Is to Be Done?

Vladimir Ilyich Lenin, the founder of the Soviet State, posed the most famous question in Communist history: "What is to be done?" He made
that question the title of his best-known political tract. Lenin's answer to his
own question, his formula for solving Russia's horrendous problems early
in the century, was for his Bolsheviks to seize power and build communism.
The question was better than the answer. Lenin's question remains valid
today, while his answer, "Communism," is now seen to have failed. In the
spring of 1991, only months before the collapse of the U.S.S.R., I met in the
Kremlin with Aleksandr Nikolayevich Yakovlev, the last reformer on Gorbachev's Politburo, to find out how Soviet leaders expected to solve Russia's
appalling political, economic, and nationality problems near the end of the
century. My first question was phrased in suitably historic terms. "What is
to be done?" I asked Yakovlev.

Aleksandr Nikolayevich smiled and responded with a question of his own.
"Do you know the answer?" Yakovlev inquired. I admitted I did not. "Then
how do you expect me to know the answer?" Yakovlev replied.

"You are sitting at the center of power, inside the Kremlin, in the office
next to President Gorbachev," I explained. "You have access to the most privileged information in the country, and the best expert advice. If anyone
knows the answer, you should."

Yakovlev paused. Then he told me something I never forgot. "Sometimes
the picture is clearer from a distance," Aleksandr Nikolayevich said.

His remark became a prime rationale for writing this book. Perhaps even
an outsider, a foreigner, could help put Soviet and post-Communist history
in perspective. After all, as Yakovlev said, sometimes the picture is clearer
from a distance.

That is true not only for Russia, but also for America. Throughout these
pages, the United States has been criticized from afar for mishandling the
Soviet threat. In this concluding chapter, suggestions will be offered on how
the United States could do better in dealing with a future Russian challenge.
It may seem presumptuous for an outsider, someone who has never held a

government post, to criticize past U.S. policy and suggest improvements for the future. But once again, Yakovlev's remark provides a rationale. Sometimes the picture is clearer from a distance.

There were, of course, other reasons for writing this book. Among them was a desire to share the lessons learned in thirty years of reporting on Soviet affairs from Russia and abroad. I first arrived in Moscow as a young journalist, open-minded, anxious to hear the Soviet side of the Cold War arguments, hopeful that the two superpowers could somehow reason together, compromise, and live in peace. However, over the years, the longer I remained in Moscow, the longer I listened to Soviet officials, the more I saw how they exploited their own people economically and deprived them of basic human rights, the more I saw them threaten the outside world, and the more I put all that together, the more I understood that Western goodwill was just another weapon in Moscow's hands. Soviet officials toyed with Western concepts like compromise or fair play, making sure that in any negotiation, the West did the giving and they the taking. Brezhnev's double game of "détente," relaxing Western defenses while conducting the biggest arms buildup in history, was but one example.

I watched in Moscow as the best-informed senior American officials let Brezhnev get away with it. Despite all the classified intelligence reports available to them, I began to realize, the Washington elite did not sufficiently understand the Russians or how to deal with the Kremlin. Over the years, the Soviets used disinformation, distortion, ruthless repression, and obsessive secrecy to mask their record and designs, then came to the conference table claiming to negotiate with the United States in good faith. More often than not, as each generation of well-intended U.S. negotiators sat down, they seemed to have learned little from the mistakes of their predecessors. Thus, as we have seen, they let Gorbachev play the weakness card as effectively as Brezhnev did, again to Soviet advantage.[1]

Nor did the performance much improve with the collapse of the Soviet Union. American officials still came to Russia blinded to the realities on the ground by their hopes for progress. As but one example of this continuing syndrome, Secretary of State James Baker attended a human rights conference in Moscow in 1992 and publicly praised Yeltsin's new Russia as a "democracy," which it manifestly was not yet then, and may never be. Bill Clinton and Warren Christopher did no better downplaying the Chechnya war as an internal Russian affair at a time when an outraged Chancellor Helmut Kohl of Germany, a wiser hand at dealing with Moscow, was phoning Yeltsin and telling him the bombing of civilians was unacceptable behavior. In the end, I concluded that Washington insiders have not done so well handling Moscow that they can afford to ignore suggestions from the outside.

Some of the best suggestions the U.S. government chose to discount came from Russian democrats. Attempting to put that right is perhaps the best justification for presuming to advise Washington from afar. For years

I listened to Russians like Andrei Sakharov explain how the wiser use of relative U.S. strengths could be more effective in dealing with Moscow. These people understood that in the long run Russians would determine the fate of their own country, but they also believed the United States could do more to help democratic forces win the continuing power struggle in Moscow. They were not asking for charity. Instead they were asking for stronger U.S. policies that would help them—and help the West at the same time. They thought that by standing firm against any Russian aggression or rollback on human rights, the United States could promote irreversible reform in Russia and help the West by making the world a safer place. Unfortunately, their message rarely got through to U.S. decision-makers. For Sakharov's sake, it is worth another try.

In the pages that follow, the reader will find specific suggestions for improving U.S. policy toward Russia. All summarize positions taken earlier in this book. All have two goals in mind—to encourage irreversible democratic reform in Russia and, at the same time, to discourage a return to dictatorship there. No claim is made that these suggestions are perfect. Instead, they are presented with an open invitation to cut, replace, amend, or otherwise improve them. My intent is to encourage debate on "What is to be done?" rather than offer definitive answers.

For America, such a debate is essential, and long overdue. The crucial first step is to start asking the right questions. Until we do, there is no hope of finding the right answers. The proof of that is the way we look at the collapse of communism. America has yet to start asking the right questions about how and why the Cold War ended.

George Bush, Ronald Reagan, and their aides would have the world believe the West won the Cold War. True enough, Soviet communism disintegrated on their watch. And, as we have seen, long-term Western resolve played a major role in pressuring communism toward its eventual collapse. But it is nonsense to say the West won the Cold War.

The truth is that the Soviet Union lost the Cold War. It lost because the U.S.S.R. never overcame a series of fatal internal contradictions. Those contradictions, each recounted at chapter length in this book, include a divided Soviet leadership, an unworkable economic system, an ideology that could be imposed only by ruthless police terror, a nationalist rebellion that could not be contained, a quest for freedom and human rights that would not be denied, and an irreparably split world Communist movement.

Responsible Soviet officials admit they lost the Cold War, that their system collapsed from internal contradictions rather than from Western pressure. Among them is Anatoly Dobrynin, the longtime Soviet ambassador to Washington and later a key Gorbachev foreign policy adviser as head of the international department of the Soviet Communist Party's Central Committee. "The years 1985–1991 were very good years for us in foreign policy," Dobrynin told me in an interview. "Reagan cooperated with us in his second term. So did Bush. On disarmament questions these years were better for us than the Nixon presidency. Nothing in foreign policy hurt us except Germany. Our system was brought down by internal economic collapse, not by international pressure."[2]

Rather than gloating over a victory they did not entirely earn, U.S. leaders would be better advised to see where the West went wrong, where it missed earlier opportunities to exploit communism's fatal contradictions and bring down the system decades earlier. The gloating suggests all is well and that no Western policies need improving. Nothing could be further from the truth. Lessons drawn from mishandling the Soviet threat during the Cold War could well make a vital difference in defeating any future challenge from an economically and militarily resurgent Russia. If the West faces an aggressive nuclear-armed Russian dictatorship again, the margin for error next time is likely to be smaller.

Naturally, improving U.S. policy will involve more than simply drawing the appropriate lessons from the past. Another essential requirement is a better understanding of post–Cold War reality. Here again, there is much to learn.

In Bill Clinton's Washington, for example, it became fashionable to talk about "the simpler times" of the Cold War. Then the greatest threat to America was clearly from Moscow. After the fall of the U.S.S.R., the world was said to have grown more complex. The major global threats remaining were no longer a single nation such as the Soviet Union. Instead they were now international dangers like terrorism, the drug trade, and nuclear proliferation. These threats were everywhere, often invisible, and therefore harder to fight. Nor was there a generally accepted solution in sight for policymakers to build a public consensus on, like higher defense spending to win the arms race against Russia.

At the same time, the end of the Cold War saw older regional conflicts resume with a vengeance, on killing fields from Bosnia to Rwanda, with no effective new world order to stop the slaughter. To many, the post–Cold War world had become a more dangerous place, with tougher problems and fewer answers. Instead of the superpower nuclear stalemate, which had largely kept the peace for four decades, there was now a more unpredictable, unmanageable world and an expanding club of nuclear powers. The primary new threat was now likely to come from places like Iran, which, according to Western intelligence sources, was five years or less away from making nuclear bombs to promote the spread of Islamic fundamentalism.

One should not underestimate the problems of the post–Cold War era, but it is absurd to suggest that handling the Soviet threat was ever "simpler." Anyone who lived through the 1962 Cuban missile crisis knows that Cold War policy choices were always exceedingly complex. The stakes then were nothing less than global survival. No problem in the Clinton era yet comes close to that. Indeed, it is precisely because Cold War decisions were so difficult—and so dangerous—that America and its allies so often erred on the side of caution.

Instead of minimizing the difficulties of Cold War policymakers, we should learn from them. The first need is to recognize the problem. It is that the West mishandled the Soviet threat, but has yet to draw the appropriate lessons. Next, these lessons need to be arranged in some coherent framework under the leadership of the United States. America emerged from the Cold War as the world's only superpower. No other country can begin to match its military might. No other force can turn back a new nuclear challenge from a revived Russian dictatorship or any other potential threat to global peace. No other nation can lead the way to a more stable new world order. But if any of that is actually "to be done," America must remain the key player fully engaged on the world stage.

Thus before Washington can decide how to handle the new Russia, or any specific foreign policy challenge, there needs to be a clear vision of the proper U.S. role in the post–Cold War world. Naturally, America alone cannot play world policeman. It should not even try to resolve all global problems on its own. Instead, what is needed now most of all is strong U.S. leadership, to rally the Western democracies first, and then the world community at large, toward the construction of a lasting era of global peace.

Unfortunately, the United States is now moving in the opposite direction. It is using the end of the Cold War as an opportunity to withdraw from foreign affairs, to turn inward and focus instead on resolving problems at home. This is no great surprise. America has turned isolationist before. U.S. domestic problems are serious and have for too long been neglected. The American public at the end of the Cold War, no longer afraid of nuclear annihilation from abroad, demanded that its leaders make domestic issues the top priority. Voters punished George Bush for concentrating too much on foreign policy and elected Bill Clinton in his place to put the emphasis back on progress at home.

While this shift in U.S. priorities is understandable, it is also dangerous. World problems don't stop growing simply because Americans no longer pay much attention. Worse, when the United States turns inward, it creates a power vacuum other nations, often the more tyrannical ones, are only too happy to fill. They seize the initiative and expand their appetites, influence, and territory until eventually they threaten vital U.S. interests. At that point the U.S. wakes to a new crisis—or even a new war involving American troops—that might well have been avoided if Washington had been properly engaged on the world stage all along.

Being properly engaged, for the United States, means continually taking leadership positions in the effort to solve problems abroad before they get out of hand. Creating an international force, anchored by U.S. troops, to prevent Saddam Hussein from seizing Kuwait and threatening vital U.S. oil interests in the Middle East is a good example of what America must do.

But one such good show, no matter how well conducted, is not enough, if at the same time U.S. preoccupation with domestic concerns lets other foreign threats continue to escalate. Bosnia, for example, was left by Bush and Clinton for the Europeans and the United Nations to solve. Without strong U.S. leadership, however, the war in the former Yugoslavia continued. Belatedly, Clinton seized the diplomatic initiative three years into his presidency, with a policy that put U.S. peacekeeping troops in harm's way on the ground there, a danger that stronger U.S. leadership earlier on could have avoided.

Bosnia also raised other dangers. For one thing, frustration over the long and bloody conflict there encouraged Americans to believe more strongly than ever that withdrawing from the world stage and concentrating instead on the home front was the wisest course. For another, the more visible flash points of the moment, like Bosnia, Somalia, Rwanda, and Haiti, were also distractions. They dominated the reduced interest Americans gave to foreign affairs in the first years of the post–Cold War era, and diverted U.S. attention from more disturbing dangers abroad.

In the long run, instability in Russia still represents the most serious danger of all. Democratic reform and market economics are failing there, while the threat of renewed dictatorship is rising, and, with that, the menace of resumed aggression. For all its problems, Russia remains a formidable nuclear power today, and with proper management it could become an economic power tomorrow. Indeed, the United States has no more important priority than to meet Moscow's multifaceted challenge, first by encouraging stable democracy in Russia and then, if that fails, by containing any new Russian threat. Washington, however, is in no position to do so, with a reduced priority given to foreign affairs generally, and, within that context, even less attention to the continuing power struggle in Moscow over Russia's future course.

The U.S. focus on the home front is overdone. Important as domestic issues are, they cannot be resolved by ignoring the rest of the world. Any aggressive new Russia would inevitably force a rise again in U.S. defense spending, taking money from efforts to solve domestic problems. Thus in that way, the Russian challenge and U.S. internal policy are related. The one affects the other. The United States can resolve its problems at home only if it limits the Russian challenge abroad.

In sum, in answering the question "What is to be done?" the United States needs to assume the proper global leadership role and then focus that role on meeting the Russian challenge. There are a number of policy decisions the U.S. government and its allies should take in order to do that job properly.

There is, of course, no one magic formula for solving all crises. A Russian attack on Poland, for example, or another nation in Eastern Europe, is likely to provoke a different Western response from a Russian attack on

Kazakhstan or some former Soviet republic in Central Asia. Each individual Russian threat requires its own specific response, depending on the geographic location of the country menaced, the timing, the balance of military forces there, the strengths and weaknesses of the political leaders involved, historical relationships, and many other variables. Nonetheless, early overall preparation can be vital to Western success, wherever the next crisis develops.

The optimal preparation will involve learning from Cold War mistakes so that in future, U.S. assets can be more effectively used to pressure Moscow away from renewed dictatorship at home or aggression abroad. Fortunately, America and its allies have a broad array of assets to deal from a position of strength with any future Russian challenge. These assets are discussed below in groups, beginning with political and continuing in order through economic, diplomatic, military, and moral strengths. In each group, specific policy lines are recommended.

I. POLITICAL

1. Take the Long View

Any effective Western policy toward Moscow has to begin with a realization of what has not changed since the fall of communism. Russia remains a prisoner of its past. The Stalinist legacy haunts the nation. The Kremlin power struggle begun at Stalin's death continues to this day, with brute force often still the decisive factor. None of the remarkable changes of recent years is yet irreversible, should dictatorship again take hold, as it may.

For decades, one of the West's gravest errors has been to overrate the pace and extent of change in Moscow. Thus in 1968, during Dubček's Prague Spring, British Foreign Secretary Michael Stewart told me, "The Russians will not invade Czechoslovakia. They have changed too much since Hungary in 1956." Similarly, the West later concluded that first Gorbachev, then Yeltsin were irreversibly committed to democracy, when in fact both proved capable of turning authoritarian and reneging on reform in order to keep power. The Western tendency to magnify positive change in Moscow is an old mistake, often repeated. It is long past time to admit that tendency and correct it.

In this context it is worth remembering that one of Russia's contributions to world culture is the concept of the Potemkin Village, containing clean new building fronts with nothing behind to back them up. In some ways, reform in Russia is still a Potemkin Village.

When the United States exaggerates democratic progress in Russia, Kremlin leaders think they can relax or even roll back reform and still retain broad international support. Only when the West insists that further substantial

democratic progress remains an essential condition for East-West cooperation does reform in Russia stand a real chance of becoming irreversible.

The long view—measuring recent reform against what must still be done
to overcome centuries of dictatorship—is the wiser course for the years ahead.

2. Exploit the Splits

By definition, the continuing power struggle in Moscow means the Kremlin leadership is divided. Such divisions can and should be exploited to Western advantage. Instead, these opportunities were often wasted in the past.
Examples cited earlier in these pages are instructive. Better use of the trade
weapon could have helped Kosygin push Brezhnev toward fundamental reform from the mid-1960s. Better use of diplomatic pressure could have discouraged a divided Soviet leadership from invading Hungary and
Czechoslovakia. The image of unity in the Politburo, propagated by the
Kremlin and swallowed abroad, was as false as the myth of a monolithic world
Communist movement.

In post-Communist Russia, rival conservative and progressive forces bat-
tled to push Yeltsin and the nation their way. The relative success of the conservatives testifies to the poor job the West did in attempting to manipulate
this split to democratic advantage through the use of aid and other policy
tools. One opportunity that the United States did not use, for example, was
to invite Russia's leading progressive politician, Grigory Yavlinsky, to Washington for talks at the White House and to address Congress, in an early effort to build up his presidential credentials, as a promising successor, or even
an alternative, to the newly authoritarian Yeltsin. Russian democrats expressed regret to me in Moscow in 1994 that this was not done. It remains
to be seen whether U.S. policymakers can do any better to enhance the
prospects of progressive candidates before the Russian presidential election
scheduled for 1996.

Should dictatorship return to Russia, and again threaten aggression
abroad, it could be a divided collective leadership or a one-man rule with divided senior advisers. Either way, opportunities will exist for the West to manipulate the divisions to contain any future threat. Exploiting divisions in
the Kremlin leadership is one of the strongest cards in the Western deck, potentially decisive in any crisis. Studies should already be under way now on
how to do that more effectively.

3. Isolate the Hard-Liners

Throughout the Cold War, the Soviet Union constantly sought to split the
Western alliance, exploiting differences between the United States and Europe or the United States and Japan. America, however, wrongly accepted
the Communist bloc as monolithic, making no concerted effort to manip-

ulate the tensions between Russia and China or Russia and Eastern Europe into an earlier collapse of communism. This error squandered a colossal opportunity. It should be corrected to meet a future Russian challenge.

Any resurgent, aggressive Russian dictatorship will launch a major effort to split the Western alliance. This time the West cannot reciprocate by working the fault lines of a Communist bloc that no longer exists. But the United States must still learn to respond more effectively here. Defense, meaning an effort to maintain alliance solidarity, is not good enough. Instead, Washington should take the initiative, rallying the allies and the rest of the world community to isolate any new hard-line dictatorship in Russia. As the world's only remaining superpower, the United States has that potential, and isolating Kremlin hard-liners could have a profound effect. If unable to claim support from other nations, a new dictatorship in Moscow is less likely to conduct military aggression abroad, more likely to be pressured into meaningful reform at home.

4. Oppose Colonialism

Incredible as it sounds at the end of the twentieth century, colonialism remains one of Russia's great weaknesses. On perhaps no other issue is Russia more vulnerable to effective Western pressure. For decades, the Soviet Union denounced the Western democracies as colonialist and imperialist, long after they had granted all their former colonies independence. Meanwhile, the Soviet Union itself maintained the world's last remaining colonial empire, covering one-sixth of the earth's surface. While posing as the champion of colonized peoples abroad, Moscow ruthlessly retained all foreign territory seized by tsars and commissars, from Eastern Europe to the Pacific. The doublethink specialists in the Kremlin essentially told the outside world, "What's mine is mine, and what's yours is negotiable." Rarely has a major power been so obviously hypocritical.

Worse, the West let the Kremlin get away with it. For decades Moscow supported "wars of national liberation" throughout the Third World, in reality nothing more than pro-Communist rebellions against Western interests, disguised as anticolonial crusades. Yet the West did not respond in kind, despite manifold opportunities to do so. The West did little to encourage Eastern Europe's rebellion within the Soviet empire. When rebellion came anyway, as in Hungary or Czechoslovakia, and Western aid could have made a difference, the West still did nothing. No other Western shortcoming contributed more to the prolonged life of the Soviet empire. Had independence movements throughout the Soviet Union and Eastern Europe received the political, economic, and even arms aid they deserved—judiciously applied, of course—communism would have collapsed decades earlier.

The West need not repeat the same mistake with the new Russia. Should dictatorship return to Moscow and again promote aggression abroad, the minority nationality regions will be its Achilles' heel. The West could then promote anti-Russian independence movements, starting in Chechnya and the Caucasus, as the most effective way to deter the Kremlin from foreign adventurism. No leadership in Moscow can afford aggression abroad at a time when Russia's national fabric is breaking apart.

Indeed, the argument can be made that just as the breakup of the Soviet Union into fifteen republics served Western interests by ending the Cold War, so would a breakup of Russia into smaller mini-states serve Western interests by leaving the Kremlin in control of little more than the greater Moscow region and thus far too small a power to conduct aggression abroad. In that case a Western policy of encouraging dissolution of the former Russian tsarist empire would be in order, on the high moral grounds of putting an end to nineteenth-century colonialism according to the universally accepted principles of the UN Charter. Nothing as crudely provocative as direct arms aid to the Chechens or other minority nationalities need be undertaken. More subtle options are available to encourage regional autonomy first, then independence, for example by substantial Western trade deals directly with Russia's increasingly powerful regional authorities, from St. Petersburg in the West to Yakutia in eastern Siberia, rather than indirectly through national officials in Moscow.

At this writing, however, Russia appears more likely to expand than to break up. In that case, decisions on the troubling question of Russian colonialism may soon be forced on Western leaders anyway, whether they are ready for them or not. Strong forces are at work in Russia demanding that the U.S.S.R. be reconstituted, bringing former Soviet republics back into the fold, by tanks if necessary, and then expanding further. Should these conservatives take power in Moscow, they are likely to act on such publicly stated aims. Then the West will have to ask itself whether it is willing to oppose such renewed Russian aggression with military force, and if so, where. In Kazakhstan? In Ukraine? In the Baltics? In Poland? If they are wise, Western democracies will draw the line sooner rather than later to contain the threat while it is still relatively small. If not, their appeasement will only increase the danger of a larger war.

5. Widen the Margins

Soviet experience shows that Western influence on Russian behavior is rarely decisive and often marginal. In the end, only Russians decide their own future. However, even marginal Western influence can be important. History is made on tiny margins. Pivotal national elections are often decided by votes like 50.5 percent to 49.5 percent, a margin of only 1 percent. In Russia, a presidential election determining whether the country moves toward further democracy or back toward dictatorship could also be decided by only 1 percent, and Western influence could well make that much difference. Furthermore, the West's marginal influence can be widened considerably.

One effective way to do this is for the West to depersonalize its approach by backing democratic reform, the policy, rather than any one top Kremlin leader alone. First Gorbachev, then Yeltsin showed the dangers of the personalized approach. The West backed each of them as as individuals, then discovered each had turned authoritarian and started rolling back reform. In both instances, Western nations were stuck, supporting the wrong man who was pushing the wrong policies, because they had denied themselves better alternatives.

A far more productive course would be to broaden the use of Western political endorsements, trade, and aid, in order to support all those Russian leaders seeking to make democracy and the market economy irreversible. By using this wider approach, the West could spread its backing among influential forces in both the capital and the regions. As one result, Yeltsin, or any other top man, would understand that his room for maneuver, his ability to roll back reform and still keep Western support, was limited, because the West would have options to back other progressives instead. As a consequence, Yeltsin would thus be encouraged to champion reform more consistently himself. Another benefit of backing reform, the policy, rather than Yeltsin, the man, would be to help unite and strengthen Russia's democratic forces, which have always been too weak and divided. For all these reasons, this broader Western approach to promoting reform in Russia should be applied well before the scheduled 1996 Russian presidential election, and then be reinforced afterward regardless of who wins.

Broadening Western support also means extending it from the presidential arena to other power centers, in order to encourage a system of checks and balances in Russia. Democracy will be healthy and secure in Russia only when there are a truly independent parliament and a truly independent court system, each sufficiently strong to prevent the presidency from taking on dictatorial powers. Neither is yet a fact of life in Moscow. A major aim of American and Western policy should be to encourage the establishment of such democratic institutions in Russia to assure proper checks and balances. The present U.S. tendency of supporting only the president encourages both the top man's dictatorial impulses and the military, security, and bureaucratic forces that support them. It is thus counterproductive and should be discarded for a more balanced approach.

6. Promote the Law-Based State

No other factor is likely to be more important in making democratic reform in Russia irreversible than adherence to law. Western experts should be provided free of charge to help Russia restructure its court, tax, police, and parliamentary systems. The goals of such restructuring would be to make fair trials, equitable taxation, oversight against police abuse, and stable democratic institutions all hallmarks of the new Russia. As part of that process, Western economic aid should be tied to progress in creating a law-based state.

II. ECONOMIC

7. Go Slow on Economic Aid

Large-scale aid grants to Russia are a bad idea for many reasons. Often economic aid ends up in the pockets of corrupt officials, rather than helping the people who need it. What does get properly invested in government programs tends to be wasted in an inefficient transition economy still suffering from holdover Soviet contradictions. And even if such corruption and waste could be eliminated, substantial economic aid is still no guarantee that democracy or market economics in Russia will be promoted. The reform leader who collects the aid can always be pushed aside by a new dictator, who then can use the Western aid funds already in the country to promote a new Cold War arms race.

For all these reasons, technical assistance, or free advice, is far more cost-effective than big cash gifts. In the long term, specialist help on how to create a proper banking or legal system will go much further in promoting irreversible reform in Russia, at far less cost. The wisest up-and-coming democratic leaders in Russia, like Boris Nemtsov in Nizhni Novgorod, favor this approach, preferring technical help in creating small businesses or in improving management structures to billions of dollars in cash aid.[3] These are the very Russian leaders that Western aid should be designed to help most. Their requests are both affordable for the West and most likely to work in Russia. By targeting technical assistance to people like Nemtsov, the West can accomplish two goals at the same time—promoting the progressive side of the power struggle and enhancing the prospects of long-term economic recovery.

8. Encourage Humanitarian Aid

Charity is a good thing, as long as it gets to the right people. Food, medicine, and other humanitarian aid can do wonders in Russia. The need is enormous, the gratitude boundless. Ordinary people and officials of good faith don't forget such kindness. Humanitarian aid in times of economic crisis, natural disaster, or civil war should be a constant of the Western approach to Russia, untied to any policy considerations. But it should come in as food, clothing, or medicine, not as cash. Most important, Western donors must arrange to oversee all transport of such goods down to the local level and into the apartments of the people it is designed to help.

That means Western guards on the planes or trains taking donated goods from Moscow into the provinces, and then on trucks within cities to the individual recipients. All too often in the past, as after the December 1988 earthquake in Armenia, generous Western relief shipments sent through Moscow have been pilfered by corrupt national or local officials and never got to the intended end user. Russia is still a country where some officials steal from their own people. Humanitarian aid should help the victims, not the vultures who prey on them.

9. Emphasize Education

Scholarships are the best aid idea of all. If the ancient Israeli parallel is true—that post-Communist Russia must wander in the wilderness for forty years waiting for a new generation of leaders to show the way to the promised land—then education is crucial.

The people who will lead Russia in forty years are now in their twenties. The best of them are studying at universities and graduate schools. America and its allies should be offering them as many scholarships as possible to study in the West. There is no finer long-term investment of foreign aid. The West now has a unique chance—never possible during the Soviet era—to educate Russia's leaders of tomorrow and show them how to bring their country into the community of truly democratic nations. It is an opportunity the democracies cannot afford to waste.

10. Use the Trade Weapon

Western economic superiority makes trade an invaluable weapon. Russia desperately needs to buy advanced Western technology and to sell in Western markets. Access to both should come at a price, as it did during the Cold War, often with effect. The Jackson-Vanik legislation in the United States made improved Soviet-American trade dependent on increased Jewish emigration from Brezhnev's Russia—and proved such linkage could produce the desired results. NATO successfully blocked technology transfer of military value to the U.S.S.R. during the Cold War under its COCOM arrangements, and will have to revive them if Russia turns back to aggressive dictatorship.

Despite such successes, however, the trade weapon was always underused. The West could have done far more. As we have seen, an oil embargo in the mid-1960s could have pushed Brezhnev toward Gorbachev-type reforms two decades earlier. The trade weapon had huge potential. Here was an option with enormous leverage for the NATO allies, because the Soviet Union could not begin to match Western economic strength. Here was also an option of minimal risk, because there was no way Moscow could retaliate in trade or economic terms. The Russians were neither an essential market nor an essential supplier for the West. At the same time, the U.S.S.R. could find no adequate substitutes for the Western markets or supplies it needed. Thus in trade wars, Moscow had almost no cards to play. The Western allies, provided they stuck together, had an unbeatable hand.

In containing any future long-term Russian threat, the allies need to do a better job exploiting the trade weapon to its full potential. Starting down that road is easy. Increased East-West trade can help Russia move toward stable democracy and a successful market economy. It should be encouraged by NATO governments and Japan as long as Russia continues in that direction. Indeed, no one in the big leagues of world trade has trouble with that concept. It is mutually beneficial. The stronger the trade relationship and the larger the Russian dependence on commerce with the West, the greater the potential leverage in Western hands.

The problem comes later on, if Moscow heads back toward dictatorship, an arms race, and Cold War. At that point, powerful Western interests will minimize the dangers and press for a policy of "business as usual" with Russia. For them, trade has become a double-edged sword. Any trade embargo on Russia would also hurt their companies. Nonetheless, at this point vital national interests have to take precedence over individual business interests. Western governments will need to deploy the trade weapon clearly and decisively, then make sure any embargo is upheld across the board. Just the threat of trade sanctions can give Moscow pause and discourage military adventurism abroad. Should that fail, the firm application of a trade boycott can substantially weaken Russian prospects for making aggression pay. No other economic option in the Western arsenal has as much potential. U.S. leadership on this front, convincing the European allies and Japan to remain on board, is absolutely essential in turning back any future Russian challenge.

III. DIPLOMATIC

11. Take the Initiative

For too long during the Cold War, the United States let the weaker Soviet Union set the rules for East-West relations. That mistake helped prolong the Brezhnev leadership and put off the ultimate failure of Soviet communism. The lesson could hardly be clearer. If given the opportunity, the Russians will seize the diplomatic initiative, despite their relative weakness, set the agenda on their terms, and force the stronger West to react within limited and unsatisfactory response options. For example, a new dictatorship in Moscow will be capable of using military pressure to incorporate Ukraine in Russia again, and then daring the West to do anything more than condemn the action in irate speeches. It should be equally clear that a top Western priority in the face of any new Moscow challenge must be to make sure Russia no longer has the opportunity to set the East-West agenda. Instead, the United States and its allies have to seize the initiative and keep it.

Fortunately, the West has every opportunity to do so. The NATO allies are far stronger than the new Russia politically—in terms of stability of institutions, public support, unity of purpose, and international backing, to name but a few crucial factors. The allies hold similarly huge advantages over Russia on every other yardstick of measurement, economically and militarily. As an overriding principle, NATO nations should tell Moscow that all future Western trade, aid, and political support depend on proven Russian performance in protecting human rights at home and promoting peace abroad. On specific individual issues, the United States and its allies can consult the Russians and listen to their views with an open mind. But at the end of the day, it is the West which should set the terms and then invite the Russians to cooperate.

Despite all its advantages, the stronger West has still not sufficiently seized the initiative. Instead the weaker Russians often continue to set the terms of East-West relations. As but one illustration of this, the world is treated to the curious spectacle of Boris Yeltsin with one hand out for Western aid and the other hand attempting to dictate the terms under which the West should be allowed to expand its own alliance. The arrogance of the aid recipient's telling the donor how to act is astounding. Nonetheless the Russian president has largely succeeded in shaping the conditions for bringing former Communist nations of Eastern Europe into NATO. He has done so by employing a long-favored Soviet tactic, the weakness card. Unless NATO expands on terms Moscow can accept, Yeltsin has warned, hard-liners may kill democratic reform and return Russia to dictatorship. Like Brezhnev, he has essentially said, "Do it my way or get someone worse."

There is nothing wrong with NATO's taking Yeltsin's concerns into account. But ultimately the Western allies themselves must decide how and when to expand NATO, what terms to grant the East Europeans—and former Soviet republics like the Baltic states—and what sort of cooperation to offer Russia. They cannot be blackmailed by Yeltsin's threats of a "cold peace" if his warnings go unheeded. Western governments must resist such pressure for many reasons, not the least of them the fact that Yeltsin himself cannot guarantee continued democratic, peaceful policies in Russia. It is, in short, a crucial test case. If the West cannot seize and keep the diplomatic initiative for the expansion of its own NATO alliance, then it is unlikely to be able to set the agenda across the board for East-West relations in the years ahead.

The way ahead for the West on NATO expansion is clear. The Western nations should decide first how to enlarge their alliance. Then and only then should they give Moscow security guarantees as an incentive to agree to an accommodation with a larger NATO. For example, it would be wrong for NATO to assure Moscow before NATO expansion that no NATO nuclear weapons or soldiers will be stationed on the soil of Poland or Czechoslovakia. However, once NATO is expanded to include these two East European nations, it would be right to offer those guarantees as part of a new security agreement between Moscow and an expanded NATO.

An accommodation between an enlarged NATO and the new Russia should be a major goal of Western policy, part of the effort to bring Moscow into the civilized family of nations. In this connection it is important for the West to show sensitivity to Russia's history, traditions, and peculiar circumstances, and to exercise patience and allow the time needed for Moscow to build a genuine democracy. In short, just as it is wrong for the West to succumb to Russia's blackmail campaigns from a position of weakness, it is equally wrong to ignore Russia's genuine concerns and refuse to help. In this connection, sentiment building in the U.S. Congress to scrap the ABM treaty and build a space-based missile defense system—because a weakened Russia can no longer do so—is particularly unfortunate. Any such action would create a new atmosphere of mistrust in Moscow and imperil implementation of other arms control treaties and future negotiations on arms reductions. Once Moscow decides it can no longer trust the West, it is likely to move closer to other world troublemakers, among them Iran, Iraq, and North Korea. In that way Russia can still be dangerous even without being a superpower. Thus, rather than ignoring Moscow, attempts to accommodate Russia, in a way that promotes Western interests, are the way to go.

12. Learn from Russia's Neighbors

Russians have a different mentality, their own psychological makeup, often difficult for Americans to understand. Part of it is the Asian influence on the Russian character. Part of it is the fundamental legacy of the Soviet era, the Stalinist terror, horrors no American can begin to comprehend. Of course, Russians and Americans have some similarities. Both are from continental-size nations, both are nuclear powers, both tend to be outgoing, warm, and generous in their personal relations. But the differences far outweigh any such superficial common ground.

These differences are crucial in decision-making. Russians factor in an awesome respect for authority that appears unhealthy to Americans. What Americans regard as normal courtesy Russians see as weakness. The Russian capacity to cope with suffering is light-years ahead of anything Americans can imagine. The list of differences is long. Suffice it to say that in most decisions, the behavior of the one surprises the other.

Such differences of approach also go into questions of war and peace. Russians react differently from Americans to the same pressures or incentives. In a crisis, that can be crucial. Peace offerings or threats designed in an American context simply may not play in Moscow, or may produce unexpected and dangerous reactions.

Happily, however, help is at hand from neighbors on Russia's borders. Neighboring nations understand the Russian mentality far better than Americans or most West Europeans ever will. The neighbors also know much more about how and when to resist Russian pressure or to fight back. They had to learn all this in order to survive as independent nations on Russia's borders despite occupation, partition, or loss of territory. Neighbors learned the hard way, over centuries, often at a cost of lives, but learn they did. Today these border nations have a richer experience in handling the Russian threat than anyone else, a better understanding of the risks involved and the best tactics to overcome them. Most important, they are willing to share their knowledge with the United States and its allies. Among them are China, Turkey, and Poland.

Such neighborly advice was an asset America ignored through the Cold War. No other mistake in handling Russia is so easy to correct. In the long run, in avoiding future crises or defusing them peacefully, no other lesson may prove more important. The United States has every opportunity now to learn from Russia's neighbors and factor that into policymaking. There is no excuse for doing otherwise.

13. Two-Track the Russian-American Dialogue

American diplomatic expertise can and should be better used. All too often the United States preferred to do Cold War business exclusively through the Soviet ambassador in Washington. The U.S. president, or his secretary of state, regularly dealt on a private basis with Anatoly Dobrynin, leaving the U.S. embassy in Moscow out of the information loop on key issues. The practice was followed by both Republican and Democratic administrations. There are times when such an approach is useful. But to institutionalize it as the preferred and only channel most of the time is a big mistake.

For one thing, it wastes the talents of some of America's best-informed specialists on Russia. More often than not, U.S. ambassadors to Moscow have been fluent Russian speakers, highly knowledgeable about the country's political struggle, economic prospects, military strength, cultural heritage, and psychological makeup. They have also been well traveled in Russia and up to speed on all segments of public opinion across the country. To keep such people out of the information loop so their advice cannot be properly factored in makes no sense at all.

The best way to take advantage of America's top diplomatic experts on Russia is to make sure that one of them rather than some unqualified political operator or presidential campaign contributor continues to hold the ambassador's post in Moscow. Then all business with the Russians should be two-tracked—it should go through the U.S. embassy in Moscow as well as the Russian ambassador in Washington. This is not duplication or an insurance policy. It is simply a far more effective way of conducting relations.

A Russian-speaking U.S. ambassador in Moscow can make sure the Kremlin leadership gets the desired American message directly, rather than a distorted one filtered through the Russian ambassador in Washington. At the same time, the American ambassador in Moscow can get authoritative reaction directly from the top Kremlin leadership, far superior to anything brought to the White House by a Russian diplomatic messenger. Both advantages should help improve U.S. policymaking. Furthermore, two-tracking through Moscow allows the U.S. ambassador there into the information loop, so that he can offer his much-needed advice. Once again, correcting this past mistake is simple, and the potential benefit enormous.

IV. MILITARY

14. Don't Hype the Threat

The Soviet military threat was overrated by the Pentagon through most of the Cold War. That was the more prudent stand, and it justified the bigger defense budgets NATO armies sought for themselves, but it was ultimately wrong.

Kremlin leaders were never prepared to risk direct military confrontation with the United States, conventional or nuclear, for the very good reason that they knew the West was by far the stronger.

Just how badly equipped, trained, and led the Russian army could be was most recently put on display in Chechnya. Many in the West saw that as an aberration, as the result of horrendous problems affecting the former Red Army since the fall of the U.S.S.R., among them budget, manpower, and weapons cuts, inadequate housing, and low morale. All those factors played roles, but they were far from the entire story. In fact, the history of the Soviet Union shows that the much-feared Red army almost never distinguished itself in combat outside the Russian heartland. It was humiliatingly resisted by tiny Finland in 1939–40, and decades later it bogged down in Afghanistan. In between it succeeded in putting down rebellions in Hungary and Czechoslovakia largely because resistance was pathetic, on the order of civilians throwing rocks at tanks. In short, the Russian army's performance in Grozny was perfectly consistent with the Soviet record over the last half century on foreign soil, ever since the Finnish War. As the Chinese always said in the face of the Soviet military threat, the Russian bear was a paper tiger.

None of this detracts from the Red Army's absolutely stellar performance defending the Russian motherland in World War II. The forces Hitler ordered to invade Russia in 1941 were the strongest in history. Yet they were defeated by the Soviet army in battles that ensured the Allied victory over Nazi Germany. The point here, however, is that the bravado performance of the Soviet army in World War II came in defense of their own soil. It was a special case of national survival, and could not be faulted. But it had nothing in common with the far less successful performance of Soviet armed forces sent on offensive combat missions abroad. That distinction is crucial. Since NATO was not about to invade Russia, it did not have to worry about suffering Hitler's fate. Instead the NATO concern was the threat of a Soviet attack on the West. And there the record was always much less ominous. The Soviet army that could not crush little Finland just across the border was not about to take on the United States of America across the ocean.

Exaggerating the Soviet military threat had serious consequences for the West. It produced overly cautious policies. As one result, the United States was loath to take the diplomatic offensive. It had ample opportunity to exploit the Soviet-Chinese split in order to cripple the world Communist movement decades earlier. Instead, Washington held back. Defensively the story was much the same. When diplomatic support and arms aid could have saved the Hungarian or Czechoslovak rebellion against Moscow's rule, America again held back. In both cases the reason was largely an exaggerated fear of Moscow's military might. In both cases the result was that an overly cautious response to the Soviet military threat only served to prolong it.

This lesson will have to be recalled quickly should Russia return to aggressive dictatorship. In that event, the Kremlin's top priority will be rebuilding economic and military strength as rapidly as possible, a process increasingly apt to succeed with time. Inevitably it will include an early test of Western resolve, probing across borders with military force. Then any caving in by NATO, any decision to look the other way because of a renewed exaggeration of Russian military might, would be disastrous. Once again, it would prolong and extend the threat, until a new crisis made it even harder for the West to intervene or to contain aggression. Exaggerating Russian military strength is always a mistake, never more so than early on, when a new dictatorship is at its weakest.

15. Don't Downplay the Dangers

It is comforting to recall that Western mistakes in handling Russia during the Cold War were always correctable, even exaggerating the Soviet military threat. Opportunities and time were lost, but the world survived. A worse mistake by far would have been to underrate the dangers. Ultimately that could have exposed the Western democracies to Communist takeovers or global destruction. Fortunately, throughout the Cold War, the West never fell into that trap.

Unfortunately, the West now tends to underrate the dangers of a new Russian military threat in the post-Communist era. Moscow is often dismissed as a has-been superpower, a crippled economic giant, a busted military machine, preoccupied with domestic crises it can no longer manage. These assessments are not a million miles from the truth. But current circumstances are not permanent. Possibly within a decade, certainly within the lifetimes of most people under fifty today, a resurgent Russian dictatorship could again haunt the world as a military superpower. Thus it would be the height of folly for the West to allow NATO to disband, or to stop or even slow development of more advanced weapons technology in the mistaken belief that the Russian military threat is over.

16. Make Arms Control the Key Test

There is no great mystery about the best way to measure Moscow's future military intentions. It is Russia's performance on existing East-West arms control agreements, nuclear and conventional. Any Kremlin delays in implementation schedules, any shortfalls in promised cuts of weapons or manpower, any Russian rollback on agreed on-site verification procedures, has to be taken as a military threat and immediately rejected by the West as unacceptable behavior. All future Western aid, trade, and political support should be conditioned on proven Russian implementation of existing arms control accords.

In return, the West must be just as constant in its commitments to the new Russia. Promised U.S. financial and technical aid to dismantle nuclear weapons of the former Soviet armed forces must be delivered on schedule in full, whatever the problems of the moment in the East-West relationship. Similarly, the Western side must just as scrupulously abide by all its commitments in existing arms control agreements. Whatever else happens—whatever human rights outrages are committed in Russia, whatever new majority emerges in the U.S. Congress—pulling back on arms control obligations cannot be a permitted response option. Only if all provisions of these accords are completely fulfilled can a future Russian military threat be limited and a stable global security system created.

V. MORAL

17. Insist on Human Rights

Andrei Sakharov set a moral tone for dealing with Russia that could long survive both his death and the collapse of the Soviet Union. Western governments should make sure it does. Sakharov urged the United States to make support for basic human rights an essential element in East-West relations. If the Kremlin could not be trusted to fulfill its human rights obligations under international agreements, he argued, then it could not be trusted to honor arms control accords either. Sakharov wanted Western trade, aid, and political cooperation with Russia clearly linked to Moscow's actual performance on human rights. There is still no better guideline for the West today on this set of issues.

Boris Yeltsin or a successor may call Russia a "democracy," but words are not enough. The sort of deeds that count—and are so far still undone—are disbanding and dissolving all agencies that replaced the former KGB security police and ending all their extralegal powers of intimidation, search, and arrest, as in most of the former Communist nations of Eastern Europe. KGB excesses in the ruthless suppression of human rights in Russia are in no way consistent with Moscow's public pledges to honor the Universal Declaration of Human Rights enshrined in the United Nations Charter. The West has every right to insist that the Kremlin honor those obligations. This is not interference in Russian internal affairs. This is perfectly legitimate monitoring of Moscow's voluntarily accepted international duties.

There is every reason for the West to follow such a stand. Russian leaders have far more respect for Western statesmen who insist on basic human rights than they do for foreign leaders who compromise on those principles in order to smooth relations with Moscow. It is but one more example of Russia's obsession with signs of strength. The Western leader who demands progress on human rights displays a strength that can force Russian concessions, as Jimmy Carter did early in his presidency. The Western leader who weakens on human rights will be pushed around by the Russians in other areas of the relationship, as was Carter's lot later on. At the same time, ordinary Russians are extraordinarily grateful for all Western support on human rights issues. Thus Russians at all levels are profoundly influenced by strong Western backing for basic human rights. As a policy line it is both morally correct and politically correct.

18. Continue Truth in Broadcasting

America should think twice about phasing out radio programs beamed to the new Russia. The Cold War is over but the need remains. Truth is the first casualty in any dictatorship, meaning the press inevitably gets muzzled. The only permitted media line sings the praises of the regime and denies any shortcomings. This was always true in Russia and will be again should dictatorship return. In that atmosphere, Western stations broadcasting to Russia in the Russian language, among them the Voice of America and the BBC, are a godsend, a highly prized link to the outside world and a unique source of objective news. Among other things, they carry the words of dissident Russian opinion and can be an effective force in rallying a political opposition to dictatorship.

To do so, however, these stations need proper funding, and, above all, total credibility. VOA, for example, must report crime or race riots in America accurately if it is to maintain a reputation for impartiality in Russia. The last thing Western stations must do is become propaganda outlets for the democracies, no more truthful than Moscow radio. In the past, both the funding and the objectivity of Western stations have been political footballs. This is a terribly shortsighted error. What is needed above all is consistency, in both funding and reliability, on a permanent basis.

19. Keep the Faith

The American motto "In God We Trust" can help manage a future Russian threat. On this issue it is wrong to separate church and state. America's interest is to combine them. Religion was a major force behind the nationalist rebellions—from Catholics in the Baltics to Muslims in Central Asia—that helped break up the Soviet Union. Should dictatorship return to Russia, religious faith will again be a major source of opposition among Russian Orthodox, Catholic, Jewish, and Muslim believers alike. Western commitment to freedom of religion is a beacon of inspiration to them. Western support in everything from shortwave religious broadcasts to prayer books smuggled to Russia helps both the faithful and the political opposition.

During the Cold War, this asset was sometimes discussed but rarely used to full potential. In one known case, Alexandre de Marenches, then head of the SDECE, the French CIA, proposed what he called "Operation Mosquito" to William Casey, then head of the CIA. The idea was a series of steps to harass the Russian bear with "insect bites," among them the circulation of Bibles in Cyrillic, to Russian occupation troops in Afghanistan, to turn them against the war on moral grounds. The idea never got off the ground, de Marenches claims, because Casey could not assure him that the secret French role in the affair would not be leaked to the American press.[4] Keeping the faith does not have to descend to the level of dirty tricks. But like so many other Western advantages insufficiently tapped during the Cold War, it could be better used in any future crisis with a new Russian dictatorship.

Anyone drawing up a list of policies has got to know when to stop. Going on too long is a sure way to invite ridicule. That principle applies even to American presidents. Woodrow Wilson was the classic example, at the Versailles Peace Conference ending World War I. Wilson tried to impose a new improved world order with a list of fourteen points. "God only had ten," French Prime Minister Georges Clemenceau noted at the time.

In that sense, the above list of ideas for containing a new Russian threat—one for each chapter in this book—is already too long. It is nonetheless offered as a preliminary draft, to encourage debate and improvement by wiser heads. Humility is useful in dealing with Russia. No Russia specialist in or out of government has all the answers. The experts proved that when none of them was able to forecast how or when the Soviet Union would collapse.

At best, they only saw the system as fatally flawed, with an uncertain future. Thus no program for managing a new Russian challenge can be fully guaranteed in advance. But even an imperfect framework is preferable to having no coherent game plan at all, as at present, when America is largely turning its back on the real world beyond its borders.

The United States and its NATO allies cannot afford to repeat Cold War mistakes. Nor can it afford to let any new threat of Russian aggression develop. More effective policies are needed now, to help salvage democratic reform in Russia and beat back the danger of renewed dictatorship.

The key to aiding Russian reform and to resisting any new dictatorship is one and the same—learning from the mistakes of the Cold War and then applying those lessons as soon as possible. This is the only way to meet the Russian challenge ahead. Anything less is dangerous folly. Nor is there any time to waste. The clock is ticking. The grim lesson of Russian reform since 1985 could not be clearer. The transition to democracy, under Gorbachev and Yeltsin, was always literally under the gun of conservative opponents. That remains true. Genuine democratic reform in Russia can still be snuffed out by an election or a new hard-line coup. Should that happen while the United States is looking inward and conducting a policy of benign neglect abroad, we will have only ourselves to blame.

ACKNOWLEDGMENTS

H undreds of people in Russia and abroad made this book possible by generously sharing with me their time and their insights in interviews over the past thirty years. Some are mentioned by name in the text. All have my gratitude.

Special thanks go to my family for encouraging this book over the years, starting with my parents, Ira and Muriel Coleman, who first stimulated intellectual curiosity and then provided a fine education. My mother-in-law, Georgette Tartavez, who lived in Russia from Stalin to Brezhnev, working at the French embassy in Moscow for twenty-nine years, was a superb source of oral history. My children, Cynthia and Eric, added another dimension to the project with the views of their generation. Above all, my wife, Nadine Tartavez Coleman, who grew up in Moscow speaking perfect Russian and knowing the country as well as any foreigner ever could, was my invaluable guide and constant helpmate from 1965 on in gathering material, in evaluating it, and in producing the manuscript.

Robin Knight, my colleague at *U.S. News & World Report* and a distinguished former Moscow correspondent, read the manuscript and provided valued suggestions for improving it, as did John Sowels, a shrewd and knowledgeable British businessman with many years of experience in the U.S.S.R. My agent, Wendy Lipkind, was instrumental in bringing this project to fruition. My editors at St. Martin's Press, Robert Weil and Becky Koh, raised the quality of the writing. To each of them, heartfelt thanks. Needless to say, any shortcomings remaining in the text are my responsibility alone.

NOTES ON SOURCES

M ost of the material in this book comes from notes taken during the fourteen years I spent as a journalist in Moscow and around the former Soviet Union. My notebooks include personal interviews, group press briefings, and my own observations and analyses. Material gathered in these notebooks was first used in preparing articles from Moscow as a permanent correspondent for the Associated Press (1964–67) and *Newsweek* (1976–79 and 1987–92), and as a visiting correspondent for *U.S. News & World Report* (1993–95). The relevant articles have not been footnoted individually because the responsibility for the accuracy of the material used is mine alone. Individual interviews from Russia and from reporting trips to more than fifty other countries are cited in the text, where appropriate.

In the relatively few cases where the work of others was used in the preparation of this book, the relevant citations have been provided below. In addition, these notes include some explanatory material excluded from the text to avoid slowing down the narrative.

Chapter 1—The October Surprise

1. Russians traditionally use the first name and the middle name or patronymic as the polite form of address. In conversation, Nikita Sergeyevich Khrushchev would normally be addressed as "Nikita Sergeyevich." Throughout this book, Soviet leaders will frequently be referred to in this way. Thus Nikita Sergeyevich Khrushchev will be called either Khrushchev or Nikita Sergeyevich, Leonid Ilyich Brezhnev will be called either Brezhnev or Leonid Ilyich, and so on.

2. The "Politburo," Stalin's name for the top Soviet leadership group, was changed under Khrushchev to the "Presidium." The name change was part of the symbolism that went with Khrushchev's de-Stalinization. Brezhnev, in scaling back the Khrushchev reforms, restored the name "Politburo," which remained in effect through the Gorbachev era. By definition, the two names are interchangeable. For the sake of simplicity, no usage is made in this book of the short-lived name "Presidium." Instead the more familiar name "Politburo" is used throughout to describe the top policymaking body of the Soviet Communist Party.

3. Stalin called himself the "general secretary" of the Soviet Communist Party. Khrushchev changed the title to "first secretary." Brezhnev changed it back to "general secretary," a title which all subsequent Soviet leaders, including Gorbachev, retained. Once again, the titles are interchangeable. In this case, however, in the interest of historical accuracy, Khrushchev is referred to in the text by the revised title he awarded himself.

4. In the early Brezhnev years the chief designer and head of the space program was identified as Sergei Korolev, and monuments were later constructed in his honor.

5. The author visited the dacha at Pitsunda in 1965, after Khrushchev's fall from power.

6. Michel Tatu, *Power in the Kremlin: From Khrushchev to Kosygin* (New York: Viking, 1969), p. 412.

7. Roy Medvedev, *Khrushchev* (New York: Doubleday, 1983), p. 245.

Chapter 2—Stalin's Legacy

1. Nadezhda Mandelstam later wrote one of the most powerful memoirs of the Stalin era, published in English as *Hope Against Hope* (New York: Atheneum, 1970).

2. Robert Conquest, *The Great Terror: A Reassessment* (Oxford: Oxford University Press, 1990), p. 486.

3. Aleksandr Solzhenitsyn, *The First Circle* (London: Collins, 1968), p. 112.

4. Bertram D. Wolfe, *Three Who Made a Revolution* (New York: Dell, 1964), p. 437.

5. Ibid., p. 371.

6. Under the old calendar used in Russia in 1917, the Bolshevik Revolution took place in October, and has been hailed by Communists ever since as "the Great October Socialist Revolution." Under the modern calender used in the Soviet era, the anniversary was celebrated each year on November 7.

7. This letter, known as Lenin's testament, is quoted by Khrushchev in his "secret speech" on Stalin's crimes to the 20th Party Congress in February 1976. In the English-language text of the speech published by the Bertrand Russell Foundation, the references to Lenin's testament are on p. 22.

8. See Chapter 13.

9. The quote is a paraphrase of a thought Lenin voiced many times, but never in his published works in those exact words. Lenin did say the capitalists "will work on the preparations for their own suicide," among many other similar phrases. See I.U. Annenkov, "Remembering Lenin," *Novy Zhurnal,* September 1961, p. 141.

Chapter 3—The Permanent Power Struggle

1. Nikita Khrushchev, *Khrushchev Remembers* (New York: Little, Brown, 1970), pp. 337–38.

2. Winston Churchill, *The Second World War,* vol. 1, *The Gathering Storm* (London: Cassell, 1950), p. 403.

3. CIA document quoted in *Le Monde,* Oct. 23, 1993, p. 1.

4. N. S. Khrushchev, *The Secret Speech* (Nottingham, England: Russell Press, 1956), pp. 47, 79.

5.   For the purposes of this analysis, Andropov and Chernenko are omitted. Both were transition leaders who had no time to get started before dying in office.

6.   The source for this incident was Ambassador Toon.

7.   See Chapter 11.

8.   See Chapter 17.

9.   See Chapter 19.

10.   Medvedev, p. 117.

11.   See Shelest interview in *Argumenty i Fakty,* Jan. 14–20, 1989, pp. 5–6.

12.   See *Moscow News* no. 37, p. 16.

13.   Voronov interview in *Izvestia,* Nov. 17, 1988.

14.   Sergei Khrushchev, *Khrushchev on Khrushchev* (Boston: Little, Brown, 1990), p. 135.

15.   Shelest interview.

16.   Sergei Khrushchev, p. 121.

Chapter 4—All That Jazz

Material for this chapter came entirely from the author's notebooks for articles produced for the Associated Press in Moscow and in Tallinn in 1965 and for *Newsweek* in Leningrad in 1989.

Chapter 5—Comrades

Much of the material in this chapter comes from the author's notebooks compiled in Moscow and Prague. In addition, an unpublished study by two Russian researchers, A. D. Chernov and M. L. Korobochkin, entitled "New Documents About the Soviet Invasion of Czechoslovakia in 1968," was generously made available to the author in 1993 and proved to be an invaluable source. This study discussed both Central Committee and foreign ministry documents then available to Russian specialists, but not to foreign researchers.

1.   Stalin's heirs were involved in a bitter power struggle up to June 1957, when Khrushchev finally removed his chief rivals from the leadership, among them Malenkov and Molotov. For a detailed account of this episode, see Chapter 3. The point is, this political showdown came the year after the 1956 Hungarian crisis. It is therefore one more piece of evidence backing the contention that the divided Kremlin leadership would have been vulnerable to stronger Western pressure over Hungary.

2.   Tibor Meray, quoted by Agnes Heller and Ferenc Feher, *From Yalta to Glasnost: The Dismantling of Stalin's Empire* (Oxford: Basil Blackwell, 1990), p. 71.

3.   Dobrynin's quotes come from recently declassified but still unpublished documents of the former Central Committee of the Soviet Communist Party, now housed in Moscow in the Modern Documentation Storage Center (MDSC). The specific reference is MDSC, file 60, case 469, pp. 57–69. Dobrynin's report, entitled "The main directions of American propaganda in connection with events in Czechoslovakia," is dated March 10, 1968.

4.   MDSC, file 60, case 301, p. 140.

Chapter 6—Dissent Comes Out of the Closet

1. Solzhenitsyn, *The First Circle,* p. 361.
2. *Pravda,* April 2, 1966.
3. Peter Reddaway, *Uncensored Russia: The Human Rights Movement in the Soviet Union* (London: Jonathan Cape, 1972), p. 99.
4. Ibid., p. 125.
5. Ibid., p. 100.
6. Many other dissidents, among them Andrei Amalrik and Andrei Sinyavsky, were pushed into emigrating. Still others, including Yuli Daniel, refused all pressures to leave and died in Russia.
7. Eventually, some Soviet Jews in the crowd outside the Shcharansky trial showed their defiance by singing the Israeli national anthem, but none of them said a word in protest about the brutal police treatment of Shcharansky's mother.
8. Andrei Sakharov, *Memoirs* (London: Hutchinson, 1990), p. 432.
9. When Sakharov returned to Moscow from Gorky he had an opportunity to move into a larger apartment in another building. The KGB, however, was anxious to keep him at his previous residence. To discourage Sakharov from moving, the KGB arranged to vacate an apartment on the floor below which Andrei Dmitriyevich could then use as additional space for his study. The KGB chief of the day, Viktor Chebrikov, explained all this to the Politburo by saying it was desirable to keep the Sakharovs where they were because their apartment was, as he put it, "fully equipped," meaning full of listening devices. Tatyana Yankelevich, Sakharov's daughter-in-law, told me this story. She said the quote from Chebrikov came from the official minutes of the Politburo meeting that discussed Sakharov's return from Gorky. Elena Bonner is the source of Sakharov's last words and the detailed account of his death.
10. Elena Bonner told me in a 1995 interview that she opposes any Sakharov monument built with Russian government funds. She is, however, ready to approve a Sakharov memorial financed by funds from private citizens, groups, or foundations.

Chapter 7—Economic Madness

1. In 1995, the average life expectancy for the Russian male was 57, the lowest of any country reporting to the World Health Organization. The comparable figure for the United States was 72. Factors responsible for the low figure in Russia include poor diet, inadequate health care, and unsafe atomic energy installations and waste disposal. See the *International Herald Tribune,* August 3, 1995, p. 1.
2. Andrei and Nina Smirnov are the only Russians given fictitious names in this book to protect their identity. Elsewhere Russian sources are either given their full real names or protected by being referred to by first name only, as in the case of Sonya in Chapter 2 and Zhenya in Chapter 8.

Chapter 8—The Soviet Threat

1. See David Binder interview with Keegan, *New York Times,* Jan. 2, 1977.
2. *North-South: A Program for Survival,* Report of the Independent Commission on International Development Issues, Willy Brandt, Chairman (London: Pan Books, 1980), pp. 117–18.

3. See International Institute of Strategic Studies, *The Military Balance* (London, 1980–81).

4. Andrew Cockburn, *Inside the Soviet Military Machine* (New York: Random House, 1984), p. 416.

5. Ibid., p. 299.

6. Interview May 4, 1978, in the German newspaper *Vorwärts*.

7. Quoted in William Hillman and Alfred Wagg, *Problems of the Presidency* (New York: Farrar, Strauss, 1952), p. 23.

8. Harold F. Gosnell, *Truman's Crises: A Political Biography of Harry S. Truman* (Westport, Conn.: Greenwood Press, 1980), p. 302.

9. Harry S. Truman, *Years of Trial and Hope* (Garden City, N.Y.: Doubleday, 1956), p. 95.

10. Herbert F. Druks, *Harry Truman and the Russians, 1945–53* (New York: Speller, 1966), p. 125.

11. See Michael R. Beschloss, *The Crisis Years: Kennedy and Khrushchev 1960–63* (New York: HarperCollins, 1991), pp. 328–29.

12. Peter Deriabin and T. H. Bagley, *The KGB: Masters of the Soviet Union* (London: Robson Books, 1990), pp. 115–16.

Chapter 9—The KGB

1. Christopher Andrew and Oleg Gordievsky, *KGB: The Inside Story* (New York: HarperCollins, 1990), p. 17.

2. Andrew and Gordievsky, p. 38.

3. Aleksandr Solzhenitsyn, *The Gulag Archipelago* (New York: Harper & Row, 1973–78), vol. 3, p. 507.

4. *New York Times*, June 1, 1989.

5. The big exception in Eastern Europe, Romania's Securitate, like the KGB was reorganized and survives to this day.

6. Deriabin and Bagley, pp. 88–89.

7. Andrew and Gordievsky, p. 645.

8. John Barron, *The KGB Today: The Hidden Hand* (London: Hodder & Stoughton, 1984), pp. 169–82.

9. Andrew and Gordievsky, p. 470.

10. British officials estimated that about two-thirds of the Soviet correspondents accredited in London also worked as KGB agents. Perhaps more interesting, they say the proportion remains about the same now in the post-Communist era. As recently as 1995, a Russian TV journalist in London was expelled for espionage—this time for the industrial variety.

11. The arrest of Daniloff, the last Cold War incident, occurred before the author arrived in 1988 for a third journalistic assignment in Moscow.

Chapter 10—Détente

1. As noted in Chapter 7 on the economy, Georgy Shakhnazarov, a top Gorbachev aide, told the author that Brezhnev hid the true extent of Soviet economic weakness from other Politburo members. Other senior Russian officials made the same point on security issues.

2.   The 7:1 ratio was a conservative U.S. estimate at the time. At a Soviet-American meeting in Moscow in January 1989 reviewing the Cuban missile crisis, the Soviet side revealed that according to Soviet estimates the U.S. advantage in 1962 was better than 15:1. Both ratios are cited by Dino A. Brugioni in *Eyeball to Eyeball: The Inside Story of the Cuban Missile Crisis* (New York: Random House, 1990), p. 254.

3.   After leaving Eisenhower in Washington, Castro stopped in Princeton to speak to students there, among them the author, and explain why calling an early election would make no difference.

4.   Walter Isaacson, *Kissinger* (New York: Simon & Schuster, 1992), pp. 165–68.

5.   Henry Kissinger, *White House Years* (Boston: Little, Brown, 1979), p. 141.

6.   Ibid., p. 144.

7.   Ibid., p. 159.

8.   Ibid., p. 305.

9.   Some 35,000 Soviet soldiers were injured in the Afghan War. U.S. State Department estimates are that one million Afghan combatants and civilians died in the war and five million Afghan refugees fled the country.

Chapter 11—Reform from the Top Down: Perestroika

1.   The source is Gorbachev adviser Anatoly Chernyayev, in a two-hour interview with the author in the Kremlin on Nov. 29, 1991.

2.   See Strobe Talbott and the editors of *Time, Mikhail S. Gorbachev: An Intimate Biography* (New York: Time/Life Books, 1988), pp. 59–60.

3.   Zhores Medvedev, *Gorbachev* (London: Basil Blackwell, 1986), pp. 62–65.

4.   Translation of verbatim transcript of Politburo meeting, March 11, 1985.

5.   Judgments in this chapter on Gorbachev's thinking come from the author's interviews with senior Gorbachev aides and a 1995 interview with Gorbachev himself.

6.   Chernyayev interview.

7.   Volkogonov speech to RSFSR parliament, Oct. 25, 1990.

8.   Boris Yeltsin, *Against the Grain: An Autobiography* (New York: Simon & Schuster, 1990), p. 191. Gorbachev aides deny Yeltsin's "guns blazing" explanation. They say Yeltsin hoped to win full voting membership in the Politburo by playing the "democratization card" and criticizing hard-liners at the plenum, but he lost, since Gorbachev was in no position to change the Politburo balance at that time. They also claim that Yeltsin's frustration over losing this gamble was so big that he attempted to commit suicide by piercing his chest with a pair of scissors in his office after he returned from the plenum. This account is depicted in memoirs by Gorbachev and by former Soviet Prime Minister Nikolai Ryzhkov.

9.   Vadim Medvedev is no relation to dissident historian Roy Medvedev or Roy's twin brother, the biologist Zhores Medvedev.

10.   Gorbachev's maneuvers with the presidency began in 1985 when he "promoted" longtime foreign minister Andrei Gromyko into that largely honorary job. The purpose was both to trim the conservative Gromyko's powers and to make way for the appointment of the more progressive Eduard Shevardnadze as foreign minister. Gorbachev then pushed Gromyko into retirement in 1988 to take the presidency for himself.

11.   The presidency that Gorbachev awarded himself in September 1988 was officially called "Chairman of the Supreme Soviet" or parliament, but it served the role of the country's president or ceremonial head of state.

12.   At this stage, Kryuchkov attended Politburo meetings, but not yet as a voting member.

Chapter 12—Reform from the Bottom Up: Democratization

1.   Some of the one hundred seats went to Party-controlled institutions like the Academy of Sciences and were used to assure the election of relatively liberal Party members such as the historian Yuri Afanasyev, the economist Gavriil Popov, or the space-program scientist Roald Sagdayev.

2.   Marshall Goldman of Harvard was a rare exception in accurately calling early attention to Gorbachev's economic plight.

3.   See Chapter 7.

Chapter 13—From Reform to Rebellion: Nationalism

1.   This chapter is based on the author's reporting in all fifteen Soviet republics between 1964 and 1994 looking at the problems of minority nationalities and the eventually successful struggle of national independence movements. Many republics, among them Lithuania and Ukraine, the author visited several times over the years, and was thus fortunate to be on scene at several historic turning points, from Lithuania the week the pope visited Poland in 1979 to Kiev for Ukraine's referendum on independence in 1991.

2.   At best, Gorbachev's knowledge of minority nationality problems during his rise to power was secondhand. As the Communist Party first secretary in the Stavropol region of Southern Russia, Gorbachev gained experience dealing with Chechens, Osetins, Ingushes, and other ethnic minorities in nearby regions. In short, he had to learn how to get along with neighbors of different ethnic backgrounds. But that is a far cry from firsthand experience managing a region where Latvians or Uzbeks or some other non-Russian nationality held the numerical majority and deeply resented what amounted to Russian colonial rule. Unlike Khrushchev or Brezhnev, Gorbachev never had the essential learning experience of running a non-Russian republic.

Chapter 14—Foreign Surprises

1.   Yakovlev was speaking in New York to a group of Americans, including the author.

2.   The Group of Seven includes the United States, Canada, Japan, Britain, France, Germany, and Italy.

3.   Yegor Ligachev, *Inside Gorbachev's Kremlin* (New York: Pantheon Books, 1993), p. 322.

4.   Tass, May 25, 1988.

5.   The Mujahedin rebels finally toppled Najibullah in April 1992, more than three years after the Soviet Union pulled its troops out of Afghanistan, but as these

lines were written in 1995, the Mujahedin were still fighting among themselves in a
continuing civil war for control of the country.

6.   "The Disappearing Act," *New Republic*, Jan. 6, 1992, p. 41.

7.   See Chapter 18.

Chapter 15—Countdown to a Coup

1.   Although the plan was named after Shatalin, many of its ideas came from
Grigory Yavlinsky and other reform economists.

2.   According to Gorbachev aides, Shevardnadze's resignation was not simply
a warning about dictatorship but also a result of personal slights. Aleksandr Likhotal, Gorbachev's spokesman since retirement, told the author, "According to my personal knowledge, Shevardnadze's resignation was also motivated to a certain extent
by hurt ambition." Likhotal noted that Gorbachev had given Yevgeny Primakov some
delicate diplomatic missions in the Middle East, outside the control of Shevardnadze's foreign ministry, leading to speculation that Primakov was being groomed
to replace Shevardnadze. In fact, that did not happen. After Shevardnadze resigned,
Aleksandr Bessmertnyk, the Soviet ambassador to Washington, became foreign minister. Primakov continued in his role as Middle East troubleshooter and later became
head of Russian foreign intelligence. He finally became Russian foreign minister
under Yeltsin in 1996.

3.   At this point Yeltsin was acting decisively, and largely on his own. Even his
closest advisers were often informed about major decisions only at the last minute.
Gennady Burbulis, then Yeltsin's top aide, told the author he had not been given
advance notice of Yeltsin's decision to name Rutskoi as the vice presidential running mate. Only later, as Yeltsin's physical health and public standing declined, did
he appear manipulated by close advisers.

Chapter 16—The Death of Communism

1.   This incident was later confirmed by several published Russian sources. The
same is true of all other episodes in the account of the August 1991 coup given in
this chapter.

2.   One of the plotters, General Varennikov, refused to be pardoned and insisted on a judicial hearing to defend himself. He wanted the opportunity to declare
in a court of law that he and the plotters had acted against Gorbachev to save the
U.S.S.R. from breaking up. Without getting into whether the coup was justified or
not, the hearing acquitted Varennikov of treason on a legal technicality. The court
ruled that he had been charged under the laws of a state, the Soviet Union, that no
longer existed. During the hearing, Gorbachev testified as a witness and answered
some questions. The judgment handed down at the end of the hearing said Gorbachev had not been involved in the plot. Neither this hearing, nor the judgment,
can be regarded as conclusive, however. This was not the kind of full scale trial that
would have subjected all the plotters and Gorbachev to the intensive cross-
examination necessary to uncover the full truth.

3.   For a more detailed account of this episode, see David Remnick, *Lenin's Tomb*
(New York: Random House, 1994), pp. 454–6.

4.   Boris Yeltsin, *The Struggle for Russia* (New York: Times Books, 1994), p. 67.
5.   Interview with the author, Dec. 24, 1994.
6.   Formerly Byelorussia.
7.   See Chapters 11–12.

Chapter 17—The Battle for Russia's Soul

1.   In an encouraging sign for reform, Chubais was promoted to first deputy prime minister in November 1994 and given broader responsibilities for running the Russian economy. Yeltsin forced him to resign in January 1996 in what could be a death blow to the reforms.

2.   On Feb. 26, 1995, the Russian interior ministry announced that $50 billion had been illegally exported from Russia in 1994, at a time when Western nations were talking about an aid package of some $6 billion.

3.   See the discussion of Germany in Chapter 14.

4.   This account of Yeltsin's long and difficult effort to get army support in his showdown with parliament came from several different senior Russian sources in a position to know. It differs slightly from Yeltsin's own account, published later in his autobiography, in that it includes details Yeltsin preferred to leave out. Yeltsin's account mentions several phone calls to Grachev on that Sunday, demanding the army be brought into Moscow to help, and the president's rising frustration that no army troops had entered the capital by 2:30 A.M. Monday. Yeltsin also confirms that he went to the defense ministry personally to address the collegium, that he was still there at 3:00 A.M., and that Grachev demanded written orders from the president before agreeing to use tanks against the parliament. Yeltsin says he then went back to the Kremlin and issued the appropriate orders. The president's account, however, makes no mention of Grachev's polling the entire collegium before agreeing to Yeltsin's demands, perhaps because this was an embarrassing defiance of presidential authority. See Yeltsin, *Struggle for Russia*, pp. 274–79.

5.   Juppé later recounted Yeltsin's prediction to the author.

Chapter 18—The Waiting Game

1.   An opinion poll published on July 3, 1995, in the newspaper *Obshchaya Gazeta* showed Lebed beating Yeltsin by 38 percent to 8 percent, and either liberal economist Grigory Yavlinsky or extreme nationalist Vladimir Zhirinovsky, two other leading presidential hopefuls, by similarly wide margins.

2.   As head of the former KGB, Stepashin still had a *vertushka*, a direct phone line to Yeltsin, but it no longer did him much good. In December 1994, Yeltsin fired one of Stepashin's key deputies, further weakening the security service. Stepashin picked up the *vertushka* to complain and urge Yeltsin to reconsider, but according to Russian intelligence sources, Yeltsin never took the call. The same sources say that after this incident, Stepashin had to report to Yeltsin through the president's chief bodyguard, Korzhakov.

3.   See *Argumenty i Fakty* no. 3, January 1995.

4.   See Chapter 10.

5.   After independence, the Ukraine changed its name to Ukraine, dropping "the." Similarly, Moldavia became Moldova.

6.   *Newsweek International,* May 2, 1994, p. 35.

7.   *Le Figaro,* Oct. 29, 1994, p. 3.

8.   Tatyana asked the author not to use her last name so that her famous family would not be implicated.

9.   The Afghanistan war took 13,000 Soviet lives. The Chechen war killed more than 20,000 Russian citizens—1,450 servicemen and the rest civilians.

10.   The quotation is from an interview with Havel in the French daily *Le Figaro,* Jan. 23, 1996, p. 6. The Havel quote in the introduction about the return of former Communists to power in Eastern Europe comes from the same interview.

Chapter 19—What Is to Be Done?

1.   See Chapter 10.

2.   Interview with the author in January 1995.

3.   See Chapter 17.

4.   Roger Falicot and Remi Kauffer, *Les Maîtres Espions* (Paris: Robert Laffont, 1994).

BIBLIOGRAPHY

Aganbegyan, Abel. *The Economic Challenge of Perestroika*. Bloomington: Indiana University Press, 1988.

Aksenov, Vasili. *A Ticket to the Stars*. New York: Signet, 1963.

Alliluyeva, Svetlana. *Twenty Letters to a Friend*. New York: Harper & Row, 1967.

Amalrik, Andrei. *Involuntary Journey to Siberia*. London: Collins, 1970.

——. *Will the U.S.S.R. Survive Until 1984?* London: Penguin, 1969.

——. *Notes of a Revolutionary*. New York: Knopf, 1982.

Andrew, Christopher, and Oleg Gordievsky. *KGB: The Inside Story*. New York: HarperCollins, 1991.

Arbatov, Georgi. *The System: An Insider's Life in Soviet Politics*. New York: Times Books, 1992.

Aslund, Anders. *Gorbachev's Struggle for Economic Reform*. Ithaca, N.Y.: Cornell University Press, 1989.

Barron, John. *The KGB Today: The Hidden Hand*. London: Hodder & Stoughton, 1984.

Bialer, Seweryn. *The Soviet Paradox: External Expansion, Internal Decline*. New York: Vintage, 1987.

Billington, James H. *The Icon and the Axe: An Interpretive History of Russian Culture*. New York: Vintage, 1970.

Borovik, Artyom. *The Hidden War: A Russian Journalist's Account of the Secret War in Afghanistan*. London: Faber, 1991.

Bourdeaux, Michael. *Patriarch and Prophets: Persecution of the Russian Orthodox Church*. London: Mowbrys, 1975.

Breslauer, George W. *Khrushchev and Brezhnev as Leaders: Building Authority in Soviet Politics*. London: Allen & Unwin, 1982.

Brezhnev, Leonid. *Peace, Détente and Soviet-American Relations: A Collection of Public Statements*. New York: Harcourt Brace, 1979.

Brown, Archie, and Michael Kaser, eds. *The Soviet Union Since the Fall of Khrushchev*. London: Macmillan, 1975.

Brugioni, Dino A. *Eyeball to Eyeball: The Inside Story of the Cuban Missile Crisis*. New York: Random House, 1990.

Burlatsky, Fedor. *Khrushchev and the First Russian Spring*. New York: Scribner, 1988.

Carrère d'Encausse, Hélène. *Decline of an Empire: The Soviet Socialist Republics in Revolt.* New York: Newsweek Books, 1979.

Cockburn, Andrew. *Inside the Soviet Military Machine.* New York: Random House, 1984.

Colton, Timothy J., and Robert Legvold, eds. *After the Soviet Union: From Empire to Nations.* New York: Norton, 1992.

Conquest, Robert. *The Great Terror: A Reassessment.* Oxford: Oxford University Press, 1990.

Crankshaw, Edward. *Russia Without Stalin.* New York: Viking, 1956.

———. *Khrushchev.* London: Sphere, 1968.

Custine, Marquis de. *Empire of the Tsar: A Journey Through Eternal Russia.* New York: Doubleday, 1989.

Dawisha, Karen. *Eastern Europe, Gorbachev and Reform: The Great Challenge.* Cambridge: Cambridge University Press, 1988.

Deriabin, Peter, and T.H. Bagley. *KGB: Masters of the Soviet Union.* London: Robson Books, 1990.

Djilas, Milovan. *The New Class: An Analysis of the Communist System.* New York: Praeger, 1961.

Doder, Dusko. *Shadows and Whispers: Power Politics Inside the Kremlin from Brezhnev to Gorbachev.* New York: Penguin, 1988.

Dornberg, John. *Brezhnev: The Masks of Power.* London: Andre Deutsch, 1974.

Druks, Herbert F. *Harry Truman and the Russians, 1945–53.* New York: Speller, 1966.

Dubček, Alexander. *Hope Dies Last.* New York: Kodansha, 1991.

Feiffer, George. *Justice in Moscow.* New York: Simon & Schuster, 1964.

Ginzburg, Evgenia. *Journey into the Whirlwind.* New York: Harcourt Brace Jovanovich, 1967.

Gittings, John. *Survey of the Sino-Soviet Dispute.* London: Oxford University Press, 1968.

Goldman, Marshall I. *What Went Wrong with Perestroika.* New York: Norton, 1992.

Gorbachev, Mikhail. *Perestroika: New Thinking for Our Country and the World.* New York: Harper & Row, 1987.

———. *The August Coup: The Truth and the Lessons.* New York: HarperCollins, 1991.

Gosnell, Harold F. *Truman's Crises: A Political Biography of Harry S. Truman.* Westport, Conn.: Greenwood Press, 1980.

Grigorenko, Gen. P.G. *The Grigorenko Papers.* Boulder: Westview Press, 1976.

Handelman, Stephen. *Comrade Criminal: Russia's New Mafiya.* New Haven, Conn.: Yale University Press, 1995.

Heller, Agnes, and Ferenc Feher. *From Yalta to Glasnost.* Oxford: Basil Blackwell, 1990.

Hillman, William, and Alfred Wagg. *Problems of the Presidency.* New York: Farrar, Straus, 1952.

Hopkirk, Peter. *The Great Game: The Struggle for Empire in Central Asia.* New York: Kodansha, 1992.

Hough, Jerry F. *Opening Up the Soviet Economy.* Washington: Brookings, 1988.

———. *Russia and the West: Gorbachev and the Politics of Reform.* New York: Simon & Schuster, 1988.

Isaacson, Walter. *Kissinger.* New York: Simon & Schuster, 1992.

Kaiser, Robert G. *Russia: The People and the Power.* London: Secker & Warburg, 1976.

Khrushchev, Nikita. *Khrushchev Remembers.* Boston: Little, Brown, 1970.
——. *The Secret Speech.* Nottingham, England: Russell Press, 1976.
Khrushchev, Sergei. *Khrushchev on Khrushchev.* Boston: Little, Brown, 1990.
Kissinger, Henry. *White House Years.* Boston: Little, Brown, 1979.
Kopelev, Lev. *To Be Preserved Forever.* Philadelphia: Lippincott, 1977.
Kuzichkin, Vladimir. *Inside the KGB: My Life in Soviet Espionage.* New York: Pantheon, 1990.
Kuznetsov, Anatoli. *Babi Yar.* London: Jonathan Cape, 1970.
Labedz, Leopold, and Max Hayward, eds. *On Trial: The Case of Sinyavsky and Daniel.* London: Collins, 1967.
Ligachev, Yegor. *Inside Gorbachev's Kremlin.* New York: Pantheon, 1993.
Mandelbaum, Michael, and Strobe Talbott. *Reagan and Gorbachev.* New York: Vintage, 1987.
Mandelstam, Nadezhda. *Hope Against Hope.* New York: Atheneum, 1970.
Massie, Suzanne. *Land of the Firebird: The Beauty of Old Russia.* New York: Simon & Schuster, 1980.
McCauley, Martin. *The Soviet Union, 1917–1991.* London: Longman, 1991.
Medvedev, Roy. *Khrushchev.* New York: Doubleday, 1983.
——. *Let History Judge.* New York: Vintage Books, 1973.
Medvedev, Zhores. *Andropov.* New York: Penguin, 1984.
——. *Gorbachev.* London: Basil Blackwell, 1986. New York: W.W. Norton, 1987.
Page, Martin, and David Burg. *Unpersoned: The Fall of Nikita Sergeyevich Khrushchev.* London: Chapman & Hall, 1966.
Parker, John W. *Kremlin in Transition.* Vol. 2, *Gorbachev, 1985–1989.* Boston: Unwin Hyman, 1991.
Pipes, Richard. *The Russian Revolution.* New York: Vintage, 1990.
Reddaway, Peter. *Uncensored Russia: The Human Rights Movement in the Soviet Union.* London: Jonathan Cape, 1972.
Reed, John. *Ten Days That Shook the World.* London: Boni & Liveright, 1919.
Remnick, David. *Lenin's Tomb: The Last Days of the Soviet Empire.* New York: Random House, 1993.
Rybakov, Anatoli. *Children of the Arbat.* New York: Dell, 1989.
Sakharov, Andrei. *Alarm and Hope.* New York: Knopf, 1978.
——. *Memoirs.* London: Hutchinson, 1990.
Salisbury, Harrison E. *The Coming War Between Russia and China.* London: Pan Books, 1969.
Schapiro, Leonard. *The Communist Party of the Soviet Union.* New York: Vintage, 1971.
Schmidt-Hauer, Christian. *Gorbachev: The Path to Power.* London: Pan Books, 1986.
Shipler, David K. *Russia: Broken Idols, Solemn Dreams.* New York: Penguin, 1984.
Simis, Konstantin. *USSR: The Corrupt Society.* New York: Simon and Schuster, 1982.
Smith, Graham, ed. *The Nationalities Question in the Soviet Union.* London: Longman, 1990.
Smith, Hedrick. *The Russians.* New York: Times Books, 1976.
Sobchak, Anatoly. *For a New Russia.* New York: Macmillan, 1992.
Solovyov, Vladimir, and Elena Klepikova. *Boris Yeltsin: A Political Biography.* New York: Putnam, 1992.
——. *Inside the Kremlin.* London: W. H. Allen, 1987.

Solzhenitsyn, Aleksandr. *The First Circle*. London: Collins, 1968.

——. *The Gulag Archipelago*, Vols. 1–2. London: Collins, 1974.

——. *The Gulag Archipelago*. Vol. 3. New York: Harper & Row, 1973–78.

Talbott, Strobe, and the Editors of *Time*. *Mikhail S. Gorbachev: An Intimate Biography*. New York: Time/Life Books, 1988.

Tatu, Michel. *Power in the Kremlin: From Khrushchev to Kosygin*. New York: Viking, 1969.

——. *Gorbatchev: L'U.R.S.S. va-t-elle changer?* Paris: Centurion, 1987.

——. et Bernard Feron. *Au Kremlin comme si vous y étiez: Khrouchtchev, Brejnev, Gorbatchev et les autres sous les feux de la Glasnost*. Paris: Le Monde-Editions, 1991.

Taubman, William. *The View from the Lenin Hills: Soviet Youth in Ferment*. London: Hamish Hamilton, 1968.

Tertz, Avram (Andrei Sinyavsky). *The Makepeace Experiment (Lyubimov)*. London: Fontana Books, 1977.

Trifonov, Yuri. *The House on the Embankment*. London: Sphere, 1985.

Troyat, Henri. *Nicolas II: Le Dernier Tsar*. Paris: Flammarion, 1991.

Truman, Harry S. *Years of Trial and Hope*. Garden City, N.Y.: Doubleday, 1956.

Tsipko, Alexandr. *Is Stalinism Really Dead?* New York: HarperCollins, 1990.

Vaksberg, Arkady. *The Soviet Mafia*. New York: St. Martin's Press, 1991.

Voinovich, Vladimir. *The Life and Extraordinary Times of Private Ivan Chonkin*. New York: Penguin, 1978.

Walker, Martin. *The Waking Giant: The Soviet Union Under Gorbachev*. London: Sphere, 1987.

Willis, David K. *Klass: How Russians Really Live*. New York: Avon, 1985.

Wolfe, Bertram D. *Three Who Made a Revolution*. New York: Dell, 1964.

Yeltsin, Boris. *Against the Grain: An Autobiography*. New York: Simon & Schuster/Summit, 1990.

——. *The Struggle for Russia*. New York: Times Books, 1994.

Zaslavskaya, Tatyana. *The Second Socialist Revolution*. Bloomington: Indiana University Press, 1990.

INDEX

ABOUT THE AUTHOR

FRED COLEMAN has been a foreign correspondent for thirty years, fourteen of them in Moscow, for the Associated Press, *Newsweek,* and *U.S. News & World Report.* He is now the only American correspondent to have worked in Russia under Khrushchev, Brezhnev, Gorbachev, and Yeltsin. In 1977, his articles on human rights in the U.S.S.R. won the Page One Award of the New York Newspaper Guild for best magazine reporting from abroad. Mr. Coleman is a graduate of Princeton University. He and his wife live in Paris, where he is bureau chief for *U.S. News & World Report.*